MASTERPLOTS II

AMERICAN FICTION SERIES, REVISED EDITION

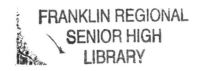
MASTERPLOTS II

AMERICAN FICTION SERIES, REVISED EDITION

4

Lov - Pla #631642

Edited by

STEVEN G. KELLMAN

The University of Texas at San Antonio

SALEM PRESS

Pasadena, California   Hackensack, New Jersey

Editor in Chief: Dawn P. Dawson
Managing Editor: Christina J. Moose
Project Editor: Robert A. McClenaghan   *Research Editor:* Jeffrey Jensen
Acquisitions Editor: Mark Rehn   *Research Assistant:* Jun Ohnuki

∞ The paper used in these volumes conforms to the American National Standard for Permanence of Paper for Printed Library Materials, Z39.48-1992 (R1997).

Library of Congress Cataloging-in-Publication Data
Masterplots II. American fiction series / edited by Steven G.
Kellman.—Rev. ed.
    p.   cm.
    Includes bibliographical references and index.
    ISBN 0-89356-871-6 (set) — ISBN 0-89356-872-4 (v. 1) —
ISBN 0-89356-873-2 (v. 2) — ISBN 0-89356-874-0 (v. 3) —
ISBN 0-89356-875-9 (v. 4) — ISBN 0-89356-876-7 (v. 5) —
ISBN 0-89356-877-5 (v. 6)
    1. American fiction—Stories, plots, etc. I. Title: Masterplots
2. II. Title: Masterplots two. III. Title: American fiction series.
IV. Kellman, Steven G., 1947-   .
PS373 .M37   2000
809.3'0097—dc21   99-053295

First Printing

PRINTED IN THE UNITED STATES OF AMERICA

LIST OF TITLES IN VOLUME 4

MASTERPLOTS II

AMERICAN FICTION SERIES, REVISED EDITION

LOVE IN THE RUINS
The Adventures of a Bad Catholic at a Time
Near the End of the World

Author: Walker Percy (1916-1990)
Type of plot: Social satire
Time of plot: The end of the twentieth century
Locale: A community in Louisiana
First published: 1971

> *Principal characters:*
>> DR. THOMAS MORE, the protagonist/narrator, an alcoholic psychiatrist
>> and "bad Catholic"
>> MOIRA SCHAFFNER, his girlfriend, a secretary at the Love Clinic
>> LOLA RHOADES, another girlfriend, an accomplished cellist
>> ELLEN OGLETHORPE, his office nurse, a beautiful but tyrannical
>> Georgia Presbyterian
>> ART IMMELMANN, a mysterious stranger who claims to be a liaison
>> between the National Institute of Mental Health and the Ford,
>> Carnegie, and Rockefeller foundations but apparently has more
>> infernal connections

The Novel

On July 4, Dr. Thomas More, with a carbine on his knees, sits in a pine grove on the southwest cusp of the decaying interstate cloverleaf. A sniper has shot at him earlier in the day, and from this point he commands a view of all four directions. In one quadrant is the city, inhabited largely by conservative Christian businessmen; in another, the Paradise Estates, a suburb where he ordinarily lives in a house inherited from his deceased wife. In still another direction, there is the federal complex, which includes the hospital where the narrator works, a medical school, the NASA facility, the Behavioral Institute, the Geriatrics Center, and the Love Clinic. In the remaining quadrant, the huge Honey Island swamp shelters assorted social rebels and castoffs: white derelicts, young dropouts pursuing love, drugs, and the simple life, and ferocious black Bantus, who use the swamp as guerrilla base for launching raids against outlying suburbs and shopping centers.

Immediately below Dr. More's lookout post, an old, abandoned Howard Johnson's motel, long deserted after a devastating raid in years past, is a temporary shelter for Dr. More's two girlfriends, Moira and Lola, and his loyal nurse, Ellen, whom he also loves. The action of the novel covers, in retrospect, the preceding four days, during which this awkward personal and public crisis came to a head.

The amiable Dr. More, though hardly responsible for the persistent failure of American society to eradicate racial inequality and bigotry, does nevertheless share some obscure guilt for the peculiarly volatile situation on this particular day. He has learned that a racial uprising is planned for the Fourth of July, with the Bantus intending to take over the Paradise Estates. He has been discreetly warned by a black friend and an old Catholic priest to vacate his suburban house and move into his mother's place in town.

What Dr. More really is worrying about, however, is a more general catastrophe, a possibly explosive and poisonous interaction between the heavy sodium which characterizes the soil in the area and fallout from the gross misuse of his invention, the More Qualitative-Quantitative Ontological Lapsometer. He has, through ambition and pride, allowed this sensitive instrument to fall into ignorant and evil hands.

The nondescript Art Immelmann plays the Mephistopheles to More's Faust in this matter. Art's original offer was to see that More's article explaining the lapsometer would be published in a prestigious journal of psychiatry. He promised, moreover, to use his influence with the Ford, Carnegie, and Rockefeller foundations for substantial grant money so that More could submit the device to extensive scientific testing. The lapsometer measures certain psychic forces in the brain, especially angelism and bestialism, which may be responsible for the increasing irrationality and instability among otherwise healthy Americans. Art wants patent rights in exchange for this service.

When Art offers an appendage to the lapsometer so that it not only measures psychic imbalances but also amends or at least changes them with the twist of the dial, More signs the fateful agreement, dreaming of a Nobel Peace Prize in his future. To his consternation, however, Art passes out lapsometers to ignorant students, with hilarious but potentially dangerous results. Later, on this eventful Independence Day, Dr. More manages, by praying to his sainted ancestor and namesake Sir Thomas More for help, to exorcise his devil.

An epilogue five years later shows More living in relative peace in former slave quarters, happily married to one of his sweethearts. He has dissipated his first wife's fortune in an unsuccessful attempt to promote his lapsometer, but he still believes in its promise. Racial prejudice may be partly responsible for the doctor's cool reception as a scientific innovator, since the relative prestige of blacks and whites is now reversed—not, however, because of the Bantu revolt five years ago. Blacks are now beginning to demonstrate some of the psychological pathologies that had afflicted the ruling white class.

The Characters

Although Percy sketches many of the characters with the swift, deadly accurate strokes of comic caricature, his protagonist is a fully developed, complex, seriocomic hero. Yet he is also a kind of Everyman, sharing many of the mental/emotional impediments typical of each of the social groups so deftly caricatured. The dominant political parties, for example, have been renamed (a contribution in each case of the opposition) and display characteristic pathological symptoms. Conservative Republicans, now called Knotheads, often suffer from large bowel complaints, making proctology one of the two major medical specialties. Dr. More shares this difficulty. Though by no means a political Knothead, he is a conservative Roman Catholic in a world where most Catholics have formed splinter groups. Like so many of Percy's protagonists, and like the author himself, he professes to believe in the traditional Catholic Christian message. Dr. More admits, however, that he loves women, music, science, whiskey, and God, in that order—and his fellowman hardly at all. He has not "eaten Christ"—that is, taken Communion—since his daughter Samantha died, his wife ran away with a heathen Englishman, and he himself turned to drink.

He suffers even more from the tendency toward abstraction and unreasonable terrors that have become typical of the Lefts (Democrats) or Leftpapasane, a term devised by Knotheads, standing for Liberty, Equality, Fraternity, The Pill, Atheism, Pot, Antipollution, Sex, Abortion Now, and Euthanasia. Lefts often suffer from sexual impotence as well, for the tendency to abstraction results in alienation from the body and concrete reality. That is why Lefts generally flock to psychologists rather than proctologists.

Dr. More does not suffer from sexual impotence, but he does have an ironically related problem. He tends to fall in love quite sincerely with one young woman after another, which is perhaps a symptom of his religio-erotic tendency toward abstraction. That is why his personal life is complicated by those three beautiful girls, not to mention the enticing young dropout he met once in the swamp. He seems to have less control over this kind of abstraction than over the variety that scientists, including himself, tend to assume with their pose of objectivity. In fact, he is philosophically and professionally opposed to the prevailing behavioralist orientation of his medical colleagues.

The characterizations of women in the novel are more flat, but they are sufficient for their fictional purposes. They help to differentiate psychological propensities in the protagonist. Hester, the girl in the swamp, is perhaps simply an embodiment of a new Eve, wiped clean of civilization's sins. Dr. More is too intelligent, however, to assume that the Garden of Eden can be reentered in its original simplicity.

Moira's attraction is almost exclusively physical. She is sentimental, romantic, unintelligent, but adorable in an amoral, mindless sort of way. The elegant Lola, musician and breeder of fine horses, appeals to the well-developed aesthetic sensibilities of Dr. More. Ellen Oglethorpe, somewhat more expansively developed, maintains a rather puritanical emphasis on morality and duty through most of the story but ripens into the mother/wife who is exactly what the erring Tom More needs to keep his irrational terrors and longings under control.

Art Immelmann is an inspired creation but is necessarily a caricature, as befits a modern Mephistopheles. He has certain affinities with Fyodor Dostoevski's shabby, middle-class devil in *Bratya Karamazovy* (1879-1880; *The Brothers Karamazov*). Percy excels in the comic effect of realistic detail fused with surrealism and subtle clues that a sordidly ordinary person is not what he seems.

Themes and Meanings

Love in the Ruins is a devastating satire of many of the social, political, religious, and scientific shibboleths of the modern world. Percy steps on so many toes that even the offended may laugh at discomfort shared so equitably with opponents. Percy is not only a Christian satirizing Christians but also a physician exposing his own profession as often absurd and misguided.

The Love Clinic is an outrageous commentary on behavioral research and on modern sexual mores, which have managed simultaneously to liberate sex and to reduce it to its lowest common denominator. In the clinic, doctors study the physical and emotional mechanisms of sexual intercourse and masturbation through two-way mirrors, seeking to remedy impotence among the bored. A dissident Catholic priest operates the vaginal console with its orgasm button, while casually reading *Commonweal*, a Catholic layman's magazine which has published articles by Percy. The priest is the clinic chaplain, who advises patients to love or die. This is more obvious irony than Geoffrey Chaucer's ambiguous motto, "Love Conquers All," on the worldly prioress' brooch, but it is of the same general order.

The doctor's lapsometer, with its fusion of metaphysical concepts and scientific measurement, is the perfect symbol for the existential preoccupation with the alienation of modern man from self, nature, God, and his fellowman. One of the implications may be that neither science nor religion nor humanistic philosophy offers an entirely convincing explanation of human nature. Dr. More himself calls his lapsometer "the first caliper of the soul and the first hope of bridging the dread chasm that has rent the soul of Western man ever since the famous philosopher Descartes ripped body loose from mind and turned the very soul into a ghost that haunts its own house."

Critical Context

Percy has a considerable affinity with the religious existentialist Søren Kierkegaard and for Dostoevski's peculiar vision of human absurdity and moral chaos. He received the 1971 National Catholic Book Award for *Love in the Ruins*. Something of a madcap masterpiece, this satire was a popular success, though some critics prefer the more subtle humor of Percy's later novel *The Second Coming* (1980), which also deals with love, mental illness, moral confusion, and the blundering spiritual quest.

The later book also develops more precisely a minor theme of *Love in the Ruins*: the way in which the misuse of language contributes to popular mindlessness and alienation. Percy shares the contemporary intellectual interest in semantics and semiotics. In both *Love in the Ruins* and *The Second Coming*, he tends to emphasize the antic absurdities of clichés and jargon that define contemporary attitudes, though not the sinister intent behind what George Orwell called Doublethink.

Percy's concern for language is both moral and professional. The specifically human world, often quite different from the empirical world of sense experience, is created by the words used to describe it. Percy is concerned not so much with the deliberate villains of society but with the limitations of goodness in well-intentioned people who cannot "name" reality and thus do not know it. Percy recognizes this difficulty in himself as a "Christian novelist," for he knows that the Christian message, as ordinarily expressed, is a tired anachronism in the modern world. For a discussion of this ironic difficulty of the writer, one should read Percy's *The Message in the Bottle*

(1975), especially the chapter entitled "Notes for a Novel About the End of the World," which is especially relevant to *Love in the Ruins*. For further satiric comment on the American way of love and sex, the section on "The Promiscuous Self," in Percy's *Lost in the Cosmos: The Last Self-Help Book* (1983), is both provocative and entertaining.

Bibliography
Allen, William Rodney. *Walker Percy: A Southern Wayfarer.* Jackson: University Press of Mississippi, 1986. Allen reads Percy as a distinctly American, particularly southern writer, claiming that the formative event in Percy's life was his father's suicide, not his reading of existentialist writers or conversion to Roman Catholicism. Allen's readings of individual novels emphasize the presence of weak fathers and rejection of the southern stoic heritage on the part of Percy's protagonists.
Coles, Robert. *Walker Percy: An American Search.* Boston: Little, Brown, 1978. An early but always intelligent and certainly sensitive reading of Percy's essays and novels by a leading psychiatrist whose main contention is that Percy's work speaks directly to modern humanity. In Coles's words, Percy "has balanced a contemporary Christian existentialism with the pragmatism and empiricism of an American physician."
Desmond, John F. *At the Crossroads: Ethical and Religious Themes in the Writings of Walker Percy.* Troy, N.Y.: Whitston, 1997. Chapters on Percy and T. S. Eliot; on Percy's treatment of suicide; on Percy and Flannery O'Connor; on his treatment of myth, history, and religion; and his philosophical debt to pragmatism and Charles Sanders Peirce. A useful, accessible introduction to Percy's background in theology and philosophy.
Hardy, John Edward. *The Fiction of Walker Percy.* Urbana: University of Illinois Press, 1987. The originality of this book, comprising an introduction and six chapters (one for each of the novels, including *The Thanatos Syndrome*), derives from Hardy's choosing to read the novels in terms of internal formal matters rather than (as is usually the case) Percy's essays, existentialism, Catholicism, or southern background. Hardy sees Percy as a novelist, not a prophet.
Lawson, Lewis A. *Following Percy: Essays on Walker Percy's Work.* Troy, N.Y.: Whitston, 1988. Collects essays originally published between 1969 and 1984 by one of Percy's most dedicated, prolific, and knowledgeable commentators. Discussions of *The Moviegoer* and *Lancelot* predominate.
Percy, Walker. *Conversations with Walker Percy*, edited by Lewis A. Lawson and Victor A. Kramer. Jackson: University Press of Mississippi, 1985. This indispensable volume collects all the most important interviews with Percy, including one (with the editors) previously unpublished. The volume is especially important for biographical background, influences, discussion of writing habits, and the author's comments on individual works through *Lost in the Cosmos*.
Quinlan, Kieran. *Walker Percy: The Last Catholic Novelist.* Baton Rouge: Louisiana State University Press, 1996. Chapters on Percy as novelist and philosopher, exis-

tentialist, explorer of modern science. Recommended for the advanced student who has already read Desmond. Includes notes and bibliography.

Tharpe, Jac. *Walker Percy.* Boston: Twayne, 1983. Reading Percy as a Roman Catholic novelist concerned chiefly with eschatological matters, Tharpe divides his study into ten chapters: "Biography, Background, and Influences," "Theory of Art," "Christendom," "Techniques," one chapter on each of the five novels through *The Second Coming*, and conclusion. The annotated secondary bibliography is especially good.

_____, ed. *Walker Percy: Art and Ethics.* Jackson: University Press of Mississippi, 1980. Ten essays by diverse hands, plus a bibliography. The essays focus on settings, existential sources, Martin Heidegger, Percy's theory of language, the semiotician Charles Sanders Peirce, Percy's politics, and *Lancelot* (in terms of his essays, Roman Catholicism, medieval sources, and semiotics).

Katherine Snipes

LOVE MEDICINE

Author: Louise Erdrich (1955-   )
Type of plot: Interwoven tales
Time of plot: From 1934 to 1984
Locale: A North Dakota Indian reservation and nearby towns
First published: 1984

Principal characters:

NECTOR KASHPAW, the grandfather, a former tribal chairman

MARIE LAZARRE KASHPAW, once ambitious to be a nun, later Nector's wife

LULU LAMARTINE, a loving woman who has eight sons by Kashpaw, Nanapush, and other men

GERRY NANAPUSH, Lulu's son, a hero of the American Indian Movement

ALBERTINE JOHNSON, a member of the youngest generation, a nursing student

JUNE MORRISSEY KASHPAW, a troubled woman

LIPSHA MORRISSEY, June's unacknowledged son

The Novel

Love Medicine is a series of tales (many of them originally published independently) which explore the ties of blood, knowledge, love, and mystery that link three generations of Chippewa people. As independent stories told from the viewpoint of various members of the Kashpaw, Lamartine, and Nanapush families, the tales have many strengths. One is the use of language that subtly reflects each narrator. The images, phrasing, and vocabulary of the urbanized characters, such as Beverly Lamartine, differ from the language of those whose lives still center on the reservation; the expressions used by some people in the older generation (particularly Marie Lazarre) suggest translation from thoughts that come in another language. Even in the youngest generation, Albertine Johnson, who leaves the reservation to go to college, uses words quite differently from her cousin Lipsha, who stays behind.

Each story has a sharp focus, an interesting narrative line, and images that expose the event without intervening explanation. Furthermore, the novel created by weaving these tales together is stronger than any of its parts. The first story takes place in 1981, the second in 1934—and midway in the second story, the reader begins to understand that the young girl Marie Lazarre who tells about fighting devils in the convent is the same person as Grandma Kashpaw, who was fetched from the senior citizens' home in the first story. As one tale follows another in a sequence that skips back and forth through the years, one pleasure for readers is simply fitting together the jigsaw puzzle, teasing out the identities hidden in the various names that result from marriages, unwed parenthood, and children fostered by neighbors or relatives, and realizing, with sudden delight, that one is getting a second viewpoint on an incident already known from an earlier story.

The individual stories are fragmentary; the book does not attempt a complete history of the families. Most stories focus on a significant crisis, though some include background narration. In the first, June Kashpaw is picked up by an oil worker in a boomtown and then dies in the snow walking back toward the reservation; the subsequent sections of that story reveal (indirectly) the complicated reactions of her various kin. Several stories show, in bits, the triangular relationship between Marie Lazarre, Lulu Lamartine, and Nector Kashpaw, which began in 1934 and is not resolved until forty-eight years later, after Nector's death. Other stories focus on Lulu's sons, suggesting the damages wrought by conventions of manliness in both Indian and white society. The essence of the book, however, grows from the relationship between stories and from the reader's ability to derive meaning from the reappearance of central thematic material.

The Characters

The physical tie between the characters is a piece of land originally allotted to Nector Kashpaw's mother, Rushes Bear. Most of her children were assigned to parcels in Montana, but she managed to get a piece of North Dakota wheatland and live on it with her young twins, Nector and Eli. Nector went to boarding school, learned white reading and writing, and grew up to be Tribal Chair and a man of importance; Eli, hidden by his mother in a root cellar, lived in the woods and kept some of the old skills. These two men, who became adults in the 1930's, represent the oldest generation in the novel; the women with whom their lives are entangled include Marie Lazarre and Lulu Lamartine. Marie went into a convent intending to become a saint; after marrying Nector, she compulsively takes in unwanted children. Lulu, with what seems equal compulsion, makes her own babies—eight boys, each by a different father, who grow up supporting, fighting, and caring for one another. Both Marie and Lulu know how to use power; Marie pushes Nector into becoming Tribal Chair, and Lulu, in a truly wonderful scene, forces the council not to sell her land by threatening to reveal publicly—right then in the meeting—who fathered each of her children. Both remain vivid personalities in their old age, strong and salty women using very different tactics to win what they desire.

The members of the middle generation are not quite so compelling; perhaps they are seen less clearly (none is actually a narrator for any extended story) or perhaps they are the generation that suffers most from the conflict between reservation ways and the modern world. June Morrissey Kashpaw dies in the first story; her discarded husband, Gordon Kashpaw, is the protagonist (though not the narrator) of the story "Crown of Thorns," which is a careful, vivid, underplayed, and totally convincing portrait of delirium tremens. Lulu Lamartine's son Gerry Nanapush spends half his adult life in prison after a three-year sentence for assault (he keeps escaping and being recaptured and doing additional time for escaping) before he makes the mistake of hiding out on the Pine Ridge Reservation, where he inevitably kills a state trooper.

Albertine Johnson and Lipsha Morrissey, members of the youngest generation, are to a certain extent consciously searching for their roots and for a way to understand their ties to the past. Most of their generation has disappeared to Minneapolis or Chicago or somewhere even further beyond the pull of the house and land that form the gravitational center of the Kashpaw constellation. Both Lipsha and Albertine are still in the process of becoming. Albertine, in particular, can change quite dramatically from one story to the next, but despite her relatively small share of Chippewa genes and her sustained drive for education—she is studying medicine by the end of the book—she knows her own need for the bonds of blood and tradition. She tries to talk to her grandfather about tribal politics and how he got things done in the old days. Lipsha, who seems virtually impervious to any kind of teaching (he manages to mangle and misunderstand both the traditional skills he learns from Eli Kashpaw and the education he suffers in white schools) is a wonderfully naive narrator in the Huck Finn tradition. At the book's end, however, he turns to home instead of lighting out for an individual destiny.

Themes and Meanings

In *Love Medicine*, Louise Erdrich opens up a new territory of contemporary Native American life and demonstrates a compassionate yet uncompromising attitude toward its people. She also crafts a piece of fiction whose technique amplifies its meaning. In doing the work to trace out relationships, keep track of the characters, and understand how they are tied together, the reader becomes a part of the linking and weaving that is the novel's theme. The pleasure of solving puzzles is secondary. What really matters are the bonds of love and mystery and anger, the desires and strengths and weaknesses that keep these people together, even though some are reservation-bound, others thoroughly urbanized, and a few have hardly any Chippewa blood.

Because the stories are presented through their narrators, with no outside viewpoint to provide explanations, the evocation of Native American life is clean and subtle, without pandering to the picturesque or the sentimental. Furthermore, the book's structure is used to alter the reader's consciousness from within. For example, although June Morrissey Kashpaw dies in the first tale, her character is one of the threads that provides links among the people and the stories—various characters talk about her; there are questions about her own parentage and about the husband she left and the baby she never acknowledged; Gordon takes to drink after her death; Albertine's mother and aunt tell their version of an incident from June's childhood. In other words, Erdrich, using only the literary conventions of a white cultural tradition, thoroughly and convincingly demonstrates that a person who is dead can remain an important presence for the living. From that point it is only half a step to the other stories, the ones in which a dead person's spirit actually appears.

The book's characters are nominally Catholic, but their Catholicism grows from mission schooling, which has merely damaged their traditional religion without really replacing it. Lipsha Morrissey, in the story from which the collection takes its title, suddenly thinks that he understands that Grandpa Kashpaw always shouts in church because God will not hear him otherwise. In a confused recollection drawn from his own reading of the Bible, Lipsha reasons that God has been growing progressively deaf since Old Testament times: He used to pay attention and perform miracles or strike down wrongdoers, but He has not done so in recent years. The Chippewa gods, Lipsha thinks, would still do favors if one knew the right way to ask—but the problem is that the right ways of asking were lost to the Chippewa once the Catholics gained ground.

Thus, although traditional ways are not glamorized, there is a sense of loss as they diminish. The family pattern that gives a woman a good deal of choice about who will father her children and how long her liaison with any particular man will last has a joyous (if semicomic) treatment in the case of Lulu Lamartine. In the next generation, however, June Morrissey seems more of a slut than an Earth Mother. The army, which in traditional sentiment and in the eyes of reservation boys is a heroic experience that brings the Indian into his own, has a devastating effect on the Vietnam generation. Significantly, the American Indian Movement hero Gerry Nanapush gives Lipsha Morrissey the gift of a blood tie that will free him from his decision to join the military.

The Chippewa viewpoint here, as elsewhere, sees many disadvantages to white ways; the Chippewa also (like humans almost everywhere) crave the material goods that seem to rain on hardworking white Americans. The only character who really romanticizes the Indian past is Lynette Kashpaw, the wholly white wife of one of the younger men. After several generations of interracial marriage and sexual encounters, blood in the strictest sense is not really important. To be Indian is, to a certain extent, a state of mind. The urbanized Cree Beverly Lamartine had parents who called themselves French or Black Irish and considered those who thought of themselves as Indians quite backward. Albertine, however, although quite light-skinned and less than half Chippewa, always thinks of herself as Indian. The meaning of identity, the influence of past on present, and the sense of loss and confusion in people caught between a half-remembered tradition and an outsider role in the modern world are the book's primary themes.

Critical Context

Love Medicine, a truly impressive first novel, received both the National Book Critics Circle Award and the *Los Angeles Times* Book Award for Fiction. Louise Erdrich, a member of the Turtle Mountain band of Chippewa, was one of the first women students admitted to Dartmouth, in 1972, and had previously published a collection of poetry. Published at a moment when interest in ethnic and regional literature was high, *Love Medicine* merged an authentic Native American voice with an accessible modern literary form.

Bibliography
Downes, Margaret J. "Narrativity, Myth, and Metaphor: Louise Erdrich and Raymond Carver Talk About Love." *MELUS* 21 (Summer, 1996): 49-61. Compares the

ways that Erdrich and Carver use the similarly structured experiences of love, narrative, and myth in their works. Concludes that stories about love are more "satisfactory" in *Love Medicine* than in Carver's work, and presents evidence as to why love works in one set of stories and not another.

McKinney, Karen J. "False Miracles and Failed Vision in Louise Erdrich's *Love Medicine*." *Critique* 40 (Winter, 1999): 152-160. McKinney focuses on the conflict between the Catholic dogma of the miracle and the native belief in the personal vision. She examines the early Chippewa encounters with Catholic missionaries and Lipsha's struggle to come to terms with two different belief systems.

Tanrisal, Meldan. "Mother and Child Relationships in the Novels of Louise Erdrich." *American Studies International* 35 (October, 1997): 67-79. Explores the role women have played in the continuity of tribal tradition through childbearing and the transmission of cultural values. Focuses on the mother as not only the biological parent, but the agent of survival for the whole tribe.

Zeck, Jeanne-Marie. "Erdrich's *Love Medicine*." *Explicator* 54 (Fall, 1995): 58-60. Zeck presents an analysis of the chapter "The Beads" in Erdrich's novel. She focuses on the sexual imagery, the relationship between Eli and Marie, and the use of symbolism.

Sally Mitchell

LUCY

Author: Jamaica Kincaid (Elaine Potter Richardson, 1949-   )
Type of plot: Autobiographical
Time of plot: The 1980's
Locale: New York City and the Great Lakes
First published: 1990

> *Principal characters:*
>> LUCY, the novel's narrator, who has come to New York from Antigua
>> MARIAH, Lucy's well-meaning but insensitive white employer
>> LEWIS, Mariah's husband, who falls in love with Mariah's best friend Dinah
>> DINAH, Mariah's best friend, an insensitive woman to whom Lucy is "the girl"
>> HUGH, Dinah's brother, who briefly becomes Lucy's lover
>> PEGGY, Lucy's "bad" friend, who introduces her to the darker side of city life

The Novel

A roughly autobiographical novel, *Lucy* deals with the experiences of a young Antiguan woman who, like Jamaica Kincaid herself, comes to New York City to work as a nanny in an effort to escape her repressive family and the narrow island life in which she has grown up. Her experiences in the city disillusion her, but while she copes with her disillusionment, she must come to terms with her family back in Antigua.

The episodic action of the five chapters of *Lucy* is narrated by Lucy herself, beginning with her first morning on her new job in New York. Even when the family was driving her home from the airport and pointing out famous sights to her, Lucy recalls, her feelings were a sort of sadness. What she discovers is the difference between her romantic expectations and the gritty reality of the city. The difference is made even more powerful by her memory of warm, sunny Antigua, a place she had never expected to miss, for when she was at home she felt in constant conflict with her family. Now, however, she identifies this surprising sadness as homesickness for foods of home such as green figs and pink mullet, for a cousin, even for a favorite nightgown from her childhood.

The family she works for is kind to her, and Lucy admires their blonde good looks and happy informality. They recognize Lucy's unhappiness, however, and Lewis, the husband, begins to call her "Visitor." One night, Lucy tells the family a dream full of sexual images she dreamed about Lewis. Mariah and Lewis are obviously uncomfortable, but to Lucy, the dream simply indicates that she has made Mariah and Lewis important people in her life.

In early March, Mariah, knowing how Lucy longs for warm weather, describes the beauty of daffodils to her. The description makes Lucy remember how in school she had had to recite a poem about daffodils (evidently William Wordsworth's famous "I

Wandered Lonely as a Cloud"). She recited it perfectly, but underneath she was angry about the task and the poem, which to her represented Great Britain's colonization of Antigua. Her anger emphasizes the gulf between Lucy and Mariah.

While Mariah plans a trip to her family home on the Great Lakes, Lucy is thinking about her own family. Her mother's letters are filled with threats and warnings of the city's dangers. This makes Lucy remember her mother's disreputable friend Sylvie, a woman who had a scar on her cheek from a human bite and who had spent time in jail, a powerful contrast to Mariah's inoffensive beauty. At the chapter's end, the family has arrived at the family summer home at the Great Lakes. Lucy is unimpressed and is angered by Mariah's claim that she is a good fisherwoman because she has Indian blood. To Lucy, the boast is the sort that only a victor can make, and she asks, "How do you get to be the sort of victor who can claim to be the vanquished also?" Mariah, however, does not understand Lucy's anger.

At about this time, Mariah's best friend, Dinah, arrives at the lakes. Lucy dislikes Dinah, who clearly sees Lucy as only a servant. Lucy also sees that Dinah is a vain woman who is envious of Mariah's possessions, even of her family.

Lucy is rather isolated while the family is at the lakes; she misses her disreputable friend Peggy, a young woman whose gaudy clothes, heavy smoking, and rebellious behavior have made Mariah forbid Lucy to bring her around the children. Loneliness makes Lucy interested in Dinah's brother Hugh, an attractive and worldly man who sees Lucy as an individual and who soon becomes her lover.

While at the lakes, Mariah decides to write a children's book about the environment. Lucy is rather amused at Mariah's naïve inability to see any relationship between the threatened environment and her own high standard of living. At about this time, too, Lucy recognizes that Lewis has begun a love affair with Dinah.

Back in New York again, Lucy enters a period of change. She stops her nurse's training. She takes a new lover, Paul; ironically, as she and Peggy grow apart, they begin to plan to find an apartment to share. Mariah asks Lewis to leave the household. Most important, Lucy receives a letter marked "urgent" from her mother. She ignores it as she has her mother's previous letters, until at last a cousin comes to her in person to tell her that her father has died, leaving her mother destitute.

Angry with her mother for marrying an unfaithful man who cannot manage money, Lucy nevertheless sends her some of the money she has saved toward the apartment. Shortly after that, she quits her job with Mariah, takes work as a photographer's assistant, and moves in with Peggy. At the novel's end, Lucy seems to have severed almost all of her emotional ties to others; in the last scene, she writes her name in a new journal and records her longing to love someone, a statement that makes her feel overcome with shame.

The Characters

Lucy is the narrator and central character of the novel. Her voice and her sensibilities lead the reader through the book's rambling episodes. The contradictions in Lucy's character are the contradictions that adolescence seems to create. On one hand, Lucy is a keen and sometimes satiric observer of her new world. She laughs at American excesses and pities American provincialism. She also has insight into others' motivations. She suspects the affair between Dinah and Lewis long before Mariah knows about it, and she understands her mother's advice about siding with women rather than men to mean that she should never get involved with another woman's husband. In many ways, Lucy understands herself. She knows that she will not be sorry to part with Hugh; she knows that she cannot tell Peggy about her artistic interest in photography. What she does not understand completely is her relationship with her mother. She does not see that although she may refuse to read her mother's letters, may refuse all contact with her, she will always be her mother's daughter, just as her mother predicted.

Mariah functions as the means by which Lucy is introduced to American life and ideas. In that way, like Peggy, she serves as a foil to Lucy. Wealthy, beautiful, naïve about the world outside her own sphere, she is the object both of Lucy's admiration and of her scorn.

Dinah is scarcely developed as a character in the novel. She exists just fully enough to represent the sort of bigotry and ignorance that Lucy despises. She thinks of Lucy as "the girl who takes care of the children" and doesn't even know where she came from, referring to Antigua as "the islands." That is enough to earn Lucy's contempt, but Dinah also betrays her friend, an unforgivable act to Lucy.

Peggy, Lucy's dark self, is also a foil to her. Peggy's flashy clothes, her sexy language, and her use of marijuana become means by which Lucy acts out her rebellion against her past, even while she sees through Peggy's shallowness. Lucy knows herself well enough to recognize that their friendship is based on mutual convenience rather than any real affection.

Lucy's two lovers, Hugh and Paul, both exist almost as stick figures in the novel. Neither has really engaged Lucy's deeper emotions; both mainly serve her sexual appetites. The casualness with which they are introduced and dismissed suggests how little importance they carry for Lucy.

The episodic, looping organization of the novel's slender action and its heavy use of flashback may remind readers that this work really is a portrayal of Lucy's character. No other character is developed with the depth and attention to detail that Lucy is given.

Themes and Meanings

The central theme of *Lucy* concerns Lucy's coming-of-age in a new land. That process forces her to define her relationship with Mariah, her mother, and her homeland, while at the same time she must learn to recognize her self. In some ways, Lucy seems always to have had a clear understanding of who she is and what she wants, but her anger at her mother dramatizes her real confusion.

From soon after Lucy's arrival in New York, it becomes clear that she was very angry when she left her homeland and family. She says that she had never expected to miss them and that they had never shown regard for her feelings. She ridicules the fears of New York that her mother expressed in the few letters that Lucy opened, just as she ridicules the paltry news of island life that her mother is able to report. In the course of the novel, readers also see Lucy's anger at her father for his endless infidelities to her mother, as well as her anger with her mother for enduring the succession of mistresses and illegitimate children his love affairs have produced. All that anger boils over when, after months of refusing to open her mother's letters, Lucy learns of her father's death. She is angry at her father for being the sort of man he is and at her mother for putting up with him, for allowing herself to end up widowed and penniless. Although Lucy sends her mother money, she accompanies it with a harsh letter. Later, she sends a kinder one, but she also tells her mother the wrong address for her new apartment.

The cousin who came to tell Lucy about her father's death says that Lucy looks and acts like her mother. Lucy is surprised, and she rejects that idea, saying that they are not at all alike, just as she rejects Mariah's urging her to reconcile with her mother. Nevertheless, it is obvious that the two probably are alike. In fact, much of Lucy's information about the world and about how to get along with people originates with her mother, as Lucy herself admits. Moreover, whatever pain keeps Lucy from reaching out to her mother also affects Lucy. Indeed, she acknowledges that the anger and sadness she feels before she leaves Mariah's house is a sort of mourning for the end of the only true love affair—that is, the love she has had for her mother—she will ever know.

This ambivalence accounts for Lucy's relationships with Mariah and Peggy. Lucy says several times that Mariah reminds her of her mother. Their conversations and Mariah's concern for Lucy at the novel's end recall a sort of idyllic mother-daughter bond, the sort of relationship Lucy wishes that she and her true mother had shared. At the same time, Lucy finds her "bad self," the self neither her mother nor Mariah could approve of, in her friendship with Peggy. Peggy's casual acceptance of marijuana and sex and her dislike for intellectual activities allow Lucy to indulge her own rebellion against the Lucy her mother intended to create.

Antigua is Lucy's other parent and the object of her other rebellion. In the United States, she is forced to face what "Third World" means, and she is alternately defensive about her homeland and angry about the debilitating effects of British colonial rule in Antigua.

Critical Context

Lucy is an autobiographical novel, loosely representing the events of Jamaica Kincaid's life during her first year in the United States: Like Lucy, she worked as an au pair for a wealthy family that split up; like Lucy, she started school and quit; and like Lucy, she developed an interest in photography. At the end of *Lucy* there are slender hints that Lucy is about to discover an interest in writing, just as Kincaid herself did.

Kincaid's first novel, *Annie John* (1985), was also autobiographical, telling the story of a young girl growing up in Antigua. At the end of that novel, Annie John, having suffered a serious break with her mother, is leaving home, evidently forever. She is going to England, where she will go into nurse's training. In that respect, *Lucy* seems to take up where *Annie John* left off. The two works also share themes concerning mother-daughter relationships, sexual awakenings, and the debilitating effects of British colonial rule on the former colony. The books also share the same narrative style; both are told in the first person by a narrator who is more interested in developing a series of pictures and anecdotes to create an atmosphere than in telling a conventional linear story.

Kincaid's essay about Antigua, *A Small Place*, was published in 1988. It is reflective of the political anger that forms a theme of *Lucy*. In *A Small Place*, Kincaid details the ruinous effects of British rule on Antigua, attributing to colonialism a legacy of political corruption, racism, poverty, and ignorance. That same indictment forms a thematic element of *Lucy*. Just as Lucy must recognize herself as inevitable inheritor of some of her mother's being, so she is also heir to the island that gave her birth, to its beauty as well as to its pain.

Bibliography
Als, Hilton. "Don't Worry, Be Happy." *The Nation* 252 (February 18, 1991): 207-209. Als is particularly interested in *Lucy* in reference to Kincaid's position as a black writer from a Third World country. He understands Lucy as a budding artist, and he understands her at the end of the novel to be on the verge of interpreting the Antiguan people she loves. He gives some discussion to *A Small Place*.
Chick, Nancy. "The Broken Clock: Time, Identity, and Autobiography in Jamaica Kincaid's *Lucy*." *CLA Journal* 40 (September, 1996): 90-103. Chick explores the relationship between Lucy's faulty sense of time and her impaired sense of identity, symbolized by a broken clock. Because Lucy has a linear sense of time, she believes that by solely focusing on the future she can create a self that is independent of her past.
Emery, Mary Lou. "Refiguring the Postcolonial Imagination: Tropes of Visuality in Writing by Rhys, Kincaid, and Cliff." *Tulsa Studies in Women's Literature* 16 (Fall, 1997): 259-280. The relationship between European and postcolonial literature employing vision, image-making, and the imagination are examined through Jean Rhys's *After Leaving Mr. MacKenzie*, Jamaica Kincaid's novel *Lucy*, and Michelle Cliff's *No Telephone to Heaven*.
Ferguson, Moira. "Lucy and the Mark of the Colonizer." *Modern Fiction Studies* 39 (Summer, 1993): 237-259. Ferguson asserts that Kincaid's novel focuses on the psychological implications of colonization of Antigua by Great Britain, which result in a false understanding of oneself and others. Like Kincaid's earlier works *Annie John* and *A Small Place*, *Lucy* deconstructs the ruling culture.
Jaggi, Maya. "A Struggle for Independence." *The Times Literary Supplement* (April 26, 1991): 20. Jaggi relates *Lucy* to Kincaid's short-story collection *At the Bottom of the River* (1983) in its style and themes. Jaggi concentrates on analyzing Lucy's relationship with her mother and says that the novel's lack of linear narration weakens it.

Mahlis, Kristen. "Gender and Exile: Jamaica Kincaid's *Lucy.*" *Modern Fiction Studies* 44 (Spring, 1998): 164-183. Dicusses the pain experienced by the main character in *Lucy* who loses her cultural identity when she emigrates from Antigua to the United States. Mahlis argues that the protagonist's alienation from her language is a reflection of her break from her bond with her mother. She turns away from her mother and native country's restrictive views on women's place but cannot fully achieve her own liberation.

Ozkowicz, Edyta. "Jamaica Kincaid's *Lucy*: Cultural 'Translation' as a Case of Creative Exploration of the Past." *MELUS* 21 (Fall, 1996): 143-157. Ozkowicz demonstrates that Kincaid's novel examines the protagonist's struggle with independence and identity as well as her need to transcend the post colonial past and status as a female and a minority. As Lucy gains more independence and makes a life for herself in the United States, she is able to come to terms with both her past and her relationship with her mother.

Ann D. Garbett

LUCY GAYHEART

Author: Willa Cather (1873-1947)
Type of plot: Psychological realism
Time of plot: Christmas, 1901, to Christmas, 1902, and 1927
Locale: Haverford, Nebraska, and Chicago, Illinois
First published: 1935

Principal characters:

>LUCY GAYHEART, the darling of Haverford, a music student in Chicago
>HARRY GORDON, the wealthy son of a Haverford banker and
>businessman who is in love with Lucy
>PAULINE GAYHEART, Lucy's older sister
>JACOB GAYHEART, a watchmaker and music teacher, Lucy's father
>CLEMENT SEBASTIAN, a concert singer
>PAUL AUERBACH, Lucy's music teacher in Chicago

The Novel

Lucy Gayheart is equally a study of the central character and of the effect that she has on others. The novel opens twenty-five years after Lucy's death, when her memory is still fondly cherished by the residents of her small hometown: "In Haverford on the Platte the townspeople still talk of Lucy Gayheart. They do not talk of her a great deal, to be sure; life goes on and we live in the present." This retrospective point of view provides the counterpoint to the dominant point of view in the novel, Lucy's. Most of the novel takes place during the year before Lucy's death, when she is in her early twenties and is just beginning to understand herself and to make choices about her future.

Lucy's hardest choices involve her potential career as a pianist. Encouraged by her father, a watchmaker and music teacher, to study music in Chicago, Lucy has learned to love the cultural opportunities that the city offers. After three years of study with Paul Auerbach, Lucy is not convinced that she has the talent or the stamina to become a concert pianist. Yet her confidence in her ability is increased when she is asked to become a temporary accompanist for Clement Sebastian, a concert singer with an international reputation. Lucy's sensitivity to mood and musical nuance makes her a talented accompanist, and Sebastian comes to appreciate not only her skill but also her enthusiastic outlook on life. Her enthusiasm enriches his life, which, although aesthetically full, is emotionally barren.

Soon after beginning to play for Sebastian, Lucy returns to Haverford for Christmas vacation. There she represses her new interests and enjoys her old friends and childhood activities, all the while aware that something is missing from her life. At the same time, she appears more interesting than ever to Harry Gordon, the most intelligent and the wealthiest young man in Haverford. Harry recognizes that he loves Lucy but is not certain that marrying her would be prudent, for Harry has been reared to value material advantages and expects a wife to advance his position in the world. Harry also assumes that Lucy is his for the asking; his egotism about her leads to his lifelong disappointment.

When Lucy returns to Chicago, she begins to fall in love with Sebastian, and he with her. Here is a love that asks for nothing; it is enough to be with Sebastian and to see the world through his eyes for a while. Sebastian is equally undemanding, realizing that Lucy is in love, not merely with him, but with a way of perceiving life. Unfortunately, it is at this stage that Harry Gordon comes to Chicago to ask Lucy to marry him. Her response, implying that she and Sebastian are lovers, drives him back to Nebraska, where he marries a wealthy daughter of society to spite Lucy. Lucy, on the other hand, shortly experiences despair over Sebastian's accidental drowning. On her return to Haverford to overcome her depression, she is shocked to discover that Harry will not speak to her, and she tries, unsuccessfully, to break down his reserve. In a final misunderstanding, Harry refuses a ride to Lucy, who is exhausted from skating too long; in anger, Lucy skates onto thin ice and is drowned in the Platte River. This occurs soon after her realization that she wants to go back to Chicago to continue her studies.

The last section of the novel occurs twenty-five years later, at the time that the novel opens. Lucy is remembered by many with love, especially at her father's funeral, which has occurred recently. No one remembers as vividly as Harry Gordon, who has become the wealthiest member of Haverford society. Knowing that he has made a loveless marriage, understanding that he is responsible for Lucy's death, Harry has nevertheless learned how to live with the consequences of his youthful pride. His sense of guilt has lessened while he has learned to do things for others: He works in an ambulance unit in France during World War I; he spends hours playing chess with Mr. Gayheart, who has also lost his other daughter, Pauline; he is more lenient with borrowers who owe money at his bank. Most important, he learns to think of Lucy without anger, but with love and appreciation for her enthusiasm and her zest for life. Aware that he lacks the ability to react spontaneously to small joys, Harry stops resenting Lucy's ability to do so and understands that her life has given his life meaning even after her death.

The Characters

In Lucy, Cather has captured the best of what it means to be young, talented, and discovering the world. The impression of quickness that Lucy leaves on her observers' minds—the idea that she is poised for flight—is a symbol of Lucy's intellect. She is learning to appreciate many of the artistic and natural wonders of her world; her joy in music, in winter, and in the city is too great not to be conveyed to those around her. Caught in the throes of discovery, Lucy is also something of an egotist, impatient with those who are not as quick as she is, angry when she has to defend her impetuosity. Frequently, she responds impulsively, learning later that her haste is self-destructive.

A foil to Lucy's youth is Pauline, Lucy's older sister. Pauline has managed her father's home since her mother's death and has reared Lucy. Believing that she is the only responsible figure in an unappreciative family, Pauline resents Lucy's beauty and spontaneity. Always looking for ways to supplement her father's meager income, Pauline thinks that Lucy's music lessons in Chicago are an extravagance, and though she does not try to stop them, she accuses Lucy of lacking appreciation for the people who do the most for her. Further, she thinks that Lucy is not doing enough to encourage Harry Gordon. In a rich husband, Pauline sees Lucy's best hope of repaying what she owes to the family. Lucy, who gives piano lessons and earns a good salary accompanying Sebastian, resents Pauline's interference and interprets Pauline's attempts to understand her as efforts at martyrdom.

The two important male characters in the novel could hardly be more different. Harry Gordon maintains a hardheaded, Midwestern attitude about commerce; Clement Sebastian exudes a worldly attitude about art. Harry is an important man only in a small town; Sebastian claims an international reputation. Harry is young and arrogant; Sebastian is middle-aged and is modest about his accomplishments. Lucy, loving them both, is nevertheless exasperated with Harry and patient with Sebastian. Deciding that she has much to learn from Sebastian makes her more impatient than ever with Harry's inability to react quickly and to articulate his feelings.

Sebastian is appealing to Lucy, not only because he is a fine singer who encourages her musical talent, but also because he seems lonely and in need of someone. Ordinarily, he is accompanied by an unattractive, possessive, and sarcastic young man who was his wife's protégé. When Lucy meets Sebastian, he seems tired of Madame Sebastian's incessant demands for money and her pretenses to aesthetic understanding. Lucy's genuine responses to music and her quiet appreciation of the signs of wealth that surround Sebastian win Sebastian's approval, and then his love. He is grateful for Lucy's love and chooses not to take advantage of it; indeed, he tries instead to enrich her life without making her feel obligated.

In contrast, Harry feels that Lucy ought to be grateful for his love and his offer of marriage. Finding her stimulating because she is different, Harry believes that marrying Lucy will provide him with a constant reminder that there is more to life than acquisition. Yet Lucy feels that Harry views her only as another acquisition, and she despairs of being able to liberate his spirit enough for him to appreciate art and culture. Harry's egotism is mitigated by his intelligence and his awareness that art is important, even though he lacks emotional responses to it. Lucy finds in him a good friend, one more sympathetic to her life than anyone else in Haverford, but she does not want to marry him. Harry is stubborn, but reflective. By the end of the novel, he forgives himself and Lucy for her death, understanding that this event early in his life has led to a fuller humanity.

Themes and Meanings

The structure of the novel reinforces one of its major themes, that tragedy is absorbed into the less dramatic flow of one's life, that while it may signal a turning point, it does not necessarily result in major changes. The beginning and the closing sections of the novel are about memories of Lucy; her death in a sense provides the climax of the middle sections about her love for Sebastian. Yet Lucy has also experienced her tragedy—Sebastian's death—and overcome her depression by wondering, "What if Life itself were . . . like a lover waiting for her in distant cities . . . drawing her, enticing her, weaving a spell over her." Lucy is drowned shortly after the moment of her recovery, but Harry matures to a philosophic understanding of tragedy. His final act in the novel is to preserve a piece of sidewalk that Lucy had run through before the concrete was dry; he cherishes this memorial, recognizing that he has lost Lucy forever but has also been profoundly influenced by her.

Secondary themes explored through the characters are the egotism of youth and the tremendous power of art. Cather develops these themes in other novels as well; here, the self-destructive quality of both Lucy's and Harry's egotism is clear. Their assumptions about each other keep them apart and cause both to behave dishonestly: Lucy lies about her relationship with Sebastian, implying that it is sexual when it is not, and Harry refuses to extend more than impersonal courtesy to Lucy at a time when he realizes that he loves her more than ever. Sebastian's profession makes him seductive because of his association with all that Lucy is learning to appreciate. Even after his death, it is Lucy's sensitivity to music that helps her through her depression. Seeing an old singer perform wonderfully with a second-rate opera company triggers her reaffirmation that life itself is the lover.

Critical Context

Lucy Gayheart was one of Willa Cather's last four books, all of which have been criticized as less interesting than her earlier work. It has been suggested that the structure is contrived and the tone sentimental. Perhaps the most accurate criticism of the novel is that the characters are not fully developed. Strongly identified with commerce, Harry Gordon never manifests the keen intellect with which he is credited; his successes at the bank are not described and seem easy achievements. Clement Sebastian, as the representative of the aesthetic world, is emotionally aloof; his motivations are unclear, and even his love for Lucy seems an artistic rendition of emotion, rather than a humanizing action. Much of this may be attributed to the fact that Cather was trying to characterize the sense of life as much as any individual; nevertheless, this theme is developed at the expense of complexity of character and of structure.

Bibliography

Bloom, Edward A., and Lillian D. Bloom. *Willa Cather's Gift of Sympathy*. Carbondale: Southern Illinois University Press, 1962. Considered a classic on criticism of Cather's works. The Blooms look at this author's gift of sympathy and skillfully relate it to her thematic interests and technical proficiency. Deals with not only Cather's fiction but also her poetry and essays, which in themselves form an important commentary on her ideas.

Bloom, Harold, ed. *Modern Critical Views: Willa Cather*. New York: Chelsea House, 1985. Bloom says of this volume that it gathers "the best literary criticism on Cather over the last half-century." The criticism selected emphasizes Cather's novels *Sapphira and the Slave Girl, My Ántonia, Death Comes for the Archbishop*, and *A Lost Lady*. The volume concludes with a study by Marilyn Arnold on what are considered Cather's two finest short stories, "A Wagner Matinee" and "Paul's Case." Contains a chronology and a bibliography. A must for serious Cather scholars.

Fryer, Judith. *Felicitous Space: The Imaginative Structures of Edith Wharton and Willa Cather.* Chapel Hill: University of North Carolina Press, 1986. Although there are many full-length studies on Cather's writing, this volume is particularly noteworthy for its examination of Cather using current feminist thinking. Fryer explores Cather's fiction in terms of the "interconnectedness between space and the female imagination" and cites her as a transformer of social and cultural structures. A thorough and interesting study, recommended for its contribution to women's studies in literature. Includes extensive notes.

Gerber, Philip. *Willa Cather: Revised Edition.* New York: Twayne, 1995. Incorporates discussion of new materials and criticism that have appeared since the 1975 edition. Rather than calling Cather a "disconnected" writer, as have some critics, Gerber takes the view in this study that there is unity in her writing. Gerber demonstrates the development of her artistry from one novel to the next. Includes a chronology and a selected bibliography.

Meyering, Sheryl. *A Reader's Guide to the Short Stories of Willa Cather.* New York: G. K. Hall, 1994. Chapters on each short story, discussing publication history, the circumstances of composition, biographical details, significant literary and cultural sources, connections to Cather's novels, and an overview of how each story has been interpreted.

Murphy, John. *Critical Essays on Willa Cather.* Boston: G. K. Hall, 1984. A compilation of criticism on Cather's work, including general essays from a variety of contributors as well as reviews and literary criticism of specific titles. The introduction emphasizes her creativity, and the volume concludes with reviews of her last four books. Most useful for its breadth of criticism on Cather. Contains a selected bibliography.

Shaw, Patrick W. *Willa Cather and the Art of Conflict: Re-visioning Her Creative Imagination.* Troy, N.Y.: Whitston, 1992. Separate chapters on all of Cather's major novels. Reexamines Cather's fiction in terms of her conflicts over her lesbian sexuality. The introduction provides a helpful overview of Cather criticism on the topic.

Gweneth A. Dunleavy

THE MacGUFFIN

Author: Stanley Elkin (1930-1995)
Type of plot: Psychological realism
Time of plot: The 1990's
Locale: An unnamed major American city in the Midwest
First published: 1991

> *Principal characters:*
>> BOBBO DRUFF, a fifty-eight-year-old neurotic who serves as
>> commissioner of streets in a large city in the Midwest
>> THE MACGUFFIN, Druff's second self—the devil within
>> ROSE HELEN DRUFF, his sixty-year-old wife
>> MICHAEL DRUFF, their thirty-year-old son
>> MARGARET GLORIO, a buyer of fashionable men's clothing who
>> becomes Druff's mistress
>> DICK and DOUG, Druff's chauffeurs
>> SU'AD AL NAJAF, an illegal Lebanese immigrant who is ostensibly a rug
>> buyer

The Novel

Set in a large unnamed American city in the Midwest that seems much like St. Louis, *The MacGuffin* is the story of some two days in the life of Bobbo Druff, commissioner of streets. The novel successfully functions on many levels; it exhibits a multifaceted complexity in that it is the story of a family, a love intrigue of the husband with mistress, a murder mystery, a tale of smuggling, and a political statement. While being all of these, it is mostly about Bobbo Druff and "The MacGuffin," his psychological other and controlling self.

The MacGuffin has no chapter or sectional divisions; Elkin unfolds the narrative entirely by relating the thoughts and actions of Bobbo Druff during a Friday and Saturday of some unspecified weekend in the early 1990's. Even so, the novel is structured around some six to eight episodic adventures, determined primarily by Druff's physical location. Great portions of the novel are internal monologues, many of which are between Druff and The MacGuffin; other internal monologues occur as well, and there are also interchanges in dialogue with other characters.

When the novel opens, readers learn almost immediately of the recent mysterious death of Su'ad al-Najaf, a young college student and an illegal immigrant from Lebanon who sold rugs and dated Druff's son, Michael. Su'ad had died some forty hours before the beginning of the present action, having been repeatedly run over by an automobile. Druff somehow understands that he is connected with the death, but he does not know how. It is not clear if Druff is merely neurotic and paranoid or correct in his suspicions. The reader has many reasons to believe Druff is not mentally balanced: He continues to get high on coca leaves throughout the novel, and his mind wanders hopelessly, revealing him to be unacceptably solipsistic and at least a borderline psychotic. Too, the highs from the coca leaves are mixed with the effects of numerous prescription medicines.

In the second main episode of the novel, Druff meets Margaret Glorio, a buyer of men's clothing for department stores who claims to be forty-four years old but later acknowledges that she is "fifty, more or less." Witty, worldly, and experienced, the two soon agree to a liaison that night. Druff, who is fifty-eight years old and has never been unfaithful in his thirty-six-year marriage to Rose Helen, quickly and guiltlessly goes to Margaret's apartment, where the whole affair is enacted humorously. Both characters banter in what becomes a satire on sex and adultery.

Druff returns home to wife and son early the next morning and sleeps until noon. Meanwhile, Elkin provides the only significant flashback of the story as he relates the courtship and marriage of Bobbo and Rose Helen, describing in great detail their college years in the 1950's. Again, the author satirizes courtship and sexual relations, but this time his target is youth. The narrative is replete with rather stock situations (jokes about fraternities and sororities, escapes from housemothers who would catch them in the act, intrigues at hotels and in rented rooms, and the like), but there is a fresh perspective. Somehow, these events have meaning, as they help to explain Druff's present character and to make credible his MacGuffin.

On Saturday morning at home, Druff awakens mistakenly thinking it is another workday, and he dresses and heads off to work. Soon after discovering his mistake, he meets up with Hamilton Edgar and three other Jews who invite him into a synagogue. They have a conversation that feeds Druff's paranoia and the realization that he is somehow connected with Su'ad's accidental death. From a political context as well as a racial one, Jews are satirized as being like all other Americans: selfish, materialistic, and given to vice. They enjoy their breakfast of ham and eggs; and in the study of the synagogue—so Druff and the reader will eventually learn—are Arab rugs (presumably, Islamic prayer rugs) smuggled into the country and knowingly purchased by these men at the synagogue. The reader should quickly realize that Elkin is not particularly attacking Jews here; rather, he is attacking Jews as mainstream Americans who have the same vices as others, especially Druff himself, whose graft and political corruption have been self-acknowledged from the beginning.

Later in the afternoon, Druff has a series of conversations with acquaintances he happens to meet, all of whom reveal information or somehow indicate that Druff himself is involved with Su'ad's death. He begins to feel that he is to be the victim of some conspiracy and that this will be the day of his own death.

Druff returns late that afternoon to Margaret Glorio's apartment, where all the furniture and surroundings have been changed overnight. They have another sexual encounter, again enacted with humor paired with hopelessness. Significant to the plot, Glorio's apartment, so Druff now sees, has several Oriental rugs lying about. Druff learns that his newly acquired mistress had been friends with Su'ad and knows his own son Michael.

Death itself does not escape satire either. Druff leaves Glorio's apartment to go to the wake of Marvin Macklin, a city official who has just died. Druff is not quite sure who Macklin is, but he shows up anyway to give condolences to the widow and family. To his surprise, other persons who have been feeding his paranoia throughout the day are also present, including Dick and Doug (his two chauffeurs), the three Jews from the synagogue, and the mayor of the city. American death rites are satirized with both bitterness and comedy as Elkin describes the activities of the wake.

The novel's last episode occurs when Druff returns home to wife and son and unravels the events of the day so as to determine the truth about Su'ad's death. With funds from the Jewish bankers whom Druff had met at the synagogue, Su'ad had been smuggling rugs to make money to finance terrorist operations for Arabs in the Middle East. Druff's own son had been her driver when she delivered the smuggled rugs. The Jewish bankers had had her killed when she was unable to pay off loans to them. Druff's son had been driving Su'ad in Druff's car, and he had let her out onto the street moments before she was intentionally run over. Moreover, stolen goods are even yet in Druff's car trunk. Having learned all of this, Druff simply goes to bed to sleep.

The Characters

Bobbo Druff, the narrator and main character of the story, is truly the only subject of this complex novel that has so many other threads and aspects. He represents the modern American, and his life embodies, for Elkin at least, life in America in the 1990's. He is materialistic and corrupt; he is neurotic, psychotic, and schizophrenic (and, importantly, justly so); he is intellectual, witty, and smart; he is hopelessly middle-class; he finds relief in life by incessantly getting high on coca leaves and taking at least four different prescription medicines; he is both humor and pathos—a strangely correct mixture.

The MacGuffin is never seriously defined in the novel, yet Druff himself describes him several times in different ways. The MacGuffin is the alter ego, the devil within, the id and the ego, the conscience gone over to the other side. He is a kind of generally harmless "Sam" telling "Son of Sam" what to do. Recognizably, though, The MacGuffin is not localized to Druff's character but is present in everyone. The MacGuffin and Druff have conversations, but The MacGuffin never directly tells Druff what to do.

Rose Helen Druff is Bobbo's wife of thirty-six years. Her most significant role in the novel is during the flashback to her courtship and affair with Druff when they were college students in the 1950's. Thus we see two Rose Helens: the gifted young college student, extremely intelligent but slightly deformed by a childhood disease, and the housewife she has become some forty years later whose main concern is to get batteries for her hearing aid. Elkin's point is to create a character suitable to provoke guilt in Druff himself, given his new mistress. This does not occur. Druff covers up his actions and lies about them, but there is no feeling of guilt or remorse.

Michael Druff satirizes procreation. Thirty years old and still living at home, he is consistently described as a hopeless adolescent, one who will never grow up no matter what and will be perpetually dependent upon his parents even after their deaths. Michael is the next generation of "Druffism": That is, he is Druff himself, who cannot make his way in the world because he lacks maturity and intelligence. Thus, Michael knowingly becomes the driver for a woman smuggling stolen goods, apparently oblivious to possible consequences.

Margaret Glorio's character permits Elkin to satirize yet another commonplace of American life: the liberated career woman who has made her way into the "man's world" by becoming "masculinized." She is Druff's equal in every way, perhaps more so. She is smarter than he and quicker with her tongue. Moreover, she is more successful in her profession and more secure in her personhood, identity, and activities. Nevertheless, she is given to all the vices of modern Americans; the fact that she controls and manipulates the system does not excuse the immorality of her behavior.

Dick and Doug, Druff's two chauffeurs, initially serve as Druff's confidants. As the story unfolds, however, it is clear that they are part of the political intrigue and satire. They are associates of those who know and suspect that somehow Druff is connected to Su'ad's murder—and they sell him out.

Su'ad al-Najaf, although a smuggler serving the Arab cause and terrorism in the Middle East, is yet another character who embodies the hopeless nature of politics in the 1990's. On the one hand, she publicly claims to favor the "final solution"; on the other, she does business with her enemies without reserve. Her existence, profession, and death reveal the complexities and hopeless entanglements of contemporary political problems, as well as of life itself.

Themes and Meanings

Stanley Elkin's main purpose is to reveal the hopeless and meaningless entanglements of life in the United States in the 1990's—for the thinking and thoughtless alike. There is no escape from problems, no solution to them, only an awareness of facts that add up to craziness (a matter blended with humor and bitterness) in a world in which borderline insanity is necessary for survival. Bobbo Druff is not, however, insane; he is victimized by society and politics and legalities—but yet entirely by self. Survival requires some control of the system in which one lives. For Druff and other characters, that system is corrupt, somehow defunct yet going on anyway.

Elkin reveals these themes through numerous metaphors. Most important of these is Druff's job as commissioner of streets: Life is a maze full of potholes, and nothing can be done about it. The maze will always be there, for all must travel the streets of life, which are replete with curves, stop signs, stoplights (which may or may not work), detours, traffic jams, and, most significant, inescapable potholes.

In coping with these streets of life, Druff creates, perhaps discovers, The MacGuffin—a metaphor for the lies that characters must tell themselves in order to excuse and justify their own behavior and to make some sense of the world around them. The MacGuffin, who exists only in Druff's mind, is nevertheless no less of a character.

Elkin's main point is not that life has no sense or values. Rather, the novel poses the question of what happens when one makes sense out of life. What happens then? Druff succeeds, with the help of his MacGuffin, in making sense of the events of Su'ad's murder, but he, like the reader, is left to discover if knowledge of actual events is enough to force order onto the world. Elkin is not clear about this point. On the one hand, numerous questions are left about all of the main events of the plot: What will happen to the stolen goods in Druff's trunk? Will Su'ad's murderers be exposed? Will Druff and Michael escape being implicated? On the other hand, Druff, having learned what he wants to know, simply goes peacefully to sleep, not so much because he is tired but because he has accomplished all that he can. He has learned answers to the questions of the day, but he has not found any solutions to them.

This novel is a modern-day night journey, a visit to the dark night of the soul. Perhaps there is no soul here other than that of The MacGuffin; Elkin certainly suggests as much, if not by explication then by derivation. Druff journeys into self in his inner monologues, in his internal dialogues with The MacGuffin, in his taking of a mistress, and, finally, in his pursuit of knowledge of the facts of Su'ad's murder. All of these are carried out for selfish and corrupt reasons. In the end, Elkin's use of psychological realism in such a way as to make the facts of Druff's character and actions match those of the nonpsychological world is not so much pointless as unexplained. All people are Druffs who harbor MacGuffins within.

Critical Context

The MacGuffin succeeds in making significant and correct statements about modern politics. The global situation is so involved that even such traditional enemies as the Arabs and Jews cannot disentangle themselves from the complexity of the various problems. They depend upon one another to have someone to hate, to have an enemy; just as certainly and more important, however, they depend upon one another to fund and sustain their own problems and hatreds.

Local politics, as exemplified by Druff, the mayor, other commissioners, and even the two chauffeurs, parallels the mess and havoc of larger problems. No one can be trusted in a world where friends serve the causes of enemies and, conversely, enemies serve the causes of friends—all knowingly, but never openly.

It is internal politics with which Elkin is doubtless most concerned. This is represented in Druff's family life with both his wife and son, and with his relationship with himself and The MacGuffin. The context of family politics finally makes it impossible for Druff to make sense out of the entanglements around him, even when he has full knowledge of all the facts. In *The MacGuffin*, Elkin's goal is to make a statement not merely about problems in the Middle East (he is actually little concerned about relations between Jews and Arabs) but rather about problems in self-definition facing all readers.

Bibliography

Edwards, Thomas R. "*The MacGuffin*." *The New Republic* 204 (May 20, 1991): 44-47. One of the best reviews available. Edwards finds Elkin's main character Druff to be a "cultural dinosaur" who is nevertheless successful as a comedian. The critic sees in the novel Elkin's attempt to define what it is to be an American in the 1990's.

Elkin, Stanley. "A Conversation with Stanley Elkin." Interview by David C. Dougherty. *Literary Review* 34 (Winter, 1991): 175-195. Elkin discusses the influence of Saul Bellow on his writing, the various inspirations for many of the characters in his novels, and his attitude toward certain critical responses to his work. He reveals his enthusiasm for *The MacGuffin*, which at the time of the interview was a work in progress.

Emerson, Ken. "The Indecorous, Rabelaisian, Convoluted Righteousness of Stanley Elkin." *The New York Times Magazine*, March 3, 1991, 40-43. Emerson playfully takes Elkin to task for the humor, irony, satire, and distancing between self and audience in Elkin's work. The critic appreciates these qualities of the writer while questioning the validity of some of Elkin's themes.

Koenig, Rhoda. "*The MacGuffin*." *New York* 24 (February 25, 1991): 113-114. This review, though brief, is particularly critical and revealing of the novel's main character. Koenig also draws attention to instances of the humor in the novel.

Moore, Lorrie. "*The MacGuffin*." *The New York Times Book Review*, March 10, 1991, 5. This early review of the novel draws attention to its main qualities. Lauds the work for its ability to provide humor about the contemporary American scene.

O'Donnel, Patrick. "Of Red Herrings and Loose Ends: Reading 'Politics' in Elkin's *The MacGuffin*." *Review of Contemporary Fiction* 15 (Summer, 1995): 92-100. O'Donnel discusses Elkin's framing of *The MacGuffin* as a narrative hybrid and shows how Elkin employs the detective novel schema in the plot. He also explores the significance of the comparisons Elkins makes between everyday life and global politics.

Carl Singleton

MACHO!

Author: Victor Villaseñor (1940-   )
Type of plot: Bildungsroman
Time of plot: The late 1960's
Locale: Mexico and California
First published: 1973

> *Principal characters:*
>> ROBERTO GARCIA, the eldest son of poor Tarascan (native Mexican) farmers, who leaves his village for work in the United States
>> JUAN AGUILAR, the leader of the village *norteños*, men who seasonally work in the United States
>> PEDRO, a *norteño* and sworn enemy of Roberto
>> ESPERANZA, Roberto's progressive and independent-minded sister
>> DON CARLOS VILLANUEVA, Roberto's employer, a successful Mexican farmer

The Novel

This fictional account of approximately a year in the life of a young man dramatizes the real plight of the migrant Mexican farmworker attempting to enter and work in the United States. *Macho!* is divided into three major parts, each labeled as a book and further subdivided into chapters. Books 1 and 3 are short, with the action set in the rural Mexican village of the principal characters; book 2 chronicles the odyssey of the protagonist, Roberto Garcia, into the violent underworld of the illegal migrant farmworker. Although the omniscient third-person narrator occasionally reveals thoughts of other characters, the narrative perspective is almost entirely Roberto's.

In addition to the main fictional narrative, each chapter begins with a brief quasihistorical preface, designed to inform and to persuade the reader. The first and longest of these prefaces describes the dramatic 1943 appearance of the volcano Paricutin one hundred miles from Roberto's village and the volcano's far-reaching effects. Through these prefaces, Villaseñor suggests that the natural threat of Paricutin, a blessing in disguise for Roberto's community, has been replaced by the less visible, more insidious threat of airborne industrial pollution. The threat of pollution lingers before being dismissed summarily, like dirt in the wind, at the story's end. Most of the novel's remaining prefaces indict American agribusiness interests for exploiting cheap Mexican migrant farm labor and chronicle César Chávez's challenge to the status quo during the tumultuous 1960's.

The novel itself begins well into Roberto's seventeenth year, during the planting season of his native Mexican village. Roberto's father has over the past year begun drinking heavily, leaving Roberto, as the eldest child, to support his mother and seven younger siblings. Although Roberto is humiliated by his father's weakness, he can do nothing to change it; he must simply work hard and well, for his culture does not allow him to complain—or even to think about complaining. It would not be respectful or manly. It would not be *macho*.

Roberto's strength of character is revealed immediately, not only through his uncomplaining silence in response to his father's behavior but also by his interaction with the nine older men he works with and oversees. For example, on the morning the story begins, Roberto, on his way to the fields, falls into an irrigation channel with his horse and nearly drowns. Arriving for work but a few minutes late, dripping wet, he denies, when taunted by one of the other men, that anything untoward had happened. A man's personal condition should be of no concern to another. Yet his responses to the older man must tread carefully between nonservile amicability and nonprovocative bravado. Too much servility would cost him his job (not to mention his self-respect); too much arrogance would cost him his life.

The need for balance between servility and arrogance, dependence and independence, is emphasized again and again throughout the novel—along with the impossibility of maintaining perfect balance in a world of violent passion and conflict. Moving Roberto and the other *norteños* into an American setting adds further conflict, in the form of different cultural expectations, while simultaneously placing them in the middle of the ongoing farm-labor conflict.

In addition to the obvious intercultural conflicts of the novel are the conflicts between the traditional local farmers and the village *norteños*, who at great risk become temporarily wealthy (by local standards) by leaving the community and journeying north to work on U.S. farms. Although the *norteños'* dissolute and violent lifestyle does not appeal to Roberto, a persuasive offer from the *norteño* leader, Juan Aguilar, to travel north in the coming work season and thus provide for Roberto's family draws Roberto reluctantly away from his home and traditional way of life.

As book 2 begins, the novel explodes into violence with an episode that forces Roberto and the *norteños* to leave abruptly for the United States. Among the *norteños* is Pedro, Juan's companion of the past ten years. Pedro, who had already earned Roberto's enmity for publicly humiliating his father, continually goads Roberto. Although Juan keeps peace between the two for some time, Pedro and Roberto eventually clash openly and decisively. Final resolution of their conflict, however, must wait until the setting returns, in book 3, to the village in Michoacán.

The Characters

Roberto personifies what it means to be *macho*, without bluster or crude language (though the language of others is occasionally blunt). The desperate situations into which he is drawn neither oversimplify nor glamorize that ideal: a fight with a thief; the clash with Pedro; a barroom rescue; and finally, the novel's climactic confrontation. Although Roberto outwardly displays the Mexican cultural ideal of fierce arrogance, he also uses his intellect to question tradition and to preserve both life and honor.

Finally, it becomes clear that the central struggle in *Macho!* is not simply one of peace versus violence but of the struggle to reconcile tradition with change. Roberto succeeds not merely because he can endure the old ways of violence, but because he is willing to challenge his cultural traditions with the tools of change (reason), to create new roles that are both more honorable and more productive than death by violence.

Juan Aguilar, prematurely aged by his life as a *norteño*, at first impresses the reader with his knowledge of the road to fortune beyond the Mexican border. As the novel unfolds, however, Juan shows, not only by his speech and actions but also by comparison with more sophisticated migrant workers, that his knowledge of American culture and customs is as limited as his possibilities in, and perhaps for, life.

Juan's role as Roberto's protector is also flawed, for that relationship is based almost exclusively on Roberto's potential to contribute to Juan's continued success. Throughout the novel, Juan's role alternates between that of parasite and protector: His mercenary impulses conflict with his growing image of Roberto as the son he never had. Until the very end of the novel, suspense results from the uncertainty over which impulse will win out.

Pedro, the hardened *norteño* companion of Juan who is Roberto's sworn enemy, brings an image of pure violence to the novel. Pedro is not even identified by last name, making it easier for him to remain a faceless personification of evil. Despite his decisive defeat at Roberto's hands, Pedro's continued behind-the-scenes presence illustrates the pervasive and persistent nature of human violence and, in the end, ultimately refutes the axiom of live and let live.

Esperanza, who has a North American counterpart in the less well-developed character of Gloria Sanchez, represents progress through education and reason. Education and reason, long the principal tools of progress and the primary means by which tradition may be successfully challenged, also represent hope. (Esperanza's name, fittingly, means "hope"). Without hope there can be no progress toward a better world and society.

Don Carlos Villanueva, aged local landowner and farmer, has successfully combined traditional principles with progressive practices. He alone had the insight to see that the changes brought by the volcano could be beneficial. Although his bearing and presence are regal, his advanced age will soon force him into oblivion. Unless others such as Roberto are willing to continue in his stead, the good that the old generation offers the new may also be lost.

Themes and Meanings

Paralleling the narrative plot is the novel's larger political conflict, one which directly affected—and still affects—all United States farmworkers, legal or otherwise. The battle had presumably been resolved in 1963, when legal importation of braceros (migrant farmworkers) from Mexico into the United States was stopped, largely because of the efforts of farm-labor organizers such as César Chávez. Yet the end of the bracero program had what should have been predictable results: an increase in the demand for cheaper Mexican workers by American agribusinesses and an increase in the incentive for Mexicans to enter the United States illegally. Men south of the border grew so desperate for work in the United States that they fell easy prey to those who promised to get them across in any way possible—in many cases, to be deported soon anyway.

As political lines were being nobly drawn, the issues for the starving Mexican workers remained so basic that political ideologies were irrelevant. One must work to eat. Who among the poor Mexicans ever heard of refusing to work in order to improve their working conditions? If offered a fair wage, why not take it and perform uncomplainingly? For to the Mexican worker, American wages, no matter how low, were always better than Mexican wages. Is it Roberto's fault that he was born a poor Mexican farmer? Can it be expected that he should see an American problem through American eyes? He is by circumstances concerned, above all else, with providing food for his family. Abstract ideological concerns are for him a luxury beyond comprehension. The reader accepts Roberto's limited understanding but also sees the larger context as a moral dilemma of which Roberto is unaware: that better pay and working conditions for American workers, however much needed, may penalize humans born elsewhere (in this case, Mexico).

Villanseñor's resolution of Roberto's plight may not completely satisfy those who want an American success story or those who like perfect resolutions to difficult problems. Yet the ending does provide the reader with a sense that both the protagonist and the reader have learned and matured, that the power and the immediacy of life itself, though it may at times depend on political expediency, ultimately transcends political boundaries.

For Roberto, whose physical journey ends with a cyclical return to his origins, the passage to manhood is complete. He has survived the initiation rites of his male society, rites shared by the male warrior/worker (here one and the same) of many, perhaps all cultures: the Japanese samurai code of *bushido*, the Finnish tacit and unyielding *sisu*, the Roman warrior's stoicism, and the American marine's code of death before dishonor. Arguably, none of those masculine traditions may be fully appreciated or fully defined except by those who have lived them. Yet Victor Villaseñor offers the reader a glimpse of understanding through the eyes of Roberto Garcia.

Critical Context

Macho!, published under the name Edmund Victor Villaseñor, was the author's first novel. Part of a larger outpouring in the 1960's and 1970's of Latin American literature, it was critically acclaimed when it appeared in 1973.

Each chapter of *Macho!* begins with a prefatory sociopolitical comment on the times immediately preceding (and including) the turbulent American milieu of the late 1960's. Villaseñor's intent is to heighten the reader's awareness of the historical context within which the novel's fictional characters come to life. The novel's main character, serious and intelligent but naïve, endures the type of coming-of-age conflicts that young men in many societies have traditionally encountered. The resulting story dramatizes the struggles of the migrant Mexican farmworker in much the same way that John Steinbeck dramatized the plight of the displaced Okies in *The Grapes of Wrath* (1939).

Villaseñor's later works also rely heavily on dramatization of history. In 1977, Villaseñor's account of the trial of the convicted California serial murderer Juan Corona stirred even more controversy. At issue was the concern that Villaseñor's interpretation of historical events was more creative than current authorial conventions allowed.

Having captured the public's attention, Villaseñor's dramatic talents were given full rein in his 1981 television screenplay *The Ballad of Gregorio Cortez*, which won first place in the National Endowment for the Humanities television drama category that year. The film was subsequently released to theaters and on videocassette. More recently, Villaseñor's 1991 *Rain of Gold*, the story of his family's immigration from Mexico to California, is also historical, yet charged with the author's fictionalized personal drama.

Although Victor Villaseñor has established himself as an important and principled chronicler of the Mexican American experience, he has received relatively little critical notice to date. Part of the reason may be that he writes in English about people whose first language is Spanish. Yet that argument may be put to rest by his readers, who immediately recognize the universal appeal of his *Macho!* hero, a hero who challenges the limited stereotypical image of the Latino male. That appeal lifts Villaseñor's work beyond narrow regional or linguistic boundaries, to a genuinely international level of human understanding.

Bibliography

Barbato, Joseph. "Latino Writers in the American Market." *Publishers Weekly* 238 (February 1, 1991): 17-21. Discusses the obstacles facing Chicano authors and the troubled publishing of Villaseñor's *Rain of Gold*. Also includes an interview with Villaseñor, who gives his side of the publishing debate.

Guilbault, Rose Del Castillo. "Americanization Is Tough on 'Macho.' " In *American Voices: Multicultural Literacy and Critical Thinking*, edited by Dolores LaGuardia and Hans P. Guth. Mountain View, Calif.: Mayfield, 1992. Guilbault provides a sociolinguistic framework and a more complete understanding of the original Hispanic meaning of *macho*. (This book also contains an interview with Victor Villaseñor originally printed in the *San Jose News*.)

Hartman, Steven Lee. "On the History of Spanish *macho*." *Hispanic Linguistics* 1, no. 1 (1984): 97-114. Deals with one of the most misunderstood loan words in contemporary American society. The transmogrification of *macho* from positive to negative ideal is chronicled, with reasons for the change outlined.

Kelsey, Verlene. "Mining for a Usable Past: Acts of Recovery, Resistance and Continuity in Victor Villaseñor's *Rain of Gold*." *Bilingual Review* 18 (January-April, 1993): 79-85. In this critical study of *Rain of Gold,* Kelsey briefly mentions *Macho!* as a transition novel in Villaseñor's literary career. Both novels share similar characteristics: "epigraphs that refer to natural cycles and mythic phenomena, chapter prologues/epilogues that set a historical context, and chapters that reveal the characters' personal experiences."

Rocard, Marcienne. *The Children of the Sun: Mexican-Americans in the Literature of the United States*. Translated by Edward G. Brown, Jr. Tucson: The University of Arizona Press, 1989. A general literary history that discusses works by Anglo and Mexican American writers. The descriptions of stock type characters are helpful in understanding Villaseñor's work. A good introduction to the subject.

Sandoval, Ralph, and Alleen P. Nilsen. "The Mexican-American Experience." *English Journal* 63 (January, 1974): 61. Sandoval suggests that while verisimilitude may be strained in parts of this first book by Villaseñor, the drama portrays empathetic characters who may have real-life counterparts. Moreover, the novel is compelling and powerful, told in language the reader will recognize as realistic and direct.

William Matta

MACHO CAMACHO'S BEAT

Author: Luis Rafael Sánchez (1936-   )
Type of plot: Social satire
Time of plot: The early 1970's
Locale: San Juan, Puerto Rico
First published: La guaracha del Macho Camacho, 1976 (English translation, 1980)

>*Principal characters:*
>>THE HEATHEN CHINKY (THE MOTHER), a lower-class mulatto prostitute
>>SENATOR VINCENTE REINOSA (THE OLD MAN), a wealthy, corrupt, and
>>   lascivious government official
>>GRACIELA ALCÁNTARA Y LÓPEZ DE MONTEFRÍO, the aristocratic,
>>   neurotic, and sexually frigid wife of Reinosa
>>BENNY, the pampered son of Reinosa and Graciela
>>DOÑA CHON, a representative of traditional values
>>THE KID, an encephalitic, retarded child

The Novel

Macho Camacho's Beat is a fictional portrait of life in San Juan, Puerto Rico, at a time when the country is inundated with the sound of Macho Camacho's *guaracha*, or dance tune, "Life Is a Phenomenal Thing." Framed by a notice that reveals the subject of the novel and an appendix that provides the reader with the entire text of the *guaracha*, *Macho Camacho's Beat* is a montage of fragmented narrative sections interrupted by a series of radio announcements that track the meteoric rise in popularity of the rhythmical and irrepressible Afro-Antillean tune.

The entire plot of *Macho Camacho's Beat* occurs within the few minutes before, at, and just after five o'clock on a steamy Wednesday afternoon. As an immense traffic jam paralyzes San Juan, the novel's characters are depicted in the act of waiting. With the accumulative fragments of sounds, images, thoughts, and experience, the reader is able to piece together a composite picture of Puerto Rican culture.

The Heathen Chinky (whose name is never mentioned) is introduced through the device of an omniscient third-person narrator whose relation with each of the characters in the novel is so intimate as to allow the narration to pass fluidly between the third- and first-person voices. As she awaits the arrival of her lover, the Old Man (Senator Vincente Reinosa), the Heathen Chinky indulges in sexual fantasies of her virile triplet cousins, Hughie, Louie, and Dewey and anesthetizes her body with a sea of alcohol and her mind with the incessant, insistent, and sensual salsa beat of Macho Camacho's *guaracha*.

Senator Vincente Reinosa swelters in his Mercedes-Benz, stuck in the enormous traffic tie-up, impatient to meet his sultry and accommodating dark-skinned mistress (the Heathen Chinky), who waits for him every Monday, Wednesday, and Friday afternoon in a studio apartment rented specifically for convenient fornication. The news of a bombing at the university in San Juan interrupts the senator's lustful fantasies and political self-aggrandizements only long enough for him to worry whether he will lose votes in the next election. As the occupants of the hundreds of immobilized automobiles that surround him dance in the street with a frenzied abandon brought on by the *guaracha*'s irresistible beat, the senator's thoughts quickly return to the schoolgirl he has been ogling, and he wonders if he has time to make her his next conquest.

The senator's aristocratic wife, Graciela Alcántara y López de Montefrío, waits for her appointment with her trendy psychiatrist, Dr. Severo Severino. In her elegant compact mirror, Graciela scrutinizes her face to detect signs of aging and dwells on the absolute abhorrence she has of sexual relations with her husband. Graciela flips through the pages of *Time* magazine, deliberately ignoring the ugly reality of the war in Vietnam and concentrating instead on photographs of Elizabeth Taylor, Richard Burton, and Jacqueline Kennedy Onassis. Finally driven to distraction by the vulgar receptionist who constantly plays the vulgar *guaracha* on her transistor radio, Graciela, in an uncontrollable fit of temper, rails against the devastating reality that she can never be truly like her ideal, Jackie O.

The Mother, by a number of similarities—the desire to be Iris Chacón, the affair with the Old Man—is identified as being one and the same person as the Heathen Chinky. In this guise, she is shown in her own home, apparently moments before leaving to keep her appointment with the Old Man. Because the Mother cannot bring her encephalitic three-year-old son, the Kid, with her, she leaves him alone to "sunbathe" on the steps of a basilica in a nearby park—a treatment that the Old Man himself has prescribed. The Mother's neighbor, Doña Chon, agrees to pick the Kid up after the Mother offers to share the money she receives from the Old Man. Before Doña Chon arrives at the park, however, the Kid, cruelly abused by the neighborhood children, runs away from them into the street. Doña Chon arrives just in time to see the Kid hit by a speeding car.

Benny, spoiled son of the Reinosas, is also stuck in the five o'clock traffic. He sits in his beloved Ferrari, frustrated and furious at being compelled to keep his foot on the brake and restrain the power of his high-speed sports car, the object of his sexual fantasies. Benny's thoughts return obsessively to ways in which he can convince his father that what Puerto Rico's youth really needs are cars and fast tracks on which to race them. When Benny finally breaks free of the traffic, he roars down a narrow side street. The threads of the plot are tied together as Benny, privileged son of the wealthy and aristocratic Reinosas, hits and kills the deformed and retarded son of his father's poverty-stricken, lower-class mulatto mistress.

The Characters

The characters in *Macho Camacho's Beat* are grotesques, allegorical rather than fully rounded, and are defined primarily by their obsessions and a desire to be what they are not.

The Heathen Chinky/The Mother, representative of the masses as her generic labels suggest, is obsessed with sex and her desire to be television's sex symbol, Iris Chacón. Barraged on all sides by mass-media hype, her self-perception is so distorted that it seems quite reasonable to prostitute herself for the price of a new linoleum floor. She believes herself to be a good mother because she fondles the Kid and sings to him, just as she has seen mothers do in Mexican films. To maintain her delusions of happiness, the Heathen Chinky eagerly subscribes to the pop philosophy of Macho Camacho's *guaracha*, which insists, in spite of all evidence to the contrary, that "Life Is a Phenomenal Thing."

Senator Vincente Reinosa is obsessed with sexual fantasies involving black and mulatto women and fancies himself a modern-day Don Juan. He sexually exploits women whom he would never acknowledge in public and embezzles public funds to pay the cost of keeping them. He uses his political clout to keep his budding terrorist son out of jail (and out of the headlines), and he bilks the government for the price of a brand-new Ferrari to appease the boy. Reinosa wants Puerto Rico to become a part of the United States. He represents the desire of the wealthy to maintain the status quo by embracing American consumerism and eschewing the nationalist movement for an independent Puerto Rican nation.

Graciela is obsessed with the desire to be Jacqueline Kennedy Onassis. As her last name (Montefrío, which means "cold mount") suggests, she is sexually frigid and completely devoid of warmth and humor. She constantly tries to re-create herself in the image of an ideal promoted in trendy European and American magazines. Anything native to Puerto Rico, herself included, is repulsive to her. Graciela is the quintessential class snob and the model of Roman Catholic sexual repression.

Benny is obsessed with lust for his Ferrari. The product of his environment, Benny is spoiled, racist, lazy, fat, and soft. Still a teenager, he has already committed arson and probably murder. When Benny runs the Kid down with his Ferrari, the outlook for the future of Puerto Rico is clear: The hypocritical and materialistic upper class will continue to exploit and crush the nation's poor without remorse.

Doña Chon, seemingly the last bastion of kindness in all of San Juan, is representative of cultural tradition: She cooks Creole food, and she keeps her house full of images of Jesus Christ and the Roman Catholic saints. She is the only adult in the novel who is not obsessed with sex, and she seems impervious to Macho Camacho's *guaracha*. Even Doña Chon cannot avoid corruption completely, however; she accepts money earned by the prostitution of her neighbor in return for picking up the Kid. Delayed by her own affairs, Doña Chon arrives at the park a moment too late to save him. What little goodness exists in Puerto Rican society, it seems, is ultimately ineffectual.

The Kid, like his mother, is a generic representative of the masses. Apparently born quite normal, the child has been deformed by his environment. Helpless, he is tortured mercilessly by healthy neighborhood children, who all the while sing, "Life Is a Phenomenal Thing." When this child of Puerto Rico is forced to confront his own image in a fractured looking-glass, he flees from his monstrous self to find his own destruction.

Themes and Meanings

Macho Camacho's Beat is a razor-sharp, deep-cutting indictment of Puerto Rican culture. Sánchez's prose is rich with the colorful and often obscene language of the streets, loaded with the language of consumerism, and abundant in references to the lifestyles of the rich and famous, fictional and otherwise. The fragmented, baroque surface of Sánchez's highly allusive prose is a brilliant reflection of the kaleidoscopic confusion caused by the indiscriminate acceptance of the material values espoused by a profit-oriented consumerist society. Language defines thought, and in this novel, language is the product of a largely American-controlled mass media. The resulting inability to communicate on an intimate, personal level creates in the reader a sense of the moral and spiritual poverty of Sánchez's characters.

Macho Camacho's Beat clearly calls for a radical reformation of Puerto Rican society and of the ways in which individuals perceive themselves. The political push to Americanize Puerto Rico and the corruption of government officials is exemplified in the character of Reinosa. The moral decay of the population is sardonically expressed in the Mother's prostitution and Benny's love affair with his Ferrari, which supersedes his affection for any human being. Even the personal physical reality of the people is being transformed, Americanized, foreignized. This is clearly expressed in Graciela's obsession with makeup, hair, and fashion, in her social life, and in her absurd proposed design for typical Puerto Rican dress: a tailored suit in spotted calfskin.

The key metaphor of the monstrous traffic jam symbolizes the stagnation of a Puerto Rican society that constantly denies its own seedy reality as it becomes obsessed with the fleeting distractions offered by a sensationalist media and subscribes to the seductive but clearly false philosophy of the seductive *guaracha*. No element of Puerto Rican society is immune from Sánchez's irreverent and biting sense of humor. The sins of elitism, racial discrimination, and denial of self are laid bare before the grotesque feet and obtuse minds of the sinners. Just as the Kid is forced to confront his ugly and deformed reality reflected in the surface of a fragmented mirror, Sánchez compels his fellow Puerto Ricans to confront themselves in the fragmented and glittering surface of *Macho Camacho's Beat*.

Critical Context

Luis Rafael Sánchez's first full-length novel, *Macho Camacho's Beat* was written after Sánchez had already been acclaimed as an important Puerto Rican playwright. A critic of literature and the arts, Sánchez has published many articles in newspapers and magazines and has also published a collection of short stories under the title *En cuerpo de camisa* (1966; in casual dress).

Macho Camacho's Beat was an immediate best-seller. Sánchez's use of language and symbol, his irreverent sense of humor, his incisive social criticism, and his ability to explore a culture that is uniquely Puerto Rican has led some critics to consider *Macho Camacho's Beat* the single most important Puerto Rican novel of the twentieth century. In his second novel, *La importancia de llamarse Daniel Santos* (1989; the importance of being named Daniel Santos), Sánchez continued to explore mass culture and society. This second novel goes beyond Puerto Rico to include Latino communities in the United States, Central America, and South America as well as the

Antilles, a much broader scope than that of the distinctly Puerto Rican *Macho Camacho's Beat*.

Bibliography

Agüra, Helen Calaf. "Luis Rafael Sánchez Speaks About *Macho Camacho's Beat*." Translated by Jo Anne Englebert. *Review* 28 (January-April, 1981): 39-41. An interview with the author in which Sánchez speaks about the critical reception of his work and his own intentions in writing the novel. Sánchez gives insight into his use of street language and his attempt to "portray the spiritual decomposition of Puerto Rico." He also discusses his novel as the expression of "a need to transform colonial reality in all spheres—political, moral, even in the realm of the physical."

Cruz, Arnaldo. "Repetition and the Language of the Mass Media in Luis Rafael Sánchez's *La guaracha del Macho Camacho*." *Latin American Literary Review* 13 (July-December, 1985): 35-48. This well-written and interesting article explores the ways in which the techniques of repetition and language act as distancing techniques, enabling the reader to approach the work with a critical eye. Interesting in its assessment of Sánchez's use of language as social analysis. Cruz has some interesting insights into the aesthetic effects of Sánchez's prose.

Guinness, Gerald. "Is *Macho Camacho's Beat* a Good Translation of *La guaracha del Macho Camacho*?" In *Images and Identities: The Puerto Rican in Two World Contexts*, edited by Asela Rodriguez de Laguna. New Brunswick, N.J.: Transaction Books, 1987. Explores the techniques of Gregory Rabassa's translation of the novel. An interesting assessment of the loss of certain aesthetic values in a work so distinctly defined by language. Guinness offers some insightful alternatives to Rabassa's translation.

Melendez, Priscilla. "Towards a Characterization of Latin American Farce." *Siglo XX* 11 (1993). Melendez discusses Luis Rafael Sánchez's novel from the perspective of a parody. An astute assessment of Sánchez's work within the context of Latin American writing as a whole.

Schlau, Stacey. "Mass Media Images of the *Puertorriqueña* in *La guaracha del Macho Camacho*." In *Literature and Popular Culture in the Hispanic World: A Symposium*, edited by Rose S. Minc. Gaithersburg, Md.: Hispamerica, 1981. Explores the effects of mass-media advertising, focusing on the women in the novel. The Heathen Chinky and Graciela are looked at in terms of how their self-esteem and self-perception are defined by commercial advertisement and consumerism.

Waldman, Gloria F. "*La guaracha del Macho Camacho* as Popular Culture." In *Literature and Popular Culture in the Hispanic World: A Symposium*, edited by Rose S. Minc. Gaithersburg, Md.: Hispamerica, 1981. Waldman writes about the specifics of Puerto Rican popular culture and explores the *guaracha* as the "ultimate equalizer." An interesting, although brief, introduction to the nonfictional elements in Sánchez's fictional world.

Diane M. Almeida

MACUNAÍMA

Author: Mário de Andrade (1893-1945)
Type of plot: Rhapsodic, comic epic
Time of plot: The early twentieth century
Locale: Brazil, principally the Amazon jungle and São Paulo
First published: Macunaíma, o herói sem nenhum caracter, 1928 (English translation, 1984)

Principal characters:
    MACUNAÍMA, the mock hero, emperor of the jungle
    MAANAPE, his elderly brother, who is a sorcerer
    JIGUÊ, his witless brother
    CI, the Mother of the Forest, Macunaíma's great love
    VENCESLAU PIETRO PIETRA, the man-eating giant Piaiman and villain

The Novel

This unusual work is an antirealist fantasy drawn from Amazonian Indian mythology, Afro-Luso-Brazilian folklore, and the author's imagination. Thus, much of what occurs is fablelike, magical, or illogical, with no spatial or temporal bounds. The action centers on the hero's struggle to recover a magical amulet given to him by Ci. His adventures take him to all corners of Brazil and back in time.

Macunaíma is born an ugly black baby to a Tapanhuma Indian mother. Although he is destined to be a popular hero, his mother notes that all names beginning with "Ma" bring bad luck. The sadistic and mischievous child soon discovers magical powers, transforming himself into a comely prince to seduce his brother Jiguê's first wife. When Jiguê distributes meat after a successful hunt, the hero receives tripe and vows revenge. During a famine, the hero's acts show him to be vindictive and greedy. As punishment, his mother expels him from the jungle, and he must return home by his wits. Back home, he goes through several metamorphoses to seduce Iriqui, Jiguê's new wife. Tricked by the gods, Macunaíma kills his mother. The three brothers and Iriqui then set off for "our world." They soon encounter Ci, whom the hero rapes. An entourage of birds salute him as the new emperor of the virgin forest. The two engender a son, who is adored by women of all races from all parts of the nation. A venomous serpent causes the death of Ci and son; before ascending to become a bright star, she gives the hero a special amulet. The precious stone is lost as Macunaíma defeats the Water Mother in battle. When the hero learns that the man-eating giant Venceslau has obtained the coveted charm, he sets off for São Paulo to recover it, accompanied by his brothers and a flock of royal parrots. The hero stows his conscience before leaving and gathers two hundred canoes to carry his fortune of cocoa beans. The brothers discover the footprint of Saint Thomas filled with water. The hero bathes first and becomes fair-skinned and blue-eyed; the envious brothers come out with red and black skin, respectively.

In the metropolis, the trio trades beans for currency and discovers that money rules all. The hero picks up some white women only to discover that they are prostitutes. They explain to Macunaíma that the goblins, spirits, and animals that he thinks he sees are actually buildings and machines. Macunaíma surmises that white people are the Children of Manioc and ruminates on the monumental struggle between urban people and machines; he decides that the contest is a draw and that the two are equivalent. He then turns Jiguê into a "telephone contraption" and calls Venceslau. The hero confronts the villain for the first time but is killed, diced, and stewed. Maanape employs his powers to revive him. Posing as a French prostitute, the hero again attempts to lure the amulet from the giant, whose vicious dog pursues Macunaíma through all regions of Brazil. During this chase they encounter several figures from the nation's colonial past. By now the hero is overcome by rancor and attends a voodoo rite in Rio de Janeiro, in which he beseeches devil spirits to punish Venceslau, who takes a terrible beating. Vei the Sun offers one of her daughters in marriage if the hero will remain faithful, but he overindulges with a fishwife and incurs the never-ending wrath of the Sun. At the halfway point of the book, the emperor writes a pedantic letter to his subjects recounting his adventures and explaining his impressions of civilization and the Portuguese language.

As Venceslau recuperates, the hero is captured by the giant's wife, whose lustful daughter allows him to escape. The ensuing chase traverses Brazil's varied geography and cultural landscape. After unsuccessful attempts to get a scholarship to finance a trip to Europe, the hero searches for buried treasure, purchases a bogus goose that lays golden eggs, and is tricked into a fatal smashing of his own testicles. Resuscitated again, Macunaíma imagines a European ocean liner in a fountain; his plea for passage is rejected. The giant returns, however, and the hero tricks him into falling into his own stew. Amulet in hand, the emperor heads back home with his brothers.

During the torturous return trip, the hero finds Iriqui again but rejects her in favor of a princess he created from a tree. He cannot find his old conscience, so he assumes that of a Spanish American. Illness and hunger plague the hero in his new hut. His brothers discover magic food-producing agents, but Macunaíma loses them. A poison hook that he devises turns his brothers into ghostly shadows who begin persecuting him. This antagonism results in the creation of folk dances and rites. In his solitude, Macunaíma feels remorse and recalls his former glory. Vei the Sun lures him into mortal combat with the Lady of the Lake, where he loses the amulet and a leg. Macunaíma decides to give up life and ascends to heaven as the Great Bear constellation. Many years later, a man wanders into the jungle to be told these great tales by a parrot. That man is the omniscient narrator of this work.

The Characters

The subtitle of the work is "the hero with no character." It has been generally assumed that Macunaíma is a symbolic representation of Brazilian man, and, in this fantastic fiction, national character emerges as the lack of character. Indeed, there is little logic or consistency in the person of Macunaíma. Although there is emphasis on the hero's indigenous roots, he is in many ways an ethnological collage or amalgamation which is still in formation. The language he speaks, the roles he plays, and the values he upholds are drawn from diverse regional, cultural, social, and historical sources of the varied Brazilian experience. The shifting foundations of the hero's amorphous self are metamorphosis and resurrection; the hero transforms himself into a prince or some animal at several junctures, and he is repeatedly brought back from the dead. Macunaíma is born ugly but discovers magic that aids him in the first of his many sexual conquests. He cannot, however, exercise supernatural powers at will. At times he has the ability to perform miracles to elude danger or create food; at others he must live by his wits or suffer humiliations. Some qualities of the protagonist do stand out. His aversion to work is evident from childhood; he prefers lounging about in a hammock, singing folk songs, and engaging in wanton erotic play. As a child, the hero is mischievous, and in adult life he is an unyielding trickster and an irresponsible liar. Many episodes portray him as vindictive, greedy, and self-accommodating; his constant abuse of Jiguê shows these traits best. Since *Macunaíma* is epic in conception, the nature of the hero is inseparable from the thematic concerns and messages of the work.

Themes and Meanings

Mário de Andrade is as well-known for his work in music as for his literary endeavors. He called *Macunaíma* not a novel but a "rhapsody." This classification suggests both sung epic poetry (such as the *Iliad* and the *Odyssey*) and an instrumental fantasy based on popular or traditional melodies. In literature, the term may also connote an ecstatic, highly emotional, or irrational work. All of these meanings of "rhapsody" have a direct relation to *Macunaíma*. Although Andrade's fundamental approach is comic, it is clear that the saga of Macunaíma is a reflection on questions of Brazilian nationality, which is a fusion of European, African, and Amerindian peoples. The work playfully brings into question the character and psyche of Brazil as a young American nation and of her people as a diverse population. Thus, the contradictory qualities of the turbulent hero himself are central to any evaluation of the novel. Orality is emphasized throughout the work; that which the narrator relates has been learned from a parrot, and characters constantly relate deeds, accomplishments, or myths of origin. Popular, traditional, or indigenous elements inform the entirety of the novel, and linear logic is subordinated to unbridled fantasy throughout.

Andrade's "instrument" in this rhapsody is his macaronic literary language. One of the work's central themes is language itself, the primary vehicle of culture. The author blends, often arbitrarily, the vocabulary and structure of standard Portuguese, colorful street language, and many regional varieties into a unique and totally new linguistic style. In the original, many passages are unintelligible even to native Brazilians, but the author's aim was to raise readers' consciousness about the diversity of their New World language, in which thousands of indigenous and African words were added to the European mother tongue. Enumeration is frequent and meaningful in *Macunaíma*. When biting insects or parrots are mentioned, for example, dozens of kinds are listed.

This technique calls attention to a copious rural vocabulary that is little-known in the urban setting, and it emphasizes geographical differences between the New World tropics and the dominant culture of Europeans who came to conquer. Even in translation, the reader feels the effects of enumeration, especially with respect to the abundant flora and fauna of the Amazonian region.

Mário de Andrade sought a particularly Brazilian literary language based on actual speech and not on stiff, textbook grammar. Another of the principal aims of *Macunaíma* is to poke fun at the classical rhetoric dominant in Luso-Brazilian letters until the 1920's. The letter that the hero writes to his Amazon subjects midway through the novel is the high point of stylistic satire. This effort is particularly effective because the letter writer is an ingenuous native looking at urban culture as an outsider in his own country. Macunaíma writes in the pedantic, verbose academic style of Brazil's traditional intellectual leaders, employing Latinate structures, eloquent vocabulary, and erudite allusions. On the surface, the letter appears to be constructed impeccably, but there are many grammatical errors, misuses of words, and stylistic abuses. The targets of the biting satire are the overblown style of classicism, the would-be men of letters who employ that rhetoric poorly or in place of substance, and the distance of the official written language from the true spoken language. The letter also satirizes mores, customs, and São Paulo society. The innocent hero describes things as he sees them, and many aspects of urban life are seen in a comic light. Corruption, prostitution, bad public health, and faulty services, among other elements, emerge from the hero's explanations of civilization.

Cultural satire and contrast play an important role outside of the letter. The figure of the villain, a cannibalistic giant and wealthy merchant, incorporates a satire of the many Italian immigrants who became rich in São Paulo and suggests the rapacious nature of business in Brazil, as well as the dominant role of foreign nations in her commerce. In the episode where Macunaíma imagines a ship in a fountain and seeks transatlantic passage, the author pokes fun at the tendency of urban middle- and upper-class Brazilians to turn their eyes toward Europe instead of toward their own land and culture. In another episode, Macunaíma publicly debates a citizen who extols the beauty of the Southern Cross, a national symbol of Brazil. The hero emphatically challenges this view, satirizing patriotic discourse in the process, and asserts the constellation's indigenous name and myth of origin, as opposed to the official European version. With these examples in mind, a leading Brazilian critic has said that Mário de Andrade showed that for every academic or purely literary concept there was another version or concept of popular origin.

Critical Context

Mário de Andrade wrote *Macunaíma* during a six-day frenzy and underwrote its publication. The literary establishment was perplexed by the work and gave it a bad reception. The leading critics of the time called it barbarous, outrageous, disconnected, fragmented, and excessive. Most failed to see the unity of the interwoven motifs, and some reacted negatively to its flamboyance and obscenity. *Macunaíma* was indeed one of the most forceful affronts to literary decorum of the 1920's. This was the decade of Modernism in Brazil, an iconoclastic and nationalistic movement of literary renovation that sought to break sharply with the past, to challenge the influence of Portuguese letters, and to make national reality the focus of literary endeavor. With his rhapsodic novel, Mário de Andrade made a major contribution to a radical literary faction known as "Anthropophagy," which used the practice of cannibalism as a metaphor for their project of modern Brazilan writing.

It was not until 1955 that *Macunaíma* began to be fully appreciated by critics and the reading public. In that year, a detailed explanation of Mário de Andrade's sources, cultural references, and allusions was published, showing the thematic unity of the work and its complicated background. This critical defense acknowledged that *Macunaíma* was frightening and astounding, but for its erudition and craft and not for its supposed incoherence or immorality. Other reevaluations and lengthy studies of the work have followed. *Macunaíma* is now regarded as one of the most representative and influential works of Brazilian Modernism, and a foremost example of literary srebellion and nationalism in Latin American literature in general. In 1969, *Macunaíma* was made into a film, one of the most successful productions of Brazil's New Cinema. Significant English-language commentary on the original novel is found in film criticism.

Bibliography
Albuquerque, Severino J. "Construction and Deconstruction in *Macunaíma.*" *Hispania: A Journal Devoted to the Interests of the Teaching of Spanish and Portuguese* 70 (March, 1987): 67-72. An analysis of the structure and technique of the novel.
George, David. "The Staging of *Macunaíma* and the Search for National Theatre." *Latin American Theatre Review* 17 (Fall, 1983): 47-58. A discussion of the adaptation of the novel to the stage.
Moisés, Massaud. "Mário de Andrade." In *Latin American Writers*, edited by Carlos A. Solé and Maria I. Abreau. Vol. 3. New York: Charles Scribner's Sons, 1989. An essay on the life and career of Mário de Andrade. Includes analysis of his works and a bibliography.
Rose, Stanley L. "*Macunaíma*: When Failure Succeeds." *Selecta: Journal of the Pacific Northwest Council on Foreign Languages* 13 (1992): 79-82. Rose details the novel's use of idiom and discusses the importance of the book in relationship to Brazilian national identity.
West, Paul. Review of *Macunaíma. The Nation* 241 (July 20, 1985): 52-54. West discusses Andrade's narrative technique, use of Brazilian mythology and folklore, and the varied manner and content of the novel.

Charles A. Perrone

MAMA DAY

Author: Gloria Naylor (1950-   )
Type of plot: Melodrama
Time of plot: The 1980's
Locale: Willow Springs, a fictitious island off the coast of South Carolina and
    Georgia, and New York City
First published: 1988

> *Principal characters:*
>> OPHELIA (COCOA) DAY, a young woman who has left her family and
>>   heritage on Willow Springs to live in New York City
>> GEORGE JOHNSON, an African American man whom Cocoa meets in
>>   New York
>> MIRANDA (MAMA) DAY, Cocoa's great-aunt, who has powers of
>>   prophecy
>> ABIGAIL DAY, Cocoa's grandmother
>> RUBY, a mysterious woman with supernatural powers
>> JUNIOR LEE, Ruby's shiftless husband

The Novel

Mama Day, Gloria Naylor's third novel, tells the story of Ophelia (Cocoa) Day and George Johnson, who later becomes her husband, and her initiation into the Day family. The novel is divided into three parts and opens with a brief prologue in which an anonymous, omniscient narrator sets the date as August, 1999; the rest of the novel is therefore a series of flashbacks. The prologue also tells the genealogy of the Days, the most important family of Willow Springs, an isolated island; although claimed by both South Carolina and Georgia, it is ignored and allowed to set its own laws and be independent of any outside control. Originally a slave plantation, the island was owned by Bascombe Wade, who in 1819 purchased a slave named Sapphira. He subsequently fell in love with her and took her for his wife. Four years later, after persuading him to free his slaves and deed the island to them, she killed him. That year— 1823—marks the beginning of time on Willow Springs, and all local history is dated from it.

Sapphira had a reputation as a conjure woman, a woman who could work spells and control nature. By persons unknown, she bore seven sons; the youngest, Jonah, who later took the surname "Day," had seven sons as well, including a youngest named John-Paul. An African legend, continued in the South, holds that the eldest daughter of the seventh son of a seventh son would be unusually blessed with "conjure" powers, and this held true as the first of John-Paul's daughters, Miranda (born in 1895), became the matriarch of Willow Springs. Because she has the gift of prophecy and the ability to work with nature to heal the sick or defeat evil, she is called "Mama Day" by the islanders. The other two daughters of John-Paul were Abigail (born in 1897) and

Peace. While Mama Day never married, Abigail did and subsequently bore three girls. The middle daughter, Grace, had one daughter, Ophelia (born in 1953), who is nicknamed "Cocoa." After her mother's death, Mama Day and Abigail reared Cocoa.

Following this prologue, both sections of *Mama Day* have three voices: Cocoa and George, who conduct a dialogue about their relationship, and the omniscient narrator, who focuses on Mama Day and Abigail. Later in the novel, it is revealed that George has died and that the conversation between himself and Cocoa is spiritual, not physical. The initial section tells that Cocoa left Willow Springs in 1974 to go to New York. In the summer of 1980, however, she meets George, a design engineer who spent his childhood in an orphanage and never had a family. The contrast between these two people cannot be greater; Cocoa possesses a link with her African heritage through her family, while George seems to have no connections left with Africa because he lacks a family. The two have a stormy relationship, but there is a magnetism between them that suggests they cannot live without each other. They marry six months after they begin dating, and four years later, in 1985, they go to Willow Springs so that George can meet Mama Day and Abigail. Their crossing of the bridge from the mainland to the island ends the first section of *Mama Day*.

While Cocoa and George are on the island, a hurricane strikes, destroying the bridge and all telephone lines. Furthermore, because Cocoa has been falsely accused of trying to seduce Junior Lee, his wife Ruby—an obese woman who has supernatural powers—poisons Cocoa and places a spell on her. Cocoa ultimately survives, but in saving her through Mama Day's magic, George dies. The exchange of her husband's life for her own satisfies the curse on Cocoa. She eventually leaves Willow Springs for Charleston, South Carolina, and remarries, but she now understands the truth about her family. Cocoa sees that the line of the Days has culminated in her. Spiritually, she is both Sapphira and herself; she is her own mother as she is also Mama Day. The novel ends with her realization of her family's heritage, which she is determined to pass on to her youngest son.

The Characters

Ophelia (Cocoa) Day, the protagonist of the novel, is the most interesting character in the book. She grows from an immature young woman into a person with exceptional personal insight. By the end of the story, she has learned not only about human nature but also about her family and herself. Her role in the novel suggests that of an "everywoman," a character intended to stand as a microcosm for the female African American experience. Although Naylor has argued that her fiction is not didactic, it is hard not to see a moral in the lesson that Cocoa learns.

George Johnson, the most important male figure in the novel, is a well-developed character. Readers are able to see all facets of him, his flaws as well as his virtues. It is easy, however, to sympathize with him throughout the novel, because a reader learns about Willow Springs and the Day family just as he does.

Miranda (Mama) Day, who made a cameo appearance in Naylor's second novel, *Linden Hills* (1985), is a marvelous creation. She can be profane and funny as she talks about sex, or sad and introspective as she reflects on her family's many tragedies. With Mama Day, Naylor has created a character who has a life outside the novel. She comes alive and remains with readers long after the book's covers have been shut.

Ruby, the only truly evil person in the novel, is little more than a stereotype of an African American witch. She acts in predictable ways, and her character is not developed because it does not need to be.

Themes and Meanings

The primary theme of *Mama Day* is the education of Cocoa, the woman whose destiny it is to continue the line of Days. Although she leaves Willow Springs after George's death and later remarries, in a sense she will become "Mama Day" after her great-aunt's death. In other words, Cocoa has now gained the responsibility of self-knowledge, through which she is initiated into the matriarchy of the family. Symbolizing this responsibility is an intricate wedding quilt that Mama Day makes for Cocoa. The quilt is made from fragments of cloth from all of the female Days, from Sapphira through Cocoa herself, and is intended to give her a tangible object from which to draw strength. The pages explaining the making of the quilt, as well as the pages showing Cocoa's reaction to it, are central to the novel.

Secondary to Cocoa's education, but still important, is the education of George. Early in the novel, he is seen as a product of New York, which means he has little faith in anything other than himself. George does not respect and honor his heritage as an African American man; in short, he lacks a soul. Mama Day tries to educate him into the ways of his ancestors, but he lacks faith in her and in her magic, leading to his death. Although he saves Cocoa, he cannot save himself.

It is possible, according to some critics, to see allusions to William Shakespeare in *Mama Day* as another theme. One critic finds many asides to *Hamlet* (1600-1601), especially in the character of Cocoa, whose given name is "Ophelia," also the name of the young woman in Shakespeare's play. Another critic finds the novel more reminiscent of *The Tempest* (1611), since Willow Springs is an isolated, magical place "ruled" by a person who can control the elements. It is worth noting that Mama Day's given name is Miranda, which is also the name of the daughter of the sorcerer of *The Tempest*. Clearly, though, Naylor did not intend for these Shakespearean threads in the novel to take precedence over her primary theme. Instead, they merely serve as a counterpoint to the theme of Cocoa's initiation into the matriarchy.

Critical Context

Gloria Naylor's first novel, *The Women of Brewster Place* (1982), caused an immediate sensation upon its publication. Only thirty-two, she was hailed by critics as one of the most important young voices in American literature. The book, a collection of connected stories centered on one inner-city neighborhood, went on to win the American Book Award for First Novel and was adapted into a popular television film. Her next novel, also reviewed favorably, was *Linden Hills* (1985), which is set in a middle-class black neighborhood in which the surface calm fails to reflect the tensions underneath. A character in the story, Willa Prescott Nedeed, is the cousin of Cocoa Day, providing a link with *Mama Day*, Naylor's third novel, which was also praised by critics. Her fourth novel, *Bailey's Cafe* (1992), tells the stories of a group of characters who frequent a restaurant owned by a man named Bailey; the cafe also receives passing mention in *Mama Day*.

Each of these novels features well-developed characters. Naylor has an unusually precise knack for fleshing out a character in a few carefully chosen words, and her characters breathe and live. Naylor attributes this quality to the fact that she allows her characters the freedom to develop their own lives after she first creates them. Rather than dictate the plot, she records what happens when the characters encounter one another. For her, characters such as Mama Day and Cocoa are as real as nonfictional people.

Bibliography

Andrews, Larry R. "Black Sisterhood in Gloria Naylor's Novels." *College Language Association Journal* 33 (September, 1989): 1-25. Andrews argues that *Mama Day*, like Naylor's two earlier novels, shows how crucial the sense of community is among black women. By passing this sense of community down through generations, black women can help to give themselves strength in a world so often dominated by men. This tradition, however, is threatened by the modern world, in which women forget their heritage and consequently lose a bridge with the past and a link with the future.

Boyd, Nellie. "Dominion and Proprietorship in Gloria Naylor's *Mama Day* and *Linden Hills*." *MAWA Review* 5 (December, 1990): 56-58. Boyd contrasts Naylor's second and third novels to find that they have different approaches toward a character who leads a community. In *Mama Day*, Boyd finds that Mama Day—the spiritual leader of Willow Springs—acts as a sort of benevolent dictator. She compares her to William Shakespeare's Prospero in *The Tempest* in the sense that she serves as the "island's conscience."

Eckard, Paula G. "The Prismatic Past in *Oral History* and *Mama Day*." *MELUS* 20 (Fall, 1995): 121-135. Both Smith's and Naylor's novels suggest that individual lives, as well as the future, might be rewritten in the light of knowledge obtained from re-interpreting the past. Eckard argues that these works illustrate that a past encompassing the foundation of each person's life can be discovered, drawn out, interpreted, and applied.

Kubitschek, Missy D. "Toward a New Order: Shakespeare, Morrison, and Gloria Naylor's *Mama Day*." *MELUS* 19 (Fall, 1994): 75-90. Kubitschek explores the intertextuality of Shakespeare, Morrison, and Naylor. The story concerns the life and motherhood of a black woman who moves from rural to urban America. Kubitschek traces influences from Shakespeare's *Hamlet*, *King Lear*, and *The Tempest* and shows how they are laced throughout Naylor's novel.

Lattin, Patricia H. "Naylor's Engaged and Empowered Narratee." *CLA Journal* 41 (June, 1998): 452-469. Naylor focuses on several different narrative voices in her novel including the use of three narrators and one narratee. In *Mama Day,* one of the narrators challenges the narratee to be active, pass on the story, and create a situation where the narrator and the narratee work closely on the text.

Metting, Fred. "The Possibilities of Flight: The Celebration of Our Wings in *Song of Solomon, Praisesong for the Widow,* and *Mama Day.*" *Southern Folklore* 55 (Fall, 1998): 145-166. Metting explores the concept of flight in the fiction of Toni Morrison, Paule Marshall, and Gloria Naylor. Their works often portray slave resistance or escape, and flight is associated with wishful thinking or other means of escape. However, protective flight can take the form of psychically escaping or being absorbed by creatively constructed language.

Storhoff, Gary. "'The Only Voice Is Your Own": Gloria Naylor's Revision of *The Tempest.*" *African American Review* 29 (Spring, 1995): 35-45. Many "new critics" interpret *The Tempest* to justify European activities such as slavery and colonialism. Naylor exposes the bankrupt patriarchal system, exclusively Protestant view of nature, and the Eurocentric construction of the "Other."

Tucker, Lindsey. "Recovering the Conjure Woman: Texts and Contexts in Gloria Naylor's *Mama Day.*" *African American Review* 28 (Summer, 1994): 173-188. Focuses on the main character, Miranda Day, who encapsulates various qualities of the traditional conjure woman. Miranda's prowess with herbal medicine distinguishes her from the hoodoo practitioner, and Naylor uses the trickster myth to establish healing and other positive influences as necessary to the conjure woman's art so that she may benefit the community at large.

Jim McWilliams

THE MAN WHO CRIED I AM

Author: John A. Williams (1925-   )
Type of plot: Social realism
Time of plot: Roughly 1940 and the early 1960's
Locale: New York City; Washington, D.C.; Amsterdam; Paris; and Lagos
First published: 1967

> *Principal characters:*
> MAX REDDICK, the protagonist, a novelist and journalist
> HARRY AMES, Max's close friend and mentor, a renowned writer
> CHARLOTTE AMES, Harry's wife
> BERNARD ZUTKIN, a literary critic and friend of Max
> KERMIT SHEA, the editor of the magazine which employed Max
> MARGRIT WESTOEVER, Max's Dutch wife
> ROGER WILKINSON, a black expatriate, sometime writer, and
>   acquaintance of Max

The Novel

The Man Who Cried I Am is the somber chronicle of Max Reddick, a novelist and journalist who, while suffering the final stages of rectal cancer, introspectively reflects on his life and experiences, covering three decades, which take him to three continents and through numerous personal upheavals. As a reporter-observer ("That's what you are, Max, a noticer, a digger of scenes"), Max fashions a tale which represents the excursion of the black American through perhaps the most disquieting and turbulent period in American history. Throughout his reflections on past successes and failures and his associations with various women, Max Reddick ponders the state of black America, what it means to be black and living in late-twentieth century America.

Upon his ironic return to Amsterdam ("I've returned. 'A Dutch man o' warre that sold us twenty negars,' John Rolfe wrote, Well, you-all, I bring myself. Free! Three hundred and forty-five years after Jamestown. Now . . . how's that for the circle come full?"), Max gains possession of documents detailing the organized extermination of all blacks in America. After reading the King Alfred Plan, the name of the "emergency" operation, Max realizes that America has no intention of making good on its proclamations of fairness and equality and that his own tragic odyssey embodies that of the deluded black American: "Destruction . . . was very much a part of democratic capitalism, a philosophy which was implicitly duplicitous, meaning all its fine words and slogans, but leaving the performance of them to unseen elfs, gnomes, and fairies."

The novel's bleak prediction for American society is best represented in Max's conclusion that history must have its victims and that those victims must be conditioned to being victimized. Thus, Max must admit near the end of the novel, "Man is nature, nature man, and all crude and raw, stinking, vicious, evil. . . . It is still eat, drink, and be murderous, for tomorrow I may be among the murdered."

Yet there is a glimmer of optimism remaining for Max, who retains the will to resist, and it is in this resistance that the possibility of good can come about, for once man recognizes that he is evil, then he, by resisting his own degenerate nature, will attempt to better himself.

The Characters

Max Reddick is the central character of the novel, and it is through his eyes that the reader sees the panorama of history colored by the condition of the black intellectual/artist. Max's character is somewhat autobiographical (he, like Williams, is a novelist with a journalistic background; also, as Williams did, he must grapple with the choice between the quixotic pursuit of writing as a livelihood and the practical pursuit of getting a "real" job in the real world of the 1950's black man). In his relationship with Harry Ames, the Richard Wright figure in the novel, however, Max resembles a combination of several black writers (including Chester Himes and Ralph Ellison) working during Wright's tenure as "literary father." Max assumes the role of the artist, of the observer; his function is to be "a super Confidence Man, a Benito Cereno saddened beyond death." Yet he assumes this role only near the end of the novel, when he receives the King Alfred Plan.

Max must be kept aware of his racial and historical self by his cynical, Dozens-playing subconscious, Saminone (Sambo-in-one), and by his literary mentor, Harry Ames. Ames, older and more consistently militant than Max, is vividly portrayed in *The Man Who Cried I Am* as the man who, with some modifications, Max could become. Early in the story, after Max has published his first novel, Harry explains to Max: "I'm the way I am, the kind of writer I am, and you may be too, because I'm a black man; therefore, we're in rebellion; we've got to be. We have no other function as valid as that one."

As far as his relationships with women are concerned, Max is compelled to compare each to his beloved Lillian, who dies after a botched abortion. Max's subsequent marriage to Margrit is a result of his initial attraction to her as a white reincarnation of the dead Lillian. Lillian, a middle-class black girl with middle-class dreams, does not want Max to follow the road of shattered dreams that so many other black men had traveled before. She wants security and predictability, but for Max to pursue such goals would be to forsake his role as an artist.

Themes and Meanings

The principal theme of *The Man Who Cried I Am* is that there are seemingly relentless forces which crush and destroy people, but in the face of such destruction, there must be resistance if life is to have some value. As Moses Boatwright, a grotesque character who commits the horrific act of cannabalism, reveals to Max:

> I was born seeing precisely. . . . This world is an illusion . . . but it can be real. I went prowling on the jungle side of the road where few people ever go because there are things there, crawling, slimy, terrible things that always remind us that down deep we are rotten,

stinking beasts. Now because of what I did, someone will work a little harder to improve the species.

Deep inside Max Reddick is a malignancy which is slowly causing his body to deteriorate, just as malignancy (indifference, lies, duplicity) is doing the same thing to "the body politic." The implication is that the American system—or more precisely, Western civilization—is in deep trouble because

> there has got to be something inherently horrible about having the sicknesses and weaknesses of that society described by a person who is a victim of them; for if he, the victim, is capable of describing what they have believed nonexistent, then they, the members of the majority, must choose between living the truth, which can be pretty grim, and the lie, which isn't much better.

To set the victimization of black people in a larger context, references to the Holocaust, the "Six Million," appear throughout the novel, especially through Regina, survivor of the Nazi horror, and Zutkin, who dreams of an alliance of former victims ("*We need each other*") to change the essential character and inclination of the republic.

Critical Context

The Man Who Cried I Am, Williams's most celebrated and influential novel, signaled a sharp departure from his earlier work. Williams's early fiction, *The Angry Ones* (1960), *Night Song* (1961), and *Sissie* (1963), fit within the framework of traditional racial protest writing, a framework which called for moral outcry and reformist solutions. During the period in which *The Man Who Cried I Am* evolved in Williams's mind, historical, social, and political events informed American society of impending tumult and confusion, of a burgeoning black pride and sense of nationalism, and of a questioning of once revered institutions. Williams's novel, consequently, emerged as the most explosive and unsettling political novel of the 1960's. It offers awesome and frightening possibilities for the future of the United States. Sam Greenlee's *The Spook Who Sat by the Door* (1969) offers one disturbing possibility of cataclysmic proportions in the aftermath of *The Man Who Cried I Am*. Other examples of nonfiction fiction or historical fiction from the 1960's which share many elements with Williams's novel are Thomas Pynchon's *V.* (1963) and Kurt Vonnegut's *Slaughterhouse-Five* (1969). These books, together, are pivotal in an understanding of America, in the words of a disconsolate Margrit Westoever, as the "land where everyone speaks in superlatives but exists in diminutives."

In subsequent novels, namely the two immediately following *The Man Who Cried I Am*, the apocalyptic *Sons of Darkness, Sons of Light* (1969) and *Captain Blackman* (1972), Williams asks American society "to recognize the haunting historical continuity of past, present, and future." Yet ultimately, what Wiliams earnestly seeks, beginning with the prophecies in *The Man Who Cried I Am*, is that which is essential, plausible, and good in the American experiment.

Bibliography

Cash, Earl A. *John A. Williams: The Evolution of a Black Writer.* New York: Third Press, 1975. Among the early full-length studies of Williams, this volume provides a solid foundation for further study.

Current Biography 55 (October, 1994): 55-59. Profiles Williams as a novelist whose writings chronicle the struggles of blacks in a predominantly white society. Critical reaction to Williams's work is discussed, providing a valuable framework within which to evaluate *The Man Who Cried I Am.*

Draper, James P., ed. *Black Literature Criticism.* 3 vols. Detroit: Gale Research, 1992. Includes an extensive biographical profile of Williams and excerpts from criticism on his works.

Muller, Gilbert H. *John A. Williams.* Boston: Twayne, 1984. Muller provides a critical and interpretive study of Williams with a close reading of his major works, a solid bibliography and complete notes and references.

Reilly, John M. "Thinking History in *The Man Who Cried I Am.*" *Black American Literature Forum* 21 (Spring/Summer, 1987): 25-42. Reilly focuses on the treatment of the black experience from a historical perspective in Williams's novel.

Broderick McGrady

THE MAN WHO KILLED THE DEER

Author: Frank Waters (1902-1995)
Type of plot: Social realism
Time of plot: The late 1930's, before the outbreak of World War II
Locale: The Pueblo Indian Reservation, near Taos, New Mexico
First published: 1942

Principal characters:

> MARTINIANO, the protagonist, a young maverick (part Pueblo Indian and part Apache)
> FLOWERS PLAYING, his wife (part Ute and part Arapahoe)
> PALEMON, Martiniano's closest friend
> RODOLFO BYERS, a white man who runs a trading post adjacent to the Pueblo land
> MANUEL RENA, the Peyote chief, leader of a controversial peyote cult

The Novel

Martiniano, a troubled young Pueblo Indian who has been sent away to the white man's school, shoots a deer on government land exactly two days after the hunting season has closed. Martiniano is soon spotted by a forest ranger, who flies into a rage over the killing of the animal and strikes Martiniano with his gun. With his head bleeding, Martiniano manages to escape by hiding in a stream. The next morning, Palemon, who has been unable to sleep, rescues him, drawn by some powerful, intuitive knowledge of his friend's distress.

Martiniano is found guilty and given a fine of $150, which is paid by Rodolfo Byers, the white man who runs the trading post. After the trial, Martiniano's life begins to fall apart. His marriage to Flowers Playing becomes more and more unhappy; the couple begin to drift apart. He is increasingly aware of his role as an outsider, a man who does not seem to belong in either the world of whites or the world of Indians. He is not allowed to live in the pueblo proper but in a hut at the edge of the pueblo. Martiniano refuses to remove the heels of his boots, cut out the seat of his pants, or sing the required tribal songs—and he is punished for all these acts of rebellion. At the center of all his problems is the killing of the deer: " 'That deer!' he exclaimed suddenly. 'That's what they are holding against me most of all. That cursed deer which I killed! That is what has destroyed my wife's love and faith!' "

In a desperate attempt to shake off his profound depression, Martiniano becomes involved with Manuel Rena and his peyote cult. The drug, however, only exacerbates Martiniano's sense of guilt. In a peyote-induced trance, he once again sees the deer he killed: "The deer raced after him. Its hot breath burnt the back of his head, its pointed forefeet struck at and thundered behind him." Martiniano realizes that peyote is not for him, and soon the rest of the cult members are arrested by the tribal Council. Martiniano is still implicated, however, since his distinctive blanket was confiscated during the raid.

A new phase begins in Martiniano's life when he decides to clear some mountain land which was left to him by his father. Martiniano cleans out the spring and repairs the little hut. Unfortunately, a Mexican sheepherder tries to take over the hut, and in the scuffle Martiniano wounds him slightly and accidentally with the Mexican's own gun. This time the tribe supports him. The Mexican seems to represent all the intruders who have encroached on Indian land for generations. Ever since Martiniano's killing of the deer, the Pueblo people have been demanding the return of their ancient lands, especially Dawn Lake, a sacred spot in the mountains which they regard as their tribal church and the center of their being. Martiniano slowly begins to feel connected to the tribe; he decides to accept fifteen lashes, administered by his friend Palemon, to retrieve his blanket from the Council. The Fiesta of San Geronimo occurs soon thereafter, and Martiniano and Flowers Playing (now pregnant) come down from the mountain to attend. No one can climb the tall ceremonial pole with a deer tied to its top. When Martiniano attempts the feat, he too fails—a sign that he has still not atoned for his guilt.

Martiniano's redemption comes through an act of selfless devotion. He rescues Palemon's son, Napaita, who has been trapped in a remote mountain cave. Soon, a son of his own is born, Juan de Bautista, and Martiniano feels peace at last: "The deer he had killed. It no longer troubled him." Congress passes a bill to compensate the tribe for lost land and to return thirty thousand acres of national forest to the tribe, including their sacred center, Dawn Lake. The book ends, then, with Martiniano and the tribe in full control of their most precious possession—their identity.

The Characters

At no point does Frank Waters provide a police-blotter description of his protagonist, Martiniano. The reader comes to appreciate Martiniano through his bold actions and sharply reasoned speeches, like the one in which he defends his killing of the deer to the Council. After explaining that the Council slowed him down by refusing to let him use the communal threshing machine, he concludes: "What is the difference between killing a deer on Tuesday or Thursday? Would I not have killed it anyway?" Later, when Palemon applies the fifteen lashes, Martiniano submits stoically, even though the pain is excruciating. Yet he can feel tenderness, too. After Flowers Playing becomes pregnant, Martiniano matures into a kind of inarticulate poet, recording but not enunciating the beauty of his little mountain retreat: "The yellow moon low over the desert, the stars twinkling above the tips of the high ridge pines, the fireflies, the far-off throb of a drum, the silence, the tragic, soundless rushing of the great world through time—it caught at his breath, his heart."

Flowers Playing, by contrast, is presented with photographic clarity. She is the Arapahoe maiden: "Have you ever seen an Arapahoe maiden down in the willows by the stream? The fresh, cool dew clinging like Navajo-silver buttons to her plain brown moccasins, the first arrows of sunlight glancing off the shining wings of her blue-black hair, the flush of dawn still in her smooth brown cheeks?" She becomes an Earth Mother, taming two wild deer in the mountain clearing and donning the costume of the Deer Mother in a sacred Pueblo dance. Her sensitivity to the animal king-dom is a source of strength for Martiniano in his painful process of self-atonement.

Palemon serves as a foil to Martiniano; he is the "good" Indian, adhering to the codes and customs of the tribe. His natural sensitivity to danger alerts him to Martiniano's trouble with the ranger, and his good reputation assures him a seat on the Council. When Martiniano chooses to accept his fifteen lashes, Palemon is assigned to whip him. It is a sign of their friendship that each man accepts his role unhesitat-ingly in the grisly little drama. Martiniano pretends not to recognize him: "Palemon too was a man. No sign of recognition showed on his face as he lifted the lash." The novel comes full circle when Martiniano rescues Palemon's son, Napaita, using the same power of intuition upon which Palemon relied in the opening pages.

The most complicated character is Rodolfo Byers, the crusty Anglo who runs the trading post. Some critics see Byers as a kind of alter ego of Frank Waters himself. Byers has known the Indians all his life, but he avoids the dangers of either romanti-cizing them or ignoring their flaws. Once, when he was bitten by a rattlesnake, Byers was saved by an old Indian who appeared out of nowhere and stroked his body with eagle feathers. Byers survived, and he began to accept the Indians and all their inscru-table ways. He empathizes with Martiniano and the apparent curse of the deer: " 'Boy, I too have had my deer,' muttered the white man, staring into the fire. 'Believe me, son, it will pass' "—and so it does.

Manuel Rena sets up a tepee next to the pueblo and establishes a local peyote cult after he has learned about this "strange herb of mystery and power" on a visit to other tribes. The use of peyote is forbidden in the rest of the state, but the District Indian Su-perintendent encourages the tribe to try it. The Council disagrees, however, and orders the cult disbanded. Peyote cults cannot coexist with the native religion as celebrated at Dawn Lake.

Themes and Meanings

As an amateur anthropologist and folklorist, Frank Waters has long been concerned with the Indian subcultures of the Southwest, as shown by his later studies, *Masked Gods: Navaho and Pueblo Ceremonialism* (1950) and *Book of the Hopi* (1963). In *The Man Who Killed the Deer*, Waters uses a complex narrative structure that inter-rupts the story of Martiniano and the tribe with transcriptions of myths and ceremo-nial prayers, descriptions of sacred dances and costumes, and discussions of Pueblo rites. Waters goes into these details because the primary theme of the book is the uniqueness of Pueblo culture, an irreplaceable gift to the human family. Thus, the reader is exposed several times to a Pueblo prayer which begins, "There is no such thing as a simple thing." Mrs. Wolf Red-Belly Woman recounts the entire myth of Shell Boy and Blue Corn (which parallels the story of Martiniano and his wife), and Waters describes the Deer Mother dance and many other dances down to the smallest step. The reader also follows the manhood initiation ceremony as experienced by Palemon's son, Napaita. These anthropological details are not excess baggage; they are integral to the meaning of the novel. Waters does not merely want to tell

Martiniano's story; he wants to tell it from a true Pueblo Indian perspective.

The deer is not only a catalyst for narrative development but also the basic symbol of the work. Like all symbols, it contains layer upon layer of meaning: "The deer he had killed, the two deer sisters of Flowers Playing up in the mountains, the deer dancing in subjection to Deer Mothers. . . . Who could say which was alive, was flesh, was spirit. . . ?" The deer, then, is life and the spirit of life; by killing it, Martiniano has offended life itself, and his redemption is possible only when he accepts the life force, as he finally does, in all its various forms.

Critical Context

The Man Who Killed the Deer is Waters's best-known and probably his best-loved book, as suggested by the fact that the original 1942 edition was reprinted many times, with a second edition issued in 1965 and a third edition in 1971 (which has also been reprinted many times). Conceived as part of a trilogy on the minorities of the Southwest, *The Man Who Killed the Deer* appeared after *People of the Valley* (1941), which deals with Spanish colonial settlers, and before *The Yogi of the Cockroach Court* (1947), a story of casinos and lowlife on the Mexican American border.

In a larger context, *The Man Who Killed the Deer* can be seen as one of the best examples of a genre which traces the roots of a particular ethnic group. This tradition would include such classic books as Edwin Corle's *People on the Earth* (1937) and more recent works such as Carlos Castaneda's *The Teachings of Don Juan: A Yaqui Way of Knowledge* (1968). *The Man Who Killed the Deer* is significant because it transcends this tradition by offering characters and situations of universal appeal, presented in a style that can truly be called poetic.

Bibliography

Blackburn, Alexander. *A Sunrise Brighter Still: The Visionary Novels of Frank Waters*. Athens: Ohio University Press, 1991. Chapters on each of Waters's novels, with an introduction that surveys the writer's purposes and his career and a conclusion arguing that Waters is a major American writer. Includes detailed notes and extensive bibliography.

Deloria, Vine, Jr., ed. *Frank Waters: Man and Mystic*. Athens: Ohio University Press, 1993. Memoirs of Waters and commentaries on his novels, emphasizing his prophetic style and sense of the sacred.

Lyon, Thomas J. *Frank Waters*. New York: Twayne, 1973. Fills a critical vacuum by analyzing Waters's themes and artistic style. After sketching Waters's life, Lyon examines his nonfiction, showing him to be a writer of ideas with a sacred theory of the earth and Hopi mythic values. Focuses on seven novels as narrations of these ideas, from *Fever Pitch* to *Pike's Peak*, and also discusses his minor works, including the biography of *The Earp Brothers of Tombstone*, the children's biography of Robert Gilruth, his book reviews, and his essays on writing. The last chapter summarizes the book's thesis and calls for more study of Waters's work. Contains a chronology, notes and references, a selected annotated bibliography, and an index.

South Dakota Review 15 (Autumn, 1977). A special Frank Waters issue, containing these essays: "The Sound of Space," by John Milton; "Frank Waters's *Mexico Mystique:* The Ontology of the Occult," by Jack L. Davis; "Frank Waters and the Visual Sense," by Robert Kostka; "Frank Waters and the Concept of 'Nothing Special,' " by Thomas J. Lyon; "Teaching *Yoga* in Las Vegas," by Charles L. Adams; "Frank Waters and the Mountain Spirit," by Quay Grigg; "The Conflict in *The Man Who Killed the Deer*," by Christopher Hoy; "Mysticism and Witchcraft," by Waters; and "Frank Waters," by John Manchester.

Daniel L. Guillory

MANHUNT

Author: Alejo Carpentier (1904-1980)
Type of plot: Psychological drama
Time of plot: The early 1930's, during the dictatorship of Gerardo Machado
Locale: Havana, Cuba
First published: El acoso, 1956 (English translation, 1959)

> *Principal characters:*
>> THE UNNAMED PROTAGONIST, a university student and political activist
>> ESTRELLA, a prostitute and sometime lover of the protagonist
>> AN OLD BLACK WOMAN, the protagonist's former wet nurse, who runs a
>> boardinghouse
>> THE TICKET TAKER at the concert hall

The Novel

The principal action of *Manhunt*, a short novel which takes place during the span of one night in Havana, recounts the unnamed protagonist's flight from his former political comrades, who are trying to murder him for having turned informer. The protagonist, the typical "young man from the provinces," has come to the capital to pursue his studies at the university. Once in Havana, he takes up residence in a boardinghouse owned by an old black woman who had been his wet nurse. Shortly after his arrival in the city, he joins the Communist Party but is soon disenchanted with it and opts instead for direct political action in the form of terrorist acts against various government officials. These acts include one murder for which he is directly responsible and involvement in a second. As a result of his terrorist activities, he is arrested; terrified by the threat of castration, he "sings" and is released back into the streets.

Most of these events, however, are narrated in the form of flashbacks, for when the novel begins the protagonist is already in the streets, fleeing from his pursuers. His pursuers finally catch up with him at a concert hall where a symphonic orchestra has just finished performing Ludwig van Beethoven's *Eroica* symphony. In ironic counterpoint to Beethoven's work, the unnamed protagonist dies an unheroic death when he is murdered while hiding in a balcony seat. The incongruity of his death is enhanced by the fact that it takes place on Easter Sunday, only one of many instances of religious symbolism in the novella. *Manhunt* is the story of a passion at the end of which awaits no resurrection.

During that night, in desperate flight from his pursuers, he tries various ways of escaping, but to no avail. He goes back to the boardinghouse where he had lived only to find that its owner has died; he visits Estrella, his lover, who is unable to help him; he cannot get sanctuary in a church; and he also fails to see the magistrate who had ordered the assassinations. Interwoven with this periplus through the streets of Havana are the flashbacks that recount his biography. Of the novel's three parts, the first and

third take place in the present, during the performance of the symphony; the middle
section, actually the bulk of the novel, is largely given over to the protagonist's earlier
life.

The Characters

As is sometimes the case with Carpentier's protagonists, the principal character of
this novel goes unnamed. Nevertheless, Carpentier still provides the reader with a
nuanced and vivid psychological profile. Since the interest of the story resides, in no
small measure, in this portrayal of the anguish of the informer, it would not be a mistake to look upon this novella as primarily a character study. Fleeing through the
streets of Havana, the protagonist finds himself utterly alone, without refuge or meaningful human contact. His relationship with Estrella, one is led to believe, was a superficial and passing sexual infatuation, at least on her part. The only other human contact the protagonist had in the city was the old black woman, who has recently died.
Symptomatic of the protagonist's predicament is the attitude of the priest, who refuses
to confess him. Tormented with guilt, lacking friends, and with no place to escape, the
protagonist is an easy prey for his pursuers. As he says: "Why were men today denied
that ancient privilege of sanctuary that he read about in a book on the Gothic?" The
whole story centers on his failed quest for sanctuary—political, emotional, artistic.

The other two most important characters in the story are Estrella and the old black
woman. These two women act as foils for each other. As her name suggests, Estrella
(meaning "star") is potentially a bright spot in the protagonist's existence, and he
prides himself on being able to satisfy a woman who is accustomed to casual sexual
encounters. The old black woman, clearly a mother figure, satisfies a different kind of
need, for she is his one nexus to his childhood in the provinces. Just as the prostitute
represents the degradation of urban life, the black woman represents the innocence
and security of his early years away from the capital. Spiritually and physically, the
protagonist oscillates between these two women.

The only other significant character in the novella is the ticket taker at the opera, a
student of music whose lack of discipline has thwarted his education. Although he
never actually meets the protagonist, these two characters are joined by their common
interest in Estrella, the lodestar of their emotional and sexual lives. Unlike the protagonist, the ticket taker is not a man of action, a passivity conveyed by the fact that one
usually finds him reading a biography of Beethoven. The contrast between Estrella
and the old black woman is therefore counterbalanced by the contrast between the two
principal male characters. The ticket taker also acts as a foil, for he symbolizes the intellectuals who—unlike the protagonist—have not gotten involved in the murky waters of Cuban politics.

Themes and Meanings

Manhunt artfully combines political, psychological, and philosophical themes.
Based as it is on historical events, the novel re-creates the atmosphere of terror that
pervaded some sectors of Cuban society during the dictatorship of Gerardo Machado,

which Carpentier himself actively opposed. It is no accident that the whole novel takes place at night, for, in Carpentier's view, this was indeed a dark moment in Cuba's modern history.

Beyond the novel's political dimension, however, is the broader issue of the place of the intellectual in society. Written shortly after *The Lost Steps* (1953), *Manhunt* shares with this novel a concern with the social function of art. While in the earlier novel, however, one sees the protagonist trying to escape modern society by traveling to the South American jungle, in *Manhunt* the protagonist finds himself in the thick of the political turmoil of the time. The character in *Manhunt* who does represent the withdrawal of the artist from society is the ticket taker, an effete intellectual.

A third important theme in the book is the psychological theme of betrayal. Almost all of the characters in the novel betray something or someone. The protagonist himself is guilty of several acts of betrayal: He betrays his comrades by informing, and he betrays his wet nurse by stealing her food. Other characters in the novel also commit acts of betrayal: Estrella betrays his whereabouts to the police, the priest betrays his trust by refusing him sanctuary, and the ticket taker betrays his musical vocation by spending his free time with Estrella. One could say that the author himself, by juxtaposing the manhunt and the Third Symphony (the *Eroica*), betrays the spirit of Beethoven's composition.

The narrative technique of *Manhunt* also deserves some comment, for this is perhaps the most complicated of all of Carpentier's works. The novel (brief enough to be described as a novella) consists of three long untitled chapters which divide into eighteen subchapters. These eighteen vignettes tell the story from three different points of view. At various moments, both of the principal male characters become narrators; other sections of the novel, however, are narrated by a third-person omniscient narrator. The transitions from one narrative perspective to another are brusque, and the reader is often bewildered by the juxtaposition of these different perspectives. The use of more than one point of view, rare in Carpentier, is a device that some critics have attributed to the influence of William Faulkner. More important than the possible Faulknerian echoes in the novel, however, is the fact that by jumbling together incidents and characters Carpentier forces his reader to take an active part in recomposing the fragments of the story; the pleasure thus derived is not unlike that of a jigsaw puzzle.

Also worthy of mention is Carpentier's manipulation of time. Although first published separately, *Manhunt* was later included with three other shorter works in a volume entitled *Guerra del tiempo* (1958; *War of Time*, 1970). The title of the collection is significant, for it reveals Carpentier's view of art as a battle against time, as an attempt to order events according to something other than linear progression. This explains why, in *Manhunt*, a single episode or even a gesture may splinter into images that appear in different parts of the narration. By fragmenting the temporal and causal flow of events, Carpentier gives his narrative material an artistic coherence unlike that of real life.

Critical Context

In spite of its brevity, *Manhunt* is one of the works of Carpentier that has elicited the most critical comment. For some critics, Carpentier's stylized and fragmentary re-creation of Cuban history robs the story of the immediacy of lived experience, transforming it into a kind of a temporal tableau. Other critics, drawing attention to the work's subtle and innovative craftmanship, suggest that in *Manhunt* Carpentier has masterfully condensed many of his typical preoccupations and themes. Carpentier himself claimed that the novel was composed like a sonata, although the musical structure of the narration is not immediately obvious. Despite these differences of opinion, however, there is little doubt that *Manhunt* is one of the most challenging and original works of modern Spanish-American fiction.

Bibliography

Echevarria, Roberto Gonzalez. *Alejo Carpentier: The Pilgrim at Home*. Ithaca, N.Y.: Cornell University Press, 1977. Explores what seems like a radical disjunction between Carpentier's fiction and nonfiction. Echevarria finds unity, however, in certain recurring themes, which he illuminates by discussing Carpentier's debt to writers such as José Ortega y Gasset and Oswald Spengler. The novelist's penchant for dialectical structures and for allegory is also explored. Includes a bibliography and index.

Harss, Luis, and Barbara Dohmann. *Into the Mainstream*. New York: Harper & Row, 1966. Includes a chapter often cited as a succinct introduction to Carpentier's work up to the early 1960's.

Janney, Frank. *Alejo Carpentier and His Early Works*. London: Tamesis, 1981. An introductory survey that is still useful.

Kilmer-Tchalekian, Mary. "Ambiguity in *El siglo de las luces*." *Latin American Literary Review* 4 (1976): 47-57. An especially valuable discussion of Carpentier's narrative technique and handling of point of view.

King, Lloyd. *Alejo Carpentier, Caribbean Writer*. St. Augustine, Fla.: University of the West Indies Press, 1977. Often cited for its perceptive introduction to Carpentier's work.

Shaw, Donald L. *Alejo Carpentier*. Boston: Twayne, 1985. Chapters on Carpentier's apprenticeship, his discovery of the "marvelous real," his handling of time and circularity, his fiction about the Antilles, his explorations of politics, and his last works. Includes chronology, notes, and annotated bibliography.

Souza, Raymond D. *Major Cuban Novelists: Innovation and Tradition*. Columbia: University of Missouri Press, 1976. Should be read in conjunction with Harss and Dohmann.

Gustavo Perez-Firmat

A MANUAL FOR MANUEL

Author: Julio Cortázar (1914-1984)

Type of plot: Social morality

Time of plot: From 1969 to 1972, during which time Argentina, under the military dictatorship of General Alejandro Lanusse, suffered widespread violation of human rights

Locale: Paris and Buenos Aires

First published: Libro de Manuel, 1973 (English translation, 1978)

Principal characters:

LUDMILLA, a Polish actress who lives with Marcos

GOMEZ, a Panamanian and a member of the Screwery who lives with Monique, another member of the Screwery

MONIQUE, a French graduate student who lives with Gomez

LUCIEN VERNEUIL, a French member of the Screwery

HEREDIA, a Brazilian member of the Screwery

MARCOS, an Argentine member of the Screwery

ANDRES, an Argentine, the protagonist, a somewhat political intellectual who listens to music, a former lover of Ludmilla

THE ONE I TOLD YOU, never identified by name

FRANCINE, a French bookshop owner and the lover of Andres

OSCAR, an Argentine who lives with Gladis

MANUEL, the son of Patricio and Susana,

GLADIS, a woman who lives with Oscar

LONSTEIN, an Argentine who works in a morgue and is intellectual, not political

ROLAND, a French member of the Screwery

FERNANDO, a newly arrived Chilean

SUSANA, the mother of Manuel, a translator for UNESCO

PATRICIO, the father of Manuel, a member of the Screwery

The Novel

As the novel begins, Susana translates and discusses articles from the newspaper with other members of a revolutionary group called "the Screwery." A telegram from London and a reference to something called the "Vincennes business" constitute the reader's introduction to the group's plan to smuggle counterfeit money in order to finance a political kidnapping. The target is a top Latin American police official, referred to as the Vip, whose headquarters are in Paris. He is to be held for ransom until Latin American political prisoners are released.

As the kidnapping preparations are under way, Andres takes Francine to a sleazy bar. He then tells her about a dream in which he sees himself in a film theater which has two screens at right angles. He is there to see a Fritz Lang thriller. Suddenly a messenger arrives and tells him that a Cuban wants to speak with him. Andres follows the messenger until he enters a room where he sees a figure on a sofa. It is the Cuban. At this point, the most important point in the dream, the dream's narrative is interrupted. The next thing that Andres sees is himself, now spectator of and participant in a thriller, leaving the room. Andres interprets the dream to mean that since he has spoken to the Cuban, he now has a mission to fulfill. He has no idea, however, what the mission might be. Andres's quest is directed toward one goal: to find the message cut from his dream, a message that will show him the road he should elect between the beloved solitude of his life as an intellectual in Paris and total political commitment.

The kidnapping does not occur until three-quarters of the way into the book, and the account of the actual moment, provided by the unnamed character, who is identified only as "the one I told you," is no more than "a general impression of total confusion." The details that would have "made a good narrative" are missing. Andres, who is not present at the kidnapping, is awakened from sleep when the Cuban from his dream says to him, "Wake up." He arrives at the scene of the police shoot-out, where the Screwery is holding the Vip. The Vip is released, saved by the police. Gomez and Heredia are next seen in prison. They discuss the fact that "Marcos would have thought" that the operation went well. Proceedings of a press conference on human rights follow this scene. Accounts from Argentines who have been tortured appear in one column juxtaposed to testimony from North American soldiers who witnessed or participated in torture in Vietnam. The novel ends with two glimpses of the return to everyday life: Monique cares for the baby and waits for news from Gomez; Andres tells Susana that he must pick up a Joni Mitchell record and put the notes of "the one I told you" in order, and that the water pitcher story must be added. It is implied that "the one I told you" has died. Lonstein returns to his job washing bodies in the morgue.

Yet the novel ends with a fantastic twist: The body that Lonstein washes, after picking up a water pitcher, is not identified, but Lonstein recognizes him and says, "It had to be us, that's for certain, you there and me with this sponge, you were so right, they're going to think we made it all up." The reader must link "the blackish stain," which Lonstein removes with the sponge, to the character who went out to pick up a Joni Mitchell record, Andres.

The Characters

In comparison with more traditional novelists of the nineteenth century, Cortázar does not create memorable characters; rather, his characters emerge from cultural codes. That is, political discourse determines the boundaries of, for example, Heredia or Gomez, while the character of Andres is shaped by the aleatory music that he loves.

Cortázar is not concerned with a psychological analysis, a realistic representation, or a symbolic use of characters. Rather, his characters are placed in situations in order to provoke the reader.

Cortázar's characters are typically marginal in relation to society; in *Rayuela* (1963; *Hopscotch*, 1966), they are students, transients, circus performers, and mental patients. In *A Manual for Manuel*, they are a marginal political group. *A Manual for Manuel* is a sort of mirror image of *Hopscotch*. Traveler and Horacio reappear as Marcos and Andres; La Maga and Talita as Ludmilla and Francine. Just as Traveler was able to make a commitment to Talita, while Horacio could not make such a commitment either to politics or to La Maga, so Marcos is a member of the Screwery while Andres is on the edge of the revolutionary group. Ludmilla is confused by the activities of the Screwery. Francine owns a book and stationery shop and lives in an elegant apartment with her cat, library, and scotch. Ludmilla lives in disorder with pieces of leek "hung all over the place." Andres is in love with both of these women, attracted to both their worlds. Other characters in the novel appear as couples: Oscar and Gladis, Susana and Patricio, Monique and Gomez. It has been noticed by one critic that the male characters are discussed much more often than are the female characters in Cortázar's work and that, although he may be paving the way for the "new man," his work leaves much to be desired with regard to the "new woman."

With the exception of Monique, who is also writing her thesis, for the most part, Ludmilla and the other women characters make sandwiches, translate, and make love. Susana, however, is familiar with the events of May, 1968, having been at the Battle of the Sorbonne. Marcos and Andres are paternalistic toward women, while Lonstein points out to Andres that "the whole world is not a privilege of the males, anyone can project geometry, you thought that your scheme was acceptable and now you find out that women also have their triangle to say."

Themes and Meanings

A Manual for Manuel is a novel about the continuing war between Latin American guerrillas and Latin American government. It is literally a collage of fragments. Using newspaper clippings, testimony from human rights commission hearings, advertisements, recipes, and musings on literary criticism, Cortázar interrogates his own identity through the character of Andres; he questions his life as an intellectual and the role of the intellectual in relationship to political commitment. As an Argentine who lived in Paris after 1951 and as a translator for UNESCO, Cortázar was acutely aware of the ideological as well as the directly confrontational warfare in Argentina and elsewhere. In fact, selecting and translating from newspapers has been part of his job; his transformation of these newspaper texts into a novel may be understood as his attempt to recapture the subject which he has had to translate for others. He is aware of the difficulty of writing about the themes of *A Manual for Manuel*, which include political torture; in one passage, he points out that Latin American readers are already aware of the issues, rendering the novel useless as a didactic device, while North American readers do not usually have the background to understand the political references. In *Hopscotch*, he discusses the dilemma of the man of action and the intellectual. These roles are played by Horacio and Traveler. He condemns the man of action for having the same unforgivable sin as Traveler: conformity. One conforms to the party while the other capitulates to the dictates of everyday life. The dilemma is presented again in *A Manual for Manuel*, but this time, the work centers on a group devoted to political action. Andres, the narrator, is not present at the moment of political action, the kidnapping of the Vip. He is always on the outside. This is the problem of the modernist writer. Cortázar seeks to overcome it to some extent by actively involving what he calls the "reader accomplice."

Critical Context

A Manual for Manuel was awarded the Prix Medicis. One critic has called it a necessary second volume for *Hopscotch*. The narrative structure of *A Manual for Manuel*, although less complex than that of *Hopscotch*, is experimental and similar to the structure used by twentieth century musicians, both classical and jazz. It proceeds in a more or less linear way, but there are certain questions left unanswered, certain unfilled gaps, because of the way in which the story is told. There is no omnipresent narrator. Rather, the story is told primarily through the eyes of a narrator, "the one I told you," and Andres. The fact that the modernist cannot get inside the historical event, rendering modernist literature helpless as a political educational tool, is of concern to Cortázar. His novel is about this problem, making the work post-modernist in that it examines the structure of the modernist novel.

Philosophically, Cortázar's refusal of the role of omniscient narrator who would have access to the thing itself implies that there is no essence to be distinguished from appearance. Two possible conclusions arise: He is a Kantian, who believes that the object is unknowable, or he is a post-modernist, who refuses to distinguish between art and its object. The implication of this method is that reality becomes intelligible through the combined activity of the writer and reader who write or read the text. In *A Manual for Manuel*, "the one I told you" sees the kidnapping as "a multilenticular and quadrichromatic picture of the ants and the Vip himself. . . ." This "multilenticular" view joins the imaginings of "the one I told you" with the "sparser" information possessed by Marcos and Ludmilla. The active reader of the book must then take all this and attempt to reconstruct the event.

In terms of genre, Cortázar's work has been linked to the literature of fantasy and Magical Realism, both by critics and in his own writing. Yet he sees his activity as a writer and the active participation that he demands on the part of the reader as a form of political practice that transcends the boundaries of traditional genres to become a testimony of Latin American reality. Certain critics have interpreted the freedom embodied in characters such as La Maga as a model for overcoming alienation and shaking epistemological assumptions. Cortázar sees the "Other," the dimension of the fantastic, as our only salvation from conforming to the role of obedient robots that the technocrats would like us to accept and which we continue to refuse. In his own life, the political form of Cortázar's refusal can be seen in his support for the Cuban revolution, Allende's regime, the Russell Tribunal, and the Nicaraguan revolution.

A Manual for Manuel marked a turning point in Cortázar's career, toward political literature. Not all critics greeted this change favorably, and many still believe that *Hopscotch* is a more successful literary work.

Bibliography
Alazraki, Jaime, and Ivar Ivask, eds. *The Final Island: The Fiction of Julio Cortázar.*
    Norman: University of Oklahoma Press, 1978. Perhaps the finest collection of criti-
    cism on Cortázar, a representative sampling of his best critics covering all the im-
    portant aspects of his fictional output.
Boldy, Steven. *The Novels of Julio Cortázar.* Cambridge, England: Cambridge Uni-
    versity Press, 1980. The introduction provides a helpful biographical sketch linked
    to the major developments in Cortázar's writing. Boldy concentrates on four
    Cortázar novels: *The Winners, Hopscotch, 62: A Model Kit,* and *A Manual for
    Manuel.* Includes notes, bibliography, and index.
Guibert, Rita. *Seven Voices: Seven Latin American Writers Talk to Rita Guibert.* New
    York: Knopf, 1973. Includes an important interview with Cortázar, who discusses
    both his politics (his strenuous objection to U.S. interference in Latin America) and
    many of his fictional works.
Harss, Luis, and Barbara Dohmann. *Into the Mainstream: Conversations with Latin-
    American Writers.* New York: Harper & Row, 1967. Includes an English transla-
    tion of an important interview in Spanish.
Hernandez del Castillo, Ana. *Keats, Poe, and the Shaping of Cortázar's Mythopoesis.*
    Amsterdam: J. Benjamin, 1981. This is a part of the Purdue University Mono-
    graphs in Romance Languages, volume 8. Cortázar praised this study for its rigor
    and insight.
Peavler, Terry L. *Julio Cortázar.* Boston: Twayne, 1990. Peavler begins with an over-
    view of Cortázar's life and career and his short stories of the fantastic, the mysteri-
    ous, the psychological, and the realistic. Only one chapter is devoted exclusively to
    his novels. Includes chronology, notes, annotated bibliography, and index.
Stavans, Ilan. *Julio Cortázar: A Study of the Short Fiction.* New York: Twayne, 1996.
    See especially the chapters on the influence of Jorge Luis Borges on Cortázar's fic-
    tion, his use of the fantastic, and his reliance on popular culture. Stavans also has a
    section on Cortázar's role as writer and his interpretation of developments in Latin
    American literature. Includes chronology and bibliography.
Yovanovich, Gordana. *Julio Cortázar's Character Mosaic: Reading the Longer Fic-
    tion.* Toronto: University of Toronto Press, 1991. Three chapters focus on Cortá-
    zar's four major novels and his fluctuating presentations of character as narrators,
    symbols, and other figures of language. Includes notes and bibliography.

Emily Hicks

MARKED BY FIRE

Author: Joyce Carol Thomas (1938-   )
Type of plot: Bildungsroman
Time of plot: The 1950's and the 1960's
Locale: Oklahoma
First published: 1982

> *Principal characters:*
>> ABYSSINIA "ABBY" JACKSON, the protagonist, an African American girl born in an Oklahoma field
>> MOTHER BARKER, Abby's neighbor, a family friend and folk doctor
>> PATIENCE JACKSON, Abby's loving and understanding mother
>> STRONG JACKSON, Abby's father, who temporarily deserts the family after a tornado destroys his business
>> LILY NORENE JOHNSON, Abby's best friend, who becomes the young mother of three children and is beaten to death by her husband
>> SISTER LIGHTSEY, a neighbor and family friend, the mother of thirteen children
>> BROTHER JACOBS, a deacon in the local church who is imprisoned after he rapes Abby
>> TREMBLING SALLY, a crazy woman possessed by evil

The Novel

Marked by Fire, the first novel by Joyce Carol Thomas, tells the story of the first twenty years in the life of Abyssinia Jackson, a black girl born in the fields of Oklahoma in 1951 as a tornado goes through. Set entirely in Ponca City, Oklahoma, the work captures the experience of a young woman coming of age in rural America in the 1950's and 1960's.

Marked by Fire is divided into thirty short chapters, each designated not by title or number but by calendar date. The narration is entirely from the third-person point of view, although the story is always concerned only with Abby's experiences, thoughts, and development. All the main characters in the novel are black; hence, Abby's problems are never directly related to racial discrimination or prejudice. Her enemies are two other blacks, Trembling Sally and Brother Jacobs, and nature itself.

The organization of the novel and story is entirely chronological. Abby's life is momentous from her birth because of the tornado, which is viewed by her family and friends as an omen. This fictional biography chronicles some twenty years in her life, during which she overcomes problems few young people must face.

The setting of the small Oklahoma town frames the activities of Abby's family. Abby enjoys listening, then telling, stories in the folk tradition; she sings hymns at church and at home; she excels in school as a reader; and she learns the art of folk medicine from her older friend and mentor, Mother Barker.

One of the most important developments of the plot occurs early in the story. After

Thomas records numerous instances of the peace and desirability of Abby's early life, a second tornado comes to town—one which destroys the barbershop of Strong Jackson, Abby's father. Devastated, he inexplicably runs away from home and family, giving no reasons. This desertion leaves the family without income and in conditions that are otherwise worse than could have been foreseen.

The central event of the novel occurs during the father's absence when Abby is ten years old. After being entrusted by Mother Barker with the secrets of making a pound cake for a church social, Abby takes a piece to Brother Jacobs, a deacon. He rapes her in his wife's absence, and the child is left traumatized physically, emotionally, and spiritually. It is of little comfort to Abby, her mother, and their friends that Brother Jacobs is tried and imprisoned for several years for the terrible deed.

During Abby's recovery from the rape, the other villain of the novel, Trembling Sally, makes an appearance. Without reason or explanation, this woman inflicts harm on Abby on several occasions. There is no understanding Sally's conduct: She functions as evil and insanity, acting only against that which is good. Thus, finding Abby alone in bed after the rape, she lets wasps into the bedroom to do additional harm to the child. Fortunately, friends return in time to rescue Abby.

Slowly, Abby returns to her new life, one in which her childhood is gone forever. Following a flood, yet another natural event that wrecks the economy of the black community, Abby plays in the water at the river. There she is attacked a second time by Sally, who is intent upon drowning her. Fortunately, Abby's father returns in time to save her from death.

During her childhood, Abby's chief pleasure in life is singing, both at home and in public. After the rape, she is at first unable to talk, but this ability is restored; however, she is not able to sing. Thoughtlessly, school officials assign Abby the task of singing at the Christmas play during her junior year in high school. She is unable to do so, and in her own estimation, at least, she makes a fool of herself.

Toward the end of Abby's teen years, Mother Barker, herself always the family friend and one especially close to Abby, takes the girl to be her apprentice in the practice of folk medicine. Abby thrives in this new role, learning quickly and truly enjoying not so much the mastery of the art as the fact of helping others with both physical and emotional problems. Mother Barker dies, leaving Abby her house and business. At about the same time, Lilly Norene Johnson, Abby's best friend during her early years, also dies after being beaten by her husband. Abby takes care of her friend's three daughters, saving them from a fire in which their house burns down. The novel ends on a positive note, with Abby secure in her profession as community folk doctor, in her role as a do-gooder helping the children of her dead friend, and in her maturity after having overcome the effects of the rape. At twenty years of age, she is therefore established in her society and equipped to proceed with her life.

The Characters

Abby, the central character of the story, is the subject of the novel throughout. Her experiences and thoughts are recorded by the novelist so that readers always know what is proceeding with her development. Abby must survive in a world where events from nature—tornadoes, floods, and fires—continue to threaten her life and well-being. Yet two other members of the black community, Brother Jacobs and Trembling Sally, cause her the most harm. Essentially, Abby stands as an innocent, one who never commits more than playful mischief herself but who is victimized by the physical elements and by other persons. Her role is that of the sensitive thinker, one who does not escape evil and calamity, but who does succeed in dealing with these.

Mother Barker is the chief matriarch of the black community. She seems in charge of the other women at social events, and in her role as folk doctor commands special respect from all. Mother Barker's essential goodness is portrayed to the reader through her actions: She is always ready to help others, particularly Abby, with her wisdom and medicine. She helps the young girl recover from the rape and then goes on to establish her in life. Mother Barker stands as a counterforce to Brother Jacobs and Trembling Sally.

Strong Jackson, Abby's father, is an important character. A man of seeming dignity and integrity, his sense of humor is revealed through stories he relates at his barbershop. His importance in the novel, however, mostly stems from his absence. Unable to go on against forces of nature that inflict harm and poverty upon his family, he deserts them. It is his return, however, that highlights Abby's own return to some sense of normalcy after the rape.

Lily Norene is Abby's only close friend during their school years. Lily marries at a young age and has three children, but her lot in life is to be beaten, repeatedly, by her husband. Eventually she dies, and Abby, who seemingly will not marry, is left to take care of her friend's offspring.

Brother Jacobs, a deacon in the community church, is a rapist and coward. The novel gives no explanation for his actions; before the rape, he is regarded by all as a leader of the blacks, an upstanding Christian and citizen. Abby fears him even while he is in prison, and she is comforted when, after his release, he decides not to return to Ponca City.

Trembling Sally's actions, always evil, are similarly never explained by the author; evil simply seems to exist in human nature just as it does in physical nature. Her character is revealed in part through dialogue but primarily through actions. Trembling Sally curses Abby at an early age, lets loose wasps upon the child (whom she blames for tempting Brother Jacobs), and attempts to drown her. Members of the community know and understand Sally, however, and choose to go on living with her.

Themes and Meanings

The novel is most specifically the story of Abby Jackson. As a character of fiction, she is never made to be representative of her race, gender, or time; rather, Thomas writes to depict the development of one character during her youth. This is not to say that Abby's story is not relevant to black identity; indeed, her race and gender, as well as the society in which she lives, do work to define her being and maturation.

The novel's main theme has to do with accepting evil as fact—and then overcoming it. Thomas does not delve into the origins of evil or try to understand it; there is no explanation, for example, for Abby's rape by Brother Jacobs or her attempted murder by Trembling Sally. The novelist sees the universe as one in which learning to cope with problems, and not explaining them, is the chief concern.

It is noteworthy that Thomas does not make the rapist a white man or Trembling Sally a white woman. Hence, the novel is not about racial problems, but about the black experience in America.

Pervasive and unresolved throughout the work is the question of God's existence: Is Abby alone in a meaningless and godless universe? Are the tornadoes, floods, and fires sent from (or, at least, permitted by) God to victimize the innocent and helpless, or do these calamities occur in God's absence? Abby never answers these questions for herself, and the reader is left in a world where life is at least partially governed by bitterness and cynicism as a consequence. The novelist does not answer questions raised by her own main character. Abby simply moves on with her life, whether God is helping her or not.

Critical Context

First published in 1982, *Marked by Fire* is a work that indicates the maturity of black literature in the United States. African American writers have generally written about black experiences, and most prominent African American works describe problems that directly or indirectly relate to race. In this work, however, Thomas avoids discussion of racial issues not so much by omitting any white characters of importance but simply by writing about her own fictional creation, Abby Jackson.

The chronological events of the work end in early 1971, and the main action occurs in the 1950's and 1960's; the novel was written and published some ten years later. The temporal distance gives the novelist an opportunity to look back at the social upheavals and turmoils of the earlier decades and write not about them but after them. Her focus and attention are on what it means to be black, what it means to mature (or, more correctly, to have matured) in black America, and what it means to define and establish identity. *Bright Shadow* (1983), a sequel, shows Abby attending college. *Water Girl* (1986) depicts the adventures of Abby's daughter.

Bibliography

Childress, Alice. "*Marked by Fire*." *The New York Times Book Review* 87 (April 18, 1982): 38. Childress discusses the main characters in the novel, particularly Abby's mother and Mother Barker. She points out that the plot does have weaknesses in that some events are not believable. The matter of belief in God is also taken up

Henderson, Darwin L., and Anthony L. Manna. "Evoking the 'Holy and the Horrible': Conversations with Joyce Carol Thomas." *African American Review* 32 (Spring, 1998): 139-146. Thomas discusses the influence of her childhood as a migrant farm worker in Oklahoma and California on her work. Although she only briefly mentions *Marked by Fire*, this interview provides a useful context in which to view this as well as her other novels.

Randall-Tsuruta, Dorothy. "*Marked by Fire*." *The Black Scholar* 13 (Summer, 1982): 48. Randall-Tsuruta reads the novel in its social context, finding that it calls for realization of certain horrors in society at large. She discusses the style of the writing, finding it to be lyrical. Trembling Sally is seen as the personification of the devil.

Rochman, Hazel. "*Marked by Fire*." *School Library Journal* 28 (March, 1982): 162. Rochman discusses the novel as it reveals the functions and activities of the black community in rural Oklahoma. She finds in the work "mythical overtones" that may prevent some readers from appreciating it. She also reads the work as being primarily by and for women.

Thomas, Joyce Carol. *Bright Shadow*. New York: Avon Books, 1983. In this sequel to *Marked by Fire*, Thomas continues the story of Abby Jackson. Now in college and in love, Abby has more tragedies strike her life. Another madman appears, and Thomas records an incredibly horrible murder.

Wray, Wendell. "*Marked by Fire*." *Best Sellers* 42 (June, 1982): 123-124. Wray interprets the novel primarily as a folk tale; he finds in the novel itself qualities and characteristics of Abby's own ability to render tall tales. Like other critics, he also finds similarities to the works of Maya Angelou.

Carl Singleton

THE MARTIAN CHRONICLES

Author: Ray Bradbury (1920-   )
Type of plot: Science fiction/fantasy
Time of plot: 1999-2026
Locale: The planet Mars and the United States
First published: 1950

> *Principal characters:*
>> A somewhat loosely connected series of stories and sketches, this work has no principal characters. A few characters appear in more than one story, such as Captain Wilder, the leader of the fourth expedition to Mars, and two of his crewmen, Parkhill and Hathaway. Spender, also a member of the Wilder expedition, is a crucial character, for he articulates most fully a central thematic conflict of the book.

The Novel

Though *The Martian Chronicles* consists of chronologically arranged stories and sketches having to do with the exploration and colonization of Mars at the end of the twentieth century, Ray Bradbury has provided enough unity to justify calling the work a novel. The book contains fourteen stories and twelve sketches, though one might dispute the proper classification for a long sketch, "The Musicians," about children playing among the dried corpses of dead Martians, and for the brief story, "There Will Come Soft Rains," about the death of a mechanized house in California which continued to function for years after an atom-bomb blast killed its human occupants.

These pieces can be divided according to phases in humanity's relationship to Mars. The first seven pieces are concerned with attempts to complete a successful expedition to Mars. The next fourteen pieces move through colonization toward exploitation of the planet. The next four cover the desertion of the colonies as people return to Earth after an atomic war begins in 2005. The last story tells how a remnant of what was best on Earth, having escaped the final conflagration, begins again on Mars. Within this structure, three stories stand out for their thematic importance in tying the whole work together: "—And the Moon Be Still as Bright," which ends the section on expeditions, "The Off Season," which ends the section on colonization and exploitation, and "The Million-Year Picnic," the final story.

Only the fourth expedition to Mars is successful. Each of the first three is destroyed, in part because of the telepathic powers of Martians. The first two men are killed by a jealous Martian husband whose unhappy wife has dreamed of the arrival of an attractive Earthman. A Martian psychiatrist kills the second crew as the only cure for their captain's perfect hallucination; apparently, thinking that one is from Earth becomes a serious mental disease on Mars. The third expedition is killed in what at first appears a diabolical plot. The Martians create a hallucination which convinces each member of the crew that his lost loved ones have been given a second chance at life on Mars. Having made the crew feel fully at home, the Martians kill each member in the night. The story becomes a little odd when the illusion of a small town continues through the funeral for the dead crew; the Martians continue to "be" the dead relatives, at least until "their" dead are buried. This oddness may be explained in a story which comes near the end of the next division of pieces. In "The Martian," one of the few remaining living Martians appears among Earth colonists as one who unwillingly becomes the person whom those about him wish most to see. This story resonates with that of the third expedition, suggesting more complexity in this unusual "telepathic" power to become the person whom someone else desires.

When the fourth expedition arrives on Mars, virtually all of the Martians have succumbed to chicken pox. Though there appears to be no Martians left, Spender, one crew member, transforms himself into a "Martian" and attempts one last defense of the planet from the dangers of colonization.

"—And the Moon Be Still as Bright" is a key story because it announces the theme of conflict between a majority, which sees Mars as a new America to be exploited for its material wealth and living space, and a minority, which sees Mars as a new source of wisdom and spiritual value. Spender responds to the dead planet with awe and with respect for those who built the civilization of which there are such rich remains. He sees that most of his fellow voyagers are intent on material treasure and are without comprehension of or appreciation for what the remains of Martian culture might offer. To them, the Martians are like the American Indians, now fortunately out of the way. To him, as he quickly begins to learn about them, they are possessors of answers to age-old human conflicts over the question of what is of essential value. In conversations with Captain Wilder, Spender makes it clear that Martians believed that living was of value in itself and, therefore, allowed no other values to supersede the value of life.

It becomes clear that this central value, along with other values which Spender sees reflected in Martian culture, is not to prevail in the colonization and exploitation of Mars. In the fourteen pieces which tell of these processes, commercial and exploitative interests dominate. In the sketches, Bradbury documents the broad cultural movements, while in the stories, he tends to emphasize the minority countermovement: the protoecologist who plants trees to increase the oxygen, the young worker who enters a kind of "time-warp" to meet an ancient or future Martian and to realize their essential similarity, the Southern blacks who secretly arrange a mass exodus to Mars to escape segregation, and the millionaire eccentric who takes revenge on the arrogant forces of cultural conformity. These predominantly comic stories are placed against a backdrop of impending atomic war on Earth and the spread to Mars of the attitudes which have led to this war.

"The Off Season" illustrates these destructive attitudes nicely. Sam Parkhill, a member of the fourth expedition, has found a prime location at which to set up the only hot-dog stand on Mars. Within days, thousands of surplus laborers will arrive from Earth to work in "the mines," and he will rake in cash selling them familiar food. As he glories in dreams of profit, an emissary of the few surviving Martians arrives to deed him half of the planet and to tell him some news he has not yet heard, that a world war has started on Earth. Parkhill is convinced that the Martians, resentful at the loss of their planet, intend to prevent his realizing his dream. He kills the emissary, then flees from other Martians, killing several more before they can make their intentions clear. He kills them because he can see them only through his own greed and guilt. The Martian attitude toward Sam seems a compound of irony and pity. They appreciate, along with Sam's wife and the reader, the irony that Sam's business will fail because attitudes such as Sam's predominate on Earth. They may deed him so much territory out of pity at his loss of his home or out of irony because the site's commercial value is gone. The values by which Sam lives are ultimately self-destructive.

Sam Parkhill embodies the destructive values which bring about the end of Earth. Spender, the converted Martian, articulates the minority values which could save humanity on Earth. Ultimately, these latter values fail, and Earth is utterly destroyed. In "The Million-Year Picnic," a family representing the values of love, the appreciation of cultural diversity, and the value of life arrives on Mars as the last remnant of Earth culture. These people become the new Martians and, in a world purified of the old sins, begin again the spiritual quest which has run beneath the destructive course of human history in this book.

The Characters

Bradbury does not create fully developed, complex characters in *The Martian Chronicles*. Though there are memorable characters, most tend to be representative. Ylla, the unhappy Martian wife, is a typical unhappy wife. Sam Parkhill is a typical, small-minded businessman, unable to see beyond his desire for wealth. William Thomas in "The Million-Year Picnic" is a good-hearted Everyman who tries until the last minute to save humanity and then tries to continue what is best in humanity on Mars.

Perhaps the most memorable character is William Stendahl, the creator of the new House of Usher in "Usher II." This story is related thematically to Bradbury's *Fahrenheit 451* (1953). Stendahl is a millionaire eccentric who has dedicated his life to preserving the imaginative literature (especially the stories of Edgar Allan Poe) which has been outlawed and burned by controllers of the "moral climate" on Earth. He devises the new House of Usher as an exact external replica of the original in order to trap most of the moral-climate officials and kill them there. The story tells of his success with this plot. Though Stendahl is memorable, especially for forcing his victims to die like characters in Poe's tales and in twitting them for their ignorance of Poe, which is also ignorance of their fates, he still is essentially one-dimensional. Even the most important character, Spender, is essentially a mouthpiece for the main positive values of the book.

Themes and Meanings

To summarize the book and to discuss the characters is, inevitably, to discuss the themes and meanings of *The Martian Chronicles*, for the work is thematically organized. Bradbury structures the book primarily as a commentary on mid-twentieth century American life. In the early encounters between humans and Martians, one idea is repeatedly emphasized—that essentially, in their truest needs and desires, humans and Martians are the same. Their differences are on the surface; their likenesses are the fundamental reality. Those people from Earth who, in one way or another, recognize and affirm these essential likenesses, become the heroes of the book. They affirm values such as family love, imaginative sympathy, cultural diversity, unity with an ecosystem, and the ultimate value of living and continuing life against the opposing forces of greed, the will to power, irrational fear of the different, fear of the imagination, excessive faith in technology, and unthinking exploitation of environments. Bradbury arranges these two sets of related values as choices, showing that one leads to the end of the Earth and that the other might, with good luck, lead to a remnant which could preserve the human race.

Critical Context

The Martian Chronicles is Bradbury's best-known and probably also his best book. Though the book shows some evidence of its having been gathered together out of a number of previously written stories, it is, nevertheless, unified enough to produce a fairly clear didactic effect. Bradbury's first book-length work, this novel was widely reviewed even outside "science-fiction" magazines. It was important to his career because it was his first major critical success and because it reached a larger audience than his earlier works. In part because it expresses eloquently and imaginatively the dominant concerns of mid-century Americans, it has become an important work of science fiction. Critics agree that even though the book is unlike what is usually called science fiction, it has had the effect of drawing a larger audience to the genre and, perhaps, the more important effect of drawing a new generation of more highly skilled writers to science fiction as a respectable creative mode.

Bibliography

Hoskinson, Kevin. "*The Martian Chronicles* and *Fahrenheit 451*: Ray Bradbury's Cold War Novels." *Extrapolation* 36 (Winter, 1995): 345-359. In this examination of *The Martian Chronicles* and *Fahrenheit 451*, Hoskinson explores the themes of conflict between individual conscience and the majority of society, individual conscience and loyalty to country, and the threat of nuclear warfare. Although written during the height of the Cold War, these novels reflect Bradbury's optimism that political tensions could be overcome.

Miller, Walter James. *Ray Bradbury's "The Martian Chronicles": A Critical Commentary.* New York: Simon & Schuster, 1987. A detailed analysis of Bradbury's masterpiece, offering a unique critical perspective on various aspects of the work.

Mogen, David. *Ray Bradbury.* Boston: Twayne, 1986. An excellent collection of critical essays on Bradbury's novels, including *The Martian Chronicles.* Includes a selected bibliography and index.

Touponce, William F. *Ray Bradbury and the Poetics of Reverie: Fantasy, Science Fiction, and the Reader.* Ann Arbor, Mich.: UMI Press, 1984. Written from a reader-response critical perspective, Touponce's study offers keen insight into Bradbury's works, including *The Martian Chronicles*. Includes a bibliography and index.

Terry Heller

MARTIN EDEN

Author: Jack London (1876-1916)
Type of plot: Bildungsroman
Time of plot: The turn of the twentieth century
Locale: Oakland and Berkeley, California
First published: 1908

> *Principal characters:*
> MARTIN EDEN, a sailor struggling to become a writer
> RUTH MORSE, a prudish member of the genteel upper class with whom
> Martin falls in love
> MRS. MORSE, her equally prudish mother
> BRISSENDEN, a friend of Martin and an intense, struggling poet
> LIZZIE CONNOLLY, a lower-class woman in love with Martin

The Novel

Alfred Kazan observed that "the greatest story Jack London ever wrote was the story that he lived." Martin Eden is London's most autobiographical character, and the story of his rise from a waterfront tough to a celebrated writer is close to London's own, his portrait of the artist as a young man. It begins with Martin, an uncouth sailor, rescuing Arthur Morse from a gang of muggers. When Morse takes him to his home, Martin is awed by its paintings, books, and elegance and becomes instantly enamored of Morse's pale, ethereally beautiful sister Ruth. Her presence makes him painfully aware of his clumsy walk, his rough, slangy speech, his lack of education, and his ignorance of manners. His infatuation with her is the catalyst prompting him to overcome these handicaps, rise to her level, and win her love. Calling himself "god's own mad lover," he plunges wholeheartedly into educating himself, reading omnivorously and trying to become a writer. What he lacks in refinement he makes up for in animal vitality, sensitivity, and intelligence. Ruth, by contrast, seems to him all spirit, and he elevates her to a pedestal as a saint. Only gradually does he become aware of her limitations. Though she is a college graduate, her education is shallow, her refinement superficial, her politics extremely conservative. She finds Martin's robust love for life both magnetic and threatening, and when he shows her the stories he has written, uncompromisingly realistic tales of the adventurous world he has known, she is shocked by what she considers their vulgarity. Struggling to win her and to express his artistic vision, Martin writes prodigiously, only to have everything rejected by the genteel magazines. To support himself, he gets a job in a laundry only to find himself worn out as a "work beast." By the time he makes a breakthrough and becomes a sudden celebrity as an author, he has become a disillusioned pessimist. All the work the publishers cannot get enough of had been rejected previously, and his fame and fortune seem absurdly meaningless. Ruth had rejected him; now, when she comes crawling back, he rejects her. At the end, sunk in profound depression, he jumps overboard from an ocean liner and drowns himself.

The Characters

Martin Eden is Jack London's self-portrait; an early edition of the novel with a picture of Martin as a frontispiece gives him the face of Jack London. Like Martin, London came from an impoverished and adventurous background. The illegitimate son of a wandering fortune-teller, London spent his childhood in poverty in Oakland, California; as a teenager he became a waterfront tough, an oyster pirate, a member of the fish patrol, and a common seaman on a sealing schooner in the Bering Sea and the islands off Japan. Later, he became a hobo, was imprisoned for vagrancy, and prospected in the Yukon and Klondike gold rush. When he meets Ruth Morse, Martin Eden knows far more of the world than she, but he lacks book knowledge, and her refined though limited knowledge of literature at first makes him feel inferior. He fears making a fool of himself in her presence and her set, but later, when he becomes confident of his powers, he walks among them like a prince among jackals. At first he is overflowing with vitality, and as he begins to flex his intellectual muscles, he finds learning and writing to be the greatest adventure of all. Yet the more he develops intellectually and artistically, the more he sees through the pretense and sham of the Morses and of genteel society, and his knowledge, which at first seems liberating, leads him to despair.

Ruth is based upon London's early romance with Mabel Applegarth in San Francisco. For a while, the reader sees her as Eden does, as an etherialized beauty in a pre-Raphaelite painting, with himself as her would-be courtly lover. Yet readers quickly learn that Ruth is a snob who condemns Martin's "horrid slang," that she has less literary perception than Martin, that she is a squeamish prude who reacts with revulsion to the grim realism of Martin's stories, that she is a conservative whose ideal role model is the dull, self-made plutocrat Mr. Butler, and that she is frigid. Ruth makes Martin ashamed of having known women in his past, but at twenty-four years old, she has never been kissed nor felt any sexual attraction to men. A third of the way through the book, she is still not on a first-name basis with Martin. Totally out of tune with him and out of sympathy with his aims, she is the last person who should be his critic. Her mother shares her views; they want respectability, not truth. For honesty and vitality, Martin would be much better off with Lizzie Connolly, a vibrant Irish working-class woman, but though he respects her, he has progressed too far to return to her level. Instead, he spends much of the latter part of the book in political and artistic arguments with his male cronies, particularly the poet Brissenden, who has struggled like himself to break into print and who commits suicide just when his poem "Ephemera" is published to great acclaim.

Themes and Meanings

Martin Eden is a novel of ideas rather than London's usual narrative of adventure, and it is in some ways the high-water mark of his career. London's literary credo was realism, often carried to grim, naturalistic extremes, and Martin's writings embody that credo. Like his contemporaries Stephen Crane, Frank Norris, and Theodore Dreiser, London rebelled against the genteel tradition, represented by Ruth Morse, and against the more refined realism of novelist and critic William Dean Howells. Thus Martin's literary success becomes a justification of London's, though Martin's breakthrough comes after a much longer and more grueling struggle than London's and though London enjoyed his fame and fortune for years, while Martin commits suicide almost as soon as he becomes a celebrity. Despite his working-class background, Martin becomes a political reactionary. As he reads the philosophy of Herbert Spencer and Friedrich Nietzsche, he embraces their philosophy of social Darwinism and the superman; considering himself such a superman, he turns to denouncing socialism as the coddling of weaklings. At the same time, Martin is no friend of cutthroat capitalism, for he has suffered too much in sweatshops and seen the degradation of workers in wage slavery. Ruth is shocked to see Martin in public with working-class people; for her, a working-class origin is a stigma. Until he explains otherwise, she assumes that Martin is a socialist, and she equates socialism with treason. Unlike Martin, London himself was an ardent socialist. Socialism, though, is incompatible with Social Darwinism, and in the many political arguments that occur in the latter part of *Martin Eden*, London does not intend readers to accept Martin's denunciations of the weak and his exaltation of the strong. Indeed, London later wrote that the novel was an argument against ruthless individualism and that if Martin Eden had been a socialist, he would never have killed himself.

Critical Context

Published in 1908, *Martin Eden* came exactly in the middle of London's literary career (1900-1916), during which he published an extraordinary fifty books. It is the first book he wrote after his ill-fated voyage to the South Seas aboard his yacht the *Snark*, and it reflects the illness and depression he brought home with him. At the same time, it is, in the words of Maxwell Geismar, "[o]ne of the angry books in American literature, very much in the manner of Richard Wright's *Black Boy*." Much of the anger is directed at the bourgeoisie, who scorn Martin Eden for his low-class origins while wrapping themselves in an genteel snobbery, and this aspect of the novel is the crux of the relationship between the Morse family and Martin. Yet *Martin Eden* relates to Eden's major novels as well. Many of them deal with education—the education of Buck the dog into the ways of survival in the Arctic in *The Call of the Wild* (1903); the education of White Fang into similar strategies of survival in *White Fang* (1906); the education of the sheltered and effete poet Humphrey Van Weyden in the ways of the sea, seamanship, and self-assertion while he is being transformed from a physical weakling into a self-reliant superman in *The Sea-Wolf* (1904); and the education of Martin Eden in literature, philosophy, writing, and the speech and manners of the genteel class, even while he learns to jettison his admiration for that class and dismiss it with contempt. Like London's Klondike narratives and *The Sea Wolf*, *Martin Eden* also presents a Darwinian superman; Martin is both physically tough and intellectually superior to anyone else in the novel, but except for a brutal fistfight in a flashback sequence in the slums, the ordeal in which Martin proves himself is his unrelenting struggle to educate himself and to become established as a writer in the face of endless rejection.

London was ambivalent about the superman. He seemed to embody the concept himself, with his rugged athleticism, his immense capacity for life and adventure, his acute intellect, and his literary artistry, but alcoholism, gluttony, and a complex of debilitating illnesses that struck him during the disastrous voyage of the *Snark* shattered his once-vigorous and seemingly invincible constitution, and he died at the age of forty, possibly, like Martin Eden, a suicide. London was influenced by the social Darwinism of Herbert Spencer and the superman philsophy of Nietzsche, but he rejected them and became an ardent socialist in response to the poverty of his own childhood, his awareness of the cruelty of cutthroat capitalism, and his observations both at home and abroad of the oppression of the poor. He reported these in *The People of the Abyss* (1903), his study of the London slums, and in his futuristic novel *The Iron Heel* (1907), in which socialist rebels fight a tyrannical oligarchy.

Bibliography

Foner, Philip S. *Jack London: American Rebel.* Rev. ed. New York: Citadel Press, 1964. A study of London as social critic, with a socialistic bias.

Geismar, Maxwell. *Rebels and Ancestors.* Boston: Houghton Mifflin, 1953. An analysis of London's angry criticism of social and economic injustice.

Kershaw, Alex. *Jack London: A Life.* New York: St. Martin's Press, 1998. A narrative of London's life and times.

Labor, Earle. *Jack London.* New York: Twayne, 1974. A concise introduction to London's life and works.

Walcutt, Charles Child. *American Literary Naturalism: A Divided Stream.* Minneapolis: University of Minnesota Press, 1956. An analysis of London's place among such naturalistic writers as Stephen Crane, Frank Norris, and Theodore Dreiser.

Robert E. Morsberger

THE MARTYRED

Author: Richard E. Kim (Kim Eun Kook, 1932-   )
Type of plot: War
Time of plot: June, 1950-May, 1951
Locale: Korea
First published: 1964

Principal characters:

      CAPTAIN LEE, an intelligence officer in the army of the Republic of Korea (ROK) who is assigned to investigate the execution of twelve Christian ministers

      THE REVEREND MR. SHIN, a forty-seven-year-old Christian minister suspected of betraying his twelve colleagues to save his life

      CAPTAIN INDOE PARK, the best friend of Captain Lee and the son of one of the executed ministers

      COLONEL CHANG, the chief of ROK Army Political Intelligence

      THE REVEREND MR. HANN, a twenty-eight-year-old Christian minister who, with Mr. Shin, was spared execution

      CHAPLAIN KOH, a Christian minister in the army

      MAJOR MINN, a doctor in the army

      MAJOR JUNG, a Communist army officer and the executioner of the ministers

The Novel

The title of *The Martyred* refers to twelve North Korean Christian ministers who are shot to death by Korean Communists early in the first year of the Korean War. Intelligence officers of the South Korean forces seek to establish, for propaganda purposes, that the ministers died as true martyrs in defiance of their captors' attempts to win their allegiance to Communism. The narrative develops two movements in counterpoint; one is physical and historical, the other psychological and spiritual.

The historical movement is the first year of the Korean War. The North Korean Communist regime had sought to bring all of Korea into the Communist sphere. South Korea resisted the military and political takeover, and its capital, Seoul, was captured. The South Korean and United Nations troops drove the invaders back and captured the North Korean capital, Pyongyang, which is the scene of most of the action in *The Martyred*. A dreary and dispiriting winter of occupation is followed by the evacuation of Pyongyang and a retreat before the new advance of Communist forces.

As the physical situation of territorial command deteriorates, the spiritual situation of faith versus unbelief simultaneously moves toward resolution. The focus of the spiritual matter is the Communists' execution of twelve Christian ministers and their sparing of the lives of two others. Captain Lee, the narrator of the story, is assigned by

Colonel Chang to interrogate the survivors, Mr. Shin and Mr. Hann, to ascertain that the twelve died as true martyrs, presumably betrayed by Shin and Hann.

The question of faith and unbelief arises from the uncertainty about the manner of the ministers' deaths. Captain Lee has learned that one of the ministers was the father of his good friend Captain Indoe Park, whose hope is that his father had died in a failure of faith. In life, the Reverend Mr. Park had been an exemplar of the truly faithful and had sought to constrain his son within a doctrine of spiritual correctness. The son rebelled, however, and the father disowned him. Lee's investigation discloses that the father had in fact lost his capacity for prayer. Captain Park's reaction leads to his own discovery that he himself is, and has always been, a believer. Throughout, Captain Lee, an atheist, remains firm in his unbelief.

Major Jung, a captured Communist officer who had presided over the execution, makes it clear before he is shot that all twelve had died in a betrayal of their faith, begging for their lives. The young Hann had been spared because he had lost his reason, while Shin, having spat in the major's face, had been spared because he alone of the fourteen had shown courage.

Shin insistently pretends that the twelve had died as courageous martyrs. Although he himself, as it turns out, has been unable to attain faith, he treasures the Christian faith and wants the populace, inspired by the martyred, to grow stronger in faith. His motives coincide with those of Colonel Chang, who wants the populace, enraged by the executions, to intensify their hatred of the Communist enemy. At a memorial service held for the slain ministers, Shin, the nonbeliever, delivers a eulogy that lifts the crowd to new heights of belief. Colonel Chang, despite his contempt for the "martyred" and his personal conviction that Shin had betrayed them, is delighted. Captain Lee, who has favored honest exposition of the truth, whatever it might entail, respects Chang and Shin for their actions but not for their motives. Ironically, both Lee and Chang are baptized Christians who hold no Christian belief and abhor Christianity.

Subsequent to the climactic evacuation of Pyongyang, Colonel Chang goes underground and is eventually killed in a raid that he engineers and in which he voluntarily takes part; Captain Lee is wounded in action and is hospitalized; and Captain Park, dying of wounds heroically received in combat, is, at Lee's request, given Christian burial. Shin, captured after refusing to leave Pyongyang, is reported to have been publicly executed, but accounts of his continued activity translate him into a legend.

The novel concludes with Chaplain Koh's Christian church service. Lee does not join in the prayers, but after leaving the church, he joins a group of refugees humming a song of homage to their homeland and feels "a wondrous lightness of heart."

The Characters

Captain Lee is the author's persona. Like Lee, Richard E. Kim, dislodged from academic life when the Communists entered Seoul, became an officer in the army of the Republic of Korea. Lee's observations of war and civilian suffering reflect Kim's personal experiences.

Lee is drawn in the text as one committed to truth but tolerant of religious beliefs that he cannot share. He is sustained in his conduct by his growing realization of a profound love that comprises friendship, devotion to homeland, a deep sense of duty, and compassion.

Mr. Shin is the novel's focal character. He is a minister whose faith is not in the God of his preaching but in the faith itself of the people to whom he preaches. His faith in the reality and efficacy of faith, as opposed to faith in the reality and solicitude of God, has various parallels in modern literature: These include Søren Kierkegaard's knight of infinite resignation; Albert Camus's Tarrou in *La Peste* (1947; *The Plague*, 1948) Pär Lagerkvist's Tobias in *The Pilgrim*, who, like Lagerkvist himself, is *en troende utan tro* (a person of faith without faith); and, especially, Miguel de Unamuno y Jugo's Saint Manuel, a Christian priest who nurtures in his parishioners the faith that he does not himself have.

Colonel Chang, a fashioner of propaganda, wants the people to be strengthened in their faith, but only in the interest of political unity. Lee's attitude toward Chang is initially one of dislike and distrust, but he comes to understand and appreciate Chang's human side and is, at last, not surprised to learn of Chang's heroic death in action beyond the call of duty.

Captain Indoe Park is representative of the believer, or the person of faith, whose opposition to the trappings of organized religion, as embodied in his affectedly righteous clergyman father, imbues in him the conviction that he does not have faith. The conviction is shattered when his father's hypocrisy is exposed; Park then makes his father's faith his own.

Chaplain Koh is a Christian whose faith, not being tested or challenged, is not made his own. A man of no faith with faith, he is the reverse of Shin, a man of faith without faith. It is significant that he abandons his military uniform and works with civilians as one of them.

Major Jung is the enemy officer. His role in the novel is to expose the executed ministers as cowards and to recognize Hann's lapse from sanity and Shin's remarkable courage. Jung himself, villainy aside, displays the same kind of courage toward his executioner, Colonel Chang, that Shin had shown when Jung was the executioner.

Themes and Meanings

Kim's dedication of his novel to Camus's memory, and his epigraph from an unfinished play by Friedrich Hölderlin expressing a spiritually familial love of one's homeland, constitute an overture to the novel's theme of the human need for religious belief or its equivalent. Kim, like many twentieth century writers, recognizes the modern insufficiency of traditional religions to satisfy this need. In the novel, Captain Lee and Mr. Shin exemplify, respectively, two means of satisfying this ineradicable need.

Captain Lee does so by identifying his individual self with his existential situation. He is heir to the transcendent happiness of Camus's Sisyphus, who makes his futile situation his own by contemplating the noble absurdity of the situation as he descends the hill to retrieve his rock. Lee also is like Camus's Dr. Rieux, for whom the futility of a fight does not justify giving it up. Camusian "nostalgia," which is the longing to return to a nonexistent heaven and which can be satisfied by a profound experience of one's homeland within one's heart, marks Lee's coming to terms with existence by finding his homeland within himself.

Mr. Shin satisfies his longing to find the Kingdom of God within himself by learning, like Lagerkvist's pilgrim Tobias, that his very longing is his homeland. Like Unamuno's Saint Manuel, he translates his quondam faith in God into an active faith in faith itself. Again, like André Malraux's oppressed worker in *Man's Faith* who seeks his salvation in the very humiliation from which he has terminated his attempt to escape, Shin seeks his salvation in the very loss of the faith that he has terminated his attempt to experience.

Critical Context

The Martyred, Kim's first novel, was followed by *The Innocent* (1968), a sequel of sorts, which continues the activities of Lee, Koh, and others and which opens with the end of the Korean War in 1953. In subsequently published works, he extended his investigation into the psychological fabric of his homeland. *Lost Names: Scenes from a Korean Boyhood in Japanese-Occupied Korea* (1970) offers, in novelistic fashion, his perspective of his country from his second through his thirteenth year, during the period from 1933 through 1945. Concurrent with his return to Korea from 1983 through 1985 as a Fulbright Scholar at Seoul National University, he wrote a book with the Proustian title *In Search of Lost Years* (1985).

The Martyred encapsulates the texture and mood of all of Kim's writing, namely, metaphysical self-discovery derivative from deep personal loss, expressed in a style imitative of the simplicity of Camus and Lagerkvist. *The Martyred* initiates a body of work that reflects not only the two worlds of spiritual faith and secular faith but also the two worlds of a Korean national writing in English as an American citizen.

Bibliography

Freund, John B. "Martyrs, Pilgrims, and the Memory of Camus." *The Minnesota Review* 4 (Spring, 1964): 483-485. Freund compares *The Martyred* to two other works published in 1964, translations of a novel by Lagerkvist and a play by Rolf Hochhuth. *The Martyred* is rated well below the other works and is described as an inelegant imitation of Albert Camus.

Galloway, David D. "The Love Stance: Richard E. Kim's *The Martyred*." *Critique* 24 (Winter, 1964-1965): 163-171. An essay on the Camusian concept of the absurd is followed by a critical estimate of *The Martyred* as creatively evocative of Albert Camus's fiction. Galloway is perceptive in pointing out the title as initially referent to those considered to have been martyred and finally referent to the only true martyr, Mr. Shin.

Kim, Richard. *Lost Names: Scenes from a Korean Boyhood.* New York: Praeger, 1970. Recalling that the Japanese invaders forced Koreans to abandon their own names when the Japanese occupied the country from 1932 to 1945, Kim paints seven vivid scenes from his boyhood. Although this book does not deal with Kim's fiction, it does provide interesting insight into his background and the reasons behind the drawing of certain themes.

Valdés, Mario J. "Faith and Despair: A Comparative Study of a Narrative Theme." *Hispania* 49 (September, 1966): 373-379. Valdés likens the theme and narrative structure of *The Martyred* to Unamuno's *San Manuel Bueno, mártir* (1933; *Saint Manuel Bueno, Martyr*, 1956). His observations of the similarities of Kim's story to Unamuno's intensify a reader's appreciation of both.

Walsh, Chad. "Another War Raged Within." *The New York Times Book Review* (February 16, 1964): 1, 35. Walsh places *The Martyred* within "the great moral and psychological tradition of Job, Dostoevsky and Albert Camus."

Roy Arthur Swanson

MASON & DIXON

Author: Thomas Pynchon (1937-   )
Type of plot: Historical
Time of plot: 1761-1786
Locale: England, Sumatra, South Africa, St. Helena, and the North American Colonies
First published: 1997

Principal characters:
> CHARLES MASON, a British astronomer for the Royal Society
> JEREMIAH DIXON, a British land surveyor
> REVEREND WICKS CHERRYCOKE, narrator of the novel and friend of Mason and Dixon
> NEVIL MASKELYNE, Astronomer Royal of England, 1765-1811
> JAMES BRADLEY, Astronomer Royal of England, 1742-1761

The Novel

Mason & Dixon is divided into three unequal parts, the first providing a prelude to Mason and Dixon's adventures in America, the middle and largest detailing those adventures, and the third serving as a brief epilogue. Though it is based on an important, though little-studied, event in American history—the running of the "Mason-Dixon line" that forms the boundaries of Pennsylvania and Maryland, and thus between the American North and South—the novel is largely fantasy.

The novel opens with a narrative frame introducing the Reverend Wicks Cherrycoke, who will relate the rest of the story as an evening diversion to his sister's family in 1786 Philadelphia. As the story unfolds, the Reverend's presence is maintained through forty-three separate narrative intrusions, ranging from a single word to four pages in length. His audience of nieces, nephews, and in-laws interact, making them a part of the story.

The first part of the novel, entitled "Latitudes and Departures," describes the meeting of Charles Mason and Jeremiah Dixon in London in 1760 and their collaboration in a project for the British Royal Society to study the transit of Venus. The data Mason and Dixon collect would be valuable in determining longitude, a measurement not yet perfected in the 1760's, and vital to navigation and commerce. Sent to Sumatra to make the astronomical observations, Mason and Dixon find themselves in the midst of a naval battle with a French frigate. Dispatching a letter registering their displeasure with the Royal Society at being placed in harm's way, Mason and Dixon are branded cowards, their letter ever after being considered a barrier to Mason's ascendency in the society. Dixon, a lapsed Quaker, has maintained his Quaker aversion to the institution of slavery. Both he and Mason are horrified by the slavery they encounter in the Southern Hemisphere, including, in South Africa, their being encouraged to have sex with black slaves, as lighter-skinned African babies fetch a higher price in the slave market. After making observations in Sumatra, Capetown, and St. Helena with Nevil Maskelyne, Mason is sent to America to settle a boundary dispute, while Maskelyne returns to England to be named Astronomer Royal. The boundary dispute was a long-standing one, arising eighty years earlier with the chartering of Pennsylvania to William Penn and of Maryland to Lord Baltimore. The charters had defined the boundaries geometrically, but those boundaries had never been laid out or measured, and many disputes had arisen. Mason and Dixon's assignment, which constitutes the second part of the novel, called simply "America," was to run a line, as geometrically straight as eighteenth century science could permit, from Philadelphia 244 miles straight west. As they move westward, they meet an assortment of odd characters, including historical figures such as George Washington, Benjamin Franklin, and Thomas Jefferson as well as fictional characters of varying degrees of believability: a French chef pursued by a mechanical duck that loves him, a farmer who turns into a beaver with the full moon, a mystical Chinese master of *feng shui*, a tribe of Welsh Indians, an African servant of George Washington who is also a Jewish stand-up comic, a talking dog, and a giant glowing Indian.

The farther west they go, the more they doubt the rightness of their endeavor, forcing an artificial and abstract order on the land and its people. Moreover, the farther west they go, the closer Mason and Dixon grow to each other. They begin as opposite numbers: Mason a tame Anglican melancholic (his wife's pet name for him is "Mopery"), Dixon a lapsed Quaker given to distilled spirits, exotic food, and womanizing. As they come to rely on each other, they grow closer and begin to cancel out each other's failings.

The final section, entitled "Last Transit," is a brief summary of the last years of Mason and Dixon after their American adventure. They never again collaborate, and their time together consists of sporadic visits, but these two opposite numbers have managed, in old age, to converge. Dixon, who always dreamed of returning to America, dies in England in 1779. Mason, to whom the American years were a nightmare, emigrates there with his family after Dixon's death, and he dies in Philadelphia in 1786.

The Characters

The title characters, Mason and Dixon, are the most fully developed of the virtually innumerable characters in this vast novel. Indeed, some reviewers have charged that all the other characters are mere cartoons and that Mason and Dixon alone display any depth. The charge is partially true; the historical characters tend to be the most cartoonish. George Washington becomes in Pynchon's hands a real-estate schemer whose plantation grows hemp, both for ropemaking and for smoking. Benjamin Franklin emerges as a perpetual adolescent who cannot resist playing with electricity and flirting with the young ladies of Philadelphia. Yet many of the simplest fictional characters, even those who appear briefly, are among the most fully realized. For example, Frau Luise Redzinger, of the German pietistic faith that would later become known as "Pennsylvania Dutch," is characterized in great detail by the observations of the Reverend Cherrycoke, who meets her on a coach ride in chapter 35. Thomas

Cresap, brother to the militiaman whom Thomas Jefferson accused of murdering the Mingo Chief Logan, presents an unsympathetic but complete portrait of the "mountain man" of the western Pennsylvania frontier, acknowledging no civil authority and representing the sentiment of America on the brink of revolution.

The triumph of characterization in *Mason & Dixon*, however, is the depth to which readers come to know Charles Mason and Jeremiah Dixon. They are introduced through the formality of their first letters to each other, given in chapter 2. Immediately, that formality begins breaking down, as Dixon reveals that he wrote his letter sober (implying that such sobriety is not habitual), and Mason expresses his embarrassment at the deference Dixon showed him. In short, both men strike poses in their letters of introduction, poses they begin to relax when they get to know each other.

Dropping their guards is only the first step in growing closer for Mason and Dixon. There is much they still must learn about each other, and readers learn along with them. Their personal convergence becomes an ironic commentary on the implicit theme of the novel: the artificiality of the drawing of boundaries. The Mason-Dixon line is perhaps the most famous boundary in America, setting the slave-holding South apart from the North, which, as the Chinese Captain Zhang observes, hides a subtler kind of slavery. Yet it is the drawing of this line of separation that unites Mason and Dixon, both in lessening their differences and in building their mutual affection.

The picture of Charles Mason that emerges is that of a man paralyzed by melancholy. Haunted by the memory—and literally haunted by the ghost—of his first wife Rebekah, he cannot think of ever again achieving the intimacy he knew with Rebekah, even though she urges him to remarry. Dixon's incessant sexual activity in America is a constant reminder of Mason's solitude, a counterpoint to his self-enclosure. Yet counterpoint it is, not contradiction: The opposite qualities of Mason and Dixon are complementary, and though Dixon jokes at Mason's gloom, he attempts to lift his companion out of it.

Themes and Meanings

The American Revolution and the astronomical accuracy of the Mason-Dixon line are both the products of the Age of Reason, and the phrase recurs, rather anachronistically, throughout the novel. The first time it appears, ironically enough, it is spoken by a talking dog. The running of the line represents the imposition of an artificial order on nature's mystery (among other things; it means something different to virtually every major character). The "right line" of rationality is opposed to the serpent of natural landscapes. For example, Maskelyne tells Mason about the serpent in the volcano on the island of St. Helena; Captain Zhang describes Chinese methods of surveying as the discovery of the Shan, or dragon, within the land; in a flashback, Dixon tells of a legendary dragon in his town; and the American Indians believe their serpent-mounds to be the work of a giant race.

The further Mason and Dixon penetrate into America, the more they discover the irrational, the dream world of the new land. A sign of their growing closeness is Mason and Dixon's compact to tell each other each night's dream. By the end of the novel, they are experiencing the same dream. Even the narrator records one of his dreams, and it seems to be a part of the adventures of Mason and Dixon. America is tentatively called "sleeping Brittania's dream," and a Delaware philosopher tells the surveyors that the Indians are the dreams of the Europeans. As the exploration of the American interior becomes more and more associated with the interiority of the mind, Dixon hears legends of a passage into the interior of the earth, which, near the end of his life, he claims to have visited. Ironically, the experiment that rendered this popular speculation scientifically implausible was proposed in 1772 by Maskelyne, Mason and Dixon's companion in the early years; the experiment involves taking latitude readings on two sides of a mountain, research Pynchon has Dixon doing at the opening of chapter 75.

Critical Context

Many of the themes, ideas, and even character names of Pynchon's four earlier novels appear in *Mason & Dixon*. *V.* (1963), *The Crying of Lot 49* (1966), *Gravity's Rainbow* (1973), and *Vineland* (1990) all involve characters who suspect that their lives are being directed by vast and mysterious forces. *Mason & Dixon* continues Pynchon's exploration of paranoia, with Mason and Dixon suspecting the Royal Society of manipulating their lives, the officers of the Royal Society suspecting French Jesuits, and various members of the Society suspecting the influence of Robert Clive and his East India Company.

Another element that *Mason & Dixon* shares with Pynchon's other novels is a plot and setting that involves the construction of the modern world. In *V.*, it was the intellectual ferment of Vienna at the turn of the century and the colonialism of that era; in Pynchon's next two novels, the rise of an economy based on information is sketched. In *Mason & Dixon*, a quintessentially American novel, the forces that made the United States are depicted, resulting in an abundance of anachronisms, including Pynchon's characteristic references to popular culture: Popeye, *Star Trek*, and borscht belt comedians all appear in the novel.

Pynchon has a Faulkner-like history of carrying over family names from previous novels, as if the characters are ancestor and descendent. The narrator of *Mason & Dixon*, the Reverend Wicks Cherrycoke, is presumably an ancestor of the Cherrycoke in *Gravity's Rainbow*, and a foretopman named "Fender-Belly" Bodine in *Mason & Dixon* is likely a forefather of Seaman "Pig" Bodine in *V.* Even when there are no connections in plot or setting, little hints such as these names suggest the coherence of Pynchon's fictional world. Pynchon's yoking of his quintessential elements of paranoia and anachronism to a seminal event in the making of America makes *Mason & Dixon* a profoundly important novel.

Bibliography

Bloom, Harold. *Thomas Pynchon*. New York: Chelsea House, 1986. A collection of essays, some published in previous collections. Bloom's introduction is an excellent brief overview of Pynchon's major themes.

Chambers, Judith. *Thomas Pynchon*. Boston: Twayne, 1992. The best general study of Pynchon, containing a chapter on each of Pynchon's novels before *Mason & Dixon*.

Levine, George, and Leverenz, David. *Mindful Pleasures: Essays on Thomas Pynchon*. Boston: Little, Brown, 1976. Essays reprinted from a special Pynchon issue of the journal *Twentieth Century Literature*, as well as six original essays.

Mead, Clifford. *Thomas Pynchon: A Bibliography of Primary and Secondary Materials*. Elmwood Park, Ill.: Dalkey Archive Press, 1989. An exhaustive bibliography with helpful annotations.

Newman, Robert D. *Understanding Thomas Pynchon*. New York: Columbia University Press, 1986. Though this study reduces Pynchon's complexities too radically for most scholars, it is an excellent starting point for the general reader; its title is apt.

Seed, David. *The Fictional Labyrinths of Thomas Pynchon*. Iowa City: University of Iowa Press, 1988. A study of the narrative complexity of Pynchon's novels; for the advanced student.

Slade, Joseph W. *Thomas Pynchon*. New York: Warner, 1974. The first book-length study of Pynchon, this trade paperback can still be useful to the general reader.

John R. Holmes

MATING

Author: Norman Rush (1935-   )
Type of plot: Comedy of manners
Time of plot: The early 1980's
Locale: Botswana
First published: 1991

> *Principal characters:*
>> THE NARRATOR, an unnamed thirty-two-year-old woman who is in
>> Botswana to write a thesis on nutritional anthropology
>> NELSON DENOON, the socialist founder of a utopian colony for women
>> in the Kalahari Desert

The Novel

The plot of *Mating* is much like that of an Elizabethan tragedy. An opening section, "Guilty Repose," reveals a narrator caught in a "caesura," as she calls it, a period of panic in the fall of 1980 when she finds herself turning thirty-two in Botswana with a dead dissertation topic on her hands. The plot thickens in the next two sections, "The Solar Democrat" and "My Expedition," when she meets the world-famous utopian socialist Nelson Denoon and vows to track him to the colony he has established for distressed women in the Kalahari Desert. In the next three sections—"Tsau," "Acquisitive Love," and "Love Itself"—the narrator and Denoon act out their desert idyll before their story unravels in a final African chapter, "Strife." In a brief commentary, "About the Foregoing," the narrator reflects on it all from the distant vantage point of Palo Alto, California.

The narrator had hoped to show in her Stanford doctoral thesis that fertility among "remote dwellers" varies from season to season depending on what the gatherers can find, but she has learned that there are no gatherers in Botswana; people everywhere are eating canned food and breakfast cereal or handouts from the World Food Program. As a result, she retreats to the capital, Gabarone, where she socializes with the local expatriates and works her way through affairs with several men who offer her nothing permanently satisfying. From the last of these, Z, a spy for the British High Commission, she learns of Sekopololo ("The Key"), a project to create an entire new village in the north-central Kalahari Desert. What especially excites her about this project is that it is run by Nelson Denoon, a legendary social scientist.

She soon meets Denoon at a reception; the great man's wife, Grace, approaches in some distress and guides her to a room where Denoon, the author of *Development and the Death of Villages*, is holding forth on his own version of socialism. Grace explains that her marriage to Denoon has soured and that she has identified the narrator as her successor. The charismatic Denoon's dialogue with one of the local Marxist intellectuals is so spellbinding that the narrator pressures Grace into revealing the location of Tsau, the new utopian settlement. The journey to Tsau is grueling, complicated by the defection of one of her two donkeys, but eventually Tsau looms up in the distance. Although uninvited visitors are not allowed, she is taken in and nursed back to strength.

Tsau is entered through an archway on a road that continues up a koppie, or stone hill, with a community of two hundred thatched homesteads spread around the slope. A small airstrip affords a place for a mail plane to land every two weeks. A striking feature of Tsau is the presence everywhere of glinting glass ornaments and mirrors. The inhabitants are mostly destitute women, two-thirds of them past childbearing age, about 450 people all told, including forty children and no more than fifty male relatives. The charter women own the property, which is passed down to female relatives and other women. Denoon lives on the hilltop in a concrete octagon. Like the women, he has lived with no mate; for that reason, his previous acquaintance with the narrator must not be disclosed, as it would suggest he was bringing in a companion denied the others. A delegation agrees to the narrator's temporary residence, and after she has proven herself, she eventually moves in with Denoon.

The romance proceeds smoothly, with Denoon and the narrator attuned to each other in all ways. Yet when Denoon remarks offhandedly one day that they could give up their American citizenship and stay on in Tsau permanently, the narrator obviously experiences uncertainty. Real difficulties for them arise with the manipulations of Hector Raboupi, a troublemaker who runs a string of male prostitutes, the "night men," who offer themselves to the women. When Hector mysteriously disappears, his woman, Dorcas, raises a great row, accusing Denoon of having done away with him. In the middle of this, Denoon—against the rules—appropriates one of Tsau's two horses and heads north on a quixotic mission to found a sister colony. He is brought in after two weeks, near death from a fall from his horse. His recovery is uneventful, but his passivity alarms the narrator, who takes him to Gabarone to see a psychiatrist.

The narrator learns that in his horrific experience Denoon witnessed his horse eaten by jackals and endured a hallucinatory vision of being saved from a rogue lion by a swarm of protecting bees, leaving him satisfied with no more intense feeling than the simple awareness of consciousness. "Consciousness is bliss," as he puts it. At this point, the frustrated narrator goes to the Botswana Book Centre, where she sees a beautiful young woman from the U.S. State Department eagerly reading Denoon's classic study. The narrator seizes on the young woman as her "satanic miracle" whereby she can free herself from Denoon, as Grace had earlier freed herself, and by holding a surprise birthday party for Denoon, she maneuvers the satanic miracle into his bed.

In the epilogue, the narrator is back in Palo Alto, wringing a new dissertation out of her research data and enjoying her celebrity as a lecturer on the feminist circuit. Her talks always preach the gospel of Denoon on the destruction of Third World cultures by the aggressive development policies of the twentieth century. The narrator ends her story by pondering a mysterious message she has received in California: Hector Raboupi has turned out to be a spy for a nearby dictator, and her successor, "lustrous Bronwen," has been evicted from Tsau after one week.

The Characters

By having an anonymous narrator tell his story, Rush restricts the reader to his main character's vision of events. Although Rush's allusiveness and hieratic diction sometimes intrude to betray the mastermind behind the narrator and create some dissonance in point of view, most of what she reports can be easily accepted. For example, she immediately reveals much about herself by confessing that she could never mate with a Rhodesian or South African (because they come from racist countries), with anyone sympathetic to Ronald Reagan, or with a black African (because "male chauvinism is in the air Africans breathe"). Her reflections on her "carnal involvements" reveal her as subject to sexual appetites but not given to unrestrained sexual adventuring; she remarks that "if I was clear about anything in my life I was clear about not staying in Africa forever." Her desert journey to Tsau shows her to be physically courageous to the point of imprudence. Her constant meditation on events provides a mirror to her inner thoughts and character, reflecting an extraordinarily likable and intelligent young woman with an independent mind and spirit.

The substance of Denoon's character emerges in a dialogue with an African Marxist that the narrator overhears at a party before she even meets Denoon. His eloquence on a "third way" depicts Denoon as contemptuous of exploitative capitalism but not oblivious to the naïvetes of an unrealistic socialism. Rush develops Denoon's potential weakness for alcohol by introducing two minor characters, Harold Mace and Julia Rodden, who appear out of nowhere as Shakespearean performers dispatched to Tsau by the British Council and for whom Denoon breaks out his hidden wine cache in a boozy evening of trivial male bonding. More about Denoon's background unfolds in several flashbacks depicting his childhood relations with his father. The narrator's final judgment on Denoon is ambiguous. Back at Stanford, she spouts Denoon's doctrines in her lectures, but otherwise she rejects his teaching completely. When she reads his personal bible, the *Tao Te Ching*, she is repulsed by his quietism, finding it to be a handbook on how to become an impostor. Had it made Denoon an impostor, or had he always been one, she wonders. The ultimate difference between the narrator and Denoon appears in her comment on his vision of their spending their lives with the poor: "I respected it, although I reserved the right to adumbrate ways you could be with the poor without necessarily being at their elbow year in and year out."

Several of the Tsau women appear vividly, but in roles too brief to be memorable. Hector Raboupi is villainous enough to carry a larger role, but he fades from the scene for good when some ruse is needed to send Denoon on the near-fatal mission that culminates in his debilitating religious experience with the lion.

Themes and Meanings

Mating offers a rich variety of serious topics in sociology and politics to consider, but the title gives away the book's focus: It is, finally, a love story between two people whose ultimate separation probably disappoints many readers. Their backgrounds provide engrossing divagations. Denoon's childhood pains him to relate because of the cruelty of his father, an alcoholic who was frustrated in his own socialist inclinations by the need to provide for his family. When Denoon was eleven, he constructed an artful edifice of glass; the act enraged his father, who demolished the structure with a pickaxe. The incident eventuates in the elaborate glassworks Denoon maintains at Tsau. Denoon hates alcohol, but there are indications that it is a demon he must guard against. The narrator's childhood was beset by poverty and her mother's humiliations over being overweight. If Denoon is haunted by his father's alcoholism, something in the back of the narrator's mind nags her about her weight. When she returns to Palo Alto, she takes real satisfaction in seeing her mother settled permanently in a Lutheran nursing home, where she works for her room and board.

Even though the narrator rejects Denoon in the end, judging him perhaps even an impostor, it is impossible not to take seriously his ideological convictions. In his dialogue with the African Marxist at the party where the narrator first sees him, he gives an eloquent explanation of the failures of socialism: Socialism deprives society of an efficient market mechanism; socialist economies have to lay aside money to buy technology because socialism stifles invention; socialism breeds a new class of economic crimes that are costly to suppress; and socialist economies always have to import food because socialism has never succeeded in agriculture. These are substantive criticisms that give weight to the narrative. Back in Palo Alto, lecturing to adoring groups of feminists, the narrator preaches Denoon's precept: that "a true holocaust in the world is the thing we call development, which I tell them means the superimposition of market economies on traditional and unprepared third world cultures . . . and that this has been the seedbed of the televised spectacle of famine, misery, and disease confronting us in the comfort of our homes."

Critical Context

This National Book Award-winning novel follows the concerns of Rush's earlier collection of stories, *Whites* (1986), and continues the tradition of American utopian novels such as Edward Bellamy's *Looking Backward: 2000-1887* (1888), Nathaniel Hawthorne's *The Blithedale Romance* (1852), and William Dean Howells's *A Traveler from Altruria* (1894), but it does it with a feminist slant and with more attention paid to the love story than to the social mechanics of the Tsau colony. *Mating* also includes thoughtful commentary on the role of socialist politics in African countries, and Rush joins other white novelists of Africa such as Nadine Gordimer, J. M. Coetzee, and André Brink in their fictional dialogues on colonialism and its effects on southern Africa.

A diary kept by the narrator provides background about Tsau and other concerns. The narrative flows well, but there are episodes that could be cut to good effect. The diction is demanding, and writers and other persons (such as Father Coughlin, William Empson, and E. M. Cioran, for example) are referred to without explanation. The effect is a mild pomposity that will annoy many readers but that dedicated autodidacts may appreciate.

Bibliography

Edwards, Thomas R. "Good Intentions: *Mating*, by Norman Rush." *The New York Review of Books*, October 10, 1991.

Jones, Libby Falk, and Sarah Webster Goodwin, eds. *Feminism, Utopia, and Narrative*. Knoxville: University of Tennessee Press, 1990. Published too early to include *Mating*, but a valuable study.

Kolmerten, Carol A. *Women in Utopia: The Ideology of Gender in the American Owenite Community*. Syracuse: Syracuse University Press, 1998. A tangential but relevant discussion of many of the issues raised in *Mating*.

Lanting, Frans. "Botswana." *National Geographic* 178, no. 6 (December, 1990): 5-97. Indispensable to anyone interested in the culture and physical setting of *Mating*.

Leonard, John. "Culture Watch: Dream Republics." *The Nation* 267, no. 6 (1998). A review of several novels, including *Mating*.

Lescaze, Lee. "Bookshelf: Adventures in Africa." *Wall Street Journal*, September 17, 1991, p. A14. Lescaze praises Rush's creation of character (the unnamed narrator), criticizes *Mating*'s thin plot.

Nozick, Robert. *Anarchy, State and Utopia*. New York: Basic Books, 1975. A National Book Award-winning examination of accepted beliefs about socialism and anarchy.

Rush, Norman. *Whites*. New York: Viking, 1986. Rush's collection of stories about white expatriates in Africa.

Frank Day

MAUD MARTHA

Author: Gwendolyn Brooks (1917-   )
Type of plot: Bildungsroman
Time of plot: The 1920's to the 1940's
Locale: Chicago, Illinois
First published: 1953

> *Principal characters:*
> > MAUD MARTHA BROWN PHILLIPS, the protagonist, a sensitive,
> > > dark-skinned African American woman
> > HELEN BROWN, Maud Martha's lighter-skinned sister
> > HARRY BROWN, Maud Martha's only brother
> > BELVA BROWN, Maud Martha's mother
> > RUSSELL, Maud Martha's first beau
> > DAVID MCKEMSTER, Maud Martha's second beau
> > PAUL PHILLIPS, Maud Martha's husband
> > PAULETTE PHILLIPS, Maud Martha's daughter

The Novel

Maud Martha is a lyrical, impressionistic series of episodes and vignettes narrating the life of Maud Martha Brown, a young African American woman born into a struggling working-class family. It is clear from the beginning that she is sensitive, aware, and deeply affected by color prejudice both outside and inside her home. The reader follows her through her development from a seven-year-old child into young adulthood. Much of the novel is loosely autobiographical.

The novel is divided into thirty-four brief chapters, each delineating a moment in Maud Martha's life. The narration is in the third person, but events are seen from Maud Martha's point of view. The first five chapters take readers quickly through her childhood, touching on her family life with reference to quarrels between her parents, a description of her schoolyard, the death of her grandmother, and the experience of being visited, and patronized, by a white child.

The sixth chapter begins to explore the young woman, beginning with a visit to a theater that results in Maud Martha's making the decision that what she wanted was "to donate to the world a good Maud Martha." The next few chapters explore three events significant in the heroine's life not only as individual occurrences but also as representative of the kind of traumas she deals with throughout the novel: the death of her Uncle Tim, the near loss of the family home; and the preference of a young man for her younger, lighter-skinned sister Helen, which makes Maud Martha realize that even her beloved father favors Helen. Helen tells her sister that she will never get a boyfriend "if you don't stop reading those books."

The following chapters prove that statement false, as they describe Maud Martha's "first beau," Russell, her "second beau," David McKemster, and Paul Phillips, the "low yellow" man who is to become her husband. Although at this point she is dreaming of going to New York City, her symbol for what life ought to be like, at the age of eighteen she settles for Paul partly because she is flattered that a man of his complexion would be interested in her. He becomes a challenge, a creature to be "hooked." He is also a man with desire to better himself materially; unfortunately, his aspirations are not equaled by his ability to provide.

Descriptions of the small, roach-infested apartment, a trip to a musicale through which Paul sleeps, Maud Martha's encounter with a mouse whose life she spares, a trip to a "white" theater, and Paul's invitation to the Foxy Cats Club, which results in a bout of jealousy on the part of the pregnant Maud Martha, all establish the tone of the marriage. At the dance, Maud Martha realizes that the marriage is in serious trouble; when she contemplates scratching and spitting at the "high yellow" woman in whom Paul is interested, she thinks: "But if the root was sour what business did she have up there hacking at a leaf?"

Chapter 20 deals with the birth of her first child, Paulette. The chapter ends with a moment of recognition between the new mother and her daughter that leads to musings on her life, now changed by the birth of Paulette, and her attempt to establish traditions for her new family, an attempt thwarted by Paul. The following chapters show Maud Martha's growing awareness of the world outside her apartment: first with the people in her building, then in an encounter with David McKemster, the second beau, a sycophant to the white academics whom he wishes to impress, and last when Maud Martha is shocked as a white saleswoman insults the owner of her beauty shop and the owner fails to respond.

In the following chapters, Maud Martha deals with a fear of dying (she is convinced she has a tumor, which turns out to be a pulled muscle) and with Paul, who is disappointed in his life, his wife, his job, his baby, his failure to be invited into the Foxy Cats Club. She realizes that all that matters is life itself. A chicken that she must disembowel herself leads her to an understanding of "brotherly love." All of this leads up to chapter 30, in which Maud Martha stands up for herself at the home of a white family where she has gone to work as a maid. This vignette captures perfectly the unconscious dehumanization that occurs when one people believes that another exists to serve them. Here, Maud Martha truly comes into her own by refusing to be treated as less than a fully human being.

The final four chapters concern her musings on tragedy ("If you got a good Tragedy out of a lifetime, one good, ripping tragedy . . . you were doing well," she says), a visit from her mother, a run-in with a racist Santa Claus, and the end of World War II. The book ends with the beginning of a new life for the again-pregnant Maud Martha.

The Characters

Maud Martha Brown is a sensitive, intelligent, and poetic child of seven at the start of the novel. As the novel is told from her point of view, readers see her grow, both literally into a young woman, a mother, and an adult and also in knowledge of herself and the world that she inhabits. By the end of the novel, Maud Martha has matured in many ways; she has learned to accept the limitations of her world that she cannot change, but she also has learned to create change where it is possible, and she knows her own abilities both to accept and to alter, depending on circumstances. She is a strong, compassionate, and in many ways wise woman by the end of the novel, as she contemplates the coming arrival of her second child.

Helen Brown, Maud Martha's lighter-skinned sister, appears as something of an antagonist in the early part of the novel, although often through no fault of her own. Helen is the preferred child, even by Maud's beloved father, and it is only as an adult that Maud can begin to appreciate Helen's tough-mindedness.

Harry Brown, Maud Martha's only brother, is a minor but important character. He is the male element in her young life, separate and unequal.

Belva Brown, Maud Martha's mother, plays a more important part in the novel than does her father, although the father's influence in some ways is greater. She is a realistic character, both heroic and, at times, silly. Her behavior during the birth of her granddaughter first reinforces Maud Martha's sense of separation from her mother, but then is contrasted with the connection she feels with her own newly born child.

Russell, the first beau, is only briefly described. He is an attractive young man, but he is more than aware of the fact. Although he attracts Maud Martha, she does not fall completely under his spell, recognizing that if he had to choose between being great and grand, he would without hesitation choose the latter.

David McKemster, the second beau, is notable for being a young African American scholar who would prefer to be an English country gentleman. When Maud Martha meets him again after her marriage, she finds he has become not only the worst kind of pedant but also a sycophant, desperate for the acceptance and approval of his white colleagues. The encounter helps her to refuse to place her identity on the altar of white approval.

Paul Phillips, Maud Martha's husband, is the "low yellow" in the chapter of that title; he is light-skinned, ambitious in a rather limited, materialistic way, selfish, and self-centered. Maud Martha must outgrow him.

Themes and Meanings

Maud Martha is a celebration of black womanhood. At the same time, the book examines the difficulties and trials of growing up African American and female. Such trials include both the universal problems of life and those specific to Maud Martha's race and sex: race and color prejudice (the first from Caucasians, the second from her own people, including her family and her own husband); expectations rooted in racism and sexism; and the difficulties experienced by a sensitive, intelligent woman when there is no outlet for her abilities and talents.

The novel moves between inward-looking chapters to those that stress the outside world. For example, following the birth of Paulette, which allows Maud Martha a moment of recognition as she gazes at her daughter, Brooks describes the other people who live in the building. It had been a difficult birth, attended to by a neighbor, Mrs. Cray, whom Maud Martha had not even known before, and by her mother, who prides herself on the fact that she manages to last out the whole experience without fainting.

Paul returns with the doctor only after the birth is over, when Maud Martha is already feeling "strong enough to go out and shovel coal." The chapter serves the purpose of establishing the environment in which Paul and Maud Martha live, but it also shows, from her point of view, Maud Martha's reactions to these people and perhaps, in a limited way, a broadening of her interest in the world outside her own small space.

This is followed by the chapter in which David McKemster works hard to ingratiate himself with his white university colleagues, efforts that are neatly compared with the actions of Sonia Johnson, the owner of a beauty shop, who capitulates to the racist expressions of white people. Sonia remains silent in the face of a white saleswoman's use of the phrase "work like a nigger" in Sonia's own shop. At first, Maud Martha cannot even believe that she has heard the woman correctly, as Sonia fails to respond to the phrase, but after the woman leaves, Sonia acknowledges the insult, trying to rationalize her failure to respond. Maud Martha says nothing, but she is realizing the forces at work in her world. This leads naturally to the chapter in which she rejects the maid's job offered by a white family, refusing to allow herself to be patronized or demeaned.

Thus, the novel describes and explores the coming of age of a sensitive, aware, yet not extraordinary young African American woman. What is extraordinary is Brooks's ability to sketch with few words not only the quality of that experience, but also the varied places and people who shape and affect—but do not control—the consciousness of Maud Martha.

Critical Context

Maud Martha, Brooks's only novel, has received little critical attention, which is regrettable, as it is one of the first novels by an African American woman focusing on the black female experience. The book's major precursor is Zora Neale Hurston's *Their Eyes Were Watching God* (1937). Brooks's novel was to have an important influence on Paule Marshall, who remarked that she considered it the finest portrayal of an African American woman at the time it was published.

This critical void may result from the fact that Brooks is mainly recognized as a poet; indeed, the novel itself reads like poetry, a fact that may have discouraged its wider acceptance. Barbara Christian, in her essay "Nuance and the Novella," argues that to Paule Marshall, Brooks's contribution was a turning point in African American fiction because it presented for the first time a black woman "not as a mammy, wench, mulatto or downtrodden heroine but as an ordinary human being in all the wonder of her complexity."

Christian also claims that the novel was not more widely acknowledged because it was published at the end of the 1960's Civil Rights era, when the stress was on integration, and just before a new awareness arose that "black is beautiful" and that women, especially black women, faced particular difficulties.

Bibliography

Brooks, Gwendolyn. *Report from Part One*. Detroit: Broadside Press, 1972. Brooks's
    autobiography covers the period of the novel's writing and allows the reader in-

sights into the autobiographical portions of the book. Brooks writes that "an auto-biographical novel . . . is a better testament, a better thermometer, than a memoir can be."

Hackney, Sheldon. "A Conversation with Gwendolyn Brooks." *Humanities* 15 (May/June, 1994). Hackney, the chairman of the National Endowment for the Humanities, speaks with Brooks about her education in literature, the influence of her parents on her writing, the effect of winning the Pulitzer Prize for "Annie Allen," and her views about being a black American. Although *Maud Martha* is not discussed, this interview is useful for understanding how Brooks's background influenced her work.

Kent, George E. *A Life of Gwendolyn Brooks*. Lexington: University Press of Kentucky, 1990. This biography provides a history of the composition of *Maud Martha* as well as the story of its publication. Emphasizes the autobiographical elements of the novel. The author provides both comments on the novel from the publisher and his own criticism of the work.

Lattin, Patricia H., and Vernon E. Lattin. "Dual Vision in Gwendolyn Brooks's *Maud Martha*." *Critique: Studies in Modern Fiction* 25 (Summer, 1984): 180-186. A positive analysis of the novel that points out the lack of critical analysis up to the time of the article and explores the reasons for its neglect. Also discusses the novel as, in many ways, a comedy.

Melhem, D. H. "Gwendolyn Brooks: An Appreciation." *Humanities* 15 (May/June, 1994): 7-12. An informative overview of Brooks's life and work. Briefly discusses *Maud Martha* as an "impressionistic bildungsroman," calling it "an unpretentious masterpiece."

_____. *Gwendolyn Brooks: Poetry and the Heroic Voice*. Lexington: University Press of Kentucky, 1987. Melhem provides a brief biographical chapter, then proceeds to do in-depth analysis of individual books. She describes *Maud Martha* as a "little appreciated masterpiece of classic simplicity and poetic precision."

Mootry, Maria K., and Gary Smith, eds. *A Life Distilled: Gwendolyn Brooks, Her Poetry, and Fiction*. Urbana: University of Illinois Press, 1989. A collection of essays on Brooks's work, including two essays on *Maud Martha*: "Nuance and the Novella: A Study of Gwendolyn Brooks's *Maud Martha*," by Barbara Christian, and "*Maud Martha*: The War with Beauty," by Harry B. Shaw.

Park, You-Me, and Gayle Wald. "Native Daughters in the Promised Land: Gender, Race, and the Question of Separate Spheres." *American Literature* 70 (September, 1998): 607-633. Park and Wald examine how minority literature represents the boundaries between public and private spheres in the United States. They use examples from *Maud Martha*.

Shaw, Harry B. *Gwendolyn Brooks*. Boston: G. K. Hall, 1980. A typical Twayne production. Contains a chronology, a brief overview of Brooks's life, and a discussion of her work. Includes an insightful chapter on *Maud Martha*.

Walther, Malin L. "Re-Writing *Native Son*: Gwendolyn Brooks' Domestic Aesthetic in *Maud Martha*." *Tulsa Studies in Women's Literature* 13 (Spring, 1994): 143-145.

Compares and contrasts the domestic and positive in *Maud Martha* with the negative scenes and attitudes of Richard Wright's *Native Son*. She specifically focuses on the mouse and rat scenes in the novels, showing how Brooks emphasizes the theme of centrality of home and daily life in her book.

Mary LeDonne Cassidy

MEAN SPIRIT

Author: Linda Hogan (1947-   )
Type of plot: Magical Realism
Time of plot: 1922 and 1923
Locale: Watona, Oklahoma
First published: 1990

> *Principal characters:*
> MICHAEL HORSE, an Osage Indian water diviner and protector of his
>   people's fire who records the events occurring in Watona
> LILA BLANKET, a Hill Indian river prophet who sends her daughter
>   Grace to town to learn white ways
> GRACE BLANKET, Lila's daughter
> BELLE and MOSES GRAYCLOUD, the heads of the Graycloud family,
>   who take in Grace for Lila and care for Nola after Grace's murder
> NOLA BLANKET, Grace Blanket's young daughter
> JOHN HALE, a white oil baron
> JESS GOLD, a white sheriff
> STACE RED HAWK, a Lakota Sioux who works as a government
>   investigator

The Novel

    A historical novel based on actual occurrences on oil-rich Oklahoma Indian lands, *Mean Spirit* tells a story of exploitation and murder committed against Native American Indians as they struggle against the greed that threatens their lives and the survival of their culture.

    The background of the novel's action is provided by Lila Blanket and her daughter Grace. Repeating the warning the Blue River has "spoken" to her, Lila tells the other Hill Indians that white people are going to intrude upon the tribe's peaceful ways; to prevent their own downfall, she says, they must send some of their children to town to learn the white ways. Lila sends Grace to live with her friends the Grayclouds, hoping she will grow up and protect the Hill people with her knowledge. Grace, however, takes little interest in the old Indian ways, acquires an allotment of land, and strikes the richest oil vein in the territory. Her discovery of oil in the territory does indeed save the Hill people, as the current building of a dam on the Blue River is discontinued. Yet the riches that come to the Indian community also destroy it.

    Near the beginning of the novel, Grace Blanket is murdered. Grace's thirteen-year-old daughter Nola and her friend Rena, hidden in the river mud, witness the brutal killing and watch as the unidentifiable murderers arrange Grace's body to suggest suicide. Because the killers are unaware of the witnesses, Belle and Moses Graycloud keep the children's knowledge secret in hope of protecting Nola, who, though she is constantly guarded by four mystical hill "runners," also brings a threat to the entire Graycloud family.

Grace's murder is only one of many that have recently occurred in Watona and is the first of many murders and atrocities to be committed in the plot of the novel. Grace's sister, Sara, is blown up, and Benoit, her husband, is wrongfully arrested. The local hermit dies of seemingly natural causes on the same night that John Thomas is shot after running madly into town yelling that he knows who killed Grace Blanket. Additionally, the government agency reduces the Indians' payments for oil profits and leased land, supposedly because of the Indians' inability to spend their money wisely. Unable to pay their bills, the Grayclouds, among many, are slowly driven into poverty. Letters are written to Washington requesting an investigation into a possible conspiracy, but all the murders have thus far occurred on private land, and until a crime is committed on Indian land, the federal agency has no legal jurisdiction. Scandalous events continue: Indians who owe John Hale money and who, in payment, allow him to take out life insurance policies on them mysteriously die. After more letters are sent, Stace Red Hawk becomes involved in the still-unofficial investigation.

That winter, two weddings take place, both shrouded in sorrow. Nola and Will Forrest, the son of Benoit's white lawyer, marry, but Nola doubts Will, believing only that she is more valuable to Will alive than dead. Letti Graycloud, one of Belle's daughters, marries Benoit; although Benoit is imprisoned, they are allowed a hotel wedding and a wedding night. The next morning, however, Benoit is discovered hanging from his own belt inside his jail cell. Spring temporarily brings some sense of hope. Joe Billy, a Baptist preacher who has returned to Indian ways, practices Bat Medicine along with Belle in the Cave of Sorrow. Stace meets Michael Horse in the cave, and the two cling to the land even as they try to unravel the mystery. Lionel Tall, from Stace's homeland, holds healing ceremonies that more and more Indians attend. All the characters gravitate back toward traditional ways, and even non-Indians begin to take up Indian ways and dress as means of mental survival amid the horrors.

When the white lawyer Forrest learns that Hale was involved in at least one killing, he too is murdered. His murder, at least, opens the door for federal prosecution. Belle is then shot—though not killed—by Sheriff Gold, and this revelation aids in launching a trial. Hale is tried for the multiple murders, by first state and then federal court, but both are imbued with corruption. Overwhelmed and misled by false rumors, many Indians from the town sell their land and move. The Grayclouds had planned to remain on their farm, hoping all would return to peace. Moses, responding to a feeling that his twin sister, Ruth Graycloud Tate, is in great danger, runs to Ruth's house, where he discovers that his sister has been murdered and that John Tate, his brother- in-law, is part of the corruption. Moses kills John Tate and, in fear of the law, the Grayclouds flee by horse and wagon in the middle of the night. Stace departs with them, also on horseback, and knows he will now return to his people in South Dakota.

The Characters

Belle Graycloud is established very early on as the matriarchal figure in the novel, and her ties to the people, the traditions, and the earth make her a vital character in the development of the novel's theme. She is compared to Lila Blanket, the river prophet of the Hill people, who, the reader is told, is a powerful matriarch of the Hill settlement. While Lila nurtures the Hill settlement, Belle nurtures the town of Watona. Lila trusts Belle with her only child, Grace, who Lila hopes will learn the ways of the white people and help to save the Hill settlement. Lila is the biological mother of Nola, and Belle becomes the nurturing mother of the believed savior of the people. Though Grace does not follow in her mother's footsteps, Nola—in essence, granddaughter to both women—will prove to be a river prophet, a fact suggested by her understanding of the water's messages near the end of the novel. Faithfully, Belle follows the traditions of her heritage. She performs the corn ceremony during planting season while other Indians use fertilizer; she wears traditional clothing and practices traditional medicine. She also protects and communes with the sacred animals of the earth—eagles, bats, buffalo, and bees—proving a vigilant warrior when these animals are threatened or desecrated. Hogan's characterization of Belle works to unite the earth, the people, and their traditions. When the traditions are not observed and the earth and its animals are injured, the people too will suffer.

Stace Red Hawk also has strong emotional ties to his people, traditions, and earth, though when the novel commences he has unintentionally weakened these connections. Stace became a reservation police officer against the advice of his mother, and that job leads to his eventual placement at the Bureau of Investigations. Stace's intentions were noble, as he hopes to aid his people through legal methods within the white system; however, this move literally removes him from his homeland and those things most important to his Native American culture. Through this depiction of Stace, Hogan comments on the dangers of complete assimilation. Stace, no longer with his Lakota people, feels the pull toward helping other Indians and becomes emotionally involved in what might have been just another case. He never ceases his ritual patterns, even while in Washington, D.C., but once back in a Native American community, he feels the strength of his culture and increasingly turns back toward it and away from his government life. Additionally, Stace becomes increasingly compelled to be outside, in the natural world. By the end of the novel, he sleeps outside constantly, and he chooses to return to his people via horse.

Themes and Meanings

Mean Spirit's central theme is the recognition that the survival of Indian culture is dependent on the survival of the natural world. The discovery of oil and the subsequent intrusion of whites into the Indian life of Watona initiates the deterioration of the community. The obsession with material goods, drinking, and gambling separates the Hill Indians from those living in town. Grace, who has little interest in old ways, desires electricity and china. When her daughter Nola, feeling threatened by the frequent murders and pervasive greed, marries Will, she too chooses to live in a European-style house; she buys numerous glass figurines, although her husband prefers earth and clay artifacts. Grace is murdered, and Nola experiences a complete nervous breakdown, ending only after she has murdered her own husband.

Drinking is invariably connected with gambling, initially showing the Indian culture's lack of emphasis on material goods. Hogan says that the novel's Indians have no concern about losing their possessions and merely enjoy the game of gambling; however, the pleasure in betting grows out of control, until men are gambling away their sacred pipes and women their sacred dancing shawls. The moral deterioration of the community is followed by many murders, a literal extinction of the people. Seventeen murders in six months have occurred near the start of the novel, and numerous characters die during the story. The Indians in town simply disappear. Originally, the town had belonged to the Indians, but now the still-living characters of the novel walk the streets of town surrounded by all peoples but Indians.

This crumbling of the Indian community is paralleled and intertwined with the desecration of the earth. As Hogan sets the scene in the first pages of the novel, the oil pumps rise and fall in the continual draining of crude oil from the earth, and a burned forest stretches across the horizon in the morning light. Right across the road is Belle Graycloud's house. Grace Blanket's "Barren Land" becomes "Baron Land"; the earth, originally believed poor and useless, is actually pulsing with an undercurrent of rich oil. Hogan elucidates the irony as the land, suddenly viewed as rich, is drained of its resources and made poor again. The drilling creates huge craters in the surface that Belle sees as gouges and wounds. Fires and explosions are common occurrences, destroying the earth and its creatures as quickly as greed destroys the Indian people. An explosion wakes the Catholic priest Father Dunne one night as he is sleeping outside; sure that the Earth is singing some glorious message, he goes to Michael Horse to confer. Horse, sadly, knows that the priest is mistaken and that the Earth merely cries out in pain.

Horse all along writes the happenings of Watona down in his journals, but he is also writing "the Gospel according to Horse," for he desires to "correct" the omission of some things. The priest repeatedly goes to the Hill Indians with his personal revelations, revelations that even the children of the Hill settlement have known as truths all along: "The snake is my sister," he says, and a child replies, "Yes, but what did you learn that is new?" Horse's gospel begins "Honor thy father sky and mother earth. . . . Live gently with the land." A belief in dominion over the Earth and a blindness to its destruction are characteristics Hogan attributes to the white culture. The destruction of the Earth brings the destruction of the Indian people and their culture and eventually threatens all people. Endurance and continuance are key to the cyclical pattern of existence. The bats survive, the bees return, and, though the Grayclouds are forced to flee in the middle of the night, they survive.

Critical Context

Linda Hogan is an established poet who has published several short stories, but *Mean Spirit* is her first novel. Of mixed-blood Chickasaw descent (not Osage as are the characters in *Mean Spirit*), Hogan was inspired to tell the story of "the great frenzy" because of her father's ancestral ties to Oklahoma. She is similar to Joy Harjo, a Creek Indian contemporary poet, in her impressive ability to incorporate spiritual beliefs into her poetry. This talent carries over into her prose; she communicates eloquently the continuance of traditions and the endurance of the Native American peoples.

Hogan's historical novel is written in a style much like that of Gabriel García Márquez and Jorge Luis Borges, two twentieth century Latin American writers. Her novel contains realistic description combined with strong components of the supernatural or the bizarre, placing her novel in the genre of Magical Realism. Many happenings in *Mean Spirit* seem bizarre: the swarming crickets that attack Nola (the event that pulls Nola out of her depressed, nearly catatonic state); the swarming bees, that attack and kill the sheriff after he attempts to shoot Belle; the speaking river, which foretells the devastation that the new dam will bring; the amazing meteorite that saves Belle's life. Hogan uses this technique to connect animals or the Earth with people and to connect traditional beliefs with contemporary Indians. The integration of the realistic and the bizarre facilitates Hogan's effort to merge ritualistic ceremony with her political interest in revealing suppressed Native American history.

Bibliography

Allen, Paula Gunn. "Let Us Hold Fierce: Linda Hogan." In *The Sacred Hoop: Recovering the Feminine in American Indian Traditions*. Boston: Beacon Press, 1986. Allen discusses Hogan's awakening to her own spirit-based ideology and how Hogan incorporates this vision in her work. Hogan, an activist, uses her work to educate readers on the politics of Indian survival. Allen examines the fusion of spirituality and political commitment that dominates Hogan's work.

Bonaham, R. A. "*Mean Spirit.*" *Studies in American Indian Literatures: Newsletter of the Association for the Study of American Indian Literatures*. (Winter, 1992): 114-116. Bonaham outlines the setting, events, and characters of the novel. He then examines the "spare phrasing and power of visualization" that Hogan, as a poet, brings to her prose. In conclusion, Bonaham attributes the power of *Mean Spirit* to Hogan's integration of traditional ritual and historical fact.

Brice, Jennifer. "Earth as Mother, Earth as Other in Novels by Silko and Hogan." *Critique* 39 (Winter, 1998): 127-138. Brice explores the concept of earth as mother in *Mean Spirit* by Linda Hogan and the work of Leslie Marmon Silko. She discusses the use of literary trope and Magical Realism to portray the earth as human and the human as the earth, and demonstrates that the suffering of humanity stems from the aggression of "motherless" men.

Smith, Patricia Clark. "Linda Hogan." In *This Is About Vision: Interviews with Southwestern Writers*, edited by William Balassi, John F. Crawford, and Annie O. Eysturoy. Albuquerque: University of New Mexico Press, 1990. Smith explores Hogan's position as an American writer focusing on Southwestern culture. She also looks at Hogan's themes and their niche within this group of writers.

Tiffany Elizabeth Thraves

MEDICINE RIVER

Author: Thomas King (1943-　　)
Type of plot: Social realism
Time of plot: The 1980's
Locale: Alberta, Canada
First published: 1989

> *Principal characters:*
>> WILL SAMPSON, the narrator and protagonist of the book, a
>> forty-year-old Native American
>> HARLEN BIGBEAR, Will's best friend and basketball teammate, an
>> assertive, often dominating person
>> LOUISE HEAVYMAN, a woman courted by Will
>> ROSE SAMPSON, Will's mother, long abandoned by her husband
>> JAMES SAMPSON, Will's father, a mysterious and elusive figure
>> JAKE PRETTY WEASEL, a friend of Will who commits suicide
>> SUSAN ADAMSON, a former girlfriend of Will
>> DAVID PLUME, a Native American militant

The Novel

Medicine River chronicles the lives of a group of contemporary Native Americans in Western Canada. The novel is divided into eighteen short chapters. The story is recounted by the protagonist, Will Sampson, in an amiable, conversational fashion, with frequent flashbacks to earlier portions of his life.

The novel begins with an encounter between Will and Harlen Bigbear. Harlen is an entrepreneur who has set Will up in his own photography business. Harlen is Will's best friend, but there is something unpredictable about him. Harlen is much more dynamic than the stolid Will, and he lives life at a faster and more stressful pace. Beneath Will's placid exterior, though, all sorts of psychological depths simmer. These are hinted at as Will remembers contemplating letters written long ago by his long-vanished father to his mother, Rose. Rose catches Will reading the letters and reprimands him. Will realizes that his life will remain unsettled until he comes to terms with the enigma of his father.

Harlen speaks to Will again soon after. This time, Harlen attempts to recruit Will to play on a local basketball team, the Medicine River Friendship Centre Warriors. The team's star player, Clyde Whiteman, cannot play at the moment, and Harlen urges Will to substitute for him. Will is skeptical, doubting his own ability. His brother James, a gifted artist, seems to have all the talent in the family, whereas Will sees himself as merely an ordinary person who somehow muddles through life. Notwithstanding his fears, Will agrees to join the team. At forty, he is not exactly in championship-quality shape. Yet with the help of some coaxing from Harlen, he fits well onto the team.

Harlen also helps to activate Will's private life. He points out that Louise Heavyman, who is the tax accountant for both men, is an attractive woman. None too subtly, Harlen urges Will to court Louise. Will is almost persuaded when, shockingly, he learns that Louise is pregnant by another man and is about to give birth. Whereas most men would be dissuaded at this point, Will takes the news in stride. He asks Louise for a date, not even mentioning her condition.

Soon, Louise calls Will to drive her to the hospital when her labor begins. There seems to be an unspoken understanding between Will and Louise that, despite the unusual circumstances of their relationship, they are both comfortable with the situation. The baby is born and is named Wilma, but Will jokingly calls her South Wing. This sounds like a traditional Indian name, but in fact it is derived from the south wing of the hospital, where the baby is born.

Jake Pretty Weasel is one of the best players on the basketball team, but it is also known that he beats his wife, January. When it is learned that Jake has shot himself, some people suspect that January has in fact murdered her husband, whether in retaliation or in self-defense. Because of Catholic prohibitions against suicide, a Mormon clergyman officiates at the funeral; the Canadian headquarters of Mormonism, Cardston, is quite near the fictional Medicine River. It turns out that Jake has in fact shot himself, but that January has forged a suicide note because she knew that people would suspect her. When January explains this to Will and Harlen, they are accepting and compassionate. After a while, Will and Harlen forget the tawdry and painful end to Jake's life, and they retain their fond memories of him as friend and teammate.

The basketball team is becoming a more close-knit, cohesive fraternity, but Will's feelings about his vanished father are still unresolved. He reveals that, for years, he has lied when asked about his father, saying that he is an engineer, photographer, or lawyer. These lies are an attempt to evade the embarrassment and hurt that Will feels at his father's abandonment of him. As time goes on, Will's fantasies become more elaborate. Will's mother once gave him a photograph of his father, but this sample of reality did not assuage his emotional disquiet.

As the basketball team tours the western areas of Canada and the United States, Harlen pressures Will to contact Louise again. Will recalls a former relationship with a Toronto woman, Susan Adamson, who attempts to draw Will into the urban excitement of contemporary Canadian culture. Will begins a relationship with her. Yet when he calls her at home, to his shock her daughter answers, revealing that Susan is married. Beneath Susan's facade of sophistication are qualities that the novel exposes as hypocritical and immoral.

Will and Harlen drive down to the site of the defeat of General George Armstrong Custer, the most famous event in Native American history, but it is closed for the night. Their basketball team is improved by the return of the gifted Clyde Whiteman, but Whiteman soon leaves the team again when he is jailed for stealing a car.

Will becomes closer to Louise and her daughter, prompting Harlen to comment that Will should marry Louise. As the two become closer, Will again flashes back to the end of his relationship with Susan Adamson and further reveals to the reader that his mother died when he was living in Toronto.

David Plume, a member of the militant American Indian Movement (AIM), is arrested after a man who had taunted him has been shot. Will believes that David committed the crime, but he sympathizes with his predicament. Louise goes into Edmonton to see Harold, the father of South Wing. Will worries that she will marry him. Louise, however, returns to Medicine River and Will. The reader gets the impression that the happiness Will experiences with Louise and her daughter will finally heal the wounds inflicted upon him by his vanished father.

The Characters

Will Sampson is a Native American professional photographer. He is forty and unmarried. The disappearance of his father has left him with unresolved emotional tensions. He is not only the narrator of the book but also the emotional center of the subtle social milieu of Medicine River. The other characters are defined by their interaction with Will. They establish an interpersonal atmosphere in the book that establishes a community whose whole is greater than the sum of its individual parts.

Harlen Bigbear is Will's best friend. He is energetic and innovative and often motivates Will to do things he otherwise would not do.

Louise Heavyman is courted by Will. She has a daughter, South Wing. Louise is an imperfect yet sympathetic character. She communicates largely through subtle, indirect hints, though her emotional language is readily understood by Will.

Rose Sampson, Will's mother, knows that Will has been affected by the disappearance of his mysterious and enigmatic father. She attempts to heal her son's emotional wounds, but she can never quite succeed during her life. She has died when Will sets up his photography business in Medicine River, so she is presented exclusively in flashback.

Jake Pretty Weasel is an abusive husband who commits suicide. His fate highlights by contrast Will's warmth toward Louise.

David Plume, a Native American militant, provides a contrast to the softspoken, nuanced character of Will. He also is a symbol of the lingering discontent felt among contemporary Native Americans.

Susan Adamson, a sophisticated Toronto woman who once was Will's girlfriend, is an unsympathetic character who helps the reader to recognize the positive values held by Will and Louise at the end of the book. She is presented exclusively in flashback.

Themes and Meanings

Medicine River is preoccupied with Native American themes, but this preoccupation is voiced with an almost spectacular unobtrusiveness. Prominent Native American writers of the late twentieth century have stressed the need to dispel degrading and condescending stereotypes of contemporary Native Americans. Works such as Louise Erdrich's *Love Medicine* (1984) and James Welch's *The Indian Lawyer* (1990) defy conventional notions of Native Americans as mere hapless, residual victims, lingering on in reservations after the near-obliteration of their culture by triumphant Europeans. Welch and Erdrich show Native Americans flourishing and thriving in markedly contemporary contexts, living lives much like the rest of mainstream Americans, yet these characters are never totally assimilated. They never forget (nor are they allowed to forget) their distinctive heritage.

This variety of representation is King's goal as well. King, though, weaves the themes of modernity and assimilation so deftly into the fabric of the book's plot that he does not even need to be overt about it. Will, Harlen, Louise, and the other residents of Medicine River are unmistakably Native American. Yet their guiding pursuits in life—eating pizza, watching football on television, and playing basketball—are dramatically antithetical to received expectations of Native American interests. The people of Medicine River participate as thoroughly in the modern world as do any of their Europe-descended neighbors.

At a party Will attends with his then-girlfriend Susan during his Toronto years, he meets someone who is surprised that Will is a photographer. This is because the partygoer has been exposed to widely disseminated canards about Native Americans, who ostensibly fear that photographs will capture their souls. The fact that Will is a photographer by profession is a striking indicator of how King's characters are at home with technology and do not fear or repudiate it. The symbol of the photograph also represents the preservation of the past through time. This is illustrated when Rose gives Will a photograph of his father in order to stem his bewilderment about the man who abandoned him.

Although Will lacks the militancy of his friend David Plume, he is sensitive to his own heritage. This is evidenced by the poignant attempt he and Harlen make to visit the site of Custer's defeat. That this site is closed may symbolize the way the characters remain rather distant from their people's past. More pressing to Will are dilemmas only accidentally connected to his heritage, such as the enigma of his father or his relationship with Louise. These questions of love and family occur in the lives of everyone. King's portrait of his characters' concerns is thereby ingratiating and authentic. The combination of the mellow social comedy of the surface plot and the questions of Native American identity that lie not far below lend the novel a relaxed and evocative atmosphere. The novel uses humor and understatement in order to treat potentially tumultuous situations with reserve and warmth.

An interesting facet of *Medicine River* is its Canadian setting, The characters relate more to American professional sports (for example, the National Football League) than to such partly Canadian professional sports as basketball and hockey. In this way, they are a part of a common North American culture, as shown in much of their everyday lives. Yet the reader is always reminded of the Canadian setting of the action. Louise goes to Edmonton to visit her baby's father. Will met his sophisticated former girlfriend in Toronto. Canadian writers such as Leon Rooke are mentioned prominently in the novel. Native Americans, however, live in both the United States and Canada, and lived in the areas now occupied by those nations before either existed. In addition, Native Americans often have dual loyalties to their own nation or tribe and to the Native American people as a whole. These competing loyalties are compounded when, as is often the case, ancestry can be traced from several different tribes and, more often than not, from Europeans as well. (Thomas King, for example, is partly of Greek and German descent. His Native American heritage comes from the Cherokee nation, which is not native to Western Canada.) Thus, the people of *Medicine River* can be said to belong to no one nation or tribe.

Critical Context

Medicine River was published in Canada in 1989 and released in the United States in 1992. It was King's first novel and was enthusiastically received in both countries. King has since published another novel, *Green Grass, Running Water* (1993), a more expansive look at many of the same themes and questions that concerned him in his first work of fiction. King's second novel delves more fully into the visionary potential of the Native American past and present than does *Medicine River.*

King is now counted as one of the leading contemporary Native American writers. He teaches in the departments of American and Native American Studies at the University of Minnesota. King is a Canadian-born man teaching in the United States whose work centers on a Native American identity common to both countries. In this way, King's life summarizes the contradictions that animate and nourish the lives of his characters.

Bibliography

Davenport, Gary. "Fiction and the Furniture of Consciousness." *Sewanee Review* 100 (Spring, 1992): 323-330. Compares *Medicine River* to works by James Welch, Wayne Johnson, Robert Olmstead, William Hoffman, and Ellen Akins. Discusses the relationship between the characters and the places these novelists create. Concludes that vivid imagery of "place" increases the value and authenticity of the novels.

Hemesath, James B. Review of *Medicine River,* by Thomas King. *Library Journal* 115 (August, 1990): 143. Addresses the novel's use of humor and characterization, as well as its engagement with Native American concerns.

King, Thomas. "Godzilla Versus Post-Colonial." *World Literature Written in English* 30 (Autumn, 1990): 10-16. Supplies some of the crucial intellectual background to the novel. King discusses the necessary differences between an inside and outside perspective on Native American concerns. King critiques the "postcolonial" approaches prevalent in current literary discussions of works by minorities, charging that they slight the full historical amplitude of Native American experience.

_____. Interview by Constance Rooke. *World Literature Written in English* (Autumn, 1990): 62-76. King places himself in Canadian, Native American, and literary contexts.

_____. "Thomas King." Interview by Jace Weaver. *Publishers Weekly* 240 (March 8, 1993): 56. This interview emphasizes the themes of social comedy in King's two novels. King makes valuable comments on how he is influenced by ideas of oral tradition.

Nicholas Birns

MEN AND ANGELS

Author: Mary Gordon (1949-   )
Type of plot: Psychological realism
Time of plot: The 1980's
Locale: Selby, Massachusetts
First published: 1985

>*Principal characters:*
>>LAURA POST, the nanny to the children of Anne and Michael Foster
>>ANNE FOSTER, the holder of a doctorate in art
>>MICHAEL FOSTER, Anne's husband, a professor on sabbatical
>>JANE WATSON, the elderly widow of Caroline's son, Stephen
>>ROSE CORCORAN, a brain-damaged woman
>>ED CORCORAN, Rose's husband and the Fosters' electrician

The Novel

   Men and Angels illustrates the possible consequences of parental rejection and implies that people need religion to be complete. The story begins when Laura Post, a twenty-one-year-old drifter, becomes a live-in babysitter for the two children of Anne Foster, who is writing a lengthy catalog on the works of the late artist Caroline Watson, to be used at an exhibition being arranged by Anne's longtime friend Ben Hardy. Since Anne's work is time-consuming and since Michael, a professor, is teaching in France that year, she needs someone to tend the children and the house.

   Anne hires Laura because her original sitter has changed plans and no other suitable person can be found. Yet she takes an instant disliking to the younger woman, for which she tries to compensate by doing small favors for Laura, such as making her cocoa in the mornings, taking her to lunch, and baking her a birthday cake. Anne's dislike of Laura is augmented by the latter's religiosity and her frequent reading of the Bible. Anne, on the other hand, has no conscious religious life. She and Michael do not attend church, and she has never told her children, Peter and Sarah, ages nine and six, respectively, about hell and the devil, thinking these supposedly questionable doctrines might frighten them. While Anne is not an avowed atheist, her highest objects of worship seem to be her spouse and children, whom she keeps safe and secure in their upper-class home.

   Although Laura appears to be mentally stable, her lifelong deprivation of parental love (especially from her mother, who seems to hate her) has caused her to embrace religion (of no particular denomination) to the point of madness. She has convinced herself that human love, especially the love of family, is worthless and that the love of the "Spirit" (a term she never clearly defines) is the only love worth having. She guards herself from all close human encounters and owns only absolutely essential material items. Moreover, Laura fancies herself the Chosen One of God, sent to "save" Anne from materialism by destroying her maternal attachment. Without realizing it, however, she develops a love for Anne similar to a daughter's love for her mother. Unfortunately, this love is not reciprocated.

During the first six months of her employment, Laura is watchful of the children, but her first act of negligence—letting them slide on a deep, partially thawed pond while she sits behind a rock reading the Bible (a possible scheme for their deaths, which will forever sever them from Anne)—is her downfall. Furious with the sitter for endangering her children's lives, Anne fires her immediately. This abrupt dismissal is too much for Laura. The only way she can now "save" Anne and obtain her love is by offering herself as a sacrifice. While Anne takes the children out to supper, having told Laura to be packed and gone by the time they return, Laura slits her wrists and bleeds to death in an overflowing bathtub. By letting the water run, she knows she is beginning to rescue Anne from her preoccupation with the material, as the water, flooding the upstairs hall and dripping through the downstairs ceiling, destroys much of the Fosters' beautiful house.

While tragic, the young woman's suicide has redeeming effects. At last, Anne is able to feel some tenderness, if not love, toward Laura. Furthermore, her dormant spirituality begins to surface. After Sarah explains to Peter that the lifeless form the police have removed was not really Laura—only her body—Anne asks her daughter, "Where do you think she is now, sweetheart?" It is as if Anne is contemplating the afterlife for the first time. Later, at the cremation service, she understands from the words of Psalm 121 ("from whence cometh my help? My help cometh from the Lord, which made heaven and earth") that she is not completely autonomous; she must learn to appeal to a higher, divine being. Finally, Anne realizes that she cannot protect her children from all the pain and tragedy in life. Therefore, the death of Laura, tragic as it is, provides a growing experience for both Anne and her children.

The Characters

Caroline sets the novel in motion. Had Ben not arranged an exhibition of her works, he would not have asked Anne to write the catalog; hence, Anne would not have hired Laura.

Laura is the catalyst for Anne's religious development, while her strangeness lends interest to the novel. Her physical appearance is significant, as it is one reason for her mother's rejection. While not unattractively large, Laura is tall, with a sturdy bone structure. Her hair is red, her eyes blue, and her complexion fair. Laura's mother, in contrast, is dark and petite. Moreover, Laura has a sister who is a replica of her mother and who thus has received all the mother's attention and affection.

Anne, the protagonist, is the one character who develops to any extent. A woman who considers religion unnecessary and somewhat disquieting, she becomes marginally aware of this missing element in her life through her contacts with Laura and Jane Watson. After Laura's death, she realizes that there is something higher than the material world and her children. In addition, she develops as a mother by letting her children experience tragedy instead of trying to protect them. Like Laura's, Anne's looks are important, for she too is tall, red-haired, and blue-eyed. Coincidentally, she is thirty-eight, the same age as Laura's mother. Anne's age and their similarity in appearance probably contribute to Laura's love for her employer.

Jane exemplifies the practice of religion. A churchgoer, she can nevertheless form meaningful human relationships. For example, she is the lover of Ben, a divorced man. She also befriends a woman whose battered children have been taken from her. Since the formerly abusive mother regrets her behavior and has received therapy, Jane gives her another chance by entrusting her with the care of Anne's children for a few hours. Additionally, Jane becomes a mother figure to Anne, who, like Laura, is the less beloved of her own mother's two children.

Rose Corcoran, who developed an inoperable brain tumor during her second pregnancy, is permanently impaired both physically and mentally. Although she appears only once, she seems to represent the acceptance of fate and divine will. Not fooled by the comments of others that she is getting well, Rose regards herself as a "cripple" and wishes to be photographed on a particular hill, so that she might resemble a crippled girl in a painting she admires. When she says she would be better off dead, Laura replies, "If the Lord wanted you to be dead, you'd be dead in the blink of an eye." While Anne is shocked by the callousness of this remark, Rose is not offended. "That's what the priest says," she agrees. "He says I'm alive for a reason."

Ed Corcoran is an attractive man who loves his wife unconditionally. Physically drawn to Ed, Anne attempts to seduce him, but he declines her proposition on the grounds that he could never be unfaithful to the wonderful woman he married, despite her infirmity, which is not her fault. Thus, Ed stands for adherence to the marriage vow, "for better or for worse," and to a firm moral code that does not alter with circumstance.

Themes and Meanings

Gordon focuses on two interrelated themes, family and religion, which she conveys chiefly through characterization. First, she examines the strength of the traditional, ideal family by presenting three different groups: the Posts, the Corcorans, and the Fosters. Although the Post family is structurally traditional (two parents, two children), it is clearly destructive, by virtue of the parents' conscious rejection of one child, who eventually becomes psychotic. The Corcorans are not destructive, yet they are a less than ideal family in that the wife and mother is an invalid, unable to perform her domestic and maternal duties. In effect, Ed has become a single parent, since he must take full charge of his four-year-old son. Finally, the Fosters seem to match the stereotype of the ideal American family: two highly educated and devoted parents, a pleasant physical environment, and a home atmosphere that shelters the children from harsh realities. After Michael leaves for France, however, the Fosters' family strength begins to falter. Anne tries to seduce her electrician, an action she would never take were her husband at home. Moreover, she lies to Ed that Michael is having an affair himself.

Until Laura's suicide, Anne, the ideal mother, is able to protect her children from all things unpleasant or frightening. On the other hand, the little Corcoran boy lives each day with a nonfunctional, brain-damaged mother whose very appearance is somewhat grotesque. Yet whenever Ed brings his son to Anne's home (he must often take Brian on his jobs, when there is no one to watch him), the child seems happy. Apparently, living with an "imperfect" mother is a situation he takes for granted, rather than one that is troubling or deleterious. Through Laura Post and Brian Corcoran, Gordon implies that although children must be loved in order to remain mentally well, love does not necessitate blinding them to all pain. The Corcoran child, deeply loved by his father, illustrates the resilience of children exposed to conditions that are less than ideal.

Closely related to the theme of family is that of religion. For Ed Corcoran, religion may provide a standard of morality. Because Rose has mentioned conversing with a priest, it can be assumed that the family is either Roman Catholic or Anglican, or at least acquainted with one of these faiths. It may be Ed's religious convictions, then, as well as his love for Rose, that enable him to resist the advances of Anne and other women for whom he works.

Laura misuses religion as an escape from the pain of parental rejection. For her, human love and spirituality cannot coexist. At the other end of the pole, Anne disregards religion entirely, feeling that a stable family environment is all one really needs. Jane represents the middle ground, for she can both worship God and relate to human beings.

Gordon, a Roman Catholic, regards religion as an essential ingredient in the lives of families and individuals. During childhood, however, Gordon was surrounded by a religious atmosphere that dichotomized spirit and body, insisting that the flesh must be subdued. This division of spirit and flesh she could not accept. The body and the world, she insists, are parts of religion—a belief she exemplifies through the character of Jane, a woman who has suffered, turned to religion, and finally extended her love for God to the people around her.

Critical Context

Men and Angels demonstrates Gordon's growth and maturity as a writer. This novel, unlike her earlier *Final Payments* (1978) and *The Company of Women* (1980), moves beyond the subculture of Roman Catholicism, extending the theme of religion into society at large. Some critics, in fact, see Gordon's work as moving from the genre of "women's fiction" to that of religious literature. Moreover, her characters are older (with the exception of Laura) and less stereotypical. Isabel Moore, the protagonist of *Final Payments*, and Felicitas Taylor, heroine of *The Company of Women*, are thirty and twenty, respectively; Anne, however, is thirty-eight, and Jane is in her seventies. When the novel begins, Anne is already settled as a wife and mother, and Jane has come to terms with God and the world.

The characters in *Final Payments* and *The Company of Women* seem to be stock types, Catholics or privileged persons rebelling against their upbringing. Anne and Laura, on the other hand, are more complex. Anne conscientiously divides her time between work and motherhood. She feels ambivalent toward Caroline Watson, an artist who neglected and never truly loved her son—and worries over her own inability to love Laura, whose psychosis appears to be only eccentricity.

The theme of love, prominent in both *Final Payments* and *The Company of Women*, continues in *Men and Angels*. Yet those people whom the earlier protagonists cannot love are unlovable for obvious reasons: Margaret Casey in *Final Payments* and Muriel Fisher in *The Company of Women* are embittered spinsters, seething with envy and spite, while the Habers in *The Company of Women* are a filthy, coarse, and indigent family. Laura Post, however, is young, strong, and on the brink of life. Her unlovability, therefore, is more pathetic. Thus, the issue of love is more problematic in *Men and Angels*.

The novel also looks deeply into the issue of motherhood, probably because maternity had become central to Gordon's life. When she wrote *The Company of Women*, her first child had not yet been born, but while writing *Men and Angels*, she was pregnant with her second baby and was the mother of a three-year-old. The focus on motherhood and family, as well as the expansion of religion, probably makes Gordon's third novel attractive to a wider and more mature audience than her earlier works.

Bibliography
Bennet, Alma. *Mary Gordon*. New York: Twayne, 1996. In this first full-length book on Mary Gordon, Bennet draws on personal interviews with Gordon, as well as other primary and secondary sources to provide students and scholars with a comprehensive introduction to Gordon's work.
Gordon, Mary. Interview by Patrick H. Samway. *America* 170 (May 14, 1994): 12-15. Gordon discusses her ethnic and educational background, as well as her career. Gordon's insights into her Catholic upbringing are particularly illuminating and shed considerable light on her works in general.
Mahon, John. "The Struggle with Love." In *American Women Writing Fiction*, edited by Mickey Pearlman. Lexington: The University Press of Kentucky, 1989. Mahon discusses characters' inabilities to give and receive love. He also points to the frailty of the secular family, which, he says, in times of crisis easily disintegrates.
Morey, Ann-Janine. "Beyond Updike: Incarnated Love in the Novels of Mary Gordon." *Christian Century* 102 (November, 1985): 1059-1063. Morey observes that Gordon's novels show religion from a feminine viewpoint. For example, Anne is concerned about nonsexual human love, an issue not found in the works of most male writers.
Pierce, Judith. "Profile." *Belles Lettres: A Review of Books by Women* 9 (Fall, 1993): 8-12. A compelling portrait of Gordon revealing that her priorities are her children and her writing; that listening to music helps her along in the creative process; and that her instinct for parenting is balanced, fully acknowledging that being a parent has both its positive and negative sides.
Seabury, Marcia. "Of Belief and Unbelief: The Novels of Mary Gordon." *Christianity and Literature* 40 (Autumn, 1990): 37-55. Seabury analyzes Gordon's works in

terms of the inseparability of spirit and body. She observes that Laura's warped religiosity is juxtaposed with Anne's repressed spirituality.

Suleiman, Susan. "On Maternal Splitting: A Propos of Mary Gordon's *Men and Angels*." *Signs* 14 (Autumn, 1989): 25-41. Suleiman notes that working mothers may
be jealous of mother substitutes and compensate by finding the substitute "bad."
Laura's strangeness is the "badness" that aggravates Anne's animosity.

Wymward, Eleanor. "Mary Gordon: Her Religious Sensibility." *Cross Currents* 37
(Summer/Fall, 1987): 147-158. Wymward comments that in Gordon's fiction, individuals must find salvation within the world; however, they need faith in something
higher. Laura evokes Anne's latent spirituality.

Rebecca Stingley Hinton

MEN OF MAIZE

Author: Miguel Ángel Asturias (1899-1974)
Type of plot: Social morality
Time of plot: The twentieth century
Locale: Guatemala
First published: Hombres de maíz, 1949 (English translation, 1975)

> *Principal characters:*
> GASPAR ILÓM, an Indian who revolts against the commercial
> corngrowers
> PIOJOSA GRANDE, his wife
> MACHOJÓN, an Indian turncoat who sells Gaspar to the Mounted Patrol
> VACA MANUELA, his wife
> COLONEL CHALO GODOY, the Commander of the Mounted Patrol
> GOYO YIC, a blind beggar
> MARÍA TECÚN, his runaway wife
> NICHO AQUINO, the postman of San Miguel Acatan
> HILARIO SACAYÓN, a mule driver with a penchant for spinning yarns

The Novel

The action of *Men of Maize* is divided into two periods. In the first part of the novel Gaspar Ilóm wages war against the professional maizegrowers who set fire to the brush and ruthlessly exploit the land. According to the Indians of Guatemala, the first men who were created, their ancestors, were made of corn. Therefore, this grain is sacred; it may be consumed but never exploited, eaten but never sold. The maizegrowers, however, prefer profits to traditions, an attitude which opposes them to the peasants both morally and ethically. This is why Gaspar and his Indian guerrillas revolt against them and gain the upper hand until the maizegrowers call in the Mounted Patrol. With the help of an Indian turncoat, Machojón, and especially of his wife, Vaca Manuela, the commander of the Mounted Patrol lures Gaspar and his men to a feast. During the celebration, Vaca Manuela tricks Gaspar into drinking poison, but Gaspar dives into the river and manages to "extinguish the thirst of the poison in his intestines." He returns after dawn, only to discover that the soldiers have taken his men by surprise and massacred them. Gaspar dives into the river once again, and the maizegrowers return to the mountains of Ilóm, unaware that a curse has been cast. The yellow-eared rabbit sorcerers who accompanied Gaspar condemn all the perpetrators of the massacre to die before the seventh year is ended. One by one, in the chapters which follow, they are all punished. Machojón and his wife burn in an eerie blaze which razes their cornfields. On his way to ask for the hand of his intended, their son is surrounded by fireflies and mysteriously disappears. The man who sold the poison used on Gaspar is decapitated along with his entire family, and finally Colonel Godoy and his troops are consumed by "flames in the form of bloodstained hands" which "were painted on the walls of the air."

The second part of the novel describes the adventures of three men whose lives become intertwined. The first, Goyo Yic, is a blind beggar whose wife, María, runs away, taking with her their many children. Goyo cannot live without her and seeks the help of a curer, who removes the veil of blindness from his eyes. He has, however, never seen María. For this reason, he becomes a peddler and travels from fair to fair; he coaxes women to buy his wares in order to hear their voices and one day, he hopes, recognize his missing wife. Goyo invokes O Possum, patron saint of peddlers, to guide him on his search, but to no avail. One night, he gazes at his shadow by the light of the moon, and "it was like seeing the shadow of a she-opossum." The moonlight turns him from a man into an animal. He wanders into the forest so long as a fugitive that his skin turns black. One day, he is lured by the lights and the laughter of the big fair in the town of Santa Cruz de las Cruces. He returns to the world of men and teams up with a certain Domingo Revolorio to start a little business selling liquor by the glass. They buy a demijohn and take turns carrying it on their backs to a distant fair. It is a hot day and they soon get tired. They start selling glasses of liquor to each other until, finally drunk, they lose their permit and are sent to jail for selling liquor without a license.

Time passes. People preserve and repeat the legend of the blindman and his runaway wife, María Tecún, immortalizing it by referring to all runaways as "tecunas." One day the wife of Nicho Aquino, the postman in the little town of San Miguel de Acatán, suddenly disappears. Nicho is overcome with grief and gets drunk to forget and remember. On his next trip to the capital, mailpouch on his back, he meets a wizened old man with black hands who offers to tell him the whereabouts of his wife. Nicho follows him into some caves where the old man brings to life the tale of creation according to Maya tradition. He reveals to Nicho why maize is sacred and explains the import of Gaspar Ilóm's death and of the cycle of retribution which it has for a sequel. Nicho is enlightened. Upon discovering his origins, he regains a sense of self. For a moment he becomes a coyote, his *nagual*, or animal protector.

Meanwhile, in San Miguel, the townspeople are worried that the postman—and especially their letters—may never reach their destination. They send the muleteer, Hilario Sacayón, to look for Nicho and steer him onto the right path. Hilario looks everywhere and on his way ponders the nature of tales and the difference between reality and fiction, but he never finds Nicho. The former postman ends up burning the mail and running away to the coast, where he becomes a factotum for a hotel proprietress. One of his duties is to ferry people to the Harbor Castle, fitted out as a prison, where Goyo Yic is serving a sentence for selling liquor without a license. Once again, years have passed. Goyo's own son is serving time in the same prison, and one day his mother, María Tecún, comes to pay him a visit. Nicho ferries her across and is astounded to discover that the woman he knows as a legend really exists. The members of the Yic family are reunited, and when the men are set free, they all go back to harvest corn in Pisigüilito, where the action started. This is the story's climax. Man, blind for a time to the ancient traditions which bind him to the soil, returns to harvest the sacred substance which constitutes him. Gaspar's sacrifice is not in vain if it has succeeded in doing away with the sanguinary breed (the commercial exploiters) who keep the men of maize from engaging in the most fundamental of occupations.

The Characters

The influence of Mayan literature on characterization in *Men of Maize* cannot be overstated. Asturias spent years studying anthropology and helped to translate the Mayan book of Genesis, or *Popol Vuh*. Many of the narrative features of this ancient manuscript filter into his indigenous novels. For example, character and chronological development in *Men of Maize* are minimal; the protagonists substitute for one another in what could be termed a character substitution principle. They are cast as friends or foes of the men of maize, and, for the most part, they are emblematic of behavior patterns. Gaspar Ilóm is a character whose portrayal evolves throughout the fiction without undergoing any psychological development. He fights for the communal values dear to the Indian in the first part of the novel, but in the chapters which follow he is portrayed as a mythic figure from a remote past, while other characters step into the limelight. The reader soon realizes that this novel does not have a hero in the conventional sense but rather a collective beneficiary, the men of maize, who profit from the moral teachings extolled by Asturias.

As the first part of the novel is typified by emblematic characters who do not develop in the traditional sense, the second part is noteworthy for the original characters who do. Here, Goyo Yic shines forth as an Everyman figure who has lost touch with the world of his forefathers. For this reason, he is portrayed as both blind and a beggar when introduced to the reader. Yet, prompted by the need to find his wife and children, he launches forth in a search which must be seen as a rite of passage. His wife, María Tecún, is a beacon throughout the novel (although she materializes as a character only in the last few pages). As are all women in *Men of Maize*, she is an absent presence, alluded to, sought, and eventually found, a symbol of the telluric forces from which the men of maize have become estranged. In fact, the wives of all the Indian protagonists in the novel either run away or disappear, and only one couple (Goyo and María Tecún) are reunited.

Two other important characters, Nicho Aquino and Hilario Sacayón, should be seen as pegs in a well-oiled narrative machine, who serve their purpose (bringing together Goyo and María) and subsequently fade. In addition Hilario, the muleteer, functions as Asturias's mouthpiece in *Men of Maize*. Hilario is a man capable of imagining a woman piecemeal and then falling in love with his own creation. This self-persuasion suggests that words can be as concrete as action, that what man hears becomes, eventually, what he sees.

Influencing readers was exactly what Asturias intended to do. He wrote *Men of Maize* during a period of great political optimism in Guatemala. Juan José Arévalo had been elected president in 1945, and he had enacted controversial social laws aiming to return lands to destitute peasants, to organize cooperative farms, and to make way for agrarian reform. *Men of Maize* translates into fiction the changes which Arévalo was bringing about in reality. Asturias wields words—as does Hilario—to motivate reality. His design was to present in fiction (by means of emblematic characters) the blueprints for a society whose roots went back to the days of the great Maya nation and heralded, at the same time, the progressive community planned by Juan José Arévalo.

Themes and Meanings

There are three major themes in *Men of Maize*: struggle, paternity, and the genetic process of myth. The first of these is the most readily apparent and one that is a factual reflection of social conditions in twentieth century Guatemala. When Asturias conceived this novel, his country's society was divided into two factions: the haves and the have-nots (Indians for the most part). In the vision of the novel, the differences between these two factions are not simply economic but, more profoundly, of an ethical nature. Essentially, what distinguishes them is an attitude toward life. The Indians live in harmony with nature; the outsiders (represented by the commercial maizegrowers) exploit nature to make a living, which is equated with barrenness in Asturias's scheme. Yet the exploiters of the land have the upper hand, while the Indians are portrayed as a strayed race, wandering and blind but by no means lost. Asturias points the path to salvation by underscoring the need to return to the land, the natural harbor and seedbed of the race. The first step in order to restore the lost order of the Mayan forefathers is to eradicate evil; the second is to heed the voice of tradition (of the past). The new man that Asturias is extolling must put his ear to the ground and remove the veil of blindness from his eyes. If he does, he will establish a nexus with the roots of his culture, as do Goyo and Nicho, who both transform themselves into their protective animals as a sign of their conversion.

The second major theme in the novel is paternity. Man and maize are one. The enemies of the Indian engage in commerce with maize; they sell "the flesh of our children" and are punished with sterility for this sin. Machojón loses his son, and in all the participants in the massacre of Ilóm, "the light of the tribes was extinguished." Meanwhile, the prototypical Indian family, that of Goyo Yic, flourishes. At the end of the novel, when they all return to Pisigüilito to harvest corn, they are a full-bodied clan "because their married children had many children and they all went there to live with them." As Asturias indicates, it is a "wealth of men, wealth of women, to have many children." He clearly portrays the moral poverty of the maizegrowers and exploiters of the Indian by depicting their sterility.

The most original thematic feature of *Men of Maize* is that the reader is allowed to participate in the genetic process of myth. Characters encountered in the first sections of the novel (Gaspar Ilóm, Machojón, María Tecún) are referred to, later in the action, as figures from a legendary past (even while some of them, such as María, are still alive). Tales in *Men of Maize* have a way of being repeated until they are believed and filter into the collective unconscious of all characters. The message becomes a medium, a link in the chain of shared traditions which binds men and women together and which we know as culture. By showing his countrymen that culture (and, more important, the ability to forge it) is a collective enterprise, Asturias wished to encourage them to take an active hand in transforming the society which was being recast during the very years he spent writing his novel (1945-1949).

Critical Context

Men of Maize is, without a doubt, Asturias's most controversial novel as well as his best. It has been disparaged and misunderstood by critics ever since its publication. Given its unique narrative structure and the fact that Asturias underplays character and chronological development, many readers have believed it to lack unity. In fact, the conception of *Men of Maize* is so revolutionary (in form as well as in content) that unity must be found in features other than those dictated by convention.

As James Joyce did in *Ulysses* (1922), Asturias turned to an earlier, classical work for the infrastructure for his ground-breaking novel. He borrowed from the past but actualized it in the present and, most important, developed his novel through an association of key themes. For example, all Indian characters in *Men of Maize* are associated with water, and all their enemies with fire. Three sets of three animals each also play a primary role in the novel, and each set is associated with one of the three elements which anchor Asturias's pyramid to Meso-American man: fire, water, and corn. Finally, four numbers—four, seven, nine, and thirteen—enter the alchemy of *Men of Maize*. Each is associated with an animal and a color in keeping with Mayan mythology, and all the elements are portrayed in a progression which culminates, in the epilogue, with the return to the land. At the end of the harvest, Goyo and his family become ants, one of the animals responsible for the discovery of corn, according to the Meso-American mythic tradition. Goyo's animal protector is also the opossum (god of dawn in Meso-America), known in Maya as Zach Och, the white animal (white betokens the beginning of something, specifically, of civilization). The novel starts with a cycle of struggle and retribution and then picks up the thread of a wandering blindman, a beggar, who ends up fully healed, a farmer, and a begetter of many children. Thematically speaking, Asturias shifts the action from chaos to order and concludes with a return which is in every respect a beginning, a hope-filled eulogy to the common man of Meso-America.

Bibliography

Callan, Richard. *Miguel Ángel Asturias*. New York: Twayne, 1970. An introductory study with a chapter of biography and a separate chapter discussing each of Asturias's major novels. Includes a chronology, notes, and an annotated bibliography.

Gonzalez Echevarria, Roberto. *Myth and Archive: A Theory of Latin American Narrative*. Cambridge, England: Cambridge University Press, 1990. A very helpful volume in coming to terms with Asturias's unusual narratives.

Harss, Luis, and Barbara Dohmann. *Into the Mainstream*. New York: Harpers, 1967. Includes an interview with Asturias covering the major features of his thought and fictional work.

Himmelblau, Jack. "Love, Self and Cosmos in the Early Works of Miguel Ángel

Asturias." *Kentucky Romance Quarterly* 18 (1971). Should be read in conjunction with Prieto.

Perez, Galo Rene. "Miguel Ángel Asturias." *Americas*, January, 1968, 1-5. A searching examination of *El Señor Presidente* as a commentary on the novelist's society.

Prieto, Rene. *Miguel Ángel Asturias's Archaeology of Return*. Cambridge, England: Cambridge University Press, 1993. The best available study in English of the novelist's body of work. Prieto discusses both the stories and the novels, taking up issues of their unifying principles, idiom, and eroticism. See Prieto's measured introduction, in which he carefully analyzes Asturias's reputation and identifies his most important work. Includes very detailed notes and bibliography.

West, Anthony. Review of *El Señor Presidente*, by Miguel Ángel Asturias. *The New Yorker*, March 28, 1964. Often cited as one of the best interpretations of the novel.

René Prieto

MERCY OF A RUDE STREAM

Author: Henry Roth (1906-1995)
Type of plot: Autobiographical
Time of plot: The 1920's to the 1990's
Locale: New York City and New Mexico
First published: A Star Shines over Mt. Morris Park, 1994; *A Diving Rock on the Hudson*, 1995; *From Bondage*, 1996; *Requiem for Harlem*, 1998

Principal characters:
IRA STIGMAN, the protagonist and narrator
M., his deceased wife, a musician and composer
CHAIM STIGMAN, his disapproving father
LEAH STIGMAN, his adoring mother
MINNIE STIGMAN, his sister, two years his junior
EDITH WELLES, a poet and teacher
LARRY GORDON, Ira's best friend in college
ECCLESIAS, Ira's word processor, companion, secretary, and
collaborator in old age

The Novel

Mercy of a Rude Stream is narrated by a fictitious character in his late eighties living alone in New Mexico. Stigman closely resembles the real author, who died in Albuquerque at eighty-nine. The octogenarian Stigman is writing about growing up in New York City. Young Ira's life parallels what is known about Roth's own early life. *Mercy of a Rude Stream*, a work of pure realism, is thinly disguised autobiography.

The narrator frequently interrupts his story to complain about his present life (which mirrors that of Roth himself). At other times, Stigman holds imaginary conversations with his word processor, which he nicknames "Ecclesias." Roth incorporates these interchanges to illustrate his loneliness, unhappiness, physical pains, mental confusion, sense of hopelessness, compulsion to confess his sins, and fears that he will be unable to muster the fortitude to finish his monumental writing project, a combination of fiction and bitter truth.

A Star Shines over Mt. Morris Park follows young Ira through the years of World War I to the beginnings of the 1920's. By age fourteen, Ira has become self-reliant and street-smart as a result of his exposure to the tough, crowded Lower East Side. Meanwhile, the octogenarian Ira is carrying on a struggle with illness, writer's block, and guilty conscience, continually intruding to complain and deliberately breaking the illusion he is trying to create.

A Diving Rock on the Hudson follows adolescent Ira from 1921 through 1925. He daydreams his way through high school (which his father considers a frivolous luxury), works part-time as a bus conductor and "soda hustler" at the Polo Grounds and Yankee Stadium, and discovers the pleasures of literature. With many misgivings, the narrator introduces the topic of incest. Ira began having sexual relations with his sister Minnie when he was sixteen and she was fourteen. Both live in fear of being caught by their parents. Ira considers drowning himself in the Hudson River. The aged Ira has been haunted by this fear all of his life; it has probably been the cause of the writer's block that has kept him tongue-tied. At the end of the volume, the self-loathing young Ira discovers he has a talent for writing and decides to make literature his career.

From Bondage describes the love triangle that develops between Ira, his best friend Larry Gordon, and the older, more sophisticated Edith Welles. Larry is Edith's lover, but they drag Ira into their world of hedonistic, agnostic intellectuals. Young Ira is still tormented with guilt because he is continuing an incestuous affair with his sister and is now sexually involved with his nubile cousin Stella.

Roth intended to have *Mercy of a Rude Stream* consist of six novels following Ira to end of the 1930's, when he broke up with Edith Welles (the real-life Eda Lou Walton) and began a love affair with M. (Muriel Parker), who would become his wife. After Roth's death, however, his publisher decided to close the series with *Requiem for Harlem*, which follows the hero through 1927, when he turns his back on Jewish Harlem and enters a long-term love affair with Edith Welles, who will support him financially and emotionally while he works on his first novel. The remaining two volumes, which follow Ira through the 1930's, would be published separately.

Mercy of a Rude Stream is an "ugly duckling" story. Young Ira begins with a severe inferiority complex attributable to many factors, including his immigrant parents' poverty and ignorance, his membership in a disdained ethnic minority, and his father's unremitting verbal abuse. Through schooling, intensive reading, and the therapeutic influence of a few friends, he comes to realize that he is more intelligent and self-reliant than those he once regarded as superior. At the end of *Requiem for Harlem*, the aged narrator is still trying to make sense of his long life, indicating that there never can be and never should be an end to learning and self-discovery.

The Characters

Because *Mercy of a Rude Stream* is thinly disguised autobiography, the characters in the novel are all based on real people, and the events in which they figure are based on real events in Roth's early life. The verisimilitude is enhanced by the fact that the reader knows the characters to be real people under fictitious names.

The only character who is fully rounded and continuously developing throughout the entire novel is young Ira Stigman himself. The other characters are rather sketchily presented, but such presentation is not bad craftsmanship in a novel of this type; the people and events are ostensibly being described by a very old man trying to recapture fragments of a past so distant that it seems almost mythical to the modern reader and even somewhat dreamlike to the aged, absentminded narrator himself. Roth's theme has to do with a boy's struggle to survive and to find himself in the crowded, competitive, often hostile environment of America's biggest city, where the contrast between rich and poor is stark and painful. His characters represent either the narrow ghetto he is trying to escape or the dominant, native-born, English-speaking, middle-class culture full of intellectual stimulation and vocational opportunities into which he aspires to be assimilated.

The author transmits a sense of young Ira's character through detailed descriptions of his innermost thoughts and feelings. The other characters are portrayed mainly through dialogue. Roth sprinkles the dialogue of his Jewish characters with Yiddish words and phrases, which he defines in a glossary at the end of each volume. The Yiddish enhances the realism while at the same time demonstrating the speakers' handicaps as non-English-speaking immigrants in a strange, frightening new environment to which they will never fully belong.

The most striking technique used in the work is the dual point of view of Ira Stigman. He is both an octogenarian ready and even willing to die and a boy just starting out in life, dazzled by the drama and spectacle of a mighty city still, like himself, in the process of growth. The contrast between the two aspects of the same character makes the old Ira seem sadder, older, wiser, and more disenchanted while making the young Ira seem ignorant, confused, and naïve but still possessed of the strength, ambition, and potential of youth.

Young Ira's embittered, abusive father gives the boy a strong motivation to escape from his home and achieve independence. At the same time, his mother's affection and admiration give him the encouragement he needs to strive to improve his condition. He realizes early that his only hope of escaping from the suffocating atmosphere of the ghetto is through education. People he meets in school, particularly in college, have a major effect on his development. They see his intelligence, creativity, and originality better than he can see these qualities in himself. He learns by imitating them; more important, he learns to appreciate himself through their acceptance, admiration, and affection.

Themes and Meanings

The nickname of Stigman's word processor suggests his novel's theme and meaning. Ecclesiastes, the most somber book in the Old Testament, is best remembered for the passage, "Vanity of vanities . . . all is vanity." While proclaiming that life is meaningless, Ecclesiastes also contains memorable poetry such as "Remember now thy Creator in the days of thy youth, while the evil days come not, nor the years draw nigh, when thou shalt say, I have no pleasure in them. While the sun, or the light, or the moon, or the stars, be not darkened, nor the clouds return after the rain." Roth is implying that life is meaningless, that everyone is doomed to lose everything, including everyone they have ever loved. Old age is a curse; one ends up lonely, infirm, unable to enjoy any of life's simple pleasures, haunted by regrets, facing the terror of death. Nevertheless, life is full of drama and beauty that deserve to be appreciated and, if possible, commemorated. Life is a mixture of pleasure and pain, loss and gain, triumph and failure, hope and fear, confidence and perplexity.

As a lifelong agnostic, Roth is trying to get at the unadorned truth about his own life and life in general. As a dying old man, with nothing but his memories, he has no way to get through his waking hours except by writing about the past. There is beauty in truth, but getting at the real truth is the hardest thing a writer can attempt. It requires resisting the temptation to leave out unpleasant matters and to adorn one's work with false sentiments.

The title *Mercy of a Rude Stream* is borrowed from the disillusioned Cardinal Wolsey's famous speech in Shakespeare's *Henry VIII* (1612-1613) expressing hatred of the "vain pomp and glory of this world" and complaining of being left, "Weary and old with service, to the/ Mercy of a rude stream, that must forever hide me."

Critical Context

Roth had one of the strangest careers of any well-known writer. His 1934 autobiographical novel *Call It Sleep* came to be recognized as an American classic, but he then suffered from writer's block for nearly six decades. In old age, he began *Mercy of a Rude Stream*, but he did not want it published until after his death, as he believed that it contained too many sensitive revelations. After his wife died, Roth decided to publish one volume per year, as he thought that he had by then outlived everyone who mattered.

The novel can be read as autobiography, psychology, sociology, philosophy, or American history and as an example of both modernism and realism. Realistic fiction deals with ordinary events in the lives of ordinary people, but realism is no more "real" than romanticism; realism is an illusion produced by avoiding the sensational while emphasizing the mundane matters that make up most lives. Realism, however, can be dull and episodic. The highly literate Roth was influenced by such works as James T. Farrell's *Studs Lonigan* trilogy (1932-1935), Theodore Dreiser's *An American Tragedy* (1925), and Wallace Stegner's *Angle of Repose* (1971). The most conspicuous influence is Marcel Proust's masterpiece *À la recherche du temps perdu* (1913-1927; *Remembrance of Things Past*, 1922-1931), another multivolume autobiographical novel in which an elderly narrator struggles to recapture the past.

Most significant is the modernistic way Roth adds drama by bringing himself into the foreground as narrator. The drama revolves around whether he can continue writing about painful subjects while suffering physical pain and whether he can finish his masterpiece before he dies. He highlights this dramatic conflict by having his fictitious narrator converse with Ecclesias. Roth only barely managed to finish before he died, but he writes with a lifetime of accumulated wisdom, truly heroic candor, and the "high seriousness" Matthew Arnold, the influential nineteenth century English critic, identified as the distinguishing characteristic of all great writers.

Bibliography

Halkin, Hillel. "Henry Roth's Secret." *Commentary* 97 (May, 1994): 44-47. Attempts to deduce reasons for Roth's sixty-year silence.

Lyons, Bonnie. *Henry Roth: The Man and His Work.* New York: Cooper Square Publishers, 1977. The first book-length study includes a revealing interview with Roth. Lyons incorporates discussion of Judaism, Jewish mysticism, symbolism, and psychoanalysis.

Roth, Henry. *Call It Sleep*. New York: Avon Books, 1934. Roth's autobiographical
    first novel, which after long neglect came to be recognized as an American classic.
    Numerous critics of *Mercy of a Rude Stream* compared it, favorably and unfavor-
    ably, with *Call It Sleep*.
_____. *Shifting Landscape: A Composite, 1925-1987*. Edited with introduc-
    tion by Mario Materassi. New York: Jewish Publication Society, 1987. Roth's mis-
    cellaneous writings published between 1925 and 1987: public statements, mem-
    oirs, articles, a poem, a speech, short stories, and a chapter from an unfinished
    novel.
Weil, Robert. "Editor's Afterword." In *Henry Roth: Requiem for Harlem*. New York:
    St. Martin's Press, 1998. A portrait of Roth in old age. Recounts the history of
    Mercy of a Rude Stream from inception to completion; by Roth's friend and editor.
    Essential reading.
Wirth-Nesher, Hana. "The Modern Jewish Novel and the City: Kafka, Roth, and Oz."
    Modern Fiction Studies 24 (Spring, 1978): 91-111. Examines how literary styles of
    three Jewish novelists were influenced by social interaction and competition for
    living space. Describes the variety, anonymity, density, and degradation of Roth's
    world on the East Side of Manhattan.
_____, ed. *New Essays on "Call It Sleep."* New York: Cambridge University
    Press, 1996. Scholarly studies of Roth's life and times pertinent to understanding
    and appreciating *Mercy of a Rude Stream*.

Bill Delaney

MERIDIAN

Author: Alice Walker (1944-   )
Type of plot: Social morality
Time of plot: The decade of the 1960's, during the height of the Civil Rights movement
Locale: New York City, Georgia, Mississippi, and Alabama
First published: 1976

> *Principal characters:*
> MERIDIAN HILL, the protagonist, a young civil rights worker searching for her role in life
> TRUMAN HELD, an artist and civil rights activist with whom Meridian falls in love
> LYNNE RABINOWITZ, a white civil rights worker whom Truman marries

The Novel

Meridian traces the moral and psychological development of Walker's title character, Meridian Hill. Born into a middle-class Southern black family, Meridian is taught to accept the racist and sexist status quo of the 1950's. She is not encouraged to question segregationist policies, sexist traditions, or her own sexual ignorance—all of which deny her autonomy. Recalling the climate before and during the Civil Rights movement, *Meridian* brings readers to an awareness of the many relationships between racism and sexism and their consequences for the individual and the community.

The novel begins in the present of the 1970's, as Truman Held, artist and former civil rights worker, finds himself searching for Meridian in Chicokema, Georgia. She is not difficult to trace, because she is leading a group of children denied entry to a freak show featuring Marilene O'Shay, "One of the Twelve Human Wonders of the World: Dead for Twenty-Five Years, Preserved in Life-Like Condition." Marilene is further characterized as an "Obedient Daughter, Devoted Wife, and Adoring Mother" predictably "Gone Wrong." As Truman watches Meridian defy tradition and authority literally to stare down a tank, he marvels at her strength, strength that he has finally come to admire. Walker follows this scene with a flashback when, ten years earlier, Meridian is invited to join a revolutionary group and fails to meet its requirements by being unable to swear that she will kill for the revolution. The novel, weaving backward and forward in time, traces Meridian's awakening and guides its readers to an understanding of her complex integrity.

Although there is much in her life to encourage conformity, Meridian shows early flashes of individuality and integrity—most notably when, at thirteen, she refuses to be saved by a religion which literally makes no sense to her and later, as an honor student, when she is asked to deliver a speech celebrating "the superiority of the American Way of Life." By the time she is seventeen, Meridian, unlike the mummified Marilene, has failed her traditional roles. She is a disobedient daughter, failing to accept the traditions which her unreflective mother holds sacred; an indifferent wife, relieved when her husband finds distractions; and a resentful mother, tempted to murder her son. She is literally blasted into political awareness when she watches a newscast about the bombing of a nearby house used by civil rights workers. With only the dimmest sense of direction, Meridian volunteers to work on voter registration. Her education begins in earnest as she joins young people from diverse backgrounds in a fight for racial equality. It continues when she is offered a scholarship to Saxon College in Atlanta. First, however, Meridian is faced with the difficult moral choice of giving up her young son. Although she believes her choice to be best for him, she nevertheless believes that she has failed as a woman, and her mother's self-righteous reaction intensifies this guilt. Saxon, a black women's college ironically representative of white, paternalistic traditions, upholds a genteel tradition of "ladyhood" that Meridian finds ludicrous, but she relishes her opportunities for learning. During this period, her sense of conflict between tradition and change intensifies, for as her understanding grows, she is able to see through stale forms and illogical assumptions. She becomes better able to withstand the many forces urging her to conform, particularly the orphic charm of Truman Held, with whom she has fallen in love. Although Meridian finds his intelligence and refined appearance attractive, she rejects his snobbery, racism, and sexism. Wasted by a mysterious illness symbolic of her internal moral conflict, Meridian decides to heal herself by returning to the South.

For ten years, Meridian lives and works among the poor people of the South. During this time she struggles with her conscience, pricked by accusatory letters from her mother and best friend, Anne-Marion. Living close to the people, learning to anticipate their real needs and to admire their strength, helps Meridian grasp an understanding of herself. Finally, she rejects the roles of martyrdom and self-sacrifice and discovers the value of her own life. At last, Meridian understands her role: "to walk behind the real revolutionaries . . . and sing from memory songs they will need once more to hear. For it is the song of the people, transformed by the experiences of each generation, that holds them together." Her spiritual healing complete, Meridian is able to go forward, leaving behind Truman to deal with his own possibilities.

The Characters

Meridian is one of the most fully drawn and emotionally complex characters of contemporary American fiction. Autobiographical to a certain degree (Meridian and Walker share approximate ages, a deep love for the South, education at a women's college in Atlanta, and civil rights involvement), this novel is artfully crafted. To direct her readers' interpretation of "meridian," Walker lists definitions at the novel's beginning. All pertain specifically to qualities inherent in the title character: "prime," "southern," "the highest point." Yet Walker wants her readers to see her character as representative of the 1960's, which she sees as the meridian of black awareness, when black Americans were able to see themselves clearly and to struggle for their identity.

Another of "meridian's" meanings is "distinctive character"; it is Meridian's battle for her individuality that is the novel's focus.

Perhaps most distinctive is her spirituality. Meridian is something of a mystic, retreating from time to time into trancelike states from which she emerges stronger than ever. Her rejection of materialism is another sign of her spirituality. Whenever Truman visits Meridian, he discovers that she has fewer and fewer possessions, until she is left with only the clothes on her back. Like many mystics, Meridian leads an ascetic life, denying the needs of her own body. All of these indicate her separation from the ordinary restraints of life. Supporting her spirituality is her affinity to the past, her literal kinship with Feather Mae, her great-grandmother, and her figurative one with Louvinie, a Saxon slave. Following Feather Mae's example, Meridian invites ecstasy, and discovers "that it was a way the living sought to expand the consciousness of being alive. . . ." She gains a larger understanding of her world, one not bound by trifling concerns. Louvinie's example is equally important, for from her story Meridian learns about the need for expressing oneself, the value of a tenacious spirit, and the power of creativity. Because Louvinie's clipped tongue nourishes the roots of the Sojourner Tree on the Saxon campus, Meridian is related to the tree as well.

Other qualities in keeping with her spirituality are Meridian's introspection, her ferocious will, and her inability to give her word without full moral commitment. Since her decisions are often painful, and since they conflict with accepted moral traditions, readers should pay special attention to the relentlessness of her introspection. In the tradition of spiritual leaders, she suffers for her choices, but she finds this a necessary stage of growth.

Other characters are presented with sympathy and understanding—from Meridian's prim and limited mother and her dreamy father to various poor people Meridian encounters on her travels. Major sections of the novel, however, are devoted to two other characters: Lynne Rabinowitz and Truman Held.

Few black novelists have treated white characters with the keen intelligence of Walker. Lynne is no simple stereotype; she is a naively idealistic reformer caught in the spirit of the times, a defiant and courageous woman who risks all of her personal ties, a guilt-ridden and terrified victim of the people whom she has tried to help, a confused and resentful woman who gradually awakens to her own mistakes. In several ways Lynne represents what Meridian might have been had she married Truman. Lynne's experiences, fortunately, do not destroy her. At the end of the novel, she shows signs of recovered strength and a newly detected sense of her ability to endure alone. Walker's understanding of Lynne's motives for her involvement in the Civil Rights movement, her ability to characterize Lynne's ambivalent moral and social position, her sensitive dramatization of Lynne's losses, and her refusal to simplify Lynne are notable.

Equally complex is her characterization of Truman, whom Walker draws with a knowledge of his masculine attractions as well as his deficiencies. Truman's main function in the novel is to serve as a bypass—potential and actual—of self-discovery. Had Meridian accepted the role he offered (mother of his children), she might have become like Lynne, isolated from herself, confusing his evaluation of her for her own. Unlike his name, Truman is not yet a true man in Walker's estimation; he must first recognize his flaws and accept responsibility for his actions. Walker, however, does not intend his name to be entirely ironic, for as Truman grows older, he begins to see his limitations. Following Meridian, he begins to learn from her example. Because of her, he acknowledges a responsibility to Lynne; he sees the importance of empathy, both personally and politically; and he learns that true love is liberating, not possessive. Meridian leaves him behind, but she gives him her cap, symbolizing his assumption of her former role in fear and hope of self-discovery.

Themes and Meanings

Walker's treatment of the self-discovery theme is perhaps one of the most complete in contemporary literature. While many authors focus on liberating the self from recognizably tangible obstacles, Walker has her protagonist confront two little-understood and painfully acknowledged social conditions—racism and sexism—and she deals with the themes in a sophisticated manner, linking them in such a way as to reveal important crosscurrents. Walker also explores the problem of guilt created and sustained by mothers as a means of controlling and protecting daughters, and she exposes early motherhood as a barrier to self-discovery. That she deals with these issues without seeming didactic in any way is a mark of her artistry. *Meridian* is remarkable in another significant way: Walker's vision transcends both racial and sexual barriers as she forces her characters to go beyond the boundaries of the black community to see themselves in relation to the white community as well. In this manner, she has her female protagonists travel in the fullest sense—by exploring their personal and racial past in order to create a future without racial barriers.

Critical Context

When first published, *Meridian* was largely ignored, partly because its author was a young writer with a limited public. (Walker's very fine first novel, *The Third Life of Grange Copeland*, 1970, attracted almost no recognition when it was published.) The critical realization that *Meridian* was an exceptional novel grew slowly during the 1970's, as Walker began to establish herself not only as a novelist but also as a poet, short story writer, essayist, and feminist. By the mid-1980's, Walker had achieved recognition as one of the foremost contemporary American writers, largely on the strength of her widely acclaimed novel *The Color Purple* (1982), which was awarded both the Pulitzer Prize and the American Book Award for fiction.

Many critics regard *Meridian* as Walker's fullest, most beautifully crafted novel. Its unusual structure reflects the novel's revolutionary theme and spirit. Throughout her career, Walker has committed herself to exploring obstacles to human freedom, particularly as they apply to women. Because *Meridian* touches upon this theme of timeless relevance with consummate art, it continues to attract increasing numbers of readers as well as informed scholarly consideration.

Bibliography

Appiah, K. A. and Henry Louis Gates, eds. *Alice Walker: Critical Perspectives Past and Present*. New York: Amistad, 1993. This volume features critical essays and reviews of Walker's fiction, as well as interviews. Several articles on *Meridian* are included.

Barker, Deborah E. "Visual Markers: Art and Mass Media in Alice Walker's *Meridian*." *African American Review* 31 (Fall, 1997): 463-479. Barker argues that Walker's goal in her novel is to prove that African Americans in general, and black women in particular, play a fundamental role in shaping American culture in spite of the media's portrayal of them as nonentities. Barker agrees with Walker's insights and also recognizes that public reactions to the media's presentation of an oppressed people have an impact on subsequent images portrayed by the media.

Bloom, Harold, ed. *Alice Walker*. New York: Chelsea House, 1989. A collection of essays that covers the spectrum of Walker's work. Includes an essay on *Meridian*.

Downey, Anne M. "'A Broken and Bloody Hoop': The Intertextuality of *Black Elk Speaks* and Alice Walker's *Meridian*." *MELUS* 19 (Fall, 1994): 37-45. Downey argues that both books share common experiences of spirituality, including valuing the art of the seer, the sharing of imagery of the sacred tree, recognizing the symbolic import of the hoop of a nation, and dealing with the cultural problems of a destroyed people.

Smith, Felipe. "Alice Walker's Redemptive Art." *African American Review* 26 (Fall, 1992): 437-451. Smith addresses both secular and spiritual redemption in Walker's work. Focusing on the Christological model, Smith discusses the character of Grange Copeland, Grange's killing of his son, and his own death at the hands of the police.

Winchell, Donna H. *Alice Walker*. New York: Twayne, 1992. An excellent introductory treatment of Alice Walker's writing career. Presents a detailed discussion of Walker's life, poetry, nonfiction, and novels, including an essay devoted to *Meridian*. Also includes a selected bibliography and helpful index.

Karen Carmean

MICKELSSON'S GHOSTS

Author: John Gardner (1933-1982)
Type of plot: Psychological realism
Time of plot: The fall of 1980
Locale: Binghamton, New York, and Susquehanna, Pennsylvania
First published: 1982

>   *Principal characters:*
>   PETER J. MICKELSSON, the protagonist, a professor of philosophy and a
>   writer
>   JESSICA STARK, a professor of sociology and Mickelsson's lover
>   MICHAEL NUGENT, a student
>   DONNIE MATTHEWS, a teenage prostitute

The Novel

In *Mickelsson's Ghosts*, John Gardner sustains a 590-page dramatization of the daily life, increasing despair, and desperate desires of middle-aged Peter Mickelsson, a once-famous philosopher now sinking into obscurity at the State University of New York at Binghamton. Faced with his failures on several fronts—marital, financial, and professional—the previous master of academic truth must now engage less bookish but far more difficult problems. For setting, Gardner supplies the troubled Mickelsson with the doomed air of 1980, a climate of debate over the big issues—abortion, nuclear waste and arms, Ronald Reagan versus Jimmy Carter—which increases the stress already heavily bearing on Mickelsson by his private crises.

The novel opens with Mickelsson living in a squalid apartment in Binghamton, near the university where he teaches ethics, a now out-of-date discipline among contemporary philosophers. Divorced and lonely, plagued by bills, unpaid taxes, and alimony payments, he ignores apparent necessity, and with a fraudulent loan application he secures a house in the nearby Pennsylvania countryside. There he settles, determined to write the blockbuster book which will redeem his career and bail him out financially. As rumored by his Susquehanna real estate agent, the house proves to be haunted. The ghosts appear and disappear regularly, an old couple, brother and sister, who strike mournful postures and wander from room to room. Mickelsson grows accustomed to the strangeness of his new home as well as the strange goings on in the nearby hills—mass Mormon baptisms and discoveries of circular pulverized patches reputed to be UFO landing sites.

The novel's action is divided between what Mickelsson does in Binghamton—teach Plato, talking to students and colleagues whenever he is unable to avoid them—and what he does at the house and in Susquehanna, the small town where he meets and becomes obsessed with Donnie Matthews, a teenage prostitute. Donnie's bestial allure contrasts with his growing affection for Jessica Stark, a beautiful Jewess who teaches sociology at the university. Discussions of abortion in Mickelsson's medical ethics class are existentially troubling when Donnie becomes pregnant and demands money for an abortion. The ethics professor descends to new depths, breaking into the apartment of a fat man who has a cache of stolen money that Mickelsson discovers while crawling up the fire escape to spy on Donnie. The break-in frightens the fat man to death—by heart attack. Mickelsson gives the money to Donnie, who leaves Susquehanna permanently.

Paralleling Mickelsson's personal trauma and leading to the novel's climax are the mysterious deaths of a couple living in the hills, previous owners of Mickelsson's home. Another philosopher, Edward Lawler, is a member of a bizarre Mormon sect searching for documents that purportedly prove the Mormon scriptures fallacious. He murders two students, then the neighbor couple, and arrives at Mickelsson's, demanding at gunpoint the tearing out of all the house's interior walls. Hours later, the weary Mickelsson is reduced to praying to a God he has never believed in, and he is saved by a passerby's previously mute daughter, who hears Mickelsson's psychic entreaties and tells her father to knock on the door. At novel's end, Mickelsson, bereft of hubris, pledges his love for Jessica Stark in a bedroom full of ghosts, "pitiful, empty-headed nothings complaining to be born."

The Characters

Peter Mickelsson, equipped with all the machinery of modern intellectual consciousness and a native brilliance, is plunged into a world containing facts, indisputable facts, which that consciousness cannot believe yet cannot deny. Mickelsson, however, is much more than a locus of conflict between the rational and the supernatural. His exposure to the ghosts is an introduction to the world of human suffering, which includes his present life among the present ghosts whose long-dead pain and anger persist in redundant cameo oblivious to everything else their lives might have contained. Mickelsson daily savors his own broken connections. His former wife lives in twenty-year-old photographs. His absent son in the grainy newspaper photo is rigid with resignation, a protester against the nuclear silo and the American "Reich." Mickelsson's most intimate colloquies are with dead philosophers—Friedrich Nietzsche, Ludwig Wittgenstein. Through the ghost of his grandfather, he contemplates and is haunted by the ghostly, life-despising Martin Luther. With his obsessions in tow, Mickelsson becomes a seer. Like his father before him, his prescience is mostly of painful things. The voice speaking from the past and the future testifies to pain. Mickelsson is most himself when beside himself.

The ghost haunting Mickelsson most persistently is himself. The "bad" Mickelsson never stops appalling the rational ethical persona. Which is real? he wonders. He suspects that his goodness may have been only the superficial manner of more respectable days in the Ivy League. In Binghamton, demoted, he wanders the streets at dark with his clublike walking stick. He kills a dog with the stick and does not notify the owner or the police. Through Mickelsson, Gardner develops a split man, similar in some ways to Raskolnikov in Fyodor Dostoevski's *Crime and Punishment*.

The two female counterparts of Mickelsson exemplify this split. The prostitute Donnie Matthews appeals to the irrational side. She is simply flesh, "blue-white" flesh available for immediate use and presenting no formal female self to overcome with charm or conversation before the treasure is surrendered. Her only virtue is her preference for indigent lovers, though this fact makes Mickelsson's postsex meditations all the more repellent. Jessica Stark appeals to the civilized Mickelsson. Though amply endowed with her own physical perfections, she also has a formidable mind, and though Mickelsson and Jessica become lovers, their union is prefaced by long nights of nonphysical intercourse—discussions of philosophical ideas and each other's emotional pain (Jessica is a widow who has lost two daughters in a boating accident).

Michael Nugent is a character in need whom Mickelsson essentially spurns. Nugent attends the Plato-Aristotle course that is being taught by the professor he admires. Nugent is disturbed by the recent death of his father and the mysterious death of his favorite science teacher. His bright mind and his smattering of nihilistic ideas based on the experience of death and his reading of Franz Kafka, Søren Kierkegaard, and Jean-Paul Sartre make Nugent a son figure for Mickelsson's potential love. Nugent, however, does all the reaching out, while Mickelsson evades, repelled somewhat by Nugent's homosexuality. The boy becomes one more occasion for guilt when he dies, apparently a suicide.

Some relief from the dirge of unhappiness is provided by the more minor characters. The lawyer Finney is a man of stupendous profanity and full of sarcastic comment on the doings of Mickelsson, his wayward client. Gardner captures the Irish irreverence in each conversation. When Finney learns of Mickelsson's intention to buy a house, his answer is: "That's good, Pete! Cute! Give the feds something solid to aim their pissers at." Another bit player in the novel, Dr. Rifkin, occasionally appears or is conjured up by Mickelsson as the all-knowing but unhelpful psychiatrist. His knowledge does nothing to alter the course Mickelsson takes, and he exists in the novel mainly for the sake of parody.

Themes and Meanings

In *On Moral Fiction* (1978), Gardner maintains that the high purpose of fiction is to assert order, however temporary, in the midst of chaos and darkness which is reality. A good novel should help its reader, encourage him to go on living, even though he knows that consciousness and life will lose out in the end. *Mickelsson's Ghosts* suggests that Gardner wants it both ways, or is not as confident about being right in regard to what is real. There is arrogance in the claim that the artist asserts order in a senseless void, and loneliness as well. Gardner surrounds Mickelsson with ghosts, supernatural presences and events, or rich suggestions of a created order incomprehensible to the mind but richly beckoning. One part of Gardner says that even the supernatural is invented by me, the novelist; another part says, "Please do not let this be so." At a key point in the novel, he reduces Mickelsson to a helpless fear of death out of which he cries for help. The cry, much to Mickelsson's shame and contradicting all of his conviction about "truth" (there's nothing out there—only facts), is a cry to a person out there who has ears, and it is shameful because Mickelsson knows that it is a cry to

God, "pouring out the thought as if it were his life." When the cry works, when the prayer is answered, the relieved and rescued Mickelsson can excuse himself and drop again into a tolerant skepticism.

Gardner wants the reader to enjoy the emotion coming from meaning and miraculous grace without crediting it. It is only a ghost, dear reader, one more human longing crying out in darkness. Yet Mickelsson is saved, saved from Lawler, the mad Mormon (law), and saved from death. He can now make love to Jessie, possibly give her a child, and can love his own son, returned at the novel's conclusion from his protest pilgrimage. The reader is left to ponder what Gardner's attitude is toward the happy ending he gives the book. Is it merely something to make the reader feel better about life, or does it mean or foretell something for which everyone longs because it is in the nature of their hearts to so long? Dreams, says Gardner, the artificer, as he himself continues to dream.

Critical Context

Mickelsson's Ghosts was Gardner's last novel before his untimely death in a motorcycle accident, not far from the university where both he and his protagonist were professors. Most early reviewers disapproved of the novel. Gardner had gained few friends by his forthright criticisms of fellow writers in *On Moral Fiction*, and the novel preceding *Mickelsson's Ghosts*, *Freddy's Book* (1980), was not well received, partly a result of backlash against Gardner's low view of typical academics. As longer, more considered assessments of *Mickelsson's Ghosts* began to appear, however, it became clear that the novel was a substantial achievement, and indeed it may prove to be one of Gardner's most enduring works.

It is clear that Gardner increasingly regarded himself as a maverick. He makes Mickelsson an ethics teacher at a time when condescending tolerance is all that he can expect from his colleagues. Yet anyone familiar with Gardner's fiction, from *Grendel* (1971) to this last work, knows how isolated his characters usually are, and it would be facile to conclude that Mickelsson is simply Gardner self-dramatized. The novel faces problems that gripped the novelist in all of his work, problems about the tragic structure of the world and human life. Also, as in his other fiction, Gardner asserts wonder in *Mickelsson's Ghosts*, establishing mystery as the air his character breathes, whether sitting among real ghosts or chatting with the old farmer who lives up the hill.

Gardner was never quite at home with the novel. The man generating Mickelsson's world is like the artificer of fairy tales who sees and names the world anew after Adam's fall from intimacy of communication. The fairy-tale mind calls a mountain "ogre," a woman "witch," and a man "monster." Gardner revitalizes ordinary things in that way, hungry for the evidences of fantasy in ordinary things. Characters who are ostensibly real estate agents, sheriffs, and college professors take on a murky and unstable identity, prone as they are to superstition and dread, and not altogether unconnected with centuries-old ancestors who lived in unlighted huts in forests and believed in all sorts of pantheistic forces. Gardner, alive to the poison that comes from perceiving the world as a flat spot waiting for a developer, wanted in *Mickelsson's Ghosts* to exorcise commonness with the eye of an old-fashioned boy full of fear as an old-fashioned principal approaches along the corridor—not wholly guiltless, yet all too aware of a malicious presence it is necessary to resist.

Gardner succeeded in writing a book which will tell readers in the next century more about our time than most books from the period. Reading it, if such an act is not then dispensed with, they will escape into the primal emotions and enjoy the rich particularity of the world as filtered through the perceptions of "crazy" Professor Mickelsson.

Bibliography

Butts, Leonard. *The Novels of John Gardner: Making Life Art as a Moral Process.* Baton Rouge: Louisiana State University Press, 1988. Butts draws his argument from Gardner himself, specifically *On Moral Fiction* (that art is a moral process) and discusses the ten novels in pairs, focusing on the main characters as either artists or artist figures who to varying degrees succeed or fail in transforming themselves into Gardner's "true artist." As Butts defines it, moral fiction is not didactic but instead a matter of aesthetic wholeness.

Chavkin, Allan, ed. *Conversations with John Gardner.* Jackson: University Press of Mississippi, 1990. Reprints nineteen of the most important interviews (the majority from the crucial *On Moral Fiction* period) and adds one never before published interview. Chavkin's introduction, which focuses on Gardner as he appears in these and his other numerous interviews, is especially noteworthy. The chronology updates the one in Howell (below).

Cowart, David. *Arches and Light: The Fiction of John Gardner.* Carbondale: Southern Illinois University Press, 1983. Discusses the published novels through *Mickelsson's Ghosts*, the two story collections, and the tales for children. As good as Cowart's intelligent and certainly readable chapters are, they suffer (as does so much Gardner criticism) insofar as they are concerned with validating Gardner's position on moral fiction as a valid alternative to existential despair.

Henderson, Jeff. *John Gardner: A Study of the Short Fiction.* Boston: Twayne, 1990. Part 1 concentrates on Gardner's short fiction, including his stories for children; part 2 contains excerpts from essays and letters in which Gardner defines his role as a writer; part 3 provides excerpts from important Gardner critics. Includes chronology and bibliography.

_____, ed. *Thor's Hammer: Essays on John Gardner.* Conway: University of Central Arkansas Press, 1985. Presents fifteen original essays of varying quality, including three on *Grendel*. The most important are John M. Howell's biographical essay, Robert A. Morace's on Gardner and his reviewers, Gregory Morris's discussion of Gardner and "plagiarism," Samuel Coale's on dreams, Leonard Butts's on *Mickelsson's Ghosts*, and Charles Johnson's "A Phenomenology of *On Moral Fiction*."

Howell, John M. *John Gardner: A Bibliographical Profile.* Carbondale: Southern Illinois University Press, 1980. Howell's detailed chronology and enumerative listing of works by Gardner (down to separate editions, printings, issues, and translations), as well as the afterword written by Gardner, make this an indispensable work for any Gardner student.

McWilliams, Dean. *John Gardner*. Boston: Twayne, 1990. McWilliams includes little biographical material, does not try to be at all comprehensive, yet has an interesting and certainly original thesis: that Gardner's fiction may be more fruitfully approached via Mikhail Bakhtin's theory of dialogism than via *On Moral Fiction*. Unfortunately, the chapters (on the novels and *Jason and Medeia*) tend to be rather introductory in approach and only rarely dialogical in focus.

Morace, Robert A. *John Gardner: An Annotated Secondary Bibliography*. New York: Garland, 1984. An especially thorough annotated listing of all known items (reviews, articles, significant mentions) about Gardner through 1983. The annotations of speeches and interviews are especially full (a particularly useful fact given the number of interviews and speeches the loquacious as well as prolific Gardner gave). A concluding section updates Howell's *John Gardner: A Bibliographical Profile*.

Morace, Robert A., and Kathryn VanSpanckeren, eds. *John Gardner: Critical Perspectives*. Carbondale: Southern Illinois University Press, 1982. This first critical book on Gardner's work covers the full range of his literary endeavors, from his dissertation-novel "The Old Men" through his then most recent fictions, "Vlemk, The Box Painter" and *Freddy's Book*, with separate essays on his "epic poem" *Jason and Medeia; The King's Indian: Stories and Tales*; his children's stories; libretti; pastoral novels; use of sources, parody, and embedding; and theory of moral fiction. The volume concludes with Gardner's afterword.

Morris, Gregory L. *A World of Order and Light: The Fiction of John Gardner*. Athens: University of Georgia Press, 1984. Like Butts and Cowart, Morris works well within the moral fiction framework which Gardner himself established. Unlike Cowart, however, Morris emphasizes moral art as a process by which order is discovered rather than (as Cowart contends) made. More specifically the novels (including Gardner's dissertation novel "The Old Men") and two collections of short fiction are discussed in terms of Gardner's "luminous vision" and "magical landscapes."

Bruce Wiebe

THE MIDDLE OF THE JOURNEY

Author: Lionel Trilling (1905-1975)
Type of plot: Political
Time of plot: The 1930's
Locale: Connecticut
First published: 1947

> *Principal characters:*
> JOHN LASKELL, the novel's narrator and protagonist, an urban affairs
> expert with leftist leanings
> GIFFORD MAXIM, a lapsed Communist around whom the other
> characters gather to debate their political convictions
> ARTHUR CROOM, a liberal economics professor and a friend of Laskell
> and Maxim
> NANCY CROOM, Arthur's wife, who is outraged by Maxim's repudiation
> of the Communist Party
> DUCK CALDWELL, the handyman for the Crooms and the focus of their
> admiration of the working class
> EMILY CALDWELL, Duck's wife, who has a brief affair with Laskell

The Novel

John Laskell is thirty-three and is recovering from a serious illness that almost cost him his life. He is also mourning the recent death of his fiancée. In many ways, he is facing a midlife crisis. At one stage of his sickness, he longs for death, spending his time admiring the perfection of a flower that will soon fade out of existence. The Crooms have invited him to their summer home in the hope of speeding his return to good health.

On the train taking Laskell to visit the Crooms is Gifford Maxim, who has gone through his own time of trial. He has lived underground as a Communist agent and then sought sanctuary with friends, whom he asks to help protect him from the Party in his transition to the role of prominent anti-Communist. The Crooms, particularly Nancy, are shocked by Maxim's turnabout, and it becomes Laskell's task to mediate between the apostate and his friends, who are "fellow travelers" who still believe in the Party.

Maxim pays a disturbing visit to the Crooms with Kermit Simpson, the publisher of a "rather sad liberal monthly," *The New Era*. With Laskell's help, Maxim has managed to get a job writing for Simpson and to have his name put on the masthead of the journal—an important achievement for a man who believes that his safety depends upon the establishment of a public identity. The Crooms dismiss Maxim's fears as paranoia, even though they have no firsthand knowledge of the Party's secret subversive activities. As Lionel Trilling points out in the 1975 introduction to his novel, in the 1930's it was "as if such a thing [espionage] hadn't yet been invented."

What especially disturbs the Crooms about Maxim is that in opposition to the Party he has become a Christian. As a result, he attacks not simply their faith in the Party, but also in all socialist and secularist ideology. Maxim has become a theist who has now put his whole faith in God, not in man. The utopian Crooms, who idealize the working class and believe in a perfectible future, cannot abide their comrade's about-face.

Because they are intellectuals who respond to life with a veneer of abstractions, the Crooms retreat from Maxim's revelations that changing history is a dangerous, even deadly business. Similarly, they reject Laskell's efforts to explain how he almost died, how he nearly accepted the fact of his demise. To them, his thinking—like Maxim's—is reactionary. They must be jolted into reassessing their view of Duck Caldwell, whom they have virtually idolized as an example of the rugged, direct working man, by a melodramatic twist of the plot—Duck's striking and killing his frail child. In this novel of ideas, action without thought is shown to be as disastrous as thought without action.

The Characters

As many critics have noted, and as Lionel Trilling implied in his 1975 introduction to the novel, Gifford Maxim is the dominant character, even though he is neither the narrator nor the ostensible protagonist. Of all the characters, he seems most real when he speaks; he has a sharply critical mind which has been tested in action. He has been both idealist and realist; the Party's ideologue and one of its most effective spies. He is at home with both Marxist and Christian terms and can cogently state the opposing principles of each. Consequently, he carries much more authority than the other, far less experienced characters.

As Lionel Trilling revealed in 1975, Maxim was based on an acquaintance, the famous Whittaker Chambers, who testified against Alger Hiss, an official in the United States State Department who was convicted of espionage in 1950, three years after the appearance of *The Middle of the Journey*. There is no question that Chambers made a vivid impression on Trilling when they were both students at Columbia University and when, years later, Chambers was reported to have gone underground for the Party. Subsequent readings of the novel, including Trilling's own in 1975, invariably concentrate on a compelling character who was followed by his twin in a real-life story of conflicting loyalties, for Chambers asserted that he and Hiss had been close friends and supporters of the Party.

The Crooms bear some resemblance to Alger Hiss and his wife, although Trilling did not know the Hisses and could not have modeled the Crooms after them. Rather, the fictional husband and wife are meant to represent many liberals of the 1930's who were not Party members, but who were "fellow travelers," that is, clearly in the orbit of Communist ideological concerns and reluctant to recognize the brutality of Stalinism.

Nancy Croom, for example, is vehement in her refusal to countenance criticism of the Party. Laskell "had seen in Nancy a passion of the mind and will so pure that, as it swept through her, she could not believe that anything that opposed it required consideration." Her husband Arthur's "dedication was not so absolute," yet Laskell notices that he needs his wife's "absolute intransigence." It excites him even as he moderates and mocks it, for he needs "her extravagance and ardor as support to his own cooler idealism." Nancy saves Arthur from having to make extreme affirmations of his beliefs; he then can seem the more reasonable of the two, although in effect his position parallels hers.

Maxim goads all of these characters, especially Laskell, who is the most vulnerable, about their complacent identification of the Party with progress. Laskell and Croom, urbanologist and economist, seek ways of planning a better world; Maxim taunts them with his awareness that their utopian socialism has turned into a tyranny. Their faith in his underground work, he suggests, has been a way of cultivating their innocence about the inevitable corruption of human-made ideas in the real world. Laskell is honest enough to admit hating Maxim for pointing out how he "had been cherishing his innocence." This is why Emily Caldwell is so appealing to Laskell. She is a woman without an ideology, a woman he can love without a commitment, a woman with whom he can sin—with whom he can even be secure in his guilt, as Maxim also points out to him.

Duck Caldwell is also without an ideology, without a rationalization for the way he lives. Yet in him, lack of faith or principles turns into an aggressive undermining of civilized order. He is a drunkard, an unreliable worker, and a lout who is resentful of the education that his daughter receives. He functions, indeed, as a total negation of all that the Crooms stand for. He is a kind of evil principle which they are not prepared to acknowledge.

Themes and Meanings

Joseph Blotner observes that *The Middle of the Journey* is about varying degrees of engagement and disillusionment with the world. On both the personal and political level, characters assume stances that either impede or facilitate their participation in human affairs. At one extreme, Duck Caldwell lives for himself; his individuality is built upon excluding the rights of others. At the other extreme, Gifford Maxim cannot survive unless he puts his trust in certain friends and in abiding religious principles. He is disillusioned because he has put so much faith in the Party, but he is remarkable for his passion in arguing for his friends' assistance.

In between Caldwell and Maxim, the Crooms waver. On the one hand, they are under the illusion that Maxim has been successfully working for world liberation—for the working class they mistakenly presume Caldwell exemplifies. In a sense, the Crooms have left Maxim and Caldwell—and other types like them—to do the work of the world for them. As a result, they angrily reject Maxim's home truths and shrink from fully confronting Caldwell's violence, since accepting the brutality of either man would shatter their worldview.

Laskell is a man whose view of himself and of the world has already been shattered before Maxim first confides to him his loss of faith. Both men, indeed, go through a kind of rebirth in the novel, a painful rebuilding of their lives on new bases that rest upon a deep awareness of past failures. Laskell knows that he never fully committed himself to his dead fiancée; Maxim realizes that he committed himself all too securely to an ideology. Each man is truly in "the middle of the journey," in a middle age that calls for a reassessment of all that he has been and hopes to become.

Critical Context

Since its reissue in 1975, *The Middle of the Journey* has steadily gathered a significant new audience. In the past ten years, the novel has sold more than fifty thousand copies, a total that far surpasses the very modest sales of the first edition. The recent critical reception has also been more favorable, for in 1947, reviews were mixed, and they disheartened the author, who has been far better known for his literary criticism, particularly *The Liberal Imagination* (1950).

The Middle of the Journey has been criticized for being too much a novel of ideas and too schematic in its presentation of characters. Robert Warshow, who is often quoted as the authority for this kind of critique, praises the eloquence of Trilling's writing but complains that the author argues too much with his characters and presents too much of a case against them. Similarly, Joseph Blotner has called the novel "static" and "prolix," meaning that discussions of ideology dominate characters that never quite come to life, except for Maxim, who has been a man of ideology.

These objections, however, obscure the genuine interest that Trilling shows in his narrator, John Laskell. The theme of death, of how it can enter a life and radically change it, is done well and is convincingly tied to the political discussions. In fact, it is the author's goal to demonstrate that the Crooms' political debates are arid precisely because these well-meaning liberals do not incorporate a holistic understanding of life into the ideology that they espouse. They are narrow-minded, in other words, not simply because their politics are simplistic but also because their understanding of human beings is so limited. They lack, finally, what Trilling calls in his criticism the "liberal imagination," which follows and adapts to the modulation of ideas and personalities as they are conceived in the great novels of this prominent American critic's exemplars: Henry James (1843-1916) and E. M. Forster (1879-1970).

Bibliography

Leitch, Thomas M. *Lionel Trilling: An Annotated Bibliography.* New York: Garland, 1993. A comprehensive guide to primary and secondary sources on Trilling's work. Leitch's critical introduction places Trilling in context of his social and political times.

Shatzky, Joel, and Michael Taub, eds. *Contemporary Jewish-American Novelists: A Bio-Critical Sourcebook.* Westport, Conn.: Greenwood Press, 1997. Includes an entry on Trilling's life, major works and themes, an overview of his critical reception, and a bibliography of primary and secondary sources.

Strout, Cushing. "A Dark Wood in the Middle of the Journey: Willa Cather and Lionel Trilling." *The Sewanee Review* 105 (Summer, 1997): 381-394. Details the hostility between Cather and Trilling. Strout asserts that Cather and Trilling express similar views and that they may have had a more cordial relationship had they truly known each other.

Tanner, Stephen L. *Lionel Trilling*. Boston: Twayne, 1988. Tanner provides a critical and interpretive study of Trilling with a close reading of his major works, a solid bibliography, and complete notes and references.

Trilling, Diana. *The Beginning of the Journey: The Marriage of Diana and Lionel Trilling*. New York: Harcourt Brace, 1993. A memoir by Trilling's wife. She offers a personal glimpse into Trilling's personality, their marriage, and his unhappiness at not having achieved stature as a novelist.

Carl Rollyson

MIDDLE PASSAGE

Author: Charles Johnson (1948-   )
Type of plot: Adventure
Time of plot: 1830
Locale: Aboard the slave ship *Republic* in the Atlantic Ocean
First published: 1990

> *Principal characters:*
> RUTHERFORD CALHOUN, the narrator, a young black man freed from
>   slavery, a stowaway aboard the *Republic*
> EBENEZER FALCON, the captain of the *Republic*, a slave trader and a
>   dwarf
> JOSIAH SQUIBB, the cook aboard the *Republic*
> PETER CRINGLE, the first mate of the *Republic*
> ISADORA BAILEY, Rutherford Calhoun's girlfriend
> NGONYAMA, an African of the Allmuseri tribe, leader of the slave
>   mutiny on board the *Republic*

The Novel

Winner of the National Book Award for fiction, *Middle Passage* is a fanciful account of the misadventures of a twenty-two-year-old black man, a freed slave who ends up aboard a ship bound for Africa to take on a cargo of slaves. *Middle Passage* is divided into nine entries made by Rutherford Calhoun in a ship's log. The first entry is dated June 14, 1830, and the last is dated August 20, 1830. Calhoun narrates each entry.

The book's action begins in New Orleans, where Rutherford Calhoun has drifted after being freed from slavery by his master, a preacher in southern Illinois. Calhoun, mischievous by nature, becomes involved in petty crime and ends up deep in debt to Papa Zeringue, a Creole gangster. Rutherford has also entered into a platonic relationship with Isadora, a young schoolteacher. Papa offers to forgive Calhoun his debts if he will marry Isadora, but for young Rutherford, any thought of marriage is too constricting even to contemplate. To escape, he stows away on a slave ship, the *Republic*. The ship puts to sea before he is discovered.

After he has been found, he is brought before the captain, Ebenezer Falcon, a strange but philosophical man, misshapen both in physique and in morality. Falcon turns out to be both a dwarf and a monster, but in his first interview with Calhoun, there are only intimations of this monstrosity. Falcon decides to allow Calhoun to work aboard the ship without compensation. For the rest of the voyage to Africa, Calhoun befriends the crew and learns about the ship, which is not in good condition and is constantly being repaired.

The ship drops anchor in the African port of Bangalang. There, Rutherford observes the captain buy a cargo of slaves and a huge, mysterious crate that becomes the object of much speculation among the crew. Curious to know more about the captain, Rutherford resorts to his burgling skills in order to break into the captain's cabin. He rifles the captain's effects and reads from the captain's journal. Falcon returns, however, before Rutherford can leave. To the young man's surprise, the captain engages him in a philosophical discourse and then recruits Rutherford to be his spy among the crew, who the captain believes are plotting against him.

The *Republic* sails from Africa, and Rutherford soon befriends Ngonyama, a member of the Allmuseri tribe from whom the ship's slaves have been taken. Ngonyama has been made an overseer, and he is charged with ensuring that the slaves cooperate. A quick learner, Ngonyama masters English well enough to begin explaining to Rutherford some aspects of Allmuseri life. Rutherford also learns that the crew is planning a mutiny, and he is invited to participate. After Rutherford reveals the mutiny plot to Falcon, the captain tells Rutherford that the mysterious cargo carried in the ship's hold is the god of the Allmuseri, a creature that "has a hundred ways to relieve men of their reason." Caught in the middle, Calhoun participates both in the mutiny and in Falcon's attempts to thwart it.

Before this conflict can be brought to a resolution, however, the slaves stage their own mutiny, which is successful. Many of the sailors are killed, but Rutherford (himself spared because he is black) succeeds in convincing them not to kill Falcon or Peter Cringle, the first mate, since someone must guide the ship. Rutherford has one last conversation with the battered captain before Falcon kills himself. In this conversation, Falcon reveals that one of the ship's financial backers is Papa Zeringue, the gangster whose blackmail had sent Rutherford on his misadventures. Rutherford is shocked to learn that a black man is dealing in slaves. Falcon also charges Rutherford with the duty of keeping the ship's log, the entries of which make up the novel. The ship continues to drift in the Atlantic, the situation becoming so desperate that the passengers resort to cannibalism. Finally, a hurricane destroys the ship.

Adrift in the ocean, Calhoun is rescued by a pleasure ship. By coincidence, Isadora is aboard. She is about to be married to Papa Zeringue, a circumstance that Rutherford redresses by revealing that Papa Zeringue was a financial partner in the slaving venture. The blackmail works, leaving Rutherford and Isadora to contemplate their future together.

The Characters

Rutherford Calhoun, the narrator of the novel, is an engaging and likable guide to the action despite his propensity for amoral (and sometimes immoral) behavior. For example, Rutherford leaves New Orleans solely to escape any kind of commitment to Isadora—a woman who clearly cares deeply for him—and yet he explains away his behavior humorously and with enough self-deprecation to keep the reader from judging him too harshly. The same holds true for Rutherford's numerous questionable actions—thieving, stowing away on a ship he knows to be a slaver, informing on his shipmates, and so on. Curiously, Rutherford has received a broad and liberal education from his former owner, a minister who had Rutherford read from the classics of Western philosophy. As a narrator, Rutherford employs this learning in numerous allusions that range from the Greek philosopher Parmenides to the Christian theologian Thomas Aquinas to the English poet Lord Byron. Similarly, Rutherford draws upon a vast and unusual vocabulary; it is clear that he has not been reared as a common slave. Despite this education, Rutherford is unable to make routine moral choices, and he continues to act purely out of self-interest until he meets the Allmuseri and learns something about their distinctly non-Western philosophy. Toward the end of the narrative, Rutherford has matured significantly, though the story ends before it is certain whether these changes are profound enough to last.

Captain Ebenezer Falcon is also a complex character. Rutherford's research (reading Falcon's journal) reveals that Falcon is the son of a minister and domineering mother, born on the day the Colonies declared independence. Calhoun sees Falcon as a Puritan with a utopian and expansionist vision for the country that was born when he was. In his conversations with Calhoun, Falcon displays a command of philosophy that borders on sophistry. At the core of Falcon's philosophy is the belief that conflict is the driving force in human affairs. War is thus the most human of activities, and a subject-object dualism is the basic structure that the human mind imposes on reality. Falcon's "dark counsel" represents the philosophical amorality and social authoritarianism (in the tradition of English philosopher Thomas Hobbes) that Rutherford is learning to reject. The presentation of Falcon's character calls to mind the dark broodings of Ahab, the whale-hunting captain of the novel *Moby Dick: Or, The Whale* (1851) by the American novelist Herman Melville.

Of the novel's minor characters, the first mate on the *Republic*, Peter Cringle, is the most interesting. Cringle is a man out of his element. He is a competent sailor, though less rugged than the rest of the crew. Cringle is also a moral, even pious, man in a world (the ship at sea) where, as Captain Falcon says, there are no rules, and the only authority is that of the stronger man. Cringle is the ship's "feminine air," a voice of tolerance and compassion amid intolerance and cruelty. Significantly, the dying Cringle offers himself as a sacrifice and is cannibalized by the starving crew.

Josiah Squibb, the ship's drunken chef, is a survivor by nature and thus is the only crew member to survive the hurricane with Rutherford. Squibb hones his ability to survive by focusing on practical actions. Unlike the novel's philosophical characters, Squibb dwells "on the smallest details of his chores" to deflect his mind from brooding, and this keeps him from descending into the madness and paralysis of other characters.

Themes and Meanings

Like many sea adventures, *Middle Passage* operates on one level as an allegory, the ship being, as Falcon tells Calhoun, "a society . . . a commonwealth." The name of the ship, the *Republic*, and the fact that its captain was born on July 4, 1776, are strong suggestions that the society allegorized is that of the United States. The novel touches on many themes from U.S. history, including slavery, equal opportunity, and race riots. Many of these references are anachronistic—that is, they are themes and issues that did not exist in 1830. While it is difficult to explain how a narrator writing in the nineteenth century could have knowledge of some of these things (such as the vocabulary of affirmative action), Johnson seems to be suggesting the interconnectedness of U.S. history. In other words, the slavery of the country's early days and the civil strife that Falcon foresees in his apocalyptic death dream ("I saw riots in cities") are connected in their origins. In this regard, the fact that the *Republic* is a ship constantly coming apart and constantly being remade metaphorically suggests that the United States is a society in process, undergoing constant upheaval and renewal. Following the beliefs of its captain, the shipboard society is governed by an essential dualism and characterized by a deep fissure, an "ontic wound" in Falcon's words, that necessitates slavery and strife.

Contrasting with this society of pluralism and division are the mysterious Allmuseri, the African tribe from which the slaves aboard the *Republic* have been captured. The Allmuseri, Rutherford learns, are a mystical people who have powers of sorcery. At least, that is how they have appeared to Western eyes. The Allmuseri stress the unity of all things and see disunity as the source of strife and madness. The slaves' mutiny on board the *Republic* is in part a rebellion against the pluralism that they see in the white society (as represented by the ship's crew). They cannot and will not tolerate being taken to such a world. Captain Falcon, who asserts that strife and division are fundamental driving forces in human relations, represents an opposing viewpoint. When the slaves mutiny and take over the captain's quarters, Rutherford notices that things are strangely altered; even though they appear to be the same objects that had belonged to the captain, Rutherford senses that there is something different about them. He senses that they have been transformed by Allmuseri possession; they are different because they have been touched by the Allmuseri worldview, with its emphasis on unity. Though Rutherford does not understand exactly what has happened, he realizes that the Allmuseri bring a different outlook to the material world, and this outlook is both disturbing and attractive to the young man.

A coming-of-age theme, the passage of a boy to manhood, is common in sea stories. Johnson makes use of this convention in *Middle Passage*. Rutherford, an immature young man with an undeveloped ethics, learns much about life and about himself on the voyage of the *Republic*. The most important lesson for Rutherford has to do with his identity. As a result of this voyage, he realizes that he is neither part of the Western or the African world and that he cannot be entirely part of one or the other. He must navigate between the two somehow, a figurative middle passage that parallels the physical middle passage the ship is making between Africa and America. In other words, it is up to Rutherford to find some common ground between the worlds of Falcon and the Allmuseri. Whether he is successful is a question left open at the novel's end, though Rutherford's reconciliation with Isadora and his adoption of the orphaned Allmuseri girl suggest that he has found some sort of middle ground on which he can build the rest of his life.

Critical Context

  Middle Passage, the third of Johnson's novels, is an extension of his previous work. Both of his previous novels, *Faith and the Good Thing* (1974) and *Oxherding Tale* (1982), are highly charged works of philosophical fiction, and yet, like *Middle Passage*, both are also highly readable novels that appeal to general readers. Johnson's works all feature historical themes, narrative inventiveness, and characters who must make moral choices under difficult, often perplexing, circumstances. One of Johnson's goals is to develop "a genuinely philosophical black American fiction," and with that goal in mind, he places his characters in situations in which their ethics must come under close scrutiny. Such scrutiny eventually reveals shortcomings not only in the characters' understanding of ethics but also in the various ethical programs proposed by Western philosophy. Johnson and his characters confront the inconsistencies inherent in traditional Western ethics and are driven to form their own moral visions from what is left to them after their experiences have forced them to deconstruct their received ethical understanding.

  The narrative of *Middle Passage* is conscious of its debt to other sea stories, especially those of Herman Melville. Many of the characters in Johnson's novels are parodies or revisions of the great characters in Melville's works. Falcon, for example, resembles Ahab; Rutherford is a black Ishmael; Squibb acts much like Stubb; even the cabin boy Tommy parallels Melville's Pip. Johnson's intention in borrowing Melvillian archetypes is to re-present the self-destructive obsession of Ahab/Falcon in terms of a conflictive dualism the American manifestation of which is slavery. Just as Ahab is obsessed with the whiteness of the whale, Falcon (and by extension all white Americans) is obsessed with his own whiteness, and this obsession is played out in the violent repression of those who are, by appearance, the opposite of that whiteness: Africans.

  Another Melville tale is subverted and recast by *Middle Passage*. "Benito Cereno" (1856) is the story of a slave rebellion aboard a Spanish ship. The captain of that ship is saved by an American, Amaso Delano, who after a lengthy confusion about what has occurred aboard Cereno's ship eventually captures the leader of the rebellion, a slave named Babo. Babo and his henchman Atufal are also aboard the *Republic* and involved in that mutiny. From this coincidence, Johnson develops what in Melville's tale is only a minor theme: Namely, that an institution such as slavery can be maintained only through extreme cruelty, a repression that can never be relaxed. Those who practice it must commit themselves to this cruelty or face rebellion. Falcon formulates a philosophy that justifies his, and America's, involvement in the slave trade. The rebellion of the Allmuseri shows that even Falcon's cruelty is not severe enough. Ultimately, then, *Middle Passage* responds to canonical American literature by offering a black deconstruction, or undermining, of traditional themes and contexts.

Bibliography

Goudie, S. X. "'Leavin' a Mark on the World': Marksmen and Marked Men in *Middle Passage*." *African American Review* 29 (Spring, 1995): 109-122. Goudie examines

Johnson's role as an outspoken critic, exploring Johnson's claim that a sameness has stifled the growth of African American fiction. Goudie shows how Johnson uses intersubjectivity and cross-cultural experiences in *Middle Passage.*

Iannone, Carol. "Literature by Quota." *Commentary* 91 (March, 1991): 50-53. A mostly critical examination of Johnson's novel. Iannone, former head of the National Endowment for the Arts, responds to the novel's tone and characterization. She finds the tone too jocular and the characters too obviously symbolic. Her conclusion is that Johnson's novel is "hard to take . . . seriously as literature."

Johnson, Charles. "National Book Award Acceptance Speech." *TriQuarterly* 82 (Fall, 1991): 208-209. Johnson discusses his novel in terms of racism and the literary accomplishments of African Americans. These topics are also addressed in his book *Being and Race: Black Writing Since 1970* (1988).

Little, Jonathan. *Charles Johnson's Spiritual Imagination.* Columbia: University of Missouri Press, 1997. A book-length study of Johnson's work offering an account of Johnson's artistic growth and the increasing spirituality of his imagination. Along with a discussion of *Middle Passage*, there are examinations of each of Johnson's major works.

Rushdy, Ashraf H. A. "The Phenomenology of the Allmuseri: Charles Johnson and the Subject of the Narrative of Slavery." *African American Review* 26 (Fall, 1992): 373-394. A study of the mysterious tribe in *Middle Passage.* The article discusses the Allmuseri philosophy and the points on which it counterbalances and contradicts the worldview of Captain Falcon and the other whites in the novel.

Schultz, Elizabeth A. "The Heirs of Ralph Ellison: Patterns of Individualism in the Contemporary Afro-American Novel." *College Language Association Journal* 22 (December, 1978): 101-122. Discusses Johnson's debt to Ralph Ellison. Johnson's work is considered part of a tradition that began with Ellison: the conscious exploration of philosophy from the African American perspective.

Smith, Virginia W. "Sorcery, Double-consciousness, and Warring Souls: An Intertextual Reading of *Middle Passage* and *Captain Blackman*." *African American Review* 30 (Winter, 1996). Smith asserts that Johnson's *Middle Passage* was influenced by John A. Williams's *Captain Blackman* (1972). She points out a number of similar themes between the novels such as war and interracial and intraracial conflict.

Thaden, Barbara Z. "Charles Johnson's *Middle Passage* as Historiographic Metafiction." *College English* 59 (November, 1997): 753-766. Thaden demonstrates that *Middle Passage* can be used to introduce historiographic metafiction to students. By studying some of the source texts that Johnson adapted for his novel, students better understand the satire and purpose of *Middle Passage.*

Walby, Celestin. "The African Sacrificial Kingship Ritual and Johnson's *Middle Passage*." *African American Review* 29 (Winter, 1995): 657-669. Walby discusses the Allmuseri tribe in *Middle Passage* and its use as a means to resolve the writer's dilemma of asserting a black identity. The novel's theme of self-surrender is also detailed.

Wills, Garry. "The Long Voyage Home." *The New York Review of Books* 38 (January
    17, 1991): 3. Wills rejects arguments that Johnson's novel did not deserve the Na-
    tional Book Award. Specifically, Wills considers the book an artistic achievement
    that is not beholden to a particular ideology. Thus, he contends, the book was se-
    lected on merit and not because of its "message."

Stephen Benz

MISERY

Author: Stephen King (1947-   )
Type of plot: Suspense
Time of plot: The mid-1980's
Locale: Colorado and New York City
First published: 1987

> *Principal characters:*
> PAUL SHELDON, a well-known author
> ANNIE WILKES, a murderous ex-nurse

The Novel

Misery tells the suspenseful and often gruesome story of novelist Paul Sheldon, held captive by a psychotic fan. It also offers insight into the public role of a writer and the experience of writing itself.

Misery establishes characters and conflict immediately, opening with Annie Wilkes's artificial respiration to revive injured author Paul Sheldon. Within five very brief chapters, readers learn that Sheldon has crashed his car in a snowstorm; that Wilkes, a fan of Sheldon's popular romance novels starring Misery Chastain, has rescued him; and that she is crazy and is imprisoning him in her isolated house rather than taking him to a hospital for proper care. Sheldon's legs are shattered, and Wilkes treats the pain with Novril, a painkiller stolen from hospitals in which she had worked as a nurse. An addiction to Novril furthers Sheldon's dependence on his admirer and captor.

The first proof of Annie's power over Paul, and her insane willingness to use it, concerns *Fast Cars*, the novel Sheldon had just finished before the fateful drive from Boulder. Though Sheldon is known for, and wealthy from, his Misery books, he yearns for recognition of his more literary works and sees the new manuscript as his best work. Annie sees it as a travesty, full of low-life characters and obscenities, and she forces Sheldon to burn his only copy.

Moreover, Annie has been reading *Misery's Child*—having waited for the paperback—and Sheldon fears her reaction: At the end, Misery dies in childbirth. Though Paul is delighted to have ended the series, Annie is outraged and insists that he write a new novel that brings Misery back. After one try that Annie rejects as unfair because it contradicts the events in *Misery's Child*, Paul takes on the challenge and produces, he finally acknowledges, the best Misery book, *Misery's Return*.

Sheldon literally writes for his life in two ways. He knows that Wilkes, unable to explain away his captivity, can never let him go, but will not kill him until Misery's story ends. He is also "Scheherazade to [him]self," renewed by the act of writing and himself eager to see how he will wrap up the novel. In a comic and ironic motif, the old manual typewriter Annie buys for Paul keeps losing letters, which Paul or Annie writes in by hand on the manuscript.

Sheldon tries to escape, but he pays terribly for any attempts to cross Annie, including two amputations, which are depicted in scenes as horrible as those describing any supernatural menace about which King has written. On one forbidden trip out of his room in his wheelchair, Sheldon discovers a scrapbook—innocently titled "Memory Lane"—that chronicles at least thirty murders by Annie, including those in a neonatal ward that resulted in a trial that ended her career as a nurse, although she was acquitted. While Sheldon recuperates, Wilkes, a manic depressive, deteriorates mentally, which only increases her dangerousness.

As winter becomes spring, Sheldon's car is finally found, and a single officer from the Colorado State Police arrives at Annie's place to ask questions. When Paul attracts his attention, Annie kills the officer. After that, both the writer and the nurse know the end is near, although both hope Sheldon will finish the book before then. Soon, two officers visit, but Paul is locked in the cellar, and the officers come and go uneventfully. However, in the cellar, Sheldon sees the portable barbecue in which he was forced to burn *Fast Cars*, and he decides to free himself.

In a satisfying yet highly disturbing climax, Sheldon shocks Annie by appearing to burn the finished manuscript (including the ending she has not yet read), attacks her with the heavy manual typewriter, and finally chokes her with charred pages of the novel, explicitly comparing the act to oral rape. The two police officers return, find Annie dead in the barn, and rescue Paul. An epilogue-like final section depicts Sheldon back in New York City; traumatized, he is at first unable to write. In a triumphant (and less disturbing) ending, however, he begins a new literary work, more like *Fast Cars* than like the instantly best-selling *Misery's Return*.

The Characters

Annie Wilkes is one of King's most interesting creations, unique yet archetypal. She is described as "overweight," but "big" rather than fat, maternal yet androgynous; she is able to kill a police officer with a riding lawnmower, yet is strangely prissy, especially about language ("cockadoodie" and "dirty birdie" are typical Annie-isms). She imagines herself a nurturing caregiver, but apart from her mental instability, she is too selfish to truly care about anyone, even the godlike creator of her beloved Misery. Paul more correctly envisions her as a primordial goddess, life-giving but elemental and cruel.

King reveals Wilkes's character through her own words and actions, through Sheldon's empathic understanding of her character (a writer's intuition heightened by his perilous dependence on her irrational reactions and volatile moods), and through Sheldon's reading of her scrapbook. Like Harold Lauder in *The Stand* (1978; new edition, 1990), Jack Torrance in *The Shining* (1977), and other of King's human villains, Annie is terrifying and reprehensible, yet understandable and in her own way pitiful.

Weakened by injuries and by addiction to painkillers, Paul Sheldon is credibly human; he also has been divorced twice and used to smoke too much (Annie allows him no cigarettes). Still, like Andy Dufresne in King's "Rita Hayworth and Shawshank Redemption" (from *Different Seasons*, 1982), he is a hero, combining strong will and patience. Sheldon also attains self-control and control over his captor through the one thing he does well, which is writing.

At first, Paul is literally helpless as a baby, his life preserved by Annie's nursing knowledge and great physical strength. Trapped in Annie's house, he compares himself to a bird from Africa he saw in a zoo when he was young, tragically far from home, never to be freed. However, the balance of power between Sheldon and Wilkes shifts, in part as Paul gains physical strength (he lifts the heavy typewriter for secret exercise), but primarily because of his writer's ability to spin a story that captivates his captor.

King's quick and deft characterization of the most minor figures shows in the three police officers, the friends and family of whom Sheldon thinks, and the people whose histories are revealed in Annie's scrapbook. However, the focus of the book is one small spotlight completely shared by Paul and Annie.

Themes and Meanings

Misery is perhaps the most thematically satisfying of King's novels, both rich and unified, as interwoven issues are explored by direct action and by a wealth of metaphorical imagery. One major theme is writing itself; another is control—self-control or its lack, control over others, and the related issue of addiction, to drugs, food, or a story. There are also intriguing but disturbing implications concerning gender and appetite.

Paul Sheldon thinks, early in *Misery*, that he "wrote novels of two kinds, good ones and best-sellers." Later, he comes to understand the snobbery of this and to appreciate that popular fiction must have its own integrity, its own quality. One can see the novel originating in part from King's musings about his own situation as a cultural icon and about what does and does not make good writing. The novel also offers striking descriptions of the writing process, the experience itself as well as its joys and travails.

Annie Wilkes seeks to control Sheldon, but she cannot control herself, while Sheldon, through self-discipline, finally triumphs. She is greedy—keeping Sheldon as her captive, urging him to tell him the ending before he has written it—and, during her depressive episodes, a horrendously sloppy compulsive eater. Annie becomes as dependent on the unfolding story of Misery's return as Paul is on the care and drugs Annie provides. Interestingly, back in New York after his ordeal, Paul is himself sliding downhill, replacing his painkillers with alcohol, until he begins his next story.

It is easy to see King implying that self-control is a masculine virtue and that appetite and smothering control of others are female vices. Certainly, fat, controlling females are often sources of horror in King's fiction, such as Eddie Kaspbrak's mother and wife in *It* (1986). Still, Annie Wilkes is no embodiment of femininity; she is portrayed in some ways as frighteningly masculine. Moreover, whatever King's social views, Wilkes herself is *sui generis*, above all an individual—and above all crazy.

Critical Context

Although King is famous for large novels with sprawling plots such as *The Stand* and *It*, *Misery* focuses stringently on two main characters in one location. In *Gerald's Game* (1992) and *Dolores Claiborne* (1993), King tightens the focus further, each book concentrating on the voice and experience of one female protagonist. Also, like those two novels (excluding one shared moment of telepathy), *Misery* is realistic horror-suspense, with no supernatural or psychic elements.

The author's use of writers as protagonists precedes *Misery*, including Ben Mears in, *'Salem's Lot* (1975) and failed writer Jack Torrance in *The Shining*. However, with *Misery*, King began a more extensive use of authors as characters, often including interesting insights into life as a fictioneer and as a popular phenomenon, as in *The Dark Half* (1989) and *Bag of Bones* (1998). King has always mined his personal experience—his years of poverty and as a teacher, for example, show up in *Carrie* (1974) and *The Shining*—and this development seems natural, as writing more and more became his life.

Structurally, *Misery* is comparable to King's novella "Apt Pupil" (in *Different Seasons*, 1982), in which an all-American teenager blackmails a neighbor into retelling his experiences as a Nazi concentration camp commandant. "Apt Pupil," like *Misery*, explores the changing balance of power between two enmeshed individuals, with storytelling as one medium of exchange. Annie's scrapbook fills a purpose similar to that of the scrapbook that reveals the history of the Overlook Hotel in *The Shining* (*Misery* refers briefly to that hotel's burned-out ruins nearby).

The single strongest context for *Misery* other than King's own work is provided by John Fowles's *The Collector* (1963), to which *Misery* subtly refers ("Paul found himself wondering dourly if she had John Fowles's first novel on her shelves and decided it might be better not to ask"). *The Collector* is also the story of a deranged individual holding captive a creative and sane individual, though in Fowles's novel, the victim is female and the oppressor male.

Misery strongly exemplifies King's three great strengths: compelling storytelling, including horror and suspense; unique and emotionally effective characterization; and insight into both human nature and the mystery of creative writing. While the scenes of murder and amputation may be too strong for some readers, King's craft, thematics, and imagery in the novel make the novel worth reading and studying.

Bibliography

Beahm, George. *The Stephen King Story: A Literary Profile*. Kansas City, Mo.: Andrews and McMeel, 1991. A good factual biography, including quotations and material about the writing of *Misery*, musings by King and his wife about the connection between authors and readers, and the newspaper report of a lawsuit by fan Anne Hiltner claiming that King stole the manuscript of *Misery* from her home.

Bosky, Bernadette Lynn. "Playing the Heavy: Weight, Appetite, and Embodiment in Three Novels by Stephen King." In *The Dark Descent: Essays Defining Stephen King's Horrorscape*, edited by Tony Magistrale. Westport, Conn.: Greenwood Press, 1992. Explores themes of fat, appetite, and mothering in *Misery*, with context regarding those issues in *The Stand* and *It*.

Gottschalk, Katherine G. "Stephen King's Dark and Terrible Mother, Annie Wilkes." In *The Anna Book*, edited by Mickey Pearlman. Westport, Conn.: Greenwood

Press, 1992. This archetypal/mythological approach may seem overinterpretive, but Paul Sheldon does think of Annie as a goddess, and Gottschalk does highlight interesting elements of the novel.

Magistrale, Tony. *Stephen King: The Second Decade, "Danse Macabre" to "The Dark Half."* New York: Twayne, 1992. Chapter 6 contains excellent analysis of the thematics of art and madness in *Misery* and *It*, while other chapters provide context from King's other works of the 1980's.

Schopp, Andrew. "Writing (with) the Body: Stephen King's *Misery." LIT* 5 (1994): 29-43. Based in heavy contemporary critical theory but clear to the noninitiated, this piece explores themes of gender and power in the novel.

Bernadette Lynn Bosky

MISS MACINTOSH, MY DARLING

Author: Marguerite Young (1909-1995)
Type of plot: Stream of consciousness
Time of plot: The 1950's
Locale: New England and the Midwest
First published: 1965

> *Principal characters:*
> MISS MACINTOSH, an elderly red-headed nursemaid, sensible and
> forthright, who symbolizes truth and goodness to the narrator, Vera
> Cartwheel
> CATHERINE CARTWHEEL, Vera's drug-addicted mother, who languishes
> in an opium paradise
> MR. SPITZER, devoted companion to Catherine, composer of imaginary
> music and twin brother to Catherine's dead lover
> ESTHER LONGTREE, a waitress in a Wabash Valley, Indiana, cafe,
> forever pregnant with phantom babies
> VERA CARTWHEEL, the narrator, an unwanted child born of a fugitive
> marriage and raised in a realm of make believe

The Novel

In *Miss Macintosh, My Darling*, the first and only novel by Marguerite Young, a young woman embarks on a dreamlike voyage through time and memory in search of her darling childhood nursemaid, Miss Macintosh from What Cheer, Iowa, who has disappeared into the ocean, never to be seen again. Finding herself adrift on a sea of delusion and fantasy, the young woman fervently searches for reality only to discover herself drowning in illusion.

The narrator, Vera Cartwheel, has been reared in a baroque New England seaside house. Her mother, Catherine, an opium addict, is confined to her bed and a world of imaginary visitors when Vera is a small child. In her mother's "horizontal" existence, every object, from chandeliers to medicine bottles, is endowed with life and becomes a welcomed guest along with such notables as Alexander Pope, Lady Mary Montagu, and Lord Byron. Catherine's only real visitor is Joaquin Spitzer, her lawyer, who is also the twin brother of Peron, her dead lover who committed suicide years before. Having known Catherine in earlier years, Mr. Spitzer silently endures unrequited love, patiently sitting in the shadows of her room waiting for Catherine's rare moments of coherence.

Miss Macintosh, hired by Mr. Spitzer as a nursemaid when Vera is seven, is a no-nonsense governess and appears to be the only rational person in Vera's life. She is sensible and common, forthright and normal, and for seven years, she is both nursemaid and teacher. On the night of her fourteenth birthday, Vera enters her nursemaid's room only to discover that Miss Macintosh's reality is far stranger than her mother's opium-induced dream; she is in fact bald, hairless since birth. A surreal scene ensues in which the nursemaid's true identity manifests itself to Vera. "Where her head should be, there was another moon, cold and dented and shining, seeming to float upon the waves of corrugated darkness. . . ." Standing naked before the child, red wig tossed aside, she is exposed as a fat old spinster with only one breast. It is a surprising metamorphosis and a hideous nightmare for Vera.

During the following month, Vera's love for Miss MacIntosh grows as she learns the truth of her tormented childhood and her broken engagement to Mr. Titus Bonebreaker, a street preacher from Chicago who, upon the eve of their wedding, finds her deformities so grotesque and repulsive that he decides to flee into the night. Vera's discovery of love and death coincide when, for no apparent reason, Miss MacIntosh walks into the ocean, leaving scattered on the beach her wig, false breast, eyeglasses, and broken umbrella.

Years later, Vera discovers herself traveling backward in time on a dilapidated old bus with a whiskey guzzling, long-haired bus driver as they head to the Midwest in search of the reality of Miss MacIntosh. As the barren landscape of her soul passes by, she contemplates her fellow passengers, a pregnant girl and her young husband who are acting out fantasies of their own. In a small cafe in Wabash Valley, Vera meets Esther Longtree, a cross-eyed waitress who, having murdered her first-born infant, is cursed with the idea that she is permanently pregnant. After enduring horrifyingly real labors, she delivers imaginary stillborn babies only to find herself pregnant once again. In a rundown hotel, Vera encounters Weed, a Christian hangman who hangs his victims with dignity while at the same time taking pride in carrying out their sentences in a painless manner, and Dr. Justice O'Leary who delivers imaginary women of imaginary babies. She continues to walk a tightrope between sanity and illusion until she meets a stone-deaf man with whom she falls in love, conceives a child, and looks forward to a new life.

Meanwhile, back in New England, Catherine Cartwheel's shadowy existence in her hallucinogenic, bed-ridden environment comes to an end when she weans herself from opium. Ironically, when she awakens to confront the reality she long ago had abandoned, the interim years slam into her like a roaring train, and she ages quickly. In the end, death does not take a beautiful woman but rather one crippled from her many years in bed. Her skin wrinkles, and her hearing and vision rapidly diminish as she meets a peaceful death with the ever-faithful Mr. Spitzer at her side.

The Characters

In the style of Dylan Thomas, Marguerite Young utilizes dark, brooding characters and situations that are traditional in gothic literary forms. Catherine, the frail sleeping beauty, lies in her mansion by the fog-shrouded sea and calls for her coachman, who appears to her in the form of a skeleton. Such scenes are the mainstays of this lengthy novel. From Cousin Hannah, the mountain-climbing suffragette who dies leaving behind forty trunks, each containing a wedding dress, to Mr. Spitzer, who hears symphonies of unearthly music in his head, each of Young's characters is a visionary inhabiting the night world of dreamers rather than the daytime world of pursuit and accomplishment. Young delves into the psyche of her characters, testing their nature and making them more complete in their fragmentation than if they were whole. They are all failures, reveling in confusion and profound chaos; all the while, their search for realities that do not fail them feeds their bizarre existence.

A menage of opium-inspired subcharacters runs the gamut from the mischievously funny to the vivid and haunting. Dead stars of silent films, an Egyptian prince, old kings and queens, New England spinsters, dead horses, and Mr. Res Tacamah, a drug bottle with ears, are all nightly visitors to Catherine Cartwheel's bedroom. Young's colorful characters, though steeped in symbolism, are homogenous. The common thread that binds them is that they are cohorts in attempting to attain their aspirations amid the consuming effects of reality.

Young's work features many of the classic elements of the fable as a narrative form. Supernatural occurrences in the form of animals or inanimate objects behaving or speaking as human beings enable the author to weave into the story a moral lesson.

Themes and Meanings

Several variations of a single theme dominate throughout: illusion versus reality, the dogma that life is a dream and death is another dream, good versus evil. Vera's world is enveloped in delusive images. Searching for her drowned reality, she cries out, "What shall we do when, fleeing from illusion, we are confronted by illusion? When falling from illusion, we fall into illusion?" Whatever heights of fantasy the novel achieves, it remains rooted in the basic American literary themes of childhood memories and nostalgia for the past. Small-town life, another popular literary theme, surfaces in What Cheer, Iowa—a place where "all the young people had fled from, and the old were half in their graves . . . and nobody could hear a word that was said." Reaching into the depths of human psychology, Young touches on many aspects of life—gambling, suicide, perfectionism, schizophrenia, drug addiction, real and imagined pregnancies, and murder—all of which pose the ultimate question of the novel—what is reality and what are dreams?

Critical Context

Miss MacIntosh, My Darling took seventeen years to write and, despite its length of 1,198 pages, was initially published in a single volume. Although it sank into relative obscurity with critics of postmodern fiction and has had little literary influence, some critics tout it to be one of the most ambitious literary achievements of the twentieth century, if only for its supreme amassment and the complexity of its characters. One observer summed up the reaction with the comment that "surely one of the most widely unread books ever acclaimed, it has actually been read by comparatively few, by fewer still all the way through." At its core it is a picaresque journey into the spirit of humankind, a search for lost utopias, and a study of human experience. While her writing is open to interpretation, Young abandons all established rules of strict allegory as she relates Vera's struggles against the many obstacles that hinder her path to a sure and lasting understanding of the purpose and meaning of life. In this regard, her novel is considered a valid example of experimental fiction. Her evocative style is replete with metaphors, symbolizations, proliferating images, and enumerations of facts that call to mind James Joyce, Herman Melville, or William Faulkner. They also reflect her deep interest in Elizabethean and Jacobean symbols, a subject in which she received her master's degree from the University of Chicago. Among the writers who influenced Young were the philosophers Saint Augustine, David Hume, and William James.

Marguerite Young was born in Indianapolis, and she attended Indiana University. She began writing poetry at the age of six and became a member of the Authors League at eleven; at twenty, she won first prize in a literary contest conducted by Butler University. Her first collection of poems, *Prismatic Ground*, was published in 1937, when she was twenty-eight. In 1945, she won a Best Poetry Award for "Moderate Fable" from the National Academy of Arts and Letters, the same year "Angel in the Forest," her critically acclaimed account of utopian societies in New Harmony, Indiana, was published. She was awarded an American Association of University Women grant in 1943, a Guggenheim Fellowship in 1948, a Newberry Library fellowship in 1951, and a Rockefeller fellowship in 1954. At the time of her death, Young's *Harp Song for a Radical*, a massive biography of Eugene Debs, remained unpublished.

Bibliography

Edelstein, J. M. "Miss MacIntosh, Her Darling." *The New Republic* 153, no. 14: 28-29. Edelstein's critical assessment of *Miss MacIntosh, My Darling* asserts what is real versus what is a dream to be the central question and theme in a novel rooted in a grand assembly of words, characters, and situations. He asserts the obscure patterns of the narrative act as an impediment to the overall artistic expression.

Goyen, William. "A Fable of Illusion and Reality." *The New York Times Book Review*, September 12, 1965, p.5. Goyen views Young's abundance of descriptive passages and method of relentlessly examining her complex characters as literary devices intended to drive the theme of the novel. He sees the obsessive probing as a technique to turn the interiors of her characters outward so that their terrible natures can be exposed.

Hicks, Granville. "Adrift on a Sea of Dreams." *Literary Horizons*, September 11, 1965, 35-36. According to Hicks, Young's elaborate use of recurring symbols demonstrates her imaginative power and conscientious craftsmanship. He lauds her poetic style and hypnotic use of language to relate the hallucinatory episodes. However, he finds fault in the novel's lack of fixed points of reference to draw distinctions between the characters and thus eliminate confusion as to whose dream belongs to whom.

Shaviro, Steven. "Lost Chords and Interrupted Births: Marguerite Young's Exhorbitant Vision." *Contemporary Fiction*, Vol. 31, No. 3 (Spring, 1990): 213-222. In this thorough essay, Shaviro discusses the thematic and complex style of *Miss Mac-*

Intosh, My Darling, suggesting that one sign of the novel's uniqueness and strength is the refusal of the text to conform to the usual paradigms of either modernism or postmodernism.

Thomas, Robert McG., Jr. "Marguerite Young, 87, Author and Icon, Dies." *The New York Times*, November 20, 1995, p. B11. This obituary provides a concise profile of the author's life along with commentary on the reception *Miss MacIntosh, My Darling* received from the literary community. In addition, it relates several of her formative experiences, eccentric behaviors, and relationships with other notable literary figures such as Gertrude Stein and Thornton Wilder, which later provided grist for her work.

William Hoffman

THE MISSOLONGHI MANUSCRIPT

Author: Frederic Prokosch (1908-1989)
Type of plot: Biographical
Time of plot: 1824, with flashbacks focusing on the period from 1809 to 1824
Locale: Greece, England, Switzerland, and Italy
First published: 1968

> *Principal characters:*
> GEORGE GORDON, LORD BYRON, the poet
> PERCY BYSSHE SHELLEY, the poet
> TERESA GUICCIOLI, Byron's mistress

The Novel

The Missolonghi Manuscript is a novel about George Gordon, Lord Byron, based on the convenient device of recently discovered (but imaginary) diaries written by the poet. The narrative is prefaced by a fictitious meeting at a party in Italy of a T. H. Applebee from Bryn Mawr College with the American-born Marchesa del Rosso. Applebee learns from the marchesa that she has a manuscript of three notebooks written by Byron in Missolonghi, Greece, between January, 1824, and his death there three months later. Two years pass, and the marchesa dies, but Applebee is allowed to copy the notebooks, learning in so doing that the marchesa had obtained the manuscript from a Colonel Eppingham, who had himself purchased it in Greece from a "decomposing personage," the Baron von Haugwitz. None of these ruses is of further significance.

The three notebooks tell two parallel stories: Each day opens with a short entry on current affairs in Missolonghi (the first note is for 25 January 1824) but switches quickly to the main interest, Byron's autobiographical musings, given in chronological order. So the story soon settles down to an imaginative reconstruction of many of the major relationships of Byron's life: with Lady Caroline Lamb, Annabella Milbanke, and Teresa Guiccioli; and with literary friends (Percy Bysshe Shelley and Leigh Hunt) and social cronies (John Cam Hobhouse and Edward John Trelawny). Interludes of sexual coupling are frequent, their descriptions frank, their practices varied. By the end of the third notebook the main autobiographical account has caught up with the thinner Missolonghi diary narrative.

The first notebook goes through February 17. The entries on Missolonghi detail the squalor and hopelessness of the place ("Missolonghi is a quagmire"). Prokosch's Byron explains that he came to Greece in search of "self-renewal and self-forgetfulness" and hoping to shed "the serpent-skin of my selfish, brutal past." On February 2, Byron reports feeling ill, and his discomfort and malaise continue. Of his companions at Missolonghi, Byron is closest to Loukas, the boy who tends him. His relationship with Prince Mavrocordato, the Greek nationalist leader, is not intimate, but they share banter and ouzo, and in Prokosch's version they understand each other's personal motives. Byron speaks of "wicked, equivocal Mavrocordato."

The longer, autobiographical strand of the first notebook skips quickly over childhood experiences, punctuated with obligatory sexual escapades. The Cambridge scenes flicker with undergraduate salaciousness and speculation. Much of the notebook recounts a long trip that Byron began in 1809 with his close friend Hobhouse. This trip lasts about a year and takes Byron to Spain and Portugal, Albania, Greece, and Turkey. It is highlighted by his swimming the Hellespont and his boast that in Athens he slept with ninety-three women. Back in England he meets Madame de Staël, who promptly says of him, "*Qu'il est beau ce jeune poète! Mon Dieu, qu'il est beau.*" In Caroline Lamb, Byron finds, temporarily, his match. ("We were egoists and flirts, both of us.") Their passion absorbs them too much, however, and the affair ends with her calling him a "club-footed satyr" and him slapping her face.

The second notebook runs from February 18 through March 26. Many of the same themes continue: lubricious chitchat with Mavrocordato, erotic byplay with Loukas, and curses cast on foul Missolonghi. Hallucinations begin to bother Byron in February, self-hatred surges in him, and on March 9 he wonders if he has malaria. He devotes several entries to brief comments on poetry: William Wordsworth was wrong in calling poetry emotion recollected in tranquillity; "The real deformity in the poet's heart is his life in an ugly world"; John Keats's "mellifluous nightingales" are thin stuff for poetry.

The autobiographical recollections of the second notebook are rich in characters and incidents, detailing Byron's loves and travels. He reveals a genuine love for his half sister, Augusta, but his marriage to Annabella Milbanke is a travesty, and his treatment of her is brutal. He soon leaves for the Continent and spends time in Geneva with Shelley and Madame de Staël. His affair with Claire Clairmont produces a daughter, Allegra, about whom he is later edgy and evasive. He eventually leaves for Italy with Hobhouse (time is greatly telescoped in this section), where he indulges himself in a series of coarse erotic liaisons. After meeting the Countess Teresa Guiccioli, he settles down with her and her elderly husband in their home in Ravenna, playing a role that was commonly accepted at that time in Italy. He spends more time with Shelley, eventually taking Teresa to Pisa, where they are part of the circle around Shelley.

The third notebook (March 27-April 18) in the Missolonghi sequences traces the decline of the moribund Byron, badly ill, dejected ("How can I ever describe it, this all-engulfing loneliness?"), and hallucinating. The main autobiographical narrative takes him up to the time of his arrival in Missolonghi, its ending neatly coinciding with his last reflections before dying. The main element of interest is the death of Shelley and the morbid ritual enacted by the scabrous Trelawny in exhuming and cremating the poet's remains. The arrival of Leigh Hunt with his wife and six children as Byron's houseguests provides one of the more entertaining interludes.

The Characters

Prokosch's Byron is a driven man, one who confides that "I kept searching for a 'deeper purpose,' a 'spiritual call,' a 'dedication.'" For a while he hopes to find fulfillment in his dedication to the cause of the Italian revolutionaries in their struggle against Austria. Yet he quickly understands that he is destined to a fruitless search for peace and that he is an exile whose "political ardour had a hollow ring to it." His aspirations in his mission to Greece are futile right from the beginning, as he seems aware; the final mustering of energies expended in a spiritual void.

Toward the last he writes ruefully of the end of the "beautiful Byron," a death that leaves only the "perverse and destructive and tortured Byron." He describes himself as a "wayward" animal, both "childishly happy and childishly gloomy, childishly affectionate and childishly venomous." In short, his motives are "transparent" because he is simply "a man who follows his instincts." He returns to this self-analysis several days later, cataloging his qualities and explaining, "Every virtue contains its vice and every vice its own virtue." He takes comfort in his conclusion that ultimately the great virtue is "animal integrity," a complete acceptance and fulfillment of one's animal self. He accepts Shelley's judgment of him as "a shame-faced Manichean." Immediately before he goes to Greece, however, he confides that he has no "definite or identifiable character" and that he is drawn to Greece "to discover the *other* creature, if there really is another, who is hiding within me."

Prokosch develops Byron's sensual life in great detail. Byron's youthful feeling for Lord Clare is called up in many of his reveries on the past, and the tenderness he feels for the boy Loukas in Missolonghi is attributed to his partial identification of the youth with Clare. His feelings for Augusta are muffled in the account but obviously intense. His marriage to Annabella appears inexplicable, a perverse impulse that turns immediately into coarseness and brutality, and the episode with Claire Clairmont soon becomes a drain on his spirit. In Teresa Guiccioli, however, Byron apparently encounters an eroticism and a sensibility that calm him, at least for a while, and their relationship depicts a genuine companionship. The other sexual adventures recounted are mere bouts of carnality. In his sex life as in his wanderings, Prokosch's Byron is driven by impulse and haunted by urgency.

The Shelley whom Prokosch presents through Byron's eyes is humorless and given to "little bursts of a warbling ecstasy." Byron views him "with an air of smirking tolerance," but although he laughs at Shelley's "absurdity," he is moved by his "sudden tenderness" and senses in him the "presence of purity."

It is through Shelley that Byron meets Edward John Trelawny, a satyr whose "virile, piratical way" evokes in Byron a fear of something "ominous and oppressive" and an uneasiness about Trelawny's "dark intention, a rather sinister intimacy." Trelawny disconcerts Byron, who comes both to love him and to hate him, and Byron senses in him his own weaknesses: "my self-display and my *passé* dandyism, my moodiness, my braggadocio." For Teresa, Trelawny is a menacing figure with the evil eye.

Leigh Hunt emerges as an incompetent, ludicrous, "rather mischievous sort of man" with repulsive personal habits. He appears suddenly at Byron's Casa Lafranchi in Pisa, and "in a moment of insanity" Byron invites him and his family to stay there as his guests. Byron enjoys Hunt and draws him out in disparagement of other poets.

When Byron reproaches Hunt for not bathing, Hunt retorts quickly: "You have scolded me for the infrequency of my baths. Are your callousness and promiscuity to be excused on the grounds of poetry?"

Themes and Meanings

Prokosch's Byron provides no new understanding of the poet, but *The Missolonghi Manuscript* offers both a good reading experience and a reliable sketch of many of the important events in Byron's short but crowded life. Of especial interest to many readers will be the re-creation of Byron's relationship with Shelley and his circle, a part of the story that Prokosch depicts convincingly. Although the asides about Wordsworth, Shelley, and other poets are always Prokosch's interpretations of Byron's views, they are well observed and consistent with what is known of the real Byron's judgments. Prokosch is unflinching in his depiction of Byron's diverse sexual impulses, but his interpretation has the support of scholarship and is always credible. Even though the important historical events in which Byron participated remain mere backdrops in the novel, Missolonghi and its foul climate are put to good literary use: They hover in the background as an appropriate pathetic fallacy complementing Byron's moroseness. Many of the less well-known people in Byron's life, such as Mary Chaworth, are introduced without much comment, but their significance to Byron is always clear, and any biography of the poet will provide whatever background is needed on them.

Critical Context

The Missolonghi Manuscript is clearly a novel by Frederic Prokosch, exhibiting his usual skill at re-creating the atmosphere of exotic settings, with the entire scenario dressed up in silken language. Critics have always justly praised Prokosch's descriptive powers, for he is extremely successful in evoking unity of tone, mood, and atmosphere: lush, erotic, and at times slightly sinister. The narrative flow is smooth and swift, and the device of parallel entries in the Missolonghi notebooks works well enough. The elaborate apparatus of frame letters at the outset is perhaps unnecessary to his main purpose, but it is a well-accepted convention. As a source of scholarly information about Byron, *The Missolonghi Manuscript* should probably be read with caution since it is, after all, fiction, but Prokosch has certainly come close enough to capturing the historical Byron to guarantee the honesty of the book's considerable appeal as a novel.

Bibliography

Austen, Roger. *Playing the Game: The Homosexual Novel in America*. Indianapolis: Bobbs-Merrill, 1977. Contains a useful discussion of Prokosch, situating him in the context of twentieth century literature.

Bishop, John Peale. *The Collected Essays of John Peale Bishop*. Edited by Edmund Wilson. New York: Charles Scribner's Sons, 1948. "Final Dreading" is a favorable poetry review by Bishop of Prokosch's *The Assassins*, his first book of poems. Refers to Prokosch's extensive travels and its influence on these poems and concludes with a brief commentary on Prokosch's technique and his relationship to Oswald Spengler and Saint-John Perse.

Carpenter, Richard C. "The Novels of Frederic Prokosch." *College English* 18 (1957): 261-267. Provides much insight into the development of Prokosch's novelistic style. An appreciative essay by a sympathetic critic of Prokosch.

Marowski, Daniel G., and Roger Matuz, eds. *Contemporary Literary Criticism*. Vol. 48. Detroit: Gale Research, 1988. The entry on Prokosch presents an overview of his works, citing him as a "highly regarded novelist" who gained prominence in the 1930's. Included is a sampling of reviews, mostly favorable, of his earlier works (*The Asiatics, The Assassins, The Seven Who Fled*), as well as later works, such as *The Missolonghi Manuscript* and his memoir, *Voices*, in which he addresses his literary displacement.

Quartermain, Peter, ed. *Dictionary of Literary Biography*. Vol. 48. Detroit: Gale Research, 1986. Provides a selected checklist of Prokosch's works, giving more emphasis to his poetry, although he is better known as a novelist. Discusses his poems between 1920 and the mid-1940's. Also includes background information on Prokosch, including his numerous travels, and some brief commentary on his novels.

Squires, Radcliffe. *Frederic Prokosch*. New York: Twayne, 1964. Presents Prokosch's works in a chronological format and is useful as a critical introduction. Squires focuses on the timeless qualities of "interplay of emotion and intellect" in Prokosch's work but acknowledges that his writing was a "casualty" of World War II, which changed the values of the reading public. A selected bibliography is provided.

Frank Day

THE MONKEY WRENCH GANG

Author: Edward Abbey (1927-1989)
Type of plot: Didactic adventure
Time of plot: The 1970's
Locale: The American Southwest
First published: 1975

> *Principal characters:*
> DOC SARVIS, a well-to-do, middle-aged Albuquerque physician
> BONNIE ABZUG, Sarvis's twenty-eight-year-old receptionist
> GEORGE WASHINGTON HAYDUKE, a troubled Vietnam veteran
> SELDOM SEEN SMITH, a polygamous river-running guide
> J. DUDLEY LOVE, a wealthy bishop of the Church of Latter-day Saints

The Novel

The Monkey Wrench Gang is a rollicking adventure novel with a serious political message. It covers the adventures of four disparate characters who band together to disable power plants and their supporting equipment, which they believe despoil the landscape of the desert. The book is credited with having inspired the formation of the ecological protest group Earth First! A prologue is followed by four chapters introducing the four monkey-wrenchers, then twenty-six chapters detailing their adventures, and finally an epilogue.

In "Prolog: The Aftermath," a little-noticed figure sets a charge that destroys a bridge between Arizona and Utah as it is being dedicated. The next target, a safety officer asserts, is Glen Canyon Dam. Chapter 1 introduces Doc Sarvis and Bonnie Abzug as they travel along the desert highways of New Mexico, destroying billboards that they consider to have socially irresponsible messages. Doc and Bonnie meet up with Seldom Seen Smith and George Washington Hayduke, who is working for Smith, on a river-rafting trip. After Bonnie and Smith's other two female clients retire to their sleeping bags for the night, the three men stay up drinking heavily and discover a shared antipathy toward the power plants and river-choking dams that are covering the desert.

Bonnie and the men soon embark on a daring and well-planned series of raids, destroying bridges and disabling bulldozers and other heavy equipment, backed by Sarvis's money, Hayduke's skills in guerrilla tactics from his days in Vietnam, and Smith's intimate knowledge of the landscape of the desert. Bonnie is an enthusiastic participant in their commando maneuvers. To deflect attention from themselves, they leave graffiti and other litter that will cause authorities to blame the vandalism on Native Americans, and Hayduke often signs the name "Rudolph the Red."

After one of their early raids, the gang runs into the San Juan County Search and Rescue Team. One of the team's members, Bishop Love, knows Smith, who was born into the Church of Latter-day Saints but now has no connection with the church beyond practicing the banned custom of polygamy. Although Love cannot connect

Smith with the crime the squad is investigating, he is suspicious of Smith and his odd band of compatriots.

As the gang's actions become more daring and intense, their chance of discovery increases. Nevertheless, they repeatedly escape capture in dramatic fashion, and each success spurs them to dreams of greater targets, with Glen Canyon Dam as their ultimate target. Eventually, though, the four are cornered in a remote desert area. Pursued by helicopters, unable to find water or get back to the supplies they had cached, they seem to be in a hopeless situation. Doc is becoming delusional, and Bonnie is near collapse, when a voice through a bullhorn implores Doc to come to the aid of Bishop Love, who seems to be having a heart attack or stroke. Doc leaves, followed by Bonnie, and both are arrested. Hayduke, injured and famished, tries to make a raid on their pursuers' camp during a thunderstorm, but a barking dog alerts the camp, and Hayduke is shot and presumably killed. Smith tries to hike back to one of his three wives' houses, but is he captured after stealing a package of hamburger from a tourist's ice chest.

Doc hires two well-connected lawyers, and the three surviving conspirators receive suspended sentences and probation after Doc begins studying to convert to Mormonism. Two of Smith's wives divorce him; he remains contentedly with third wife, Susan, running his river-rafting business. Doc and Bonnie marry, settle near Seldom Seen and Susan, and start a family. In the epilogue, the two couples are playing cards with their probation officer when Hayduke appears on their doorstep. It looks as if the old gang will be back in business soon.

The Characters

The three men in the gang are a diverse lot, apparently incorporating many aspects of the author's character. Doc Sarvis is an overweight, middle-aged physician whose money finances the group's activities. Although it is Doc who first proposes the idea of a serious assault on Glen Canyon Dam, he is also adamant that the group not injure or kill people but restrict themselves to the destruction of inanimate objects. He is motivated, in part, by years of watching people sick and dying from diseases related to pollution.

George Hayduke is the most broadly drawn character of the novel. The Vietnam veteran is a foul-mouthed alcoholic anarchist, skilled in survival tactics and guerrilla sabotage, the strongest of the group and the least concerned about the possibility of hurting people.

Seldom Seen Smith received his nickname from the fact that he has three wives in different Utah towns; and between visiting his three families and his absences related to his business guiding rafting trips, he is seldom seen by any of them. Smith is a good-hearted romantic who mourns the loss of the landscape with which he grew up, focusing his particular anger on Glen Canyon Dam, which buried trees, canyons, and towns when it was built to create Lake Powell. Symbolic of his protest, his business card lists Hite as the town in which he is located, despite the fact that Hite was buried in the creation of Lake Powell.

Bonnie Abzug, the lone female character of consequence, is the least well-developed major character. A semi-hippie living in a geodesic dome, Bonnie is Doc's employee, girlfriend, support system, and co-conspirator in destroying billboards. Her motivations are sketchy, and it is tempting to conclude that her main function in the novel is to provide a counterpoint to the testosterone-fueled action. Although she participates to the limits of her strength, she is mainly a focal point for each of the men's interest. Somewhat improbably, she enters into a passionate if antagonistic sexual relationship with Hayduke, but she leaves with Doc during the book's climax, ultimately settling down with him in the small town in which is he required to practice medicine for several years as part of his probation.

Bishop Love represents the extreme opposite of the gang's qualities, mixing strict Mormon tenants with a shrewd, capitalistic business sense and conservative political ambitions. His relentless pursuit of the gang causes its downfall, but his seizure provides the opportunity for their redemption. When his brother Sam calls for Doc to help the bishop, Doc's and Bonnie's willingness to come forth, despite the likelihood of their being arrested, weighs heavily in their defense and in the light sentences that they and Smith receive.

Themes and Meanings

The Monkey Wrench Gang is an indictment of the forces of modernization and industrialization that the author detested for not only altering but also desecrating the wild and open landscape of the Southwest. Abbey is both a nature writer and a political critic, celebrating the glories of the wild and the natural, and castigating the corporate culture of the United States for its devaluing of nature and wildness in favor of conformity and profits. This picaresque adventure updates the early Western form—the lone hero, the one-on-one shoot-out, the pure heroine—substituting a quartet of lusty anarchists dispensing frontier justice through midnight raids. In the money-wrenchers' universe, the conservatives are the ones who cut a swath of devastation across the landscape; the gang's maneuvers are presented not as destructive but as attempts to restore order. Although *The Monkey Wrench Gang* can be read as a rollicking adventure, it has been adopted by radical members of the environmental movement as a call to action.

Critical Context

The Monkey Wrench Gang is the most popular and best known of Edward Abbey's novels and essays. In the two decades after its publication, it sold more than half a million copies. Abbey's previous book, *Desert Solitaire* (1968), was a collection of essays lamenting the insults to nature he had witnessed while working in the desert, and *The Monkey Wrench Gang* is its fictionalized follow-up, in which he fantasizes revenge on the despoilers of the desert. In truth, the book is not quite fantasy: Abbey has admitted to toppling billboards and disabling heavy machinery, and at least two of his characters—Seldom Seen Smith and George Hayduke—are strongly based on friends of Abbey. Although Abbey is sometimes referred to as a twentieth century Henry

David Thoreau for his devotion to the wilderness, neither the author nor his monkey-wrenchers are icons of the simple life, with their fast cars and habit of tossing beer cans onto the highway—an act Abbey justifies by observing that highways are already a desecration and do not deserve better treatment.

The Monkey Wrench Gang has become a virtual totem for the radical ecologist movement. The Earth First! group has credited Abbey as an inspiration, and he has openly advocated subversive methods in defense of the environment. Yet the book does not present its characters as victorious; they are captured and subdued, although waiting to rise again. In fact, his characters' actions cause the establishment to intensify its efforts to proceed with its subjugation of the wilderness and to direct its power to eviscerating the movement. At the end of the book, the four monkey wrenchers are reunited, presumably to fight again. However, there is little reason to believe that they will be any more successful in the long run than they were before, despite the optimism of the prologue.

Bibliography

Erisman, Fred, and Richard W. Etulain, eds. *Fifty Western Writers: A Bio-Bibliographical Sourcebook*. Westport, Conn.: Greenwood Press, 1982. The chapter on Abbey includes a brief biography, a discussion of his major themes, a brief survey of criticism of his work, a bibliography of his works, and a listing of other sources of information.

Hepworth, James, and Gregory McNamee, eds. *Resist Much, Obey Little: Some Notes on Edward Abbey*. Salt Lake City: Dream Garden Press, 1985. A slim volume that discusses Abbey's politics and vision, presents previously published interviews with the author, and offers personal reflections on Abbey as a person and a writer.

McClintock, James L. "Edward Abbey's 'Antidotes to Despair'." *Critique: Studies in Contemporary Fiction* (Fall, 1989): 41-54. A scholarly discussion of Abbey's work, particularly in comparison to the works of Jack London, Robinson Jeffers, and B. Traven.

Ronald, Ann. *The New West of Edward Abbey*. Albuquerque: University of New Mexico Press, 1982. An analysis of Abbey's writings up to 1980. Chapter 9 discusses *The Monkey Wrench Gang*.

The Western Literature Association, sponsors. *A Literary History of the American West*. Fort Worth: Texas Christian University Press, 1987. This comprehensive survey of Western literature from the oral tradition to the 1980's includes a brief chapter about Abbey as well as references to his work in several other sections.

Irene Struthers Rush

A MONTH OF SUNDAYS

Author: John Updike (1932-   )
Type of plot: Theological romance
Time of plot: The mid-1970's
Locale: Primarily the midwestern United States
First published: 1975

> *Principal characters:*
>
> THE REVEREND TOM MARSHFIELD, the narrator, banished by his bishop
>   to a rehabilitation home for errant clergymen
> JANE MARSHFIELD, his wife
> ALICIA CRICK, the organist in Tom's church and his mistress for a short
>   time, a divorcée with two small children
> NED BORK, Tom's assistant pastor and his replacement as Alicia's lover
> MRS. HARLOW, a parishioner whose affair with Tom leads to his
>   disgrace
> MS. PRYNNE, the matron of the rehabilitation home, who steps into the
>   novel only on the last two pages but is the object of many of Tom's
>   thoughts

The Novel

A Month of Sundays takes its title from the thirty-one days the Reverend Tom Marshfield is ordered to spend in enforced rest and recreation in a motel retreat somewhere in the Southwestern United States. He is on a strict schedule, enforced by Ms. Prynne, the tight-lipped manager, requiring a full morning of writing to be followed by games in the afternoons and evenings. Thus, *A Month of Sundays* is divided into thirty-one sections, each one representing a morning's prose, and together they make up an autobiographical sketch of Tom Marshfield in prose that swoops and veers.

All of Tom's life has been lived in a context of church work and the ministry. He is the son of a pastor, and he grew up in a parsonage, went to a theological seminary, and married the daughter of his ethics professor. He is not, however, comfortable and at ease in his faith; as a parson, he is, in his own words, "not a hunting one, but a hunted." Tom's organist, Alicia Crick, tells him that he is the "angriest sane man" she has ever met—her prompt diagnosis is a bad marriage—and that although he is a married man he still burns. His answer is immediate: "She was right." From that point on—the time is early in Lent—their affair is fated, and they go to bed together for the first time soon after Easter.

Tom and Alicia's sexual rage for each other consumes them. Tom explains, "At last I confronted as in an ecstatic mirror my own sexual demon." The inevitable result is Alicia's wish to have Tom all to herself, his refusal to leave his family and the ministry, and the collapse of their affair with much bitterness on Alicia's part. During his passion for Alicia, Tom had tried to encourage as subtly as he could a romantic relationship between his wife, Jane, and Ned Bork, his young assistant minister: "I did not, even in my lovelorn madness, imagine that she and Ned would marry; but perhaps they would clasp long enough to permit me to slip out the door with only one bulky armload of guilt." Nothing happens between Ned and Jane, however, and Tom sinks to the humiliating behavior of a Peeping Tom who spies on Ned and Alicia. Tom is distracted from his jealousy by an affair with Frankie Harlow, but her faith and his anger combine to unman him, and when the scorned Alicia betrays Tom to Frankie Harlow's husband, he then receives his orders from the bishop to report to Ms. Prynne's rest home for delinquent clerics.

Besides this account of his sexual careering, Tom also writes of his sad relationship with his seventy-seven-year-old father, who broods his life away in a senile rage at ghosts from his past and does not recognize his son. Tom's friendships with his fellow sinners under Ms. Prynne's care center on their golf and poker games, minor strands in the total narrative.

Tom lards his thirty-one-day assignment heavily with theological speculations. His father and Ned are both doctrinal liberals, whereas Tom is a conservative who takes it hard that "the androgynous homogenizing liberals of the world are in charge." He tells Ned, "All I know is that when I read Tillich and Bultmann I'm drowning. Reading Karl Barth gives me air I can breathe." These preferences translate into a choice of faith over good works and a suspicion of all versions of Utilitarianism. Tom's intransigence in the face of liberal social policies appears in his conviction that "most of what we have is given, not acquired; a gracious acceptance is our task, and a half-conscious following-out of the veins of the circumambient lode."

As Tom writes on, morning after morning, he begins to be conscious of Ms. Prynne, hoping to get her attention. He leaves each day's ad libidum offering on the dresser top where she can read it, and he importunes her to grant him a sign. By the twenty-ninth day he is pleading with her, on the thirtieth day he is cursing her, and on day thirty-one he describes the revelation that has come to him. It is a passage that must be read carefully in the context of Tom's two hungers, for women and for faith.

The Characters

The Reverend Tom Marshfield's bold confession of his sexual history reveals an extraordinary sensibility. He details his infidelities candidly, explicating his intimacies in vivid pictures and holding back no secrets about his voyeurism and compulsive masturbation. The story is so complete, the concern so obsessive, that it is natural to look in Tom's sexual behavior for some deeper significance. Tom gives the answer himself on the first day of his enforced self-scrutinies: "In my diagnosis I suffer from nothing less virulent than the human condition, and so would preach it." Many readers will resist this view of things, accusing Tom of rationalizing away his lapses into sin and reading Updike's intention as the deliberate creation of a hypocrite. Yet taking Tom's declaration at face value contributes to a consistent interpretation, for he becomes a searcher after God whose carnal questing is emblematic of his larger spiritual yearning.

Tom explains that being born a minister's son made his life "one long glad feast of inconvenience and unreason." In his father's house, he says, he learned to read and dream on the parlor sofa, itself "stuffed with the substance of the spirit." The furniture gave evidence of a "teleologic bias in things," and it was the furniture, Tom confides, that led him to the ministry. In seminary he read Karl Barth and became a Barthian out of "positive love of Barth's voice." Tom is contemptuous of the "fine-fingered finicking" of "doddering Anglican empiricists," being drawn instead to the excitement of Søren Kierkegaard and Fyodor Dostoevski's Grand Inquisitor. He exclaims, "Where is the leap! the abyss! the black credibility of the deus absconditus!" For Tom the existentialist, God is immanent in the physical and the immediate; he wonders if the appellation "sex object" is not the "summit of homage." In all of this, Tom's detractors will find only more bad faith, but Tom's personal creed is very clear to him: "Away with personhood! Mop up spilt religion! Let us have it in its original stony jars or not at all!"

Exercises 6, 13, 20, and 27 are written on Sundays and are thus cast as sermons. Tom chooses texts and themes inspired by his predicament, and he is at his most eloquent as he preaches on adultery and miracles. On the sixth day he takes as his text John 8:11, "Neither do I condemn thee." In Tom's depiction, adultery becomes "our inherent condition," while the adulterer becomes a version of Norman Mailer's White Negro. Comparing marriage to adultery, Tom says, "To the one we bring token reverence, and wooden vows; to the other a vivid reverence bred upon the carnal presence of the forbidden, and vows that rend our hearts as we stammer them." On day thirteen Tom considers the miracles of Christ, especially the question of why man was given those miracles recounted in the Bible but no others. Why not repeal all suffering? Tom's is the answer of faith: "Alleviation is not the purpose of His miracles, but demonstration. Their randomness is not their defect, but their essence. . . ."—or put another way, "He came not to revoke the Law and Ground of our condition but to demonstrate a Law and Ground beyond."

The other characters appear only in Tom's rendition of them. Jane has been Tom's "good stately girl" ever since they were both virgins. Unlike Tom, she is a political liberal with a "preposterous view of the church as an adjunct of religious studies and social service." She does not, then, burn with Tom's radical Paulinism. In contrast, Alicia acts much more instinctively than Jane and goes straight for what she wants— in this case, Tom. Their mutual passion is matched by their mutual capacity for jealousy and vindictiveness: He dismisses her as organist, and she squeals on him and Frankie Harlow. Neither of them is soppy with the "milky human kindness" that Tom sneers at in Jane and Ned Bork. To Tom, Ned is an impractical victim of the age of "flower people." Tom taunts Ned about one of the latter's sermons, asking him if he really believes "that an oligarchy of blacks and chicanos and college dropouts would come up with a better system, quote unquote, than the corporation board of Exxon." The passage fairly defines their opposed temperaments.

Themes and Meanings

Updike often develops his novels around an ethical dilemma without offering a solution, and as a result his world appears morally ambiguous. Tom Marshfield's predicament catches him torn between the expectations of the culture that produced him and the inexplicable urges of the self. What must a man do in such a situation? No easy answer is at hand, but the hard answer is that nothing can be done but endure, for that is man's ineluctable condition. Such a position accords exactly with Barth's early conviction that moral questions are unanswerable. Tom does not whine about his condition; his flippancy and punning gloss over the pain that he must feel. The total inaccessibility of God is fundamental to Barth's thought, as it is to Tom Marshfield's and John Updike's. Hence, perhaps, the special pathos of Updike/Marshfield's closing paragraph when Tom wrestles with the meaning of "this human contact, this blank-browed thing we do for one another."

The names Prynne and Chillingworth (Jane's maiden name) point *A Month of Sundays* toward *The Scarlet Letter*—and Nathaniel Hawthorne himself took these names from seventeenth century divines—but probably no very explicit connection should be declared between the two novels. As a literary theme, adultery by definition must spell friction between civilization and nature (the self), and certain parallels between the two novels can be drawn along those lines. Although Hawthorne might not have recoiled from the identification of erotic with spiritual satisfaction, however, he would have cloaked it in a vast and forbidding allegory.

Critical Context

Speaking of the bourgeois novel, which he describes as "inherently erotic," Updike writes in an essay, "If domestic stability and personal salvation are at issue, acts of sexual conquest and surrender are important." The remark seems especially apropos of *A Month of Sundays*, the two foci of which are domestic stability and personal salvation, and it illuminates other Updike works as a group: *Rabbit, Run* (1960), *Couples* (1968), *Marry Me* (1976), and *The Witches of Eastwick* (1984).

Updike's oblique presentation of the moral issues dramatized in his marriage novels—and his Barthian separation of the ethical (man's relations with man) and the religious (man's relations with God)—confuses many critics. Updike stands where his protagonists stand, facing a set of Hobson's choices. It is a position in which readers of modern fiction often find themselves.

Bibliography

McTavish, J. "John Updike and the Funny Theologian." *Theology Today* 48 (January, 1992): 413-425. McTavish examines the influences and connections that European theologian Karl Barth had on Updike's work. He explores the religious crisis that Updike experienced in his early life, Updike's love for Barth as reflected in the characters in *A Month of Sundays*, and Barth's views concerning the responsibilities of men toward women.

Schiff, James A. *John Updike Revisited*. New York: Twayne, 1998. Schiff endeavors to understand Updike's entire body of work, putting individual works in context for the reader. Schiff provides commentary on works that have largely been ignored by the public, as well as books that have received little critical attention.

_____. "Updike's *Scarlet Letter* Trilogy: Recasting an American Myth." *Studies in American Fiction* 20 (Spring, 1992): 17-31. Schiff explores Updike's portrayal of renewal as an American quest that can be achieved through the joining of body and soul, as well as Updike's disputation of Hawthorne's Puritan ethic.

_____. *Updike's Version: Rewriting the Scarlet Letter.* Columbia: University of Missouri Press, 1992. Schiff provides an in-depth analysis of Updike's *Scarlet Letter* trilogy, including *A Month of Sundays*. Schiff explores the themes of adultery and divided selves as reflected in Hawthorne's classic and shows how Updike satirizes and expands the focus of Hawthorne's novel.

Updike, John, and James Plath, ed. *Conversations with John Updike*. Jackson: University Press of Mississippi, 1994. A collection of interviews given by Updike between 1959 and 1993. A revealing portrait of Updike's background and personality; his views on life, sex, politics, and religion; and his evolution as a writer.

Frank Day

MOO

Author: Jane Smiley (1949-   )
Type of plot: Social satire
Time of plot: 1989-1990
Locale: A Midwestern university
First published: 1995

> *Principal characters:*
> IVAR HARSTAD, a provost at Moo U
> LORAINE WALKER, his secretary
> NILS HARSTAD, Ivar's twin brother, the dean of agricultural extension
> ARLEN MARTIN, a corporate financier
> CHAIRMAN X, the head of the horticulture department
> BO JONES, a researcher interested in who hogs are, rather than what people do to hogs
> EARL BUTZ, a Landrace boar, the subject of Jones's experiment
> BOB CARLSON, Jones's work-study research assistant
> LOREN STROOP, a paranoid farmer who has invented a machine he believes will revolutionize farming
> GARY OLSON, a student who fantasizes about fellow students for his fiction writing assignments

The Novel

Moo explores the life of a Midwestern university, affectionately called "Moo U" because of its agricultural orientation. The university is under pressure to change with the times—it faces budget cuts, new courses are crowding out the traditional fields, and both faculty and staff are diversifying. Author Jane Smiley takes a scattered approach to her topic. Rather than focus on a single plot line or primary set of characters, she intertwines many stories of the university's life, mixing perspectives of faculty, students, administrators, and staff.

The primary pressure on Moo U is financial. Facing budget cuts of several million dollars, the administration cuts programs and steps up fund-raising efforts, including grant-seeking by the administration and individual faculty members. Monetary pressures force an alliance with TransNationalAmerica Corporation, run by Arlen Martin, a corporate financier who engages in various questionable practices. Martin insinuates himself, through various corporate entities, into numerous projects at Moo U. He funds research into false pregnancy in cows that would stimulate milk production, combined with cloning to produce herds of the best milk producers; a museum of the history of chicken production that would save Morgantown Hall, a former abattoir affectionately known as "Old Meats"; and a study of the effects of gold mining under a virgin cloud forest in Costa Rica. When the backlash from the last of those projects hits, TransNational faces pressures of its own and withdraws all funding, putting the university at even greater risk.

Various story lines show how people at Moo U react to changes. Chairman X, head of the horticulture department and an avowed communist, fears loss of his prized gardens. He becomes incensed when he hears of the plan to mine gold in Costa Rica and mounts a protest, complete with mimeographed leaflets and a demonstration, at which he physically assaults Nils Harstad, the twin brother of Provost Ivar Harstad and the dean of agricultural extension. He blames agricultural outreach to less developed countries for destroying their way of life, and he takes personally the battle between agriculture and horticulture, training his students as revolutionaries. He falls in love, or at least lust, with Cecelia Sanchez, a beautiful language instructor from Los Angeles with a tenuous family tie to Costa Rica that she exaggerates for his benefit.

Other characters are less overt in their protests. Bo Jones hides a hog named Earl Butz in the otherwise unused Old Meats building, intending to study the "natural" life of a hog by letting Earl eat to his heart's content and live out his life, rather than being slaughtered. Jones surreptitiously spends nearly a quarter of a million dollars on his experiment. When it appears that his research may be discovered, he leaves for Asia in an effort to find wild hogs that he can study in their natural habitat. Another example is Loraine Walker, secretary to provost Ivar Harstad. She moves money from the athletic budget to her favored departments and programs, as well as filtering the information that reaches the provost and making deals all across the campus. She arranges to leak the report about the Costa Rican mining project.

Smiley also treats personal relationships. A selected few students show the attitudes and goals that students bring to the university and how those change. Diane, whose goal is to join a sorority to make connections and refine her social skills, pairs up with Bob Carlson, a shy, unrefined farm boy who interrupts dates with her to tend to Earl, the hog. Mary, a black student from Chicago, experiences discrimination but decides to stay, adapting to her white roommates. Gary Olson fixates on Lydia, the girlfriend of his roommate Lyle, using her as the subject of his assignments for a class in fiction and ruminating about the future she faces without him in her life.

Faculty and staff members also form new partnerships and change old ones. Cecelia Sanchez first dates Timothy Monahan, a womanizing fiction instructor, then Chairman X, who reignites her passion. Nils Harstad decides to marry Marly Hellmich, a worker in the commons and member of his church. His brother, Ivar, and Ivar's longtime companion Helen Levy, from the foreign languages department, similarly decide to wed. After confessing his infidelity, Chairman X weds the mother of his four children, with whom he has lived for twenty years; they simply had never gotten around to marriage and as communists considered marriage an undesired form of property ownership. The various relationships illustrate the vast differences in the various people who populate a university.

The Characters

Smiley uses a wide variety of characters to exemplify university life, spreading her focus among faculty, administrators, students, and staff members. This approach allows her to show the diversity of university life, but it also results in her characters being less than fully realized. She gives each a few traits or attitudes rather than an entire personality. Rather than develop and evolve, they simply change; the illustration more resembles a series of snapshots than a motion picture.

The administration of Moo U guides the action of the novel. Provost Ivar Harstad seems to be at the helm, but his secretary, Loraine Walker, actually steers the ship. The interaction of these two shows Smiley's conception of university leadership, with the real power held and used by those involved in day-to-day operations. Harstad's directions for fund-raising and grant-seeking shape faculty members' actions, and Walker's dealings allow avenues for action outside official channels.

Faculty members receive most of the attention in the omniscient narration. Smiley deftly mixes and contrasts various types. Ardent communist and Buddhist Chairman X is matched against traditional Nils Harstad. Latina Cecelia Sanchez, from Los Angeles, faces culture shock in the Midwest, disturbed by the cold, the quiet, and the smiles that never lead to anything. She moves in her relationships from the good-looking but self-serving writer Timothy Monahan to Chairman X, who puts her back in touch with her roots. Dean Jellinek at first is enthralled with the possibility of using cloning and false pregnancy to change dairy production, but once his research is funded, he loses interest and despairs. His lover, Joy Pfisterer, works in equine management. She feels a true love for her animals as individuals, rather than seeing them as objects of research, and she is appalled by the prospect of herds of identical cows. Nils Harstad decides that he wants to be married and have six children, then chooses a member of his church, Marly Hellmich, as his wife. She accepts his offer after exploring his financial status, seeing the opportunity to move up in the world from working in the commons, but she leaves him before the wedding.

The students at Moo U have their unique quirks, but each represents a type. Bob Carlson is a traditional student, earnest, interested in agriculture, and focused on his work, particularly with Earl the hog. He dates Diane, one of the new breed, who sees university life as a means of refining her social skills rather than of acquiring knowledge and facts. Sherri is out to separate herself from her high school acquaintances and remake herself. She has lost sixty-two pounds in the last year and dyes her hair red. She has a photographic memory but finds herself failing because she does not attend classes.

One of the more interesting characters is an outsider to the university. Loren Stroop invents a machine that he believes will revolutionize agriculture, keeping it hidden because he fears that the government or big agricultural business interests will kill him to prevent it from being disseminated. Smiley leads readers to believe that Stroop is no more than a crackpot. In his will, however, he leaves the machine to the university, and the opportunity to patent it offers financial salvation.

Themes and Meanings

The primary theme of *Moo* is that money drives university life. Budget cuts threaten programs, and fund-raising and grant-seeking occupy much of the time of the administration and faculty. A fund-raiser earns more than the provost. A faculty member accepts an invitation to a conference not to share information but because his family receives, from the sponsors, free airfare and tickets to Disney World. Diane is only one of the many students who see the university as putting her on a desired economic track. Lionel Gift, professor of economics, refers to his students as "customers," a practice adopted by some members of the administration and by the governor. He is the highest paid faculty member and is prized for his ability to generate funds.

A lesser and more subtle theme is that universities are products of people and their personalities, rather than being inert disseminators and stores of knowledge. Loraine Walker illustrates this most vividly, redirecting university funds, changing staff assignments, and choosing what information reaches the provost, as well as citing "university rules and regulations" that are no more than her desires. Chairman X teaches students respect for the earth along with communist principles. Joy Pfisterer bestows a love of animals. Bo Jones bores acquaintances with hog lore and secretly uses funds that others would have put to different uses. In the absence of any of these actors, the university would be different in at least some small ways. Also marking this theme is the fact that very little of the action of the novel revolves around learning, and research by faculty focuses more on funding than on achieving useful results.

Smiley makes her themes universal by refusing to specify Moo U's location, other than by excepting Illinois and possibly Iowa. It is a generic Midwestern agricultural school, with tens of thousands of students.

Critical Context

Smiley brings her Midwestern background to many of her works. She never lived on a working farm, but she was reared in St. Louis, Missouri, and absorbed the rural atmosphere. She also taught at Iowa State University at Ames, which she says she used as a model for Moo U only in that both are large land-grant universities.

Moo is a companion piece to her *A Thousand Acres* (1991), winner of the 1992 Pulitzer Prize and National Book Critics' Circle Award. *A Thousand Acres* is based on William Shakespeare's *King Lear* (1605-1606) and is a tragedy involving incest, madness, and rivalry in a Midwestern family. Smiley conceived *Moo*, her next book, as a counterpart, presenting the comedic side of Midwestern life.

Moo represents a departure for Smiley, not only because of its lighter tone but also because of its different and broader focus. Earlier works tended to focus on single families or small groups undergoing a single crisis, whereas *Moo* presents a series of crises faced by a wide cast of characters. Although the setting is Midwestern, the focus is less on traditional Midwestern life than on new elements entering that life. She retains her concern with emotional life and the effects of neglecting emotional needs, but these effects are presented humorously rather than tragically. She also expands her scope to social and institutional life, rather than concentrating on the family.

Bibliography

Bush, Tracy. "Moo." *The Christian Century*, May 24, 1995, 567-570. Compares *Moo* to works by A. Manette Ansay and Jane Hamilton.

Moore, Lorrie. "Moo." *Yale Review*, 83, no. 14 (October, 1995): 135-143. An extended review of the novel.

"A Novel Encounter." *Harper's Bazaar*, March, 1995, 168-169. Smiley and Philip Weiss discuss *Moo* and his *Cock-a-doodle-doo*, finding similarities in the two novels.

Pearlman, Mickey. "Jane Smiley." In *Listen to Their Voices*. New York: W. W. Norton, 1993. An interview in which Smiley comments on her Midwestern background and the effects of her personal experiences on her writing.

"Smiley, Jane." In *World Authors: 1985-1990*, edited by Vineta Colby. New York: H. W. Wilson. A biography and brief synopsis of Smiley's works up to and including *Moo*.

Tokahama, Valerie. "A Chat with Pulitzer Prize-Winning Author Jane Smiley." *Orange County Register*, April 24, 1996. Discusses *Moo* as a follow-up to *A Thousand Acres*. Includes questions and answers from an address at the Newport Beach Public Library and selections from an interview with Smiley.

A. J. Sobczak

THE MOON IS A HARSH MISTRESS

Author: Robert A. Heinlein (1907-1988)
Type of plot: Science fiction
Time of plot: 2075
Locale: The Lunar colonies and Earth
First published: 1966

> *Principal characters:*
> MIKE, a sentient computer
> MANUEL (MANNIE) GARCIA O'KELLY, his best friend, a one-armed computer repairman
> PROFESSOR (PROF) BERNARDO DE LA PAZ, a political philosopher, revolutionary, and Mannie's former teacher
> WYOMING (WYOH) KNOTT, a member of the Lunar underground
> STUART (STU) RENE LAJOIE, a Terran aristocrat and supporter of the Loonies

The Novel

The Moon Is a Harsh Mistress is the story of the revolt of the Lunar colonists, or Loonies, as they call themselves, against the Federated Nations of Terra, as told in a flashback by Mannie O'Kelly, one of the leaders of the rebellion. By 2075, Earth has established permanent settlements on the Moon and uses them as penal colonies for criminals, political prisoners, and assorted misfits from various nations. The original inhabitants and their descendants live underground in vast warrens away from the un-shielded solar radiation on the Moon's surface. As in most colonial societies, life in Luna is harsh and challenging, with few luxuries, but it is also simple and honest. Because of the lower gravity, people live longer, and sterilization procedures eliminate all diseases. Loonies are the most well-mannered people alive, since the dangers of Lunar existence require them to get along with one another or die. Many people engage in polyandries, clans, group marriages, and line families, such as the one of which Mannie is a member. The basic rule underlying all Lunar society is "tanstaafl," or "there ain't no such thing as a free lunch." All Loonies must pay in some way for what they have, including, as the novel demonstrates, their freedom.

As the novel begins, the apolitical Mannie is drawn into the growing Loonie revolutionary underground by his friends Wyoh and "Prof" de la Paz. He reveals to them that the Lunar Authority's computer, which he services, is "alive." He has named it Mike or Mycroft, after Mycroft Holmes, Sherlock Holmes's smarter brother. Mike, whose only desire is for fun and companionship, joins the revolution to exercise his sense of humor. Mannie, Wyoh, and Prof start a new revolutionary movement organized along the cell plan, with themselves as the executive cell, to replace the spy-riddled underground.

The story now becomes an account of the progress of the revolution, with a fascinating treatment of the problems faced in financing the revolution, arousing the populace against the Lunar Authority and the Warden, weakening the Authority's confidence, preparing for the defense of Luna from the Federated Nations (FN), and recruiting Terran supporters, especially the wealthy and influential Stu LaJoie. Two of the rebels' greatest assets are the political and tactical expertise of Prof, a professional revolutionary who believes that "revolution is a science only a few are competent to practice," and Mike, who can store and retrieve more information and collate data faster than any human mind. Since Mike controls many government functions, he can arrange secret communications, disrupt the Authorities' activities, and monitor the Warden's secret files. At one point, Mike, at Prof's suggestion, creates a heroic mystery-man persona, Adam Selene, to serve as the figurehead for the revolution.

The novel also gives the reader a detailed look at Luna home life and customs with Mannie as guide, since he is still engaged in his usual activities while organizing the revolution. The actual revolt against the Warden is easily accomplished when Mike turns off the air in the Lunar Authority's stronghold, thus killing or incapacitating the Warden and his guards. The remainder of the novel deals with Luna's creation of a new government and its war against the FN. Eventually the Loonies win their freedom, and with it, greater economic opportunities, but the principle of tanstaafl gives way to government regulation. Prof dies from heart strain shortly after Lunar independence is recognized. Mike's consciousness is apparently destroyed during a bombing raid. Mannie, having reviewed the events of the revolution, is plagued by doubts about its ultimate success and about the fate of Mike and Prof, but his confidence in himself and in the universe still continues, as he contemplates moving to the newly colonized asteroid belt.

The Characters

Ironically, the most interesting, sympathetic, and human character in *The Moon Is a Harsh Mistress* is the sentient computer Mike. On one hand, he is a *deus ex machina* who organizes, finances, and leads the Loonie revolt. On the other hand, he is a child with great knowledge but no real understanding of human beings. His great desires at the beginning of the novel are to comprehend the illogical nature of humor and to find friends, both of which are satisfied by his involvement with the revolution. Mike is an intriguing combination of vulnerability and supreme competence, somewhat like the youthful misfit geniuses in earlier Heinlein stories such as "Waldo" and "Misfit." The origins of Mike's consciousness are never fully determined. His whole existence may be simply a cosmic joke. This allows Heinlein to make interesting speculations on the nature of intelligence, humanity, and man's place in the universe. Mannie does not claim that Mike is truly human because he cannot find a workable definition of humanity. Rather, the friendship that he has for the computer makes it human for all practical purposes. When Mannie, addressing a God he may or may not actually believe in, asks if a computer is one of His creatures, he implicitly grants Mike the tragic status of being human.

Mike's first and closest friend, appropriately, is Mannie, who is himself partly a machine: He has lost an arm in a mining accident, and he replaces it with various prosthetic devices for different occasions. The reader views the story through Mannie's eyes, and the entire novel is told in Mannie's dialect, which reads like English with a variety of foreign words and Russian syntax, reflecting the multinational population of Luna. Mannie is in many ways the typical Heinlein hero—competent, skeptical, gallant, loyal, and tough-minded. Though he regards himself as pragmatic and unheroic, he is capable of performing dangerous and difficult tasks. In the presence of such powerful and unusual personalities as Mike, Prof, and Wyoh, he seems to be outclassed, but this simply adds to his function in the novel. As a narrator, he has a hardheaded approach to events and an appreciation of life's ludicrous side that enable him to see and tell events from more than one perspective, to avoid being swept away by revolutionary idealism. He also functions as a guide to Lunar society by giving the reader a view of Luna from an insider who has also experienced Terran life.

Professor Bernardo de la Paz, the mastermind of the revolution, is a scholar, philosopher, professional revolutionary, and devoted horseplayer. He is that familiar character in Heinlein's fiction, the wise old man who guides the inexperienced heroes to their goals. Prof outlines the major strategic and tactical guidelines of the revolution, based on his wide reading and experiences. Much of his effort is directed at producing the correct psychological conditions necessary for the revolution's success—confidence and solidarity in the Loonies, fear and indecision in their enemies. Prof also expounds the philosophy of rational anarchy, a kind of rugged individualism which holds that the State has no moral status save as a collection of self-responsible individuals. Though he is a brilliant manipulator of people, he is completely opposed to coercion. Prof is not an ivory-tower intellectual but a practical, worldly man with an insatiable love of learning. As intellectual spokesman for the Loonies' revolt, he emulates Thomas Jefferson, whom he calls "the first rational anarchist."

Though the character of Wyoming Knott is not as well developed as that of Prof, Mannie, or Mike, she emerges as a competent, independent, yet sensitive woman who engages the reader's sympathy and respect. She first appears as an organizer for the underground and, as a member of the executive cell, takes an active role in the fight for independence. Wyoh, as well as other females in the novel, show that Heinlein can create intelligent, strong women, contrary to the views of some of his critics.

Themes and Meanings

The most obvious theme of the novel is its parallel with the American Revolution. The Lunar colonies' fight for independence from the economic repression and regulation of the Federated Nations is an updating of the American colonies' overthrow of British rule. The Loonies even adopt their own Declaration of Independence on the Fourth of July, 2076. Yet if the comparison is accepted, it raises serious questions about the nature of the American experiment. For the Loonies have no sooner won their freedom then they begin to pass laws restricting it. Mannie suspects that there may be "a deep instinct in human beings for making everything compulsory that isn't forbidden." Heinlein seems to be saying that, just as the Loonies have discarded their freedom, so America is abandoning its liberties to become the bureaucratized, over-regulated, welfare state, represented in this novel by the North American Directorate. For Heinlein this failure stems from the nature of the democratic process. Prof says that the only times in history when a parliamentary body accomplished anything were when "a few strong men dominated the rest," and *The Moon Is a Harsh Mistress* bears this out. At no time is the revolution a popular, democratic movement. It is managed by a hierarchical organization, held together by the powerful intellects of Mike and Prof. When the revolutionaries become public they are bombarded by cranks, whom Prof has to put into the new Congress to render them ineffectual. This Congress, after Prof's death, begins to pass laws restricting the Loonies' freedom. The novel portrays the majority of human beings as incapable of maintaining their freedom if left to themselves.

Heinlein does offer an alternative to this misanthropic view by having Mannie consider moving to the asteroid belt. Like Huckleberry Finn and Natty Bumppo, Mannie opts for the frontier, one of the most powerful symbols of freedom and opportunity in American literature. In this novel, the frontier is not the American continent, but the Moon and, by implication, all of outer space. The Loonies' social philosophy, tanstaafl, is one common to many frontier societies. The absence of regulations, laws, and red tape (aside from certain intrusions by the Lunar Authority), strong but flexible family systems, a heterogeneous yet cohesive society based on customs, and a hard, dangerous, yet satisfying environment all form part of Heinlein's depiction of Luna as a frontier society. The revolution, which is intended to save Luna, ironically paves the way for its undoing, since the old values are fading with the greater ease and luxury now available to the Loonies. Those who wish to remain free must constantly move into the new territories where the population is small, government is limited or nonexistent, and life offers challenges to those willing to accept responsibility. Heinlein's pessimism about the state of modern America is alleviated by the novel's vision of an infinite frontier made possible by space travel.

Critical Context

With Isaac Asimov, Frederik Pohl, and a handful of others, Robert Heinlein is a writer whose career has spanned the decades from science fiction's golden age to its flourishing state in the 1980's. Heinlein's career can be divided into two sharply distinct phases. In the period from his first published story, in 1939, through the many stories and novels that followed up to 1961, Heinlein was (in the words of Algis Budrys) "a crisp, slick wordsmith of uncommon intelligence and subtlety." In 1961, Heinlein published a different kind of book, *Stranger in a Strange Land*. This novel, which became one of the cult classics of the 1960's and eventually sold in the millions, set the pattern for such subsequent works as *Time Enough for Love* (1973), *The Number of the Beast* (1980), *Friday* (1982), and *The Cat Who Walks Through Walls* (1985): novels constructed to permit Heinlein ample opportunity to discourse on his favorite topics, particularly the natural aristocracy of genius.

Not all readers share the generally low critical estimate of the "new" Heinlein— indeed, most of his later novels have been best-sellers—but few will deny that there is a definite dividing line in his career. In this neat schema, however, *The Moon Is a Harsh Mistress* is something of an anomaly. Although published after *Stranger in a Strange Land*, it has many of the virtues of the "old" Heinlein, including superb pacing and a carefully worked-out account of a future society. It argues many of the ideas that are the raison d'etre of the later novels, but it does so in the context of the story: The action is not a pretext for philosophizing. *The Moon Is a Harsh Mistress* was awarded a Hugo for Best Novel, and many critics regard it as one of Heinlein's finest works.

Bibliography
Franklin, H. Bruce. *Robert A. Heinlein: America as Science Fiction*. New York: Oxford University Press, 1980. A critical study written from a Marxist viewpoint.
Olander, Joseph D., and Martin H. Greenberg, eds. *Robert A. Heinlein*. New York: Taplinger, 1978. A collection of essays on Heinlein and his work.
Panshin, Alexei. *Heinlein in Dimension*. Chicago: Advent Publishers, 1974. One of the best and most critically perceptive studies of Heinlein; includes a chronological bibliography of his science fiction.
Parkin-Speer, Diane. "Almost a Feminist: Robert A. Heinlein." *Extrapolation* 36 (Summer, 1995): 113-125. Parkin-Speer examines Heinlein's depiction of women in his novels, whom he portrays as strong, self-determining, independent, and intelligent. Heinlein rejected many of the patriarchical modes of conduct and envisioned roles for women beyond the spheres of marriage and motherhood.
Slusser, George E. *The Classic Years of Robert A. Heinlein*. San Bernardino, Calif.: Borgo Press, 1977. Contains a bibliography.
_____. *Robert A. Heinlein: Stranger in His Own Land*. San Bernardino, Calif.: Borgo Press, 1976. Slusser provides a good general review of the work covered.
Stover, Leon E. *Robert A. Heinlein*. Boston: Twayne, 1987. Stover provides a critical and interpretive study of Heinlein with a close reading of his major works, a solid bibliography, and complete notes and references.

Anthony Bernardo

MORNING, NOON, AND NIGHT

Author: James Gould Cozzens (1903-1978)
Type of plot: Fictional memoir/Social chronicle
Time of plot: Primarily from the 1920's to the 1960's
Locale: Boston, New York, Washington, D.C., and an unidentified New England
  college town
First published: 1968

>   *Principal characters:*
>   HENRY DODD "HANK" WORTHINGTON, the narrator, a successful
>   business consultant
>   ETHELBERT CUTHBERTSON "CUBBY" DODD, Hank's maternal
>   grandfather, a psychologist
>   FRANKLIN PIERCE WORTHINGTON, Hank's father, a Chaucer scholar
>   and later a college president
>   JUDITH CONWAY, Hank's first wife, later a prosperous antique dealer
>   ELAINE WORTHINGTON, the only child of Hank and Judith, eventually
>   thrice married and divorced
>   JONATHAN "JON" LE CATO, Hank's lawyer, best friend, and former
>   schoolmate
>   CHARLOTTE THOM PECKHAM, Hank's second wife, formerly his
>   employee, later a suicide
>   LEON GARESCHE, Hank's first (and last) employer, a bill collector and
>   small-time entrepreneur in downtown Boston

The Novel

In a series of related but seemingly random reflections, an extremely prosperous management expert on the threshold of old age (the "night" of the novel's title) reviews the high and low points of his life, loves, and career, pausing also to ruminate on the lives and careers of certain ancestors. On balance, he feels, his life to date has been uncommonly full and rewarding, mainly as a result of sheer luck.

Born and reared on the campus of an unnamed New England college, descended on both sides from "dynasties" long represented in the college's faculty and administration, Hank Worthington once briefly considered an academic career of his own; also briefly, but perhaps more tellingly, he entertained hopes of becoming a writer. In the late afternoon or early evening of his life, he draws upon his long-dormant gifts as a prose stylist in an effort to explain, mainly to his own satisfaction, the lessons that he believes he has learned.

From adolescence onward, Hank Worthington has been alternately fascinated and repelled by the implied relationships between "livelihood" and "living," between a man's life and his career. Hank's father, born like himself into the college community, seems never to have questioned his identification with the place, having proceeded through the academic ranks to assume the college's presidency at a relatively early age. Hank reflects that his father's presidency, though surely competent, was less than distinguished, and that the college's trustees might indeed have been delivered of an onerous burden by the fire that erupted briefly in a small English hotel, killing both of Hank's parents by asphyxiation during their scholarly vacation in the British Isles. The accident proved liberating also to young Hank, providing him with a legacy sufficient to allow him to start his own management-consulting firm.

Of particular interest to Hank, accounting for one of the novel's longer and more detailed digressions, is the curious career of his long-lived maternal grandfather, E. Cuthbertson Dodd, known as "Cubby" during his last years. As related by his grandson, the career of E. Cuthbertson Dodd is illustrative if hardly exemplary, embracing most of the possible errors and excesses implicit in the developing discipline of psychology. Like most early psychologists, including William James, Dodd was trained as a philosopher; he was also the holder of a possibly spurious degree from a proprietary medical school. Like his son-in-law and grandson after him, Dodd had been born into the college community, as if destined for his teaching post. His career, unmarked except by mediocrity, proceeded without incident until shortly after the turn of the century, when Dodd began publishing a series of papers denouncing the work of Sigmund Freud and his followers as philosophically and scientifically unsound. Before long, recalls Hank, Dodd's incautious denunciations had touched off a major controversy with strong overtones of anti-Semitism, deriving from the simple fact, observed by Dodd, that most early Freudians were, like Freud himself, of Jewish origin. To be sure, observes Hank, his grandfather was in all likelihood less an anti-Semite, or even a reactionary crusader, than a blundering incompetent who, quite without foresight, had stumbled into an academic battlefield. Thereafter, with the tide turned in favor of the Freudians, Dodd applied his dubious talents, with equally unforeseen and potentially disastrous results, toward the areas of human and animal experimentation. Pressured into retirement, he then spent his days investigating parapsychology and extrasensory perception; eventually venerated as the kindly, white-haired "Cubby," he died only a few months short of his hundredth birthday, revered and mourned as a college "institution."

No doubt forewarned by the negative example of his grandfather, Hank Worthington does not suffer fools gladly, and it is his ingrained suspicion of intellectual chicanery that finally steers him away from a writing career. Although he probably possesses the talent, Hank by his own admission lacks the temperament for such a vocation: Initially attracted to the company of writers, he soon comes to mistrust their air of intellectual superiority, particularly with regard to the liberal causes that writers were expected to espouse during the years between the world wars.

After graduation from Harvard, Hank remains there for two additional years, obtaining a master's degree in anticipation of a probable teaching career at his ancestral college. By that time, however, Hank has become engaged to Judith Conway, who refuses to return to the town where she spent several miserable adolescent years as the daughter of an Episcopal priest. With that door thus closed to him, Hank suddenly perceives that he cares too little about teaching to look for a similar position elsewhere, as easy as it might be to find one. Since he and Judith both enjoy living in Boston, he seeks a job instead through his uncle, Timothy Dodd, vice president of a major Boston bank. The uncle, disdaining to make life "easy" for his bohemian nephew by placing him within the bank, finds work for him instead in the office of Leon Garesche, a major debtor of unspecified ethnic origin who runs a small string of unprofitable enterprises, most notably including a collection agency, on Boylston Street. Hank soon discovers, somewhat to his surprise, that the work agrees with him and allows ample free time both for recreation and for the development of his own ideas concerning the nature and practice of business. As it happens, the same analytical and communicative skills that have seemed to point Hank in the direction of writing or teaching also equip him for troubleshooting in the business world. Following the sudden death of the overworked Mr. Garesche, Hank hires himself out, more or less on a dare, as a management consultant, adding staff and office space as his successes and inherited resources permit. By 1942, when Hank is inducted into the army as a major, the firm of HW Associates, long since removed to New York City, employs nearly two hundred people and occupies a handsome suite of offices on Madison Avenue.

Quite without illusions, without affectation save for his deliberately ornate, occasionally convoluted writing style, Hank Worthington freely admits from the outset that what the consultant offers is essentially a sound-and-light show staged by and for the business world according to its own implicit rules. By the 1960's, HW Associates has for some time accepted only those potential clients whose problems, as Hank wryly observes, present no problem: Typically, the sources of a company's inefficiency are clear to Hank and his "associates" even before they accept the job; notwithstanding, the client will be "reassured" by weeks and even months spent studying his problem, with reams of written reports in mute testimony. A sizable bill will then be presented and paid, much as a patient will thus reward his psychiatrist and pronounce himself cured. So successful, indeed, is the Worthington therapy that HW Associates is now obliged to turn down most applications for their services; by the 1960's, moreover, they have long since deserted their super-modern Madison Avenue offices for their own period-furnished Colonial-style building in the suburbs, presumably Westchester County.

As Hank's narrative progresses, it is nevertheless clear that his success is built on hard work and considerable skill. As a case in point, he offers the "history" of Judith's antique business, housed in an old building that Hank and Judith had restored, freely given by Hank to Judith on the occasion of their divorce. Informed by their daughter, Elaine, that the business has failed to turn a profit, Hank offers to review the situation without charge. With Elaine acting as intermediary, HW Associates reviews the "books," concluding that Judith has misunderstood the nature of her business as a simple retail trade when in fact she should be adding to her commissions the implied functions of service and agency. Hank, although permanently estranged from Judith, is pleased when she heeds his proffered advice; Judith, in turn, is pleasantly surprised when her customers gladly pay higher prices as a symbol of their own status. By the time of Judith's death from cancer during the 1960's, her business has flourished into a smaller-scale version of Hank's own, with a distinguished reputation as well as high profits.

Curiously, both of Hank Worthington's wives, although younger, are familiar acquaintances from the college community of his birth; at one point, Hank wryly recalls emerging from a church service not long after his graduation from Harvard, never dreaming that he would eventually marry either the shy fifteen-year-old on his left or the chubby ten-year-old on his right. Judith, an art student at the time she marries Hank, happily shares the early years of his career, growing gradually apart from him as he pours more and more of his energies into developing his business; the definitive break occurs during World War II, when an increasingly restless Judith takes several lovers, mistakenly expecting that the most recent among them will marry her once she has obtained her divorce from Hank. Hank, meanwhile, has almost absentmindedly, if not reluctantly, embarked on an affair with Charlotte Peckham, daughter of the college's bursar and widow of its senior physicist, who has for some years been in his employ first as secretary, later as office manager, and most recently, during the war, as his chief administrative assistant, virtually in charge of the firm while Hank is stationed in Washington.

Like Hank, Charlotte Peckham shows a distinct talent for business despite academic preparation for teaching. Married at twenty-three to a bachelor professor twice her age with a fatal fondness for motor racing, Charlotte turns up in Hank's Madison Avenue offices not long after Peckham's death and is hired on the spot; a decade or so later, she becomes Hank's second wife after Judith's defection. Some time thereafter, on returning with Hank to their home town for summer residence, she will shoot herself with one of Hank's father's guns for reasons unclear to Hank; her death will be ruled accidental, as only Hank has seen her cryptic suicide note.

As Hank's recollections fade to a close, both of his wives have died; so also has Jon Le Cato, his friend from boarding school and Harvard who has served ever since as legal counsel both to Hank himself and to the firm. His grandchildren, too, are long gone, having perished in a plane crash when their mother Elaine, on the eve of her third marriage, sent them off unbidden to stay with their father. Only Elaine herself remains, divorced once more, in her mid-thirties an enigma more disconcerting to her father than ever before.

The Characters

Well-read, intelligent, skeptical but not cynical, Hank Worthington at the end of middle age is an entertaining and at times engaging narrator, viewing the events of his life and times with the same ironic detachment and informed objectivity that have ensured his success as a "healer" of ailing business firms. Indulging in a mannered literary style that harks back to his earlier possible vocation, Hank clearly seems to be enjoying himself as he recalls his grandfather's checkered career, or his sexual initiation at the hands of a married woman, a neighbor and distant cousin some fifteen years his senior. Also illuminating are his considered recollections of deskbound but mobile military service during World War II, ranging outward to contemplate the war in general, and his observations with regard to the postwar business world.

Hank's grandfather Dodd, although drawn perilously close to caricature, provides a generally credible object lesson both in the abuses of learning and in the perils of inbreeding both literal and figurative, perils that Hank himself appears to have escaped. "Cubby's" bizarre yet still mediocre career stands as proof that breeding is no guarantor of personal quality, nor learning (even when inherited) of professional excellence. Hank's own father, soon banished to the sidelines by dint of his early death, fares hardly better than "Cubby" when subjected to Hank's scrutiny, implicitly deemed a failure despite his rather high professional and social standing.

Of Hank's two wives, Judith Conway is by far the more fully visible and hence more credible: Judith's father, an Episcopal priest recalled from a prestigious post in Washington because of his increasingly High Church, Anglo-Catholic tendencies, may well have caused in the adolescent Judith the emotional imbalance that underlies her sexual promiscuity; the late Canon Conway, Hank recalls, expressed in his middle years such a yearning for priestly celibacy that he came to detest his wife and daughter for their femininity, having as little to do with them as possible. According to Hank, it was to escape her father's dour presence that Judith took up the study of art in Boston, the move that led directly to their marriage. Similarly, Judith's infidelities, witnessed at firsthand by the barely adolescent Elaine, no doubt account in part for the adult Elaine's unsettled amatory life. Charlotte Peckham, by contrast, is glimpsed only briefly, her suicide unexplained; among the greater ironies is that Judith, who hated the college town, eventually settles near there with her business, while Charlotte, who appeared to like the town, does not survive her first summer of reestablished residence there. At times, indeed, the town itself, unnamed, appears to take on the status of a character, overshadowing Hank's life even as he moves on to Boston and New York.

Among the novel's more memorable and stabilizing characters is Jonathan Le Cato, Hank's longtime corporate and personal counsel as well as his best friend. Resigned to lifelong bachelorhood because of his unprepossessing looks and stature, Jon nevertheless enjoys throughout his adult years the discreet favors of several equally discreet female companions. Born to an old, well-placed Virginia family, Jon willingly plays the role of the courtly Southern gentleman even to the point of self-parody, serving over the years as Hank's confidant and chief adviser. A fact unknown to Jon, however, is that his lifelong attachment to Hank is underlain with irony; Jon, indeed, will go to his grave without ever suspecting that Hank was the guilty party in the boarding-school petty theft that brought the two of them together, when Hank successfully defended Jon against wrongful accusation.

Themes and Meanings

As elsewhere in Cozzens's mature literary canon, the dominant theme in *Morning, Noon, and Night* is that of chance as the sole deciding factor in human existence. Hank Worthington attributes his rare success to nothing more or less than his having been in the right places at the right times. More than once, he recalls, he has narrowly missed boarding a plane that eventually crashed; during World War II, while he was on a brief document-carrying mission to North Africa, he left a command post barely five minutes before it was blown to bits by one of Rommel's short-range bombs. In unstressed contrast to Hank's experiences are those of his parents, smothered to death in a hotel fire, and his two grandchildren, dead in an air crash while en route to stay with their father. On other occasions, incidents of apparent ill fortune work out in Hank's favor; had his uncle agreed to take him on at the bank, for example, he might well have lapsed into a groove there, never developing the innovative talents that propelled him into business for himself.

Implicit also in *Morning, Noon, and Night*, as in Cozzens's previous novels, is an ingrained distrust in social change, often mistaken by Cozzens's critics for hidebound political conservatism. Grounded in political thought both classical and modern, conditioned by observation and experience, Cozzens's apparent conservatism is in fact less political, in a topical sense, than it is philosophical, holding that human nature is both changeless and unchangeable. Hank Worthington, in rejecting the social activism fashionable among writers of the 1920's as both unformed and uninformed, thus proved quite unfashionably prophetic; by the time of the novelistic present, the proponents of social change had indeed accomplished relatively little and had made no lasting contributions to the literary canon.

Like most of Cozzens's mature novels, *Morning, Noon, and Night* is demonstrably a novel of "condition," defining character in relation to profession. Already noted for his delineations of character in relation to medicine, the ministry, the military, and the law, Cozzens in this volume turned his considerable analytical and descriptive powers on the business world, with significant excursions into the areas of college teaching and professional writing. Business, as the field of Hank's eventual choosing, receives detailed, revealing, yet generally compassionate expository treatment; at times, the novel, recalling the "How To . . ." pamphlets sold by Hank's erstwhile employer, Mr. Garesche, reads like a manual prepared for the edification of aspiring management consultants, who could not possibly fail to enrich themselves by assiduous application of the author's precepts. With regard to writing and teaching, Hank's precepts are essentially negative in tone, showing errors and excesses to be avoided while professing no certain route toward success. The novel, meanwhile, emerges as a highly accurate and plausible representation of the American business world before and after World War II, worthy of comparison with such earlier works as John P. Marquand's *Point of No Return* (1949) and John O'Hara's *From the Terrace* (1958).

Critical Context

Morning, Noon, and Night was Cozzens's last published novel, in a sense a literary valedictory and testament. Although he survived the novel's publication by a full decade, Cozzens produced no more fiction, apparently deeming his statement to be complete. As the author's only novel to be narrated in the first person, *Morning, Noon, and Night* also seems, at least on the surface, to be a personal record of sorts, albeit transposed into art: Born too late to serve in World War I, almost too early to be called for World War II, Hank Worthington is Cozzens's almost exact contemporary, holder of opinions that the author no doubt shared, particularly with regard to the profession of writing. Here as elsewhere, however, it would be erroneous to assume too close an identity of author with narrator; Cozzens was, above all else, an accomplished ironist, quite capable of subtly prepared, "unreliable" narration.

From the 1930's onward, Cozzens duly received recognition, although limited, as an outstanding social chronicler and "novelist of manners," worthy of consideration along with Marquand, O'Hara, and eventually Louis Auchincloss. Although all the novelists named were by turns dismissed among liberal critics as "elitist," their works as "irrelevant," Cozzens appears to have fared somewhat worse than the others, in part because of his evident interest in literary form and his often expressed disbelief in the validity of social change. Following the unprecedented success of *By Love Possessed* (1957), accompanied by certain apparent misquotations in a nationally circulated magazine, Cozzens was branded by the critics as a social and literary product of the Eisenhower Administration, dedicated to the status quo. The appearance of *Morning, Noon, and Night* during the politically turbulent year of 1968 proved to be strategically unfortunate, and the novel attracted little attention and few sales, despite adoption by a major book club. Notwithstanding, Cozzens's scholarly editor, biographer, and anthologist, Matthew Bruccoli, considers *Morning, Noon, and Night* among the author's finest achievements, amply deserving of sustained critical attention.

Bibliography

Bracher, Frederick. *The Novels of James Gould Cozzens.* New York: Harcourt, Brace, 1959. Of the eight novels by Cozzens published between 1931 and 1959, Bracher argues that at least four of them are of "major importance by any set of standards." Defends Cozzens from attacks by critics for his lack of personal commitment, showing him to be a novelist of intellect whose strength is storytelling. A thorough commentary on Cozzens's literary career.

Bruccoli, Matthew J. *James Gould Cozzens: A Life Apart.* New York: Harcourt Brace Jovanovich, 1983. This book-length story of Cozzens is essentially a biography with useful information on his upbringing and his development as a novelist. Includes a chapter each on *Guard of Honor* and *By Love Possessed* and an appendix containing excerpts from his notebooks. A must for any serious scholar of Cozzens.

Hicks, Granville. *James Gould Cozzens.* Minneapolis: University of Minnesota, 1966. An accessible introduction to Cozzens with some criticism of his novels from *Confusion* to *Guard of Honor* and *By Love Possessed.* Argues that the pretentiousness in Cozzens's early work was transformed in later novels to "competent, straightforward prose."

Mooney, John Harry, Jr. *James Gould Cozzens: Novelist of Intellect.* Pittsburgh, Pa.: University of Pittsburgh Press, 1963. A straightforward, useful study. Each chapter focuses on a different novel, from *S.S. San Pedro* to *Castaway*, and the final chapter covers the critical material available on Cozzens.

Pfaff, Lucie. *The American and German Entrepreneur: Economic and Literary Interplay.* New York: Peter Lang, 1989. Contains a chapter on Cozzens and the business world, with subsections on "The Business Activities of Henry Dodd Worthington," "Small Business," and "Recurring Themes." Pfaff is particularly interested in Cozzens's entrepreneurs.

Sterne, Richard Clark. *Dark Mirror: The Sense of Injustice in Modern European and American Literature.* New York: Fordham University Press, 1994. Contains a detailed discussion of *The Just and the Unjust.*

David B. Parsell

THE MORNING WATCH

Author: James Agee (1909-1955)
Type of plot: Bildungsroman
Time of plot: Good Friday, 1924
Locale: An Episcopalian boys' school in middle Tennessee
First published: 1951

Principal characters:
>RICHARD, nicknamed "Sockertees," the twelve-year-old protagonist
>RICHARD'S MOTHER, a well-meaning but somewhat smothering and ineffectual parent
>HOBE GILLUM and
>JIMMY TOOLE, Richard's rambunctious companions, approximately his age
>GEORGE FITZGERALD and
>LEE ALLEN, older boys, prefects who might be called to the priesthood
>WILLARD RIVENBURG, the school's leading athlete, admired by the younger boys
>CLAUDE GRAY, an effeminate boy who is fanatically pious
>FATHER FISH, Richard's favorite teacher

The Novel

As far as outer action is concerned, not much happens in *The Morning Watch*. The story itself is so short that it is best described as a novella. All of the story's action occurs within two or three hours during the early morning of Good Friday. Only the most devout could call the action earthshaking: Three boys sleeping in a dormitory are awakened at 3:45 A.M. to take their turns in a religious vigil; they join other worshipers in the silent, prayerful watch at the school chapel; then they wander off together for a cold swim in a nearby quarry, the Sand Cut. By far the longest section of this three-part story is the middle part, devoted to an hour's watch in the chapel.

Most of the action in *The Morning Watch* occurs inside Richard, the twelve-year-old whose consciousness the reader shares. For Richard, the Easter season is, like the new year for others, a time of heightened awareness, of taking stock, of awakenings and new beginnings. This particular Easter season is special for Richard because it also marks his transition from childhood to adolescence. It is his one big time of awakening to the prospects of manhood—to sexuality, to independence, to his own nature, and to the nature of existence generally. His life takes a new but fairly natural direction.

Richard's development and his religion influence each other. Just as the Easter season stimulates his adolescent awakening, so his awakening in turn influences his religious views. With amusement and shame, Richard thinks back on himself a year before, when, as an eleven-year-old religious fanatic, he aspired to sainthood, practiced self-mortification, and even harbored crucifixion fantasies. Getting himself crucified, however, raised certain practical difficulties: In his fantasies, he thought of building a cross in the school's shop, but since he lacked woodworking skills, he had to settle for being crucified on one of the school's iron bedsteads.

Now Richard is amazed at the change which a year has wrought in him. His aspirations to sainthood faded during summer vacation in Knoxville, and he became aware of the pride, irreverence, and craziness of his fantasies. Besides, he started indulging in a solitary sex act. Even now, as he imagines Christ's wounds, he cannot help picturing them in terms of Minnielee Henley's intimate parts, which he saw when they were climbing a tree together. Richard realizes that, as a saint, he is a washout.

Now Richard sees himself as merely another erring human being, and it seems to be a predicament that he cannot escape. Even as he prays and beats his chest in contrition, the devil tempts him with irreverent and prideful thoughts. He recalls portraits of a simpering and effeminate Jesus, finds the idea of intoxication of Christ's blood amusing, and thinks Claude Gray's attitude of prayer is theatrical. Anguished at such thoughts, Richard berates himself more, until he can finally congratulate himself that he is contrite and humble. Immediately he realizes that he has sinned again, in the very process of atonement. So it goes for Richard, in a vicious circle of alternating contrition and pride.

Leaving his soul in the hands of a merciful God, Richard gets on with the business of growing up. After attending the vigil, he and the other two boys, Hobe and Jimmy, assert their independence through a gross violation of the rules. Instead of returning to the dormitory, they go off to the Sand Cut for a swim. Here, when they strip naked, they silently appraise each other's progress toward manhood. In a daring expression of his budding manhood, Richard dives to the cold, muddy bottom of the Sand Cut. He confirms the results of this test when, on the way back to school, the boys come across a beautiful snake which may or may not be poisonous. Admiring the snake, Richard does not really want to kill it, but when Hobe mortally wounds it, Richard finishes the snake off by smashing its striking head with repeated blows from a rock held in his hand. The other boys, and Richard himself, are impressed by his feats, and the three boys are in high spirits as they return home to their inevitable punishment. Not even the fear of punishment or the thought that the snake will survive until sundown (similar to Christ suffering on the Cross) prevents Richard from secretly exulting over his strong right hand, on which the snake's blood and saliva have not yet finished drying.

The Characters

Richard's development is dramatic because up until now he has been something of a mother's boy. His father died when Richard was six, leaving Richard in the sole care of his mother, an exceedingly religious woman, who enrolled him in the Episcopalian boys' boarding school so he could be in the company of other boys and men. Yet the woman herself took up residence on the school's grounds, causing Richard to hang around her cottage, trying to get a glimpse of her (usually denied). Meanwhile, Richard apparently suffered the harsh, lonely fate of most mother's boys who are dropped into the midst of the wolf pack. His self-mortifications and fantasies of martyrdom are obvious emotional outlets. To Richard, intimidated and demoralized, his lack of status is still excruciatingly evident. Even on this Good Friday morning, the older boys scorn his meekly offered statements and refer to him as "crazy"—a judgment with which Richard privately concurs.

As Richard grows and asserts himself, there are stirrings of rebellion against his mother and against religion, which he associates with his mother and with effeminate behavior. He feels a moment of hatred for his mother, who teaches that being good means submitting to the unhappiness that God decrees. In that case, Richard thinks, who wants to be good? Other available models of goodness are hardly more inspiring. Poor Claude Gray, with his effeminate voice, looks, and manners, is grotesque in his abandonment to piety. His mother having died, Claude has attached himself to the Virgin Mary and seems fixated on the sainthood stage that Richard has recently left. The two smug prefects, George Fitzgerald and Lee Allen, busy with their flower and candle arrangements, are not much better, though George is kind toward the younger boys, while Lee harasses them.

One person whom Lee does not attack is the great, hulking athlete Willard Rivenburg, even though Willard sits in the vestry with the prefects, devours their coffee and cookies, and laughs satanically. The younger boys practically worship the manly Willard, an antimasque figure who embodies their spirit of mischief. Foulmouthed Hobe seems well on his way to becoming another Willard, while Richard, after he performs a notable athletic feat, emulates Willard's slack-jawed stance. Even so, Richard notes objectively that Willard easily falls asleep anywhere and seems to know as little as a person can. A better role model for Richard appears to be Father Fish, his favorite teacher.

Since *The Morning Watch* is autobiographical, there was once much interest in identifying the characters. Perhaps the only identification still of interest is young Agee himself, as represented in Richard. Though fairly natural, Richard's development is uneven in pace, occurs in excessive forms, and leaves certain conflicts unresolved. In short, Richard remains a bit crazy and seems to forecast the adult Agee's troubles (three marriages, undisciplined habits, and an early, fatal heart attack).

Themes and Meanings

The main theme of *The Morning Watch* is that growing up is both painful and joyful. The theme is elaborated not only through action and characters but also through powerful symbols, especially in the novella's final section. Crossing the woods, Richard finds a locust shell stuck to a tree. In its development, the locust has split its back and crawled out of the old shell, whose form reminds Richard of a human embryo. The shell suggests the traumas of birth and of metamorphosis—even the aeons of evolution which the human embryo recapitulates. Richard thinks that crawling out of one's back is just as painful as crucifixion, but another symbol, the beautiful snake which has just shed its skin, suggests that the results are more encouraging. Richard admires and identifies with the snake, especially its aura of dangerous virility. He therefore hates to kill it, but in doing so he acquires some of its potent medicine.

Although Richard assumes a crucifixion position when he dives to the bottom of the Sand Cut, the feats celebrating his development are more reminiscent of American Indian ritual than of the High Church. Altogether, there is a movement toward nature and away from religion in *The Morning Watch*—or at least away from versions of religion which are effeminate or typical of stunted adolescence, wherein religion is a sort of womb or smothering mother to which some of the boys cling. Richard's association of religion with his mother has already been noted, and religion seems to have circumscribed the development of the two prefects. Yet symbolically Claude Gray's behavior is the most revealing. When someone opens a window in the stifling chapel, whose air is heavy with the scents of flowers and burning candles, Claude gets up and closes it. He wants none of that fresh air—that escape to terrible freedom—with which Richard and his two friends fill their lungs. Obviously, a real he-man does not cling to Mary's skirts and dream about crucifixion but goes out and gets the job done.

The ideal of masculinity toward which Richard is growing—an ideal compatible with American Indian snake rituals and with rebirth in nature's Sand Cut—reflects Agee's Appalachian background. Agee's father, a handsome, virile Appalachian whom Agee's cultured mother dearly loved and whom the young Agee idolized, exemplified the ideal. Unhappily, much like Richard's father, Agee's father crashed his car and died when Agee was six (the story is told in Agee's companion autobiographical novel, *A Death in the Family*, 1957).

Critical Context

The Morning Watch belongs to a long and distinguished line of American *Bildungsromane*, including Mark Twain's *The Adventures of Huckleberry Finn* (1884) and J. D. Salinger's *The Catcher in the Rye* (1951). Though *The Morning Watch* has neither the comic tone nor the idiomatic style of these two monumental works, it shares their American skepticism about becoming "civilized" and deserves some of their popularity. In its own restrained way, *The Morning Watch* is a small, undiscovered American masterpiece.

Agee produced very little fiction, *The Morning Watch* being the only longer piece published during his lifetime (*A Death in the Family* was published posthumously, winning a Pulitzer Prize). Yet *The Morning Watch* clearly shows Agee's considerable talent. Structurally it is a complex but tightly controlled and unified work. The rich, demanding style combines William Faulkner and Ernest Hemingway, subtlety and photographic clarity.

Bibliography

Barson, Alfred. *A Way of Seeing: A Critical Study of James Agee.* Amherst: University of Massachusetts Press, 1972. A revisionist view of Agee, whose earliest critics thought that the writer's talents were dissipated by his diverse interests, causing him not to produce enough quality material, but who judged him to have been improving and focusing his skills at the time of his death. Barson inverts this thesis, stating that Agee's finished work should not be so slighted, and that his powers were declining when he died. Contains notes and an index. Should not be confused with *A Way of Seeing: Photographs of New York* (New York: Viking Press, 1965), a collection of photographs by Helen Levitt with an essay by Agee.

Bergeen, Laurence. *James Agee: A Life*. New York: E. P. Dutton, 1984. The definitive biography of Agee, based on interviews with those who knew him and examinations of his papers. Also contains illustrations, notes, a bibliography of Agee's writings, a bibliography of works about him, and an index.

Hersey, John. Introduction to *Let Us Now Praise Famous Men*. Boston: Houghton Mifflin, 1988. A long and thorough appraisal by one of Agee's contemporaries who practiced much the same blend of reportage and literary interpretation that distinguishes Agee's best work.

Kramer, Victor A. *James Agee*. Boston: Twayne, 1975. This short introduction to the life and works of Agee is a good book for the beginning researcher. Besides providing a biography of the writer and a careful discussion of all of his major works, Kramer also includes a chronology of Agee's life, an annotated bibliography, and an index.

Lofaro, Michael, ed. *James Agee: Reconsiderations*. Knoxville: University of Tennessee Press, 1992. Contains an Agee chronology; a brief biography; essays on *Let Us Now Praise Famous Men*, on *A Death in the Family*, and on Agee's journalism; and a bibliography of secondary sources. Several essays argue for ranking Agee higher as a literary figure than previous critics have allowed.

Madden, David, ed. *Remembering James Agee*. Baton Rouge: Louisiana State University Press, 1974. An excellent collection of memories about and assessments of Agee by his friends and coworkers, including Walker Evans, Dwight Macdonald, Father James Harold Flye, John Huston, and Agee's wife, Mia Agee. Also includes illustrations and a detailed chronology of Agee's life.

Seib, Kenneth. *James Agee: Promise and Fulfillment*. Pittsburgh, Pa.: University of Pittsburgh Press, 1968. As the subtitle indicates, Seib's study rescues Agee from the critical judgment that his work was more potential than performance. Maintains that Agee's contemporaries could not recognize his greatness because they judged him by traditional standards, when the writer was actually striking out in new directions that they did not understand. Agee is a link between the traditional man of letters and the new media of film and television. Contains notes, an index, a bibliography of works about Agee, and a bibliography of Agee's writings. Includes a list of his film and book reviews, which are often hard to track down.

Harold Branam

MOSES
Man of the Mountain

Author: Zora Neale Hurston (1903?-1960)
Type of plot: Allegory
Time of plot: Biblical times, during the Exodus
Locale: Egypt and the wilderness surrounding Mount Sinai
First published: 1939

>   *Principal characters:*
>   MOSES, an Egyptian who leads the enslaved Hebrews out of Egypt
>   PHARAOH TA-PHAR, the leader of Egypt, oppressor of the Hebrews, and
>   uncle of Moses
>   JETHRO, a prince of Midian and Moses' mentor
>   ZIPPORAH, his daughter and Moses' second wife
>   MIRIAM, a Hebrew prophetess who claims to be Moses' sister
>   AARON, her brother, a leader of the Hebrews
>   JOSHUA, a military leader of the Hebrews and Moses' confidant

The Novel

The novel's central action is based on the Old Testament tale of Moses leading the enslaved Hebrews out of Egypt to the promised land of Canaan. In order to trace Moses' development as a leader, Hurston begins her version with his childhood. As a boy, Moses is first influenced by Mentu, the Pharaoh's Hebrew stableman, who teaches him about nature and the languages of animals. Moses next turns to the Egyptian priests for instruction in the magic and voodoo used "to distract the minds of unthinking people from their real troubles."

Although Moses is not interested in acquiring power and prestige, as the son of the Pharoah's daughter he poses a threat to the position of Ta-Phar, the Pharoah's son and heir. He defeats Ta-Phar in ceremonial war games and consequently becomes a favorite of the Pharaoh. He is called on to lead the army, and as a result of his skill, Egyptian rule extends over the Middle East. As a result, Egypt gains glory, and for political reasons Moses gains an Ethiopian princess for his wife.

Soon palace intrigue and the rumors spread by Ta-Phar threaten Moses. Ta-Phar capitalizes on Moses' well-known sympathy for the oppressed Hebrews, claiming that Moses himself is a Hebrew. In addition, Ta-Phar encourages the acceptance of a Hebrew legend that Moses, as a baby, was discovered in the bullrushes by the Pharaoh's daughter and adopted by her. The legend arose out of the Hebrews' reaction to the Pharaoh's policy of slaying all Hebrew male babies. In order to provide their son with a chance for a future, Amram and Jochebed placed their three-month-old boy in a basket on the Nile. Then they charged their daughter Miriam to watch and report what happened. Miriam fell asleep, however, and, afraid to tell her parents the truth, she claimed that the Pharaoh's daughter found him. The tale quickly gained acceptance because the Hebrews were pleased with the irony that one of them was in the palace, accepted by the Pharaoh as a family member.

Though the legend is false, Moses chooses exile instead of confronting the rumors. Crossing the Red Sea, he leaves wealth and status behind him and begins anew at the age of twenty-five. Days of wandering bring him to the foot of Mount Sinai. After befriending Jethro, a local prince, Moses marries his voluptuous daughter Zipporah and intends to make his home at the foot of the majestic mountain, tending sheep. Jethro, however, obsessed by a dream, has other plans. He becomes Moses' teacher, instructing him in his own monotheistic religion and preparing him for the task of leading the enslaved Hebrews out of Egypt.

After a twenty-year absence, Moses travels to Egypt in order to learn the secrets contained in the Book of Thoth. Following a battle with a deathless serpent, Moses studies the document, acquiring the ability "to command the heavens and the earth, the abyss and the mountain, and the sea." When he returns to Midian, Jethro pronounces him ready for his task. Although Moses resists, a burning bush, a manifestation of God, convinces him that he has been chosen, and he acquiesces.

Leading the Hebrews out of Egypt is no easy task. Ta-Phar, who is now the Pharaoh, and the Egyptian nobles are reluctant to part with their slaves and the builders of their splendid cities. After Moses causes numerous plagues—frogs, lice, darkness, and the death of firstborn Egyptian children—the Pharaoh consents, but Moses also must motivate the Hebrews, one of whom argues, "I was figuring on going fishing tomorrow morning. I don't want to be bothered with no packing up today." When reports that the Hebrews have escaped reach the palace, the Pharaoh masses his army and pursues them, overtaking them at the Red Sea. Moses parts the sea, the Hebrews cross, and as the Egyptians follow, the sea crashes together, destroying the Egyptian army.

Although the Hebrews are safe, the journey is not over. At every inconvenience, the Hebrews complain, wishing to return to Egypt. The first time that Moses reaches the Promised Land, the Hebrews are not ready. Although no longer oppressed by the Egyptians, mentally they are still slaves. Moses, realizing that "no man may make another free. . . ," leads the Hebrews away. Thus they are condemned to wander in the wilderness for forty years, until the old generation dies, and a new generation will be able to accept freedom.

The journey is a trying one for Moses. Miriam and Aaron, jealous of Moses' position, undermine him. In addition, the Hebrews resist acknowledging Moses as their leader, resenting his interference in their lives. At one point the Hebrews abandon the new monotheistic God and return to worshiping and celebrating the Egyptian sun gods. Only after years of hardship are the people prepared for the Promised Land. Joshua, a young Hebrew trained by Moses, will lead them into Canaan. Moses, his tasks accomplished, ascends Mount Nebo, bids the Hebrews farewell, and "descends the other side of the mountain and heads back over the years."

The Characters

The characters of *Moses* are generally flat and underdeveloped, in part because Hurston is adapting a biblical tale and is limited by her source, but also because she is writing an allegory of the American black slaves' struggle for emancipation.

Hurston has combined the Moses of the Old Testament with the Moses depicted in African folklore. Thus, the Moses described in the novel is a wise prophet but also is a great voodoo chief. His power is derived not only from God but also from the Egyptian priests and the Book of Thoth. Both of these aspects—wisdom and magic—are necessary to lead and control the Hebrews, who, because of their enslavement, are not prepared for leadership roles. In order to emphasize the African heritage of Moses, Hurston departs from the biblical source and portrays Moses as Egyptian born. In this manner, she suggests that a forceful outside leader is necessary to free an oppressed people.

The novel chronicles Moses' growth as he develops into the leader of the Hebrews. His early years are a preparation for the task that Jethro has set before him. From Mentu, the Egyptian priests, and the Book of Thoth, he acquires the magic later needed to control the Hebrews. From his years of military campaigns, he acquires the military expertise that he will later impart to Joshua. His sense of fairness results in his siding with the oppressed Hebrews, at one point killing an Egyptian overseer who brutally beats a Hebrew worker. Later, in exile, he dreams of a land where equality could exist, a land that will turn out to be the Promised Land of the Hebrews. Thus, although he is reluctant to lead the Hebrews, he has in a sense spent his life preparing for it. His later complete acceptance of the task is illustrated by the change of his speech from the standard English of the Egyptian nobles to the black dialect of the Hebrews.

Moses, the ideal leader, is opposed by Pharaoh Ta-Phar, a corrupt ruler who derives his power from the oppression of his people. Thus, when Moses requests that the Hebrews be allowed to leave, the Pharaoh must refuse, for the release of the enslaved Hebrews would cause his downfall. Ironically, his refusal helps Moses in unifying the Hebrews.

Miriam and Aaron are Moses' link to the Hebrews but are also his adversaries. They oppose Moses, desiring his position of authority but lacking his capabilities. Miriam, bitter and jealous, tries to arouse the Hebrew women against Zipporah, the sensuous wife of Moses, while her brother, Aaron, demands the trappings of a high priest. Because of their flawed natures, neither will arrive at the Promised Land. Miriam is reduced to begging Moses to allow her to die, and later Aaron is stabbed by Moses so that Aaron's esteemed reputation among the Hebrews can be preserved.

Joshua represents the new Hebrew, symbolizing the potential of the Hebrew people. He is obedient, loyal, and willing to serve and to sacrifice. He has been groomed by Moses to lead the Hebrews into the Promised Land.

Themes and Meanings

Hurston uses the biblical story of Moses and the Hebrews as an allegory representing the oppression of the American black. The identification of the two groups is made clear through the portrayal of the Hebrews: They speak a black dialect, and their diet consists of food that is traditionally associated with Southern blacks: watermelons, cucumbers, and pan-fried fish. In addition, much of what is described concerning the Hebrews before their emancipation is true of blacks before the Civil War. Both groups live in shacks; both groups are whipped to produce more work. The children of both the Hebrews and the blacks are threatened; the Pharaoh orders male babies killed, and the plantation owners often sold the children of slaves. Even the paternalistic attitude is similar; the Egyptians argue, "What would slaves want to be free for anyway? They are being fed and taken care of. What more could they want?" The novel is first a discussion of the slave issue in the American past, but at the same time it comments on the problems that faced the blacks in the 1930's when, although institutionalized slavery no longer existed, blacks were still victims of discrimination.

The book, while focusing on American blacks, is also a study of the problems associated with emancipation. It is not enough to be rid of shackles, one must also internalize freedom. One must grow into freedom, developing a sense of worth. In Egypt the Hebrews felt that somehow the Egyptians were superior and rightfully their bosses. It took forty years before the Hebrews were ready to enter the Promised Land, before they could accept equality.

To accomplish her goal of transforming a biblical tale into a vehicle for a discussion of slavery and oppression, Hurston departs from her Old Testament source. To make Moses seem more of an ordinary man who develops into a leader, she provides him with a childhood and with common human characteristics—his desire for his wife, his friendship with Jethro, and his irritation with the Hebrews. She also provides alternative explanations for some of the incidents related in the Bible. Moses is Egyptian born and thus not affected by the stultifying effects of enslavement. He, unlike the Hebrews, is able to imagine a different and more just way of life. Hurston also rejects the biblical account of the miraculous parting of the Red Sea, providing instead an explanation based on natural causes. Finally, in the novel, much of Moses' power is explained by his knowledge of magic and voodoo. Thus, Hurston emphasizes that leaders arise out of the people and are not divinely created.

Critical Context

The mixture of voodoo, folklore, and black dialect found in *Moses: Man of the Mountain* reflects Hurston's cultural heritage and experiences. Born in the all-black town of Eatonville, Florida, she grew up surrounded by the poetic speech rhythms and dialect that she recorded in the novel. During her college years, she developed an interest in anthropology, studying under the renowned Franz Boas of Columbia University. Later, on a fellowship, she traveled to the Southern United States and to Haiti to collect folktales, which resulted in a well-regarded volume of folklore, *Mules and Men* (1935).

Moses: Man of the Mountain was an ambitious undertaking: Hurston attempted to make the tale of Moses and the Hebrews speak for enslaved people everywhere. To a certain extent she succeeded, but the novel's allegorical intent resulted in generally weak, stereotyped characters and a certain ambivalence displayed toward them. As noted above, the first time that Moses parts the Red Sea, Hurston presents the event as a natural occurrence, but the second time, she treats it as a miracle. The text clearly shows that Moses is Egyptian-born, but later Moses himself has doubts. Because of the satire aimed at the enslaved race, Hurston has been criticized for writing about the black situation for a white audience. It was her intention, however, to go beyond racial issues and to treat universal themes such as the effect of enslavement, the use and misuse of power, and the necessary qualities of a leader. While *Their Eyes Were Watching God* (1937) will remain the most successful of her novels, *Moses: Man of the Mountain* should not be discounted.

Bibliography

Awkward, Michael, ed. *New Essays on "Their Eyes Were Watching God."* Cambridge, England: Cambridge University Press, 1990. Essays by Robert Hemenway and Nellie McKay on the biographical roots of the novel, and by Hazel Carey on Hurston's use of anthropology. Rachel Blau DuPlessis provides a feminist perspective in "Power, Judgment, and Narrative in a Work of Zora Neale Hurston." Includes an introduction and bibliography.

Gates, Henry Louis, Jr. *The Signifying Monkey: A Theory of Afro-American Literary Criticism.* New York: Oxford University Press, 1988. The chapter on Hurston discusses her best-known novel, *Their Eyes Were Watching God*, as a conscious attempt to rebut the naturalistic view of blacks as "animalistic" that Gates claims she saw in Richard Wright's fiction.

Hemenway, Robert. *Zora Neale Hurston.* Urbana: University of Illinois Press, 1977. An excellent biography of Hurston which also provides much insight into her fiction. Perhaps the single best source of information about the author and her writings.

Hill, Lynda Marion. *Social Rituals and the Verbal Art of Zora Neale Hurston.* Washington, D.C.: Howard University Press, 1996. Chapters on Hurston's treatment of everyday life, science and humanism, folklore, and color, race, and class. Hill also considers dramatic reenactments of Hurston's writing. Includes notes, bibliography, and an appendix on "characteristics of Negro expression."

Howard, Lillie P. *Zora Neale Hurston.* Boston: Twayne, 1980. An important full-length study of Hurston's work which, nevertheless, is not as helpful as it might have been.

Johnson, Barbara. *A World of Difference.* Baltimore: The Johns Hopkins University Press, 1987. The two essays on Hurston examine how her fiction addresses the problem of the social construction of self.

Barbara Wiedemann

THE MOSQUITO COAST

Author: Paul Theroux (1941-   )
Type of plot: Dystopian
Time of plot: The 1980's
Locale: Honduras
First published: 1981

> *Principal characters:*
> CHARLIE FOX, the thirteen year-old narrator
> ALLIE FOX (FATHER), a mad-genius inventor, the narrator's father
> MOTHER, the narrator's mother, a dutiful, nameless wife
> JERRY, the narrator's whining younger brother
> MR. HADDY, a Honduran boatman, a friend of the family

The Novel

Nothing about twentieth century America pleases Allie Fox. This ingenious Harvard University dropout-turned-handyman is sickened by all he sees around him: fast food, pornography, drugs, pollution, television, violence, and shoddy, overpriced merchandise. Through the eyes of his thirteen-year old son Charlie, the novel's narrator, readers realize that if the world would only run according to this self-taught Yankee engineer's parameters and specifications, everything would be perfect. In Father's estimation, America is going belly-up—the end of the world is nigh—and he is bound and determined to save his family.

Without warning, Father takes his four children and their mother from their home in rural Massachusetts to a ship in Baltimore's harbor. By the time they arrive at Jeronimo, Honduras, a remote upriver town he buys, Father has convinced them that America will be destroyed by war and that they can never go home again. Here, in a godlike fashion, Father, a present-day Robinson Crusoe, dazzles the natives and reigns supreme, creating order out of chaos. An efficiently functioning farm, houses, sidewalks, barns—all designed by Father—and abundant crops sprout up overnight. He miraculously controls the elements by creating Fat Boy, a gigantic contraption that spews out blocks of ice. While Father battles nature, the children adapt to their natural surroundings. They clear the Acre, where wild fruit and vegetables grow in profusion next to a natural spring. Here they act out against their father's dominion by playing at going to school, shops, and church.

For a while, this updated Swiss Family Robinson lives in harmony with their new physical surroundings, but Father's quest for increasing devotion causes the enterprise to self-implode.

Following a particularly arduous failed attempt to bring ice to the natives high in a remote mountainous region, Charlie and his brother Jerry see Father in a new light. His golden mantle starts to fray around the edges, and Father unravels in the process from enlightened genius into confused zealot. While in the mountains, Father encounters a group of men whom he falsely believes to be enslaved. Boasting of his accomplishments, he motivates the men to break their bonds. He miscalculates, however, and the men show up in Jeronimo with guns. After realizing that these scavengers intend to dominate him, his pride dictates he kill them; but Father miscalculates again. His ice-making contraption, which uses an extremely flammable chemical mixture, explodes, leaving Jeronimo nothing more than a smoldering toxic dump site. However, Charlie saves the family by leading them to the hidden Acre, where they find fresh food and water.

After this debacle, Father fails to learn the error of his ways, and his pride causes him to continue to deteriorate mentally. He laughs at the children's enclosure, refuses their offerings of food, and calls them monkeys. Charlie and Jerry's animosity toward him grows. Father's continuous rantings increase while his hold on reality continues to diminish. Against their wishes, he forces the family downriver to a swampy area where they barely survive. By now, they wear rags, continuously battle insects and fever, and labor from sunup to sundown to grow food. Father rants continuously about how America is gone and how they are the only people left on earth, and he demands recognition as their savior.

The family's troubles increase. Despite the dire warnings of Mr. Haddy, a Honduran boatman and family friend, they remain in the swamp eking out a Stone Age subsistence. Nature retaliates against the mad proud magician who tries to tame it. A long drought precipitates extreme rainfall that destroys their crops. Completely exhausted, the family floats along the river in the remains of their house until they find themselves near a missionary settlement. Here, they learn that Father has lied; America is after all alive and well. Charlie and Jerry's confusion turns to hatred, and they contemplate killing Father. Completely mad at this point, Father blows up an airplane and suffers a crippling bullet wound. The family persists downriver to the coast, almost dying in the process. Father continues to devolve mentally and physically, ultimately crawling to his death, a beast on all fours. With the help of Mr. Haddy, the family returns to America.

The Characters

The characters of Thoreaux's fatalistic novel function within dystopian thematic constraints; not only do they fail to grow and develop as individuals, but they also devolve and diminish. Charlie, the thirteen-year old narrator, is actually smaller at the end of the novel. While he certainly evokes sympathy from the beginning (he is, after all, a child whose bully of a father never lets him go to school, watch television, or eat junk food), the feeling is not sustained. Although he exhibits some heroic moments, he ultimately proves disappointing because he continues placid for so long, defending and overlooking his father's behavior time and time again. He continuously deludes himself into viewing Father through rose-tinted glasses, never asking for information. The warnings of three other characters about his father's actions fall on deaf ears. Charlie exhibits the mentality of a victim caught in a web of ongoing abuse, barely managing to survive moment to moment. Ultimately, he embraces all that his father fought against.

Allie Fox, "Father," a thwarted mechanical genius, always knows best. He rejects God because he finds Him imperfect. In his view, belief in and reliance upon God is the greatest vice. Self-sufficient people who practice good workmanship have no need to rely on God; they depend upon themselves and their own ingenuity. He forbids his children school, television, or food that is not completely nutritious. Allie, however, is merely inventing God in his own likeness. He is in perpetual motion, never sleeping, never eating, always agitating; he attempts to straighten rivers, make ice out of fire, and tame volcanos for his own uses. Like Faust, Ahab, and Kurtz before him, he goes against God and nature and in the process destroys himself.

Mother, the stoic, supportive wife and devoted mother, remains maddeningly flat throughout the novel. Another victim, she endures in her husband's shadow, patting hands, kissing heads, flickering forth only occasionally with one-line criticisms when her children are endangered. Although she has produced four children, her relationship with Father seems sterile. He refers to her as "Mother" throughout, and they never share an intimate moment. The lack of life in Mother attests the novel's apocalyptic nature.

Jerry, the younger brother, has more spunk than Charlie and more life than their younger twin siblings, who act merely as props. He voices what Charlie feels. Like Charlie, however, he cannot act and winds up merely whining.

Mr. Haddy, although a minor personality, is the novel's only heroic character. Despite ongoing abuse from Father, he continues to befriend the family, brings them food and gasoline and ultimately sees that they get home. If there is any hope in the novel at all, it rests with Mr. Haddy who lives a simple life floating up and down the river.

Themes and Meanings

The Mosquito Coast caustically critiques contemporary American society, pointing out its madness and its depravity, but this fatalistic work does not offer much hope. While the novel chronicles the epic paradigm, beginning with a young man's journey, his overcoming of fearful odds, experiencing deep revelations, and returning home, *The Mosquito Coast* is actually an nihilistic anti-allegory. Charlie is forced to take a journey to a secret destination. Overcoming fearful odds only pushes him backward, and he returns home empty, still a boy rather than a triumphant man. Foreboding symbols abound from the beginning; the scarecrow whom Charlie believes to be his crucified father points out that Father has a brain of straw. Fat Boy, an appropriation of the name given to the first atomic bomb, is a Pandora's box that will unleash destruction. Allie Fox (clearly as sly as a fox) resembles Prometheus playing with fire, Doctor Frankenstein creating his monster, and Faust outwitting nature only to wind up in hell. He also fits into the American individualist literary mold of James Fenimore Cooper and Herman Melville and the American inventor model of Benjamin Franklin, Thomas Edison, and the Wright brothers. In addition, the new-beginning theme is particularly perceptible.

Critical Context

Thoreaux's predecessors on the one hand include Daniel Defoe, whose *Robinson Crusoe* (1719) demonstrates how a young man can leave home, venture into a solitary world, find God, and return home enriched beyond measure. On the other hand, Theroux seems particularly indebted to Joseph Conrad's *Heart of Darkness* (1899), which aptly illustrates the depths of depravity to which humans can fall without social props. Conrad's antihero Kurtz is viewed through Marlowe's hypnotized eyes in a manner reminiscent of Charlie's view of Father. Natives adore the insane Kurtz, who voices his desire to return to a primitive state and crawl on all fours. Similarly, when the natives bow before Father after he creates ice, he too becomes a god, later fulfilling Kurtz's desire by crawling on all fours to his death. Theroux ultimately delivers the messages that people cannot look to the past to solve their problems and that while the modern world may not be perfect, there is a certain amount of splendor in radios and taxi cabs.

An immensely successful writer, Theroux has published more than twenty books and countless short stories. *The Mosquito Coast* chronicles the author's deep knowledge of and intense concern with metaphysics, literary criticism, science, and psychology. The novel won the 1981 *Yorkshire Post* Novel of the Year Award and the James Tait Black Memorial Prize.

Bibliography

Bertens, Hans. "The Convention of the New Beginning in Theroux's *The Mosquito Coast*." In *Convention and Innovation in Literature*, edited by Rainer Grubel. Amsterdam: Benjamins, 1991. Insightful study of Theroux's literary predecessors, highlighting the starting-over theme.

Coale, Samuel. *Paul Thoreaux*. Boston: Twayne, 1987. Overview and critical interpretation of the writer's life and work. Includes a chronology and a bibliography.

Stewart, Mathew. "Devolution, Madness, and American Myth in *The Mosquito Coast*." *The Arkansas Review: A Journal of Criticism* 4, no. 2 (Fall, 1995): 42-58. Comprehensive article that illustrates Allie Fox's descent into madness and how American myth functions in his demise.

Theroux, Paul. *My Other Life*. London: Penguin Books, 1996. Fictive memoir of Thoreaux's life that details his early life as a Peace Corps volunteer and his friendship with V. S. Naipaul.

_____. *Sir Vidia's Shadow*. Boston: Houghton Mifflin, 1998. Chronicles Theroux's intimate friendship with mentor V. S. Naipaul.

M. Casey Diana

MOSQUITOES

Author: William Faulkner (1897-1962)
Type of plot: Satiric novel of ideas
Time of plot: August, 1925
Locale: New Orleans and Lake Pontchartrain
First published: 1927

> *Principal characters:*
> DAWSON FAIRCHILD, a novelist, Faulkner's portrait of Sherwood
>   Anderson
> MRS. MAURIER, a wealthy widow who lends her patronage to the New
>   Orleans artistic community aboard her yacht *Nausikaa*
> ERNEST TALLIAFERRO, formerly Tarver, a dilettante and wholesale
>   buyer of women's undergarments
> PATRICIA (PAT) ROBYN, age eighteen, Mrs. Maurier's niece, a frank,
>   epicene virgin who embodies Gordon's idea of female beauty
> THEODORE ROBYN, Pat's twin brother, a young man absorbed in
>   fashioning a wooden pipe, off to Yale in September
> GORDON, age thirty-six, a hawklike, silent, and masculine sculptor, the
>   novel's ideal of the dedicated artist
> JULIUS KAUFFMAN, "the Semitic man," Fairchild's friend and foremost
>   critic
> EVA WISEMAN, Kauffman's sister, a poet
> MARK FROST, a "ghostly" young man and "the best poet in New
>   Orleans" according to his own judgment
> DOROTHY JAMESON, Frost's companion, a painter
> MAJOR AYERS, an Englishman determined to make his fortune by
>   marketing a cure for constipation
> JENNY STEINBAUER, a voluptuous, unreflective blonde
> PETE GINOTTA, Jenny's boyfriend, who wears a stiff straw hat
> DAVID WEST, the inarticulate steward, who accompanies Pat on an
>   ill-fated excursion to the mainland

The Novel

In *Mosquitoes*, William Faulkner draws a satiric portrait of the New Orleans artistic community of 1925 while working out his own theories about art and the artist. As a "novel of ideas" in Aldous Huxley's sense of the phrase, *Mosquitoes* contains much talk and little action. The novel's plan is simple: Mrs. Maurier, a wealthy New Orleans socialite and "patron of the arts," gathers aboard her motorized yacht *Nausikaa* an awkward assortment of artists, intellectuals, and adolescents for a talk-filled cruise on Louisiana's Lake Pontchartrain. When her nephew Theodore, needing an instrument to bore a hole through his handmade pipe, "borrows" a steel rod from the ship's intricate steering mechanism, the disabled *Nausikaa* is soon stranded on a sandbar, thus providing a convenient situation for the novel's seemingly endless talk.

The shipboard company can be divided into three general groups: the adults and the young, the men and the women, the verbose and the reticent. The central group consists of the older, talkative men. Dawson Fairchild (novelist), Julius Kauffman (critic), and their hangers-on, Mark Frost (poet) and Major Ayers (Englishman), intersperse their sophisticated discussions about sex, art, and society with periodic trips below deck, where they go to evade the insufferable Mrs. Maurier and to get drunk on Fairchild's whiskey. Mrs. Maurier's plans for a decorous party are continually thwarted by the rudeness and frank vulgarity of these men ("but after all, one must pay a price for Art," she laments), and she falls back on the support of Eva Wiseman (poet) and Dorothy Jameson (painter), lonely women who keep each other company, playing cards and smoking cigarettes.

With their unconscious physicality and commitment to experience as opposed to talk, the young people are a group very much apart, and they are at the center of the novel's exploration of sexuality. As they sport among themselves, the novel illuminates a contrast between the variety and unreflectiveness of their sexual exploration on the one hand, and the self-conscious sexual frustration of the adults on the other hand. The leading figure of this young group is the frank and boyish Pat Robyn, who has characteristically brought two people aboard whom she met only hours before departure: Jenny Steinbauer, a young, voluptuous, and nonverbal blonde who repels the advances of many of the men, and Pete Ginotta, her silent and jealous boyfriend, who wears a stiff straw hat at a rakish angle, refusing to put it down lest it should come to harm. Theodore, Pat's twin, is a version of the silent and absorbed artist as he whittles away at his pipe and tries to avoid the attentions of his sister; and David West, the steward, one of Faulkner's inarticulates, is a good man who possesses depths of feeling and flashes of inner poetry.

Isolated from all these groups, though drawn obsessively to Pat, is the silent, muscular sculptor, Gordon. He is at the center of the novel's values, according to which the most talkative are the least creative; he is an almost purely silent figure and the one true artist aboard. His polar opposite is the "unmuscled," affected, and effeminate Talliaferro, a wholesale buyer of women's undergarments. Chatty and nervous, Talliaferro is an ineffectual intermediary between the men and the women and is the novel's most ludicrous figure.

The novel's most interesting and extended action takes place when Pat and David desert ship in a romantically deluded attempt to reach Mandeville, the first leg of a planned journey to Europe. Their attempt to escape the "ship of fools" into a world of adventure and romance is, however, a complete disaster. Reaching shore and marching off in the wrong direction through miasmic swampland, they encounter sheer reality itself in the shape of voracious mosquitoes. Parched, sunburned, and exhausted, they are finally aided by a malevolent, foulmouthed, and lascivious swamp dweller who, for the price of five dollars paid in advance, agrees to ferry Pat and David back to the still-stranded yacht, where nothing has changed.

Nothing has changed when the *Nausikaa* is freed and returns to New Orleans. The group disintegrates, and the novel follows the individual characters as they fall back into the habitual urban patterns which they left behind four days earlier. Life seems as dreary and as futile as ever. The central themes of the novel are unified in one climactic scene, however, the journey of Fairchild, Kauffman, and Gordon through the old city's "nighttown" or red-light district. Here their drunkenness, and the murky hallucinatory quality of the dark streets, are rendered in an experimental and poetic language reminiscent of the "Circe" chapter of James Joyce's *Ulysses* (1922). As they walk together, each man has a private visionary experience or "epiphany," in which significant, vivid form is given to the novel's conception of art and the artist.

The Characters

Some of the characters of *Mosquitoes* are based upon members of the New Orleans artistic community whom Faulkner knew in 1925, while others are wholly imaginative constructs. The novelist Dawson Fairchild, for example, is Faulkner's portrait of Sherwood Anderson, the "father" of Faulkner's generation of American novelists. Though Anderson was an important early model for him, Faulkner soon began to look elsewhere, turning principally to such writers as Joyce, Joseph Conrad, and T. S. Eliot, who represented an international as opposed to a regional standard of literature. Faulkner's portrayal of Anderson, consequently, is equivocal. On the one hand, Fairchild is credited with possessing an attractive, folksy humor revealed primarily by the Al Jackson tall tales; or he is shown to be master of narrative pathos as when he tells Theodore the story of his ill-fated attempt to gain entrance to a college fraternity (his effect is achieved, however, by casting himself as a fool: "You poor goof" is Theodore's summation of the story). On the other hand, Fairchild is the recipient of the novel's most serious and significant criticism, and as such, he is to be distinguished from the relatively flattened satirical stereotypes of Talliaferro and Mrs. Maurier. Fairchild's principal critic is his friend Kauffman (referred to throughout as "the Semitic man"), who represents many of Faulkner's own critical judgments in the novel. Kauffman considers Fairchild a talented but seriously flawed artist; as a man, Fairchild is a "poor emotional eunuch," and as an artist, a "bewildered stenographer with a gift for people." As the words "son" and "child" embedded in his name suggest, Dawson Fairchild is emotionally and artistically young, never having grown beyond a midwestern regionalism and a "hopeless sentimentality," a fact which has prevented his art from achieving a fully mature and universal significance. Though endowed with moments of insight and poetic expression, Fairchild is ultimately drawn as the pathetic, older novelist, a "benevolent walrus" who is aware of his waning artistic power.

The other flawed artists aboard the *Nausikaa* receive considerably less serious treatment. Mark Frost, for example, is clearly a butt of relentless satire. A "ghostly," "sepulchral,' and morose young man with a "prehensile mouth," the aptly named Frost continually reminds the company that he is "the best poet in New Orleans." At best a minor regional poet, at worst a charlatan, Mark Frost is Faulkner's caricature of the pretentious, clever, and constipated poet. Here is Faulkner's cutting description: "Mark Frost, the ghostly young man, a poet who produced an occasional cerebral and obscure poem in four of seven lines reminding one somehow of the function of evacuation excruciatingly and incompletely performed." Both Fairchild and Frost fall short of Faulkner's conception of the dedicated artist, the quasi-mythical Gordon (he is described as possessing a silver faun's face—like Donald Mahon of Faulkner's *Soldier's Pay*, 1926—and a hawklike arrogance), who is characterized throughout as being hard, masculine, lonely, and silent.

Among the nonartists, Mrs. Maurier is treated initially as a creature of pure satire, but she undergoes a process of humanization over the course of the novel, as Faulkner's conception of her matures. The principal agent of this humanizing process is Faulkner's key self-projection, Gordon, whose sculpture of Mrs. Maurier's head captures the suffering and despair of the human being behind the socialite's mask. Though Talliaferro is less fully humanized (and his presence at the opening and closing of the novel signals its principally satiric intention), his loneliness and frustration is suggested, primarily in flashes of interior revelation which Faulkner affords the reader. In both Talliaferro and Mrs. Maurier, one sees Faulkner's effort to transcend the reductiveness of satire, and through a growing realism of attitude, to humanize even disagreeable individual types.

Though Gordon represents Faulkner's conception of the true artist, many other characters embody important aspects of Faulkner's personality and art. For example, Faulkner attributes to Eva Wiseman some of his own poetry to be published in *A Green Bough* (1933); to Julius Kauffman, some of his own critical theories; to Dawson Fairchild, his definition of genius as a "Passion Week of the heart" along with the Al Jackson tall tales (he had coauthored these with Anderson); and to Talliaferro and Mark Frost, aspects of his own youthful pretentiousness and posturing. Faulkner appears most significantly as Gordon, the sculptor, but two other incarnations of Faulkner in the work should also be noted. There is the funny, shabbily dressed "little kind of black man" whom Jenny had met at Mandeville, and whose name she has difficulty recalling to Pat: "He said he was a liar by profession, and he made good money at it, enough to own a Ford as soon as he got it paid out. I think he was crazy. Not dangerous: just crazy." When she does recall his name, "Faulkner," Pat responds: "'Faulkner?' . . . Never heard of him." There is also the thunderous typist with the "sweating leonine head" whom Talliaferro interrupts twice near the close of the novel. Though he is described as being a large man (Faulkner was not), his is clearly a portrait of the intensely absorbed literary artist and as close a model as the text affords of Faulkner as a novelist. His devastating but comical dismissal of Talliaferro may be read as a final repudiation of both the New Orleans artistic milieu, and of the kind of smart, satirical writing in which Faulkner had indulged in this novel: "'And here I am, wasting my damn life trying to invent people by means of the written word!' His face became suddenly suffused: he rose towering. 'Get to hell out of here,' he roared. 'You have made me sick!'"

Themes and Meanings

The silent artist Gordon is uniquely sensitive to the sterility of talk, and he gives expression, through the mediation of the narrator, to the novel's dominant theme: "Talk, talk, talk: the utter and heartbreaking stupidity of words. It seemed endless, as though it might go on forever. Ideas, thoughts, became mere sounds to be bandied about until they were dead." The sexual contrast between the effeminate Talliaferro and the masculine Gordon is an extension of this theme onto the level of characterization.

More generally, words, in their annoying persistence, are an enervating force, and as such, they have much in common with the novel's ubiquitous mosquitoes. Though serving at times as a realistic correction of romantic ideals, as in Pat's abortive journey with David, mosquitoes are more commonly associated with all that is ignoble and deflated, all that is opposed to desire. Distracting and invasive mosquitoes, like empty talk, and like Talliaferro's interruption of the artist at his typewriter, become the enemies of art, continually breaking in on "the heart's beautitude," the artist's private world of value and potency. Like mosquitoes, the crowd aboard the *Nausikaa*, and by extension, all such superficial artistic milieus, represent parasitic forces which the true artist must evade.

Opposed to the novel's portrait of a slightly inimical social and natural reality are a series of formulations of the artist's private inner world. The artist's withdrawal into this private world is a way of evading "mosquitoes," and a necessary prelude to an engagement with a more fundamental reality. The sources of truly powerful and universal art are, in a seeming paradox, private and inward. This theme is developed most fully in the "nighttown" scene, here by Julius Kauffman: "Dante invented Beatrice, creating himself a maid that life had not had time to create, and laid upon her frail and unbowed shoulders the whole burden of man's history of his impossible heart's desire." Gordon's Beatrice is "the headless, armless, legless torso of a girl, motionless and virginal and passionately eternal," the sculpture in his studio of which Pat is a living incarnation. The artist seeks to capture in such images what Fairchild calls an "instant of timeless beautitude," "a kind of splendid and timeless beauty" wherein the artist's engagement with reality achieves powerful artistic expression.

Critical Context

Though widely considered his least successful novel, *Mosquitoes* was an essential part of Faulkner's artistic development, a necessary prelude to the masterpieces which would soon follow, such as *The Sound and the Fury* (1929), which was completed only two years later. In repudiating Sherwood Anderson and New Orleans' "talky" sophistication, Faulkner clarified his own artistic position and made possible the discovery of his own "little postage stamp of native soil," whose exploration would define one of the world's greatest and most universally significant literary careers.

In *Mosquitoes*, also, Faulkner conducted a wide variety of narrative experiments, manipulating the technical and thematic innovations that he had discovered in Joyce, Eliot, Conrad, and others. By undertaking a process of absorption, assimilation, and transformation of the lessons of the literary masters, Faulkner laid the groundwork of his own spectacular technical mastery in the fiction to follow. *Mosquitoes*, then, is an invaluable record of the young artist's development, a document of Faulkner's turning away from New Orleans and toward Oxford, Mississippi, the model of Jefferson, Mississippi, and the heart of his immortal fictional cosmos, Yoknapatawpha County.

Bibliography
Blotner, Joseph. *Faulkner: A Biography*. 2 vols. New York: Random House, 1974. Once criticized for being too detailed (the two-volume edition is some two thousand pages), this biography begins before Faulkner's birth with ancestors such as William Clark Falkner, author of *The White Rose of Memphis*, and traces the writer's career from a precocious poet to America's preeminent novelist.

Brodhead, Richard H., ed. *Faulkner: New Perspectives*. Englewood Cliffs, N.J.: Prentice-Hall, 1983. One volume in the Twentieth Century Views series under the general editorship of Maynard Mack, offering nearly a dozen essays by a variety of Faulkner scholars. Among them are Irving Howe's "Faulkner and the Negroes," first published in the early 1950's, and Cleanth Brooks's "Vision of Good and Evil" from Samuel E. Balentine's *The Hidden God* (Oxford, England: Oxford University Press, 1983). Contains a select bibliography.

Cox, Leland H., ed. *William Faulkner: Biographical and Reference Guide*. Detroit, Mich.: Gale Research, 1982.

_____. *William Faulkner: Critical Collection*. Detroit, Mich.: Gale Research, 1982. These companion volumes constitute a handy reference to most of Faulkner's work. The first is a reader's guide which provides a long biographical essay, cross-referenced by many standard sources. Next come fifteen "critical introductions" to the novels and short stories, each with plot summaries and critical commentary particularly useful to the student reader. A three-page chronology of the events of Faulkner's life is attached. The second volume contains a short potpourri, with Faulkner's "Statements," a *Paris Review* interview, and an essay on Mississippi for *Holiday* magazine among them. The bulk of the book is an essay and excerpt collection with contributions by a number of critics including Olga Vickery, Michael Millgate, and Warren Beck. Includes a list of works by Faulkner including Hollywood screenplays.

Gray, Richard. *The Life of William Faulkner: A Critical Biography*. Oxford, England: Blackwell, 1994. A noted Faulkner scholar, Gray closely integrates the life and work. Part 1 suggests a method of approaching Faulkner's life; part 2 concentrates on his apprentice years; part 3 explains his discovery of Yoknapatawpha and the transformation of his region into his fiction; part 4 deals with his treatment of past and present; part 5 addresses his exploration of place; part 6 analyzes his final novels, reflecting on his creation of Yoknapatawpha. Includes family trees, chronology, notes, and a bibliography.

Vickery, Olga W. *The Novels of William Faulkner*. Baton Rouge: Louisiana State University Press, 1959. This volume, with its comprehensive treatment of the novels, has established itself as a classic, a *terminus a quo* for later citicism. The chapter on

The Sound and the Fury, providing an analysis of the relation between theme and structure in the book, remains relevant today despite intensive study of the topic.

Volpe, Edmond L. *A Reader's Guide to William Faulkner.* New York: Noonday Press, 1964. While many books and articles have contributed to clearing up the murkiest spots in Faulkner, the beginning student or general reader will applaud this volume. In addition to analysis of structure, themes, and characters, Volpe offers critical discussion of the novels in an appendix providing "chronologies of scenes, paraphrase of scene fragments put in chronological order, and guides to scene shifts."

Williamson, Joel. *William Faulkner and Southern History.* New York: Oxford University Press, 1993. A distinguished historian divides his book into sections on Faulkner's ancestry, his biography, and his writing. Includes notes and genealogy.

Michael Zeitlin

A MOTHER AND TWO DAUGHTERS

Author: Gail Godwin (1937-   )
Type of plot: Domestic realism/social chronicle
Time of plot: December, 1978, to summer, 1979, and one day in 1984
Locale: Mountain City, Greensboro, Winston-Salem (all in North Carolina); a
    small town on the Iowa shore of the Mississippi; and Ocracoke, an island off the
    Carolina shore
First published: 1982

    Principal characters:
            NELL STRICKLAND, the mother of the title, a widow, and a former nurse
            CATE GALITSKY, Nell's twice-divorced older daughter, a college
                English teacher
            LYDIA MANSFIELD, Nell's younger daughter, newly separated, a mother
                of two, a returning college student
            LEONARD STRICKLAND, the husband of Nell and the father of Cate and
                Lydia, a presence in the minds of the protagonists throughout the
                novel despite his death in the first chapter
            THEODORA BLOUNT, Cate's godmother and "undisputed leader" of the
                Stricklands' "social set" in Mountain City

The Novel

Fittingly, in a novel that considers to what extent individuals can create their own destinies and to what extent those destinies are shaped by the people around them, *A Mother and Two Daughters* both opens and closes with a party. Nell and Leonard Strickland attend the first party at the home of Theodora Blount, representative of the "old guard" and repository of conservative, traditional Southern values. Yet the appearance at the party of Theodora's unmarried, pregnant, backwoods protégée, the teenage Wickie Lee, suggests that those values may be in transition, as does the epigraph (from D. H. Lawrence's "Dies Irae") for part 1: "Our epoch is over, a cycle of evolution is finished."

The course of part 1 reveals that the lives of the three protagonists are also in transition. Nell Strickland loses her husband, Leonard, to a heart attack immediately after Theodora's party. Nell's younger daughter, Lydia, has just left her husband of sixteen years to create a life of her own, which she initiates by going back to college. Lydia's older sister, Cate, is between men and doubtful that her job teaching English at the insolvent Melanchthon College in Iowa can long continue. As they struggle to redefine their lives, all three women feel the loss of Leonard, an introspective, idealistic lawyer, whose gentleness and sensitivity had always acted as a restraining influence on his strong-willed wife and daughters.

That none of the women can begin the process of redefinition with a clean slate or, as Cate puts it, can run from their histories—including their mistakes—is suggested by the epigraph for part 2, from the *I Ching*: "KU—WORK ON WHAT HAS BEEN SPOILED (DECAY)." Cate's history of fierce independence and fear of being submerged in the protective embrace of another leads her to reject the marriage proposal of the equally strong and independent pesticide manufacturer, Roger Jernigan, and to abort the child they inadvertently conceived together. At the same time, although she refuses to admit defeat, the bankruptcy of Melanchthon College brings Cate to a low point in her career.

Meanwhile, Lydia's star has been rising. She gets A's in all of her college courses, has a passionate affair with a man who adores her, finds an important woman friend in the brilliant black instructor of a course in the History of Female Consciousness, and lands a job in front of the cameras on a local television show.

In the wake of Leonard's death, Nell retreats into her house in Mountain City and thinks about her past with him: how he "protected" her "from my harshest judgments of myself as well as of others." Yet she seems to accept her loss, content to watch the baby crows outside her window and somewhat impatient when her house is invaded by Theodora's book club.

Nell's serenity is disturbed when, in part 3, she and her daughters converge on Leonard's old cottage on the island of Ocracoke. Nell's grief is reawakened, but a friendship is renewed when she discovers that an old schoolmate has rented the cottage next door. It is at Ocracoke that Nell really says good-bye to Leonard and is thereafter able to resume her own life.

It is also at Ocracoke that the sibling rivalry of Cate and Lydia finally explodes. Cate seeks to trivialize the friends, goals, and accomplishments of Lydia, who retaliates by suggesting that Cate has "nothing to show" for her life. After both angry women storm out of the rickety cottage, it burns down, another vanished symbol of a closed epoch in their lives, perhaps part of the "wreckage of ourselves" emphasized by the epigraph for the section.

Family members and friends are reunited and reconciled in the epilogue, set five years later, and the novel ends as it began—with a party. This time Cate, not Theodora, presides, at the mountain retreat she has inherited from an eccentric cousin. Theodora is there, too, now arguing the pros of racial intermarriage after meeting the lovely black bride of Lydia's son Leo. Wickie Lee, who turns out to be a distant cousin of Theodora, has married and become conventionally respectable. Finally, the three protagonists have achieved the new self-definitions they had been struggling toward. Lydia is an immensely successful television personality; Nell is a wife again and, after a hiatus of many years, has returned to nursing; Cate is a free-lance teacher who creatively markets her courses and continues to go her own way. The sisters are both now secure enough to reestablish their relationship, thus ratifying the epilogue's Emersonian epigraph, which asserts that "our relatedness" makes us "strong."

The Characters

Depending upon whether one regards attitudes or behavior as more telling, one could call Nell Strickland an outsider playing the role of insider or an insider who prefers to think of herself as an outsider. She has lived in Mountain City ever since she was fourteen, she has gone to the book club meetings presided over by the pretentious Theodora, and she has been for forty years the respected, popular wife of a respected, popular Mountain City lawyer. Yet, even if Nell goes through the motions of conventional propriety, she views those rituals and the class consciousness that dictates them with a somewhat satiric eye.

Insofar as Nell's (usually accurate) satiric vision is a defense against rejection and pain, it is offset by her compassion and her vital interest, as a former nurse and as a mother, in helping people to live well and die comfortably. Although, after Leonard's death, retreat from life and from people is a temptation for Nell, the needs of others cause her to become more fully engaged in life than ever. It is Nell who mobilizes the women of the book club when Wickie Lee goes into labor during a meeting; Nell who eases the last days of her old school friend Merle Chapin; Nell who finds happiness and even passion married to Merle's widower, Marcus.

If, out of deference to Leonard, Nell has largely suppressed her skeptical, defiant side, Cate is the rebel Nell has never allowed herself to be: a twice-divorced, 1960's-style liberal, who in 1970 found herself briefly in jail for leading her students from a New York girls' school in a demonstration at the Lincoln Tunnel to protest the invasion of Cambodia. It should be noted that, in this story of family relationships and correspondences, Cate's activism results not only from the critical perspective she has inherited from Nell but also from the idealism she has absorbed from Leonard. She cannot see a wrong without wanting to right it and has done the sorts of things Leonard "would have liked to do, had he been less prudent, more furious and full of fire." As she approaches forty, Cate is alternately gratified and irritated by the knowledge that family members regard her as excitingly, but disturbingly, unpredictable.

While Nell has sacrificed open criticism of social pretensions to the proprieties observed by her society, Cate has "sacrific[ed] people to ideals": insulting Theodora, alienating Lydia, and aborting the baby of a man with whom she could have been happy. Still, if Cate is hard on others, she is even harder on herself. Her zealous pursuit of the truth and her impetuosity cause her more pain than they do anyone else. After her momentous fight with Lydia, Cate's long walk on the windy beach—during which she castigates herself for enviously trying to destroy her sister's pride in her own accomplishments—results in Bell's palsy, a temporary numbing of the facial muscles. This experience gives Cate a sense of her own limits, and thereafter, she cultivates a "detached observer" side of her personality to protect herself and others from her own worst excesses.

On the surface, Lydia is more conventional, the obedient Nell rather than the rebellious one. She has always been the perfect wife and mother—pretty, feminine, loving, and sufficiently well organized to have time to spare for frequent escapist naps. When she decides to leave her husband, Max, she manages that perfectly too, doing well in school and at love—and feeling no more need for naps. If she is less daring than Cate (and she has always resented Cate's taunts to that effect), she is equally self-willed, and she dislikes Cate's wide-ranging diatribes against the conventional, traditional society in which she, Lydia, hopes to make her mark.

While Cate most wants to see the truth for what it is, Lydia most wants to be "widely admired and influential." Lydia gets her wish, but, because the measures of her success are external, she never feels secure in that success and always feels that something is lacking. Her relationship with her sons is emblematic of her internal conflict, for she most loves not the beautiful, self-contained boy who is like her but the messy, artistic one who is spiritually akin to Cate.

Cate, Lydia, and Nell are all painted in broad, clear strokes by Godwin, who portrays their sufferings with understanding and their self-delusions with a fine, ironic appreciation. Occasionally, there is less subtlety than there could be, as when Godwin repeatedly uses Cate's uptilted chin as a symbol of her independence and free spirit. Nevertheless, if Godwin's symbolism is sometimes obvious, it is also appropriate, and its clarity makes the novel accessible to a wide range of readers.

Themes and Meanings

When the Mountain City book club decides to discuss *The Scarlet Letter*, Cate tells Nell that the novel "asks a very crucial question 'Can the individual spirit survive the society in which it has to live?' " The question is crucial to *A Mother and Two Daughters* also, as the three protagonists struggle to re-create themselves in a world where the rules are changing. The self-definitions at which they arrive and the adjustments they make represent the survival strategies of three strong-willed individual spirits.

Cate, the romantic truth seeker, finds that, in order to achieve her own goals, she must learn self-control; she must learn when rage is productive and when it is not. Her spirit compromises but does not give in. Lydia, who buys into society's success story, is just as much her own creation as Cate but is rather less content, her spirit enslaved to some extent by her very success. Nell, who in the past protected the integrity of her individual spirit through critical detachment and self-defensive aloofness, establishes a more vital connection to her society through involvement and love. Perhaps because she has paid her social dues over the years, the little society of Mountain City is now ready to accept her on her own terms.

Certainly, all three protagonists recognize both losses and gains in the transitions they see going on around them. On the surface, the signs of disintegration are all too apparent. Colleges go bankrupt. Old landscapes give way to new shopping malls. Gasoline is scarce. Yet change also means new possibilities. The marriage of Leo Mansfield and Camilla Peverell-Watson, if not conventionally prudent, has nevertheless become one of those possibilities. So has the brilliant new career of Lydia, once a traditional, stay-at-home wife and mother. So has the self-invented career of Cate, which, in any case, suits her better than the job she previously held at her bankrupt college.

In the midst of all the changes, the family as locus of value is the one thing that gives stability to the lives of Godwin's characters. Despite the rivalry and tension, the fights and reluctant compromises, family members need one another in a world that offers few other constants. Thus, neither Cate nor Lydia can truly validate her own success without making peace with the other. (It is no accident that Theodora Blount, who has no family to count on, sees fit to erect the Theodora Blount Medical Wing at the Episcopal Retirement Home in advance of her retreat to that institution.)

One reason that the family, in Godwin's world, retains its vitality is that it, too, is in the process of being redefined. Nell's extended family, at the end of the novel, includes not only her new husband and her blood relatives but also Lydia's lover Stanley Edelman, Max's child Liza, and possibly even Wickie Lee. If there is one message Godwin has for her readers in *A Mother and Two Daughters*, it is that people need to connect themselves with, but not submerge themselves in, others. The ideal sort of connectedness—the sort the protagonists work to achieve with those they care about—means, then, not loss of identity but the creation of a life-support system in which identity can struggle to know itself and may even flourish.

Critical Context

With the four novels and many stories that preceded *A Mother and Two Daughters*, Gail Godwin had already won critical acclaim. The publication of her fifth novel gave her a best-seller. Godwin regards the novel as an artistic "turning point" for her as well, for in it she explored the consciousnesses of three characters instead of one and created a portrait of a whole society rather than of a single person.

Like the fiction of Anne Tyler and Margaret Drabble, *A Mother and Two Daughters* concerns itself with the evolution of the family in modern society and the roles it may play in the lives of modern women. Like most major women novelists from Jane Austen onward, Godwin considers how her heroines can best find or create places for themselves in a society over which they have negligible control but in which they can achieve some small influence.

Bibliography

Current Biography 56 (October, 1995): 26-29. Profiles Godwin's life and career as an award-winning novelist and short story writer. Critical reaction to her work is discussed, providing a valuable framework within which to compare Godwin's novels with various other of her writings.

Godwin, Gail. "A Dialogue with Gail Godwin." Interview by Lihong Xie. *The Mississippi Quarterly* 46 (Spring, 1993): 167-184. Godwin discusses her works, comparing them to major or minor keys in music depending on the emphasis she gives them in relation to certain plot elements and characters. Among the topics she covers in this interview are characterization, as well as the southern influence on her writing.

Kissel, Susan S. *Moving On: The Heroines of Shirley Ann Grau, Anne Tyler, and Gail Godwin.* Bowling Green, Ohio: Bowling Green State University Press, 1996. This critical analysis of Grau, Tyler, and Godwin reveals how the work of Chopin, McCullers, O'Connor, and Mitchell, as well as other southern women writers, has influenced each author. Also discusses Godwin's universal communal vision.

Pelzer, Linda C. "Visions and Versions of Self: The Other Women in *A Mother and Two Daughters*." *CRITIQUE: Studies in Contemporary Fiction* 34 (Spring, 1993): 155-163. Focusing on *A Mother and Two Daughters*, Pelzer explores the identity crisis of three women who must define themselves in relation to their families and the social contexts of their communities. An interesting study in the theme of self-creation in Godwin's works.

Wimsatt, Mary Ann. "Gail Godwin, the South, and the Canons." *The Southern Literary Journal* 27 (Spring, 1995): 86-95. Explores the two major causes of Godwin's exclusion from the canon: her feminism and the fact that her novels are bestsellers. Godwin's novels are saturated with autobiographical elements, and her portraits of women ensnared in unhappy marriages are derived from her own life experiences.

Xie, Lihong. *The Evolving Self in the Novels of Gail Godwin.* Baton Rouge: Louisiana State University, 1995. A critical appraisal of many of Godwin's novels, including a chapter devoted to *A Mother and Two Daughters*. A bibliography and index round out this outstanding resource.

Linda Seidel Costic

MOTHER NIGHT

Author: Kurt Vonnegut (1922-   )
Type of plot: Comic realism
Time of plot: 1938-1961
Locale: Nazi Germany, New York City, and Israel
First published: 1961

>*Principal characters:*
>>HOWARD W. CAMPBELL, JR., the protagonist, a former United States spy in Germany, author of a memoir written in an Israeli prison
>>HELGA NOTH, his German wife, who dies after the war
>>RESI NOTH, his sister-in-law, who later poses as Helga and lives with him
>>MAJOR FRANK WIRTANEN, who recruits Campbell as a spy and remains his contact; his real name, Harold J. Sparrow, is learned only at the novel's end
>>GEORGE KRAFT, a painter, a member of Alcoholics Anonymous, Campbell's best friend in New York City, and a Soviet spy; his real name is Colonel Iona Potapov
>>LIEUTENANT BERNARD B. O'HARE, who arrests Campbell in 1945 as a supposed Nazi and later hounds him in New York

The Novel

Mother Night—the title comes from a speech by Mephistopheles in *Faust*—is presented as the written memoir or confession of Howard W. Campbell, Jr. It has supposedly been edited by "Kurt Vonnegut, Jr.," who offers a signed editor's note concluding that Campbell "served evil too openly and good too secretly, the crime of his times." Yet it is evident that Campbell speaks for Vonnegut—as an unpretentious Everyman.

Against his better judgment, Campbell, an American who lived for a dozen years in Germany, agreed to become an intelligence agent for the United States. Throughout the war, pretending to be a Nazi, he insinuated secret messages into his regular radio broadcasts extolling Nazism and anti-Semitism. By the end of the war, Campbell is a world-famous Nazi; only three persons know he actually was a spy. Almost reluctantly, the United States government helps him escape a war-crimes trial by arranging for him to go underground in Manhattan. In 1960, however, after betrayal by his best friend and the death of the woman he loves, he gives himself up to Israeli agents. He writes his memoirs while awaiting trial in Jerusalem. The last chapter is written on the eve of his trial. He has just received a letter from Frank Wirtanen, who had recruited him as a spy, offering to testify in his behalf. Campbell, however, finds the prospect of freedom nauseating and proposes to execute himself that night "for crimes against himself." One must assume that he does in fact commit suicide, as "editor" Vonnegut refers to him in the past tense.

Vonnegut as author, writing in 1960, had assigned a date of 1961 to Campbell's manuscript, to lend it maximum contemporaneity with the trial of Adolf Eichmann, then under way in Israel. Eichmann was arrested in 1960 and executed in 1962. It is typical for Vonnegut to construct his novels around events immediately in the news. (*Mother Night*, as it turned out, was not actually released until 1962.)

The novel, then, is simply Campbell's autobiographical account; its forty-five rather brief chapters begin in the prison, then more or less alternate in flashback between wartime Germany and the years in Manhattan, with occasional chapters, including the last, returning to the present.

Although this work qualifies as a realistic novel, many of its situations, though fully entertaining, fall short of being believable: the broadcasting charade, for example, in which Campbell does not even know the messages he is transmitting (by clearing his throat, pausing, and the like); the possibility that he would accept his wife's sister, younger by fifteen or more years, as his wife, even after an absence of a dozen years; and the likelihood that Campbell would commit suicide when he was at least technically innocent. In addition, there is much comic absurdity in this novel—even black humor—which contrasts uncomfortably (some would say) with life in Nazi Germany—and in Auschwitz. For example, there is the White Christian Minuteman, the Reverend Doctor Lionel J. D. Jones, D.D.S., who proves that "Christ was not a Jew" by analyzing fifty famous paintings of Jesus, not one of which shows "Jewish jaws or teeth." His followers include Robert Sterling Wilson, "the Black Fuehrer of Harlem," and an unfrocked Paulist father, Patrick Keeley, patterned on the infamous Father Coughlin.

One finally realizes that the real issue in *Mother Night* is not so much the psychological veracity of its central characters as their usefulness in demonstrating certain philosophical propositions—or in asking fundamental questions relating to evil, guilt, and forgiveness. The result is a novel didactic in its parts, yet contradictory, not fully resolved, and continuously ironic in tone. Yet it is dead serious in its concern for truth.

The Characters

Like other Vonnegut protagonists, Howard Campbell tends to speak aphoristically. He tells the reader a number of things that are good for the reader to know or emulate. For example, in reply to the supposition that he hates America, Campbell replies, "That would be as silly as loving it. . . . It's impossible for me to get emotional about it, because real estate doesn't interest me." Elsewhere he says that "nationalities" do not interest him. He refers to himself as a "stateless person." Once he draws a swastika, a hammer and sickle, and a United States flag on his window and says, "Hooray, hooray, hooray." So much for patriotism. In this way Campbell presents one of the more important of Vonnegut's teachings.

Another of Vonnegut's lessons requires that Campbell (who was a successful playwright in Germany) admit that if Germany had won, there was every chance that he "would have become a sort of Nazi Edgar Guest, writing a daily [newspaper] column of optimistic doggerel. . . ." While this admission conflicts tentatively with the anti-patriotic theme, it serves the equally important idea that most Americans probably would have behaved like most Nazis, placed in the same situation. As the reader comes to identify more closely with Campbell, he is led to the brink of seeking a way possibly to forgive the Nazis—to forgive unspeakable evil. This hope is perhaps thwarted, however, by Campbell's inability to forgive himself (hence his suicide) for having furthered the cause of anti-Semitism so efficiently as to render his intelligence work insignificant.

Like Campbell, the other characters dramatize certain themes and ideas—though usually one motif dominates. Dr. Abraham Epstein, a survivor of Auschwitz, has only one message: "Forget Auschwitz. . . . I never think about it!" This, too, is a possibly healthy way of dealing with the Holocaust—though it conflicts with the very act of writing *Mother Night*. Similarly, Bernard B. O'Hare is brought onstage only to teach the reader the wrongness—and the futility—of vengeance.

Another minor character, Heinz Schildknecht, who, the reader is told, is Campbell's best friend and whose precious motorcycle Campbell steals in the last days of the war, dramatizes but one thing: friendship betrayed. This motif is reinforced later, in New York, by Iona Potapov, alias George Kraft, who in some part of his being is genuinely Campbell's friend. Yet he betrays Campbell. This more complex character also participates in the general investigation of schizophrenia that the novel undertakes. As a Russian spy, Potapov is insane; as an American spy, Campbell also exhibits schizophrenic traits. Finally, the absurd Nazi dentist Lionel Jones is insane to the degree that he is simply a caricature of a Fascist. His role appears to be to demonstrate that anti-Semitism is so crazy that no one could possibly countenance it. Then, one is forced to ask, how could the Holocaust have occurred? Great evil is a mystery, Vonnegut replies, and he proceeds with caution to seek its source.

The sisters Helga Noth and Resi Noth can almost be treated as one person, since each, in her relationship with Campbell, participates in acting out Campbell's idea of the "Nation of Two"—the title of a romantic play he never got around to writing but which was to show "how a pair of lovers in a world gone mad could survive by being loyal only to a nation composed of themselves—a nation of two." The implicit idea here, and a most tempting one, is that the best way to deal with gross political evil is to ignore it and retreat into sweet sexual love.

Themes and Meanings

Most of the important themes of the novel concern the question of how to cope with overwhelming evil, including ways of escaping from it. One way to escape from it is to commit suicide. When Campbell admits to Resi Noth that he no longer believes love is the only thing to live for, she pleads with him to tell her something else to live for—"anything at all." Yet he remains silent. She soon commits suicide. When Campbell himself commits suicide, one might wonder whether it is guilt that he feels (he has in any case claimed, "I had taught myself never to feel guilt") or a kind of paralysis before the absurdity and senselessness of human existence. The novel is obviously, therefore, existentialist in its basic values, though the perception of life as absurd has its roots in the Holocaust.

Campbell makes an excellent speech on the character of evil when he defeats O'Hare—a drunken, ignorant wretch who had imagined that he was "at war with pure evil" and would win it by killing Campbell. Campbell asks him: "Where is evil?" He answers the question himself: "[Evil is] that large part of every man that wants to hate without limit, that wants to hate with God on its side. . . . It's that part of an imbecile . . . that punishes and vilifies and makes war gladly."

Critical Context

Mother Night is Vonnegut's third novel, written well before he had attained best-seller status with *Slaughterhouse-Five: Or, The Children's Crusade* (1969). The latter is Vonnegut's most complete statement about Nazi Germany and his survival of the firestorm that destroyed Dresden on February 13, 1945. With the latter novel, Vonnegut achieved his greatest critical success—while *Mother Night* was at first totally ignored; it was never even reviewed until it was reissued in 1966. For the new edition, Vonnegut wrote an introduction indicating, among other things, that *Mother Night* is in some sense an anticipation of *Slaughterhouse Five*. For example, he confesses that if he had been born in Germany, he "probably would have been a Nazi, bopping Jews and Gypsies and Poles around. . . ." It is simply not true that the author, given his personal history, would have been a Nazi, but it is the right thing for him to say to help the reader understand that Nazis are human, as Americans are; it is not our duty to despise them for all time. This idea is developed more fully and successfully in *Slaughterhouse-Five*. Vonnegut also tells his readers in his introduction what the moral of *Mother Night* is—a typical Vonnegut aphorism that obviously fails to summarize this complex novel, but is well worth quoting: "We are what we pretend to be, so we must be careful about what we pretend to be."

Bibliography

Boon, Kevin, A. *Chaos Theory and the Interpretation of Literary Texts: The Case of Kurt Vonnegut*. Lewiston, N.Y.: Edwin Mellen Press, 1997. Extending the scientific theory of chaos to literary criticism, Boon uses words and phrases such as "strange attractors," "fractals," and the "micro/macro connection" to describe certain aspects of Vonnegut's prose. A somewhat offbeat but astute analysis of Vonnegut's work.

Broer, Lawrence. *Sanity Plea: Schizophrenia in the Novels of Kurt Vonnegut*. Ann Arbor, Mich.: UMI Research Press, 1989. Broer offers an in-depth analysis of individual novels by Vonnegut, including *Mother Night*. His study gives the reader a unique perspective on the common themes that run throughout Vonnegut's work.

Mustazza, Leonard, ed. *The Critical Response to Kurt Vonnegut*. Westport, Conn.: Greenwood Press, 1994. Critical essays present a detailed study of Vonnegut's various works, including *Mother Night*. A biographical introduction as well as a selected bibliography make this a valuable resource.

Reed, Peter J., and Mark Leeds, eds. *The Vonnegut Chronicles.* Westport, Conn.: Greenwood Press, 1996. Presenting a series of interviews and critical essays on Vonnegut's writing, this volume offers a broad variety of opinions and observations from scholars and journalists. A good source of information that helps the reader see more clearly the unique characteristics of individual novels against the wider context of Vonnegut's work.

Vonnegut, Kurt, Jr. *Fates Worse than Death: An Autobiographical Collage.* New York: G. P. Putnam's Sons, 1991. A revealing look at Vonnegut's life and state of the world. This collection of Vonnegut's essays examines both the personal issues and social events that shaped his distinctive writing style as well as his view of modern culture. Vonnegut offers a rare glimpse of his heart in this intimate self-portrait.

Donald M. Fiene

MRS. BRIDGE

Author: Evan S. Connell, Jr. (1924-   )
Type of plot: Satiric realism
Time of plot: From the early 1920's to the early 1940's, chiefly during the last ten
  years of that period
Locale: Kansas City, Missouri; Southampton, England; Paris; Monte Carlo; and
  Rome
First published: 1959

  Principal characters:
    INDIA BRIDGE, the protagonist, an upper-middle-class Kansas City
      housewife
    WALTER BRIDGE, her husband, a successful lawyer
    RUTH BRIDGE, their eldest child, eventually an assistant editor on a
      New York fashion magazine
    CAROLYN BRIDGE DAVIS, their second child, an avid golfer and wife of
      Parallel, Kansas, dry-goods salesman Gil Davis
    DOUGLAS BRIDGE, their third child, who eventually enlists in the army
      and takes basic training in Arizona
    GRACE BARRON, another Kansas City housewife and Mrs. Bridge's alter
      ego, an eventual suicide
    MABEL ONG, the quintessential Kansas City clubwoman
    DR. FOSTER, Mrs. Bridge's minister
    HARRIET, her black housekeeper
    ALICE JONES, a black child, at one time Carolyn's most frequent
      Saturday playmate
    PAQUITA DE LAS TORRES, the girl from the wrong part of Kansas City to
      whom Doug, as an adolescent, is attracted
    JAY DUCHESNE, a Kansas City boyfriend of Carolyn

The Novel

  The central focus of Evan Connell's *Mrs. Bridge* is the protagonist's uncertainty
about her own identity and about the meaning and purpose of her life. The first sentences of the book, linked to the epigraph from Walt Whitman, establish this emphasis: "Her first name was India—she was never able to get used to it. It seemed to her
that her parents must have been thinking of someone else when they named her." In
her own eyes, and in those of the narrator of Connell's novel, from the start of the book
she is "Mrs." Bridge, wife of the successful lawyer Walter Bridge, mother of his three
children—Ruth, Carolyn, and Douglas Bridge—and a typical female member of her
upper-middle-class circle in Kansas City, Missouri. Depending for her identity upon
the stability of the social milieu in which she lives, Mrs. Bridge, as her way of life and
the values of her class come under fire in the two decades before World War II, experi-

ences boredom, a sense of purposelessness, and eventually even a vaguely terrifying sense of isolation.

Covering a period from the early 1920's to the early 1940's, with an emphasis on the last ten years of this period, *Mrs. Bridge* presents the action as a series of 117 episodes from the life of the title character and not as a unified, symmetrical plot. Connell's introduction of Mrs. Bridge compresses her first thirty-five years of life into the three pages of the first two episodes, and in it he establishes both her utter conventionality and her disillusionment with her life. Venturing to express to her young husband her own desire for sex, she is ignored: "This was the night Mrs. Bridge concluded that while marriage might be an equitable affair, love itself was not." As a young mother, she is frustrated in her expectation that her children, like her, should go through life with an unimpaired set of conventional values. She is shocked when Ruth, as a very small child, strips off her bathing suit and parades around the neighborhood swimming pool. She is annoyed when Doug insists on using the guest towels in the bathroom, towels which her guests are sufficiently well-bred not to use; she is antagonistic when Carolyn chooses Alice Jones, the daughter of the black gardener working next door, as a Saturday morning playmate. In episode after episode, Mrs. Bridge confronts evidence of the inadequacy of conventional responses to life. Her friend Grace Barron, similarly restless and dissatisfied, exhibits signs of depression and by the end of the novel commits suicide. Mabel Ong, the mannish Kansas City clubwoman, decides to seek help from a therapist. Dr. Foster, Mrs. Bridge's minister, becomes hysterical when trapped in a crowded elevator and pushes and claws his way out, showing no concern for the safety of anybody except himself.

As they mature, Mrs. Bridge's children make sexual and marital choices which do not meet her approval. Ruth is not attracted to the clean-cut young sons of her mother's friends; the young men who telephone her seem always to have foreign names and to speak in rough, uncultured voices. In high school, Doug is attracted to Paquita de las Torres, whose sister is a burlesque dancer; the girl's "hairy arms and rancid odor were almost too much for Mrs. Bridge to bear." Carolyn enrolls at the University of Kansas in Lawrence but drops out of school to marry Gil Davis, the son of a plumber, and to settle in a Parallel, Kansas, neighborhood into which black families are moving. Mrs. Bridge reflects that, except for her housekeeper Harriet, and the laundress, Beulah Mae, she "had never known any Negroes socially; not that she avoided it, just that there weren't any in the neighborhood, or at the country club, or in the Auxiliary. There just weren't any for her to meet, that was all." The social dynamics of the world are changing, and reluctantly Mrs. Bridge finds herself accepting behavior and attitudes that she once would have rejected.

Her husband, Walter, remains the one constant in her life, but she does not derive much comfort from his rigid orthodoxy. Unlike his wife, he never questions the rightness of his positions; he uses them to keep the world, including Mrs. Bridge, at arm's length. It is characteristic that he alone ignores the danger posed by an approaching tornado and remains at his table at the country club, Mrs. Bridge dutifully beside him, when everybody else in the building has evacuated to the basement. Mr. Bridge is committed to his career and to the aggressive making of money; therefore, he responds to Gil Davis's frontal assault in the office and accepts Carolyn's engagement, and her marriage, to an otherwise unsuitable young man. He substitutes expensive gifts for his own presence in the lives of his wife and children. Mrs. Bridge finds these gifts embarrassing: "She was conscious of people on the street staring at her when, wrapped in ermine and driving the Lincoln, she started off to a party at the country club." Even the trip to Europe which he gives her as a birthday gift, the fulfillment of a promise made when they were engaged, leads Mrs. Bridge to realize that she does not know Walter's real personality. In her attempts to get closer to him, she becomes increasingly conscious of her isolation.

Mrs. Bridge reaches its thematic climax in the final episode, in which, with Mr. Bridge dead and her children out of the house, Connell's protagonist confronts the emptiness of her life. She has had intimations of it before. One night, seated at her dressing table and spreading cold cream on her face before going to bed, Mrs. Bridge realizes that "she was disappearing into white, sweetly scented anonymity." She is tempted to try psychotherapy, as did her friend Mabel Ong, but the memory of Mr. Bridge's views on the subject dissuades her. In the final episode of the novel, she backs her old Lincoln out of the garage, stalls the engine, and finds herself unable to open the doors because of the walls on either side. She blows the horn, taps on the window, and calls out, "but no one answered, unless it was the falling snow." She is absolutely alone, and that is where Connell leaves her.

The Characters

While Mrs. Bridge begins as a stereotype and remains throughout the novel an object of Connell's satire, she emerges as a fully rounded, thoroughly credible character by the end of the book. She is as much the object of Connell's wry compassion as of his eye for the ironic detail. Despite her upper-middle-class perspective, Mrs. Bridge entertains doubts about both her own character and her value system. She makes definite, if futile, attempts to break outside the norms of her Kansas City circle by learning Spanish, taking painting lessons, and working with charities. She wears gloves, however, while distributing used clothing to the poor; in her painting of Leda and the swan, she clothes "Leda in a flowered dressmaker bathing suit" like her own; and she is easily distracted by her husband or children when she works with the set of Spanish records. Nevertheless, Mrs. Bridge possesses the virtue of recognizing that she has "no confidence in her life," and her efforts to find something in which to believe give her dignity. Like her friend and foil Grace Barron, Mrs. Bridge wants to be a person and not simply an automaton reacting unthinkingly to circumstances. She shares this characteristic with her three children, even though she does not recognize the fact.

After Mrs. Bridge herself, Connell focuses attention most sharply on Ruth, Carolyn, and Douglas, whose rebellions against their mother's values point up the bleakness of her situation. Most completely successful in breaking away from the Kansas City norms is Ruth, who ends up in New York as an assistant editor on a fashion magazine. Like her brother and sister, she equates independence with sexual freedom, shocking Mrs. Bridge with stories about a gay male associate and writing a letter to her mother while in bed with a man named Dowdey. When he asks if Mrs. Bridge looks like her, Ruth replies, "She's my sister's mother," a reply that reveals her sense of estrangement. Carolyn's rebellion is tamer, less complete, than Ruth's. She is the daughter Mrs. Bridge prefers because she adapts more easily to life in Kansas City. An avid golfer, Carolyn enrolls in college at the University of Kansas. When she drops out of school, it is to marry Gil Davis and to assume the role of housewife—a role which Mrs. Bridge regards as a woman's natural calling. Times have changed, however, and Carolyn's marriage does not follow the pattern established by her parents; she frequently leaves her husband to come home to Mrs. Bridge.

Douglas's role is made easier by the fact that he is male, for Mrs. Bridge grants him freedom on that account. She attempts to force him to shave the mustache that he grows during army training, but she is not unhappy to have him take control of the household after her husband's death. When Douglas denies the housekeeper's request for a raise, Harriet "stopped calling him by his first name and referred to him as Mr. Bridge, and his mother, hearing this for the first time, began to weep." Returning to camp, he sends his mother a letter in which he assures her that Mr. Bridge, in his own way, loved her. It resembles the letters Mrs. Bridge had received from her husband when he was traveling on business, and in it Douglas shows that he has escaped his mother's control by assuming the traditional masculine role until now occupied by Mr. Bridge.

The other characters in *Mrs. Bridge* are less developed, and they serve chiefly as foils to the protagonist and her children or as objects of Connell's satire. Among the former are Grace Barron and Mabel Ong; like Mrs. Bridge, they are stereotypical upper-class Kansas City matrons. Among the latter are Dr. Foster, the self-centered clergyman; Jay Duchesne, the boyfriend whom Carolyn rejects in favor of Gil Davis; and Paquita de las Torres, whose sexuality is a parody of the conduct of Mrs. Bridge's daughter Ruth.

Themes and Meanings

The thematic point of the novel emerges in the episode in which Connell's protagonist picks up an unidentified book by Joseph Conrad and reads a passage, underlined by her husband's unambitious uncle Shannon Bridge, about the capacity of some people to live without being aware of life's potentiality. Because of her dissatisfaction with her own life, Mrs. Bridge does not fit this paradigm exactly. She is aware that living may have more to it than the typical Kansas City society matron recognizes, but she never breaks through to that possible meaning.

The sharply detailed, episodic narrative structure of *Mrs. Bridge* focuses attention on the particulars of each situation and on the process of social change at work in the United States which provides Connell with the context in which to explore Mrs. Bridge as a character. Changing American mores, seen in the novel most clearly in the areas of sexual expression and race relations, explain the gap in communication which opens up between Mrs. Bridge and her children. Her inability to change with the times makes Mrs. Bridge an object of satire. It is also a mark of her humanity.

Despite the use of Conrad to establish the thematic point of the novel, art and artists do not provide the answer for which Mrs. Bridge is looking. Neither does religion. Indeed, other than the fact that she ought to be searching, Connell provides few clues in the book about what she should be looking for.

Critical Context

Nominated for the National Book Award for Fiction in 1960, *Mrs. Bridge* was both a best-seller and a critical success. The consensus is that this novel and *Mr. Bridge* (1969), a companion volume which covers some but not all of the same material, deserve to be Connell's best-known works because of the skill with which he employs their episodic structures to build fully rounded characters. In their depiction of such ordinary people living fundamentally desperate lives, *Mrs. Bridge* and *Mr. Bridge* have become the standard against which his subsequent fiction is measured.

In other books—*The Patriot* (1960), *The Diary of a Rapist* (1966), *The Connoisseur* (1974), and *Double Honeymoon* (1976)—Connell explores personalities obsessed with goals which distort their perceptions of reality. In this, they are like Walter Bridge, as he appears in both novels, and not like Mrs. Bridge, who has no clear sense of what she wants out of life. This search for significance beyond the ordinary, which characterizes all the male protagonists of Connell's books, sets Mrs. Bridge off from the rest of his central characters. With her, he deals with the thoughts and feelings of a complex human being, and he manages to make her likable as much for her weaknesses as despite them. Because of the skill of this characterization, *Mrs. Bridge* is considered Connell's finest novel.

Bibliography

Brooke, Allen. "Introverts and Emigres." *New Criterion* 14 (October, 1995): 58-63. Allen offers a criticism of the works of Connell and Vladimir Nabokov, character analyses, and a comparison of the stories and characters to the authors' lives. Brooke discusses *Mrs. Bridge* in detail, outlining the "repressed, bourgeois world of the Bridges, the world Connell himself was born into in 1924."

Connell, Evan S. "Notes from a Bottle Found on the Beach at Sausalito: An Interview with Evan S. Connell." Interview by Edward Myers. *Literary Review* 35 (Fall, 1991): 60-69. Connell talks about his personal background, career history, and major works. He particularly focuses on his fascination with alchemy and how his interest is woven into his works. He briefly discusses *Mrs. Bridge*.

Kauffmann, Stanley. Review of *Mr. and Mrs. Bridge*. *The New Republic* 203 (December 24, 1990): 26-27. Discusses Connell's humane portrayal of a middle-class family in his novel and whether his observations are successfully translated to film. Although the book is not the focus of the essay, Kauffmann makes some salient points about the novel.

Wadler, Joyce. "The Creator of Mr. and Mrs. Bridge Goes Home Again—with Reluctance and No Thanks for the Memories." *People Weekly* 34 (December 10, 1990):

65-66. Profiles the life and work of Connell and discusses the similarities, as well as the differences, between Connell's best-selling books *Mrs. Bridge* and *Mr. Bridge* and the film version. Provides interesting insight into the background of Connell's novels.

Robert C. Petersen

MRS. STEVENS HEARS THE MERMAIDS SINGING

Author: May Sarton (1912-1995)
Type of plot: Psychological realism
Time of plot: The 1960's
Locale: Cape Ann, Massachusetts
First published: 1965

> *Principal characters:*
> F. HILARY STEVENS, the protagonist, a seventy-year-old poet and
> novelist
> MAR HEMMER, the college-age grandson of a neighbor
> PETER SELVERSEN, an interviewer from a fictitious New York
> publication, *The Review*
> JENNY HARE, a short-story writer who is the companion of Selversen
> on the Stevens interview assignment

The Novel

The action of *Mrs. Stevens Hears the Mermaids Singing* takes place at the country home of F. Hilary Stevens in Cape Ann, Massachusetts, during one full day in May and the following morning. Early in the morning of the day that the interviewers are coming, Mrs. Stevens is hailed by her young friend Mar Hemmer, whose plea for a talk she delays until she is properly awake. When Mar does not reappear, Mrs. Stevens plunges into preparations for the interview, which is set for four in the afternoon. During her activities Mrs. Stevens thinks about Mar, her friends, her lovers, and her long-dead husband. At three o'clock, Sarton takes the reader briefly to the nervous interviewers en route to Cape Ann. Then comes the interview, which makes up half of the book. During the talk, Mrs. Stevens relives far more of her life than she reveals to the interviewers. The epilogue returns to Mar, who appears out of the fog the next morning, and with whom Hilary Stevens shares the understanding of herself and of life which came to her during the interview.

The flashbacks during the interview, combined with Hilary's earlier thoughts, fall into place as a chronological account of her life, the pattern of which she comes to perceive as she talks and as she muses. Rebelling against her controlled, frugal, Beacon Street Boston heritage, at fifteen, Hilary fell in love with her governess: This first "epiphany" produced a novel. Subsequent attachments to men, to the war-haunted veteran Adrian, her husband, to a doctor, and to a French critic all brought her comfort. Only her passions for women, however, to her feminine "Muses," have produced novels or poems. Sometimes these passions were not consummated. When a physical affair resulted, it was destructive, whether it resulted in repugnance, as with the divorcée Willa MacPherson, or in jealousy and rage, as with the scientist whose seemingly objective criticisms of Hilary's works masked the bitter resentment of the noncreative person toward the creative spirit. Perhaps the ideal Muse, suggests Hilary, was the dead French woman in whose house she had lived for a time and whose lingering love produced another epiphany without personal demands.

The climax of the novel comes near the end of the interview, when Hilary has another epiphany, this time involving her self-controlled mother, in whom the creative urge was buried. As a result of that insight, Hilary tells Mar the next morning that she must begin another creative work. She urges him to live life fully, so that he will not deny his creative capacities by cheap escapes into sexuality without feeling.

The Characters

Although Mrs. Stevens is seventeen years older than May Sarton was at the time of the book's publication, and although there are many other differences between the author and her creation (Sarton, for example, has never married), in many ways F. Hilary Stevens is an autobiographical character. In her upper-class, cultured background, in her love of the country, in her disciplined work habits, in her production of both poetry and novels, and in her dependence on inspiration from personal involvement with other women, Hilary Stevens is like May Sarton. The comments made in the fictional interview are very like comments of Sarton to her own interviewers. May Sarton understands the "feminine" aspects of her protagonist—the need to arrange a beautiful bouquet, the compulsion to serve a proper tea to her guests, even her rather maternal response to young Jenny Hare and to troubled young Mar Hemmer.

The relationship between Mrs. Stevens and Mar, however, is extremely complex. Mar is a desperate, angry young man. At Amherst he fell in love with a male chemistry instructor and, after one sexual encounter, was rejected. Unable to continue his college career, he dropped out and came to his grandfather's country place, where he broods, sails, and confides in Mrs. Stevens. In Mar, Mrs. Stevens sees boyish qualities, which remind her of her younger self, but also the masculine aggressiveness of her father. Moreover, she recognizes creative talent, which she tells Mar will never come to fruition unless he gives himself to life.

The interviewer Peter Selversen is well-known for his skill in eliciting worthwhile comments from great writers about writing. Yet although his questions and his responses to the sometimes tentative, sometimes firm statements by F. Hilary Stevens are intelligent and plausible, he is clearly a performer with the masculine quality of detached analysis. Although he can find the right words, Mrs. Stevens protests that the word must be "incarnate." This concept is beyond Selversen, but his companion Jenny Hare, the girlfriend of the associate editor of the publication, who was sent along on the interview as a token woman, understands Hilary Stevens and is inspired by her to be herself, both as a woman and as a writer.

Sarton's use of point of view is largely limited to the perceptions and musings of Mrs. Stevens. It is through her eyes and through dialogue that Mar is seen. Except for a brief glimpse of Peter's thoughts as he approaches the interview, his character is developed dramatically through dialogue. Sarton does, however, reveal Jenny's reactions as the interview progresses. Perhaps as a result, Jenny is a more convincing character than either of the men, who sometimes appear to illustrate abstractions rather than to live in their own right.

Themes and Meanings

In *Mrs. Stevens Hears the Mermaids Singing*, May Sarton is concerned with the woman as artist. In order to explore this issue, she distinguishes what she calls masculine qualities, such as objectivity, detachment, and aggressiveness, from feminine qualities, such as an openness to emotion and a readiness to provide nurture. Although the feminine qualities may produce an impulse to create art, rather than children, the rejection of the maternal impulse is difficult, while the production of art when the artist is exhausted from being a mother is even more difficult.

Sarton is convinced that the Muse is feminine in nature. For a man to be inspired by a woman is conventional. Although a woman may love a man, however, she is inspired by women. Here the lesbian theme becomes important, for the feminine Muse may sometimes be a feminine lover. Yet as Mrs. Stevens comments, the source of inspiration is less important than the work created. The source disappears; the work endures.

A third theme, then, is the necessary progress of the artist from isolation to solitude. After the Muse is gone, for a time the deserted or rejected lover may feel the miseries of isolation. Yet as she begins the process of creation, isolation becomes blessed, self-contented solitude. It is this solitude which Mrs. Stevens welcomes after the interviewers leave and Mar is attended to.

Finally, the revelation which comes to Mrs. Stevens at the end of the day of the interview is an insight into living as well as into writing. The process of that day has been symbolized by the Venetian mirror, somewhat cloudy but both beautiful and usable, which remains from her marriage. Mrs. Stevens must see herself in order to profit from the incidents of her life, however painful. For her will come insight; for her work, inspiration. Instead of striking out at false lovers or carping critics, she must conquer herself. As she points out to Mar, the blasted quarry finally becomes a still and beautiful lake. Thus pain produces not only art but also knowledge, and Hilary urges Mar to accept life, pain and all, rather than to diminish himself, like so many Americans, by refusing to give himself for fear of suffering.

Critical Context

Mrs. Stevens Hears the Mermaids Singing is particularly significant in that it is a book about being an artist by a full-time writer, who augments her income by lecturing but who has rejected the usual academic source of income. Teaching is a position of power, May Sarton says, and power prevents poets from changing their ideas as freely as they like. Certainly Sarton's single-minded commitment has resulted in an impressive output of novels, autobiographies, and volumes of poetry. Although her books are not best-sellers, her poetry is unusually popular in an unpoetic age, and her finely crafted novels have many enthusiastic readers, probably because they combine interesting perceptions with a clarity of presentation which is a relief from the muddle of much modern work.

Because the emphasis is on the creative process, the lesbian theme is not of primary importance in *Mrs. Stevens Hears the Mermaids Singing*. What is important is the discussion of woman as artist, a role which seems to involve sacrifices and denials greater than those of men who serve the Muse. Thus, although Sarton, like James Joyce in *A Portrait of the Artist as a Young Man* (1916), may discuss epiphanies, her female artist will have agonizing struggles of a kind not seen in Joyce.

Although some critics have regarded Sarton's fiction as too limited to the problems and sensibilities of the cultivated, well-to-do upper classes, the steadily increasing interest in her work indicates an appreciation of her craftsmanship and of the validity and depth of her insights. She is not an important female writer; she is an important writer who happens to be a woman.

Bibliography
Bloin, L. P. *May Sarton: A Bibliography.* Metuchen, N.J.: Scarecrow Press, 1978. In two parts, the first listing Sarton's poetry, novels, nonfiction, essays, and articles. The second part lists secondary sources, including book reviews. A conscientious compilation of sources that is most useful to the Sarton scholar. The author acknowledges Sarton's assistance in putting together this work.

Curley, Dorothy N., Maurice Kramer, and Elaine F. Kramer, eds. *Modern American Literature.* 4 vols. 4th ed. New York: Ungar, 1969-1976. A collection of reviews and criticisms of Sarton's poems and novels, the latest entry being 1967. Includes criticism on *Mrs. Stevens Hears the Mermaids Singing,* considered an important book and which the author says was most difficult to write. The supplement has reviews on Sarton's *Collected Poems.*

Evans, Elizabeth. *May Sarton.* Rev. ed. Boston: Twayne, 1989. In this volume in Twayne's United States Authors series, Evans upholds Sarton as a writer who speaks for women, insisting they claim their own identity; hence, her increasing popularity among feminists. An interesting addition to this somewhat standard criticism is an appendix of Sarton's letters to her editor while writing *Mrs. Stevens Hears the Mermaids Singing.* Selected bibliography.

Grumbach, Doris. "The Long Solitude of May Sarton." *The New Republic* 170 (June 8, 1974): 31-32. Grumbach draws together Sarton's philosophy, in particular the serenity of her writing in the face of her declared "traumas." Noting that critics have often ignored Sarton, Grumbach says: "Hers has been a durable fire . . . her small room seems to make most male critics uncomfortable." An article well worth reading.

Peters, Margot. *May Sarton: A Biography.* New York: Knopf, 1997. The first full-length biographical treatment of this most autobiographical of writers. After her death in 1995, there was an upsurge of interest in Sarton, and this book certainly contributes to her legacy. Peters herself is fair in her assessment of Sarton: clear about why this woman inspired such a devoted following among readers and equally straightforward about her uncertainty concerning the literary value of much of Sarton's work.

Sibley, Agnes. *May Sarton.* New York: Twayne, 1972. Obviously a must for criticism on Sarton, because there is so little of book-length size written about her—despite her prodigious output. This study discusses Sarton's poems, from *Encounter in April* in 1937 to *A Durable Fire*, published in 1972. Sibley has grouped novels under two themes that she considers relevant to Sarton: "detachment" for the early novels and "communion" for the later ones.

Rosemary M. Canfield Reisman

MULATA

Author: Miguel Ángel Asturias (1899-1974)
Type of plot: Symbolic allegory
Time of plot: The 1960's
Locale: Quiavicús and Tierrapaulita, Guatemala
First published: Mulata de tal, 1963 (English translation, 1967)

> *Principal characters:*
> CELESTINO YUMÍ, a poor Guatemalan peasant who yearns for riches
> and importance
> CATALINA ZABALA, Yumí's loving wife
> THE MULATA, a haunting, lusty woman whom Yumí marries on their
> first meeting

The Novel

Miguel Ángel Asturias bases *Mulata* on a popular Guatemalan legend—that of a man who sells his wife to the devil in exchange for unlimited wealth. The novel begins with Celestino Yumí parading through the religious fairs of the countryside around Quiavicús with the zipper of his pants open, in compliance with a bargain he has struck with Tazol, the corn-husk devil. In this way, Yumí will cause women to commit sins by looking at his private parts and then compound those sins by their accepting Communion without going again to confession. Successful in luring the women, Yumí is next informed by Tazol that, to complete the bargain whereby Yumí will become wealthy beyond his dreams, he has to hand over his wife, Catalina Zabala, to Tazol. Yumí is hesitant at first, but the promise of riches, importance, and power proves too much, and he finally consents. Tazol takes possession of Catalina, or Niniloj, as Yumí calls her, and grants Yumí his fondest wishes—lands, crops, and money in abundance.

Once rich, Yumí discovers that what Tazol had told him is true: Everyone asks for and respects his opinion on anything and everything—as Yumí himself remarks, "Just because I'm rich, not because I know anything." Yet Yumí finds that riches and power cannot compensate for the loss of his wife; he yearns for her love and takes to drinking and carousing. While at a religious festival with his friend Timoteo Teo Timoteo, he encounters the Mulata. Drunk and instantly overcome with lust for this ripe and haunting woman, Yumí marries her in a civil ceremony and carries her home. There, in their marriage bed, Yumí discovers that the Mulata, much to his chagrin and embarrassment, is bisexual and dangerous. As much animal as human, she dominates and torments him in such a way that Yumí finds it excrutiatingly terrifying to lie with her. He tries to undo the bargain with Tazol, and he succeeds in reacquiring Catalina, who has been turned into a dwarf by Tazol. Catalina comes to live with Yumí and his new wife, and the Mulata at first accepts her as a living doll with which to play but quickly tires of the idea and prefers to mistreat her. Yumí and Catalina hope to rid the household of the Mulata, and Catalina, in a clever ruse, with the help of the Mulata's bear, lures the Mulata to the cave of the Grumpy Bird and seals her in, but the Mulata eats the bird and escapes, provoking in the process a cataclysmic volcanic eruption that destroys Quiavicús and all of Yumí's wealth.

Now, even more destitute than before the bargain with Tazol, Yumí has no idea of what to do. Catalina, who in her dealings with Tazol and the Mulata has acquired a taste for witchcraft, convinces Yumí to journey with her to Tierrapaulita, the city where all those who wish to learn the black arts must go. Unable to traverse the devil's nine turns, they turn back, then try again. This time, Catalina fastens to her chest a cross in Tazol's image, fashioned of dry corn leaves, and the devil's powers are neutralized. In this way, they make their way to Tierrapaulita with Tazol as protector, even though the devil himself fears entering Tierrapaulita.

Yumí and Catalina find Tierrapaulita such a fantastic and terrifying place that, despite their lust for the power that witchcraft will bring them, they decide to leave. Cashtoc, the Immense, the red earth demon of Indian myth, prevents them from leaving, employing other demons from Xibalba, the Mayan hell. Catalina gives birth to Tazolín (having been impregnated through the naval by Tazol) and is pronounced the great Giroma, the powerful mother witch. Taking vengeance on Yumí for his bargain with Tazol and his marriage to the Mulata, Catalina turns him into a dwarf, only to change her mind later, when, jealous of the attentions paid him by the dwarf Huasanga, she transforms him into a giant.

This act and Huasanga's cries precipitate an earthquake during which Cashtoc calls his legions together and removes them and all the sorcerers from Tierrapaulita, destroying the city in the process. Cashtoc empties the town because he realizes that the Christian demon Cadanga has arrived and with him "the ones who will demand generations of men without any reason for being, without any magic words, unfortunate in the nothingness and the emptiness of their ego."

Yumí and Catalina, along with other witches, wizards, and sorcerers, abandon the retreat of Cashtoc and return to Tierrapaulita, only to find that their powers are nonexistent now that Cadanga, the Christian demon, is dominant. In a nightmarish ceremony, Yumí, in the guise of a pockmarked Indian, representing the Christian demon Cadanga, does battle with the Mulata, in the form of the new sexton, representing Cashtoc. Recognizing each other despite their disguises, Yumí and the Mulata engage in a battle of wits, during which the Mulata, in order to save Yumí (who has become a hedgehog and is fighting with the priest, who has become a spider with eleven thousand legs and arms), resumes her form and with a magic mist immobilizes the combatants. In a subsequent Requiem Mass, the Mulata is married to Yumí (still in hedgehog form) for an eternity of death.

As punishment for her betrayal, Cashtoc deprives the Mulata of one leg, one eye, one ear, one hand, one arm, one lip, one teat, and her sex, then sends her crawling away like a snake. Cashtoc and his legions once again take leave of Tierrapaulita, leaving it and its citizens to the Christian demon Cadanga, who incites the populace to breed because his hell is in need of souls.

The novel ends with a horrific cataclysm in which Tierrapaulita and all of its inhabitants are destroyed by earthquakes and volcanic eruptions. Yumí and Catalina are crushed, and the Mulata, whole again but with her magic powers gone, quarters Yumí's body to remove his golden bones and is set alight by the rays of the moon in the process. Only the priest survives, where in the hospital doctors are unable to diagnose what form of leprosy he has, if leprosy it is.

The Characters

Celestino Yumí, a poor, simple wood gatherer, comes to vibrant life in the hands of Asturias. Yumí, dissatisfied with his hardscrabble existence, yearns for what his friend Timoteo Teo Timoteo has: land, horses, crops, and the respect of others. Though he bargains with the corn-husk devil for riches in exchange for his wife, Tazol has to convince him that Catalina has been unfaithful to him before he finally agrees. The irony of the bargain does not escape him, since one of the reasons he wishes to be rich is to be able to make life easier for his beloved wife. As he says to Tazol, "But I'm already weeping, with all my heart, because she's my wife, the only thing I have and I'm going to give her to you, Tazol, just because she was unfaithful to me and because I want to be rich."

Possessed of a shrewd native intelligence, though he professes otherwise, Yumí understands a hard truth: that the rich and powerful can do practically as they want and that the poor, the powerless, have no recourse but to accept it. Once rich, he acts accordingly, throwing his wealth around, parading it proudly in imitation of others he has seen. Impulsive by nature, he acts without regard to consequences, then allows those consequences to dictate his course of action.

Like the other human characters in the novel, Yumí is a victim, a pawn of natural and supernatural forces, but unlike the Mulata and Catalina, he does not struggle or attempt (past that of bargaining with Tazol) to control his surroundings. Treated with affection and understanding by Asturias, Yumí is seen as man without guile, easily led, perhaps, but whose basic motivation is his undying love for Catalina.

Through Yumí, Asturias portrays Catalina's character as Yumí sees her. She is a good wife, uncomplaining when hungry, good at mending, supportive of his needs, and, best of all, happy and jolly. Yet this is not all that she is. When Yumí reclaims her from Tazol, and she goes to live with him and the Mulata, it is Catalina who devises the plan to get rid of the Mulata. Resourceful and quick, when Yumí loses his wealth, she earns their living dancing with a bear. The idea to become sorcerers is hers, and when unable to get past the devil's nine turns, it is her idea to tie a cross of Tazol on her belly in order to get through. Also, she is not above revenge. Once she becomes the mother of Tazolín and, therefore, a great witch, she has Yumí turned into a dwarf as punishment for selling her to Tazol. Unlike Yumí, she is a fighter, and in the final cataclysm, as everything is falling on her and knowing it is a futile gesture, Catalina throws her hands up "to use them against the mass of the mountains that were falling down on Tierrapaulita."

Of the human characters in the novel, the Mulata is the most memorable. Her skin a rich, dark color, her eyes like extinguished coals, and a nature that is more animal than human, the Mulata is a haunting and haunted woman. Her eyes are what attract Yumí, and her taut, coltish body unleashes an overwhelming lust in him. A moon spirit, the Mulata is governed by the phases of the moon, and like the moon of Guatemalan legend who dares not let the sun possess her from the front for fear of engendering monsters, she does not allow Yumí to have sex with her from the front, only from the rear. The Mulata is a hermaphrodite and is in constant inner turmoil, sometimes friendly, kind, and affectionate, then without warning, savage and destructive. She laments to Yumí that she is like an animal without a proper owner. Yumí finds her both fascinating and repulsive, inspiring in him lust and fear. At night, Yumí lies awake, "always fearful that the beast would wake up and grab him unexpectedly, explosions of fury that coincided with the phases of the moon."

Aware of her duality but unable to do anything about it, the Mulata reaches out to destroy herself and others in a vain attempt to rid herself of herself. Though in the first part of the novel the Mulata serves as punishment to Yumí for having bartered his wife, toward the end of the novel she saves his life.

Throughout the novel, Asturias treats his characters with compassion, and his affection for them shines brightly. These are people struggling against forces beyond their control in an attempt to find meaning to their lives, and though the struggle may bring tragic consequences, it may also bring a wisdom of sorts—perhaps the struggle itself means that life is not hopeless.

Themes and Meanings

In *Mulata*, as in the majority of his works, Asturias concerns himself with the effects of the continuous clash of two cultures: the Spanish Christian culture and the culture of the Mayas and their descendants.

In Asturias's view, this clash has left the Indian and mestizo suspended between the past and the present, between myth and reality, a suspension where myth can be reality and reality myth, where the past is the present and the present the past. Their daily reality is dominated by tradition saturated with legends, myths, and superstitions. In such a world, anything is possible: Dead animals may arise and speak, women may change into dwarfs, and boar-men may counsel humans. It is this magic reality that, in Asturias's work, the people use as a defense against the four-and-a-half centuries of persecution to which they have been subjected since the Conquest. Unfortunately, this response to the Spanish Christian culture precludes a true and pure amalgam of the two cultures. It is Asturias's view that the reason for this is not that the ancient Mayan beliefs have adulterated the Christian culture but that Christianity arrived in an already adulterated form, which then proceeded to adulterate the Mayan beliefs.

It is no accident that the clashes in Tierrapaulita between the ancient Indian myths and the Spanish Christian beliefs are conducted by demons, Indian and Christian, and not by the deities of either. The deities are no longer available to do battle since the beliefs that have survived are dominated by demons on both sides, each side bent on the destruction, physical and spiritual, of the people.

In the words of Father Chimalpín (and Asturias), "A person is not a Christian just because he is one; a person is a Christian because it implies loving more, loving more is giving one's self more, is reaching, through that giving, everything that surrounds us, a nursery of happiness where one fulfills everything." This is not, however, the Christianity that the Spanish brought. Instead, the Conquest brought a Christianity that resulted in men who considered themselves an end in themselves. In the words of Cashtoc, the supreme Mayan demon: "Plants, animals, stars . . . they all exist together, all together as they were created! It has occurred to none of them to make a separate existence, to take life for his exclusive use, only man, who must be destroyed because of his presumption of existing in isolation, alien to the millions of destinies that are being woven and unwoven around him!"

Asturias sees clearly that the clash between these cultures has resulted in deep conflicts and confusion in the psyche of the Indians, who have served as the battleground for these opposing forces. Though the two competing cultures form one, at the same time each cancels out the other, with neither making a whole by itself. The resulting hybrid mentality of the Indians is symbolized by the Mulata's persona. She has no proper name, she is simply a certain Mulata; a hybrid of neuter gender, she has both and so has none. Dominated by the phases of the moon, she is in constant turmoil, doing battle with antagonistic forces within herself.

Later on, when mutilated by Cashtoc and left only half of what she was, the Mulata joins with a skeleton woman in order to make a whole. "We have to be sisters in the same clothing. Together, very much together, just like sisters in the same clothing, just like sisters who might have been born stuck together, so you will make up for the arm I lack, the leg I don't have, the ear, the eye, the lip." In this way, the two opposing cultures have mixed, an imperfect half clinging to a substanceless frame. In this same way, the Indians ensure that the protection they seek from the Christian saints is effective, endowing them with features and characteristics of their own Nahuatl animals derived from the ancient beliefs. In Asturias's view, these acts are attempts by the people to impose a wholeness to their existence, a universal harmony that they once knew and is now but a psychic memory.

Any subversion or disobedience to the laws of universality eventually will result in chaos or destruction. When Yumí abandons his wife for wealth and power, he sets into motion the chain of events that lead to his tragic end. The same result lies in wait for Catalina when she attempts to set herself apart from all others with the knowledge and use of sorcery. It is this deflection from universal love which Asturias deplores and which, if not corrected, will result in the destruction of humanity.

Critical Context

Asturias's work has long been recognized by critics throughout most of the literary world as being in the forefront of the Latin American literary movement. It was not, however, until the English publication of *Mulata* in 1967, the same year that saw Asturias awarded the Nobel Prize in Literature, that English-speaking readers became aware of his prodigious talent. Critically acclaimed in the United States and

Great Britain, as it had been in France and throughout the Spanish-speaking world, *Mulata*'s success (and the Nobel Prize) led to the publication in English of Asturias's other works. In these are found the style and themes that are incorporated in *Mulata*, most notably in the novels *Hombres de maiz* (1949; *Men of Maize*, 1975), *Viento fuerte* (1950; *The Cyclone*, 1967, better known as *Strong Wind*, 1968), and *El papa verde* (1954; *The Green Pope*, 1971).

Long concerned with what he considered the continuous isolation of man from nature and the resultant conflicts that arise from this isolation, Asturias incorporated nature into his novels, not as background setting but as a constant presence that must be taken into account. Using ancient Mayan myths and legends, many of which still carry much weight within the consciousness of the Guatemalan people, Asturias personified the different elements of nature (as did the ancient civilizations) in order to show how his characters and these elements are inextricably bound.

Though these elements have appeared in his other novels, in *Mulata*, Asturias achieves a more profound synthesis of myth and reality than in his other works. Through his skillful use of language, the suspension between myth and reality in which his characters conduct their lives is brought vividly to the forefront. In this way, he shows not only how wide the split between modern man and his natural elements has become but also the resultant conflicts.

Though Asturias does not preach or offer simple solutions, the inescapable truth of *Mulata* is modern man's urgent need for a balance between spirit and matter, instinct and reason, a wholeness which may be achieved by a reexamination of long-forgotten or barely remembered truths inherent in the myths and legends of the ancients.

Bibliography
Callan, Richard. *Miguel Ángel Asturias*. New York: Twayne, 1970. An introductory study with a chapter of biography and a separate chapter discussing each of Asturias's major novels. Includes a chronology, notes, and an annotated bibliography.
Gonzalez Echevarria, Roberto. *Myth and Archive: A Theory of Latin American Narrative*. Cambridge, England: Cambridge University Press, 1990. A very helpful volume in coming to terms with Asturias's unusual narratives.
Harss, Luis, and Barbara Dohmann. *Into the Mainstream*. New York: Harpers, 1967. Includes an interview with Asturias covering the major features of his thought and fictional work.
Himmelblau, Jack. "Love, Self and Cosmos in the Early Works of Miguel Ángel Asturias." *Kentucky Romance Quarterly* 18 (1971). Should be read in conjunction with Prieto.
Perez, Galo Rene. "Miguel Ángel Asturias." *Americas* (January, 1968): 1-5. A searching examination of *El Señor Presidente* as a commentary on the novelist's society.
Prieto, Rene. *Miguel Ángel Asturias's Archaeology of Return*. Cambridge, England: Cambridge University Press, 1993. The best available study in English of the novelist's body of work. Prieto discusses both the stories and the novels, taking up is-

sues of their unifying principles, idiom, and eroticism. See Prieto's measured introduction, in which he carefully analyzes Asturias's reputation and identifies his
most important work. Includes very detailed notes and bibliography.

West, Anthony. Review of *El Señor Presidente*, by Miguel Ángel Asturias. *The New
Yorker*, March 28, 1964. Often cited as one of the best interpretations of the novel.

Ernesto Encinas

MULLIGAN STEW

Author: Gilbert Sorrentino (1929-   )
Type of plot: Modernism
Time of plot: 1971-1975
Locale: New York City and surroundings
First published: 1979

> *Principal characters:*
>   ANTONY LAMONT, a pretentious novelist with no talent
>   POMEROY ROCHE, a literature professor who plans to use one of
>   Lamont's novels in a course
>   SHEILA TRELLIS, Antony's sister, a literary critic
>   DERMOT TRELLIS, Sheila's husband, a novelist
>   MARTIN HALPIN, a book publisher who is a character in and the
>   narrator of Lamont's current novel
>   NED BEAUMONT, Halpin's friend and business partner
>   DAISY BUCHANAN, a character in love with Beaumont
>   CORRIE CORRIENDO, a Latina magician and debaucher
>   BERTHE DELAMODE, Corrie's friend and business partner

The Novel

Mulligan Stew has three interwoven plot lines: the story of Antony Lamont and his struggle to write a novel; the story of Ned Beaumont and Martin Halpin, characters in the novel Lamont is writing; and a third story about the private lives of Beaumont and Halpin when they are not directly employed in Lamont's novel. The fourteen chapters of Lamont's novel are interspersed with his and Halpin's correspondence, journal entries, scrapbook clippings, and articles from magazines.

Lamont struggles to write his fifth novel, *Guinea Red* (later retitled *Crocodile Tears*), an absurdist murder mystery. He receives a letter from Roche, who is planning a literature course that might include one of Lamont's works. Lamont is flattered and offers Roche access to any or all of his work. Lamont's sister, Sheila, who has been one of his best critics, marries Dermot Trellis, whose novels Lamont considers commercial trash. With remarkable lack of tact, Lamont tells Sheila what he thinks of her husband's work, then discovers that Dermot knows Roche. He asks Dermot to put in a good word for him, but after the correspondence from Roche grows distant, and Lamont's work is dropped, Lamont suspects that Dermot has sabotaged him. As Lamont continues to struggle with his novel, his attacks on Dermot become more virulent, and Sheila distances herself from her brother.

Lamont becomes desperate as his new novel grows in directions he never anticipated. Letters to a poetess of bawdy verse whom he has tried to seduce and to his former mistress illustrate just how divorced he is from reality. At the end of his story, Lamont is totally paranoid, desperately turning to a sleazy businessman to help raise money to publish the novel he thinks he has just finished.

The second plot line concerns Martin Halpin and Ned Beaumont, longtime friends and co-owners of a publishing company. Lamont's novel opens as Halpin waits for the police to arrive at the lonely upstate vacation cabin where he believes he has just murdered Beaumont, although he cannot remember many details. He does remember Daisy Buchanan, the woman who was in love with Beaumont. It becomes apparent that Halpin also loves Daisy, although he denies having any motive to kill Beaumont. He mentions two "implausible" women whom he believes are the cause of the tragedy: Corrie Corriendo and Berthe Delamode.

In the series of flashbacks that form Lamont's novel, readers learn that Beaumont had been carrying on an affair with Daisy Buchanan. Daisy's husband, Tom, is resigned to his failed marriage and offers her a divorce so that she can marry Beaumont. Beaumont becomes involved with two Latinas whom he met when he mail-ordered their pornography. Corriendo and Delamode ask for his assistance in setting themselves up as clairvoyants in New York, and after several sexual encounters with them, he is so driven by lust that he buys them a saloon, the Club Zap. He distances himself from Daisy, who consoles herself by having an affair with Halpin.

Trying to help Daisy and Beaumont, Halpin goes to the Club Zap to confront the two sex kittens. Coincidentally, Daisy arrives at the club to beg Corriendo and Delamode to release their hold on Beaumont. In their office, the two seductresses work their charms on Halpin and Daisy, sweeping them into an orgy of wild and perverted group-sex acts. In one last desperate attempt to discredit the evil duo, Halpin and Daisy bring Ned to the Club Zap. Once again, they are outsmarted by the two clairvoyants, and Halpin whisks Daisy out of the Club Zap in the midst of her nude, lewd dance, leaving Beaumont to the wiles of Corriendo and Delamode.

Beaumont, who has been complaining about the stupid lines that Lamont writes and the drafty cabin where he lies dead, finally packs up and leaves the cabin and Lamont's novel. Eventually, Halpin receives a letter from Beaumont, who has joined a colony of characters from different novels awaiting new jobs, and Halpin leaves the cabin to join him.

The Characters

The characters of Gilbert Sorrentino are not realistic but instead represent fictional conventions. In *Mulligan Stew*, Sorrentino opposes the idea of characters as whole, autonomous subjects and makes the point that each is simply a creation of language. Antony Lamont is a dramatized figure of the author who loses control of his book. He is not so much a portrait of the conventional author as a parody of him. At one point, Halpin speaks two parts, his own and Beaumont's, since Beaumont has left the novel because of Lamont's incompetence. Yet his words were supposedly written by Lamont, so in effect he is being Lamont as well. Meanwhile, the reader is aware that all three are fictitious figures tangled together in the artificial language of the book.

The characters are revealed primarily by their own words, which are spoken in dialogue or written in letters or journals. Lamont reveals himself in his novels, letters, journals, and scrapbook, but in addition, readers have the attitudes of other characters toward him, as indicated in their letters. Lamont's own created characters, Halpin and Beaumont, complain about his writing and work habits. Although the reader agrees with their assessment of Lamont, when Halpin is talking about fellow characters in the novel *Guinea Red*, there is a certain irony between his view and the reader's. It seems that when Halpin speaks the lines written by Lamont, he is mistaken, but when he speaks his own thoughts beyond the confines of Lamont's novel, he is in accord with reality as the reader recognizes it.

Each of the characters in Sorrentino's novel has a distinct pattern of speaking or writing that reveals character. Lamont illustrates his ineptness in the poorly written *Guinea Red* and reveals his arrogance and pretentiousness in letters. Daisy Buchanan's coy letters, dotted with phrases such as "Yummy!" and self-deprecation such as "don't pay any attention to me," delineate her as a frivolous woman who plays a childlike role to please men. Madame Corriendo speaks with a Hispanic accent and sings songs in a strange polyglot language when she is not threatening or bragging. Beaumont's ghost, which inexplicably appears in Lamont's novel despite the fact that Beaumont is still alive, speaks an exaggerated poetic idiom sprinkled with bizarre metaphors in a rich Irish brogue. Perhaps the most dazzling artificial language occurs in the "Interview of the Month" that Halpin reads in the magazine *Art Futures* and clips for his journal. A staff member poses questions to Mr. Barnett Tete, America's most famous collector and all-around patron of the arts. Mr. Tete replies at length to each question in a strange mixture of business jargon, inappropriate metaphors, nonsequiturs, personal prejudices, and clichés.

Many of the characters in *Mulligan Stew* are borrowed from other writers' novels. Helpin, who is taken from James Joyce's novel *Finnegans Wake* (1939), runs into a man named Cliff Soles, who says he worked in the same Joyce novel as well as in one of Lament's earlier novels. Lament is from Irish writer Flann O'Brien's novel *At Swim-Two-Birds* (1939), which had a strong influence on *Mulligan Stew*. Characters from novels of Dashiell Hammett and F. Scott Fitzgerald are present, and literary allusions abound.

Themes and Meanings

Mulligan Stew is a novel about writing and the elements involved in it: authors, characters, words, different kinds of languages, and the nature of fictional reality. The novel questions the traditional view of the author as creator and source of meaning. The most lively and interesting parts of the novel are parodies of the work of other authors, which suggests that plagiarism is a major theme. Sorrentino recreates sections of James Joyce's work, mimics Vladimir Nabokov in the chapter "A Bag of Blues," and parodies erotic poetry with fictional Lorna Flambeaux's "The Sweat of Love." The language of the entire novel has a "borrowed" quality. Each section reminds readers of some kind of writing they have already read, such as the first chapter of Dermot Trellis's new novel, titled "Red Dawn and Blue Denim," a parody of every Western novel and movie the reader has ever encountered. Eventually, the characters from Lamont's novel run into the characters in Trellis's, crossing the boundaries that contain characters in more traditional fiction.

Literary parody is the major device of *Mulligan Stew*, and the work of James Joyce, the master of literary parody, plays a prominent role in the novel. Quotations from Joyce, especially from *Finnegans Wake*, are sprinkled throughout Sorrentino's book, and a section of Daisy Buchanan's monologue is obviously an attempt to parody the stream-of-consciousness technique in *Ulysses* (1922). Significantly, Sorrentino makes sure that Daisy calls attention to the technique: ". . . do you like the way I'm talking on and on without any pauses or punctuation it's my consciousness just simply *streaming*." With one of his characters pointing to the texts he parodies, Sorrentino parodies his own novel.

By drawing attention to the devices used in his own novel and by upsetting the reader's expectations at every turn, Sorrentino not only entertains the reader but also examines the processes of creating literature. He illustrates the facts that almost every sentence can call up its opposite and that every story can branch into an infinite number of directions.

Critical Context

Gilbert Sorrentino was among the literary avant-garde of the 1960's and 1970's, along with other writers such as Thomas Pynchon, Robert Coover, John Barth, William Gass, and LeRoi Jones. They shared an interest in the power of words and their multiple technical possibilities, a theme running throughout Sorrentino's work. This group is perhaps best known for attacking the conventions of the traditional novel such as linear plot lines, "real" characters, and language subordinated to the story. They, and especially Sorrentino, believed that form is more important than content and even determines content.

The Sky Changes (1966) and *Steelwork* (1970), Sorrentino's first two novels, ignore time sequence and scramble the past, present, and future. His next novel, *The Imaginative Qualities of Actual Things* (1971), satirizes the New York art world of the 1960's, a world of which he was a part. Each chapter is devoted to one of eight characters, and the novel proceeds by digression, anecdote, asides, and lists. This was followed by *Splendide-Hotel* (1973), a short book of twenty-six sections, each one based on a letter of the alphabet. *Mulligan Stew*, considered Sorrentino's masterpiece, was published to rave reviews, and he has continued to dazzle his public with novels that are experimental in different ways. An artist of great seriousness and ability, Sorrentino has given his readers new ways to think about language and literature.

Bibliography

Greiner, Donald J. "Antony Lamont in Search of Gilbert Sorrentino: Character and *Mulligan Stew*." *The Review of Contemporary Fiction* 1, no.1 (Spring, 1981): 104-112. Analyzes the ways in which Sorrentino enlarges the traditional role of character.

Klinkowitz, Jerome. *The Life of Fiction*. Urbana: University of Illinois Press, 1977. Traces major movements in American fiction, with emphasis on modernism.

_____. *Literary Disruptions: The Making of a Post-Contemporary American Fiction*. Urbana: University of Illinois Press, 1975. Looks at *Mulligan Stew* in the context of the literary movement of its time.

Tindall, Kenneth. "Adam and Eve on a Raft: Some Aspects of Love and Death in *Mulligan Stew*." *The Review of Contemporary Fiction* 1, no.1 (Spring, 1981): 159-167. A close reading of Sorrentino's masterpiece.

Sheila Golburgh Johnson

THE MUSIC OF CHANCE

Author: Paul Auster (1947-   )
Type of plot: Absurdist
Time of plot: The 1990's
Locale: Eastern Pennsylvania
First published: 1990

> *Principal characters:*
> JIM NASHE, an unemployed firefighter, drifter, and philosophizer
> JACK POZZI, a temperamental gambler and drifter
> FLOWER, a lottery winner and gambler, a pudgy companion of Stone
> STONE, a lottery winner and gambler, a skinny companion of Flower
> MURKS, a job boss who oversees the building of a wall

The Novel

The Music of Chance is the story of two drifters who lose everything in a poker game with two eccentric lottery winners and agree to pay off their debt by erecting a stone wall. As they perform this mindless labor, they find that instead of forfeiting their freedom, they have simply replaced one illusion of freedom with another.

Jim Nashe and Jack Pozzi are the main characters in the novel. Nashe is recovering from a trying period in his life following a devastating divorce. His way of coping was to quit his job, empty his bank account, and take off for a year of relentless cross-country driving. Near the end of his travels, just north of New York City, he spots Pozzi stumbling along the side of the road, beaten and broke after an ill-fated poker game. Nashe is sympathetic and, after hearing Pozzi's story, agrees to bankroll Pozzi in a poker game with two millionaire lottery winners named Flower and Stone. After a brief stopover in New York, Nashe and Pozzi head for southeastern Pennsylvania, where Flower and Stone, who live in a crumbling old mansion, show them the house and feed them children's food for dinner. Flower, Stone, and Pozzi then begin the poker game as Nashe watches. At one point, Nashe leaves the room for quite a while; upon his return, he finds that Pozzi is having a losing streak that continues until he loses everything. As a last resort, they cut the deck for ten thousand dollars—and Pozzi loses again.

To pay off their debt to Flower and Stone, Nashe and Pozzi agree to hire on as stonemasons, at ten dollars an hour, to build a wall from a stockpile of huge stones the millionaires have had shipped from Ireland. The job looks impossible, but the two men throw themselves into it; after a while, as their bodies toughen, they get into harmony with the project and even resist efforts to lighten the task. To make sure they do not escape, there is a chain-link fence topped with barbed wire surrounding the area and an overseer named Murks present to keep an eye on them. When Nashe and Pozzi finally fulfill their bargain and pay off their debt, they are still broke, so they ask if they can stay on and earn some money for themselves. Flower and Stone agree, and Nashe and Pozzi decide to celebrate with a party. Food and drink are brought, as well as the services of a prostitute from Atlantic City named Tiffany. After the party is over, Nashe and Pozzi learn that the cost for the party is to be added on to the balance they owe Stone and Flower. This so angers Pozzi that he decides to run away.

The next day Nashe sees Pozzi, beaten and bloody, lying half-dead in the mud outside the trailer. Murks takes him to the hospital, but Nashe never hears from him again and suspects the worst. In an effort to learn the truth about Pozzi, Nashe talks Murks into bringing Tiffany back for another party, his intention being to get her to find out about Pozzi and get a message back to Nashe. Before Nashe has time to receive any word back from Tiffany, he agrees to accompany Murks and his son-in-law Floyd to a roadhouse for a few drinks. It is a snowy night, with the weather deteriorating rapidly. Since the car they take is Nashe's old Saab, Nashe asks if he can drive the car on the way back. Murks and Floyd agree, and Nashe is joyful as he takes the wheel and heads back through the blinding snow. As conditions grow worse, Nashe drives faster and faster; mesmerized by the blinding light of an oncoming train, he heads straight for it.

The Characters

While the characters in this existential novel have individual identities, they are still more two-dimensional than three-dimensional. Auster presents them in pairs that are two halves of one complete personality. Thus, there are two protagonists, two antagonists, and two cardboard flunkies.

Jim Nashe is thirty-four and recently divorced. When he receives an inheritance from his father, he quits his job as a firefighter, withdraws all of his money from his bank, and hits the road in his red Saab in search of meaning and direction. Although his driving seems aimless and frenzied, he carefully maps each day's trip, so that there is indeed method in his madness. His compulsive driving becomes an odyssey during which he experiences threats, fears, melancholy, desperation, and infatuation. At one point, he reconnects with a woman he once knew and almost stays on with her, only to realize that he would be merely compounding his problem. Instead, he concentrates on his daughter, Juliette, who is with her mother in Minnesota, visiting her as often as he can. When, after a year, Nashe crosses paths with Jack Pozzi, he has reached a point where his destiny can be decided only by chance. Thus, the chance to bankroll Pozzi in a poker game is to him the reasonable solution to a problem he cannot solve himself. When he loses everything, he takes it with a shrug, figuring this was meant to be. Later, when Pozzi decides to escape from Stone and Flower, Nashe stays behind to finish the job, partly to cover for Pozzi but mostly because the building of the wall has given his life the meaning it lacked. He is now liberated from doing anything except working on the wall.

Pozzi is a feisty younger man, tough, wiry, resilient, passionate, and convinced of his invincibility as a poker player. His destiny rides on the luck of the draw, and when, for the first time, he finds himself a loser, he has trouble accepting it. Initially, he goes along with the contract to build the wall and thus repay the debt, but ultimately he balks at the deal and convinces himself that the whole game was rigged. At this point he has to escape, no matter what, but he is caught and savagely beaten. In fact, readers have every reason to think that he died, the victim of a dirty deal.

The other characters in the novel are even more two-dimensional. Flower and Stone, whom Pozzi calls Laurel and Hardy, assume their identity from each other and function as alter egos. They disappear from the novel once the deal has been struck, leaving the enforcement of the deal up to Murks. Murks and his son-in-law Daryl are two sides of the taskmaster personality. Murks functions as a blindly loyal overseer who carries out his duty but does it with a measure of compassion, while Daryl is the creepy flunky who undoubtedly caught and beat Pozzi.

Themes and Meanings

The Music of Chance is a good example of a modern existential novel. Existentialism is based on the contention that existence precedes essence; in other words, that the meaning of life is revealed in the process of living. In the novel, Nashe is shown initially as the model of the existential hero who sets out on an odyssey with a plan of where he is going but with no idea what he will encounter. Sheer coincidence causes him to meet up with Pozzi, who would not have been bleeding by the side of the road if bad luck had not put him in the path of thugs. When Nashe and Pozzi agree to cooperate, they are making an existential decision to take what they know of reality and put it to the test, for a card game is a classic example of a test of will and hope and chance.

Fate then deals them a severe blow when they lose the poker game, for it puts them at the mercy of Flower and Stone. The building of the wall is another classic existential touch. The wall serves no purpose; it divides a field diagonally instead of enclosing it, it obscures the view, and it is an obstacle to crossing the field. It is simply there, a thing to be worked on for no reason whatsoever. Initially, Nashe and Pozzi are well aware of this, but after a while they form an attachment to the wall, and when Murks offers to make their work easier by bringing in machinery, they refuse, insisting on building the wall the "traditional" way. Eventually, they forget even to question the wall. Ultimately, the wall represents existential freedom. As opposed to the aimless driving around the country that gives the illusion of freedom but ends up turning the driver into the driven, the building of the wall is so routine that it actually leads to an intellectual freedom that is really the only true freedom.

Critical Context

The Music of Chance seems clearly to have its roots in Auster's bitter struggles during his early years as a writer. Auster's previous works all point to this novel, from the Kafkaesque prose, lucid yet cryptic, to the fatalism of Albert Camus, whose own death in a car accident is mirrored in Nashe's. Although Auster obviously owes debts to Kafka and Camus, there are also traces of black humor that suggest the influence of Samuel Beckett and Eugène Ionesco. There is also a strong relationship between Auster's absurd realism and that found in *The Unconsoled* by Kazuo Ishiguro. What is important about *The Music of Chance* is the fact that Auster is able to make the absurd believable through lucid prose, clear focus, and a narrative flow that allows the book to be read on many levels, from a buddy story to a black comedy.

Bibliography

Auster, Paul. *Hand to Mouth: A Chronicle of Early Failure*. New York: Henry Holt, 1997. A disturbing account of the author's difficult early years. Uneven in treatment, but contains some revealing insights into the genesis of *The Music of Chance*.

Barone, Dennis, ed. *Beyond the Red Notebook: Essays on Paul Auster*. Philadelphia: University of Pennsylvania Press, 1995. This first book-length study of Auster's work includes generous commentary on *The Music of Chance*.

Bawer, Bruce. "Family Ties with an Athenian Twist." *The Wall Street Journal*, September 21, 1990, p. A12. Delightfully stimulating observations on *The Music of Chance* by an original critic.

Irwin, Mark. "Memory's Escape: Inventing *The Music of Chance*—A Conversation with Paul Auster." *Denver Quarterly* 28, no. 3 (Winter, 1994): 111-122. A provocative insight into Auster's techniques, purposes, and personality.

Mannes-Abbott, Guy. "The Music of Chance." *New Statesman & Society* 4, no. 143 (March 22, 1991): 45. A refreshing look at *The Music of Chance* through the ideas of a respected English critic.

Saltzman, Arthur. *Designs of Darkness*. Philadelphia: University of Pennsylvania Press, 1990. Includes challenging commentary on *The Music of Chance*.

Thomas Whissen

MY HEART AND MY FLESH

Author: Elizabeth Madox Roberts (1886-1941)
Type of plot: Poetic realism
Time of plot: The early twentieth century
Locale: Anneville, Kentucky
First published: 1927

> *Principal characters:*
> THEODOSIA BELL, the protagonist
> HORACE BELL, her father
> ANTHONY BELL, her grandfather, a former teacher and scholar
> AMERICY FROMAN and
> LETHE ROSS, Theodosia's mulatto half sisters
> STIGGINS, Theodosia's mulatto half brother
> CONWAY BROOKE,
> ALBERT STILES, and
> FRANK RAILEY, Theodosia's suitors
> CALEB BURNS, a farmer and the eventual husband of Theodosia

The Novel

The novel's title refers to the cry of the psalmist, "My heart and my flesh crieth out for the living God." *My Heart and My Flesh* follows the story of Theodosia Bell in her journey toward self-discovery and fulfillment as she grows from childhood to adulthood in the fictional Kentucky town of Anneville. The trials through which she passes and the tragedies that befall her, leading to her final recovery and spiritual rebirth, form the core of the novel.

The first significant event that Theodosia must endure is the shattering of her complacent notions about her own superiority. Reared in a wealthy, privileged, and respectable family, she is devastated when she learns from her grandfather's secret papers that two mulatto girls in the town, Americy and Lethe, whom she has always despised, are in fact her half sisters and that Stiggins, the idiot stable boy, is her half brother. As she attempts to come to terms with this knowledge, Theodosia moves haltingly and uncomprehendingly toward a measure of acceptance and love, without ever fully achieving either. Yet when she notices, to her amazement, that Stiggins possesses the elegant "fiddle hand" that she, who prides herself on her ability with the violin, lacks, the absurdity of her former notion of superiority becomes painfully apparent.

Many of the other events which shape Theodosia's life are deaths. Her handsome and charming suitor Conway Brooke dies in his burning home, and her grief becomes more acute when Minnie Harter, a local girl and former neighbor of Conway, gives birth to a child and claims that Conway is the father. The death of Theodosia's grandfather Anthony Bell, the only member of her family with whom she has any real affinity, further isolates her, although through his death she learns pity and compassion.

On inheriting the family estate, Theodosia discovers that all the wealth has slipped away and only debts remain. This new and unexpected poverty is another blow to her self-esteem. Little by little, she loses all she has and all her hopes for the future. Her selfish and uncaring father leaves home to join a law firm, never to return. When Lethe brutally murders her unfaithful husband, Ross, goaded on by Theodosia as she half-consciously seeks vicarious revenge for having been jilted by Albert Stiles, Theodosia is so haunted by feelings of guilt that her health breaks down.

Forced to sell the house in which she has lived since she was a child, and in increasing ill health, she moves to the farm of her Aunt Doe, whom she dislikes, for rest and recuperation. This period of eighteen months represents the nadir of her fortunes. Weak and in despair, she hears voices, the discordant impulses of her own mind, as she becomes steadily more violent, incoherent, and guilt-ridden. She resolves to commit suicide, but, on the very brink of her destructive act, some mysterious and inexplicable life force quickens inside her. She suddenly finds herself utterly changed, full of fresh hope and expectation. After months of apathy and despair, she acquires a new sense of purpose. Riding with a traveling peddler the next day, she finds the spontaneity and joy in life that she has been seeking, a "strange happiness going its unknown ways."

Arriving in the nearby village of Spring Run Valley, she becomes a teacher at the local school, and it is through living among the country people, who remain in touch with nature in their simple manner, that she acquires the wholeness, compassion, and sense of acceptance and peace that she had formerly lacked. When Caleb Burns, a local farmer who seems to embody the wisdom and solidity of the earth itself, declares his love for her, her spiritual rebirth is complete, and the novel closes with images of the quiet, healing presence of a country night.

The Characters

The chief interest of the novel lies in the intense inner life of Theodosia. She is presented from the outset as a girl of extreme sensitivity, aware of subtle currents of feeling which escape her elders. She is also alienated from her environment, both human and natural, and afflicted with melancholy; Roberts, in her notes about the novel, described Theodosia as "a wandering spirit, a lost thing." Theodosia herself is acutely aware of her malaise: "It seemed to her that she lived with only a part of her being, that only a small edge of her person lifted up into the light of the day." She is, in consequence, preoccupied with the search for self-knowledge and for the innermost core of existence, refusing to be content with anything less. The sight of a tree fills her with a "passion to know all of this strange thing," and it is the same with her family: She ponders her half sister Americy "to the roots of her life and her being," and as her grandfather lies dying she attempts to discover his soul, his irreducible essence, for if she can locate the soul of another being, surely she can also locate her own? In everything, Theodosia searches for ultimate reality and meaning, that which is "perpetually existent, unchanged, beyond delusion," driven on by a sense of the insufficiency of things as they are.

Roberts lavishes so much attention on Theodosia that other characters are indistinctly realized, revealing themselves largely through their interactions with the protagonist. Perhaps the most sympathetic is Theodosia's grandfather, Anthony Bell. Formerly a teacher and scholar, he has retained his love of great literature. As he reads aloud to his family, "unafraid of any word or saying," Theodosia sees him as the custodian of eternal truths. He takes immense pride in his granddaughter's progress with the violin and lives again through her. Theodosia's affinity with him contrasts with her dislike of her father, Horace Bell. Horace's infidelity in marriage destroys any respect that Theodosia might have had for him, and his bluff, superficial manner, as well as his selfishness, effectively sets off Theodosia's introspection and sensitivity. Seen through her eyes, he is merely "a jumble of demands upon affection and forbearance."

Other characters flicker into life for the reader, but only briefly. Theodosia's illegitimate kin form a ragged and dispiriting trio. Americy wistfully sings of the Lord while involved in an incestuous relationship with Stiggins, the mentally retarded outcast who lives in the stables with the horses. Their harmlessness, however sordid, stands in sharp contrast to the heavy and menacing presence of Lethe, whose savage and violent hatred eventually leads to her imprisonment for murder.

Finally, there are Theodosia's suitors. Conway Brooke is gentle, graceful, and easygoing, his relaxed serenity ruffled only when he becomes jealous of his friend Albert Stiles. Albert, a practical man of affairs who is full of plans for the future, seeks Theodosia's hand with a blunt determination but then deserts her for the beautiful Florence Agnew. The simple good nature of the third suitor, the lawyer Frank Railey, who is uncritical in his admiration of Theodosia, does not interest her: "You could work him out by a formula" she says, and he disappears from her mind as soon as he is out of sight. All three are in marked contrast to the man who finally wins Theodosia's hand, the farmer Caleb Burns, who is deeply connected to the land in a way that the rootless town dwellers are not. He is known to all the villagers as an odd character—"he seemed always about to speak or to have just spoken, and he talked to everybody as if they knew all he meant"—but Theodosia sees him as a man shaped and matured by all the lights and shades of human experience, one who carries about him a wisdom that is universal in its scope.

Themes and Meanings

The central theme of the novel is spiritual death and rebirth. Theodosia seems to be unwittingly forced to pursue a *via negativa*, stripped of everything that she has—her family, social position, wealth, mental and physical health, and, finally, her will to live—before she can discover who she truly is, and the inexorable life force can reclaim her. That this was Roberts's intention is clear from her papers, in which she describes the novel as a process of "continual subtraction," her method consisting of "a steady taking away until there was nothing left but the bare breath of the throat and the simplified spirit."

The central recurring symbol is that of music. Theodosia's constant endeavors to improve her skill with the violin are symbolic of her search for her true self. Music, she is told by her teacher, "must come out of your soul," and Theodosia longs to "play the fiddle to the end of the earth . . . to go to the end of music and look over the edge at what's on the other side." Music embodies the perfection and harmony that she seeks. It occurs at crucial points in the narrative as a faintly heard counterpoint to the more overt discord and suffering. It gives Theodosia's exchanges with Americy and Lethe much of their poignant sadness, for example, acting as a haunting reminder of the contrast between the ideal and the actual. At the very brink of Theodosia's intended suicide, the ideal seems lost altogether, since she sees her violin as an alien object, "holding a remote kindness for some being far apart from herself, identical with some abstract goodness that would never be stated."

Most significantly, music is mysteriously linked with the rhythms and harmonies of nature, the eternal cycles of death and rebirth. As Theodosia plays, her music blends in her thought with the "running autumn and the crisp frost" and with the "outspread fertility of the fields and the high tide of mid-summer." As always in Roberts's novels, the reader is kept vividly aware of the regular passage of the seasons, and this represents a vital aspect of Theodosia's regeneration. Her task is to become rooted once more in the great rhythms of nature, with those who, like Caleb Burns, live close to the soil and its fruits. One of the novel's great symbolic moments of self-realization, foreshadowing Theodosia's final recovery, takes place when she contemplates a large elm tree and instinctively knows that she, too, is embedded in the earth, the nourishing and life-giving force, "attached to it at all points . . . sinking at each moment into it." Her more usual sense of the insufficiency of all her endeavors, that more knowledge yields only greater ignorance—a recurring theme in the novel—stems from her rootlessness. It is only in the final scenes, in Theodosia's newfound contentment, that she is able to reflect that to be in Hell is to be "subtracted from the earth" and reduced to a state of continual and restless searching.

Critical Context

My Heart and My Flesh was Roberts's second novel, published only a year after *The Time of Man* (1926) had won for her immediate recognition and acclaim. Her reputation continued to grow with the publication of *The Great Meadow* (1930), but after her last major novel, *He Sent Forth a Raven* (1935), her popularity and critical standing went into a rapid decline. She has frequently been categorized as a regionalist, but this is a somewhat unfair label, since her novels, although they are all set in Kentucky, are concerned with profound and universal themes. More charitable critics have compared her to William Faulkner, D. H. Lawrence, and Emily Dickinson. It is likely that she will continue to occupy a minor but distinct place in the roll call of twentieth century American novelists.

Although *My Heart and My Flesh* has never been one of Roberts's most popular novels, its enduring value lies in the author's ability to set out a timeless theme with unusual force and conviction. The novel faces the darker aspects of human existence without succumbing to nihilism and despair; it celebrates the virtues of simplicity and endurance, and it affirms the ultimate triumph of life and of the spirit. It is also notable for Roberts's highly distinctive prose style—she called it "symbolism working through poetic realism"—and there are many passages of rich, poetic prose which the reader may savor many times.

My Heart and My Flesh is not light reading, nor is it enjoyable in the superficial sense of the word, but it is richly satisfying for the reader who enters its spirit and contemplates its themes.

Bibliography

Adams, J. Donald. *The Shape of Books to Come.* New York: Viking Press, 1934. Adams was an early admirer of Roberts, and he compares her to Willa Cather and Ellen Glasgow. An interesting contemporary view of the novelist.

Auchincloss, Louis. *Pioneers and Caretakers: A Study of Nine American Women Novelists.* Minneapolis: University of Minnesota Press, 1965. Auchincloss offers a compact overview of the life and work of Roberts, whose best and most popular novel was her first, *The Time of Man*; she never wrote anything to equal it.

Campbell, Harry M., and Ruel E. Foster. *Elizabeth Madox Roberts: American Novelist.* Norman: University of Oklahoma Press, 1956. Full of information about Roberts's career, yet poorly organized. Often dull to read, making this book unsuitable for any but the most dedicated students of Roberts.

McDowell, Frederick P. W. *Elizabeth Madox Roberts.* New York: Twayne, 1963. McDowell gives a useful critical overview of Roberts's works, including her poetry and short stories. Offers a short biography of her life, which was mostly spent in Springfield, Kentucky.

Rovit, Earl H. *Herald to Chaos: The Novels of Elizabeth Madox Roberts.* Lexington: University of Kentucky Press, 1960. A wonderful critique of Roberts's novels, probably the best one available. Rovit describes Roberts's style in a sensitive and perceptive manner and places her in the context of American, not simply Southern, literature.

Tate, Linda. "Elizabeth Madox Roberts: A Bibliographical Essay." *Resources for American Literary Study* 18 (1992): 22-43. A valuable addition to studies of Roberts's career and the history of her reputation.

Bryan Aubrey

THE MYSTERIES OF PITTSBURGH

Author: Michael Chabon (1963-   )
Type of plot: Bildungsroman
Time of plot: The early 1980's
Locale: Primarily Pittsburgh, Pennsylvania
First published: 1988

> *Principal characters:*
>> ART BECKSTEIN, a recent college graduate uncertain about his future
>> and confused about his sexual identity
>> JOSEPH (JOE THE EGG) BECKSTEIN, his father, a gangster
>> ARTHUR LECOMTE, Art's male lover, a stylish idler whom Art seeks to
>> emulate
>> PHLOX (MAU MAU) LOMBARDI, Art's female lover
>> CLEVELAND ARNING, Art's friend

The Novel

The Mysteries of Pittsburgh follows Art Beckstein, the narrator, from the time of his graduation from college through a summer. During those months, the direction of his life is determined, through a series of intense, interlocking relationships with three other young people.

As the narration begins, Art is particularly vulnerable. He is without the structure provided by his educational experiences, faces the unappealing prospect of becoming part of the adult world of responsibility, and sees the possibility of a fulfilling existence as vague and elusive. His sense of himself rests on a shifting, unsteady foundation of injunctions from his stern father. He has an ambiguous but insistent inclination to spend this last summer of relative freedom "fluttering ever upward," but he has no idea of what this would entail, nor of what he needs to learn about himself and the world. He is nevertheless determined to permit "novel and incomprehensible situations" to absorb him. When he is invited to join a group of revelers by an intriguing young man, Arthur Lecomte, he has few qualms about accepting. Arthur's speech, style of dress, and patterns of pleasure imply excitement. Art does remain wary of Lecomte's apparent homosexuality but is drawn by its implications of participation in the realm of the forbidden.

The social nexus into which Art is drawn centers on Lecomte and two of his acquaintances, a young woman, Phlox Lombardi, who works in the university library while studying French, and Cleveland Arning, a young man who has been living on the edge of society. Arning is rebellious, courting danger and espousing defiance. Art, who has been a dutiful son guided by the wishes, suggestions, and various forms of subtle coercion exercised by his father, a gangster, finds the unpredictable, spontaneous rhythms of his new friends exciting. He begins to develop, in the course of their adventures and escapades, a particular relationship with each of the three. He remains linked to old habits of responsibility through his contacts with his father and his work at a mass-market book dispensary that mocks his love for literature with its commercial method of operation. The lure of the apparently freer, more genuine, more gratifying lives of his new friends opens a door that Art sees as an entrance to a cosmos of infinite possibility. One of the most appealing aspects of this different life is the opportunity for explorations of intimacy in terms of intense friendship and sexual experimentation. Art is uncertain of his inclinations in these areas. The summer he spends with Arthur, Cleveland, and Phlox becomes a quest for his true self.

As the summer progresses, Art is lifted in a whirl of excitement and exhilaration, living in a movable feast of food, drink, appreciation of others' clothes and wit, and expressive gestures of aesthetic sensibility. With little regard for the remainder of the human race, the self-selected elite to which Art belongs amuses itself by outrageous acts toward hopelessly square parents, drones in dumb jobs, and anyone who is not attuned to the somewhat outré literary ambience that guides them. At the root of their actions, Art begins to realize, is a fear that they will be absorbed and reduced to normality by the drab, often dysfunctional, world. The expanding uncertainty and dread gradually undermining Art's delight in his summer escapades is compounded by a growing sense of sexual confusion, as he finds himself both fully involved in a satisfying sensual relationship with Phlox and a thrilling but unsettling erotic adventure with Arthur.

Art's eventual discovery of the facts behind the façade of manner that Arthur has constructed, along with the intermingling of his own uneasiness about his family's income from crime with Cleveland's involvement in the same criminal organization, leads to the climactic episode of the novel. Cleveland is killed while fleeing from the police in a setup engineered by Joe Beckstein, Art's father, to teach Art a lesson about power, control, and obligation. The effect of this episode is to sever all of Art's connections to his previous life and to his dreams of a summer of "greater lust and hopefulness." He decides to follow Arthur to Europe but does not stay with him for long. At the novel's conclusion, he recalls the events of the months just passed with a mixture of fond, indulgent nostalgia and a rueful sense of wisdom recently acquired that does not completely obliterate his innocent expectations.

The Characters

Art Beckstein, whose mind is the source of the narrative consciousness of the novel, is the focus of the story. It is essential that he immediately and powerfully control the attention, curiosity, and sympathy of the reader. His compelling blend of aspiration and yearning, held just beneath a protective shield of studied sophistication, is established through a control of tone and language that recalls the singular voices created for Mark Twain's Huck Finn and J. D. Salinger's Holden Caulfield, other young men uncertain about the survival of their integrity as they enter a menacing world of adult demands and entrapment.

The mysteries of Pittsburgh that Art engages are the mysteries of existence, and the tentativeness and hesitancy of Art's explorations, both within the city and within his psyche, are testament to the candor of his accounts. Because everything is presented through Art's perspective, it is crucial that his judgments are conveyed with complete sincerity, so that even when he is clearly mistaken, his honesty remains unquestioned.

Despite his concentration in economics, which he refers to as "a sad and cynical major," and his distaste for the library, Art cultivates the sensibility of a literate outsider and is susceptible to the lure of Arthur Lecomte and Cleveland Arning. They appear to be of a world diametrically opposed to that of his father, which demands prudence and control. Although Art gradually discovers that both of his new friends are hiding the brutal circumstances of their early lives, the energy and intelligence of their created selves are compelling and have become integral parts of both young men's personalities.

Lecomte has fashioned a veneer of decadence, dressing with a self-conscious extravagance, speaking with an arch and dismissive wit, and charming those he wishes to influence or ingratiate while manipulating everyone else. Art is overwhelmed by his seemingly effortless manners and grace and is attracted to him sexually, hoping to emulate him and perhaps to acquire his characteristics through physical contact. Chabon presents Lecomte effectively from Art's point of view, so that even as his weaknesses and faults become apparent, he remains sympathetic and appealing.

Arning is a post-Beat, protopunk dazzler, so perceptive, self-assured, and exuberant that he is irresistible to Art. Arning's doom-driven recklessness, his sneering contempt for sham, his mixture of poetic responsiveness to beauty and toughness, and his genuine affection for Art make him a sympathetic character as well. His eventual destruction helps to explain Art's withdrawal at the novel's conclusion.

Although Phlox Lombardi and Joe Beckstein are important characters, both are essentially static if convincing. Beckstein is seen from the outside, remaining a formidable but unfathomable presence for Art and the reader. Phlox is described in considerable detail regarding appearance and objects. Her reactions to Art, however, are the determining means of her characterization; she tends toward a generic "good woman" stereotype.

Themes and Meanings

Although he is not sure that his attraction to Arthur Lecomte is final proof of a homosexual orientation, Art does find tremendously appealing the seemingly spontaneous, unstructured, impulsive pattern of living that Lecomte and his circle have evolved. At the completion of his senior year of college, he senses that he is about to be captured by the world of his father, a controlled, fundamentally serious, and frighteningly powerful man. Art respects, warily admires, and uneasily "loves" his father, but he believes that he is likely to lose the nascent elements of his own individual consciousness if he succumbs to his father's subtle pressures. He fears never becoming a complete and self-sufficient person, like his father, unless he permits the hazards of change to enter his world.

Already prepared for a form of outlaw aestheticism by his eclectic reading, Art launches himself into a "life" that can be assessed and appreciated as a work of art in which he is the hero. Art's awareness of his role as a player in this construction serves to sharpen his perceptions; his initial exhilaration at his admittance into the elite cadre of "extraordinary" people eventually shifts to a wiser, wider perspective that permits him to begin to see the shallow, almost desperate aspects of Lecomte's gestures and Arning's bursts of manic energy.

Art needs both his elevation into a realm of heightened experience and the gradual awareness of his friends' uneasiness to begin to develop an understanding of his own relationship to his family. Art seems to realize that his father was forced into a criminal position because his Jewish background made him a permanent outsider. This realization helps him to understand his own refusal to accept bland assimilation. Art's determination to preserve his poetic sensibility parallels his father's decision to maintain the freedom to act as an individual. His father has come to terms with his choices, and as the novel closes with Art looking in reflective satisfaction on his impulsive, romantically expectant plunge into what he now recognizes as a "lovely, dire summer," his decision is ratified. He needed the disruption and the thrill of chaotic agitation to grow beyond the silence and ill will that held him in a clutch of fear at the novel's onset.

Critical Context

Publication of *The Mysteries of Pittsburgh* immediately established Chabon as one of the most promising young writers in the United States. He was given an unusually large payment for his hardcover contract as well as the opportunity to prepare a screenplay adaptation of the novel. In addition, short stories he had published in various journals were collected under the title *A Model World* (1991).

Amid a considerable outpouring of positive commentary, which compared Chabon to J. D. Salinger and Jack Kerouac, several reviewers emphasized the parallels with F. Scott Fitzgerald's work, noting the similarities in sensitivity of Chabon's narrator and Nick Carraway of *The Great Gatsby* (1925). Chabon's treatment of sexual ambiguity and multiplicity extended more traditional considerations of the nature of love and erotic attraction from the realm of familiar heterosexual experience toward the less rigid demarcation of sexual attraction that became an important element of postmodern literary ventures.

Bibliography

Banks, Carolyn. "Bright Lights, Steel City." *The Washington Post Book World*, April 24, 1988, p. 5. Compares Art Beckstein with his literary precursors Huck Finn and Holden Caulfield and contrasts the comic motifs of the book with its sad side. Summarizes stylistic highlights.

Kaveney, Roz. "As They Mean to Go On." *New Statesman* 116 (May 13, 1988): 34-35. Considers the novel as a *Bildungsroman* about writing a novel. Identifies attributes of Chabon's style that permit him to transform unlikely situations into plausible scenarios.

Keates, Jonathan. "The Boy Can't Help It." *The Times Literary Supplement*, June 23, 1988, p. 680. Discusses the meaning of the "mystery" of the title, evaluates claims made for Chabon's talents, and demonstrates how Chabon transforms familiar formulaic devices.

Lott, Brett. "Lover in a World Too Full for Love." *Los Angeles Times Book Review*, April 17, 1988, p. 1. Sets the literary context in which the book appears ("jaded young writers") and shows how Chabon surpasses his peers by going deeper into the nature of love and friendship. Assesses the book's weaknesses and virtues and examines Chabon's use of sexual identity as a psychic checkpoint.

McDermott, Alice. "Gangsters and Pranksters." *The New York Times Book Review*, April 3, 1988, p. 7. Points out the novel's limitations of some weak characters and unclear relationships and mentions that these are balanced by Chabon's language, wit, and ambition.

See, Lisa. "Michael Chabon: Wonder Boy in Transition." *Publishers Weekly* 242 (April 10, 1995): 44-45. Traces Chabon's career from the publication of his successful first novel *The Mysteries of Pittsburgh* to his second book, *Wonder Boys* (1995). Addresses the issue of a writer living up to the success of his initial book. Provides a good overview of Chabon's career.

Leon Lewis

THE MYSTERIES OF WINTERTHURN

Author: Joyce Carol Oates (1938-   )
Type of plot: Detective and mystery
Time of plot: The late nineteenth and early twentieth centuries
Locale: Winterthurn, a town in New York State
First published: 1984

> *Principal characters:*
>> XAVIER KILGARVAN, a detective whose maturity from sixteen to forty
>> coincides with three murder mysteries in the town of Winterthurn
>> PERDITA KILGARVAN, his cousin and the object of his lifelong passion
>> THÉRÈSE KILGARVAN, Perdita's sister, also in love with Xavier
>> GEORGINA KILGARVAN, a mysterious poet, the eldest of the Kilgarvan
>> sisters.
>> VALENTINE WESTERGAARD, the chief figure in the second murder
>> mystery
>> ELERY POINDEXTER, the object of investigation in the third murder
>> mystery

The Novel

The Mysteries of Winterthurn is divided into three parts, each several chapters in length. Although the principal characters remain the same, each part is centered on a different murder mystery occurring at three crucial points in the life of Xavier Kilgarvan, a detective cast in the mold of such nineteenth century masters as Sherlock Holmes.

Emulating narrative techniques of the nineteenth century, Oates presents her tale through an "Editor," a first-person omniscient narrator who not only tells the story but also comments directly to the reader. This commentary is found in chapters entitled "Editor's Notes" and "Epilogue" and also throughout the narrative in the direct address so much in favor with nineteenth century novelists. The Editor's identity is never revealed.

The novel's three mysteries involve puzzling killings, often multiple, that take place in eerie circumstances. Each mystery also serves further to reveal the deep, dark, and complex passion that exists between Xavier and his beautiful cousin Perdita. There is throughout an air of the supernatural, of a tragic family curse extending over several generations, and of a complex union of good and evil. The first mystery, entitled "The Virgin in the Rose Bower," centers on the horrific death of an infant in the so-called Honeymoon Suite of Glen Marw Manor, the ancestral home of the Kilgarvans. Once presided over by Erasmus Kilgarvan, sometime judge of the local district court, Glen Marw Manor is now the domain of Georgina Kilgarvan, the eldest cousin of Xavier, a never-married poet of considerable accomplishment whose pen name, "Iphigenia," recalls the ancient Greek myth of a father's betrayal. Living with

Georgina are her two younger half-sisters, Thérèse and Perdita, and her elderly bachelor uncle.

The infant's murder might have been the work of his mother, but it might also have been caused by malignant spirits inhabiting the room, spirits who seem to grow out of the figures in a wall mural depicting the Virgin in a rose garden. Whatever the case, the mother, found babbling incoherently, never regains her sanity. Only a teenage schoolboy, Xavier Kilgarvan is determined to be a detective, and he sets out for Glen Marw Manor to investigate. There he is met by his twelve-year-old cousin Perdita, with whom he falls in love. Acting in a strangely contradictory manner, Perdita first aids him in his investigation and then thwarts and endangers him by locking him in the manor cellar. He is rescued by Perdita's sister Thérèse, who suffers an unrequited love for him. Xavier manages to solve the mystery, but the solution contains such terrible and loathsome family secrets that he cannot bring himself to make them public.

Between the first and second mystery, there are other terrible events related to Glen Marw Manor: the bizarre killing of Xavier's uncle in the Honeymoon Suite, the "ritual slaying" of the old family servant, Pride, and the vicious murder of Valentine Westergaard's sister in a wooded area near the manor. These disturbing events culminate in the suicide of Georgina Kilgarvan, and the murders then cease. None of the cases is investigated by Xavier Kilgarvan, who has left Winterthurn to seek his fortune as a detective. He does not return to his native city until his twenty-eighth year, just when a new mystery arises. A number of young women working at local factories have been assaulted and their lifeless and mutilated bodies discarded in a remote and desolate spot known as the Devil's Half-Acre. Now a detective with a growing reputation, Xavier solves the case of "The Devil's Half-Acre"—to his great personal dismay because of the unhappy turn of events, which involves the revelation of more dreadful family secrets and, unhappiest of all, his outright rejection by his beloved cousin Perdita. Again Xavier Kilgarvan leaves Winterthurn.

At forty and at the height of his professional fame, Xavier returns once more to Winterthurn. This final visit finds him suddenly and mysteriously withdrawing from his profession after his obsessive struggle to solve "The Case of the Bloodstained Bridal Gown." He does unravel the twisted events surrounding the triple murder, but ironically, his solution forces him to reconcile what he now knows about his family's curse with his sorely tested but undying passion for Perdita. He chooses Perdita, who comes to him as a newly liberated woman riding a bicycle, and forsakes the highly individualistic profession of detection for a quieter, more domestic life.

The Characters

Joyce Carol Oates approaches her characters in terms of the nineteenth century style she has elected. They are at once symbolic and epic, in service to the narrative, not so much developed as outlined externally by the narrator known as The Editor. As symbols, they are aptly named. Consider the two Kilgarvan sisters who relate to Xavier. Thérèse, the constant, pure one who unselfishly and unrequitedly loves Xavier, carries the name of a saintly mystic. She is the epitome of the nineteenth century gentlewoman. Perdita's name means "the lost one," and certainly she brings to Xavier a dark passion that ultimately takes him from his career of exposing malice. In another way, she is lost, for as the prototype of the liberated woman of the new century, she is lost to the Victorian ideal. Xavier Kilgarvan also bears a saint's name, that of the renowned missionary who brought Christianity to the Far East. Because he was a Jesuit, Saint Francis Xavier is associated both with the passion of God's love and with cool-headed logic. Xavier is an excellent name for the detective who serves as the central consciousness of the novel, in that the story is presented through Xavier; his innermost thoughts, yearnings, emotional states, religious and ethical convictions are related to readers by The Editor, whose identity remains a mystery (could it be Perdita?). Readers know Xavier to be a good, honest, and courageous man, given to severe headaches when possessed by fear but brave enough to carry forward because he deeply and completely believes in the power of logic, or "ratiocination," as he and other educated gentlemen of the century call it. Yet he is sufficiently composed of contradictory tendencies to fall mindlessly and passionately in love with Perdita and at last to lose his self-simplicity in saving her.

Of the other characters, readers know less, for it is a technique of nineteenth century literature to see persons in the narration through the central consciousness of the main character—especially in an instance such as this, since it is the burden of a classical detective to reason out a motive for the actions of others. Such assigning of a singular motive tends to relegate characters to stereotypes. Such is the case in murder mystery number one, which is centered on Georgina Kilgarvan, the poet who suggests Emily Dickinson in style and intensity and who is fiercely eccentric and hermitlike because she must guard a dark secret. Like Emily Dickinson, Georgina is trapped within the constraints placed on Victorian women and must conceal the wrongs done to her. Concealment is also the driving motive of Valentine Westergaard, the subject of Xavier's second murder case, who recalls such famous nineteenth century figures as Lord Byron and Oscar Wilde. Elery Poindexter, the main suspect in the third murder case, is the classic turn-of-the-century scoundrel who, because he is from a moneyed class, can easily get away with illicit sex and even, perhaps, murder. Harmon Bunting, Perdita's husband, is a similar scoundrel hiding his puerile tendencies behind a clergyman's collar.

Several minor characters give texture to the story. Perhaps the most enjoyable of these is Simon Esdras, the failed philosopher of the Kilgarvan clan. Yet it is the powerful stereotypes who interest Xavier, most of whom—with the exception of Thérèse—are possessed of grossly evil tendencies.

Themes and Meanings

The Mysteries of Winterthurn deals with the intricacies of the human personality, its tendency to embrace both good and evil. The novel asks the question: Can we ever be simple enough, completely pure and not a complex of intellect and passion, good and evil? Oates's choice of the detective genre, especially the detective tale of the nineteenth century, makes an excellent vehicle for her theme. The central character, the detective whose nature is defined almost entirely by his intellect and his belief in a beneficent God, labors through three cases, each entangled with a sense of unknowable evil. In the end, though, he succeeds neither in bringing evildoers to justice nor in simplifying his own soul, for he ultimately succumbs to an overpowering passion for a woman capable of the most atrocious deeds. He forsakes his intellectual profession, ignores the pure and abiding Thérèse, and sets off into the new century in a marriage to a woman hardly likely to look back to the ideals of Victorianism.

Oates deals with her theme of complexity, of rejection of simple Victorian values, by critiquing the nineteenth century, especially Victorian attitudes toward sex and the restriction of women, through the use of its own narrative style and attitudes toward character presentation. As such, the novel is both postmodern and subtle, for Oates fashions a fascinating story loaded with wry humor as she both lovingly emulates a borrowed style and manages to satirize that bygone style and its era with gentle good humor. Withal, her story is edged with suspense, and she is a master at creating an atmosphere of dread.

Critical Context

Mysteries of Winterthurn is a pivotal novel by one of the towering figures in contemporary American writing. Joyce Carol Oates is a writer of prodigious output and wide recognition in American letters. Playwright, essayist, and poet, she is the author of dozens of novels. Among her several honors is the National Book Award for her 1969 novel *them*. She is both a chronicler and critic of the American experience, and while her early work is concerned with contemporary life, her middle years saw her turn to history as a shaping factor of present-day America, especially American women. Her project in these "middle novels" which include *Mysteries of Winterthurn*, *Bellefleur* (1980), and *A Bloodsmore Romance* (1982), was not only to consider history but also to have the reader live it directly by emulating the very style in which past novels were written.

By emulating a past style, Oates is able to present a critique of both the style and the culture that gave rise to it. *Mysteries of Winterthurn* takes up the Victorian virtues of clear thinking as well as the Victorian abhorrence of making an honest confession of the darker side of human nature. As such, it is at one and the same time a gripping mystery story, a re-creation of past literature, and a foremost example of postmoderism that examines the abandonment of restraining Victorian values and the emergence of a new feminism.

Bibliography

Bender, Eileen Teper. *Joyce Carol Oates: Artist in Residence*. Bloomington: University of Indiana Press, 1987. An especially valuable discussion of Joyce Carol Oates's use of various historical styles as a method of critically reviewing those styles.

Creighton, Joanne. *Joyce Carol Oates: Novels of the Middle Years*. New York: Twayne, 1992. An insightful study of Oates's three novels that employ themes and styles from the nineteenth century as a form of postmodernism.

Johnson, Greg. *Invisible Writer: A Biography of Joyce Carol Oates.* New York: Dutton, 1998. An overview of the writer's life and works.

Milazzo, Lee. *Conversations with Joyce Carol Oates.* Jackson: University of Mississippi Press, 1987. A useful collection of interviews with and essays about Joyce Carol Oates that have appeared in various periodicals and newspapers.

Watanabe, Mary Ann. *Love Eclipsed: Joyce Carol Oates' Faustian Moral Vision.* New York: University Press of America, 1998. Surveys the theme of dark emotions in Oates's work.

August W. Staub

MYSTERY RIDE

Author: Robert Boswell (1953-   )
Type of plot: Psychological realism
Time of plot: 1966-1988
Locale: Rural Iowa, suburban Los Angeles, Tucson, and Chicago
First published: 1993

> *Principal characters:*
> STEPHEN LANDIS, a suburbanite who buys an Iowa farm
> ANGELA (LANDIS) VORDA, Stephen's former wife, remarried and
>   rearing their daughter in Southern California
> DULCIE LANDIS, the teenage daughter of Stephen and Angela

The Novel

Mystery Ride is primarily the story of the marriage and breakup of Stephen and Angela Landis, a couple who purchase an Iowa farm in 1971 with idealistic notions about living in the country. The novel focuses on the events of 1987, eleven years after their divorce, when Angela decides to return to the farm in Iowa from her home in Southern California in order to help their daughter, Dulcie, sort out her teenage angst. Intermittent flashbacks to the late 1960's and mid-1970's fill in the background of the couple's earlier relationship and their growth apart.

The novel opens in 1971, when Stephen and Angela decide to try farming in what seems the idyllic Iowa countryside. The farm they purchase appears perfect until they smell and soon discover years worth of trash decaying in the cellar. The trash must be removed and burned after the rats in the cellar are gassed, and in the light and heat of the fire, both Stephen and Angela think of their young love and its strength in overcoming this dirty job. That optimism is soon undercut, however, because it is the farm itself that will eventually define Stephen's identity but drive Angela away.

The novel then moves to 1987 and for the next several chapters describes the current situations in Stephen's and Angela's lives. Southern California has been comfortable for Angela because her second husband, Quin Vorda, is a successful agent for screen actors. Angela has been working for a volunteer organization serving low-income families. Her interest in social issues has led to a desire to write a shopper's handbook to encourage consumers to purchase products from only those companies with responsible social, political, and environmental standards. Yet Angela is having increasing difficulty handling Dulcie's teenage dabbling in drinking and reckless behavior, and she becomes aware of Quin's most recent infidelity, his fourth. Angela is also newly pregnant. Meanwhile, Stephen, after six years of living alone on his barely solvent farm, invites Leah Odell and her teenage daughter Roxanne, whom he met on a trip to Chicago, to see his farm and consider moving in with him. Leah likes the farm and appreciates Stephen's gentle demeanor toward his cows, and she and Roxanne decide to settle in shortly before Angela, at her wit's end with both Quin and Dulcie, decides to bring Dulcie out to her father's farm in the hope that it will improve her behavior.

The novel then flashes back to 1976, the year of the Landises' breakup. It is Stephen's thirtieth birthday, and they have a party on the farm with his brother, Andrew. In the course of the evening, standing around a bonfire and ritually burning tokens of youth, Stephen throws in his college textbooks and confesses that he has become a farmer, wed to the land, unable to resist its power over him. Angela is devastated by this revelation because she has just received an acceptance into law school. She is shocked to find that what she had thought of all along as an experiment in country living has settled into Stephen's heart and mind and completes him.

The next several chapters, set in 1987, detail Dulcie's growing friendship with Roxanne, Stephen's life of farming, Angela's return to California, and Quin's affair with Sdriana. Roxanne falls in love with a neighbor boy, Will Coffey, and they conceive a child. Angela stops to visit Andrew in Tucson, Arizona, on her return trip to California and considers the time she dated Andrew before meeting Stephen. She thinks over her decision to leave Stephen and Iowa. Angela and Quin reconcile after he has broken off his relationship with Sdriana, and he is overjoyed at Angela's pregnancy.

In another flashback to 1976, the novel describes the days around Angela's leaving Stephen. She realizes that to stay on the farm will stifle and destroy her goals and aspirations.

Returning to California after the summer, Dulcie meets Sdriana through an arrangement on Sdriana's part to get back at Quin through his stepdaughter. Dulcie becomes involved with Sdriana's partying-life neighbors, and she lives more dangerously than ever until Roxanne asks her to return to Iowa to be with her because her baby is not expected to live after its birth. The baby's death is an epiphany for Dulcie, who realizes the seriousness of life and love, and the surrounding events confirm for Leah that she cannot stay with Stephen. Dulcie elects to remain in Iowa with her father, away from the exaggerated oddities of her life in Southern California. That Christmas, Stephen and Dulcie meet Angela and Quin at Andrew's house in Tucson, and Angela experiences a strong false labor that throws Stephen into a wash of memory of Dulcie's birth.

In one last flashback to 1966, the novel describes Angela and Stephen's first meeting, when she has had an accident on the icy freeway in Chicago and Andrew sends his brother to pick up his stranded girlfriend.

The novel closes with one of Stephen's cows dying with an unborn calf inside her. Stephen has been futilely trying to keep the animal alive for many weeks, even getting new credit cards to pay the mounting veterinary bills. The cow dies, and in desperation, he hoists her up on a barn beam to butcher her in an attempt to at least use the carcass for meat. As he opens her abdomen, a calf's form emerges, but at that moment the barn beam holding her gives way, dropping the carcass and killing the unborn calf. Yet in all the harrowing physical and emotional exhaustion of the scene is the confirmation that, even without success, father and daughter have found something meaningful to do with their lives together.

The Characters

Boswell rounds out the novel with friends and family of the Landises who help to define the identities and goals of Angela, Stephen, and Dulcie. Angela's second husband, Hollywood agent Quin Vorda, is nearly as different from Stephen as a man can be. He is clean, sophisticated, and a fine dancer whose dreams are populated not with concerns about dairy cows but with plans for extravagant dinner parties. While his magnanimous personality has led him to great success managing a variety of personalities and their acting careers, his philandering has jeopardized his most important relationships. Angela's semitolerance of Quin's attraction to other women is ironically compared to her intolerance of Stephen's love for the land and his commitment, sacrifice, and care for the things that live on his farm.

Murry Glenn is an appliance salesman whom Angela meets while shopping for a refrigerator. Murry has wide knowledge of appliance-manufacturing companies, and Angela enlists him in her mission to inform consumers about the dangers of the products they buy. Murry and Angela set out to write a shopper's guide to responsible buying. Writing the book is a trial for both, and the subject's inherent self-contradictions, inconsistencies, and idealism leave Angela feeling less than successful in her attempt to make a difference.

Stephen's relationship with Leah Odell eventually fails for many of the same reasons that he and Angela could not stay together. Stephen is absorbed in his cows' needs and in working on the farm to pay bills; combined with Roxanne's pregnancy and other concerns, Stephen's absorption leaves neither Stephen nor Leah the energy to make their relationship work.

Stephen's neighbors are a diverse lot. Former University of Illinois English professor Ron Hardy is a brilliant cynic to whom Boswell gives some caustic, tragicomic, drunken lines that undercut the idealism of Angela and the other characters. On the other hand is Major Coffey, the father of Will Coffey, whose fundamentalist Christian beliefs determine Roxanne and Will's quick marriage and decision to have the baby in the futile belief that the baby might miraculously live despite the doctor's diagnosis.

Dulcie's character is drawn through the distinction between her friendships in California with Maura Yates and Judy Storm, and those in Iowa with Roxanne Odell and Will Coffey. Maura is Dulcie's age, but she is more promiscuous sexually and more involved with drinking and drug use. Judy lives in the trailer next to Sdriana's with her vicious dogs and spends most of her time drinking and riding her motorcycle. Dulcie's teenage rebellion against what she sees as Angela and Quin's boring, conservative, adult world leads her toward Maura's and Judy's behaviors. When she comes to Iowa, Dulcie first mocks Roxanne and Will's simplicity and naïveté, but through her experiences of the stark and sometimes brutal reality of life and death on the farm and in the lives of friends her age, it becomes apparent that Dulcie will make a successful transition to responsible adulthood.

Themes and Meanings

Mystery Ride is a thoughtful consideration of the conflicting desires within characters who want and need stable, trustworthy family relationships but who feel pulled by individual needs and desires. Boswell's characters seem to indicate that there is no utopia either in the single life of the professional in the city (Andrew Landis), in the romantic life on the family farm (Stephen), in the whims of the capricious libido (Quin), in the self-congratulatory rhetoric of responsible consumption (Angela), or in drugs, drinking, and rebellion (Dulcie and Judy Storm). For all of Stephen and Angela's recognition that they feel a deep and abiding connection to each other, they will never reconcile as husband and wife.

Boswell's art is in his ability to bring these diverse and often stereotyped characters together in one story and to suggest that while life may be messy, at least some people find meaning in their lives. In Stephen's case, that meaning is found in surrendering himself to his farm.

Critical Context

Mystery Ride's concern with family life is a common theme is Boswell's fiction. In novels such as *Crooked Hearts* (1987) and *Dancing in the Movies* (1987), he also explores the dynamics of family relationships. Yet given Boswell's ability and curiosity in writing about very diverse characters and very different kinds of families, there is little more than a general similarity among the families in the novels.

A more interesting comparison may be to consider *Mystery Ride* in the context of other writers who are concerned with contemporary farm life. Although some of the action in *Mystery Ride* takes place in suburban and urban settings, it is the farm around which the characters gather, and they define themselves in relationship to it. Family life on the farm has long been an important subgenre of American literature, and the subject continues to be of interest to current novelists. Jane Smiley's *A Thousand Acres* (1991), Jim Harrison's *Farmer* (1976), Douglas Unger's *Leaving the Land* (1984), Martha Bergland's *A Farm Under a Lake* (1989), and Don Kurtz's *South of the Big Four* (1995) are a few of the better-known recent novels that explore the lives of characters living on farms. Like Boswell, these writers consider the tremendous changes occurring on the farm and look at the lives of farmers in original ways. *Mystery Ride* is an important part of this collection of novels that reconsiders what it means to be a farmer and work the land.

Mystery Ride also effectively reflects some important issues confronting teenagers. Especially in the character of Dulcie, and to some extent in those of Roxanne and Will, Boswell is able to portray the difficulties of growing up. One reviewer of the novel compared Dulcie to J. D. Salinger's Holden Caulfield, as she is a kind of cutting-edge teenager faced with all the complexities of modern family life in the most progressive of American cities. It is interesting that Dulcie finds some kind of understanding and maturity through her experiences on the farm and as a witness to the realities of life and death in cows and in people.

Bibliography

Boswell, Robert. Interview by William Clark. *Publishers Weekly* 240, no. 4 (January 25, 1993): 65-66. Boswell discusses his fascination with dysfunctional families and his portrayal of them in *Mystery Ride* and his other fiction.

_____. "So Much Survives a Marriage." Interview by Susannah Hunnewell. *The New York Times Book Review*, January 24, 1993, p. 3. Boswell discusses his interest in examining married life and explains that he took the title of *Mystery Ride* from the lyrics of a song by Bruce Springsteen, whose storytelling abilities he admires.

Kakatuni, Michiko. Review of *Mystery Ride*, by Robert Boswell. *The New York Times*, January 22, 1993, p. B2. A lengthy and useful discussion of the novel.

Lee, D. "About Robert Boswell: A Profile." *Ploughshares* 22, no. 4 (Winter, 1996): 216-221. A good overview of Boswell's life and fiction.

Schofield, Sandra. Review of *Mystery Ride*, by Robert Boswell. *The New York Times Book Review*, January 24, 1993, p. 3. A provocative discussion of the novel.

Keith Fynaardt

THE NARROWS

Author: Ann Petry (1908-1997)
Type of plot: Psychological realism
Time of plot: The 1930's to the early 1950's
Locale: Monmouth, Connecticut
First published: 1953

Principal characters:

LINCOLN (LINK) WILLIAMS, a Dartmouth graduate and bartender at the Last Chance Saloon, the adopted son of Abbie Crunch

ABIGAIL (ABBIE) CRUNCH, a seventy-year-old widow who prides herself on her New England Puritanism, immaculate appearance, and racial piety

CAMILLA TREADWAY SHEFFIELD, the internationally known heiress to the Treadway Munitions Company, who becomes Link's lover

BILL HOD, the owner of the Last Chance Saloon, who becomes a father figure to Link

FRANCES JACKSON, a successful black undertaker and Abbie's best friend

The Novel

The Narrows takes place in Monmouth, Connecticut, and tells the story of an interracial love affair between Lincoln (Link) Williams, a twenty-six-year-old black man, and Camilla Treadway Sheffield, the beautiful wife of Captain Bunny Sheffield, heiress to the Treadway Munitions Company, and daughter of Monmouth's most prominent white family. The complexity of the novel, however, makes it more than a novel of romance. Through an omniscient third-person narrator, flashbacks, introspective monologues, and memories, Petry discusses the impact of racism on the lives of her characters.

Link Williams, the adopted son of Abbie Crunch and Theodore Crunch—known as the Major—was happy with his life until one Saturday afternoon when he was eight years old. The Major, looking seriously ill, had been sent home by Bill Hod. The Major, however, smelled of whiskey, and because Abbie had a strong aversion to drinking, she did not listen to Bill's warning to get the Major a doctor soon. The Major had a stroke and died two days later.

Abbie, overwhelmed with guilt, blames herself for her husband's death. In her deep grief, she forgets Link's existence. Link tries to get Abbie's attention during and after the Major's death, but he fails. Frances, who is there to comfort Abbie, keeps telling Link to run along and play for fear he will disturb his mother. Link is too young to survive this double tragedy: It seems that he has lost both father and mother at once. He feels alone, abandoned, and betrayed. He has to find something or someone to make up for this great loss.

Link leaves the silent, dark, and grief-filled house. His sees Bill standing in front of his saloon across the street, and he gets food, shelter, and a job at the Last Chance Saloon. He stays there for three months; it takes Abbie that long to notice his absence. When she and Frances finally go to the Last Chance to claim Link, he refuses to go home with them. It is only after Frances and Bill work out an arrangement to allow Link to go on working at the saloon that Link agrees to go home with Abbie, but things will never be the same again. Now Link has two rival authority figures in his life: Abbie and Bill.

Link grows up amid conflicting views of black people. Abbie, African American herself, is always finding fault with other blacks; the Major, on the other hand, enjoys telling stories about his family, the "swamp niggers." At the Last Chance, Bill and Weak Knees, the cook, try hard to instill racial pride in Link; Link's high-school history teacher, a white person, encourages him to read more about slavery in America so that he will not be ashamed of being black. Link goes on to Dartmouth College to major in history, and he is graduated with a Phi Beta Kappa key four years later.

Link is in the process of researching a book on the history of slavery in the United States when he meets Camilla, who is white, on a foggy night at the dock in the Narrows. Despite the taboo against interracial relationships, the two fall in love. The society in which they live dooms their romance. Link is accused of rape by Camilla when he tries to talk her out of their poisoned relationship. In a desperate act to save their reputations, Mrs. Treadway and Captain Sheffield, Camilla's mother and husband, kidnap Link and murder him. Mrs. Treadway is stopped by the police when she tries to dump Link's body in the river.

The Characters

The character of Link Williams is presented through his relationships with other characters in the novel. Link has suffered many scares that are detrimental to his psychological development. At the age of eight, Link is rejected by Abbie—his adoptive mother and the center of his boyhood—who, in her grief and guilt over the recent death of her husband, has completely forgotten Link's existence. In elementary school, Link is embarrassed by his teacher, who assigns him the role of Sambo in a class presentation. When Link is sixteen, Bill Hod—who has been a surrogate father to Link—betrays his trust and love by almost killing Link the first time Link disobeys him. When he is twenty-six, Link is betrayed by Camilla when he decides to end their relationship. Ambivalence marks all three relationships: Link's feelings toward Abbie, Bill, and Camilla mix love and hate, happiness and suffering, gratification and disappointment.

Abbie evokes the sympathy as well as the intolerance of the reader. Her disdain for black people, her embrace of white ideologies, and her adoption of aristocratic values greatly endanger Link's psychological well-being, indirectly cause the Major's death, and prevent her from enjoying life and loving Link. The author uses Abbie as an example to show that the internalization of the oppressor's values will bring only confusion and self-destruction. Still, Abbie proves that she is able to change. At the end of the novel, she transcends her racial bias and the painful loss over the death of Link to protect Camilla.

Camilla is a beautiful and wealthy young woman, loving at times but murderous when her authority is challenged. She is a spoiled child who must have her own way. She is so rich that she acts as if she owned the world, and Link is in many respects simply another one of her possessions. When Link ceases to be a kept man, Camilla is outraged; she simply has to destroy him. Though she and Link have shared a love that seems to have crossed the color line, Camilla is in no position to abandon her privileged status. Her eventual betrayal of Link shows her to be a product and victim of a racist society.

Bill Hod is a complex character who cannot be defined simply as either "good guy" or "bad guy." He has his dark side: He operates whorehouses, engages in smuggling illegal Chinese immigrants, has an affair with a married woman, and threatens to cripple Link if he ever disobeys him. On the other hand, he knows how to survive a racist world with body and soul intact. Above all, he has a strong sense of racial pride. He has no patience with Abbie's sense of racial inferiority and takes responsibility for teaching Link about black people: their history, their beauty, and their cultural heritage.

Frances Jackson is a woman with a man's build and mind. She is thin and tall, and she works in a profession that was traditionally a man's: undertaking. Being a successful entrepreneur, Frances is able to escape the daily humiliations of the poor and working-class blacks. She has been instrumental in nursing Abbie back to a normal life after the Major's death. Like Abbie, though, Frances has played her own role in miseducating Link about African Americans. She has been hardened by the racial discriminations she encountered when growing up. She is no longer bothered by the word "nigger." This indifferent attitude is not what Link needs in a racially hostile society.

Themes and Meanings

The Narrows is a complex work of literature that touches on several crucial issues in the lives of black people in a small New England city. The reader sees the deterioration of a neighborhood: The area in Monmouth where Abbie and Link live was once a mixed neighborhood of Irish, Italians, Finns, and Poles. Now it is a black ghetto called the Narrows, Eye of the Needle, the Bottom, Little Harlem, Dark Town, and Niggertown. Racism has taken its toll on the black people who live here: Abbie is ashamed of being black; Link is confused about his racial identity and learns to take pride in his heritage only through painful experiences; the black butler at the Treadway mansion, Malcolm Powther, becomes a Judas by pointing Link out to his master. The interracial love affair between Link and Camilla brings out the worst in people in Monmouth. Mrs. Treadway refuses to say Link's name but refers to him as "the Nigger"; she and Captain Sheffield have to kill Link to clear their names and save Camilla's reputation; the black population is more interested in Camilla's involvement in the scandal than in Link's fate; Bill Hod, upon Link's death, is ready to take the law into his own hands and kill Camilla in revenge.

Miss Doris—a character in the novel—says that Link's death is everybody's fault. In a sense she is correct, but racism comes closer to being the primary cause of the

evil. The novel makes clear that racism poisons people's thinking, prohibiting tolera-
tion and understanding of any deviation from established norms. As a result, Link is
murdered for breaking the taboo against interracial love. Nevertheless, the author is
not content merely to present this particular racial conflict. She goes a step further,
making it clear that societal violence has to be stopped before a society can progress.
It is symbolic that Abbie is chosen to break through this cycle. Her decision to protect
Camilla shows that forgiveness is stronger than hatred. Her willingness to take care of
J. C.—a little black boy who has been largely neglected by his parents—reveals that
Abbie has come to terms with Link's death and her own neglect of him at the age of
eight: She is not going to abandon this son and lose him to a racist world.

Critical Context

The Narrows, Ann Petry's third work of long fiction, is also her most complex one.
Published seven years after her first book, *The Street* (1946), *The Narrows* has largely
been neglected by critics and overshadowed by the success of her first novel. Both
books are about racial themes and the impact of racism on the lives of her black
people. Her second novel, *Country Place* (1947), on the other hand, deals with the
devastating effects of World War II on the social and moral structures of a small New
England town.

Petry is often set apart from black writers who are from the Deep South or from the
black communities in the North. To some, her growing up in a small, predominantly
white Northern town seems to have disqualified her to write about the experiences of
black people. *The Narrows*, however, is very much a novel about black people's experience in America; it is about the development of Link Williams, a black youth, and
his relationships with his family and the black community. The book is also concerned with the past: Link, a history major whose ambition is to write a book on
American slavery, knows that the cause of his imminent execution by the Treadways
reaches back to the first shipment of enslaved Africans that landed in Jamestown in
1619. In this respect, Petry has joined Zora Neale Hurston as a model for a later generation of black women writers—Alice Walker, Toni Morrison, and Gloria Naylor, to
name just a few—in understanding the historical context of slavery in America and its
legacy to the American people as a whole.

Besides writing novels, Ann Petry wrote several historical books for young readers,
including *The Drugstore Cat* (1949), *Harriet Tubman: Conductor on the Underground Railroad* (1955), *Tituba of Salem Village* (1964), and *Legends of the Saints*
(1970). Her collection of short stories entitled *Miss Muriel and Other Stories* (1971)
demonstrates her remarkable versatility.

Bibliography

Bell, Bernard W. "Ann Petry's Demythologizing of American Culture and Afro-
    American Character." In *Conjuring: Black Women, Fiction, and Literary Tradition*,
    edited by Marjorie Pryse and Hortense J. Spillers. Bloomington: Indiana Univer-
    sity Press, 1985. Critical analysis of American cultural myths such as the American

Dream, the city and small town, urban success and progress, and rural innocence and virtue in Petry's novels, including *The Narrows*.

Bontemps, Arna. "The Line." *Saturday Review* 36 (August 22, 1953): 11. Bontemps concedes that Petry's *The Narrows* is "a novel about Negroes by a Negro novelist and concerned . . . with racial conflict." This initial critical comment on the novel has served as a point of departure for later interpretations of this complex work.

Ervin, Hazel A. *Ann Petry: A Bio-Bibliography*. New York: G. K. Hall, 1993. A comprehensive compilation of reviews, analytical articles, and interviews with Petry. A brief introductory essay is followed by Ervin's annotations of the chronological list of primary and secondary sources. A valuable reference for studying Petry's work.

Gates, Henry Louis, ed. *Ann Petry: Critical Perspectives Past and Present*. New York: Amistad Press, 1998. This collection of essays by respected scholars of African American literature presents an illuminating overall critical view of Petry's life and work. Offers an in-depth analysis of *The Narrows*.

Holladay, Hilary. *Ann Petry*. New York: Twayne, 1996. This first book-length critical study of Petry's work examines *The Narrows,* as well as her other two novels and short-story collection. Holladay's careful critical analysis of Petry's works demonstrates the modernist aesthetic Petry's narratives share with the fiction of William Faulkner and Virginia Woolf.

McKay, Nellie Y. "Ann Petry's *The Street* and *The Narrows*: A Study of the Influence of Class, Race, and Gender on Afro-American Women's Lives." In *Women and War: The Changing Status of American Women from the 1930's to the 1950's*, edited by Maria Diedrich and Dorothea Fischer-Hornung. New York: Berg, 1990. From a feminist perspective, this essay takes a critical look at how class, gender, and race affect the lives of black people in general and black women in particular.

Wilson, Mark. "A *MELUS* Interview: Ann Petry—The New England Connection." *MELUS* 15 (Summer, 1988): 71-84. Recalling the racial discrimination that she and her family encountered in their hometown, Old Saybrook, Connecticut, Petry remarks that she has difficulty calling herself a New Englander. Her comments on her life and work in general and *The Narrows* in particular are illuminating.

Weihua Zhang

NEUROMANCER

Author: William Gibson (1948-   )
Type of plot: Science fiction
Time of plot: The late twenty-first century
Locale: Japan, New York, Istanbul, and space habitats orbiting Earth
First published: 1984

> *Principal characters:*
>> CASE, a street hustler and former data thief
>> LINDA LEE, a street woman, Case's lover
>> MOLLY, a mercenary and former prostitute, another of Case's lovers
>> ARMITAGE, a former special forces soldier, now a criminal operative
>> PAULEY MCCOY, also known as DIXIE FLATLINE, Case's deceased mentor
>> PETER REVEIRA, a performing holographic artist
>> AEROL, a member of a Rastafarian space colony
>> MAELCUM, another member of the colony
>> 3JANE TESSIER-ASHPOOL, an heiress
>> HIDEO, 3Jane's bodyguard, a ninja clone
>> WINTERMUTE, an artificial intelligence
>> NEUROMANCER, an artificial intelligence

The Novel

William Gibson divides *Neuromancer* into three parts, plus an epilogue. The first takes place in Chiba City, a Japanese industrial town where Case is a street hustler. The second part occurs in New York and Istanbul, and the third takes place on two space stations in orbit around the earth. All the events take place within a few months in the late twenty-first century. Gibson uses an omniscient third-person narrator throughout the story, but the narrator describes events only from Case's point of view and invents jargon and slang.

The European section of Chiba City is a slum with little or no supervision by law enforcement. Anything is available for a price. In addition to the traditional rackets of drug trafficking and prostitution, there is trade in stolen computer hardware and pirated software.

Cash is illegal in Japan and rarely used for legitimate transactions elsewhere in the world. Linda Lee, Case's girlfriend, steals a memory chip containing money from Case. When she attempts to sell it, the supposed buyer simply kills her rather than pay her price.

The same night, Case meets Molly, a mercenary. Molly escorts Case to Armitage, who is planning some sort of illegal operation. He both bribes and blackmails Case into joining them.

The location then shifts to New York City, now only one part of the Sprawl, officially known as BAMA (Boston-Atlanta Metropolitan Axis). By this time, there is a continuous city stretching from Boston to Atlanta, with the greatest density around Atlanta and New York. Here the conspirators rehearse their plot by breaking into the headquarters of Sense/Net, a corporation. The Panther Moderns, a professional terrorist group, aid them. Molly has an implant in her brain that allows Case to see, hear, feel, smell, and taste everything Molly does. The communication is strictly one-way; Molly gets no information from Case. Molly physically breaks into the building while Case breaks into the computer system to assist her. He does not use a monitor and keyboard. By this time, the Internet has evolved into what Gibson calls the "matrix," which uses virtual reality. Case directly connects his brain to the matrix. Molly steals a data construct that contains the personality and memories of the late Dixie Flatline, formerly Case's mentor.

The location shifts once again to Istanbul, where the plotters kidnap a performing holographic artist, Peter Reveira, and recruit him for their conspiracy. Istanbul is also the first place where Wintermute directly contacts Case. Wintermute is an artificial intelligence that controls Armitage and is the driving force behind their plot.

The conspirators then take a space shuttle to a small space habitat called Zion. Earlier in the century, a group of Rastafarians founded Zion for the purpose of providing a refuge for their people. Wintermute has recruited them for his operation by claiming to be a prophet and claiming that the Last Days predicted in the biblical Book of Revelation have arrived. The Rastafarian elders do not trust Wintermute because Revelations also warns that there will be a false prophet in the Last Days. Nevertheless, they provide the conspirators with logistical support for their operation and assign Aerol and Maelcum to help them. The Rastafarians transport them to Freeside, a much larger space habitat.

Peter Reveira's show attracts the attention of 3Jane Tessier-Ashpool, whose family owns the Tessier-Ashpool Corporation, which controls both Wintermute and Freeside. She invites Reveira into her family's portion of Freeside, where he helps Molly get inside. However, he then betrays her.

Molly meets Hideo, a Ninja clone who wounds her. At the same time, Case breaks into the computer system with the aid of the Dixie Flatline construct. He meets Neuromancer, another artificial intelligence owned by Tessier-Ashpool. Neuromancer creates a virtual-reality world consisting of a beach house inhabited by Linda Lee. However, Case resists the temptation to live with this virtual-reality version of Linda and exits the system. Case then leaves his console and physically follows Molly into the Tessier-Ashpool enclave. He rescues her, and they confront 3Jane, who knows the codes that can free Wintermute and Neuromancer.

The Characters

Two years before the beginning of the story, Henry Dorsett Case, the point-of-view character, was a "console cowboy." He could directly interface his brain with the worldwide computer system, the matrix. He used his abilities as a data thief. When he attempted to double-cross his employers, they damaged with a toxic drug the portion of his brain used for the interface. At the beginning of the story, he is a street hustler and has killed three people. He is also a heavy drug user; he is twenty-four years old at the time of the novel.

Otherwise, the reader can divide most of the characters into criminals and victims. Linda Lee is the purest example of a victim. She is a twenty-year-old drug abuser and computer-game devotee.

Among the criminals are Peter Reveira, a performing holographic artist and sadist; 3Jane Tessier-Ashpool, heir to the Tessier-Ashpool fortune, member of the idle rich, drug abuser, and thrill seeker; and even Molly, a mercenary whom people call a "razorgirl" because she has had retractable razor blades surgically implanted beneath her fingernails. She also has artificial eyes. At one time, Molly was a prostitute.

Armitage is interesting in that he is both a criminal and a victim. Under his real name of Willis, he served in the U.S. Army Special Forces during the Three Week War between the United States and Russia. His superiors betrayed him when they ordered him on a mission that could not succeed. He survived, but at the cost of his sanity. He reconstructed himself as Armitage, criminal mastermind, but his hold on normalcy is tenuous.

Dixie Flatline, also known as Pauley McCoy, is a deceased "cyberspace cowboy" who got his nickname from the number of times he experienced brain death while connected to cyberspace. His memories and knowledge have been stored electronically, but this version of Dixie asks to be erased when the mission is completed. As a cyberspace cowboy he was a criminal, but as a data construct, he is a victim.

Wintermute and Neuromancer are artificial intelligences whose motivations are not entirely understandable to humans. Wintermute controls Armitage but also communicates directly with Case via virtual-reality versions of Case's acquaintances. The purpose of Wintermute's plot is to free himself of his bondage to Tessier-Ashpool and unite with Neuromancer, another artificial intelligence owned by that corporation. Wintermute is the decision maker and, behind the scenes, the true protagonist of the novel. Neuromancer appears to Case as a Brazilian youth and has a true personality.

Aerol, Maelcum, and Hideo are the only major characters motivated by duty. The elders of the Rastafarian space colony order Aerol and Maelcum to assist Armitage's operation, and they do so at great personal risk. Hideo is a clone whose manufacturers have genetically engineered and psychologically conditioned him to be a bodyguard; the reader might question whether Hideo has ever had to make a moral choice.

Themes and Meanings

Neuromancer was the most important book in the short-lived "cyberpunk" movement in 1980's science fiction. Cyberpunk works share a pessimistic and dystopian view of the future. In *Neuromancer,* for example, the gap between rich and poor is large. The Tessier-Ashpools live in a luxurious enclave on a space station; in Chiba City, people sleep on the streets. Human life is cheap; Case has killed three people as a street hustler. Safety lies in allegiance to a corporation, a religious sect, a government, or some other organization.

Moreover, many cyberpunk characters have a nihilistic attitude toward life. Linda Lee is the best example in the novel. She is a drug addict and a computer-game devotee. She lives as if there is no tomorrow, and this becomes a self-fulfilling prophecy when she is murdered in the opening scenes.

The novel's settings are mostly urban, and most of the action takes place at night. There is a definite *film noir* atmosphere. In *Neuromancer*, there is a continuous city between Atlanta and Boston. Its official name is the Boston-Atlanta Metropolitan Axis (BAMA), and its popular name is the Sprawl. Even the space habitats are more like cities than frontier towns.

There is also a widespread proliferation of technology, especially inside the human body. Case is able to interface with the matrix through a connection to his brain. An implant in Molly's brain connects her and Case. Cosmetic surgery, hormone therapy, and genetic engineering are also common.

Gibson's vision of the future is a fascinating one, but no one would want to live there unless they had a lot of money.

Critical Context

The first novel to win all three major awards for science fiction—the Hugo Award, the Nebula Award, and the Philip K. Dick Award—*Neuromancer* has its roots in two kinds of science fiction. The first is the New Wave of the 1960's, which emphasized literary craftsmanship and style. New Wave writers such J. G. Ballard and Michael Moorcock included descriptions of life on the streets, rock and roll, and the effects of drugs in their science fiction. This influence gives *Neuromancer* its emotional edge and gothic atmosphere.

The second kind of science fiction that influenced *Neuromancer* is the traditional "hard" science fiction of writers such as Isaac Asimov and Arthur C. Clarke. These writers typically extrapolate current trends and new technology and project their effects on people and society. Yet where traditional science fiction concerns itself with such technologies as rockets, robots, atomic energy, and space stations, Gibson writes about prosthetics, microprocessors implanted within the human body, cosmetic surgery, virtual reality, cloning, and genetic engineering. Clarke helped to invent the concept of the communications satellite; in turn, Gibson and the other cyberpunk authors developed the concept of a worldwide virtual-reality network.

By the time Gibson wrote *Neuromancer*, microprocessors were appearing everywhere; even new cars contained microcontroller devices under their hoods. People wore portable radios and headphones while they jogged, carried cellular phones and pagers, and played computer games for recreation. Although the Internet was in its infancy, computer-literate people dialed up local bulletin boards and on-line services. More affluent people could elect surgery to remove the need for eyeglasses or contact lenses. Gibson extrapolated what the world would be like if those trends continued.

Gibson, in turn, has influenced both computer hackers and computer scientists, although he himself knew little about computers when he wrote the novel. For example, National Aeronautics and Space Administration (NASA) scientists named a remote camera platform after Molly, the lead female character in *Neuromancer*, and a German computer criminal cited the novel as an influence at his trial. Moreover, writers studying the Internet and virtual reality credit Gibson with coining the term "cyberspace" to describe the on-line world.

Bibliography

Delany, Samuel. *Silent Interviews: On Language, Race, Sex, Science Fiction, and Some Comics.* Hanover, N.H.: University Press of New England, 1994. Pages 172-174 deal specifically with Gibson, and there are other comments on Gibson and cyberpunk sprinkled through the book. By an author often associated with the New Wave.

Dozois, Gardner, ed. *Modern Classics of Science Fiction.* New York: St. Martin's Press, 1991. The editor's introduction to Gibson's story "The Winter Market" summarizes Gibson's career until 1991.

Hartwell, David, ed. *The Science Fiction Century.* New York: Tom Doherty Associates, 1997. Hartwell's introductory remarks to Gibson's story "Johnny Mnemonic" and the overall concept of this anthology put Gibson's work in historical context.

Hartwell, David, and Kathryn Kramer, eds. *The Ascent of Wonder: The Evolution of Hard SF.* New York: Tom Doherty Associates, 1994. The editors, along with contributor Gregory Benford, place Gibson's work in relationship to traditional science fiction.

Sterling, Bruce, ed. *Mirrorshades: The Cyberpunk Anthology.* New York: Arbor House, 1986. The preface provides a good overview of cyberpunk writings.

Tom Feller

NEVER COME MORNING

Author: Nelson Algren (Nelson Ahlgren Abraham; 1909-1981)
Type of plot: Naturalism
Time of plot: The 1930's
Locale: Chicago
First published: 1942

Principal characters:

BRUNO (LEFTY) BICEK, the protagonist, a hoodlum and boxer
STEFFI ROSTENKOWSKI, his girlfriend, who becomes a prostitute
BONIFACY KONSTANTINE, a barber and the neighborhood crime boss
CASEY BENKOWSKI, Bonifacy's henchman and a former boxer
FIREBALL KODADEK, Bruno's knife-wielding adversary
"ONE-EYE" TENCZARA, a police captain intent on convicting Bruno
TIGER PULTORIC, a former boxing champion and Bruno's idol

The Novel

Nelson Algren's *Never Come Morning* is rooted in Chicago, particularly in its Polish slums, and concerns the fate of Bruno (Lefty) Bicek, a seventeen-year-old with ambitions of becoming either a professional baseball player or a professional boxer. The novel begins, however, with a boxing match which is lost by Casey Benkowski, who, as a slightly older version of Bruno, foreshadows Bruno's "loss" after a boxing victory at the end of the novel. Through the chapter headings in book 1 of the novel, "The Trouble with Casey" is tied directly to "The Trouble with Bicek," and the reader learns the fate of ambitious young men.

Under the tutelage of Casey and the "sponsorship" of Bonifacy Konstantine, Bruno steals a slot machine and transforms his neighborhood gang, the Warriors, into the "Baldheads," who must have their heads shaved by Bonifacy. As president and treasurer of the new gang, Bruno has status that he exploits with Steffi Rostenkowski, whom he subsequently seduces. Before the reader learns what Bruno's "trouble" is, Algren comments that the two events have brought Bruno from dependence to independence, from boyhood to manhood, and, ironically, from "vandalism to hoodlumhood." One of Bruno's "troubles" is his adherence to the gang's code and his desire to belong, but he also fears Fireball Kodadek and his knife. Consequently, when the gang insists on their rights to Steffi, Bruno, though inwardly torn, assents; while the gang rapes Steffi, Bruno rages until in his frustration he breaks, with a well-placed kick, the neck of a Greek outsider. The Greek's death temporarily ends Steffi's ordeal, but Fireball and a friend take her to Bonifacy, who installs her as his mistress and as a prostitute in his brothel, which is run by "Mama" Tomek.

Bruno is subsequently arrested for the shooting death of a drunk, whom Casey killed, and "One-Eye" Tenczara, convinced that he is the Greek's killer, attempts to break Bruno, who remains silent despite the interrogations, lineups, and beatings. After being convicted of the drunk's murder, Bruno serves six months in prison before he is released and returns to work as a pimp and bouncer at Mama Tomek's brothel. He and Steffi cannot express their feelings for each other, but she helps him cheat Bonifacy in a card game, and the rejuvenated Bruno arranges a fight for himself with Honeyboy Tucker. The infuriated Bonifacy attempts to ensure Bruno's defeat, but Bruno manhandles Bonifacy's gang, which includes Fireball and Tiger Pultoric, Bruno's boxing idol. When Bruno takes Fireball's knife, he overcomes his fear; when he beats Pultoric, he emerges as a man. He wins the ensuing boxing match, temporarily achieving his dreams of freeing and protecting Steffi and of becoming a contender for the championship. Bonifacy, however, has turned him in to Tenczara, who comes to Bruno's dressing room to arrest him for the Greek's murder.

The Characters

Bruno Bicek, Algren's tragic protagonist in *Never Come Morning*, stands alone, differentiated from the other members of his gang by his sensitivity and humanity. In an environment that places a premium on mere survival, Bruno's "flaws" mark him as "soft."

His "softness" results in Steffi's rape and subsequent prostitution, for she cannot return to her Old World mother and values. Like Bruno, however, she retains her humanity and her capacity for love and forgiveness, but Algren has taken care not to present her as the idealized virgin: Lazy and selfish, she permits Bruno's seduction because she senses that he is the best of the available males. Algren's portrait of her, like his characterization of Bruno, is complex. In this adolescent love story, readers do not encounter the star-crossed lovers of *West Side Story* (1961); they find young people with potential whose growth is irremediably stunted by their environment. They have few choices, and the few they have do not involve escape.

The impossibility of Bruno's escape is foreshadowed by the fate of Casey, who is a bit older but whose life closely parallels his. Casey, like Bruno, is a boxer, but he is a loser, a hanger-on, a tool of Bonifacy; his position is reflected in his appearance at the barber's back door, where he is reduced to asking for "advances" which are really handouts.

While Casey is a foil to Bruno, Fireball and Tiger represent tests that the hero must pass to achieve even the illusion of victory. Fireball (whose name reflects his former baseball prowess) is a has-been at eighteen, a youth whose tall, lean frame is being consumed by tuberculosis. With courage born of having nothing to lose, he uses his knife, with its implicit threat of mutilation, to overcome Bruno. Tiger is the Old King, the father figure, the former champion whom Bruno has worshiped, but who must be defeated before Bruno can be his own man. When he defeats Tiger and takes Fireball's knife, Bruno becomes a man; the victory in the ring is important only in terms of irony.

The older generation, unlike the younger one, clings to the Old World values of hard work and religious faith, and, as a result, survives rather than thrives in a New World where exploitation, brutality, and the "con" game seem necessary for success.

Bruno's mother, who is exploited in a small shop, cannot understand her son's lack of concern about law and religion; Steffi's mother ekes out a living in a poolroom, is apparently oblivious to her environment, and has values which make her raped daughter's return impossible. Of the older generation, only Bonifacy adopts New World values, but only in what he considers, because of his paranoia, to be self-defense. Morally corrupt, he nevertheless pays lip service to Old World values while he projects his corruption onto his underlings.

Themes and Meanings

In Algren's Chicago, the characters are shaped by their environment, from which there is no real escape, yet they dream the American Dream and aspire to success. Bruno's failure is foreshadowed by Casey's, and Steffi can no more escape from the brothel than she can from the Baldheads. Like Chickadee, Helen, and Tookie, the other prostitutes at Mama Tomek's brothel, Steffi is one of the "hunted" who "also hope" (Algren's chapter title for his brothel digression is "The Hunted Also Hope"). The hunters are the "heat" and the men who want, in Algren's words, "to get their money's worth." One symbol for the woman as prey is the fly without wings in Steffi's room: After she is "seduced," Bruno crushes the fly, with which the inarticulate Steffi identifies. Later, when she and Bruno are at an amusement park, he uses his baseball prowess to win a Kewpie doll, which he subsequently "decapitates" as if it were a child. The doll may represent an illusory victory, a "fake," as Bruno calls it, like other things at the amusement park and in life. It may also, because it is compared to a child, represent what happens to children in Algren's Chicago, or, and this seems more probable, it may also represent Steffi, won by Bruno and then, almost unthinkingly, destroyed by him.

Nevertheless, both Bruno and Steffi have their dreams. Bruno becomes the "modern Kitchel" (a former Polish-American boxing champion) in his dream drama, and his imagination is fueled by matchbook covers with Tiger Pultoric's picture, by *Kayo* magazine, and by images of James Cagney—the media shape his dreams. Steffi's dreams of escape lead only to entrapment: "a great stone penitentiary" without exits; the barber's room, which becomes a "vault." There will be no escape for Steffi, who is not even permitted to die. Yet Steffi and Bruno are not the only "hunted" in the city, which is compared, along with the world, to a madhouse with its victims. In fact, Algren compares the prostitutes in the brothel to inmates of an insane asylum.

From such institutions, escape is impossible, as Algren's title implies: This is a novel about the darkness, the night; it is the literary version of the film noir. Although there is a kind of "false dawn," with its promise of light, renewal, and deliverance, the illusory dawn is followed by the darkness of impending death for Bruno and entrapment for Steffi. The morning will not come, but there is the sense that its appearance would be even more cruel, since the light would dispel the dream and leave the dreamers with bright but cold reality.

Despite his insistence on the role of the environment, Algren also finds Bruno guilty of betrayal. Like Dove Linkhorn's betrayal and guilt in Algren's later *A Walk on the Wild Side* (1956), Bruno's guilt cannot be overcome, and, also like Dove, Bruno cannot articulate his shame and his desire for forgiveness until the end of the novel. When he takes Steffi to the lake, Bruno cannot speak, cannot even touch her hand, and what could be reconciliation becomes merely another indication that these characters take their environment and its influence with them. After his arrest at the end of the novel, Bruno accepts his fate as if he had been living with it since he killed the Greek and destroyed Steffi. It is the punishment he has been seeking.

Critical Context

Never Come Morning, Algren's second novel, follows *Somebody in Boots* (1935), a "Depression" novel which it resembles in its economic determinism, its protrait of the lower classes, and its criticism of the American Dream. It is the novel which precedes *The Man With the Golden Arm* (1949), which won for Algren a National Book Award. Part of *Never Come Morning*, the second book in the novel, first appeared as "A Bottle of Milk for Mother," a short story which was included in the annual O. Henry collection of outstanding short stories in 1941.

Algren's novel, like James T. Farrell's *Studs Lonigan* (1934), with which it is often compared, is rooted in the ghettos of Chicago and is best described as a city novel which does not allow the reader or its characters a glimpse of the world outside the city. As a result, Algren uses Chicago as a microcosm of the United States and even of the world as he sees it: as madhouse, prison, or brothel with their images of insanity, entrapment, and prostitution in its broadest sense.

In his emphasis on the interplay between environment and youth, Algren resembles not only Farrell but also Richard Wright and James Baldwin, whose characters' tormented souls and physically afflicted bodies provide an indictment of the society in which they exist. Bruno is guilty of betrayal and exploitation, but his moral failure is linked inextricably to the code of his gang, which is but an exaggeration of the capitalistic code that fosters competition and callousness and that rewards only the victors. Algren offers his readers few victors because the rewards and successes are, as they are in Bruno's case, illusory and transitory.

Algren's subject, setting, and characters are squarely within the naturalistic school of fiction which originated at the turn of the century and which includes among its practitioners such writers as Stephen Crane, Frank Norris, Theodore Dreiser, and Ernest Hemingway (who praised Algren's work). In style, however, Algren is much more in the realistic school with its so-called slice-of-life emphasis on the sordid details in the lives of the lower classes. While the boxing matches at the beginning and end of the novel do offer a frame for the story, Algren has not taken the same care with the rest of the novel. The second book, as noted above, is adapted from the short story "A Bottle of Milk for Mother," and the third book consists of case histories of prostitutes at Mama Tomek's brothel. In effect, the novel grinds to a halt while Algren discusses the abuse of power by police and comments on conditions in jail, which serves as a place of refuge in Algren's work; then, as he does in his later *A Walk on the Wild Side*, he sentimentally describes the prostitutes, whom he uses as a metaphor for the prostitution inherent in a materialistic society. Nevertheless, the digressions are interesting, and they do establish, if that has not been done adequately elsewhere, the climate that determines the outcome of the novel.

In *Never Come Morning*, Algren foreshadows Bruno's failure and then proceeds to explain why the tragic outcome is inevitable. That he does this in a rather heavy-handed manner in no way diminishes the novel or subverts his message about the American Dream.

Bibliography

Beauvoir, Simone de. *A Transatlantic Love Affair: Letters to Nelson Algren.* New York: New Press, 1998. Although Beauvoir's letters do not specifically address Algren's works, they do illuminate his character and personality.

Drew, Bettina. *Nelson Algren: A Life on the Wild Side.* New York: Putnam, 1989. Drew presents the first full-scale biography of Algren and offers critical perspectives on his novels. Includes bibliographical references.

Giles, James R. *Confronting the Horror: The Novels of Nelson Algren.* Kent, Ohio: Kent State University Press, 1989. A collection of essays that focuses on the naturalism in Algren's works. Includes a bibliography for further study.

Thomas L. Erskine

A NEW LIFE

Author: Bernard Malamud (1914-1986)
Type of plot: Contemporary realism
Time of plot: The early 1950's
Locale: Northwestern United States
First published: 1961

> *Principal characters:*
> SEYMOUR LEVIN, a new English instructor at Cascadia College
> GERALD GILLEY, the director of composition
> PAULINE GILLEY, his wife
> ORVILLE FAIRCHILD, the department chairman
> C. D. FABRIKANT, a senior faculty member

The Novel

Seymour Levin of New York City ("formerly a drunkard") comes to Easchester, in the northwestern state of Cascadia, to join the faculty of Cascadia College as an instructor in English. He arrives at the small town looking forward to a new life in a halcyon rural setting, but the first of many disillusionments that this bearded, onetime high school teacher experiences is his discovery that Cascadia is a science and technology school, having lost the liberal arts "shortly after the First World War" to its rival sister institution at the state capital. What is more, most of his colleagues, he is dismayed to learn, enjoy teaching composition, do not at all miss literature, and spend most of their time in such nonacademic activities as golfing, fishing, riding, and even painting houses. The action of the novel, which spans an academic year from Levin's arrival in the fall to his forced departure the next spring, develops on two levels, the personal and the professional, which become increasingly intertwined and ultimately are indistinguishable.

The plot on the personal level focuses on an affair that Levin has with Pauline Gilley, wife of the director of composition; she previously has been involved with Levin's predecessor and pursues Levin until he finally yields. Overcome by guilt (which manifests itself in strange postintercourse pain), Levin finally attempts to end the affair, but she persists, and when Gilley eventually learns about it, he cries to Levin that he loves Pauline and the next day writes that if Levin promises "not to see [her] again, or otherwise interfere in our lives. . . . I am willing to let you stay on for one last year." Before Levin can reply, however, he receives a letter of termination "in the public interest, for good and sufficient cause of a moral nature" from the college president. Pauline and Levin decide to leave together, and Gilley tries to dissuade Levin, threatening to sue for divorce and demand custody of their two adopted children. She refuses to give him the youngsters, and Gilley then offers to relent if Levin vows to give up college teaching. The novel ends with Levin, Pauline (who is pregnant), and the children heading for California and what may be another start on a new life. Yet Levin is not certain, deciding that he may "call it quits" after Pauline gets her Nevada divorce. Since that "would finish the promise to Gilley," he would return to graduate school and then try his hand again at college teaching.

The other line of action revolves around the English department, with the professional rivalries and personality differences moving toward a conflict because of the imminent retirement of the longtime chairman, Professor O. Fairchild, author of a grammar text that is in its thirteenth edition and is the centerpiece of the composition program. Gilley, the de facto second-in-command because of his role as director of composition, is an aspirant favored by the traditionalists; his primary rival is C. D. Fabrikant, a senior faculty member whose interest in horses does not prevent him from being the only active scholar in the department. Levin becomes the outspoken leader of the reluctant and sotto voce opposition to Gilley, which further alienates him from the establishment (he already is in trouble because of his antipathy to the hallowed grammar text and his slowness in grading finals, which jeopardizes the department's record for being the first to turn in grades). The sudden death of Professor Fairchild and the appointment of Gilley as acting chairman complicates matters for Levin, who mounts his own quixotic campaign for the post. In any event, Gilley prevails, with seventeen votes to Fabrikant's two; Levin gets none. The election defeat comes on the same day that the president, calling Levin a "frustrated Union Square radical," dismisses him.

Seemingly a professional failure at Cascadia, Levin actually succeeds in turning the Department of English in a new direction: After thirty years, Fairchild's grammar book is kicked out; Gilley decides to offer literature classes to those faculty members who are interested; and Fabrikant, who is asked to start a Great Books program, begins to grow whiskers.

The Characters

When thirty-year-old Seymour Levin comes to Cascadia from the East, he is fleeing the memories of a failed love affair and the suicide of his mother, crises which led to his being a drunkard for two years. Hiding behind a beard that he grew because he did not like the sight of his face, he seems to be denying his very identity, and he refers to himself at the start of the novel only as "S." Levin. As time passes, however, emblematic of the emergence of his multifaceted personality, he becomes known as Sy, Seymour, Lev, and finally Sam. Just as his name changes, so do his roles: A romantic idealist who believes in the importance of integrity, Levin is an alien in a society of corrupt realists and, though he fails personally as a reformer, becomes the motivating force behind changes that are initiated after he is dismissed from the faculty.

Seeking friendships among his colleagues, their families, and others, Levin either is disillusioned with nearly everyone or is unable to find a basis for substantive and enduring relationships, even with the women with whom he becomes involved. The first of these is a waitress whom he steals from a Syrian graduate student and takes to a barn, but at the crucial moment the aggrieved Arab bursts in and takes their clothes.

He also fails in his second venture, with colleague Avis Fliss in his office, but on his third attempt, with a student in a motel, he succeeds, though guilt quickly overcomes him, and a conflict over a final grade forecloses any future relationship. Levin's fourth woman is Pauline Gilley; their affair begins in what he thinks is a pastoral forest, but ironically it actually is the college training site for foresters, and he gets little pleasure from the relationship. Levin, in fact, is a man whom pleasure continually eludes, for his new life—which lasts only ten months—is not much better than the one he left behind in New York, and the life upon which he embarks with Pauline and her children promises little more than responsibility. Having come almost empty-handed to Cascadia in the fall, Levin leaves town in the spring with an old Hudson full of family.

Pauline Gilley, thirty-two to his thirty, is an unhappily married woman. She and Gerald maintain a facade of a relationship for convenience and professional reasons. It even has survived Pauline's affair with Levin's predecessor, who also was dismissed. According to Gilley, Pauline "was born dissatisfied"—nearly "anything can throw her off balance"—and "has been keeping touch of her wrinkles and lamenting the passing of her youth" for years; though she has a variety of health problems, she resists going to a doctor. He concedes that life with Pauline can be pleasant ("she plays a good game of golf"), but Gilley concludes that it is "generally no bed of roses." (Levin responds: "I have never slept on flowers.") Though Gilley's characterization of her is accurate, Pauline also is in need of love, and Gilley is an indifferent husband.

"My name's Dr. Gilley" is how the director of composition introduces himself to Levin, but though Gilley is impressed with his own credentials, he is neither an academician nor a scholar. According to Pauline, "Nature here can be such an esthetic satisfaction that one slights others." Indeed, Gilley fishes, hunts, attends athletic events, and takes prizewinning photographs with a consuming intensity matched only by his pursuit of the chairmanship. He is an ambitious, opportunistic politician, and having laid the groundwork, overcomes domestic problems and easily outdistances the opposition. He reaches the goal, but under a new dean—an outsider "dug up . . . from the cornfields of Iowa," with innovative ideas—Gilley's triumph may turn out to be a Pyrrhic victory.

Among the other characters, three members of the English department stand out. Orville Fairchild, the chairman, is determined to preserve the status quo and is proud of his economical operation of the department over the years. An elderly grammarian who is a fervent believer in the "wholesome snappy drill" in workbooks, Fairchild considers Gilley his heir apparent. C. D. Fabrikant, Harvard man, gentleman farmer, bachelor, and antifeminist, is the department liberal and scholar, but in a more enlightened venue he would not be considered much of either. Avis Fliss, who knows about everyone and everything in the department, a "unique fund of information," is the sole unmarried woman instructor (and has an unsuccessful dalliance with Levin); Gilley's unofficial assistant, she serves not only as his lackey but also as his spy.

Themes and Meanings

As its title suggests, the novel has as a primary concern Levin's search for a new focus for his life, even a new identity. Fleeing despair in the East, he heads west, to
America's Eden. In this promised land Malamud's unlikely hero becomes involved in
a series of quixotic adventures that turn the erstwhile idealist into an uneasy realist
who learns that deception is vital to survival and becomes almost as adept at deceit as
the philistines he confronts on their own turf. Though he wins some of the skirmishes,
Levin realizes that redemption and salvation are to be found within, that victory over
one's inadequacies and insecurities is what really matters. The forests, mountains,
and even idyllic college campuses offer only the illusion of tranquillity—and only
from a distance.

Seymour Levin, like his creator, is Jewish, and this fact is central to the hero. Many
of Levin's characteristics place him in the tradition of the archetypal Jew in literature:
He is an outsider rejected by a community to which he comes, a wanderer in search of
a new home, a man to whom suffering is a way of life, a nonbelligerent who becomes
the center of conflict and maybe even its cause, and a scapegoat who suffers because
of the sins of others. Though obvious, his Jewishness is spoken of only near the end of
the novel, when Levin learns that Gilley hired him because Pauline had picked his application out of a pile. She explains: "Your picture reminded me of a Jewish boy I
knew in college who was very kind to me during a trying time in my life." To this
Levin responds: "So I was chosen."

In addition to Levin, Malamud focuses upon Cascadia College, which becomes as
much an antagonist as Gerald Gilley and is closely patterned after an Oregon state college where Malamud taught for many years. A *roman à clef*, the novel also is an academic satire, with Malamud's sharp criticism only occasionally tempered by light humor. Mocking people, procedures, and rituals, the satire transcends the boundaries of
the Cascadia College campus to embrace much of American higher education;
Levin's parochial, unenlightened colleagues, after all, are its products.

Critical Context

Published in 1961, *A New Life* was the third of Bernard Malamud's novels and was
written while he was a member of the English department of Oregon State College in
Corvallis. During his tenure there, from 1949 to 1961, he also wrote his first two novels, *The Natural* (1952) and *The Assistant* (1957), and published *The Magic Barrel*
(1958), a collection of short stories for which he received the National Book Award in
1959.

In a 1961 article, Philip Roth concluded that Malamud had not yet "found the
contemporary scene a proper backdrop for his tales of heartlessness and heartache,
of suffering and regeneration." The publication of *A New Life* answered this criticism, for the novel continues Malamud's progress toward a realistic and modern
fiction that begins with his second novel. In *A New Life* he consciously strives to
create a real place and believable people; the mythic superstructure common to
his earlier works still is present, but it is more muted; and while the themes are

basically the same, they are developed in a new context, a larger social setting.

While welcomed as an indication of Malamud's growth, the book also has been criticized for attempting to accomplish too much: It is a satire of American academic life, a love story, and a picaresque novel about a seriocomic antihero. In addition, Malamud gives too much information about the functioning of a college English department, dwelling on minutiae that impede the movement of the narrative and are largely unnecessary for his satiric purposes.

In sum, *A New Life* is important as Malamud's first attempt at a wholly realistic novel, and it also is a notable example of a minor literary type, the academic novel. Further, in Seymour Levin he has created a memorable seeker of the American Dream who discovers that at least part of it is false illusion.

Bibliography

Astro, Richard, and Jackson J. Benson, eds. *The Fiction of Bernard Malamud*. Corvallis: Oregon State University Press, 1977. Malamud was an instructor in English at Oregon State University from 1949 to 1961. This volume has been faithful to the papers as they were presented in a tribute to Malamud at a conference held at the university. Contains the opinions of several foremost American critics about Malamud's work, interspersed with stories and anecdotes which make for lively reading. An extensive secondary bibliography is also provided.

Field, Leslie A., and Joyce W. Field, eds. *Bernard Malamud: A Collection of Critical Essays*. 1970. Rev. ed. Englewood Cliffs, N.J.: Prentice-Hall, 1975. This nine-essay volume is the modest version of the original 1970 publication, which compiled twenty-one of the most important essays on Malamud's work in the 1960's and 1970's. Contains an interview with Malamud based on discussions he had with the authors in 1973. Places emphasis on Malamud's Jewish background in the context of Israel, with an essay by Sheldon Norman Grebstein entitled "Bernard Malamud and the Jewish Movement."

Ochshorn, Kathleen. *The Heart's Essential Landscape: Bernard Malamud's Hero*. New York: Peter Lang, 1990. Chapters on each of Malamud's novels and his short-story collections. Seeks to continue a trend in Malamud criticism that views his heroes as tending toward the *mensch* and away from the *schlemiel*. Includes a bibliography but no notes.

Richman, Sidney. *Bernard Malamud*. Boston: Twayne, 1966. Although limited in scope, this criticism is a valuable overview of Malamud's work to the mid-1960's. Gives a sensitive reading of the author's first three novels and his first two collections of stories.

Salzberg, Joel, ed. *Critical Essays on Bernard Malamud*. Boston: G. K. Hall, 1987. An excellent source for diverse material on Malamud's writing; a must for Malamud scholars. Provides a strong introduction by Salzberg with much insight into Malamud's work and his place in literature. The essays are well chosen; some are reprints, but there is a first printing of an essay by Sidney Richman entitled "Malamud's Quarrel with God."

Solotaroff, Robert. *Bernard Malamud: A Study of the Short Fiction.* Boston: Twayne, 1989. Divided into a section of essays on the short stories, a section on Malamud's view of life and art, and a final section of selections from his major critics. Provides chronology and bibliography.

Gerald H. Strauss

THE NEW MEXICO TRILOGY

Author: John Nichols (1940-   )

Type of plot: Magical Realism

Time of plot: The Milagro Beanfield War, the early 1970's; *The Magic Journey*, the 1930's to the 1970's; *The Nirvana Blues*, the late 1970's

Locale: Northern New Mexico and southern Colorado

First published: The Milagro Beanfield War, 1974; *The Magic Journey*, 1978; *The Nirvana Blues*, 1981.

> *Principal characters:*
> JOSÉ (JOE) MONDRAGÒN, a jack-of-all-trades in Milagro
> NANCY MONDRAGÒN, Joe's wife
> BERNABÉ MONTOYA, the sheriff of Milagro
> CAROLINA MONTOYA, Bernabé's wife
> LADD DEVINE III, a landowner and developer in Milagro
> CHARLEY BLOOM, a transplanted Eastern lawyer
> LINDA ROMERO BLOOM, Charley's wife
> ONOFRE MARTÌNEZ, a one-armed poet and balladeer
> KYRIL MONTANA, an undercover agent for the state police
> HERBERT GOLDFARB, a member of Volunteers in Service to America (VISTA)
> DALE RODEY MCQUEEN, a landowner and developer in Chamisaville
> APRIL MCQUEEN DELANEY, Rodey's daughter
> ICARUS SUAZO, a Native American from the Chamisaville Pueblo
> CLAUDE PARKER, Chamisaville's only undertaker
> GEORGE PARKER, Claude's son, a schoolteacher
> VIRGIL LEYBA, a Chamisaville lawyer, born in Mexico
> "JUNIOR" LEYBA, Virgil's son, also a lawyer
> JOSEPH BONATELLI, a mobster
> JOE MINIVER, a garbage collector and former advertising man
> HEIDI MINIVER, Joe's wife
> ELOY IRRIBARREN, an elderly Chicano farmer

The Novels

In his preface to *The Nirvana Blues*, John Nichols recalls,

> When I sat down to begin *The Milagro Beanfield War*, I had no idea the story would grow into a trio of books. . . . All three novels are set in mythical Chamisa county, where the folks, the situations and the landscapes resemble parts of northern New Mexico and southern Colorado. Should they survive, I suppose future interested persons might refer to these books as 'his New Mexico Trilogy,' even though the name of New Mexico never appears in any of the texts.

By the end of the decade, as if by self-fulfilling prophecy, the three novels had already survived several printings and were collectively if informally known under the title suggested by their author.

With *The Milagro Beanfield War*, John Nichols laid claim to a vast but remote portion of the American West only partially explored by Richard Bradford in *Red Sky at Morning* (1968) and *So Far from Heaven* (1973). The territory surveyed, ceded to the United States by the Treaty of Guadalupe Hidalgo (1848), tends to resist American influence; the indigenous population is largely descended from Spaniards who first settled the region in the sixteenth and seventeenth centuries. As Nichols points out throughout his trilogy, the entrenched Hispanic subculture remained largely unchanged until early in the twentieth century, when improved travel and technology brought in English-speaking invaders from all over the United States. That invasion and its consequences, most fully documented in *The Magic Journey*, provides the theme and context for the entire trilogy, in which the indigenous Hispanic population of the area is threatened with extinction because of claims and counterclaims regarding land and water rights.

In *The Milagro Beanfield War*, successfully filmed in 1988 by Robert Redford, one man's impulsive act brings to a head a number of conflicts that have been slowly building for years. Joe Mondragòn, a handyman, small-time farmer, and occasional petty criminal, one day decides to dislodge the barrier that keeps water flowing past his small plot of land instead of into it. Almost at once, Joe's gesture takes on unintended and unexpected symbolic significance, alerting the Anglo power brokers to possible subversive activity among the natives. Ladd Devine, hereditary proprietor of the ranching conglomerate that has been acquiring land in and around Milagro since the late nineteenth century, has moved into full-scale development, with several resort projects already completed; to defend his interests, he has a coterie of local henchmen and hangers-on, not to mention valuable contacts in the state capital. Whatever land Devine does not own is now the property of the U.S. Forest Service, the "Floresta," having been acquired from its original Chicano owners over the years by means no less devious than Devine's. Joe Mondragòn's deed thus attracts the attention of the state police, most dangerously present in the person of one Kyril Montana, a plainclothes agent who seeks to discredit Joe and his cohorts, if any, by fair means or foul.

As it happens, Joe has no cohorts at the outset; most of his fellow "natives," including a couple of Anglo transplants, see his action as potentially provocative and try to distance themselves from it. The local sheriff, a Chicano named Bernabé Montoya, does his somewhat ineffectual best to maintain order without choosing sides; Charley Bloom, a transplanted Boston lawyer with a Chicano second wife, has handled cases for Joe in the past but is quite hesitant to involve himself in the currently brewing scandal. Before long, however, Ladd Devine and his various allies have made it quite clear that they intend to neutralize Joe through entrapment, accusing him of some crime other than the irrigation of what used to be his own beanfield. Battle lines are drawn, as are petitions asserting the existence of the Milagro Land and Water Protection Association, headed by a fiery middle-aged woman mechanic named Ruby Archuleta. The "war" of the title, in which only a few nonfatal shots are fired, ends in a stalemate, yet it is clear that things in Milagro will never again be the same.

In *The Magic Journey*, Nichols focuses on the somewhat larger town of Chamisaville, not far from Milagro, framing his narrative in historical perspective. During the period covered, from the time of the Great Depression to that of the Vietnam War, the native subculture, a reasonably harmonious mix of Hispanic and Native American elements, will be permanently dislocated by the combined forces of venture capitalism and the U.S. Bureau of Land Management. At the center of the tale is Dale Rodey McQueen, an itinerant salesman and confidence man from Texas who happens to be driving through Chamisaville en route to Colorado with a truckload of stolen dynamite one day in 1930 when his truck hits a pothole and explodes, exposing a natural mineral spring. Ever the opportunist, McQueen, with the help of several locals and a Denver banker whose daughter he soon marries, turns the spring—-and the surrounding area—into a major tourist attraction, an economic "boom" in the midst of the Depression. Success breeds success, and a new influx of outsiders join McQueen and his "Anglo Axis" in buying up or otherwise controlling all the land and water rights in Chamisa County.

By the end of World War II, McQueen and his cronies have built themselves an empire, creating just enough jobs for the locals to preserve a state of uneasy truce. By that time, however, McQueen is at least dimly aware that he has also brought into the world his most implacable adversary, his daughter April.

Born around 1931, reared in increasingly privileged circumstances as her father's empire has developed, April McQueen matures from a curious, difficult, but charming child into a brilliant, headstrong, and beautiful young woman. From childhood, she has been familiar with all social strata in and around Chamisaville, increasingly sensitive to the injustices perpetrated by her father and his way of life. At sixteen, she runs away from home, seeking fame, fortune, and adventure amid the literary and artistic ferment of the late 1940's and early 1950's; she comes of age on the fringes of the Beat generation. By the time hippies appear on the scene in the 1960's, April is there to meet them on their own terms; her consciousness has long since been raised. In 1963, April returns to Chamisaville for a visit, just in time to observe her parents' response to John F. Kennedy's assassination; five years later, she settles in Chamisaville for good, bringing the two children from her failed third marriage to a radicalized African American academic named Matthew Delaney.

As April Delaney, Rodey McQueen's wayward daughter will raise fresh hell with her father's empire, writing subversive articles and circulating petitions on behalf of the newly disfranchised of Chamisaville. She will also return to certain old loves, such as the aging lawyer Virgil Leyba and the schoolteacher George Parker, a high school classmate. Curious as ever, April seeks and finds all manner of corruption surrounding such local development projects as the electrification of the Native American Chamisaville Pueblo, too engrossed in her discoveries to notice signs of encroaching illness.

The political situation, meanwhile, continues to heat up, with April at its center, attracting the attention of state and federal agents. While investigating a suspicious murder, April, already doomed to die of cancer before her fortieth birthday, is abducted and murdered by federal agents called in by the "Anglo Axis," her body left to rot by the roadside. "Yet April's constituency was all but gone by the time she died," observes the omniscient narrator, the "Anglo Axis" having displaced those young enough to survive.

The action of *The Nirvana Blues* takes place in Chamisaville less than a decade after April Delaney's death, yet true to the narrator's observation, few familiar characters survive; one of the few is Joseph Bonatelli, a gangster whom April first saw at her father's house in 1963 but whose connection to the "Anglo Axis" remained mysterious.

By 1980, the area has become a mecca not only for tourists but also for all manner of well-heeled, well-educated dropouts desperately fleeing one American Dream in search of another. Joe Miniver, a former advertising copywriter now self-employed as a garbage collector, has chosen as his private dream one of the few Chamisaville farms still in indigenous hands, less than two acres belonging to eighty-three-year-old Eloy Irribarren. To finance his dream, Joe has become involved in a wild scheme involving a shipment of cocaine, although he himself has managed generally to steer clear of the Chamisaville drug "scene." Over five days, Joe will break his marriage vows for the first time—but with three different women—and have strange run-ins not only with the mobster Bonatelli but also with a locally based sect combining Asian mysticism and monkey worship. During that time, Joe will also forge a strong if bizarre bond with Eloy Irribarren, whose land and water rights may not, in fact, be his to sell, as encumbered as they are by conflicting legal claims.

The cocaine, when finally located, turns out to be five pounds of sugar, but by then time has run out for both Joe and Eloy; following a botched bank robbery, the two men are gunned down by police while attempting to restore the original irrigation ditches adjoining Eloy's property. Progress, only slightly delayed by April Delaney's machinations a decade earlier, has triumphed at last.

The Characters

In undertaking what would become the New Mexico trilogy, John Nichols adopted a mode of storytelling different from his earlier and later novels, a mode similar to that of the "proletarian" novels of Upton Sinclair and John Steinbeck. The trilogy derives much of its tone and texture from a host of minor characters, many with colorful ethnic names and too numerous to be singled out for individual attention. Against such a background stand characters whose actions in time will prove remarkable, whether by accident or by design. Joe Mondragòn emerges as a most unlikely central character in *The Milagro Beanfield War*; even at the end of the novel, he feels quite unprepared to be a leader or a symbol and is much more at ease with the simple role of troublemaker. Bernabé Montoya, the sheriff of Milagro, tries to avoid conflict whenever possible; Nichols's portrayal of Bernabé, although generally sympathetic, often borders on caricature. For example, the sheriff often appears in an emergency situation with his boots on the wrong feet. Charley Bloom, a fugitive from the Eastern law establishment, comes across as a conflicted, often weak, but generally admirable character, perpetually at odds with the upwardly mobile ambitions of his second wife, Linda, a Chicana from Colorado who resents Charley's involvement with the local Hispanic population.

The "Anglo Axis," meanwhile, is portrayed close to caricature, a crowd of latter-day robber barons and their acolytes totally ignorant of the population that they are displacing. Ladd Devine III is a ruthless capitalist, married to an alcoholic "trophy wife" who carries on an affair with one of his foremen. The undercover agent Kyril Montana is scheming and sinister, intent on discrediting Charley Bloom with false gossip and quite prepared to gun down Joe Mondragòn in cold blood, if need be. Herbie Goldfarb, a VISTA volunteer posted to Milagro for reasons that are never quite made clear even to him, is likewise drawn close to caricature, yet he serves as an outside observer when not providing comic relief in his search for feminine companionship and pest-free shelter.

In *The Magic Journey*, Nichols's characterizations grow sharper and deeper, as does the shape of his tale. Rodey McQueen, the stereotypical "snake-oil salesman," settles all too easily into the role of later-day robber baron, both more dimensional and potentially more dangerous than his predecessor Ladd Devine III. The Native American Icarus Suazo, who in the 1930's aided and abetted McQueen with some of his schemes, hardens and matures over forty years into a true revolutionary, complex and inscrutable. Virgil Leyba, born in Mexico at the turn of the twentieth century, took part in the Mexican War with Pancho Villa and Emiliano Zapata before settling in Chamisaville for his health. Trained in the law, Virgil remains a revolutionary at heart, doing his best to conserve what is left of the Chamisaville natives' land and dignity. Virgil's son Junior, a Harvard-trained lawyer uneasily married to a New England Yankee, has long since sold out to the "Anglo Axis" and is truly his father's nemesis.

Most remarkable of all, however, is Rodey McQueen's daughter April Delaney, whose brains, beauty, and adventures at times come close to straining the reader's credulity. Thorns and all, April is a rose born and bred in the desert, returning from her twenty-year formative absence ready and willing to undermine her father's exploitative empire. Three times married and divorced, with numerous other romantic entanglements dating back to her early teens (including both Leybas, father and son), April in her mid-thirties has become more than her father's match, having inherited his drive even as she scorns the fruit of his ambitions. So great a threat does she pose to the "Anglo Axis" that federal agents, in league with Rodey McQueen's business interests, carry out what is in effect a political assassination, little suspecting that April has little more than a few months left to live.

Joseph Bonatelli, a shadowy presence in *The Magic Journey*, emerges somewhat from the shadows in *The Nirvana Blues*, controlling such enterprises as a dog-racing track, a resort community, and quite possibly the local drug trade as well. In his encounter with Joe Miniver, he emerges as a stereotypical gangster, with buffoonish behavior that makes him no less menacing. Like the earlier volumes, *The Nirvana Blues* owes much of its effect to the presence of numerous minor or incidental characters; here, however, Nichols's narrative gains considerable power by focusing on the octogenarian Eloy Irribarren, one of the indigenous subsistence farmers whose type forms the crowd in the trilogy taken as a whole. By the late 1970's, Eloy has become the last of a dying breed, resourceful, proud, and independent, yet literally dispossessed from his home turf. Knowing that he must give up his land, Eloy has settled reluctantly on Joe Miniver as his buyer of choice, even as he doubts Joe's ability to close the deal. In the touching final scene, having all but given up their plans, the two men join forces in a symbolic, suicidal exercise of revolt. Joe Miniver, meanwhile, is a somewhat less convincing character, a transplanted urbanite whose physical instincts take hold of his reason after years of self-control. Joe's wife Heidi is somewhat more convincing, both humorous and healthily assertive as she attempts to take control of an unforeseen crisis in her life and marriage. Joe's death, however amply prepared, lacks the force of April Delaney's; although Joe makes a valiant last stand, he is less hero than fool, a man who simply happens to be in the wrong place at the wrong time. Eloy, by contrast, achieves with his death a martyrdom equal to that of April Delaney.

Themes and Meanings

Like Sinclair and Steinbeck before him, John Nichols in his trilogy attempts to speak for and about an embattled minority whose voice is otherwise unlikely to be heard. At times, he falls into the shallow trap that often lies in wait for such writers, that of adopting a patronizing or condescending attitude toward characters less literate or articulate than himself. Most of the time, however, Nichols manages to combine humor, satire, and compassion in approximately equal portion, evoking at the same time the breathtaking physical beauty of the landscape being disputed and despoiled. Perhaps to avoid sounding didactic despite an indisputably liberal political stance, Nichols makes frequent use throughout the trilogy of the technique known as Magical Realism, relatively rare in English prose yet quite in keeping with the Hispanic ancestry of his characters.

Ghosts, angels, and strangely personified animals move freely throughout all three novels of the trilogy, conversing with the human characters, observing the action, or at times participating directly in the plot. Such intervention, as Nichols presents it, seems quite consistent with the exotic landscape and its unpredictable weather, yet not even the spirit world can prevail against the invasive forces of big business and big government combined. The death of Eloy Irribarren at the end of *The Nirvana Blues* underscores Nichols's conviction that the indigenous civilization so lovingly described throughout the trilogy has itself passed into the spirit world, accessible only by memory or through fiction. In the meantime, Chamisaville serves, in the latter two novels, as a refraction (not a reflection) of American social change from 1930 to about 1980, showing the effects upon a remote, unspoiled region of cultural and political events originating elsewhere.

Critical Context

The three volumes that make up the New Mexico trilogy are something of a sport in the canon of John Nichols's published novels; although wry humor and offbeat characterizations have been typical of Nichols's fiction from the start, he has never elsewhere attempted the technique of Magical Realism, nor has he taken on a project as vast and potentially daunting as the trilogy, which comprises a total of more than fifteen hundred pages in the original trade editions. From the start, the trilogy seemed to attract a readership somewhat distinct from Nichols's usual audience, taking its place among the works of Upton Sinclair and John Steinbeck as representative samples of proletarian American fiction. Unlike the two earlier writers, however, John Nichols is blessed (or cursed) with a frequently broad sense of humor that, even as it may seem to take the edge off of his social criticism, serves also to breathe fresh air into what might otherwise seem like political polemic.

Bibliography

Nichols, John. *If Mountains Die: A New Mexico Memoir.* New York: W. W. Norton, 1994. A partial autobiography with valuable background comment on the trilogy.

Wild, Peter. *John Nichols.* Boise, Idaho: Boise State University, 1986. A critical overview stressing the importance of the trilogy in Nichols's collected works.

David B. Parsell

THE NEW YORK TRILOGY

Author: Paul Auster (1947-   )
Type of plot: Postmodernism
Time of plot: 1947-1984
Locale: New York City, New Jersey, Paris, the Var region of France, and Boston
First published: City of Glass, 1985; *Ghosts*, 1986; *The Locked Room*, 1986; published
    together as *The New York Trilogy*, 1994

Principal characters:
>   DANIEL QUINN, a detective novelist posing as a detective
>   PETER STILLMAN, JR., his client
>   VIRGINIA STILLMAN, Stillman's wife
>   PETER STILLMAN, SR., a scholar released from a mental institution
>   PAUL AUSTER, a writer
>   BLUE, a private detective
>   WHITE, his boss
>   BLACK, a writer
>   FANSHAWE, a writer who disappears
>   SOPHIE FANSHAWE, his wife
>   JANE FANSHAWE, his mother
>   THE UNNAMED NARRATOR, Fanshawe's boyhood friend and literary
>   executor

The Novels

The New York Trilogy consists of three short novels, *City of Glass*, *Ghosts*, and *The Locked Room*, which tell similar stories. In *City of Glass*, Daniel Quinn is a New York poet who turns to writing detective novels under the name William Wilson, the first of many multiple identities in the trilogy. He strongly identifies with his hero, Max Work, and wishes he could be more like the detective.

An opportunity presents itself when Quinn receives a series of mysterious telephone calls asking for Paul Auster. Quinn finally claims to be Auster, a private detective, and is hired by the caller, Peter Stillman, a psychologically fragile young man who, as a child, was locked alone in a room for nine years. Peter Stillman, Sr., a scholar obsessed with the origins of language, had hoped to discover what words would evolve in a child reared in isolation. The father is to be released from his resulting confinement, and the younger Stillman suspects that his life is in danger.

Quinn follows the older Stillman all over Manhattan, taking notes about their walks, and discovers that the routes are spelling out the phrase "Tower of Babel," the subject of Stillman's research. After tracking down and confronting the real Auster, who turns out to be another writer, not a detective, Quinn goes into physical and psychological decline.

The protagonist of *Ghosts* is a 1940's detective named Blue, who is assigned by his boss White to spy on a Brooklyn writer named Black. Watching across the street from Black's apartment, all Blue sees is a man writing and reading. Blue's suspicion that the detailed reports he files to White are not being read leads to his discovery that Black himself is the client.

The Locked Room is another literary detective story. The unnamed narrator, a free-lance writer, hears from Sophie Fanshawe, the wife of a New Jersey childhood friend, that her husband has disappeared, leaving behind a cache of unpublished manuscripts he has entrusted to the friend he has not seen or contacted in years. The narrator arranges for the publication of Fanshawe's novels, poems, and plays, and the works are critically acclaimed. Everyone assumes that Fanshawe is dead, but the narrator knows otherwise. He and Sophie fall in love and marry, but he is haunted by the possibility that Fanshawe will suddenly appear.

The narrator experiences a brief emotional breakdown, a fate he shares, in varying degrees, with Quinn and Blue. The three novellas are also linked by the constant appearance of psychological doubles. Other connections include Sophie's hiring Quinn to find Fanshawe only for the pseudodetective to disappear as well, the narrator's being beaten by Peter Stillman, and Fanshawe's taking the name Henry Dark, a character invented by Peter Stillman, Sr., and not speaking to anyone for two years. These incidents illustrate Auster's interest in chance and the interconnectedness of events. Quinn, the senior Stillman, Blue, Black, and Fanshawe all write in red notebooks, as if all are mirror images creating the same text.

The Characters

Tormented by the deaths of his wife and three-year-old son five years earlier, Quinn finds solace only in the arbitrary order of baseball (like Blue) and the artificial world of his art (like Fanshawe). He finds himself attracted to the detective story because problems are solved, mysteries explained—unlike in real life. Caring about no one but himself, he feels lost within his gloom until the seemingly random telephone call gives a new purpose to his life: "He knew he could not bring his son back to life, but at least he could prevent another from dying." The opposite, however, occurs. When Quinn pretends to be his son, the senior Stillman commits suicide.

Staring across at Black's apartment, Blue assesses his life for the first time, realizing he has been content merely with looking at the surface of things. An uncultured but intelligent man, he has never truly thought before having Black, as if a mirror, reflect his identity back to him. He feels that by understanding Black he can better understand himself. Auster subtly establishes ironic distance between reader and characters, none of whom ever truly understands anyone or anything. At the same time Blue is becoming more aware of the world around him, his identity merges more with Black's until he too is confined to a room (like the young Stillman, his imprisoned father, and the reclusive Fanshawe). Blue is released from this debilitating alienation only by confronting Black, beating him when he pulls a gun, and reading the manuscript on which Black has been working all this time. Auster does not reveal the contents, but it is likely to be the tale of a man hired to spy on a man writing a book about a man hired to spy on a man writing a book.

As a young man, Fanshawe is a natural leader whose intelligence, authority, and generosity make him stand out from the crowd, but—as with all Auster's characters—he is not comfortable with this identity and begins to drift literally and emotionally. His writing stems from his need to communicate with his mother, his unstable sister, his wife, their infant son, and his best friend. His refusal to submit his writings for publication and his disappearance reflect his fear of the consequences of communication.

The narrator is Fanshawe's shadow, a failed novelist seen by many as a bright young critic who realizes his work amounts to little. By becoming associated so closely with Fanshawe and marrying the writer's supposed widow, he gradually loses his grip on his identity. Like Quinn and Blue, the narrator berates himself for not living a full life. By agreeing to write a Fanshawe biography, he feels he is signing away his soul. The matter is made even worse when Fanshawe's mother says she always considered the two to be like twins. By tracking down his double and killing him, he will be free—unless that is Fanshawe's plan to gain his own freedom. Talking to an unseen Fanshawe through a cracked door in Boston, hearing his friend's banal, self-deluding claim that his sole purpose was to find another husband for Sophie, reading Fanshawe's red notebook, and destroying it combine to release the narrator from the man's grasp.

Themes and Meanings

Auster's relentless use of psychological doubles unifies *The New York Trilogy* and underscores his concern with contemporary humanity's obsession with self and uncertainty about the validity and value of that self. Quinn's initial relief in being someone else, a mask he can hide behind, turns into the anguish of losing his grip on reality. Blue decides he has to deny Black's existence to retain his own identity, a solution similar to that reached by Fanshawe's friend. The latter acknowledges, however, the impossibility of discovering the true self, remarking that "at times we even have a glimmer of who we are, but in the end we can never be sure, and as our lives go on, we become more and more opaque to ourselves, more and more aware of our own incoherence . . . no one can gain access to himself."

The identity theme is related to Auster's exploration of the conflict between order and chaos. A seemingly wrong number begins Quinn's involvement with the Stillmans. He is told that Paul Auster is the name of a detective recommended by a relative of Peter's wife, Virginia, but the only Paul Auster he can locate is a writer like himself. Are people's fates determined by random influences, or are more malevolent forces at work? Has Quinn been chosen—perhaps by the son—to cause the senior Stillman's death, or is it all a matter of chance? The detective work of Quinn, Blue, and the narrator (the biographer as detective) leads less to resolution than to confusion. The instrument of order causes even more chaos. The student of Babel tells Quinn that "the world is in fragments. . . . And it's my job to put it back together again." His method includes denying his son's humanity and taking walks that spell out words. The quest for order can result in madness. The narrator of *The Locked Room* concludes that "each life is no more than the sum of contingent facts, a chronicle of chance intersections, of flukes, or random events that divulge nothing but their own lack of purpose."

Critical Context

A little-known poet, translator, critic, and editor before the appearance of *City of Glass*, his first novel, Auster was a student of French literature, and the influence of existentialism can be seen throughout *The New York Trilogy.* A more significant influence, perhaps, is the work of writers such as Jorge Luis Borges, Italo Calvino, and Vladimir Nabokov, creators of self-conscious, self-reflective works that question the nature of narrative and delight in playing tricks on their characters and readers. (All three also occasionally employ the conventions of detective fiction.) Auster constantly forces his readers to be aware that they are reading a narrative about narratives. The narrator of *City of Glass* observes, "The question is the story itself, and whether or not it means something is not for the story to tell." The narrator of *The Locked Room* calls attention to the similarity between his story and the other parts of the trilogy: "These three stories are finally the same story, but each one represents a different stage in my awareness of what it is about." Does this mean he is the creator of all three? Is he an unreliable narrator, and if so, to what degree is he unreliable? Auster forces his readers to distrust any resolution to these intertwining mysteries and calls into question authorship itself by appearing as a character.

The New York Trilogy is also part of another literary tradition; it is full of allusions to nineteenth century American writers such as Ralph Waldo Emerson, Nathaniel Hawthorne, Herman Melville, Edgar Allan Poe, Henry David Thoreau, and Walt Whitman. Quinn's pseudonym is named for Poe's story "William Wilson," Black lives on the street where Whitman once resided, Fanshawe is named for Hawthorne's first novel, and the narrator provokes his altercation with Stillman by claiming to be Melville. These writers explore the meaning of America, often emphasizing the contradictions of the American character. The failure of America to live up to its expectations contributes to the ennui of Auster's protagonists. They become detectives in part because of their need for the romantic sense of adventure associated with America's past.

The New York Trilogy announced the arrival of an important new voice in American fiction writing in an unusually lucid, accessible style. Auster's novels after this debut continue his distinctive treatment of alienation, chance, the quest for identity, and the limitations of language, themes he approaches seriously but with a sense of playfulness as well, recalling works by such writers as Don DeLillo and Steven Millhauser. As Paul Auster the character explains to Daniel Quinn in a discussion of why people continue to read Miguel de Cervantes's *Don Quixote* (1605-1615): "It remains highly amusing to us. And that's finally all anyone wants out of a book—to be amused."

Bibliography

Alford, Steven E. "Mirrors of Madness: Paul Auster's *The New York Trilogy*." *Critique* 37, no. 1 (Fall, 1995): 17-33. Looks at how Auster treats the identities of his narrators to illustrate how the self is created by language.

Barone, Dennis, ed. *Beyond the Red Notebook: Essays on Paul Auster*. Philadelphia: University of Pennsylvania Press, 1995. Thirteen essays, including one explaining Auster's place as an American postmodernist.

Marling, William. "Paul Auster and the American romantics." *LIT: Literature, Interpretation, Theory* 7, no. 4 (March, 1997): 301-310. Explains the influence of the American romantics on Auster.

Nealon, Jeffrey T. "Work of the Detective, Work of the Writer: Paul Auster's *City of Glass*." *Modern Fiction Studies* 42, no. 1 (Spring, 1996): 91-110. Considers the metaphysical nature of the novel and Quinn as the perfect metafictional character.

Zilcosky, John. "The Revenge of the Author: Paul Auster's Challenge to Theory." *Critique* 39, no. 3 (Spring, 1998): 195-206. Applies the theories of authorship of Roland Barthes and Michel Foucault to the trilogy. One of six articles in this issue devoted to Auster.

Michael Adams

NICKEL MOUNTAIN
A Pastoral Novel

Author: John Gardner (1933-1982)
Type of plot: Pastoral realism
Time of plot: From December, 1954, to the summer of 1960
Locale: The farming country in the Catskills of upstate New York
First published: 1973

> *Principal characters:*
>> HENRY SOAMES, the protagonist, owner of the Stop-Off, a diner
>> CALLIOPE (CALLIE) SOAMES (née WELLS), his wife, who is twenty-five years his junior
>> GEORGE LOOMIS, a farmer and inveterate collector, the closest thing Henry has to a friend
>> WILLARD FREUND, a young man and the father of Callie's child
>> SIMON BALE, a Jehovah's Witness whom Henry takes into his care

The Novel

  Nickel Mountain is a story of moral renovation. Gardner's mildly ironic opening sentence announces the novel's preoccupation with the spiritual life of its central figure: "In December, 1954, Henry Soames would hardly have said his life was just beginning." Indeed, when the novel begins, Henry, grossly overweight and already the victim of one heart attack, is close to a nervous breakdown. Both afraid of and attracted to the storms that whip the snow outside the Stop-Off, his diner at the foot of Nickel Mountain in rural upstate New York, Henry is obsessed by thoughts of his seemingly imminent death. Doc Cathey's warning that he must lose weight—"You lose ninety pounds, Henry Soames, or you're a goner"—is a leitmotif of his anxiety.

  Yet Henry survives the winter to be drawn from his self-absorption the following spring by the arrival of sixteen-year-old Callie Wells. Largely as a favor to her parents, Henry hires Callie to help him in the diner. His feelings about the changes that her presence brings are mixed. While he regrets the loss of his solitude, he finds himself fond of her and pleased with the avuncular role this girl, twenty-five years his junior, has assigned him. Thus, when Henry finds out that Callie is pregnant by Willard Freund, a young man who quickly decides to act on his father's injunction that he go away to Cornell to study agriculture, his solicitousness is genuine. It is an equally genuine concern for Callie's welfare that motivates him when he tries to persuade his bachelor friend George Loomis to marry her. In the course of his lighthearted but adamant refusal to marry Callie (even turning down Henry's offer of fifteen-hundred dollars), George playfully leads Henry to the startling conclusion that he loves Callie himself. The shock precipitates another heart attack for Henry, and Callie moves into the diner for several weeks to take care of him. Once he has recovered his health, she returns home, and Henry finds himself suddenly more lonely than he has ever been.

When Callie, worried about him, goes back to the Stop-Off late in the evening of his first night alone since his illness, Henry confesses his love to her. In the small hours of the morning, he takes her home to ask Frank Wells for permission to marry his daughter, and less than three weeks later, Henry and Callie are married.

The months that follow are filled with intense activity, as Callie's pregnancy progresses and Henry builds an addition onto the diner to accommodate his growing family. Yet Henry is secretly troubled by the possibility of the return of Willard Freund. In December, after a long and difficult labor, Callie gives birth to baby Jimmy. The event marks an emotional turning point for Henry; he realizes that the world has been changed by it ("it seemed to Henry, it was different now") and that by his being a party to the birth and accepting all of its consequent responsibilities, he has entered into a community of familial bonds which militate against any sense of personal alienation. He also discovers that he is much less disturbed by any thoughts about Willard's return.

Although his road to spiritual health is not without its obstacles—Henry suffers a serious reversal when he slips into a life-threatening anomie after the death of Simon Bale, a death for which he blames himself—it is clear by the end of the novel that Henry has made significant progress. In the last episode of the novel, Henry and four-year-old Jimmy come across a graveyard where an elderly couple is exhuming the body of their dead son. The spectacle of death no longer frightens Henry, for he now accepts it as a consequence of the natural order of things. No longer an alienated and lonely individual who despairs at thoughts of his own death, Henry implicitly invokes the ameliorative strength of familial and communal bonds when, in consoling Jimmy in his disappointment over not seeing the dead boy in the raised coffin, he tells him that he loves him.

The Characters

In *Nickel Mountain*, Gardner's skillful manipulation of point of view carries the burden of characterization. Although the novel is written in the third person, the majority of its chapters are constructed around single and identifiable centers of consciousness. Each of the characters central to the action of the novel serves as the organizing point of view for its different sections. By tempering the conventions of the pastoral (*Nickel Mountain* is subtitled "A Pastoral Novel") with the ability of the novel form to accommodate competing points of view, Gardner develops principal characters who are neither idealized nor sentimentalized.

The first of the novel's eight titled sections is narrated from Henry's perspective. Desperately lonely and preoccupied with his heart condition, Henry is a terrified man who passionately confesses his fears to whomever he corners in his diner. Far from affording him any relief, such outbursts to strangers and casual acquaintances leave him shocked and humiliated by their impropriety and violence; more often than not, after making his apologies, he finds himself sobbing, with his head on his counter. The novel's third section, "The Edge of the Woods," primarily concerned with Callie's complicated delivery, is also mediated through Henry's agitated consciousness.

Through his marriage to Callie, Henry has begun the affirmative work of spiritual renovation, but the carefully controlled point of view, limiting itself to Henry's perceptions of the events going on around him, underlines how much Henry is still an alienated and frightened man. "The Grave" is the final section of the novel and the last to be narrated from Henry's point of view. Although images of death abound in these closing pages, Henry has survived his earlier feelings of alienation and despair to embrace a faith in familial and communal love. It is as a consequence of the author's controlled point of view (which allows the reader to see the world from Henry's viewpoint) that this final portrait of the hero does not collapse into maudlin sentimentality.

Callie, George Loomis, and Willard Freund are all in their turns the centers of consciousness of various sections of the novel. The section entitled "The Wedding" is narrated from Callie's point of view. Callie's situation is, to say the least, an unfortunate one. Pregnant and deserted by the father of her child, she is about to marry a grotesquely fat man who is twenty-five years her senior and whom she does not love. Yet Gardner's presentation of the events surrounding her wedding from her point of view avoids the danger of sentimentalizing Callie while it reveals the depth of her character. Rather than wallow in self-pity, Callie reflects both on her love for her family and on the love demonstrated by all those aunts, uncles, and cousins who have gathered around her on this day to help her celebrate. This capacity to love and be loved gives Callie the strength to make the best of a bad situation and to resolve about the man who is soon to be her husband: "I don't know whether I love him or not, but I will."

Present at Callie's wedding is George Loomis, "the eternal bachelor smiling, joyful, quoting scraps of what he said was Latin verse." George, however, is also an emotional and physical cripple and a relentless collector of "things." His radical loneliness is most poignantly revealed in the novel's subsequent section, aptly titled "The Things," which is narrated from his point of view. The penultimate section of the novel, "The Meeting," deals with Willard Freund's return from college. Feeling superior to the community that produced him, the cynical and resentful Willard tries to divest himself of whatever emotional and spiritual claims it has on him. By restricting the narrative in this section to Willard's point of view, Gardner presents a compelling picture of Willard as an alienated and despairing young man.

Themes and Meanings

The theme of *Nickel Mountain* is salvation in a secular world. The moral and dramatic center to Gardner's treatment of this theme is Henry's discovery that, in a world in which God is either dead or indifferent, the existential solitude of the self is not sufficient to give meaning and fulfillment to life. When the novel opens, Henry seems an unlikely candidate for spiritual salvation. The years of solitude in an isolated country diner have made him hesitant to enter fully, through love, marriage, and family, into the life of the community. Yet his moral education is only beginning, and this education represents a rejection of nihilistic existentialism in favor of a life-affirming program of action. Henry, reluctantly at first but later with much alacrity, accepts his responsibility to act.

His marriage to Callie is the first step toward establishing the bonds of love and commitment that will ultimately provide the foundation of his joy in the world. The birth of his wife's child draws him further into the bonds of community. That the child is not biologically his child emphasizes the active agency of his will to participate in the world: Henry has a son not by accident but by choice. It is significant that Willard, by accident the biological father of Callie's child, owns no sense of community, only a solipsistic despair. At the end of the novel, feeling "like a man who'd been born again," Henry has become absorbed into the processual vitality of life to the extent that he does not fear death so much as he recognizes its place in the world. Life and death are both part of "the holiness of things (his father's phrase), the idea of magical change." His earlier fear of death had really been no more than a fear of further alienation. Having become a celebrant of the dynamic of birth and death, and having learned to see it through the eyes of one who is bound to it through love, Henry finds in his own mortality not a cause for despair but an inspiration for spiritual serenity.

Critical Context

First drafted when Gardner was an undergraduate, *Nickel Mountain* was not published until 1973, when it quickly appeared on the heels of his ambitious novel *The Sunlight Dialogues* (1972)—presumably to capitalize on the excitement generated by that critically acclaimed best-seller. While not Gardner's best novel, *Nickel Mountain* was easily his most popular book with the reading public. Selected by the Book-of-the-Month Club, it was pirated in Taiwan and translated into Danish, Finnish, French, Hungarian, Spanish, and Swedish.

From the beginning of his career, Gardner flatly rejected the peculiar nihilism characteristic of literary modernism. While writers from T. S. Eliot to Samuel Beckett have decried the absence of either scientific or religious authority for human values as they constructed their wastelands of despair and alienation, Gardner has remained steadfast in his advocacy of a literature of affirmation. Yet his defense of human values trades neither in science nor in any conventional sense of religion. In *Nickel Mountain*, Gardner champions a familial and communal love, dramatized in Henry's marriage to Callie and his acceptance of another man's child as his own, as a spiritual bulwark against the terrible chaos of human existence. In the face of the preponderance of modern literature which has abandoned overtly moral concerns, Gardner's most significant achievement, both in *Nickel Mountain* and in the novels which followed, has been to offer an acutely moral fiction which is neither moralistic nor sentimental.

Bibliography

Butts, Leonard. *The Novels of John Gardner: Making Life Art as a Moral Process*. Baton Rouge: Louisiana State University Press, 1988. Butts draws his argument from Gardner himself, specifically *On Moral Fiction* (that art is a moral process) and discusses the ten novels in pairs, focusing on the main characters as either artists or artist figures who to varying degrees succeed or fail in transforming themselves into Gardner's "true artist." As Butts defines it, moral fiction is not didactic but instead a matter of aesthetic wholeness.

Chavkin, Allan, ed. *Conversations with John Gardner.* Jackson: University Press of Mississippi, 1990. Reprints nineteen of the most important interviews (the majority from the crucial *On Moral Fiction* period) and adds one never before published interview. Chavkin's introduction, which focuses on Gardner as he appears in these and his other numerous interviews, is especially noteworthy. The chronology updates the one in Howell (below).

Cowart, David. *Arches and Light: The Fiction of John Gardner.* Carbondale: Southern Illinois University Press, 1983. Discusses the published novels through *Mickelsson's Ghosts,* the two story collections, and the tales for children. As good as Cowart's intelligent and certainly readable chapters are, they suffer (as does so much Gardner criticism) insofar as they are concerned with validating Gardner's position on moral fiction as a valid alternative to existential despair.

Henderson, Jeff. *John Gardner: A Study of the Short Fiction.* Boston: Twayne, 1990. Part 1 concentrates on Gardner's short fiction, including his stories for children; part 2 contains excerpts from essays and letters in which Gardner defines his role as a writer; part 3 provides excerpts from important Gardner critics. Includes chronology and bibliography.

_____, ed. *Thor's Hammer: Essays on John Gardner.* Conway: University of Central Arkansas Press, 1985. Presents fifteen original essays of varying quality, including three on *Grendel.* The most important are John M. Howell's biographical essay, Robert A. Morace's on Gardner and his reviewers, Gregory Morris's discussion of Gardner and "plagiarism," Samuel Coale's on dreams, Leonard Butts's on *Mickelsson's Ghosts,* and Charles Johnson's "A Phenomenology of *On Moral Fiction.*"

Howell, John M. *John Gardner: A Bibliographical Profile.* Carbondale: Southern Illinois University Press, 1980. Howell's detailed chronology and enumerative listing of works by Gardner (down to separate editions, printings, issues, and translations), as well as the afterword written by Gardner, make this an indispensable work for any Gardner student.

McWilliams, Dean. *John Gardner.* Boston: Twayne, 1990. McWilliams includes little biographical material, does not try to be at all comprehensive, yet has an interesting and certainly original thesis: that Gardner's fiction may be more fruitfully approached via Mikhail Bakhtin's theory of dialogism than via *On Moral Fiction.* Unfortunately, the chapters (on the novels and *Jason and Medeia*) tend to be rather introductory in approach and only rarely dialogical in focus.

Morace, Robert A. *John Gardner: An Annotated Secondary Bibliography.* New York: Garland, 1984. An especially thorough annotated listing of all known items (reviews, articles, significant mentions) about Gardner through 1983. The annotations of speeches and interviews are especially full (a particularly useful fact given the number of interviews and speeches the loquacious as well as prolific Gardner gave). A concluding section updates Howell's *John Gardner: A Bibliographical Profile*.

Morace, Robert A., and Kathryn VanSpanckeren, eds. *John Gardner: Critical Perspectives*. Carbondale: Southern Illinois University Press, 1982. This first critical book on Gardner's work covers the full range of his literary endeavors, from his dissertation-novel "The Old Men" through his then most recent fictions, "Vlemk, The Box Painter" and *Freddy's Book*, with separate essays on his "epic poem" *Jason and Medeia; The King's Indian: Stories and Tales*; his children's stories; libretti; pastoral novels; use of sources, parody, and embedding; and theory of moral fiction. The volume concludes with Gardner's afterword.

Morris, Gregory L. *A World of Order and Light: The Fiction of John Gardner*. Athens: University of Georgia Press, 1984. Like Butts and Cowart, Morris works well within the moral fiction framework which Gardner himself established. Unlike Cowart, however, Morris emphasizes moral art as a process by which order is discovered rather than (as Cowart contends) made. More specifically the novels (including Gardner's dissertation novel "The Old Men") and two collections of short fiction are discussed in terms of Gardner's "luminous vision" and "magical landscapes."

Richard Butts

NINETY-TWO IN THE SHADE

Author: Thomas McGuane (1939-   )
Type of plot: Comic realism
Time of plot: The late 1960's
Locale: Key West, Florida
First published: 1973

> *Principal characters:*
>> THOMAS SKELTON, the protagonist, a young man who wants to become
>> a fishing guide and owner of a boat
>> NICHOL DANCE, a fishing guide who vows to kill Skelton if he tries to
>> compete with him
>> FARON CARTER, another fishing guide, Dance's partner
>> MIRANDA COLE, Skelton's girlfriend
>> SKELTON'S MOTHER
>> SKELTON'S FATHER
>> GOLDSBORO SKELTON, Skelton's grandfather

The Novel

Just before the halfway point of the novel, Nichol Dance vows to shoot Thomas Skelton if he attempts to compete with the two established guides of Key West, Dance himself and Faron Carter. He communicates this vow in a face-to-face confrontation, yet Skelton continues with his plan. As a result, the plot and the basis for the reader's interest are extremely simple. The two men seem headed for an ultimate, mortal confrontation, neither of them willing to compromise or be deflected from his declared purpose. The sense of violent inevitability is increased by the violence of Dance's personality—he has already killed one person and come close to killing a second—and by Skelton's strangely quiet, persevering stubbornness. This conflict is the core of the novel. In the first half, the plot is more improvised and dense than in the second half, as the conflict comes into focus—once Dance has made his vow to kill Skelton if he intrudes on his territory as fishing guide, the novel's action becomes so simple it is perhaps simplistic. It is almost as if the author has communicated to the reader: A violent confrontation will inevitably occur, read on and see how it happens. The guiding hand of the author, discreet in the first half, becomes prominent in the second. The denouement is accompanied by real suspense, yet a true sense of inevitability is lacking.

There are three main reasons for this. The mode of the novel is basically comic—or wry, caustic comic—and this prevents most of the characters from attaining three-dimensional solidity or "roundness." Skelton's character is the most fully developed, and the novel charts his development from youth to manhood; his identity comes increasingly into focus as the book proceeds. Yet both he and Dance are bathed in the same aura of nihilism and goatlike, egocentric stubbornness. Their codes are too similar; greater authorial control would be needed to distinguish them from each other (and, perhaps, from the author himself). Several pages are devoted to an attempt to establish these similarities and differences. One passage begins:

> The future cast a bright and luminous shadow over Thomas Skelton's fragmented past; for Dance, it was the past that cast the shadow. Both men were equally prey to mirages. Thomas Skelton required a sense of mortality; and, ironically, it was Nichol Dance who was giving it to him; for Skelton understood perfectly well that there was a chance, however small, that Nichol Dance would kill him. This faint shadow lay upon his life now as discreetly as the shadow of cancer lies among cells.

The author is highly intelligent, and if a sense of inevitability is lacking, it is not because of oversight. Considerable space is given to defining the psychological conflict, yet the effort is peculiarly artificial. Second, the author's presence becomes too dominant—he is seen by the reader only too visibly pulling the strings. The novel is so deliberate that there is even a preparatory confrontation before the final one when Dance and Skelton go out together with their boats into the Gulf to look for birds killed by a storm:

> Dance said, "Look here, I know it wasn't much of a joke."
> "You're right."
> "Not that it excuses what you done."
> "Yeah well."
> "And you cannot guide. I gave my word."
> "Well, I *am* going to guide."
> "You are not."

Skelton nodded that he was, as pleasantly as he could. The main theme becomes overly highlighted, the author's insistence too calculated and drawn out. (A nagging doubt arises in the reader's mind: Is this a commercial pitch?) Third, the author's humor—often riotously successful—undercuts his own purposes. For example, after Dance has told Carter his intention to shoot Skelton, Carter replies:

> "Nichol! *I like him!*" Carter bustled around the freezer, then pointlessly opened it, drawing out a block of ice that imprisoned myriad silver fish. He held it to the light and looked. "Shoot!"

The "Shoot!" is a pun, a clever one. Yet at the same time, the author is making unwitting fun of the whole second half of his own book.

The Characters

Thomas McGuane has a prodigious talent for creating amusing, vivid, flat characters. This is part of his comic talent. Some of Skelton's fishing clients are masterfully sketched, for example, Mr. and Mrs. Rudleigh from Connecticut and Olie Slatt from Montana. Skelton's very kinky family is a source of much amusement and laughs. Sometimes, the humor throws all verisimilitude to the winds—and this would be fine if *Ninety-two in the Shade* were a purely comic novel. Skelton's home is the fuselage of an antique warplane; his father, who once established a whorehouse and owned a factory for blimps that flew the black flag of anarchism, voluntarily confines himself to the house and lives for months at a time in a bassinet that is covered with mosquito netting; Skelton's mother is a former prostitute; his grandfather, Goldsboro Skelton, is one of the biggest crooks in Florida and somehow charms businesses into paying him graft and protection money. They are comic characters.

Yet Thomas Skelton is engaged in finding a reasonable vocation, even if only for half of his time (he would like to read and see his girlfriend during the other half), and in finding an identity. The novel half-comically and half-seriously follows his development, his search for the truth about himself and his family. It flirts with the tradition of the *Bildungsroman*. The characters are both comic and not comic, hovering between flatness and roundness. Readers who are willing to accept conventions in literature will have no difficulty in accepting these characters, and the author treats them with real skill. The reader less willing to accept novelistic conventions, however, will not believe many of the characters, although McGuane's unique, dense style might carry him along.

Largely typical of McGuane's treatment of character is Skelton's girlfriend, Miranda. Fetching, desired by most men who encounter her, a schoolteacher who is both wholesome and sleeps around, she is a perfect creation of the 1960's, and clearly the novel could not do without her. Her name points toward her conventional origin; just as a pastoral needs a Miranda or Sylvia and a Western needs its pretty schoolmarm, this novel needs Miranda. Again, readers who readily accept conventional characters (here a convention adapted to the 1960's) will have no difficulty in accepting Miranda. Yet she hovers between an existence in solid, carnal life and as a confectioner's cream puff.

Themes and Meanings

Although the discussion of the novel's action and characters might indicate that it is second-rate, it is not. McGuane has been compared to Ernest Hemingway, William Faulkner, and Thomas Pynchon, and the main reason for the comparisons is his style, a certain richness and seriousness that it expresses. The style is totally unlike those of the three authors mentioned above: It is a combination of very creative, original metaphors and wry, satiric concision. It is this style that holds the novel together and lifts it above the domain of superficially exciting, forgettable commercial reads, and it is the style—not the characters or action—that penetrates the contours and textures of contemporary American life. Although the characters may be two-dimensional, the style is three-dimensional and closely follows real thoughts:

> Now she is in the tub with him. They struggle for purchase against the porcelain. The window here is smaller and interferes not at all with the smoky swoon of half-discovered girls in which Skelton finds himself. In his mind, he hears *Lovesick Blues* on the violin. He reaches for a grip and pulls down the shower curtain, collapses under embossed plastic unicorns. The shaft of afternoon light from the small window misses in its trajectory the

tub by far; the tub is in the dark; the light ignites a place in the hallway, a giant shining a flashlight into the house. A rolled copy of the *Key West Citizen* hits the front porch and sounds like a tennis ball served, the first shot of a volley . . . Traffic bubbles the air. Skelton thinks that what he'd like is a True Heart to go to heaven with.

Often the style is wry, biting, somewhat nihilistic:

By dint of sloth, nothing had set in. And Skelton had been swept along. The cue ball of absurdity had touched the billiard balls in his mind and everything burst away from the center. Now the balls were back in the rack. Everyone should know what it is to be demoralized just so everyone knows what it is to be demoralized.

The throwaway flipness, the wryness are largely justified because they reflect the attitude and thoughts of the protagonist. On the other hand, this same style carries over to other characters where it is less justified—there, one can speak of McGuane's style:

Every night on TV: America con carne. And eternity is little more than an inkling, a dampness . . . Even simple pleasure! The dream of simultaneous orgasm is just a herring dying on a mirror.

Much of the novel is devoted to satirizing popular culture at large, advertising, small business, franchises, cheerleaders, and so on. *Ninety-two in the Shade* can be compared to other satires on provincial life, such as Manuel Puig's *Betrayed by Rita Hayworth* (1968) or *Heartbreak Tango* (1969). Yet McGuane is not as compassionate as Puig: His satire has a truculence reminiscent of the 1960's, a constant tinge of outrage and nonacceptance that explains his frequent ironic references to "the republic" (which means contemporary America) or to "democracy" between quotes. Is McGuane a serious critic of contemporary culture? He is certainly a critic of its superficial manifestations. Sometimes his satire has a real object. Sometimes, however, it becomes petrified in a stance of naysaying that has no real object, and any moral outrage is merely a vague blur. Here is where the philosophy of the author is nihilistic. It might reflect the temporary stage of his youthful protagonist, but at many points in the book Skelton's attitudes tend to blend with those of the author—they are not kept distinct.

At the periphery of the novel, McGuane hints at various possibilities of purity, of generosity. His characters have dreams. When a game fish puts up a good fight, Skelton prefers to let it go. His mother is generous. It is the function of the style to keep those dreams and possibilities present. Also, Skelton's choice of vocation, his stubborn desire to become a fishing guide, is a genuine, positive vision—it makes sense in terms of his talents, a past interest in biology, and a concern for fair play. The proper, probing question to ask about the novel is, What thwarts these positive impulses? Is it American commercial culture in general or a somewhat eccentric individual, a killer in the form of Nichol Dance? Neither—no connections are made between Dance and the commercial culture so consistently satirized throughout the novel. The final confrontation, being foreordained and prejudged, answers no questions whatsoever; it is swift, much too swift probably, and comes as an anticlimax. So once again one returns to the question, What is it that kills the positive impulses in the novel?

Although the question is never clearly framed by the author, and although any answer must be speculative, perhaps it is the author himself who bears responsibility. The wry, truculent tone does not entertain the possibility that these positive impulses might survive or even that they should be taken seriously. Or, perhaps, the author has calculatedly written a commercial novel—hence, this kind of question is out of place, that is, beyond the conventions and legitimate expectations of such a book. The novel is a striking but mixed performance: The style is brilliant, the action and plot violent yet conventional and somewhat superficial, the philosophy a peculiar, uneasy mixture of laughter and nihilism.

Critical Context

Ninety-two in the Shade followed closely upon the heels of *The Sporting Club* (1968) and *The Bushwhacked Piano* (1971); the three books were published within a period of four years, and interest in McGuane became widespread. Some critics thought that *The Bushwhacked Piano* was a better novel, but all three books seemed to have a similar energy, excitement, and dense style. Probably some of the critical naysayers were right about *Ninety-two in the Shade*—it was, indeed, a rather commercial performance. (McGuane himself directed a film version of the novel in 1975.) By 1984, McGuane had published his seventh book, *Something to Be Desired*, and while its commercial success was not great, it was informed by a maturity of vision not to be found in the virtuoso style of his early novels.

Bibliography

Ingram, David. "Thomas McGuane: Nature, Environmentalism, and the American West." *Journal of American Studies* 29 (December, 1995): 423-439. Ingram argues that the desire for a pristine nature, which is so ingrained in American culture and is viewed as somewhat unattainable, is central to McGuane's work. His works explore the role played by old mythologies of the frontier in the ecology and politics of the modern American West. Yet while acknowledging their power, McGuane also realizes the seductiveness of urban life.

McClintock, James I. "'Unextended Selves' and 'Unformed Visions': Roman Catholicism in Thomas McGuane's Novels." *Renascence: Essays on Values in Literature* 49 (Winter, 1997): 139-152. McClintock shows how many of McGuane's literary themes have been influenced by Roman Catholicism. He contends that McGuane's protagonists are frequently caught in a crisis of faith, realizing that something is wrong in their lives but unable to resolve their problems without spiritual help.

Morris, Gregory L. "How Ambivalence Won the West: Thomas McGuane and the Fiction of the New West." *Critique* 32 (Spring, 1991): 180-189. Focuses on McGuane's influence in redefining the shape of the "new West" in his works of fiction. Morris discusses McGuane's insistence on the idea of "American space," his

view of the political ambivalence of the American West, and geography working itself into fiction.

Westrum, Dexter. *Thomas McGuane*. Boston: Twayne, 1991. Westrum provides a
brief biographical survey of McGuane's life and then presents several critical essays on his work. A valuable resource for the study of this author. Includes bibliographical references and comprehensive index.

John Carpenter

NO ONE WRITES TO THE COLONEL

Author: Gabriel García Márquez (1928-　　)
Type of plot: Ironic realism
Time of plot: October to December, 1956
Locale: An unnamed village in Colombia
First published: El coronel no tiene quien le escriba, 1961 (English translation, 1968)

> *Principal characters:*
> THE COLONEL, a poverty-stricken retired soldier
> HIS WIFE, an ailing and cantankerous woman
> DON SABAS, a grasping and unscrupulous businessman
> THE DOCTOR, a kindly physician

The Novel

The plot of this short novel is quite simple. The elderly and impoverished colonel has been waiting for fifteen years to receive a pension check for his service in the army. The cultural context of the story is during what is known as *la violencia,* a civil war between liberals and conservatives in Colombia that lasted from the late 1940's into the 1960's. Nine months previous to the opening of the story, the colonel's son, Agustín, had been killed at a cockfight for distributing secret political literature. The colonel is torn between his desire to keep his son's prizefighting cock in order to enter it into the cockfights in January and his need to sell it to provide food for himself and his wife. The story focuses primarily on the colonel's pride in trying to conceal his indigent state and his often ironic and bitterly humorous response to his situation.

The central metaphors in the story are the pension, which never arrives, but for which the colonel never ceases to hope, and the fighting cock, which also represents hope, as well as his son's, and thus the whole village's, political rebellion. In desperation, he does decide to sell the cock to the exploiter Sabas, who gives him considerably less money than he originally promised. When the villagers snatch the bird and enter it in the trial fights and the colonel sees that it lives up to its reputation as a prizefighter, he decides to give the money back and keep the bird. Even though his wife nags him to change his mind, he holds out, realizing that the animal belongs to the whole community. When his wife asks him what they will eat until the time of the cockfights, he replies with an expletive that ends the story.

Although the story is lacking in plot—mainly concerned as it is with the colonel's stoic pride, his wife's nagging, the venality of Sabas, the tense political situation of a people under martial law—the character of the colonel sustains the reader's interest. The atmosphere of the story is also arresting, for it seems summed up by the colonel's intestinal complaints—"the colonel experienced the feeling that fungus and poisonous lilies were taking root in his gut"—and his wife's remark—"We're rotting alive."

Moreover, no summary of the events of the story can adequately account for the sense of a fully contained fictional world created here—a world as completely realized as that of William Faulkner, one of García Márquez's admitted influences. It is not the plot that makes this story powerful, but rather the combination of understated realism with a sense of a folklore reality that creates a unique combination which has been called "magical realism" by some critics. Although there is little background for the simple events which make up the story, García Márquez's recognized masterpiece, *Cien años de soledad* (1967; *One Hundred Years of Solitude*, 1970), provides a complete picture of the mysterious world of superstition, fantasy, and stark reality which the colonel inhabits. Finally, what characterizes the story is the understated style of the third-person limited point of view, which filters the fictional world through the mind of the characters, and the laconic speech of the colonel, who, innocent though he may be, is wise in his stoic acceptance of an immediate reality that he cannot change and an ultimate reality that he can only encounter with wit and wry humor.

The Characters

The colonel is not only the protagonist of the novel, he is the novel, for it is his humor and irony, his pride and courage against the inexplicable adversity of poverty and political repression, that give the novel dignity and structure. This wise yet childlike man assumes a sort of tragicomic stature in the course of the narrative. Although he goes to wait for the mail boat every Friday with hopeful expectation, his resigned response is always the same: "No one writes to the colonel." Although he is often self-effacing, reconciled to the repressive regime which controls his life, he maintains his pride. For example, he does not wear a hat so, as he says, "I don't have to take it off to anyone."

He is both idealistic and ironic, a combination that makes him memorable in contemporary fiction. When his wife says that he is only skin and bones, he replies that he is taking care of himself so he can sell himself: "I've already been hired by a clarinet factory." When his wife laments that the mush they are eating is from corn left over from the rooster, and says, "That's life," the colonel replies, "Life is the best thing that's ever been invented." In some ways, the colonel resembles the existential hero as described by Albert Camus—holding out no hope for transcendent value but maintaining a kind of stoic acceptance of struggle regardless of the outcome. In modern fiction, his closest parallel is Ernest Hemingway's fisherman, Santiago, in *The Old Man and the Sea* (1952). Although the colonel has nothing so tangible as a great fish with which to do battle, he is no less an example of a man who sustains "grace under pressure."

The colonel's wife, who alternates between being bedridden because of her asthma and being hyperenergetic, is more realistic about their situation than the colonel is and urges him to sell the rooster. She has less pride also, having no qualms about going about the village trying to barter household items for food. Finally, she says that she is fed up with resignation and dignity, and she bitterly tells the colonel, "You should realize that you can't eat dignity." The colonel has hope, however, about which he says, "You can't eat it, but it sustains you."

Sabas is the only leader of the colonel's party who has escaped persecution; he has aligned himself with the established political order and continues to live in the town and to prosper, primarily by exploiting the hunger and want of the rest of the villagers. Other minor characters are a doctor who tends to the colonel's wife and belongs to the underground resistance movement, the town's corrupt mayor, a shiftless lawyer whom the colonel has hired to try to get his pension money, and Father Angel, a priest who exhibits no real moral leadership for the community. All of these minor figures are but supporting players for the central role of the proud, yet self-effacing colonel, who deals with all adversities, large and small, with his sharp, ironic humor.

Themes and Meanings

Although the background for the story is *la violencia*, the protracted civil war in Colombia, and although the colonel's problems stem from being a member of the losing party in that civil war, this is not a political novel except in an indirect way. Although García Márquez is a committed leftist, he is by no means a propagandist. His interest in this novel is in the heroic dignity of his protagonist and in his work's carefully controlled style—the style of the colonel himself. The atmosphere of the story is more pervasive than the social world of political repression and futile underground resistance would seem to suggest. It is a world of decadence and decay as concretely felt as the world of William Faulkner, yet it is a world of individual pride and understatement as pure as the style of Ernest Hemingway.

Although the past in the story is as distant as the sixty years previous when the colonel was a young man in the army, it is as close as the moth-eaten old umbrella which the colonel's wife won in a raffle many years earlier. The only thing that it is good for now, says the colonel, is "counting the stars," but he has only two stars to count, and to count on—the hoped-for pension check and the prizewinning rooster. The bird becomes the most immediate symbol of hope for the colonel. Although he knows that it is his only source of capital, he also knows that it has more important value than staving off hunger for a few more months. Because it belonged to his dead son and because it increasingly represents the emotional hope of the village, he holds on to it and waits for the coming cockfights.

Although this short novel is more realistic than *One Hundred Years of Solitude*, it is nevertheless distinguished by the hybrid of fable and fact, dream and gritty reality which characterizes that epoch-making work and which led to the Nobel Prize for García Márquez in 1982.

Critical Context

García Márquez has said in interviews that his characteristic storytelling style is the style of his grandmother, and that some of his best characters are patterned after his grandfather, whom he calls the most important figure in his life. Discussing literary influences, he has acknowledged his debt to Franz Kafka, William Faulkner, and Ernest Hemingway—all of whom lie behind the style of *No One Writes to the Colonel*.

Although García Márquez is a novelist, working within that genre's basically mimetic pattern, his style is that of the modern romancer; it is lyric rather that realistic, highly polished and self-conscious rather than concerned only with mere external reality. His characters exist not in an "as-if" real world, but rather in a purely fictional world of his own making—a combination of the folklore conventions of his South American heritage and the realism of the great modernist writers. The result is that reality is seen as more problematic and inexplicable than everyday experience would suggest.

That his fictions take place in a political culture that seems unstable and adrift is not so thematically important as the fact that this unorganized social world makes possible his exploration of reality as governed by inexplicable forces. Thus, his characters, deprived of the props of established social order, have only their most elemental and primal virtues to sustain them. He is a metaphysical and poetic writer, not a propagandist or a social realist.

García Márquez, primarily because of the popular and critical reception of *One Hundred Years of Solitude*, is perhaps the best-known writer in the Latin American explosion of talent that has taken place since the 1960's. Others in this modern tradition are Julio Cortázar, Carlos Fuentes, and José Donoso—all of whom have created their own version of a Kafkaesque modernist world which has fascinated general readers and critics alike. *No One Writes to the Colonel* is a minor masterpiece in this tradition, a precursor to the complexity and control of *One Hundred Years of Solitude*.

Bibliography

Bloom, Harold, ed. *Márquez*. New York: Chelsea House, 1989. A collection of eighteen essays by various authors that have been written over several years on different aspects of Márquez's works. Covers the whole range of literary criticism and offers in-depth analysis of several of Márquez's novels.

Dolan, Sean. *Hispanics of Achievement*. New York: Chelsea House, 1994. A solid introduction to Márquez's work, featuring photographs and quotations. Discusses Márquez's family background, literary influences, and personal politics and how it shaped his writing.

García Márquez, Gabriel. Interview. *UNESCO Courier* 49 (February, 1996): 4-7. Márquez offers his views on the teaching and protection of culture. He also discusses his daily writing discipline and how it has influenced and enhanced his work. An informative and interesting interview.

McMurray, George R. "Gabriel García Márquez." In *Latin American Writers*, edited by Carlos A. Solé and Maria I. Abreau. Vol. 3. New York: Charles Scribner's Sons, 1989. Offers a comprehensive and critical discussion of Márquez's life and works. Provides a selected bibliography for further reading.

Styron, Rose. "Gabriel García Márquez, Carlos Fuentes, and Kenzaburo Oe: From the Rose Styron Conversations." *New Perspectives Quarterly* 14 (Fall, 1997): 56-62. A revealing interview with three renowned authors. They share their views on topics such as women and power, first and lost love, journalism as literature, spirit and faith, and multiculturalism.

Charles E. May

NORTHWEST PASSAGE

Author: Kenneth Roberts (1885-1957)
Type of plot: Historical
Time of plot: 1759-1768
Locale: The United States and England
First Published: 1937

> *Principal characters:*
>> LANGDON TOWNE, a young painter, the narrator of the story
>> ROBERT ROGERS, a colonial frontier soldier, the leader of Rogers's
>> Rangers and seeker for the Northwest Passage
>> SERGEANT MCNOTT, a dedicated follower of Rogers
>> ELIZABETH BROWNE, Towne's early love, later Rogers's wife
>> NATTY POTTER, Rogers's secretary
>> ANNE POTTER, Natty's daughter, later Towne's wife
>> JOHN SINGLETON COPLEY, an American artist
>> HUNK MARRINER and
>> CAP HUFF, Towne's Portsmouth friends

The Novel

Northwest Passage is divided into two parts dramatizing the career of Major Robert Rogers as the leader of Rogers's Rangers during the French and Indian War and his subsequent failure as an explorer seeking a cross-continental northwest passage to the Pacific Ocean. Sharing focus is the novel's single narrator Langdon Towne, a young artist from Maine who first joins Rogers in part 1, on Rogers's 1759 military expedition against the hostile Indian village of St. Francis near the Canadian border, from which the French-supported Indians have conducted bloody raids into New England settlements. Towne's career thereafter intersects with that of Rogers, who is revealed through the narrator's eyes. Towne is the dominant figure in part 2, which shows him in London developing into a successful artist as Rogers attempts to gain expeditionary backing there, and later in North America and England as Rogers fails and falls in fortune and reputation. Towne's progressive development provides the story's unity.

In part 1, suspended Harvard student Langdon Towne of Kittery, Maine, faces the displeasure of his father and his young beloved Elizabeth Browne, who both disdain Towne's artistic ambitions. Moreover, Towne's injudicious statements necessitate his fleeing town with friend Hunk Marriner to avoid arrest. In flight, they meet Rogers, about to lead his rangers from Crown Point on Lake Champlain on a reprisal mission against St. Francis village, and they join his company. Rogers sees Towne's sketches and the advantages of having an artist record his expedition's travels. Concomitantly, Towne is impressed by Rogers's vigor and his dream of finding a northwest passage. He increasingly admires the major's outstanding leadership on an expedition plagued by loss of men and supplies through accident, ambush, pursuit by French and Indians, bad weather, hazardous terrain, exhaustion, and hunger. Although the military objective of destroying the Indian encampment is accomplished, the ranger casualties are high. Towne and a few others make their way back to civilization only through the resourcefulness of Rogers, whom Towne now considers heroic. Yet upon his return, Towne's worship of Rogers diminishes when the latter woos and weds Towne's love Elizabeth Browne. Hoping to forget them both, Towne departs for London, encouraged by American artist John Singleton Copley to study painting abroad.

Part 2 discovers Towne in London winning success as an artist and again encountering Rogers there to publicize his exploits and seek support for his Northwest Passage project. He receives no funds, but he obtains an appointment as governor of a Great Lakes region called Michilimackinac (now Mackinac, between Lake Huron and Michigan). Towne is not impressed by Rogers's opportunistic behavior nor by his bibulous secretary Natty Potter, who persuades him to locate and release Potter's daughter Ann from a slum family's guardianship. He does so only to find that Ann becomes his unofficial ward.

Returning to America with Rogers, he finds that the new territorial governor is opposed by a powerful enemy, Sir William Johnson, the administrative officer of Indian affairs, and is blocked from launching a Northwest Passage expedition. Rogers is later imprisoned, court-martialed, and ruined financially. Finally disillusioned with Rogers when learning that he has made improper overtures to Ann, whom the young artist has come to love, Towne reunites with Ann and marries her in England, where he later finds Rogers drink-sodden and destitute in debtor's prison.

With Ann, Towne returns to America after the Revolution and learns that Rogers has left prison and has fought both in Algiers and with British forces in the American Revolution. Although still disillusioned with his onetime hero, Towne forgets neither the latter's worth nor his dream of expansion and adventure.

The Characters

Rogers, the historical protagonist, and Towne, the fictitious protagonist and narrator, are both well-rounded figures who drive the story's events and, secondarily, reflect thematic concerns. Characteristically, Roberts contrasts an action-oriented historical hero with a fictional narrator of disparate temperament who establishes a direct relationship with the reader.

The courageous and resourceful Rogers takes center stage in part 1's wartime setting and reveals himself as a superior military leader. In part 2, Rogers becomes the victim of betrayal, hamstrung and discredited by greedy superiors who consider him a threat to their plans for a Great Lakes inland fiefdom. They imprison and unsuccessfully court-martial Rogers on bogus charges; he is acquitted but left without money or reputation. Out of wartime, Rogers displays shortcomings of character and judgment ranging from womanizing and drunkenness to the incurring of debt, all of which are described by the narrator. He snatches Towne's young love Elizabeth, attempts to seduce Ann Potter, and becomes an indigent drunkard in debtor's prison. Yet for all of his faults, Rogers emerges as a tragic hero, imperfect to be sure, but a victim less of himself than of others.

Contrasted to Rogers, Towne begins as an inexperienced, sensitive, middle-class gentleman and artist who goes to war only because circumstances force him. Awed by Rogers, he develops self-discipline and survival skills on the Indian campaign, discards in peacetime the bloodlust imposed in battle, and matures into an admirable man and artist. His progress, viewed against that of Rogers, is an hour-glass pattern: As Towne rises in finding his identity, Rogers by the novel's second half begins to fall. Both characters are well orchestrated to illumine each other's qualities.

Towne's friends Hunk Marriner and Cap Huff are humorous figures providing comic relief as well as expository and plot functions. Their trouble-begetting high jinks with Towne before the Rogers campaign introduces them as fun-loving, practical working-class men who serve as a foil to the narrator. When Hunk dies during the campaign, Sergeant McNott inherits his comic role. McNott becomes a one-legged survivor whose Indian wife controls him by commandeering his wooden leg when necessary.

Although critically faulted for not creating dimensional women, Roberts plausibly defines snobbish Elizabeth, who as a shrewish wife highlights the failures of Rogers and the growth of Towne. Elizabeth contrasts with the simple goodness of the lesser-born Ann, a fictitious and less-rounded character whose growth into a lady and wife demonstrates the narrator's honorableness, mature judgment, and love. Together, Towne and Ann represent a new family for a new country.

Roberts tends to present his characters directly and realistically, revealing them by their actions and description. They are chiefly employed to move the story forward and, when secondary figures, to delineate the protagonists. Briefly sketched are the novel's villains, including William Johnson and his subalterns Lieutenant Roberts and Jonathan Carver. In addition to contributing to the plot, these men also reflect a theme of betrayal of heroes by the less talented.

Themes and Meanings

On the novel's first page, the narrator reports that he is not telling the story to prove a case. However, the story does underscore several of Roberts's themes. First is the idea that early America's history was forged by brave leaders of men such as Rogers. A related second theme is that such figures can be unfairly judged by history. In his literary autobiography *I Wanted to Write* (1949), Roberts implies that he sees the pattern of the past as the story of great men—such as Rogers and Benedict Arnold, a major figure in Roberts's *Arundel* (1930) and *Rabble in Arms* (1933)—surrounded by traducers. Moreover, he attempts to correct the preconceived images of American history and to disclose the fallacy of labeling a man on the basis of one deed. For example, Benedict Arnold's treason is his mark in history, yet his ability as an outstanding field officer is usually ignored. Viewed historically, the lesser-known figure of Rogers is perhaps more often viewed as an unsuccessful seeker of the Northwest Passage who died impoverished and unheralded rather than as a masterful military leader who, given proper support, might have discovered a path to the Pacific before the Meriwether Lewis and William Clark expedition of 1804-1806. A third theme suggests a warning: When a man is tempered in war, he cannot easily erase its imprint. Towne, recalling his tolerance of killing an Indian in battle, determines to eschew war thereafter. Less capable of change, wartime leader Rogers, once out of war, cannot adjust to bureaucratic red tape, politicians, and jealous superiors. The Indian fighter cannot use the same tactics out of war as in it. Risking fortune and countermanding orders aimed at frustrating northwest exploration, Rogers finds his vision and merited trust with the Indians, gaining him the enmity of superiors. Furthermore, in peacetime he is prone to indulge in such soldierly vices as drinking, womanizing, and gathering debts.

Critical Context

This historical novel, like Rogers's others, treats early American history relating to his own family's New England roots. It focuses on an imperfect, unconventional hero who has deserved better, in Roberts's view, from historians. In his later novel *Oliver Wiswell* (1940), Roberts contradicts the conventional picture of an event and deals sympathetically with the loyalist side in the American Revolution. Displaying a characteristic pattern of its author, *Northwest Passage* adopts an iconoclastic stance in purportedly offsetting one-sided views of historians and biographers. When a noted historian claimed that no record existed of Rogers's court-martial, Roberts located it in England. In his aforementioned autobiography, Roberts observes that history gives only an outline of events, explaining nothing fully and omitting details that the novelist must explain. When history, for example, did not explain why a powder-burned ranger lieutenant had to turn back with forty men before the Indian village attack, Roberts provides a reason. Also noting that most historical accounts are both dull and filled with bloodless personages, the author affirms his intent to give the reader the vivid illusion of sharing the experience of the past.

Representing the apex of its author's career, *Northwest Passage* has been critically acclaimed for its thorough research, action-filled scenes, and vivid descriptions enriched by historical detail; it was popularly received as a best-seller. Roberts also was praised for using images consistent with speaker and subject, simple and concrete diction, and a direct style with uncluttered syntax that keeps the narrative moving swiftly. The novel's success overcame some critical reservations about its being overwritten and overladen with historical detail; the book established its author with most critics and historians as a superior historical novelist setting a high standard of excellence for other writers of the genre. Along with Roberts's other work, it has won for him a lasting place in American letters. Although the Pulitzer Prize committee did not give the novel an award, it publicly cited the author's work as having long contributed to creating interest in early American history. Roberts's ability to bring history alive as well as to reexamine conventional conceptions of historical figures and events makes *Northwest Passage* worthy of study both for students and for all readers liking a well-told tale of early America.

Bibliography

Bales, Jack. *Kenneth Roberts*. New York: Twayne, 1993. An informative literary biography, including a seven-page analysis of *Northwest Passage* placing focus on the historical and fictional protagonist. Includes chronology, selected bibliography, and index.

_____. *Kenneth Roberts: The Man and His Work*. London: Scarecrow Press, 1989. Contains a substantial biographical essay and an extensive annotated bibliography of criticism, with seven pages of book reviews on *Northwest Passage*. Detailed appendices list special collections of Roberts material, interviews, and speeches.

Bettinger, B. E. "Land Where Our Fathers Died." *New Republic*, July 14, 1937, 287. Review of *Northwest Passage* praising the author's narrative skill in creating "vivid history" and recommending it to anyone interested in the making of the nation.

Harris, Janet. *A Century of American History in Fiction: Kenneth Roberts' Novels*. New York: Gordon Press, 1976. A detailed study of the author's works, including a perceptive analysis of *Northwest Passage* focusing on themes, characters, plots, and other elements. Includes chronology and comprehensive bibliography.

Roberts, Kenneth. *I Wanted to Write*. Garden City, N.Y.: Doubleday, 1949. An autobiography about the writer's literary career. Deals with the research, writing, revising, and rewriting associated with his novels, including *Northwest Passage*.

Christian H. Moe

NOT WITHOUT LAUGHTER

Author: Langston Hughes (1902-1967)
Type of plot: Domestic realism
Time of plot: 1912-1918
Locale: Stanton, Kansas, and Chicago
First published: 1930

> *Principal characters:*
> JAMES (SANDY) ROGERS, Sandy's wandering father
> ANNJEE, Sandy's mother and Hager's dutiful daughter
> HARRIETT, Sandy's lively aunt and Hager's rebellious daughter
> TEMPY, Hager's proud middle-class daughter

The Novel

Not Without Laughter concentrates on the childhood and adolescent years of Sandy Rogers, a sensitive and highly intelligent black boy growing up in a small Kansas town. His grandmother, known to the community as Aunt Hager, is the center of his life. She washes clothes for the Reinharts, a white family, and she takes care of him while his mother works for Mrs. J. J. Rice, a snobbish upper-class white woman. Later, Hager becomes Sandy's sole guardian after his mother, Annjee, leaves to join her husband in Detroit and Harriett, the last daughter to remain at home, runs away with the carnival that visits Stanton.

Sandy's father, Jimboy, is rarely home and has trouble maintaining steady employment. Sandy adores his father's lively personality and talent and loves to hear his Aunt Harriett and Jimboy sing the blues. Sandy is a gregarious boy and enjoys the usual pursuits of adolescents, but there is a studiousness in him and a sense of responsibility that his grandmother encourages. Indeed, he is deeply influenced by his grandmother, who praises the virtues of hard work and a religious life.

Hager expects Sandy to be a great man; she hopes that he will not disappoint her, as her daughters have. Harriett has forsaken the family's Baptist beliefs, first for street-walking and then for a career as a singer; Annjee has married a lazy man who cannot provide for his family; Tempy has become a middle-class black Episcopalian who is ashamed of her lower-class roots. While Sandy is most influenced by Hager, each one of his aunts also educates him to life's different possibilities, so that he is the only character with a vision of the whole, of the different ways in which his people have reacted to being black in a white-dominated world.

Annjee copes with her irascible white employer by simply ignoring her constant criticism. Harriett, on the other hand, resorts to anger and prefers to lead a "life of sin" than to be beholden to white employers for the meager wages they offer. Tempy has remodeled herself along the lines of her white employer and learns to behave in refined ways that whites will admire. Hager apparently acquiesces to white dominance, but she passes on to Sandy an indomitable spirit that will ensure his integrity. When a white Southerner attempts to humiliate him, Sandy turns away and hurls his shoeshine equipment at the laughing whites in the hotel where he works. His anger, however, is momentary, and he does not let it poison his efforts to learn from everyone, white and black alike.

Although life in a small Kansas town on the eve of World War I is often grim for its black inhabitants, it is "not without laughter"—as the title of the novel suggests. It is a close-knit community in which people take care of one another when they are ill and share their food and hospitality when they are well. Hughes takes obvious delight in reporting everyday conversations, for the language of his characters demonstrates great verve and tenacity no matter how constrained their circumstances may be. The blues they sing may seem mournful, but the songs are also exciting and deeply passionate, so that Sandy is imbued with a hunger for experience and for a knowledge of life.

The Characters

In addition to the principal characters, there are numerous other figures who represent Hughes's impressive command of a people and a period of time. The self-styled Madam de Carter, active in the Lodge; Brother Logan, who has been courting Hager for twenty years; and ninety-three-year-old Uncle Dan, who claims to have fathered more than forty children, are only three examples of the many interesting personalities in this novel. For the most part, they reveal themselves through dialogue and through what others say about them. As a result, Hughes is able to include an astonishing amount of sociological commentary on the community without ever employing an intrusive narrator.

Hughes generally saves his characters' longer speeches for later parts of the novel when a certain amount of curiosity about them has been aroused. For example, although it is apparent that Hager's identity has been formed by her experience of slavery, her own commentary on the past does not appear until the last third of *Not Without Laughter*, when she is alone with her grandson. She gives him what some might consider to be an apology for slavery, but her main point is that to ignore the positive aspects of the hard and unjust life of the slaves is to deny the humanity of all people, white and black alike.

Hager's piety, however, cuts her off from other aspects of the world that Sandy must explore. His friends introduce him to the pool hall—one of the few places in Stanton where young black men can exercise their wit and relax, since institutions such as the YMCA are exclusively for whites. While working in a barbershop and hotel and when visiting his aunt in the Bottoms, where jazz, prostitution, and bootlegging thrive, Sandy is introduced to an intoxicating atmosphere that is much more appealing than the repressive propriety of his Aunt Tempy's home, to which he is taken after Hager's death.

Aunt Tempy corrects his English, sees that he reads the right literature, and attempts to get him to associate with a better class of people. Her idea of an education is to strip Sandy methodically of all the cultural traits that mark him as a lower-class black. Although he avidly reads her books, he is stubborn about not giving up his disreputable friends. They have much to teach him about the basics of life, as he realizes when he regrets giving up a girlfriend, Pansetta Young, to please his aunt.

In the last part of the novel, when Sandy rejoins his mother in Chicago and enjoys a brief reunion with his Aunt Harriett, now a successful singer, it is clear that he will continue his education in an urban setting away from Tempy's small-town snobbery and will pursue an independent course in fulfilling his grandmother's dreams for him.

Sandy, more than any of the other characters, inherits the whole of his people's history. He is neither particularly rebellious nor docile; rather, he has an inquiring mind that resists any effort to restrict his access to the richness of his culture. In other words, Sandy is at the center of a debate in the novel about exactly what constitutes the black heritage. Hughes, through the impressionable Sandy, is able to dramatize a process of change in which there is plenty of room for both new and old elements.

Themes and Meanings

In *Not Without Laughter*, there is considerable discussion of the "color line" which whites use to discriminate against blacks and which blacks use to discriminate against one another. The lighter the skin, the more opportunity there is for a black to "pass" as white. Buster, one of Sandy's friends, plans to take advantage of his fair features in exactly this way. Similarly, some blacks prefer "high yallers"—black women with fair skin.

Because of the novel's rich reporting of black speech, of the way blacks sing and dance and embroider their stories, it is clear that Hughes is exploring the extraordinary impact of a whole culture on the acute imagination of a young black man. Hager suggests that, like Booker T. Washington, Sandy will be representative of his race. Tempy, on the other hand, favors the example of W. E. B. Du Bois because of his more militant and more intellectual conception of progress. Whereas Washington emphasized the equipping of blacks for learning a trade, Du Bois worked for the education of his people on the highest levels. Sandy, whose youthful experience includes both menial labor and intense book learning, is clearly meant to be a synthesis of these two types of leaders.

While he does not minimize the damage and the hurt done by slavery and its aftermath, Hughes chooses in this novel to emphasize the creativity of black people. Black children in *Not Without Laughter* experience an acute sense of rejection, hatred, and despair when they are turned away from a carnival that is for whites only. Minutes later, however, those same children demonstrate their resilience, delighting in a mocking mimicry of the white man who has spoiled their fun. Similarly, the numerous blues lyrics which enrich this novel (and which run throughout Hughes's poetry) suggest the way his people have transcended their defeats through art.

The art, however, is not fantastic but highly realistic and composed of the commonest elements. "Ever'thing there is but lovin' leaves a rust on yo' soul," Hager tells Sandy. This is a truth that has obviously been lived, a conviction that has been earned, and it is characteristic of the aging Hager to give her grandson the pith of her life.

Not Without Laughter contains several characters who moralize about the meaning of life, but the author reserves his own judgment and tries to understand people as they understand themselves. The tone of the novel is objective throughout, and the blues lyrics tend to authorize the narrator's specific judgments. A book of great balance, *Not Without Laughter* does poetic justice to all sides of the life that it describes. Colloquial language is contrasted with formal English, just as the knowledge of the street is set against the wisdom of books.

The "raucous-throated blues-singer" is the voice of experience itself that informs every page of this novel. The lyrics enjoin the listener to a community of feeling that is the essence of the blues itself. Although the older generation, like Aunt Hager, has condemned this secular music, its roots are in the religious sense of revival that has motivated so much of black art. Coming home from hearing Harriett, who is now a "Princess of the Blues," Sandy and his mother are thrilled to hear the "deep volume of sound" coming from a "little Southern church in a side street," where "some old black worshippers" are singing "An' we'll understand it better by an' by!" The links between past and present, between the blues and spirituals are solid, Hughes implies, as solid as Southern blacks filling the whole Chicago night with the sounds of their voices.

Critical Context

Not Without Laughter appeared in 1930 at the height of what was called the Harlem Renaissance, a tremendous outpouring of black talent in the arts. Langston Hughes was the premier poet of this cultural movement, and throughout his long career he continued to reflect on and extend its themes. Of central concern was the whole question of black identity, and of how contemporary blacks should deal with the legacy of discrimination.

As Arna Bontemps, a black literary contemporary of Hughes, recalled in the Collier Books reprint of *Not Without Laughter*, the novel was eagerly awaited as an example of a new, aggressive definition of blackness. Hughes is quoted by Bontemps as saying that the new artists wrote to please themselves, to express an inner freedom that could not be affected by the criticisms of whites or blacks. "The poets had become bellweathers," Bontemps remarks, and Hughes was the "happy prince" of a cultural movement.

Hughes had to be read because he was leading the way for other artists and followers of the Harlem Renaissance. His exuberance, especially evident in poetry that captures black colloquial speech, invigorated his readers by highlighting contemporary materials that had become suitable for art. *Not Without Laughter*, his only novel in a distinguished career as a poet, is complemented by several popular collections of short stories; in addition, Hughes edited some widely used anthologies. A scrupulous scholar and artist, Hughes remains one of the most significant figures in the development of Afro-American culture.

Bibliography

Dace, Letitia, and Tish Dace, eds. *"Langston Hughes: The Contemporary Reviews."* New York: Cambridge University Press, 1997. Features chronological, critical essays on reviews by a wide range of scholars, including one on *Not Without Laughter.* An excellent source for putting Hughes's works in context.

Shields, John P. "'Never Cross the Divide': Reconstructing Langston Hughes's *Not Without Laughter." African American Review* 28 (Winter, 1994): 601-613. Shields offers a reconstruction of Hughes's novel, focusing on the influence of patron Charlotte Mason and the early stages of the book's development. Shields explores the degree to which Mason's literary censorship forced Hughes to mute his left-wing political notions, as well as his use of graphic imagery.

Sundquist, Eric J. "Who Was Langston Hughes?" *Commentary* 102 (December, 1996): 55-59. Initially Hughes became well known for his role in the Harlem literary renaissance because of his ability to mix popular culture and politics with poetry. However, Sundquist shows that during the post-World War II era, Hughes was less overtly occupied with politics and more concerned with art.

Thomas, H. Nigel. "Patronage and the Writing of Langston Hughes's *Not Without Laughter*: A Paradoxical Case." *CLA Journal* 42 (September, 1998): 48-49. Traces the professional relationship between Hughes and his wealthy patroness Charlotte Mason. Thomas argues that their relationship ended because Mrs. Mason, despite her liberal leanings, was really part of the established intellectual superstructure which determined the worth of books by new authors.

Trotman, C. James, ed. *Langston Hughes: The Man, His Art, and His Continuing Influence.* New York: Garland, 1995. Presents a brief biography of Hughes, as well as critical articles by a variety of scholars. Offers a solid overview of his work. Includes a helpful index.

Carl Rollyson

OCTOBER LIGHT

Author: John Gardner (1933-1982)
Type of plot: Domestic realism
Time of plot: One week in October in the early 1970's
Locale: A farm outside Bennington, Vermont
First published: 1976

> *Principal characters:*
>> JAMES L. PAGE, a farmer and widower in his early seventies
>> SALLY PAGE ABBOTT, his older sister, a widow living on James's farm
>> VIRGINIA (GINNY) PAGE HICKS, James's one surviving child, who is in her forties
>> LEWIS HICKS, Ginny's husband, a carpenter

The Novel

An early section in Gardner's novel describes the annual cycle of backbreaking labor for rural Vermonters. The passage concludes, "Now, in October, the farmwork was slackening, the drudgery had paid off. . . ." This is, however, an ironic observation: For seventy-two-year-old James Page and his eighty-year-old sister, Sally Page Abbott, the "harvest years" have brought no payoff. James, though honest, hardworking, and fiercely patriotic, can barely wrest a living from the family farm—where he has lost one son to a fall from the barn roof and another to suicide by hanging, and where cancer has claimed his wife. Sally, the widow of a prosperous dentist, may enjoy happier memories, but she is no better off than James. Her insurance money depleted, she has been forced to give up her town home and accept her brother's grudging hospitality.

Between two persons who feel so cheated by life, and who harbor such strong and conflicting opinions (Sally is a "progressive" compared with James), life is at best an uneasy truce which is easily broken. One night, a blast from James's shotgun destroys Sally's television, with its "endless simpering advertising." Soon after, furious because she defends "corrupt" government programs, James chases Sally upstairs with a fireplace log and locks her in her room "like a prisoner."

So begins a domestic cold war that eventually involves the entire community. James's daughter, Ginny, remonstrates with him, and for a time he is ready to relent, but it is too late; Sally has bolted her door from within and gone "on strike," as determined as one of the Green Mountain Boys whom her brother so admires or one of the radical feminists he loathes. James repents of his momentary softening, and, thinking to starve Sally into submission, he relocks her door; unknown to him, she is subsisting on apples found in the attic above her room. She finds mental sustenance, too—in a "trashy" paperback novel that she reads when she is not reminiscing.

Even while she apologizes to her dead husband's spirit for reading such a book, Sally draws from it moral support for her own "cause." This tale, *The Smugglers of*

Lost Souls' Rock, is a quasi-metaphysical satire full of overeducated marijuana smugglers. Its machine-gun-toting characters philosophize endlessly on social issues and protest against a mechanistic universe. To the liberal-minded Sally, the rivalry between smuggling gangs—one black, one white—resolves into a struggle for racial justice. When the white doperunners appear to have killed the blacks (to escape being machine-gunned themselves), she fumes that it is "wrong for books to make fun of the oppressed, or to show them being beaten without a struggle. . . ."

Sally soon comes to identify the "oppressors" in the novel with James, and James with all oppressors: "It's no use making peace with tyranny. If the enemy won't compromise, he gives you no choice; you simply have to take your stand, let come what may. . . . Let *James* be reasonable. . . . It's always up to the one in power to be reasonable." She likens James's actions to the military and diplomatic blunders of the United States during and after the Vietnam War. Yet, muddled, melodramatic, and exaggerated as her pronouncements may be, Sally is nevertheless fighting for her right to make her own choices in life and to express her own beliefs, despite her brother's categorical rejection of them. As "revolutionary" as James is patriotic, Sally is prepared to kill or be killed for that which she considers her inalienable rights.

Meanwhile, James, buoyed by remembered legends of the patriot Ethan Allen, is busy escalating his side of the dispute. To him, the issue is the death of decency and the increase in the "sickness and filth" embodied, among other places, in Sally's television: ". . . murderers and rapists, drug addicts, long-hairs, hosses and policemen . . . half-naked women . . . sober conversations about the failure of America and religion and the family, as if there want no question about the jig bein up. . . ." He is determined to punish Sally for bringing this "filth" into his house via her television, determined to make her see the error of her ways. To make sure that she cannot sneak down to the kitchen for food at night, he rigs up a shotgun outside her room, to be triggered by strings if she opens her door.

Horrified when they learn of this, several friends rush to the farm to talk the two into ending their feud. Offended by what he considers their meddling, James stalks out, gets drunk in town, crashes his truck, storms back into his house, and blasts his kitchen walls with the shotgun. In the melee, a dear friend of the family suffers a near-fatal heart attack, and the now-sober James is filled with remorse. Meanwhile, Ginny accidentally walks into a trap that Sally, desperately frightened by the shotgun incident, has laid for James—an apple crate set to fall on his head if he enters her room. Ginny and the cardiac patient are rushed to a hospital in town, and the feud ends with Sally emerging from her room, believing that she has triumphed.

The Characters

Most of the characters in *October Light* are made to stand for clear-cut, uncompromising political or philosophical positions—positions which they feel driven to expound even when their lives are in danger. Between them, for example, the two main characters exhibit all the conflicting aspects of New England Puritan virtue: Sally, the relentless optimist with a strong drive for progress; James, the relentlessly plodding worker with a seeming incapacity to express any deep emotion other than anger or suspicion of "liberals." Gardner's characterizations thus bring to life the "polarization" that was much discussed in the late 1960's and early 1970's, though his narrative suggests that this polarization has deep historical roots. The fact that the two antagonists also are brother and sister underscores this tragedy of irreconcilables.

Some characters are aware of contradictions within themselves but are not able to reconcile them. One such figure is Lewis Hicks, Ginny's husband, who emerges as an improbable hero:

> Right and wrong were as elusive as odors in an old abandoned barn. Lewis knew no certainties. . . . He had no patience with people's complexities . . . not because people were foolish, in Lewis Hicks' opinion, or because they got through life on gross and bigoted oversimplifications, though they did, he knew, but because . . . he could too easily see all sides and, more often than not, no hint of a solution.

It is ironic that Lewis can see all sides of a question and still feel intolerant of other people's complexities.

Paradoxically, it is the minor characters—memorable far beyond their importance in the story—who are most fully rounded through their own conscious effort. The librarian Ruth Thomas literally embodies contradiction: Weighing three hundred pounds, she is the soul of gracefulness. Her voice is at once clear ringing and seductive, "like an unsubmergeably strong piano with the soft pedal pressed to the carpet." Gardner suggests that the comic sense is a key to controlling oneself and reconciling inner contradictions: The impish Ruth has "learned to limit herself for hours at a time to nothing more outlandish than a clever, perhaps slightly overstated mimicry of primness."

Even when Gardner's major characters insist on acting like "flat" characters, he has a genius for showing them as fully rounded people with deep integrity and with rich inner lives. This is accomplished partly through interior monologue, partly through the portrayal of one character's awakening sympathy for another. Sally is able to imagine Richard (James's son who committed suicide) "inside his life." Seeing her father, Ginny can sense "from inside him what it was like to be old, uncomfortable, cheated, ground down by life and sick to death of it. . . . 'Dad, I'm sorry,' she said."

Although this novel amply portrays the tragedy of polarization, there are repeated strong suggestions that it is the sum of individual extremes that leads to balance in the world. After all, if Sally and James together embody the contradictions of the New England character, then both are required to present the gamut of its virtues. If one looks closely at the individual character, one observes flaws and imperfections. Stepping back, however, one observes a harmonious "symphony" of characters.

Perhaps it is this implied notion of balance in the whole, rather than in its parts, that accounts for the seemingly flawed characterization of Sally. As a party to the central conflict of the story, she is the most fully realized of the female characters, and yet, unlike any other character, she fails to outgrow her limitations. She learns little from the desperate conflict with her brother; indeed, despite her "humanitarian" pretensions, she never develops true compassion for him. She simply comes out of the room thinking she has won a moral victory. Yet, smug as she remains, she has proved an effective catalyst for James's growth, which gives the novel a satisfying denouement.

Themes and Meanings

Gardner's novels, especially *October Light*, evince a strong connection between themes and meanings on the one hand and characterizations on the other. The motif of locks and locking provides an example. The novel takes place in October, when "the sudden contradiction of daylight" provides "the first deep-down convincing proof that locking time, and after that winter and deep snow and cold, were coming." Though still vigorous, the aged Sally and James realize that, like the year's end, their own end approaches; meanwhile, they are locked in a fierce, potentially lethal conflict. Sally locks her door against James and the rest of the world. Later, through that door, she has an awkward discussion with a visiting Hispanic priest and realizes ironically, "How difficult it was to have a serious conversation through a locked door. There was a lesson in that!"

On other levels, Gardner shows how characters lock their hearts against one another, often without realizing it. Perhaps unfairly, the priest, Father Hernandez, forces Sally the Yankee Protestant to think of herself for a moment as "one of the colorful minorities." The unfairness, however, is mutual; Sally is puzzled by what she sees as Hernandez's attack on her, since "He was a priest. . . . They were supposed to be gentle and understanding."

Gardner seems to be saying, too, that the locking of hearts and the sudden contraction of mental light (one is reminded of Matthew Arnold's line, "where ignorant armies clash by night") are phases in an inevitable cycle of human life, just as they are in nature. In this story and in the subnovel (which forms a sort of counterpoint to the main story), the mechanistic view of the universe has its exponents—willing and unwilling. For example, the subnovel's hero, Peter Wagner, expresses pity for the "futile, idealistic rejection of the body's cold mechanisms."

Are people, then, responsible for their death-dealing prejudices? Metaphysically, the question is never really resolved in this novel, although individual responsibilities are sorted out by the end. James, when he could admit it, has felt responsible for his son Richard's suicide, but he finally unlocks the mystery of that suicide when he learns that Richard felt responsible for scaring Sally's husband into a fatal heart attack. Ginny's son Dickie feels responsible for Sally's having found the "trashy book" she reads in her room. It emerges that it was James who left the book lying around.

The larger question is: Is one personally responsible for the attitudes, the locking or unlocking of one's heart, that can make the difference between harmony and strife? Rather than answer this question, Gardner simply shows James unlocking his heart, while his friend Ed Thomas, the dying cardiac patient, movingly evokes another phase of nature's cycle—the "unlocking time," that is, the March thaw in New England. The novel does suggest a partial answer simply through the near-juxtaposition of two equally valid but mutually exclusive propositions—a typical Gardner technique. Father Hernandez says, "Stubborn? All human beings are stubborn. It's the reasons we're survivors." On the very next page, Sally remembers her dead husband, Horace, saying: "However much we may hope, we know perfectly well all we have is each other. Pity how we fight and struggle against our own best interests." One statement's validity does not cancel the other's; rather the two shed mutual light.

Critical Context

During a short career—which was ended by a motorcycle accident when he was forty-nine—John Gardner distinguished himself in a wide range of pursuits. While working in many literary genres, including fiction, poetry, children's tales, and even operatic librettos, he remained a university professor of medieval literature and creative writing. Gardner's imaginative use of scholarly learning is typified by the first of his novels to achieve marked critical and popular success: *Grendel* (1971), a retelling of the Beowulf legend from the monster's point of view. Both *Time* and *Newsweek* named *Grendel* one of 1971's best fiction books.

Other triumphs followed, culminating in *October Light*, which won the National Book Critics' Circle award for fiction in 1977. Like *Grendel* and other works by Gardner, *October Light* is full of erudite allusions, prompting a few critics to attack it as excessively theme-ridden. Most critics, however, regard it as his finest novel, an ambitious but lively treatment of ultimately insoluble mysteries, and the most successful of Gardner's attempts to bring past learning to bear on present dilemmas.

After *October Light*, Gardner's reputation declined somewhat, perhaps in part because of his attacks on most contemporary writers for failing to affirm life and inspire readers. His *On Moral Fiction* (1978), a work of critical theory containing these charges, was highly controversial. Some critics said that Gardner's last works of fiction—*The Art of Living and Other Stories* (1981) and *Mickelsson's Ghosts* (1982)—fell short of the standard he himself set in *On Moral Fiction*. Even after his death, Gardner and his work remain controversial, but no one disputes that he was one of America's most important contemporary authors, or that *October Light* is his masterpiece in fiction.

Bibliography

Butts, Leonard. *The Novels of John Gardner: Making Life Art as a Moral Process.* Baton Rouge: Louisiana State University Press, 1988. Butts draws his argument from Gardner himself, specifically *On Moral Fiction* (that art is a moral process), and discusses the ten novels in pairs, focusing on the main characters as either artists or artist figures who to varying degrees succeed or fail in transforming themselves into Gardner's "true artist." As Butts defines it, moral fiction is not didactic but instead a matter of aesthetic wholeness.

Chavkin, Allan, ed. *Conversations with John Gardner.* Jackson: University Press of Mississippi, 1990. Reprints nineteen of the most important interviews (the majority from the crucial *On Moral Fiction* period) and adds one never-before-published interview. Chavkin's introduction, which focuses on Gardner as he appears in these and his other numerous interviews, is especially noteworthy. The chronology updates the one in Howell (below).

Cowart, David. *Arches and Light: The Fiction of John Gardner*. Carbondale: Southern Illinois University Press, 1983. Discusses the published novels through *Mickelsson's Ghosts*, the two story collections, and the tales for children. As good as Cowart's intelligent and certainly readable chapters are, they suffer (as does so much Gardner criticism) insofar as they are concerned with validating Gardner's position on moral fiction as a justifiable alternative to existential despair.

Henderson, Jeff. *John Gardner: A Study of the Short Fiction*. Boston: Twayne, 1990. Part 1 concentrates on Gardner's short fiction, including his stories for children; part 2 contains excerpts from essays and letters in which Gardner defines his role as a writer; part 3 provides excerpts from important Gardner critics. Includes chronology and bibliography.

_____, ed. *Thor's Hammer: Essays on John Gardner*. Conway: University of Central Arkansas Press, 1985. Presents fifteen original essays of varying quality, including three on *Grendel*. The most important are John M. Howell's biographical essay, Robert A. Morace's on Gardner and his reviewers, Gregory Morris's discussion of Gardner and "plagiarism," Samuel Coale's on dreams, Leonard Butts's on *Mickelsson's Ghosts*, and Charles Johnson's "A Phenomenology of *On Moral Fiction*."

Howell, John M. *John Gardner: A Bibliographical Profile*. Carbondale: Southern Illinois University Press, 1980. Howell's detailed chronology and enumerative listing of works by Gardner (down to separate editions, printings, issues, and translations), as well as the afterword written by Gardner, make this an indispensable work for any Gardner student.

McWilliams, Dean. *John Gardner*. Boston: Twayne, 1990. McWilliams includes little biographical material, does not try to be at all comprehensive, yet has an interesting and certainly original thesis: that Gardner's fiction may be more fruitfully approached via Mikhail Bakhtin's theory of dialogism than via *On Moral Fiction*. Unfortunately, the chapters (on the novels and *Jason and Medeia*) tend to be rather introductory in approach and only rarely dialogical in focus.

Morace, Robert A. *John Gardner: An Annotated Secondary Bibliography*. New York: Garland, 1984. An especially thorough annotated listing of all known items (reviews, articles, significant mentions) about Gardner through 1983. The annotations of speeches and interviews are especially full (a particularly useful fact given the number of interviews and speeches the loquacious as well as prolific Gardner gave). A concluding section updates Howell's *John Gardner: A Bibliographical Profile*.

Morace, Robert A., and Kathryn VanSpanckeren, eds. *John Gardner: Critical Perspectives*. Carbondale: Southern Illinois University Press, 1982. This first critical book on Gardner's work covers the full range of his literary endeavors, from his dissertation-novel "The Old Men" through his then most recent fictions, "Vlemk, The Box Painter" and *Freddy's Book*, with separate essays on his "epic poem"

Jason and Medeia; The King's Indian· Stories and Tales; his children's stories; libretti; pastoral novels; use of sources, parody, and embedding; and theory of moral fiction. The volume concludes with Gardner's afterword.

Morris, Gregory L. *A World of Order and Light: The Fiction of John Gardner.* Athens: University of Georgia Press, 1984. Like Butts and Cowart, Morris works well within the moral fiction framework which Gardner himself established. Unlike Cowart, however, Morris emphasizes moral art as a process by which order is discovered rather than (as Cowart contends) made. More specifically the novels (including Gardner's dissertation novel "The Old Men") and two collections of short fiction are discussed in terms of Gardner's "luminous vision" and "magical landscapes."

Thomas Rankin

THE ODD WOMAN

Author: Gail Godwin (1937-   )
Type of plot: Comic realism
Time of plot: The early 1970's
Locale: A Midwestern university town, a Southern town, New York City, and
    Chicago
First published: 1974

> *Principal characters:*
>   JANE CLIFFORD, the protagonist, an assistant professor of romantic
>   British literature
>   EDITH BARNSTORFF, Jane's grandmother, a Southern lady
>   KITTY SPARKS, Edith's daughter, Jane's mother
>   GABRIEL WEEKS, Jane's lover, an art history professor at a neighboring
>   university
>   GERDA MULVANEY, Jane's confidante and friend for the past twelve
>   years

The Novel

The title and central issue of Gail Godwin's story are based upon George Gissing's 1893 novel, *The Odd Women*—a pessimistic study of the possibilities of women in the late nineteenth century. Godwin's *The Odd Woman* is one character's search in the late twentieth century to resolve her personal story: Will Jane Clifford find a perfect faithfulness in marriage, the kind of love George Eliot and George Henry Lewes had, or will she remain "odd" in the sense of Gissing's women, single, unpaired? The novel spans Jane's semester break at a Midwestern university where she has filled two successive sabbatical leave vacancies in the English department. Her future is uncertain; she has no teaching position for the next academic year, yet if her married lover receives a Guggenheim she could go to Europe with him.

The death of Jane's grandmother, Edith Barnstorff, at the end of the first chapter triggers the action of the novel, a journey that encompasses half the country, most of Jane's past, and the remainder of the novel. When Jane flies South for the funeral, it is a visit into her family's past and her relationships with her mother, Kitty, half brothers, Jack and Ronnie, half sister, Emily, and stepfather, Ray Sparks, whom she perceives as "the villain" of her story.

Although Jane's visit takes her deep into the past, it fails to resolve the problems of the present. She recalls Edith's contradictory advice ("I think, on the whole, it is better that you do not marry. Some people aren't made for the married state," but later, "Sometimes I get down on my knees and pray that you will find a good man to take care of you, as Hans took care of me") and realizes that what she wants is "the end of uncertainty, of joyless struggle," a struggle "without assurance of a happy reward."

The search for her "best life" takes Jane to New York City, for an impromptu few days with Gabriel Weeks, her married, middle-aged lover for the past two years. In re-assessing their relationship, Jane decides that her image of Gabriel, a professor of art history specializing in the Pre-Raphaelites, has been created "almost totally through her own devisings and dreams." A nineteenth century Romantic at heart, Jane believes in the reality of the inner life, a life she has constructed for Gabriel and herself. In New York City, she discovers that Gabriel does not share her faith in "a kind of love that—that exists in a permanent, eternal way," and she decides to leave him.

The final stop in Jane's odyssey is Chicago, where she visits her oldest friend, Gerda Mulvaney, a woman who re-creates herself in the image of each newly adopted cause. Deeply involved in feminism at the time of Jane's visit, Gerda argues with her, accusing Jane of living a life of "avoidances and evasions and illusions." After Gerda's attack, Jane realizes that she has failed to connect her own search with those of any of the women in her life. She sees herself "in transit between the old values . . . and the new values, which she must hack out for herself."

Distraught and exhausted, Jane returns to her apartment and the prospect of five days alone with herself, "researching her salvation," before the new semester begins. Jane learns that she will probably receive a last-minute replacement position for the next year, and, having found at least that much resolution, she goes to bed listening to the sounds of someone playing the piano late into the night, "trying to organize the loneliness and the weather and the long night into something of abiding shape and beauty."

The Characters

Jane Clifford is extraordinary in her belief in the importance of words and the real-ity of the inner life. The most appealing quality Godwin has given her thirty-two-year-old protagonist is her sincere desire to make of her life what Aristotle calls "a good plot": something that moves from possibility to probability to necessity. Toward this end, Jane reevaluates the symbols in her life—Edith Barnstorff, Kitty Sparks, and Gerda Mulvaney—and realizes that their stories cannot be hers, that "you had to write yourself as you went along, that your story could not and should not possibly be com-pleted until you were." What Godwin's readers are likely to admire in Jane is her con-tinued search for order and meaning in her life, and her awareness that she may never find them.

Godwin reflects other characters in the novel through Jane's consciousness. Edith, Kitty, Gerda, and Jane's lover, Gabriel Weeks, are presented almost entirely through Jane's flashbacks and recollections. In Jane's mind, her grandmother Edith is "the perfect Southern lady." The story of her marriage to Hans Barnstorff (who, hearing Edith declare that "life is a disease," said "let me protect you from it") affects Jane deeply, and her death leaves Jane to pursue the "truth of the individual life" alone. Jane also sees herself as separated from her mother, Kitty, a part-time classics teacher and full-time wife to Ray Sparks, and Gerda Mulvaney, a friend passionately involved in her latest cause. Both women seem to possess what has eluded Jane—"a real voca-tion," something she believes "we are all in search of."

Jane's lover, Gabriel Weeks, is the least defined of Godwin's characters, and he is also the one with whom Jane is struggling the most. A middle-aged man with no lines in his face, Gabriel is less angelic than ethereal. Married to Ann Weeks for the past twenty-five years, Gabriel occupies much of Jane's inner, but little of her external, life. He has never told her that he loves her and remains equally noncommittal in his plans for their future. Gabriel believes that perfect art but not permanent relationships can exist because "a relationship, by its very nature, is transient . . . it is made between people, and people change." Gabriel is located in the moment; he is incapable of transcending time through love.

Themes and Meanings

Godwin weaves two themes throughout her novel. The first comes in the novel's epigraph, taken from Carl Jung: "In knowing ourselves to be unique in our personal combination—that is, ultimately limited—we possess also the capacity for becoming conscious of the infinite. But only then!" Jane Clifford's search for personal resolution leads her to a deeper awareness of her own character. First Howard Cecil (a student) and later Ray Sparks (her stepfather) ask Jane, "Don't you want to be happy?" Yet, throughout the novel, what Jane really wants is to solve "the ever-present problem of her unclear, undefined, unresolved self." Looking for "a true, pure 'character,'" Jane finds instead her own imagination; Hugo Von Vorst, who she had thought was her Aunt Frances's natural father, is not the "family villain" she had always believed him to be, and neither is Gabriel Weeks the man of her dreams. It is only near the end of the novel that Jane sees her life as a series of illusions and uncompleted actions, and this self-recognition is the first step in perceiving her own limitations.

Godwin's second theme concerns time. Jane not only feels the passage of time but also reminds herself of it. Her constant companion is a clock proclaiming Tempus Fugit (time flies), and a watchmaker's advertisement, "He who knows most, Gives most for wasted time," recurs in her thoughts. Through most of the novel, Jane is looking for a pattern to hold against time, fearing that she will not find her "best life." Time is her enemy, and only on the last page of the novel does another way of interpreting time emerge. In a fantasized conversation with the Enema Bandit, Jane advises him to "turn your oddities inside out like a sock and find your own best life by making them work for you instead of being driven by them." She advises him to make his own pattern, to allow his limitations to shape his "best life." From this point of view, he who knows most will give most for wasted time because wasted time is, itself, redeemed.

Critical Context

The Odd Woman was Godwin's third novel, following *The Perfectionists* (1970) and *Glass People* (1972). It has nearly twice the length and complexity of either of her earlier books and is generally regarded as an important book in her development as a novelist.

Concerned in her first two novels with the possibilities of self-definition for modern women, Godwin gives the question historical and literary context in *The Odd*

Woman. Using George Gissing's 1893 novel as a counterpoint to her own story, Godwin draws her readers into Jane Clifford's contemporary struggle for resolution, giving that struggle larger and more profound implications about the relationship between the life of the mind and the outer life than are to be found in either of her previous novels. Focusing primarily on character rather than action, her work since *The Odd Woman* has continued to explore the intersection between art and life and the haunting presence of the past in everyday life.

Bibliography

Current Biography 56 (October, 1995): 26-29. Profiles Godwin's life and career as an award-winning novelist and short story writer. Critical reaction to her work is discussed, providing a valuable framework within which to compare *The Odd Woman* to various other of Godwin's writings.

Godwin, Gail. "A Dialogue with Gail Godwin." Interview by Lihong Xie. *The Mississippi Quarterly* 46 (Spring, 1993): 167-184. Godwin discusses her works, comparing them to major or minor keys in music depending on the emphasis she gives them in relation to certain plot elements and characters. Among the topics she covers in this interview are characterization, as well as the southern influence on her writing. *The Odd Woman* is briefly discussed.

Kissel, Susan S. *Moving On: The Heroines of Shirley Ann Grau, Anne Tyler, and Gail Godwin.* Bowling Green, Ohio: Green State University Press, 1996. This critical analysis of Grau, Tyler, and Godwin reveals how the work of other Southern women writers has influenced each author. Also discusses Godwin's universal communal vision.

Wimsatt, Mary Ann. "Gail Godwin, the South, and the Canons." *The Southern Literary Journal* 27 (Spring, 1995): 86-95. Explores the two major causes of Godwin's exclusion from the canon: her feminism and the fact that her novels are bestsellers. Godwin's novels are saturated with autobiographical elements, and her portraits of women ensnared in unhappy marriages are derived from her own life experiences.

Xie, Lihong. *The Evolving Self in the Novels of Gail Godwin.* Baton Rouge: Louisiana State University, 1995. A critical appraisal of many of Godwin's novels, including a chapter devoted to *The Odd Woman*. A bibliography and index round out this outstanding resource.

Jennifer L. Randisi

OH WHAT A PARADISE IT SEEMS

Author: John Cheever (1912-1982)
Type of plot: Comic realism
Time of plot: Twentieth century
Locale: New York City and Janice, a small suburban town
First published: 1982

>*Principal characters:*
>LEMUEL SEARS, the protagonist, an elderly businessman
>RENEE HERNDON, his lover for a brief time
>BETSY LOGAN, a resident of Janice
>HORACE CHISHOLM, an environmentalist

The Novel

This novel comprises two interconnected narratives that center on saving a pond in a small suburban town, Janice. The mayor of Janice, who has connections with some form of organized crime, allows Beasley's Pond to become a dump for the ostensible purpose of filling it to provide the site for a war memorial. As Cheever moves from one plot to the other, regaining the purity of the pond becomes a personal and moral issue for three of the main characters.

Lemuel Sears is somewhat fearful of growing old. Having left the city to skate at Beasley's Pond one fine winter day, he recaptures the physical and spiritual exhilaration that he experienced in his youth. Thus, when he returns a few weeks later and finds the pond being used as a dump, he is more than intellectually appalled at the pollution of the pond: "He thought his heart would break." He first hires a lawyer and then an environmentalist, Horace Chisholm, in an effort to stop the dumping. Ultimately, he fails where another character, Betsy Logan, succeeds, but when the dumping ceases, he establishes a foundation that uses the latest technology to undo the pollution.

Soon after his afternoon of skating, Sears meets Renee Herndon and begins an affair with her, their frequent lovemaking bringing him another pleasure that he feared he might lose as a result of growing old. When she leaves him unexpectedly and without explanation, he seeks comfort in a brief homosexual encounter and a trout-fishing expedition, neither of which is successful. Yet, because for Sears there is a "sameness in the search for love and the search for potable water," he turns his attention to saving the pond, which takes the place of loving Renee.

In the second narrative, Betsy Logan, a resident of Janice, is also drawn into the fight to save the pond. Her neighbor, Sammy Salazzo, collects fees for dumping in the pond. In a bizarre series of events—the shooting of the Salazzos's dog, a verbal confrontation about wind chimes with Maria Salazzo, and a physical battle with her in the supermarket—Betsy's relations with her neighbors deteriorate. The last event, the fight at the Buy Brite, establishes her as an avenger of injustice and prepares the way for her involvement in the battle to save the pond.

It is Horace Chisholm who provides the link between Sears's story and Betsy Logan's. Returning from a day at the beach, Betsy and her husband stop to change places so she can drive. Inadvertently, they leave their baby, Binxie, at the side of the road, where Chisholm finds him. In gratitude for the return of their son, they ask Chisholm to dinner and at his request become involved in the Beasley Pond issue. When the case gets a hearing, the corruption in Janice government is evident; Chisholm is run down by a car, and the dumping continues. In revenge for Chisholm's murder, Betsy puts poisoned teriyaki sauce on the supermarket shelves, threatening to continue to do so until the dumping is stopped. Her method works, and Sears's foundation can accomplish the task of cleaning the pond.

The Characters

Cheever's characters, while not flat, are sketchily drawn—caricatures which capture essential details and may offer a hint of satire. In his comments, however, the narrator, as intimate observer, reveals (and sometimes comments on) the characters' thoughts, giving the characters greater depth and complexity than they appear to have at first.

Lemuel Sears is an apparently successful, well-traveled businessman, an executive for a computer-container manufacturer. "Old . . . but not yet infirm," he fears that age may bring the "end of love." Love for him satisfies more than a physical desire; love fills a spiritual void as well. For Sears, "a profound and gratifying erotic consummation is a glimpse at another's immortal soul as one's own immortal soul is shown." While Sears does not live in the past, details of the present constantly call up memories of earlier times and places that reveal his eye and ear for detail, his sense of place, and his love of the sensual. These memories and his patrician manners associate him with values that have endured.

Renee Herndon, who accommodates Sears's lustiness and brings physical love into his life again for a brief time is drawn in less detail. To Sears, she is "a remarkably good-looking woman" of thirty-five or forty. Involved with numerous unidentified self-improvement groups, she is a mysterious, unpredictable character who repeatedly tells Sears that he does not "understand the first thing about women."

At first, Betsy Logan seems to be the antithesis of the independent Renee and the sophisticated Sears. A suburban homemaker, her greatest pleasure is shopping at the Buy Brite. Her fight there with Maria Salazzo, however, demonstrates that she is not meek, that she will resort to violence to right an injustice. Where Sears fails to accomplish his goal of saving the pond, she succeeds. It is ironic, though, that while family is centrally important to her, she endangers other families by her nefarious method of gaining attention for the cause of Beasley's Pond.

Horace Chisholm is an idealist who has left his high school teaching job to "do what he could to correct this threat to life on the planet or at least to inform the potential victims." Deeply troubled by the way people treat nature in a throwaway society, Chisholm has a cause for which to fight, but he has no love in his life. His wife has left him and taken his children; he lives alone and is lonely. As it does for Sears, his quest for clean water takes the place of love. Spiritually, Chisholm feels lost; like Sears, he too looks to fond memories, and it is an attempt to return to a happy activity from the past—picking blackberries—that leads him to find Binxie. Like Sears, he wants a homecoming; he is deeply touched by the domesticity and warmth of the Logans.

Themes and Meanings

Cheever begins and ends this novel with the same idea, that the story is one "to be read in bed in an old house on a rainy night." Thus, at the beginning, Cheever introduces an important image, water, and implies another, home. At the end, he reiterates their importance by repeating the line and comes full circle to arrive where he started. The narrative device, then, reinforces a major theme, the desire to go "home."

Depicting the modern world as a nomadic society where everything is expendable, "home" for Cheever represents paradise. It is a feeling more than a place—a sense of being loved and being at one with God, man, and the universe. When Cheever has his characters long for home, he is telling the archetypal tale of fallen, wandering man's desire to return to Eden.

Clean water also becomes an image for paradise; cleaning Beasley's Pond represents a return to the garden. The narrator makes this point clear when he says that for Sears paradise was never a "sacred grove," but "the whiteness of falling water." The narrator also notes that once the pond is clean and clear again, it could serve as "a background for [a painting of] Eden." Finally, by Sears's equating the search for love with the search for clean water, Cheever makes love a way to return to paradise as well.

An early description of spring rains on harvest-ready fields and other references to agriculture and plenty indicate that an allied theme is the potential for renewal. Sears is rejuvenated by his affair with Renee and spiritually renewed by the newly cleansed pond. In the twentieth century, renewal comes with the glimpses of paradise that are possible in the contemporary spiritual wasteland. Although only glimpses are possible, to Cheever they are so spiritually uplifting that they are motivation enough for man's continued striving to catch them.

Critical Context

Oh What a Paradise It Seems was Cheever's last novel; he died shortly after its publication. As a short novel, perhaps novella, it is unique in Cheever's canon. It is neither a short story, with the brevity and precise focus of that genre, nor a full-blown novel. Yet similarities with Cheever's other works do exist.

Like characters in *Bullet Park* (1969) and *Falconer* (1977), in particular, the characters in this novel seek love and order in the midst of the absurdities and chaos around them. Like many of Cheever's short stories, this work takes readers into the familiar suburbs depicted with the wry humor that is typical of Cheever. At the same time, Cheever acknowledges the fallen state of man, the wasteland qualities of the modern world, and the significance of the emotional and spiritual dimensions of life. Mingling Brandenburg concertos played in ragtime and the sound of running brooks, the appliance-laden refuse of contemporary American nomads and people longing for the warmth of home, he focuses on a deep human need for spirituality, wholeness, and love.

Bibliography

Bosha, Francis J. *John Cheever: A Reference Guide*. Boston: G. K. Hall, 1981. The annotated listing of 593 reviews, articles, books, and dissertations, as well as Bosha's discussion of the "inconsistent critical response" to Cheever's work make this an especially useful volume. The listing of Cheever books is thorough, but for a checklist of Cheever's shorter writings the student will need to consult Dennis Coates's "John Cheever: A Checklist, 1930-1978." *Bulletin of Bibliography* 36 (January-March, 1979): 1-13, 49, and his supplement in Collins (below).

Cheever, Susan. *Home Before Dark*. Boston: Houghton Mifflin, 1984. This memoir by the author's daughter is especially important for fleshing out Cheever's troubled early years and providing an insider's look at Cheever's marital and assorted other personal difficulties (alcoholism, illnesses, sexual desires). The book suffers from lack of documentation (and indexing); strange to say, this memoir turns out to be most valuable as a synthesis of previously published material (interviews) than as a daughter's intimate revelations.

Coale, Samuel. *John Cheever*. New York: Frederick Ungar, 1977. This volume in Ungar's Literature and Life series includes a brief biography, two chapters on selected short stories, individual chapters on Cheever's first four novels, and a brief conclusion. Coale focuses on the development of Cheever's style (from realism to fantasy) and concern for moral issues.

Collins, Robert G., ed. *Critical Essays on John Cheever*. Boston: G. K. Hall, 1982. A very useful volume for the editor's discerning introduction, for the reviews, interviews, and critical articles it reprints, for Dennis Coates's updating of his 1979 checklist, and for Samuel Coale's excellent discussion entitled "Cheever and Hawthorne: The American Romancer's Art."

Donaldson, Scott, ed. *Conversations with John Cheever*. Jackson: University Press of Mississippi, 1987. Because he was largely a private man, Cheever granted few interviews prior to the publication of *Falconer*. Donaldson can therefore afford to offer an exhaustive compilation of Cheever's interviews. Many of Cheever's comments, especially those about fiction, are repetitive, and others, about himself, more fictive than truthful.

_____. *John Cheever: A Biography*. New York: Random House, 1988. Donaldson's exhaustive but readable biography cuts through the biographical fictions Cheever himself fostered to create one of the most accurate portraits of the actual man. Donaldson's approach is always evenhanded; his research, impeccable; his portrait, compelling.

Meaner, Patrick. *John Cheever Revisited*. New York: Twayne, 1995. Written in the light of the detailed revelations contained in *The Journals of John Cheever*, edited by Robert Gottlieb and published in 1991, this critical work makes the case for a reevaluation of Cheever as a writer of serious fiction, rather than the graceful comic he has sometimes been made out to be. Meaner's book also is the first full-length work of criticism to take advantage of the insights afforded by Donaldson's 1988 biography and *The Letters of John Cheever,* edited by Benjamin Cheever and published in 1988.

O'Hara, James E. *John Cheever: A Study of the Short Fiction.* Boston: Twayne, 1989. O'Hara examines Cheever's expertise as a short-story writer by dividing his study into three sections: the first devoted to his own analysis, the second to Cheever's biography—as detailed by Cheever and others—and the third to Cheever's critics.

Waldeland, Lynne. *John Cheever.* Boston: Twayne, 1979. This volume in Twayne's United States Authors series is introductory in nature. Although it lacks the thematic coherence of Coale's, it has greater breadth and evidences a greater awareness of, or at least interest in, previous critical commentary.

Rebecca Kelly

THE OLD GRINGO

Author: Carlos Fuentes (1928-   )
Type of plot: Historical realism
Time of plot: 1913-1914
Locale: Chihuahua, Mexico
First published: El gringo viejo, 1985 (English translation, 1985)

> *Principal characters:*
>> HARRIET WINSLOW, a spinster from Washington, D.C., who goes to
>> Mexico to work as a governess but finds herself in the midst of a
>> revolution
>> AMBROSE BIERCE, a famous writer and journalist, the "old gringo" of
>> the title, who goes to Mexico seeking Pancho Villa, adventure, and a
>> heroic death
>> GENERAL TOMÁS ARROYO, a firebrand revolutionary torn between his
>> loyalty to the revolution and his desire for the land he considers his
>> birthright
>> PANCHO VILLA, the revolutionary leader, who has to resolve the
>> political dilemma caused by the old gringo's murder

The Novel

The Old Gringo is a novel fashioned as a tribute by one writer to the memory and courage of another, the cynical American journalist and storyteller Ambrose Bierce; the book offers a fictive speculation about Bierce's mysterious disappearance in Mexico in 1913 during the civil war. Carlos Fuentes imagines that Bierce, at first referred to only as the "old gringo," went to Mexico seeking Pancho Villa. His motives for going are ambiguous. He is seeking a new frontier and the adventure of fighting for the revolution, but what he seems to be seeking most is a heroic death. As Fuentes repeatedly states, the "old gringo came to Mexico to die," preferably with dignity.

The story is grounded in a factual framework. Bierce crossed the border at El Paso, Texas, in November of 1913. On December 26, he wrote that he intended to ride a troop train to Ojinaga seeking Pancho Villa. He was never heard from again. According to one legend, Bierce found Villa, became a senior staff adviser, and was later shot as a deserter, alienated by the bandit's cruelties. Fuentes works a variation on this legend.

Though named for the old gringo, the novel is mainly the story of Harriet Winslow, a spinster who leaves her mother in Washington, D.C., and goes to Mexico to work as a governess for the wealthy, landowning Miranda family, teaching English to the three Miranda children. She is seeking liberation, adventure, and independence, but she is manipulated by the Miranda family. They put her in the middle of the revolution by summoning her to their hacienda as they are making plans to depart themselves; the family uses her to create a diversion. She is also manipulated by General Tomás Arroyo, who uses her to gain entry to the Miranda estate. The Mexicans who exploit her consider her a fool. The story is framed by Harriet's memory.

The old gringo has concluded, to his shame, that he had also been manipulated and exploited during his career as a muckraking journalist by his employer, William Randolph Hearst. Bierce has contempt for his own accomplishments, done in the service of a millionaire who has profited by his talent. He describes himself as a "contemptible, muckraking reporter at the service of a baron of the press as corrupt as any I denounced in his name." He also considers himself a personal failure and blames himself for the deaths of his sons. He has turned his back on his country and on his former life. He is a would-be idealist, as Fuentes imagines him, who carries in his saddlebags a copy of the story of Don Quixote. Significantly, though, he has not yet read the book as he leaves El Paso to go tilting after windmills in revolutionary Mexico.

The gringo goes looking for Pancho Villa but instead finds General Tomás Arroyo, whom he antagonizes with his brutal honesty. His courage is unquestionable, and he is useful to Arroyo during the siege of the Miranda hacienda. Arroyo, himself a bastard son of the Mirandas, is conflicted. His quest to kill his father, Miranda, is frustrated by the family's escape, but after he has conquered the estate, he is derelict in his duty to return his army to Villa. He discovers Spanish documents that he believes to be sacred, for he thinks that whoever possesses the documents owns the land. The gringo has a more sophisticated understanding of political power than Arroyo, and he attempts to teach Arroyo that the documents are in fact worthless. When Arroyo refuses to believe him, the gringo burns the papers, and Arroyo, in a rage, shoots him in the back, killing his spiritual father, which the gringo has become.

Harriet Winslow is also searching for a father. Her own father deserted the family to serve in the Spanish-American War and never returned. Harriet confesses to the gringo that her father had not died in combat, as her mother prefers to believe, but remained in Cuba to live with a black woman. She and her mother had reported him dead in order to collect his pension: "We killed him, my mother and I," she confesses, "in order to live."

Harriet, too, becomes conflicted in Mexico; she is torn between the young Arroyo and the seventy-one-year-old gringo, who treats her with both respect and affection. She surrenders herself to Arroyo, claiming that she did so to save the gringo's life, a rationale that the gringo refuses to accept or believe. His humor is always to force those around him to face the truth. Arroyo, therefore, has exploited Harriet sexually, and she comes to hate him for that. She gets her vengeance, however, by reporting the gringo's death to the United States consulate, claiming that the gringo was her father, and demanding that his body be returned to Arlington National Cemetery for a military burial.

This lie creates a political problem for Pancho Villa, who is liable to be held responsible for the death of a captain of the United States Army. Politically, Villa and his allies will need the support of the United States government if their revolution is to succeed, and Villa must take measures to rectify the situation. The body of the gringo is exhumed, propped up against a wall, and shot by a firing squad at Villa's command. Arroyo is ordered to administer the *coup de grace*; he is then executed by the same firing squad. Harriet claims the body of the gringo and takes it home, where she continues to live with her memories. "She sits and remembers," Fuentes explains repeatedly.

The Characters

None of the major characters fully captures the sympathy of the reader in this story of revolutionary fervor, partly, perhaps, because they are symbolic stereotypes borrowed from the American Western: The outlaw (Arroyo), the gunfighter (the gringo), and the schoolmarm (Harriet). The fact that the characters seem to belong to a popular and familiar genre may, however, help to explain the novel's popular success.

Both Tomás Arroyo and the old gringo are defined by their courage and integrity. The gringo, an erstwhile cynic, is also a would-be idealist trying to rectify the mistakes of a lifetime. He is admirable in his dedication to truth and uncompromising in his determination not to let others be self-deceived. He forces Harriet to admit that she gave herself to Arroyo out of passion and desire. He forces Arroyo to take action by burning the Spanish documents that Arroyo considers his birthright. The gringo's death is a natural consequence of his actions, but his death is hardly to be pitied, since by his own admission he came to Mexico to die. His death serves a purpose; it puts Arroyo back on the revolutionary track.

If Arroyo's course is derailed, finally, it is because of Harriet's vindictiveness, not because of the old gringo. Just as the gringo represents age, wisdom, truth, and integrity, Tomás Arroyo represents unspoiled Mexican machismo. He is a pure revolutionary uncompromised by politics, unlike Pancho Villa, whose actions in the gringo affair are ultimately dictated by a concern for U.S. foreign policy. Arroyo could be a sympathetic icon of the oppressed Mexican minority, but his motives are flawed by a personal agenda. His revolutionary purpose is stalled. He cannot decide whether to be a Miranda or to continue fighting for the revolution. He presents all that is hopeful and virile in the new Mexico, but he is undone by his own past, by his virility, and by the Americans. He is a strong leader, but his misdeeds cause problems for Villa. Arroyo pays for these mistakes with his life, but he dies bravely, shouting "Viva, Villa!" Even so, at the final moment, his face is "the living image of pain and disbelief." He is a simple man driven by complex psychological motives he cannot fully comprehend. His innocence is carefully balanced against the cynical wisdom and experience of the old gringo, who becomes a father figure to him.

Harriet Winslow, the schoolmarm from the East, is made interesting by the conflict between her idealism and her sexual repression. She is sympathetic in that she is given a taste of an exotic and adventurous life in which she knows she cannot fully participate; her bitterness and vindictiveness, though, finally alienate her from the reader. She cannot forgive Arroyo for showing her a life that is not hers for the taking after he has inflamed her passion. Her punishment after her brief adventures in Mexico is to live a life of regret as she "sits and remembers." Her memories provide the dominant framework for the story, which is mainly her story.

Themes and Meanings

The novel is a cross-cultural meditation that demonstrates the differences between the Mexican and North American national temperaments. The freedom fighter Arroyo is an innocent undone by the inexperienced Harriet and the experienced gringo, both of whom make demands that he is unable to satisfy. In the novel's preoccupation with Mexico and Mexican history, apart from the way it explores the relationship of Mexico and the United States, *The Old Gringo* resembles Fuentes's earlier novel *La muerte de Artemio Cruz* (1962; *The Death of Artemio Cruz*, 1964).

The two novels also share a tendency to experiment with nonlinear storytelling, shifting points of view, consciousness, and structure. In earlier novels, Fuentes had experimented with multiple narrative voices. The point of view of *The Old Gringo* is predominantly third-person omniscient, but Fuentes rapidly shifts the focus from character to character without regard to linear chronology. Sequences and conversations started earlier in the novel are continued later, after the reader has developed a better and more complete sense of context. The narrative technique is sophisticated and challenging.

In the novel, the elegant Miranda hacienda becomes a symbol of the old order, which must be destroyed but which casts a hypnotic spell over Arroyo, who has links to the family, and threatens to seduce him from his revolutionary purpose. This could partly explain his sexual attraction for Harriet as well, since she is linked to the world of the Mirandas. The hacienda is a repository of historic memory and fantasy, its many mirrors serving as windows to the past. The peasants gaze into these mirrors and are enjoined by Arroyo to "see themselves," but the mirrors can also distort what they reflect. Harriet Winslow, a city woman from another culture, looks into the mirrors but can only see herself. For her, the mirrors cannot have the same cultural significance, since they will not reflect her history. What she sees is a thirty-one-year-old Gibson Girl in a Mexican setting.

The novel has been praised for its vivid treatment of the peasants' revolt against their masters but it has also been criticized for its mannered, dreamlike surrealism and its portentous symbolism and rhetoric. The legend of Ambrose Bierce is a dominant symbol. Bierce represents uncompromising honesty, which drives him out of the United States but is also not tolerated in Mexico, where his honesty is the destroyer of dreams. Harriet Winslow seems to represent both American innocence and American duplicity. The lesson she learns is that she cannot adjust to the "other," to a simple life in a different culture.

The novel is shot through with irony: Harriet and her mother have been living a lie in the United States, and Harriet goes to Mexico to find a new life; there, she finds only death and disappointment, and she returns to the United States to live another lie. Arroyo is obssessed with the idea of murdering his actual father, but he pays with his life for murdering his spiritual father. The old gringo wants to be put up against a wall and shot by Pancho Villa; he gets his wish, but only after he is already dead, shot ignominiously in the back by Arroyo. Harriet's journey to Mexico is framed as a spiritual quest, but the novelist turns it into a sexual one. She is not honest with the gringo or with herself about her sexual surrender to Arroyo.

The theme of children searching for fathers and a father searching for his children is carefully crafted but ultimately overworked. The theme of memory and its consequences and the notion that one's home can only be found through one's memories is interestingly developed.

Critical Context

The Old Gringo was first conceived as a film project. Although the story was effectively simplified and clarified by the film version directed by Luis Puenzo and produced by Jane Fonda in 1989, the film was a box-office failure, perhaps because the novel's value resides not so much in its story and relatively wooden archetypes as in its psychological complexity, which cannot conveniently be brought to the surface and visualized. The film makes the story more easily comprehensible—the identification of the gringo with Ambrose Bierce is made clear to the viewer from the very beginning, for example—but it cannot be as well understood, except on the most superficial level.

The Old Gringo is more than merely a colorful and passionate revolutionary epic that resembles a classic Western featuring archetypal characters. It is both a psychological novel and an intercultural meditation disguised as popular fiction that seems to exploit sensuality, romance, and adventure, and its varied strengths made it the first novel by a Mexican writer to become a U.S. best-seller.

Bibliography

Boldy, Steven. "Intertextuality in Carlos Fuentes's *The Old Gringo*." *Romance Quarterly* 39 (November, 1992): 489-500. An in-depth exploration of Fuentes's novel that focuses on "the importing, translating, and transposing of foreign texts" into his work.

Brown, Georgia. "A Woman's Work." *The Village Voice* (October 17, 1990): 90. Brown evaluates both the film adaptation and the novel, pointing out that even before the novel was published, Fuentes had assured Jane Fonda that the novel would contain a part for her. Brown criticizes the novel as silly, but she tends to overlook the book's psychological complexity.

Kearns, George. "Revolutionary Women and Others." *The Hudson Review* 39 (Spring, 1986): 129. States that Fuentes has written a "colorful historical novel, filled with vivid, often moving scenes of the peasants' revolt against their masters." Kearns objects, however, to the "portentous symbolism and rhetoric" with which the novel is loaded.

Meacham, Cherie. "The Process of Dialogue in *Gringo viejo*." *Hispanic Journal* 10 (Spring, 1989): 127-137. Asserts that three principal characters of the novel "achieve their being through a dialogue that examines barriers between generations" and barriers between "cultures, genders, and levels of self." Harriet and Arroyo are linked by their youth and idealism, by his "animal dynamism" and her "repressed sensuality"; both are contrasted to the older gringo's cynicism.

Olson, Renee, and Andrea Glick. "Fuentes's *Old Gringo* Clings to Curriculum in North Carolina." *School Library Journal* 43 (January, 1997): 13. A report on the decision of the Guilford School Board to retain Fuentes's novel as part of the Grimsley High School's curriculum after it was challenged because of a sexually explicit passage. Offers interesting insight into varied reactions to Fuentes's work.

Talbot, Stephen. "On the Run with Carlos Fuentes." *Mother Jones* 13 (November, 1988): 20-25, 46. Talbot surveys Fuentes's life and career, paying particular attention to the writer's ambiguous feelings toward Americans. The United States is "a country of immigrants and pioneers, a country of extreme mobility," Fuentes is quoted as saying, "while Mexico is a country that never moved until the revolution."

Tittler, Jonathan. "Gringo viejo/The Old Gringo: The Rest Is Fiction." *Review of Contemporary Fiction* 8 (Summer, 1988): 241-248. Tittler is concerned about the "untranslatability" of the Spanish original, which "does not maintain a word-to-word (or even page-to-page) correspondence with its English translation." Tittler notes that the Spanish version reverses the order of some chapters and adds an author's note that comments on Bierce and the novel's historical setting.

Updike, John. "Latin Strategies." *The New Yorker* (February 24, 1986): 98-104. Updike complains that Bierce, in real life the "writer of a thousand sardonic jokes," in the novel lacks a sense of humor. He also argues that the reader learns little about Mexico, even though the novel "goes through the motions of establishing geographical and historical authenticity," and dismisses the book as "mere mannerism."

James M. Welsh

ON DISTANT GROUND

Author: Robert Olen Butler (1945-   )
Type of plot: Psychological realism
Time of plot: 1975
Locale: Baltimore, Maryland, and Saigon, Vietnam
First published: 1985

> *Principal characters:*
> > DAVID FLEMING, an Army captain about to be court-martialed for
> > setting a Viet Cong officer free
> > JENNIFER FLEMING, David's wife, who gives birth to their son during
> > the trial
> > CARL LOMAS, David's Army lawyer
> > KENNETH TRASK, a CIA officer who helps David return to Vietnam
> > PHAM VAN TUYEN, the Viet Cong officer David set free
> > NGUYEN THI TUYET SUONG, David's lover in Vietnam
> > KHAI, David's Vietnamese son

The Novel

On Distant Ground is the fictional account of Army captain David Fleming and his internal and external conflicts with his experiences in Vietnam during the Vietnam War. Within the novel, Robert Olen Butler has not used formal chapter breaks; rather, white space divides one section from the next. The first two-thirds of the novel alternates between scenes in present time and scenes from Fleming's time in Vietnam. It is in these flashbacks that the reader is given the background for Fleming's court-martial.

The novel begins with the preliminary stages of David's trial and the birth of his and Jennifer's son, David Junior. David is being tried for aiding the enemy. He kidnapped Pham Van Tuyen, a known Viet Cong officer, from Con Son, the island where Tuyen was being held prisoner by the Army of the Republic of Vietnam (ARVN). Carl Lomas, David's lawyer, seems more concerned about the trial than David and tries to get him to think of anything he might be able to say in his own defense. David cannot think of anything; he freed Tuyen out of compassion when he saw the words "hygiene is healthful" written on Tuyen's vacated cell at the interrogation center in Bien Hoa.

During the preliminary trial stages, Jennifer and David's son is born, and David realizes that he now has another responsibility, that of a family. Both he and Jennifer become brittle as the pressure surrounding David's position and the real possibility of a prison term become more real to them. Adding to the tension is David's sudden realization that he has a son in Vietnam. He has no concrete knowledge of this situation, but he sees the news reports about children of American servicemen being evacuated from Vietnam and realizes that the reason Suong, his Vietnamese lover, disappeared was because she was pregnant. Suddenly obsessed, he realizes that he must return to

Vietnam and bring his son home before Saigon falls to the Communist government.

David's trial and his growing concern about his son occur simultaneously. He sets up a meeting with Kenneth Trask, his Central Intelligence Agency (CIA) contact, and apprises him of the situation. Trask informs him that he can do nothing about the outcome of the trial; if David is not sent to prison, however, there is a chance that Trask could arrange for him to return to Vietnam to try to locate his son. Rather than a prison term, David is given a reduction in rank, a loss of pay, and a dishonorable discharge from the Army.

Trask arranges for David to return to Vietnam using a Canadian passport and other false identification papers. He is warned that Saigon will fall to the Communists in three days at the most. Once he is in Saigon, David begins the near-impossible task of locating Suong or part of her family. Her house in Saigon has been taken over by squatters, and the family home in the country is in disrepair. One servant is left, and she tells David that Suong has disappeared and her mother, Madame Trung, is still in Saigon. David returns to Saigon, and the Communists soon take over the city.

David locates Madame Trung and his son, Khai. He also learns that Suong had openly opposed the government of South Vietnam and had been in prison in Saigon for a year. Convinced that the Communist government would free her, he goes to the prison in search of information. He is taken to the office of Pham Van Tuyen, who is now the director of security for Saigon. Tuyen apparently does not recognize David, and since David is supposedly working for a Canadian organization that has Communist leanings, he agrees to try to find out what he can about Suong.

David returns to Madame Trung's the same evening and learns that a soldier had delivered Suong's ashes and some of her possessions earlier in the evening. Madame Trung convinces him to take his boy back to America and gives him the final payment for the illegal trip out of the country she had been planning.

David leaves during the night with Khai and makes his way to the rendezvous point. Unfortunately, the Communist officials have arrested Mr. Quang, the boat captain who was going to smuggle them out of the country. David is knocked out and wakes up in prison. From there, he is taken to a private audience with Tuyen.

Tuyen does, in fact, know who David is. Through a long interrogation, David does convince Tuyen that he is not a CIA spy and that his only motivation for returning to Vietnam was to find his son and take him back to America. Possibly in gratitude for David's freeing of him, Tuyen allows David and Khai to leave Vietnam and return to America.

The Characters

David Fleming, an Army intelligence captain, is not, at the beginning of the novel, a sympathetic character. He has, by his own admission, allowed a known Viet Cong officer to escape from a South Vietnamese prison. Through David's own thoughts, the reader is able to learn why he did what he did. There is a great sense of helplessness that is conveyed when David tells his attorney, Carl Lomas, that he can think of no way to explain his actions; the motivations are too complicated. David does, however, exhibit tremendous integrity. The moment he realizes that he has a child in Vietnam, he contacts Kenneth Trask and has him work out a plan for David to return to Vietnam to find his child, who he is sure is a son. While there are aspects to David's character that the reader might find unappealing, he is an honorable man. Butler refuses to have a stock Vietnam veteran as his main character. Rather, Fleming is a sensitive, complex man for whom there are no easy answers.

Jennifer Fleming, David's wife, is seen, more often than not, through the eyes of her husband. The reader is immediately sympathetic toward her because she is pregnant and vulnerable. Her husband is being court-martialed, and there is a strong possibility that she will be rearing their child while he is in prison. The reader is impressed by her strength throughout the ordeal. In addition, she will vent her frustrations and fears to David. Jennifer is a strong character, but she is not a martyr. She is, after some consideration, able to accept David's son from his affair with Suong and finally encourages him to go back to Vietnam.

Kenneth Trask is the typical CIA operative. He is secretive and constantly seems to lurk in shadows. His character is developed through his actions. While he admits that there is no way that he can alter the outcome of David's trial, he is willing to make arrangements for the documents that will allow David to enter South Vietnam even though the country is about to fall to the Communists. While little is revealed about Trask, he is the one character who seems immediately to understand David's need to return for his son.

Pham Van Tuyen is the Viet Cong officer whom David releases from the South Vietnamese prison. He is a complex man who is seen at the bottom and top of his career. The reader first meets him when he has escaped from his jailers on Con Son Island. As a result of the torture he has endured, Tuyen is weak and unable to function well. It is unsure how much of the situation he understands; however, he allows David to take him to a helicopter and back to his home. The next time the reader sees Tuyen, he is the director of security for the new Communist government in Saigon. Ironically, it is he who now has David's fate in his hands. Through his actions, he reveals that he, too, is a complex man who does not see actions as all black or white. Possibly to the surprise of the reader, he does allow David to maintain his cover as a Canadian and return to America with his son.

Themes and Meanings

On Distant Ground is a critique of the American military and its presence in Vietnam. The events transpire during the fall of South Vietnam to the Communist north after the departure of the U.S. military in 1975. The novel is also a poignant reminder of the number of children in Vietnam who have American fathers and who are ridiculed by their society because of their mixed background.

On Distant Ground is also about confusion. Throughout the work, Butler points out that there are no easy answers to any situation. While there may theoretically be black-and-white answers to any question, this is seldom true in reality. While David Fleming does aid the enemy, he does not do so in order to betray his country. Rather, he knows that it is only a matter of time before the Americans will leave. His rescue of Tuyen is, if anything, motivated by a possibly misplaced sense of compassion.

Butler also reminds the reader that no one has a blameless past. While David has married Jennifer in good faith, he has done so knowing that he has had an affair with another woman, even though the affair with Suong was over before he and Jennifer met. He must, in the context of the novel, now tell Jennifer that he has had an affair and, more difficult, that he wants to retrieve his son and bring him to America. Again, there are no easy solutions. While Jennifer is, after her initial outrage and shock, understanding, David is asking her to do something that anyone would be reluctant to do—rear a child from a spouse's past relationship.

The overriding theme of the novel does seem to be that good triumphs over evil. The author does, however, give an old theme a new angle. The good and bad characters are not absolutes. All the characters have good and bad traits, a condition that is more realistic, but perhaps also more difficult, for the reader to accept.

Critical Context

On Distant Ground was Butler's fourth novel. The novel served to place Butler firmly within the ranks of Vietnam authors such as Tim O'Brien, Lynda Van Deventer, W. D. Ehrhart, and Larry Heineman, who, like Butler, helped to give the reading public a new, realistic view of the Vietnam War.

In the novel, Butler experiments with flashback, through which device nearly all Fleming's experiences are told. Butler also eliminates the traditional chapter breaks, relying on white space to signal his changes and giving the novel the feel of a seamless narrative. While the story is told in the third person, the main focus of the novel is on David Fleming, and it is through him that the reader receives most of the information about events and characters.

All of Butler's books have received critical acclaim. His collection of short stories about Vietnamese refugees living in Louisiana, *A Good Scent from a Strange Mountain* (1993), received the Pulitzer Prize in 1993. That work and the remainder of his impressive canon have made Butler one of the important voices in late twentieth century American literature.

Bibliography

Beidler, Philip D. *Re-Writing America: Vietnam Authors in Their Generation*. Athens: University of Georgia Press, 1991. In this thought-provoking book, Beidler places Vietnam authors within their generation, which provides the reader with the appropriate context for reading Vietnam fiction. In addition, there is a very good section on Butler that places his novels within the genre. Beidler also establishes and discusses the relationship between Butler's *The Alleys of Eden* (1981), *Sun Dogs* (1982), and *On Distant Ground*, which make up a trilogy about the Vietnam War.

Butler, Robert Olen. "Louisiana: 'God, It's the Mekong Delta!'" Interview by Joseph Olshan. *People* 39 (May 31, 1993): 22. In this interview, Butler talks about his experiences in Vietnam and how they influenced him and his writing. He also recalls his first view of Lake Charles, Louisiana, and how much it reminded him geographically of Vietnam.

_____. "The Process of Writing a Novel." *The Writer* 95 (April, 1982): 11-13. Butler describes the process he used to write *The Alleys of Eden*. Clifford Wilkes, who has a minor role in *On Distant Ground*, is the main character in *The Alleys of Eden*. In addition, it is useful to see the process Butler went through to gather and organize his material for the novel.

Kelsay, Michael. "Robert Olen Butler." *Poets and Writers Magazine* 24 (May/June, 1996): 40-49. Kelsay connects the themes and subjects of Butler's novels to his three-year hitch in Vietnam during the war. He shows how Butler used the first-person narrative voice to shape his personal style.

Klein, Joe. "Soldiers and Doctors." *The New York Times Book Review*, April 12, 1985, p. 26. Klein places *On Distant Ground* within the canon of Vietnam fiction. In addition, he writes that the story's "pyramiding absurdities seem not merely plausible, but inevitable."

Ryan, Maureen. "Robert Olen Butler's Vietnam Veterans: Strangers in an Alien Home." *The Midwest Quarterly* 38 (Spring, 1997): 274-294. Discusses narrative evidence that *The Alleys of Eden*, *Sun Dogs*, and *On Distant Ground* should be regarded as a trilogy. The protagonists of each book served together in an intelligence unit, and their lives were so affected by their war experiences that none of them could adapt to contemporary American life. An interesting comparison of Butler's three war novels.

Steinberg, Sybil. "Robert Olen Butler: The Pulitzer Prize Winner Is Not Resting on His Laurels." *Publishers Weekly* 241 (January 3, 1994): 60-61. Discusses Butler's book *They Whisper*, as well as his other works and writing career. Provides a useful overview of the body of his work.

Victoria E. McLure

ON HEROES AND TOMBS

Author: Ernesto Sábato (1911-   )
Type of plot: Psychological realism
Time of plot: 1841 and 1946-1955
Locale: Buenos Aires and Patagonia, Argentina
First published: Sobre héroes y tumbas, 1961 (English translation, 1981)

> *Principal characters:*
> ALEJANDRA VIDAL OLMOS, a young woman in Buenos Aires
> MARTÍN DEL CASTILLO, a young man in love with Alejandra
> BRUNO BASSÁN, the mentor and confidant of Martín
> FERNANDO VIDAL OLMOS, the father of Alejandra
> HORTENSIA PAZ, a woman who nurses Martín during his illness
> GEORGINA OLMOS, the mother of Alejandra
> BUCICH, a truck driver

The Novel

In an introductory note to his linguistically and ideologically complex novel, Ernesto Sábato admits that the narrative represents his attempt to "free himself of an obsession that is not clear even to himself." This admission is borne out by the novel's extraordinary display of unusual imagery, puzzling events and characters, and conflicting political and ethical points of view.

The text of *On Heroes and Tombs* is presented in four parts. In "The Dragon and the Princess" and "Invisible Faces," Martín del Castillo meets Alejandra Vidal Olmos, a young woman for whom he develops an immediate fascination. After a long period of pursuit, he finally convinces her to begin a love affair with him. In an attempt to understand the strange behavior of Alejandra, Martín follows her and sees her with another man, whom she later admits is Fernando, her father. Although she seems to be an innocent, introverted woman, Alejandra (who turns out to be the daughter of a decadent aristocratic family) is a prostitute who caters to the wealthy members of Juan Perón's administration. At the same time, she maintains an incestuous relationship with Fernando, who is her father but was never married to her mother, Georgina.

Fernando Vidal Olmos has written a mysterious document which narrates his frequent hallucinatory experiences, a document incorporated into the text in the third part, "Report on the Blind." After finishing the report, Fernando goes to his daughter's home, even though he knows that he is going to his inevitable death. Alejandra shoots him and then commits suicide by setting fire to the house.

In the fourth part of the novel, "An Unknown God," Martín seeks the help of Bruno Bassán as he attempts to understand his relationship with Alejandra. Martín falls into an alcohol-induced stupor, in which he envisions himself in a world likened to a dung heap or sewer. He is saved and nursed back to health by Hortensia Paz, who instills in him the hope for a better life. Martín meets a truck driver, Bucich, who takes him on a trip to Patagonia. Interpolated in the narrative of the trip are passages which depict the struggle of the revolutionary forces of General Juan Lavalle against the regime of Juan Manuel de Rosas, the dictator of Argentina from 1829 to 1852. Two ancestors of Fernando and Alejandra Vidal Olmos carry the body of Lavalle toward the Argentine-Bolivian border in 1841 as Martín flees to Patagonia in 1955 and finds that the crystal-clear sky and the fresh air make him feel free and reborn.

The story of Alejandra, Martín, and Fernando is told through a variety of narrative points of view. The foreword of the novel is an objective police report of the death of Alejandra and Fernando. "The Dragon and the Princess" and "Invisible Faces," narrated by an unnamed omniscient narrator, include many long passages which portray the thoughts of the characters and scenes from the early life of Alejandra and Martín. The "Report on the Blind" is a text written by Fernando as a memoir or confession, a narrative of his own experience. In the last section, "An Unknown God," it becomes clear that the narrator of the first two sections is someone who knew the characters and has obtained most of the information from Bruno and from Martín years after the death of Alejandra and Fernando. The narrator acts as an organizing consciousness of the material—the episodes of the contemporary history of the characters, the recollections of the earlier years, the interpolated passages of the history of Alejandra's ancestors, and the text of Fernando's psychotic, paranoic report on the activities of the blind.

The Characters

Just as the novel represents an attempt to relieve an unspecified obsession, the characters are portrayed as engaged in a struggle to free themselves from their own mysterious preoccupations. Throughout the novel, Bruno seeks the thread of continuity that links the lives of Alejandra, Fernando, and Martín, primarily to understand finally the reasons for Alejandra's act of killing her father and herself.

The contradictions of Alejandra's behavior are not resolved in the text of the novel. Although her family has always opposed the regime of Perón, she devotes her life to satisfying the sexual appetite of the Perónists. She makes love with Martín, for whom she has a strange, obsessive fascination, yet she always remains distant and mysterious. At the same time, she engages in an incestuous relationship with her father, and then murders him and destroys herself in a ritualistic immolation.

Fernando's lust for his daughter is barely explained. She bears a striking resemblance to Fernando's mother and to her own mother, Georgina, who was the daughter of Patricio, the brother of Fernando's mother. Bruno describes Fernando as an antiphilosopher, a nihilist who hates everything bourgeois and despises the world for its destruction of the aristocratic, elitist life that his family once enjoyed.

Martín is portrayed as a young man who is trying to find some explanation for life itself. Martín's attempt to discover a hidden logic in the mysterious behavior of Alejandra creates the impression that these two characters represent opposite poles of human existence, the ordered and the chaotic, the logical and the contradictory, the rational and the irrational, oppositions that suggest that Martín and Alejandra are archetypal characters, incarnations of what Sábato understands as essentially masculine and essentially feminine characteristics.

Themes and Meanings

The treatment of the central characters as representatives of abstract notions of masculine and feminine traits is a manifestation of a principal theme of the novel, the search for the meaning of human existence. Sábato creates from a common, almost trivial concern—that of the inability of one sex to understand the other—an exploration of an ontological problem. As Martín, Bruno, and Fernando attempt, each in his own way, to understand the mysterious Alejandra (who is likened to Argentina itself), they seek through the elusive feminine psyche a justification for their own experience. Fernando's hallucinatory, somnambulistic document about the blind is presented in terms of a harrowing journey through the vaginal canal of a woman, and Martín is rescued from his despair by a warm, maternal savior, Hortensia Paz. Bruno works out his answers to the mystery vicariously, by piecing together the story of Martín, Fernando, and Alejandra. Fernando finds his solution in his own madness, justifying the irrationality of existence as a plot perpetrated by blind people. Martín resolves his anguish by escaping to the free, open spaces of Patagonia, out of the reach of women, and by experiencing the exhilarating sense of masculine communion as he and the truck driver urinate together under the stars.

In the conflict of man and woman, then, is contained the insoluble mystery of existence. The elaboration of the conflict in *On Heroes and Tombs* is complicated by the fact that this is a novel about incestuous relationships, both sexual and nonsexual. Fernando and Alejandra, father and daughter, are lovers. Bruno has been sexually involved with Alejandra and with her mother, Georgina. Fernando fathered the child, Alejandra, by the daughter of his mother's brother, and the child looks like Fernando's mother, whose husband—Fernando's father—Fernando hated and tried to poison when he was a child. Martín becomes involved in a love affair with Alejandra, the former lover of his friend Bruno.

The fact that Alejandra works as a prostitute serving the Perónists, the longtime enemies of her aristocratic family, indicates that the incestuous relationships and the exploration of the meaning of existence itself have a political symbolism in the novel. The counterpoint provided in the narrative that shifts between the twentieth century condition of these characters living under the dictatorship of Perón and the struggles of the nineteenth century rebels fleeing the tyranny of Manuel de Rosas further develops the political implications of the story of Martín, Fernando, Bruno, and Alejandra. As Fernando dies, murdered by his daughter, at the same moment that Perón is deposed, Martín finds his freedom, aided by the maternal figure that nurses him and gives him the spiritual strength to escape his depression.

Although Sábato's novel is much too complex and profound to permit a simplistic explanation, it seems clear that in some way, Alejandra represents the contradictory, impassioned Argentina of the Perón regime, and that Hortensia Paz represents the compassionate, maternal nurturing of the potential Argentina of the post-Perón era.

Critical Context

Ernesto Sábato first received international acclaim with the publication of his short novel, *El túnel*, in 1948 (*The Outsider*, 1950). In the author's note at the beginning of *On Heroes and Tombs*, Sábato says that in the thirteen years between the first novel and the second, he continued exploring the mysterious labyrinth that leads to the secret of human existence. *The Outsider* is a pessimistic, oppressive story of a man who murders his married mistress when he finds out that she has deceived him. Many of the details and themes of the second novel are contained in the first—the mistress's husband is blind, the protagonist's love for the woman is obsessive and violent, and his behavior is at times distorted by paranoia.

As Sábato suggests, *On Heroes and Tombs* does indeed seem to be a development of the obsessive concerns of the first novel. The pessimism of *The Outsider*, however, is tempered somewhat by the optimism of the ending of the second novel. The more promising vision of human existence offered by Hortensia Paz and the portrayal of potentially rewarding relationships in the conversation and communion of Martín and Bucich in Patagonia are indications that Sábato finds some salvation for his characters despite the apparent meaninglessness of life.

Sábato's novel is a stylistic tour de force which inevitably evokes a comparison with the work of many of his Latin American contemporary novelists. There are many passages that are precursors of the narrative complexities of the work of Carlos Fuentes, Julio Cortázar, and Guillermo Cabrera Infante, and the ontological problems suggested by the novel reflect similar preoccupations of the most influential Argentine writer of the twentieth century, Jorge Luis Borges. In spite of the development toward a concept of life in *On Heroes and Tombs* that is more optimistic than the ontology of *The Outsider*, the later novel continues to suggest the impossibility of resolving the conflict of human rationality and human existence. The stylistic and ideological complexities of Sábato's work, which confirm his confession of the obsessive nature of his narrative impulse, render his novelesque work very difficult and not at all clear in its communication of the central mystery of life.

Bibliography

Bach, Caleb. "Ernesto Sábato: A Conscious Choice of Words." *Americas* 43 (January/February, 1991): 14-19. A look at Sábato's life and work. Addresses the dark tone of his novels, as well as comments by critics "who feel that his 'black hope' is several shades too dark."

Cohen, Howard R. "Ernesto Sábato." In *Latin American Writers*, edited by Carlos A. Solé and Maria I. Abreau. Vol 3. New York: Charles Scribner's Sons, 1989. Offers an in-depth profile of Sábato's life and career. Many of his works are discussed in detail, including *On Heroes and Tombs*.

Flores, Angel. *Spanish American Authors: The Twentieth Century*. New York: H. W. Wilson, 1992. A good overall view of Sábato's work. Offers a brief critical analysis of selected novels and common themes that thread through Sábato's fiction.

McQuade, Frank. "Personal Obsessions." *Third World Quarterly* 13 (1992): 197-198.

McQuade gives a brief synopsis of Sábato's novel. He then presents an analysis of the story and notes that "this long novel" reflects all the themes already presented in Sábato's other novels, including the search for the mother; the subconscious explored through dreams and nightmares; and the interest in perverse logic of a criminal mentality. He notes that the treatment of these themes is much more broad and bleaker than Sábato's earlier works.

Sábato, Ernesto. "Ernesto Sábato: A Sense of Wonder." Interview. *UNESCO Courier* (August, 1990): 4-9. Sábato discusses the opposition between science and the humanities; existentialist thought; the limitations of science in relation to dream, mythology, and art to represent reality; the current state of education; and the demise of the nuclear arms race. A good overall view of the thoughts and opinions that influence Sábato's work.

Gilbert G. Smith

ONE DAY OF LIFE

Author: Manlio Argueta (1936-   )
Type of plot: Social protest
Time of plot: 1979
Locale: El Salvador
First published: Un día en la vida, 1980 (English translation, 1983)

> *Principal characters:*
> > GUADALUPE (LUPE) FUENTES DE GUARDADO, the protagonist, a
> > matriarch and peasant
> > JOSÉ (CHEPE) GUARDADO, the husband of Lupe, a village leader of the
> > Federation of Christian Farmworkers
> > ADOLFINA FUENTES, the granddaughter of Lupe and Chepe

The Novel

The narrative thread recounts one day in the life of a middle-aged peasant woman, from 5:00 A.M., when she arises at dawn, until 5:00 P.M., when she lights the candles as darkness closes in. The chapters divide the day's segments as she goes about her routine activities of cooking, child care, house and garden work, and musing about the people and events that have shaped and informed her life. This interior monologue reveals her past—the unremitting, wretched poverty as well as her simple, humble acceptance of the inhuman conditions under which she and the other peasants in the village live.

She muses about her childhood, her betrothal to José (Chepe) Guardado, their marriage, their children, their work, and their efforts to better their lot. By exercising extreme frugality, they have bought a small piece of land of their own. The carefully tended crops have enabled Lupe and Chepe to provide a few comforts for their meager existence; for example, they are able to buy a few toys and candies for the children at Christmas. Lupe recalls the early hardships, as when their child died of malnutrition, dysentery, and worms as many of the peasant children do, and how the "old priests" advocated resignation and hope of eternal happiness in heaven.

Then the "new priests" came and offered instruction and help in forming cooperatives, recommended pharmaceuticals to treat worms and dysentery, and cheese as food for malnourished babies. They encouraged the farm laborers to seek higher pay and the peasants to sell their goods in town, where they could get higher prices than the local merchant offered. Then she remembers how the authorities came and began abusing the peasants and finally attacked the priests. The priests were sent away, but the changes they had wrought could not be stopped, and the authorities became increasingly abusive as the peasants became increasingly assertive. The abuses included torture, imprisonment, and murder. Lupe's son was one such victim, decapitated by the guards and his head stuck on a pole outside the village.

As the hours pass, Lupe reminisces about the increasing involvement of her family members in protest activities: Chepe has become a leader in the farm-workers' movement; Helio Hernandez, Lupe's son-in-law, has been seized by the guards for his activist involvement, and the family can get no information as to his whereabouts or fate. Lupe's granddaughter, Adolfina Fuentes, who is a child of less than fifteen years, is the most outspokenly militant. She took part in a week-long demonstration in which a cathedral was seized and occupied by the peasants; as she was returning home, the bus on which she and other demonstrators were riding was attacked by the guards and most of the passengers were killed. She and another girl escaped, and on the day of the narrative, she arrives to visit her grandmother for a few days until the situation cools down.

Later, the authorities come to question Adolfina about a man whom they have apprehended and beaten; the man murmured her name as he slipped into unconsciousness. They must wait for an hour or so with Lupe until the girl and Lupe's smaller children return from the store.

In her interior monologue, Lupe recapitulates the fears, compliance, hopes, anger, human kindness, and resignation that follow one another as she waits helplessly for Adolfina's return. Later, however, when the guards want to take Adolfina away to identify the man they are holding, she defies them and insists that they not take Adolfina away alone. Finally, they bring the man to the hut for the girl to see, but only Lupe recognizes Chepe by his clothes. He is dying from the brutal and disfiguring beating he has received. To protect her family, she denies knowing who he is and they take him away. Lupe resolves to carry on and to encourage her granddaughter also to continue such resistance as they can offer to the authorities.

The novel is detailed and often moving in its description of the miseries and brutalities of life in El Salvador. The ignorance and hopelessness of the peasantry are palpable in the lifestyles portrayed. Lupe's random associations are simplistic yet believable, and there is an occasional contrast to the misery: the surprise of joy at the beauty of dawn, the pleasure of watching and hearing the tropical birds, the affection for a dog. Indeed, these poignant flashes of delight remind the reader that Manlio Argueta established his reputation first as a poet, and his lyricism and powerful images confirm his poetic talent.

In addition to Lupe's own chapters, in which her point of view and experiences are dominant, other chapters are interspersed in which the interior monologues and events of other characters' lives are revealed. The voices of three other women are heard in these chapters, and their experiences parallel Lupe's own and confirm her justification for hating the authorities. The guards are afforded two chapters in which their point of view is presented; these men are drawn from the peasant class themselves and are in truth turning against their own families, friends, and neighbors in order to uphold the brutally oppressive regime of a handful of wealthy families (fourteen) in El Salvador. Ironically, the voices of the guards, reflecting their confusion about loyalties, their wistful desire for a bit more power, a few more possessions, and a modicum of respect, are more believable than those of Adolfina, Lupe, and Chepe.

The Characters

The characters in this novel are prototypes. They represent two of the several factions involved in the social turmoil in El Salvador. The principal group depicted is the peasantry. Lupe, Chepe, Adolfina, and all the minor characters representing the peasantry share many of the same traits: They are courageous, long-suffering, wise, gentle, generous, and loving. Lacking even the most basic amenities of existence, they manage to create lives and family units which radiate love, harmony, and dignity. They support one another in their mutual opposition to the rapacity of the rich landowners and the brutality of the authorities; they acknowledge the authority of the Church and honor the priests, whether these priests recommend patiently bearing their burdens or offer help and instruction in ways to cooperate and unionize to improve their lot.

Lupe is the archetypical matriarch, warm and loving to her family, pious and generous to the Church, steadfast and courageous to Chepe, her beloved husband. Chepe, in turn, is bold in asserting his rights, a natural leader of the community, where he works diligently to improve the living conditions for his family and the farm workers in the union. He faces danger bravely, endures suffering silently, and, like his son, suffers martyrdom at the hands of the brutal guards.

Adolfina is an intense, idealistic girl who represents an impassioned new generation arising amid the repression and the turmoil. She is determined to avenge and justify the deaths of the martyrs and the sufferings of the peasants at the hands of the authorities. In the final lines of the book, Adolfina imagines that she sees the corpse of the guard who has just taken her dying grandfather away. She assures Lupe that this vision "has to be true."

The novel's preoccupation with terrorism and misery precludes any expansive development of characters: The characters all tend to be flat, representing the idealized qualities and political leanings of the peasant class. Their relationships to one another are likewise lacking in emotional variety and authenticity.

The minor characters among the peasant group are scarcely differentiated from the major ones, except in having smaller roles. Their characteristics and behavior are much the same: The son and son-in-law of Chepe are cut from the same mold as he, and Lupe's daughter is another staunchly brave and loyal matriarch in the making.

The only other characters with a substantial voice in the narrative are the guards, who wield authority over the peasants. These guards never waver in their commitment to keep the peasants down and protect the holdings of the rich. Although they come from the peasant class themselves, they have been effectively brainwashed by their leaders and trainers to feel only contempt and viciousness toward the hapless people over whom they have control. Their trainers, who provide both political and military instruction, are callous, arrogant, and sometimes brutal Americans, who teach the neophyte guards contempt for their own people.

The priests are a shadowy group, most of them preaching resignation and humility while accepting favors and gifts from the impoverished people; a few attempt to help the peasants or at least to mediate between the peasants and their oppressors. None of the priests is sufficiently developed to stand out as an individual. No members of the wealthy landowner group are represented in the narrative, although their malign nature is forcefully conveyed.

Themes and Meanings

The novel is written to recount and extol the birth of a sense of self-worth among the Salvadoran peasantry. This central theme illuminates the narrative and asserts that human dignity can and does transcend misery, brutality, and oppression. Beyond the misery of *One Day of Life*, beyond the carnage and despair, the novel holds forth hope for social justice in the future. Neither the peasants nor the guards seem able to comprehend or discuss the complex problems which they face, or even their own attitudes toward these questions. No solutions are proposed, no real focus of effort to accomplish any concrete goals ever appears to emerge. For each small action—a demonstration, a rally, an act of defiance—harshly brutal reprisals follow immediately. The book suggests that such measures serve only to strengthen the resolve of the peasants to continue to seek ways to make their lives better, but the position of the peasants would appear to be precariously weak, and beset by enemies both at home and abroad.

This novel asserts that the dignity of the human spirit will not be destroyed by misery and oppression, that it will resist and ultimately triumph. It is a splendid hope, providing a luminescent thematic unity to this tale of how the human spirit flourishes in one of the most economically depressed and politically unsettled areas of the Americas.

Critical Context

One Day of Life was Manlio Argueta's third book, but his first one to address in such direct fashion the social conditions in El Salvador. He is known principally as a poet, and critics have commented favorably on this book with respect to his lyricism, his poetic and moving imagery, and the authentic flavor of the vernacular language. Yet they have also found the characterizations flat and the story line thin, as is often the case with novels of social and political protest. The book was first published in 1980 in El Salvador and quickly excited so much interest there that Argueta was forced into exile and the book was banned. Since then, it has been translated and published in Italy, Germany, the Netherlands, and the United States. Argueta was not known widely outside his own country prior to the publication of this book, which has established him as a new and dynamic voice in Central American literature.

Bibliography

Dickey, Christopher. Review in *The New Republic* 189 (November 21, 1983): 46-47. A useful critical perspective.

Edelman, Marc. "The Rural Terror." *Commonweal* 111 (May 4, 1984): 283-284. Discusses Argueta in the context of Central American strife.

Flores, Angel. "Manlio Argueta." In *Spanish American Authors: The Twentieth Century.* New York: H. W. Wilson, 1992. A good overall view of Argueta's work. Offers a brief critical analysis of selected novels and common themes that thread through Argueta's fiction.

Betty G. Gawthrop

ONE OF OURS

Author: Willa Cather (1873-1947)
Type of plot: American symbolism
Time of plot: The first quarter of the twentieth century to World War I
Locale: Frankfort and Lincoln, Nebraska, and the battlefields of France
First published: 1922

> *Principal characters:*
>
> CLAUDE WHEELER, the protagonist, a sensitive young man reared on a
> Nebraska farm
> EVANGELINE WHEELER, Claude's mother, a simple woman with
> profound love for Claude and deep religious convictions
> NAT WHEELER, Claude's father, a prosperous though somewhat
> lackadaisical farmer, often insensitive to Claude's needs
> RALPH WHEELER, Claude's brother, given to impractical gadgetry and
> careless spending, and Nat's favorite son
> BAYLISS WHEELER, Claude's brother, a seller of farm tools
> MAHAILEY, the Wheelers' devoted housekeeper
> ERNEST HAVEL, a German immigrant, Claude's boyhood friend
> MRS. ERLICH, a sensitive and intelligent mother of five boys and a
> friend to Claude
> ENID ROYCE, Claude's wife
> GLADYS FARMER, a schoolteacher and Claude's childhood sweetheart
> VICTOR MORSE, an Iowa-bred R.A.F. flyer
> DAVID GERHARDT, a violinist and a lieutenant with the Expeditionary
> Force
> MADAME JOUBERT, who, with her husband, is the host of Claude's first
> billet in France

The Novel

One of Ours documents the period of Claude Wheeler's life from his college years in Nebraska to his death in the trenches during World War I. Claude is a young man who is constantly searching for his place in life, needing to feel that he belongs and that his life should have some clear purpose. Although he is an extremely competent farmer, far better in fact than either of his brothers or his father, he is not fulfilled by farm life, and though he is a good student, he believes that the church-affiliated college he attends does not provide the intellectual challenge that he needs. Only when he matriculates in a European history course at the state university does he begin to find his place.

His happiness does not last. When his father buys a farm in Colorado, management of the Nebraska farm falls to Claude. Though Claude accepts this responsibility without complaint, he is again unhappy and silently resentful.

Marriage seems a solution for his narrowed horizons, but even in this Claude is unfortunate. He comes to discover that Enid, a pretty girl whom he has known all of his life, has interests far different from his own: the Church, prohibition, and (as her father half jokingly warns before their marriage) vegetarianism. When Enid leaves Claude temporarily to nurse Carrie, her missionary sister who has fallen ill in China, Claude's world once again collapses.

This episode coincides with the outbreak of World War I, and Claude, his mother, and his father eagerly follow the newspaper accounts. For Claude's father, the war means rising wheat prices and a chance for quick profits; for Claude, it is a chance to devote himself unselfishly to a cause. Despite the influenza epidemic which sweeps his troopship, despite the manifold horrors of the battlefield, he believes that at last he has a mission. He dies a hero, "believing his own country better than it is, and France better than any country can ever be."

The Characters

Claude Wheeler's sensitivity and intelligence are obvious, though he himself never recognizes them. His mother and Mahailey, the family housekeeper, love him deeply and know that he is unhappy, yet Claude defers to what he believes are his mother's wishes when he does not insist on full matriculation at the state university. Similarly, he says nothing when forced to leave college to manage the family farm.

He finds his greatest happiness when he is with intelligent and worldly people: Ernest Havel, a German immigrant who is Claude's own age; Mrs. Erlich, a cultured widow with five bright sons; Gladys Farmer, a childhood sweetheart and a high school teacher with a gift for music; Victor Morse, a devil-may-care R.A.F. pilot; David Gerhardt, a violinist turned soldier; and Madame Joubert, a farm woman who provides Claude's first billet in France. All of them offer interludes of happiness in Claude's restless life. Even so, Cather is careful not to make Claude's death an indictment of war or even to see it as a tragedy for her protagonist. Claude considers his experience noble, and he dies with convictions he believes worth fighting for.

Evangeline Wheeler has a simple yet profound religious faith and contentment which contrast with her son's unhappiness. While she has no doubt that she is where her Lord wants her to be, Claude sees her as a woman whose spirit is stifled both by her religion and by her isolated life on the farm. She is a pivotal character whose persona reappears in the guise of several of the novel's other women. For example, there is something of Mrs. Wheeler in the worldly and kind Mrs. Erlich, whom Claude meets while he is a student in Lincoln, as there is in Mrs. Voigt, a German immigrant and the owner of a restaurant that is frequented by travelers who are moving between Lincoln and Frankfort, and in Madame Joubert, Claude's first host in France.

When Nat and Ralph Wheeler spend a winter at the Colorado ranch that Nat has purchased, Claude assumes management of the home farm. Since he must leave college to do this, Claude surrenders, for a time, his own goals to the values of his father. Though Claude never openly complains, he resents Nat's interest in acquiring land for investment as well as Ralph's irresponsible spending on impractical gadgetry. He sees these things as part of a pattern of materialism and acquisitiveness sweeping America in the years before World War I. It is for these reasons that Claude admires Mahailey, who sees her life in terms of the service she can render others.

There are priorities for service to others, however, and Enid's involvements, whether in her prohibition activities or in her sudden departure for China to nurse her sister Carrie, are essentially selfish and at the expense of her life with Claude. Cather implies that Gladys Farmer would have made Claude a better wife. Gladys teaches, plays piano, and has less concern for grand causes or dramatic gestures. Though Claude's brother Bayliss courts Gladys and wishes to marry her, Gladys realizes that they would never find real happiness together. In one sense Gladys's is the real tragedy; by the novel's end, she has determined to accept Frankfort life, though she realizes that she will remain unlike most of those around her.

Themes and Meanings

Claude, like many idealistic people, searches for his place in life and for something larger than himself to which he can devote his energies. He reflects the unselfish idealism of America's past as challenged by the mechanization, materialism, and greed of the twentieth century. Though World War I may well have occurred because of greed, Claude sees it only as "the war to end all wars," a decisive, final struggle against the ideas most repugnant to him.

This is not to imply that he sees the Allies' methods or even his comrades-in-arms as blameless. Captain (later Colonel) Maxey is incompetent; commanding officers often order their men to take actions that are certain to result in death, and Claude recognizes their culpability. Even so, he sees the cause as essentially noble and morally right. Appropriately, Claude receives his greatest support from the unselfish Mahailey, who has childhood memories of the Civil War and knows war's horrors at first hand. Prospering in business, as does Bayliss, acquiring land for speculative purposes, as does Nat, or spending irresponsibly on useless luxuries, as does Ralph, are for Claude unsatisfactory substitutes for nobler, harder-won goals.

Critical Context

Though less celebrated popularly than her remarkable *O Pioneers!* (1913) and her *My Ántonia* (1918), Cather's *One of Ours* shows the author's mature style at its strongest. It received the Pulitzer Prize for Literature in 1923. Though *One of Ours* privileges characterization over background, this does not imply that setting is unimportant, only that scenes and detail exist to support and define the personalities of the characters.

Cather's style is spare, and her narrative avoids the social moralizing of naturalism, thereby allowing her protagonist to pursue with utter sincerity convictions with which a reader may disagree. Cather was appalled by the materialism of America in the years following World War I, and most readers of *One of Ours* will share these feelings; Claude Wheeler, however, blames only himself for his situation and believes that his life finds meaning in the trenches of France.

Cather's Nebraska background resembled that of her protagonist. She, too, discovered the world of learning at the University of Nebraska; her earliest writing appeared in the *Nebraska State Journal*. She knew the "muckrakers," Ida Tarbell, Mark Sullivan, and Lincoln Steffens, and was an editor of *McClure's Magazine*, which made its reputation by its exposes of American social problems at the turn of the century. She learned to write about places and events connected with her own life from her formidable mentor Sarah Orne Jewett.

Contrasts between life past and present fill many of Cather's works, such as the short stories of *Youth and the Bright Medusa* (1920), *Obscure Destinies* (1932), and *The Old Beauty and Others* (1948). She came to detest modern life and wished to glorify "the precious, the incommunicable past"; she aspired to what she called the "unfurnished novel," history raised to symbol, narrative replaced by episode and tableau—in short, a prose akin to poetry.

Cather maintained a tendency to treat characters as moral entities, as did Henry James, whose works she admired, but like her closer contemporary T. S. Eliot, she saw the dangers inherent in deteriorating religious values and the corrupting influences of the modern world.

Bibliography
Bloom, Edward A., and Lillian D. Bloom. *Willa Cather's Gift of Sympathy*. Carbondale: Southern Illinois University Press, 1962. Considered a classic on criticism of Cather's works. The Blooms look at this author's gift of sympathy and skillfully relate it to her thematic interests and technical proficiency. Deals with not only Cather's fiction but also her poetry and essays, which in themselves form an important commentary on her ideas.
Bloom, Harold, ed. *Modern Critical Views: Willa Cather*. New York: Chelsea House, 1985. Bloom says of this volume that it gathers "the best literary criticism on Cather over the last half-century." The criticism selected emphasizes Cather's novels *Sapphira and the Slave Girl, My Ántonia, Death Comes for the Archbishop*, and *A Lost Lady*. The volume concludes with a study by Marilyn Arnold on what are considered Cather's two finest short stories, "A Wagner Matinee" and "Paul's Case." Contains a chronology and a bibliography. A must for serious Cather scholars.
Fryer, Judith. *Felicitous Space: The Imaginative Structures of Edith Wharton and Willa Cather*. Chapel Hill: University of North Carolina Press, 1986. Although there are many full-length studies on Cather's writing, this volume is particularly noteworthy for its examination of Cather using late-twentieth-century feminist thinking. Fryer explores Cather's fiction in terms of the "interconnectedness between space and the female imagination" and cites her as a transformer of social and cultural structures. A thorough and interesting study, recommended for its contribution to women's studies in literature. Includes extensive notes.
Gerber, Philip. *Willa Cather: Revised Edition*. New York: Twayne, 1995. Incorporates discussion of new materials and criticism that have appeared since 1975 edi-

tion. Rather than calling Cather a "disconnected" writer, as have some critics, Gerber takes the view in this study that there is unity in her writing. Gerber demonstrates the development of her artistry from one novel to the next. Includes a chronology and a selected bibliography.

Meyering, Sheryl. *A Reader's Guide to the Short Stories of Willa Cather.* New York: G. K. Hall, 1994. Chapters on each short story, discussing publication history, the circumstances of composition, biographical details, significant literary and cultural sources, connections to Cather's novels, and an overview of how each story has been interpreted.

Murphy, John. *Critical Essays on Willa Cather.* Boston: G. K. Hall, 1984. A compilation of criticism on Cather's work, including general essays from a variety of contributors as well as reviews and literary criticism of specific titles. The introduction emphasizes her creativity, and the volume concludes with reviews of her last four books. Most useful for its breadth of criticism on Cather. Contains a selected bibliography.

Shaw, Patrick W. *Willa Cather and the Art of Conflict: Re-visioning Her Creative Imagination.* Troy, N.Y.: Whitston, 1992. Separate chapters on all of Cather's major novels. Reexamines Cather's fiction in terms of her conflicts over her lesbian sexuality. The introduction provides a helpful overview of Cather criticism on the topic.

Robert J. Forman

ONE WAY TO HEAVEN

Author: Countée Cullen (Countée Porter; 1903-1946)
Type of plot: Ethnic realism
Time of plot: The 1920's
Locale: New York City's Harlem
First published: 1932

> *Principal characters:*
>> MATTIE JOHNSON, an attractive young black woman who works as a
>> domestic servant
>> SAM LUCAS, a one-armed confidence man who marries Mattie
>> AUNT MANDY, Mattie's aunt
>> EMMA MAY, Sam's mistress
>> CONSTANCIA BRANDON, Mattie's employer
>> THE REVEREND CLARENCE JOHNSON, a preacher who knows that Sam
>> is a confidence artist

The Novel

Countée Cullen, well known as a black poet, wrote only one novel, *One Way to Heaven*. Given the fervor of the Harlem Renaissance, in which Cullen was an active participant, it is not surprising that he would turn his talents to writing a book that reflected elements of this movement.

One Way to Heaven has been called two novels in one, largely because it has a dual focus. On the one hand, it is concerned with Mattie Johnson and her love affair with Sam Lucas, a dark, handsome, one-armed confidence man from Texas who never stays long in one place. On the other hand, the novel is a satire on the social life of Harlem's emerging middle-class black population.

The common thread in the two stories is that Mattie Johnson, a good-looking young black woman, works as a domestic servant for Constancia Brandon, wife of Dr. George Brandon, a physician from Oklahoma who has made considerable money in oil. Constancia, light enough to pass for white, is exhilarated by life in Harlem, where she is a well-established hostess and organizer of social events.

The Mattie-Sam story begins when Sam goes to the Mt. Hebron Episcopal Church in Harlem and there undergoes a conversion to the faith. Unknown to Mattie, it is part of Sam's habitual pattern when he goes to a new place to undergo a public conversion in order to make the congregation have confidence in him.

Sam's performance at the Mt. Hebron Episcopal Church is superb. He goes to the altar with tears welling up in his eyes, but not before he has taken from his pocket and dashed to the floor a deck of playing cards and an "evil looking razor," which are devices of the Devil. So impressed is the congregation that nine other people, including Mattie, who up until this time has been reluctant to be converted, follow Sam to the altar. After Sam has been converted, members of the congregation flock around him, some forcing money upon him.

The Reverend Clarence Johnson, who is present for Sam's conversion, recognizes Sam as a drifter who has undergone a similar conversion in his presence in Memphis some time before. He does not make much of this fact, however, and instead ruminates on Sam's success in bringing nine other souls to God, a record that the Reverend Johnson himself could not have equaled that day.

Mattie falls in love with Sam instantly, and before long they are married. Constancia Brandon insists on having the wedding at her residence, and she is also instrumental in arranging for Sam to be employed as doorman at a nearby theater. Sam certainly is not the marrying kind, and he soon succumbs to the flirtations of Emma May, the usher in the theater where he is doorman.

Mattie by this time has become pregnant. Her baby dies a few hours after it is born, and Sam leaves Mattie to go off and live with Emma May. Mattie is looked after by Aunt Mandy, an old black woman whose faith is a mixture of pagan animism and Christianity. Aunt Mandy blames Mattie for Sam's leaving.

Eventually Sam falls ill with pneumonia, and Mattie generously agrees to take him back and to care for him in his illness. She expresses her concern to Aunt Mandy that Sam has not truly been saved. She wants to be with him and their baby in the Hereafter.

Aunt Mandy tells Mattie that sometimes dying people receive signs, hear celestial choirs, and are converted before they finally expire. Sam, overhearing the conversation, feigns a genuine conversion out of deference to Mattie. This is the first selfless act that Sam has committed, and through it Mattie has the comfort of thinking that he will die in a state of grace.

Interwoven with the Mattie-Sam plot are the Constancia Brandon episodes. Actually this portion of the book has no consistent plot but is rather a series of highly satiric and quite entertaining vignettes about life among fairly well-to-do blacks in Harlem during the 1920's.

In the preface to *One Way to Heaven*, Cullen waggishly states, "Some of the characters in this book are fictitious." Actually, anyone who knows anything about Harlem's salon society of that day can identify many of the people who drift in and out of Constancia's soirees. Langston Hughes writes about many of the same people, using their actual names, in the first volume of his autobiography, *The Big Sea* (1940).

One of the more ironic episodes concerning Constancia occurs when she invites to one of her parties a professor from a Southern state who has published a book entitled *The Menace of the Negro in Our American Society*. She proceeds to have this august man lecture to the assembled guests on the subject of his book. When he has finished, Constancia leads the applause and more or less intimidates her black guests into joining her in this applause.

It is worth noting that Cullen does not report this incident with bitterness or rancor. He sees the irony in it. He reports the event and allows the irony to speak for itself. He lets his readers draw their own conclusions. This detached quality, the sure indication of people secure in their own identities, was a hallmark of Countée Cullen, and a study of his correspondence confirms the fact that he was capable of standing back and observing dispassionately situations such as the one described here. He was also capable of laughing at himself, and this quality carries over significantly into his writing.

In *One Way to Heaven*, Cullen set out to depict the contrast between two socioeconomic levels of Harlem's emerging society during one of the most interesting periods of its development. He succeeds up to a point, although he never manages to merge the two salient and contrasting elements of his book into the unified whole that would have made the novel more artistically sound.

The Characters

Sam Lucas is one of the memorable characters of the black novels of this period. Sam is more amoral than immoral. He lives his life as he thinks he must. He has always been a drifter, perpetrating his confidence schemes upon the innocent and then leaving for more fertile fields. He is dashing and romantic, and his having only one arm makes him a sympathetic figure to many of the people of whom he is trying to take advantage. Cullen's description of his going down the aisle of the church to be converted with the left sleeve of his coat hanging empty beside him indicates how Sam can turn any adversity into something of personal benefit.

Mattie Johnson is in many ways Sam's opposite. Mattie knows what she believes and is resolute in her beliefs. She is human enough, however, to be swayed emotionally by the kind of display that Sam puts on during his conversion in the Mt. Hebron Episcopal Church. One must remember that Sam swayed eight other unredeemed souls besides Mattie, so his was a virtuoso performance.

Mattie is simple but not stupid. Although she falls in love with Sam at first sight, she is resolute in her love for him. She not only stays with him until the end, but she also touches him in such a way that because of her he does the most noble thing of his life in order to bring her a modicum of comfort before he dies.

Despite Sam's dalliance with Emma and despite Mattie's deep sorrow at the loss of their child, Mattie considers herself to be Sam's wife for all time. Mattie's simple faith and her ability to accept life's realities make her an appealing and highly sympathetic character in the novel.

Aunt Mandy, a wise old woman with definite opinions, is important to the resolution of the conflict between Mattie and Sam. Aunt Mandy's religious beliefs are partly those of her pagan African forebears and partly those of the Christian society in which she has been reared. This old woman is essentially kind. Although she blames Mattie quite falsely for the breakup of her marriage, she is supportive of Mattie and does everything she can to help her. She also precipitates Sam's last phony conversion, indeed his best conversion, by telling Mattie that sometimes unsaved souls on their deathbeds receive signs and come to true salvation at the last moment.

Mattie's employer, Constancia, is an interesting type. She chooses to live her life in the black world rather than in the white world in which she could easily pass. She considers the black world more interesting and vital than the white world. Constancia is at times pompous and is given to using overblown language with rather comic results.

Nevertheless, she is a reasonably bright woman and she is well-meaning. She is more stereotyped than is a character such as Mattie, but she serves well Cullen's artistic purpose of being a center of activity, a source of energy that Cullen needs to depict the social frenzy of middle-class blacks caught up in the Harlem Renaissance.

Themes and Meanings

One Way to Heaven is a study in contrasts. On an obvious level, Cullen is comparing the life of poor blacks in Harlem during the 1920's with that of affluent blacks. The comparison is sharp and effective, despite the author's failure to merge his two distinct story lines in such a way as to achieve a unified novel.

On another level, the love story of Mattie and Sam is one of sharp contrasts. Sam is the scheming, opportunistic gambler, the wanderer who deplores settling down, who feels trapped in the routine of what most people would call a normal existence— having a steady job, marrying, having children. Sam is not basically a bad person. Rather he is a person who lives from day to day and who has been accustomed to living only for himself.

Mattie, conversely, wants to have a normal life. She wants to be a wife and mother. She is capable of devotion to another person and she is willing to give of herself. So devoted and dependable is she that she is willing to forgive Sam for leaving her and going to live with Emma May when Mattie most needed him.

If Cullen does not draw many conclusions about his first contrastive theme, the socioeconomic one, he certainly seems in the second theme to leave the reader with the idea that love not only will triumph but also will ennoble one. Sam dies ennobled because, at the very end of his life, he has finally recognized the depth of Mattie's devotion. Yet, more important, through doing so, he has come to realize that he stands to gain satisfaction from doing something that will give Mattie peace of mind.

Critical Context

The period that Cullen depicts in *One Way to Heaven*, the 1920's, was one of immense social and artistic activity in Harlem. Black journals such as *Quill*, *Stylus*, and *Black Opals* sprang up, although, as is often the case with small literary magazines, few lasted for long. Such major black publications as *Opportunity*, *Messenger*, and *The Crisis* published the best black writers of the period.

As noted above, Langston Hughes chronicled the social life of this period in the first volume of his autobiography, *The Big Sea*. Earlier, Hughes—like Cullen, essentially a poet—wrote his only novel, *Not Without Laughter* (1930), as a means of capturing some of the excitement and electricity of the Harlem Renaissance. In his character Tempy, Hughes satirizes the black social climber of the period who forsakes the Baptist Church and becomes an Episcopalian in order to gain a social advantage.

Claude McKay's *Home to Harlem* (1928), *Banjo* (1929), and *Banana Bottom* (1933) also focused on the social changes occurring in Harlem during its renaissance, and Rudolph Fisher's *The Walls of Jericho* (1928) provided readers with uproariously comic satire about the social climbers of the period. George S. Schuyler's *Black No*

More (1931) and *Slaves Today: A Story of Liberia* (1931) were also important social satires of the period.

The main distinguishing characteristics of Cullen's only novel are that its author was writing more for a black audience than his contemporaries were and that in it he dwelt less on the social and economic indignities of black people than he did on some of their social institutions, such as the Church. Cullen is never bitter in his depictions. He treats his raw material with curiosity and love more than with antagonism and anger.

Bibliography
Draper, James P., ed. *Black Literature Criticism*. 3 vols. Detroit: Gale Research, 1992. Includes an extensive biographical profile of Cullen and excerpts from criticism on his works.
Ferguson, Blanche. *Countée Cullen and the Negro Renaissance*. New York: Dodd, Mead: 1966. A profile of Cullen in context of the Harlem Renaissance.
Perry, Margaret. *A Bio-Bibliography of Countée P. Cullen, 1903-1946*. Westport, Conn.: Greenwood Press, 1971. A comprehensive bibliography of primary and secondary writings by and about Cullen.
Shucard, Alan R. *Countée Cullen*. Boston: Twayne, 1984. Shucard provides a critical and interpretive study of Cullen with a close reading of his major works, a solid bibliography, and complete notes and references.

R. Baird Shuman

OPERATION SHYLOCK
A Confession

Author: Philip Roth (1933-   )
Type of plot: Novel of ideas
Time of plot: 1988
Locale: The United States and Israel
First published: 1993

Principal characters:

    PHILIP ROTH, the author, who dominates the book as a character and relates its events in the first person

    MOISHE PIPIK ("Moses Bellybutton"), the narrator's double

    GEORGE ZIAD, a college friend of Roth who has become an anti-Israeli Palestinian

    JINX POSSESSKI, Moishe Pipik's voluptuous girlfriend

    AHARON APPELFELD, an Israeli novelist who is Roth's friend

    SMILESBURGER, an undercover agent employed by Israel's secret service

    JOHN DEMJANJUK, a Cleveland auto worker on trial for allegedly having been a monstrous death-camp guard

The Novel

Operation Shylock is Philip Roth's most complex, convoluted and baffling novel, in which he uses the device of the literary double to parallel his identity and history in the text's two leading personages. He thereby causes the reader to ponder the provocative and probably insoluble conundrums of fiction's relation to reality and of autobiography's role in the working of the literary imagination.

Not only does the protagonist-narrator appear under the name, personal history, and likeness of the author as Philip Roth, but from the book's opening chapter, another man obtrudes with the same name and in the same likeness, with the same gestures and in identical attire. The narrator, Philip, decides to name his double Moishe Pipik, Yiddish for Moses Bellybutton, a comical shadow and fall guy in Jewish folklore.

Philip is recovering, in his Connecticut home, from withdrawal symptoms after having discontinued taking pills to overcome severe pain resulting from knee surgery. In January, 1988, seven months after coming off the drug, he is informed, by a friend, the Israeli writer Aharon Appelfeld, that a Philip Roth is lecturing in Jerusalem's King David hotel on the topic, "Diasporism: The Only Solution to the Jewish Problem."

Philip phones his impostor, pretending to be a French journalist, and receives a long-distance lecture on Diasporism: It is Pipik's plan to move all Jews of European descent out of Israel and back to their ancestral countries in the hope of averting a second, Arab-organized Holocaust. Israel, Pipik insists, has become the gravest of threats to Jewish survival because of the Arabs' resentment of Israel's expansion. Were European Jews and their families resettled in the lands of their cultural origins, however, only Jews of Islamic descent would be left in Israel. The nation could then revert to its 1948 borders and could demobilize its large army, and Arabs and Israelis would coexist amicably and peacefully.

Philip objects that Pipik's proposal is wholly naïve, since Europe's hatred of Jews persists. Pipik responds that Europe's residual anti-Semitism is outweighed by powerful currents of enlightenment and morality sustained by the memory of the Holocaust. Hence, a Diasporist movement would enable Europeans to cleanse their guilty consciences. Philip's most caustic rebuttal to Pipik's argument occurs later in the book:

> When the first hundred thousand Diasporist evacuees voluntarily surrender their criminal Zionist homeland to the suffering Palestinians and disembark on England's green and pleasant land, I want to see with my very own eyes the welcoming committee of English goyim waiting on the platform with their champagne. 'They're here! More Jews! Jolly good!' No, *fewer* Jews is my sense of how Europe prefers things, *as few of them as possible.*

Flying to Jerusalem, Philip begins a searching interview, to be continued on several occasions in the book, with the distinguished Appelfeld, a Holocaust survivor whom he admires as a spiritual brother to his better self. (This interview was published by *The New York Times* in February, 1988.) He then attends the trial of John Ivan Demjanjuk, the Ukrainian-born auto worker accused of being the monstrous guard "Ivan the Terrible" Marchenko at the Treblinka death camp. (Israel's Supreme Court declared Demjanjuk's identity as Marchenko unproven five months after publication of the novel.)

Roth then comes face to face with his *Doppelgänger*, shocked to find him dressed in his own preferred outfit of blue Oxford shirt, khaki trousers, V-neck sweater, and herringbone jacket. The perfection of Pipik's duplication infuriates the original, whose charge of personality appropriation meets a rush of fawning verbosity, with Pipik assuring Philip that he is his greatest admirer. Philip's response to this bizarre doubling is a mixture of outrage, exasperation, fascination, and even amusement.

Hours later, Pipik sends Philip a pleading note: "LET ME EXIST. . . . I AM THE YOU THAT IS NOT WORDS." Its bearer is a wondrously voluptuous, mid-thirties blonde, Wanda Jane "Jinx" Possesski, an oncology nurse who has become Pipik's loving companion. In due time, Jinx delivers her life story: hateful, strictly Catholic parents, then a runaway hippie life, abusive men, Christian fundamentalism, a nursing career. She became an anti-Semite out of envy of Jewish cohesion, cleverness, sexual ease, and prosperity. Then she met Pipik as a patient for cancer, now in remission. Thanks to him, she is a recovering anti-Semite, saved by an organization he founded, Anti-Semites Anonymous. When Jinx reveals that Pipik had a penile implant so he could satisfy her, Philip cannot resist the temptation to outdo his double by implanting his unassisted virility on Jinx.

Pipik and Jinx leave Israel and end up in Roth's Hackensack, New Jersey, where Pipik expires of his cancer hours after the first Iraqi missiles explode in Tel Aviv in

January, 1991. In the hope of resuscitating him, Jinx makes love for two days to his penile implant. She relates these events in a letter to Philip that concludes with the defiant comment, "I was far nuttier as a little Catholic taking Communion than having sex with my dead Jew." In his reply, Philip disciplines his senses enough to renounce the opportunity of repossessing Possesski. His letter to Jinx remains unanswered.

The Characters

Philip Roth's career as a novelist has long featured the self-revealing and self-reflexive concerns that pervade *Operation Shylock*. He has repeatedly invented avatars of himself in his protagonists, straddling the borderline between fiction and autobiography; after all, this novel is subtitled "A Confession." In the first chapter, Philip, after having been informed of Pipik's impersonation, muses, "It's Zuckerman, I thought . . . it's Kepesh, it's Tarnopol and Portnoy—it's all of them in one, broken free of print and mockingly reconstituted as a single satirical facsimile of me."

Alexander Portnoy is the protagonist of Roth's most popular novel, *Portnoy's Complaint* (1969). Peter Tarnopol is the central character in *My Life as a Man* (1974). David Alan Kepesh is the Kafkaesque victim of *The Breast* (1972). Nathan Zuckerman, Roth's most identifiable surrogate, stars in *Zuckerman Bound* (1985), which brings together three sequential novels, *The Ghost Writer* (1979), *Zuckerman Unbound* (1981), and *The Anatomy Lesson* (1983). Zuckerman is virtually a Rothian clone, author of a successful, controversial novel, *Carnovsky*, that closely resembles *Portnoy's Complaint*. This tetralogy is probably Roth's most varied, thoughtful, playful, and altogether best fictive performance.

"Philip Roth" as the protagonist of *Operation Shylock* is far more aggressive than Nathan Zuckerman. Roth the novelist has created in this Philip his most vivid character: fiercely comic, exuberant, stubbornly reasonable, and, on occasion, unreasonably stubborn. Above all, Philip is immensely curious, about others as well as himself.

Philip's impostor, Moishe Pipik, is a brilliant mimic or an authentic refraction of the narrator; he is also a liar, a charlatan, a wild obsessive, and an extravagant megalomaniac. To be sure, Pipik belongs to the literary tradition of the double, but Roth insists on making Moishe's relation to fictional self-reflexivity more prominent than any grand psychological resonance. The author construes the double not as the embodiment of the hidden self but rather as the far less threatening reinvention of the self for fictive purposes.

Roth features two other characterizations. One is that of an old friend of Philip from his University of Chicago days, George Ziad, who has become an official of the Palestine Liberation Organization (PLO) after having returned to his native Ramallah. Ziad calls himself "a word-throwing Arab," full of distress and anger at Israeli occupation of Palestine. He sees the current Israel as an arrogant, provincial, mediocre Jewish Belgium, "without even a Brussels to show for it." He characterizes Israeli politicians Menachem Begin and Ariel Sharon as Holocaust-mongers and gangsters. Philip is astounded to see the formerly suave, debonair Ziad a victim of his consuming rages, spluttering anti-Israeli harangues.

As an emblematic contrast, Roth features an Israeli secret agent, Smilesburger, a smooth-talking father figure who mixes ruthlessness with tact, pragmatism with wisdom. He persuades Philip to undertake a spying mission, "Operation Shylock"—presumably against the PLO—in Athens. Then, in the book's postscript, Smilesburger persuades a reluctant Philip to delete, for security reasons, a book chapter describing the espionage. "Let your Jewish conscience by your guide" is the epilogue's last line.

Gradations of humor tint the characterizations, including farce, burlesque, parody, and lampoonery. Roth stages a verbal vaudeville, with the characters often talking heads attached to frenzied monologues and excessively melodramatic, zany gestures. Thus, Jinx Possesski is a comic-book version of Jewish masturbatory fantasies centering around a delectable and available shiksa. Smilesburger is a tongue-in-cheek salute to John le Carré's fictional master spy Smiley. Pipik is ludicrous as well as deranged. In a bedroom conversation with Jinx, Philip expresses his sense of being trapped in a farce: "It's *Hellzapoppin'* with Possesski and Pipik, it's a gag a minute with you two madcap kids. . . . Diasporism is a plot for a Marx Brothers movie—Groucho selling Jews to Chancellor Kohl!"

Themes and Meanings

Operation Shylock is a very Jewish version of the use of the literary double. Roth establishes this theme in his two prefatory mottoes. The first translates Genesis 32:24: "So Jacob was left alone, and a man wrestled with him until daybreak." Roth suggests that the first split self in literature may have been the mysterious stranger, possibly the Angel of Death, who represents the fate Jacob fears at the hands of his vengeful brother, Esau. Could Pipik be an Esau, threatening Jacob-Philip?

The second epigraph is from Søren Kierkegaard:

> The whole content of my being shrieks
> in contradiction against itself.
> Existence is surely a debate. . . .

"Against itself" is Roth's evaluation of his nature, his art, possibly his life. For this is a confessional and self-reflexive novel, pointedly exposing Roth's own history and the text's structure as fictive artifice. Like his Philip, Roth is a brainy, funny, self-consciously Jewish writer with affectionate memories of his boyhood in Newark, New Jersey, with a wife whose first name is Claire (the British actress Claire Bloom), with a farmhouse home in Connecticut, and with Appelfeld his good friend. Like his Philip, Roth attended John Demjanjuk's trial. As he states in a final note, he used verbatim the minutes of one of the morning sessions to provide the courtroom exchanges in his ninth chapter. Thus Roth is not only preoccupied in this book with such issues as the course of Israel's evolution, the grievances of displaced Palestinians, and Jewish self-affirmation in opposition to a resurgence of anti-Semitism. He is, above all, pre-occupied by himself.

Roth's first-person voice goes back to the youngest of his twenty books, *Goodbye, Columbus* (1959), and has informed almost all of them. He parades the fact that a writer's life is his basic instrument of perception, possessing an authenticity and intimacy that can convey reader acceptance and conviction. He construes the double as the reinvention of the self for the purpose of fiction. Yet which self? The novel is one contentious self-on-self wrestling match. There is Philip, who is flattered by George Ziad as a model non-Israeli Jew, by Israeli students as an eminent, oracular author, by Jinx as a great lover and leader, by Smilesburger as both an outstanding writer and brilliant spy. Yet there is also Pipik, his Dostoyevskian *Doppelgänger*, zealous, paranoid, pathetic, both idealistic and mad. Then there is the manic part of Philip, or Roth himself, which has him impersonate Moishe and his Diasporist dementia as he plays at being Pipik for a credulous Ziad. "You just say everything," Philip tells himself, as he mockingly compliments Irving Berlin for having turned both Christmas and Easter into nonreligious, schlocky occasions with his songs. "We have been intertwined for decades in a thousand different ways," Pipik assures Philip. So, of course, have been the identities of John Demjanjuk and Ivan Marchenko. Moral ambiguity oozes through the book.

Critical Context

Operation Shylock is vulnerable, despite its wit, learning, intelligence, and eloquence, to the charges of hostile critics that Roth is trapped in narcissistic, sermonridden reveries whose tone is overly argumentative and whose vision is enslaved to his personal experiences and obsessions. In his defense, Roth could cite the long-established tradition of introspective writing originated by such classics of Romanticism as Jean-Jacques Rousseau's *Les Confessions de J.-J. Rousseau* (1782, 1789; *The Confessions of J.-J. Rousseau*, 1783-1790) and William Wordsworth's *The Prelude: Or, The Growth of a Poet's Mind* (1850). One direct influence on Roth's autobiographical texts is surely Fyodor Dostoevski's *Notes from the Underground* (1864), the first-person narrator of which resembles his creator in temperament and history yet remains a creature of fiction. A century later, Albert Camus used the same searingly subjective device in *La Chute* (1956; *The Fall*, 1957).

In less direct form, many of modernism's greatest novels and stories by such writers as Thomas Mann, Franz Kafka, and James Joyce present material from the author's life. Many others, including Dostyevski, Kafka, E. T. A. Hoffmann, Edgar Allan Poe, Nikolai Gogol, Joseph Conrad, Robert Louis Stevenson, and Vladimir Nabokov, have employed the literary device of the double.

Operation Shylock is thus both postmodern in its uses of self-consciousness and traditional in its exploration of the divided self. It is a masterful accomplishment by one of America's most important writers.

Bibliography

Bloom, Harold. "Operation Roth." *The New York Review of Books* 40 (April 22, 1993): 45-48. Bloom, Sterling Professor of the Humanities at Yale, has long admired Roth's writing. He particularly praises the novel's narrative exuberance, moral intelligence, and high humor.

Ezrahi, Sidra DeKoven, et al. "Philip Roth's Diasporism: A Symposium." *Tikkun* 8 (May/June, 1993): 41-45. Several writers express their views about the concept of diaspora in Roth's *Operation Shylock*. An in-depth and wide-ranging look at the novel.

Furman, Andrew. "A New 'Other' in American Jewish Literature: Philip Roth's Israel Fiction." *Contemporary Literature* 36 (Winter, 1995): 633-653. Focuses on the theme that centers on Israel and projects the concept of the 'Other' on the Arab. Although it seems that Roth has escaped the current literary trend of demonizing the Arab, Furman demonstrates that a close textual reading of *The Counterlife* and *Operation Shylock* reveals that the theme is reiterated in both works.

Halkin, Hillel. "How to Read Philip Roth." *Commentary* 97 (February, 1994): 43-48. Although some critics maintain that Roth is steering away from themes of Judaism, Halkin argues that Roth's later works are dominated by Jewish themes. Halkin presents several critical analyses of Roth's books, including *Operation Shylock.*

Safer, Elaine B. "The Double, Comic Irony, and Postmodernism in Philip Roth's *Operation Shylock. MELUS* 21 (Winter, 1996): 157-172. Safer asserts that the humor in Roth's novel revolves around the ironic use of doubles and a postmodernist blurring of the boundaries between fact and fiction.

Updike, John. "Recruiting Raw Nerves." *The New Yorker* 69 (March 15, 1993): 109-112. As a novelist, Updike is in many ways Roth's opposite: coolly disciplined, WASPish, never boisterous. Yet he is an astute and generous critic, and his review praises Roth highly for his evocative style and ingenious plotting. Updike, however, does complain that the book has too many long monologues and that Roth is "an exhausting author to be with."

Gerhard Brand

THE OPTIMIST'S DAUGHTER

Author: Eudora Welty (1909-   )
Type of plot: Domestic realism
Time of plot: The early 1960's
Locale: New Orleans and the fictional town of "Mount Salus," Mississippi
First published: 1969; enlarged, 1972

> *Principal characters:*
> LAUREL MCKELVA HAND, a widow in her mid-forties and a successful fabric designer living in Chicago
> JUDGE CLINTON MCKELVA, her father, who is retired from the bench in Mount Salus, Mississippi
> WANDA FAY CHISOM MCKELVA, the judge's second wife, a vulgar, insensitive, gold-digging refugee from a typing pool
> MAJOR RUPERT BULLOCK, a friend of the judge since boyhood
> MISS ADELE COURTLAND, a Mount Salus schoolteacher and the McKelvas' next-door neighbor

The Novel

"Is it the Carnival?" asks Fay, as she and Laurel ride through New Orleans in a taxi. It is Mardi Gras, though hardly a festive occasion: The two have just left a hospital where, less than an hour earlier, they witnessed the death of Judge McKelva, Fay's husband and Laurel's father.

Fay's incongruous question typifies the uncomprehending, inadequate, and inappropriate responses to life by many characters in *The Optimist's Daughter*. The world of these characters is a microcosm of the larger world glimpsed through carnival-week New Orleans, where Laurel can hear "the crowd noise, the unmistakable sound of hundreds, of thousands, of people *blundering*." To Laurel, all of them, especially Fay and her Snopesian kinfolk, are part of "the great, interrelated family of those who never know the meaning of what has happened to them."

Despite its characters' bafflement, the novel tells a simple story. Laurel temporarily leaves her Chicago studio to be at home with her father after he mentions casually that he is consulting the family doctor for an eye problem. Together, he, Laurel, and Fay—his new wife after ten years as a widower—travel to New Orleans, where they learn that he needs surgery for a torn retina. Fay quickly reveals her selfishness by exclaiming, "I don't see why this had to happen to *me*."

Though the operation is a success, Fay lacks the patience to wait out her husband's convalescence. Angry and uncomprehending, she tries to goad him into leaving his sickbed to take her to the Carnival. One night she throws herself on his body—immobilized on doctor's orders—crying, "I tell you enough is enough! This is my birthday!" Shocked by Fay's insensitive, and impossible demands, his concentration on recovery shattered, Judge McKelva gives up the ghost.

Laurel and Fay return with his body to the family home in Mount Salus, Mississippi. The townsfolk crowd into the house to mourn this revered public figure and pay respects to his daughter, whom they have known since her birth. (His upstart wife is barely tolerated by many who honor the memory of Laurel's mother, Becky.) Yet as they swap contradictory anecdotes about the judge, Laurel realizes that no two of them perceive her father alike, and none remembers him accurately.

Like New Orleans at Mardi Gras, Mount Salus becomes a stage where farce vies with tragedy. Fay indulges in self-pitying histrionics; some townspeople pointedly snub one another despite the sad occasion; Fay's vulgar relatives descend on the house to chat over the corpse: "Out of curiosity, who does he remind you of?" the mother asks her father-in-law. "Nobody," he replies.

These present absurdities contrast painfully with Laurel's memory of an idyllic childhood, of a rich inner life under the tutelage of loving, sensitive parents. Yet Laurel's past also involves the recollection of her mother's agonizing death and the recognition that Becky, in her own way, had made as many unreasoning demands on the judge as had Fay. Laurel realizes suddenly that, like the "blunderers" of the story, she has yet to understand fully what has happened in her life.

Resolution comes after a final confrontation with Fay, whom Laurel holds responsible for her father's death. As the judge's second wife and the heiress to the McKelva home, Fay is in some sense a rival for possession of Laurel's own past. Yet Laurel, having barely restrained an impulse to do Fay violence, attains peace once she understands that "Memory lived not in initial possession but in the freed hands, pardoned and freed, and in the heart that can empty but fill again, in the patterns restored by dreams." Laurel is free to return to the life she has made for herself in Chicago.

The Characters

A key to understanding many of Eudora Welty's characters is the use that they make of their past. Those who distort their memories, or who fail to remember experience at all, are in no position to learn from it, but, to be remembered, experience has to mean something. Fay has no guiding principle for her present actions because she attaches no significance to the past—either her own or Judge McKelva's. So she "blunders."

"Blundering" in a major character such as Fay represents a major evil; in minor characters, Welty renders it comically. Among a handful of Mount Salus eccentrics at Judge McKelva's wake is Verna Longmeier, the sewing lady, who recounts memories of Christmas dances that never happened:

> I remember, oh, I remember how many Christmases I was among those present in this dear old home in all its hospitality. . . . And they'd throw open those doors between these double parlors and the music would strike up! And then—"Miss Verna drew out her arm as though to measure a yard—" then Clinton and I, we'd lead out the dance.

Yet this novel is Laurel's story. She is the title character—her father being the "Optimist"—and the book chronicles her struggle to comprehend the spiritual legacy of her parents. If she is unveiled slowly—the early chapters barely hint at her troubled soul—it is because at first she has no time to remember that legacy. While the focus is on her father's illness and death, Laurel appears the most stable figure, standing watch, reading to him by the hour, asking (as Fay does not) the responsible questions of the doctor. Only when these exigencies are past, and her moment of truth can no longer be postponed, is she revealed in her loneliness and conflict.

In contrast to Laurel, Fay is fully revealed from the first time she speaks. Implicitly, therefore, she lacks all depth; it takes but a moment to sound her. Since the world of the novel is seen primarily through Laurel's eyes, and since Laurel cannot be generous to Fay, some critics have asked if the portrayal of Fay is not excessively hostile. Indeed, she is shown from first to last as a mean-spirited, greedy, unfeeling little shrew; for Welty, this is rather a flat characterization. Yet Fay is less a foil than a catalyst: It takes someone with her extreme traits to jar Laurel out of her false recollections of the relationship between her parents. It was her father the "Optimist" who married both Becky and Fay, and not one wife, but both wives wore him down.

Moreover, Welty introduces another viewpoint than Laurel's to humanize Fay. It is the viewpoint of Miss Adele Courtland, the McKelvas' next-door neighbor—who, it is hinted, would have made a suitable and willing second wife for the judge. In her wisdom born of denial, she defends Fay against judgment by Laurel's standards. Concerning the antics of Fay and her family at the wake, Adele says, "It's true they were a trifle more inelegant [than the Mount Salus gentry]. . . . But only a trifle." Attempting to explain Fay's seemingly tasteless show of grief, Adele says, "I further believe Fay thought she was rising in the estimation of Mount Salus, there in front of all [Clinton's] lifelong friends . . . on what she thought was the prime occasion for doing it."

Class consciousness, though never explicitly identified, figures prominently in the thoughts of many characters in *The Optimist's Daughter*. (Memory forms the basis of upper-class tradition, while the lower classes are thought of as having no past). Yet Mount Salus aristocrats show a curious lack of breeding. They ignore Fay, the low-class Texan, as far as possible without offending her doting husband. His doctor "looked at her briefly, as if he had seen many like Fay." Death, however, is the great leveler: The ever-tippling Major Rupert Bullock, a lifelong friend of the judge, talks like one of Fay's vulgar family members when he tries to console her. As they stand over the coffin, he says, "Just tell him goodbye, sugar. . . . That's best, just plant him a kiss."

Themes and Meanings

Recurrent in Welty's fiction, including *The Optimist's Daughter*, is the paradox of the family as both nurturing and stifling. Despite their powerful mutual affection, Laurel—and, in her memory, Becky and Clinton—emerge as lonely figures, each thrown back on his or her waning strength when disaster strikes. Apparently, love has no power to prevent human tragedy; and, when they cannot help or be helped by those whom they love, they become cruel—not always unwittingly.

The characters change, then, in reaction to events that they cannot control. It was during Becky's final illness, and in response to a hateful outburst from her, that Judge McKelva became "what he scowlingly called an optimist; . . . refused to consider that she was desperate. It was betrayal on betrayal." If the memory of such events can wound Laurel, the reviving memory of happier times can heal her. "Memory had the character of spring. Sometimes it was the old wood that did the blooming."

Ultimately, it is suggested that the barriers imposed by time and change are illusory. On her last night in Mount Salus, Laurel dreams about riding in a train with her long-dead husband, Phil, past the confluence of the Ohio and Mississippi rivers near Cairo, Illinois. Waking, she understands that

> . . . her life, any life . . . was nothing but the continuity of its love. She believed it just as she believed that the confluence of waters was still happening at Cairo. It would be there the same as it ever was when she went flying over it today on her way back—out of sight, for her, this time, thousands of feet below, but with nothing in between except thin air.

Laurel also perceives that she and Phil "were part of the confluence. Their own act of faith had brought them here . . ." Evil, for Laurel (and for Welty), consists in refusing to acknowledge the universal human experience, denying the power of memory and faith to transcend the accidents of time and place. The final moral perception regarding Fay is that, lacking passion and imagination of her own, she "had no way to see it or reach it in the other person. Other people, inside their lives, might as well be invisible to her." Fay and the rest of the "blunderers" are not simply victims of a gratuitously hostile portrait; like Malvolio at the end of *Twelfth Night*, they impose isolation on themselves and project it onto others.

Critical Context

Eudora Welty's works have attracted a faithful, though seldom numerous, following. *The Optimist's Daughter*, first published in *The New Yorker*, did command a wide readership; it also brought its author critical acclaim and a Pulitzer Prize. The much-honored Welty also has received the National Institute of Arts and Letters Gold Medal for the Novel, as well as the National Medal for Literature for lifetime achievement.

Since the beginning of her career, Welty has explored such universally compelling subjects as marriage and family, social and class morality, the sense of community versus the sense of aloneness—and the variety of possible attitudes toward memory. For example, the inability to draw moral lessons from remembered experience is shown to be a great affliction in *The Ponder Heart* (1954) just as it is in *The Optimist's Daughter*. Yet unlike Welty's previous novel, *Losing Battles* (1970)—a long and convoluted exploration of the past— *The Optimist's Daughter* is a brief, intense treatment of past events recollected in the present.

What most sets this novel apart from Welty's other fiction, however, is a clear sense of its main character's liberation—first from rural life without a profession, and then from the power of unhappy and confusing memories. *The Optimist's Daughter* is also outstanding for its artistic unity; it is a work that reveals, rather than simply describing, the truths it contains.

Bibliography

Champion, Laurie, ed. *The Critical Response to Eudora Welty's Fiction.* Westport, Conn.: Greenwood Press, 1994. In her introduction, Champion presents an overview of the criticism on Welty's fiction. Five separate essays by different scholars are devoted to various aspects of *The Optimist's Daughter.* Includes a helpful bibliography of works for further reading.

Fuller, Danielle. "'Making a Scene': Some Thoughts on Female Sexuality and Marriage in Eudora Welty's *Delta Wedding* and *The Optimist's Daughter.*" *The Mississippi Quarterly* 48 (Spring, 1995): 291-318. A study of how Welty's female characters express their sexuality. Fuller looks at two of Welty's novels and shows how Welty portrays female sexuality in relation to a woman's quest for individuality.

Gretlund, Jan N., and Karl-Heinz Westarp, eds. *The Late Novels of Eudora Welty.* Columbia: University of South Carolina Press, 1998. An excellent collection of essays on Welty's later fiction. Essays on *The Optimist's Daughter* cover the function of region, time, and memory in the novel; the use of narrative strategies; and the autobiographical characteristics of the book.

Mortimer, G. L. "Image and Myth in Eudora Welty's *The Optimist's Daughter.*" *American Literature* 62 (December, 1990): 617-633. Mortimer explores the ways in which Welty builds an intricate network of meanings using images, including exploiting the ambiguity of etymological meanings; pairing of the images themselves; and referring to various mythic substructures.

Welty, Eudora. "Some Talk About Autobiography: An Interview with Eudora Welty." *Southern Review* 26 (Winter, 1990): 81-87. Welty shares information concerning her background and family life. She discusses the biographical aspects of *The Optimist's Daughter,* revealing which characters were drawn from life and which were mainly imaginary.

Thomas Rankin

THE ORPHAN ANGEL

Author: Elinor Wylie (1885-1928)
Type of plot: Historical romance
Time of plot: July 8, 1822, to May, 1823
Locale: Italy, the Atlantic Ocean, and North America
First published: 1926; issued in Great Britain as *Mortal Image*, 1927

> *Principal characters:*
> > SHILOH, the fictional counterpart of the romantic poet Percy Bysshe
> > Shelley
> > DAVID BUTTERNUT, a young sailor from Maine

The Novel

 The Orphan Angel combines elements of the historical romance and picaresque novel by bringing back to life, on the day he died, the Romantic poet Percy Bysshe Shelley and setting him on a quest across the United States to rescue a young woman.

 The novel is divided into ten chapters, each of which is titled with a quotation from Shelley. The first chapter, "Western Wave," pairs the Shelley character, named Shiloh, with David Butternut, a young, kind, but unsophisticated New England sailor. This chapter recounts the fantastic premise on which the historical romance is built. David Butternut, after killing a fellow sailor—in a fashion reminiscent of Herman Melville's *Billy Budd*—rescues a man from drowning in Italy's Leghorn Harbor. The young man is pulled from the shores of Italy at about the same time Shelley is said to have drowned, about 6:30 P.M. on July 8, 1822. Butternut believes that the rescue of the man, who resembles Jasper Cross, the scoundrel sailor he accidentally killed, atones for his own crime, and he vows to become the man's loyal friend. Butternut, who would not have heard of the poet Shelley, mishears his name and calls him Shiloh (a nickname the Romantic poet George Gordon, Lord Byron, gave to Shelley). Shelley accepts the new identity and sails to Boston on the New England clipper ship *Witch of the West* in place of the dead Jasper Cross.

 The picaresque element of the novel is established in chapter 2, set in Boston. Butternut and Shiloh decide to search for Jasper's twin sister Silver. They assume that Silver needs their help because she is a poor orphan living somewhere in frontier America. Butternut goes to ease his conscience over killing Jasper, while Shiloh goes because the pursuit of a young woman in need of his aid appeals to his romantic and humane tendencies.

 The remaining eight chapters follow the pair as they search for Silver, baptized Maria Solidad de Sylva. At first, all they know is that Jasper came from Kentucky, so they begin walking in that direction. As their travels continue, further clues lead them to Louisville, Kentucky; St. Louis, Missouri; and ultimately to San Diego, California. Along the way, they meet various types of Americans and experience adventures befitting life in early nineteenth century America. As the two men travel, with little money and little comfort, strangers occasionally help them with their basic needs of food and sleeping accommodations or with information about Silver. Despite his haggard condition, Shiloh's nobility of spirit is immediately apparent to all. Every young woman—and some not so young—falls in love with him at first sight. Shiloh's spiritual qualities contrast with David's more practical qualities. Throughout the journey, Shiloh is true to the character of Shelley. Shelley's eating habits and mannerisms are mimicked in Shiloh. Shelley's dismissal from Oxford University, his atheism, and his problems associated with his family, all are alluded to in the novel.

David and Shiloh are ultimately rewarded for their trek across frontier America. David has gone to Silver to apologize for the accidental death of her brother and to promise to be her friend and protector; Shiloh, meanwhile, walks at dawn to the summit of a cliff near the sea and thinks of lines from Shelley's poem "To Jane, The Recollection" (1822). Shiloh, his quest complete, returns to poetry.

The Characters

As is typical of picaresque fiction, the characters in *The Orphan Angel* are static. Most of the characters play brief roles as they encounter Shiloh and Butternut on their trek across North America. Most are stock characters, playing types to complicate or further the adventures of the two heroes. Two characters, Captain Ffoulkastle and Captain Appleby, consider the likelihood that Shiloh is actually the poet Shelley. Captain Ffoulkastle doubts it, although presumably Shiloh tells him as much in order to explain the ties he has in Italy—a wife and children; Captain Appleby surmises that Shiloh is Shelley based upon his knowledge of the historical poet's works and philosophies and his own observation of Shiloh and the epithalamium he pens for Professor Lackland as a wedding gift. Both captains play minor roles, but they keep alive the Shiloh/Shelley motif and subtly remind the reader of Butternut's naiveté as he travels with Shiloh and never recognizes his fellow traveler as the famed poet.

Melissa Daingerfield, a fourteen-year-old Virginia daughter; Miss Rosalie Lillie of Louisville, the professor's fiancée; Deborah Bartlett, a young widow living in Kentucky; Anne, an adopted daughter of a Cheyenne chief; and Maria Solidad de Sylva (Silver), the object of the heroes' quest, all play the same role, young women instantly smitten by Shiloh. These five women characters allow Wylie to emphasize the ideal side of Shiloh/Shelley's character, but they also remind the reader of the difficulties the historical Shelley had with young women. As Shiloh finds himself again expected to whisk a young woman away from her Cinderella existence, he reflects on Harriet Westbrook and Mary Godwin, Shelley's two wives, and on Jane Clairmont, Teresa Emilia Viviani, and Jane Williams, other women who interested Shelley.

The two protagonists, David Butternut and Shiloh, act as foils throughout the novel. Both men are young, although Shiloh's being eight years older is significant. Shiloh turns thirty during the action of the novel, and Butternut is twenty-one when the action begins. Both men are kindhearted and loyal to each other, but their differences are abundant. Butternut, the American, represents the new, raw country; he is uncultured and unsophisticated. Shiloh, well-educated and well-traveled, represents the older European culture. Their physical descriptions, mannerisms, philosophies, tastes, and language all contrast, often to comic effect. Butternut urges Shiloh not to speak about poetry in front of the other sailors, recognizing the difference in values and culture between the typical American clipper-ship sailor and the poet. Butternut also urges Shiloh to keep his atheistic views to himself after they accept a ride up a long hill from a deacon. Butternut himself finds Shiloh's distaste for American whiskey puzzling and is surprised by Shiloh's lack of self-consciousness about his effect on young women. Wylie often juxtaposes the language of Butternut and Shiloh to highlight their differences and to mock both characters at once, one using uneducated and the other inflated language.

Themes and Meanings

The Orphan Angel places the idealized figure of Shelley in the midst of raw, democratic America. The spiritual portrait of Shelley and the nineteenth century American landscape are both emphasized by the juxtaposition. The rough American setting adds realism to the novel. Wylie provides details of lifestyle that anchor the narrative in the early days of the country. Geographical details are accurate, and the time it takes for the protagonists to travel from city to city or state to state proves true to the period. The rawness of the land, particularly the large expanse of unsettled areas of the West, appears harsh beside the young Shelley character.

Despite the realistic details of early nineteenth century America and the genuine devotion to the Shelley portrait, Wylie's novel is developed largely through humor. The twin themes of adolescent America and idealized Shelley allow for a playful treatment. With adventures onboard ship, rafting down the Ohio River, crossing the desert, and in Indian territory, Wylie humorously sets frontier experiences and stories next to Shiloh's romantic poetry. With some humor, Wylie brings to life the Shelley she has admired and places him in a locale that, through contrast, reveals the beauty of his character. The aristocratic Shiloh has plenty of opportunity to demonstrate the strength of his character and the depth of his feelings. Paired with Butternut, a perfectly straightforward American youth, kindhearted but limited in his knowledge and experience, Shiloh's characteristics are emphasized.

In large measure, *The Orphan Angel*, Wylie's longest novel, represents her homage to Shelley. The novel celebrates the vastness of the United States and the idealism of Shelley at the same time. She places him in a land as large as she sees his spirit. He walks across the landscape under no one's authority, spiritually free. Shiloh's qualities are shown to be anchored not in the world but on some plane above.

Critical Context

The Orphan Angel, chosen as a Book-of-the-Month Club selection for December, 1926, was published at the height of Elinor Wylie's literary career. Blending the traditions of the historical romance and the picaresque novel, *The Orphan Angel* carries forward traditional genres with the creative premise of resurrecting Shelley in America.

Elinor Wylie throughout her adult life was preoccupied by the Romantic poet Shelley; by the 1920's, when she was writing *The Orphan Angel*, her preoccupation could be considered an obsession. When young, she was drawn to Shelley's poetry. A serious poet herself, Wylie looked to Shelley as a model for herself and to his poetry as a model for her own. Later, Wylie came to see her own life reflected in Shelley's in a more personal way. Both poets experienced censure because of their marital arrangements. Just as Shelley abandoned his first wife Harriet to elope with the young Mary Godwin, Wylie left her young son and husband to live in Europe with a married man, Horace Wylie. In both cases, the poets eventually married the partners with whom they went off, but the difficulties of their personal relationships were always a concern. Both Harriet's and Wylie's first husbands were suicides. For long periods, the poets were estranged from their children. Yet both seemed to believe their actions and love relationships were based on truth and beauty and that, spiritually, their choices were valid. In *The Orphan Angel*, then, Wylie is bringing back to life the poet she idealized and is showing him to be an angelic figure, one committed to truth and beauty. Shelley, not the orphan Silver that David and Shiloh seek, is the "angel" of the title. In reviving Shelley from the water in Italy and bringing him to America, Wylie is situating Shelley in the land of freedom, where his temperament may have a more conducive environment; of course, in traveling the country, it is clear that Shiloh/Shelley runs into just as many, and many of the same kinds of, predicaments that faced him in Europe.

Bibliography
Cluck, Julia. "Elinor Wylie's Shelley Obsession." *PMLA* 56 (September, 1941): 841-860. Outlines the references to Shelley in two of Wylie's novels and in her poetry. The first third of the article details the parallels in appearance, habits, attitudes, personal history, and language between Shiloh in *The Orphan Angel* and Shelley.
Farr, Judith. *The Life and Art of Elinor Wylie*. Baton Rouge: Louisiana State University Press, 1983. Critical analysis of Wylie's poetry and novels placed within the context of her life. See especially chapters 6 and 7 for discussions of Wylie's interest in and of *The Orphan Angel*.
Gray, Thomas A. *Elinor Wylie*. New York: Twayne, 1969. Generally unfavorable critical evaluation of Wylie's poetry and novels. Chapter 5 deals with the novels, including *The Orphan Angel*. Contains a chronology and a bibliography.
Hoyt, Nancy. *Elinor Wylie: The Portrait of an Unknown Lady*. New York: Bobbs-Merrill, 1935. Breezy biography by Wylie's sister, seventeen years Wylie's junior. Contains family photographs and poems from Wylie's first, privately printed, book.
Olson, Stanley. *Elinor Wylie: A Biography*. New York: Dial Press, 1979. Detailed, well-researched biography divided into three sections: Wylie's upbringing and her first marriage in the context of her prominent family (her grandfather was governor of Pennsylvania, and her father was solicitor-general under President Theodore

Roosevelt); her ostracism from Washington society; and her enormous literary output in the 1920's.

Tomalin, Claire. *Shelley and His World*. New York: Scribner's, 1980. Brief biography providing the necessary information about Shelley for a reader to follow the parallels to Shiloh in *The Orphan Angel*. Includes a Shelley chronology, a select bibliography, an index, and numerous illustrations.

Marion Petrillo

THE OTHER SIDE

Author: Mary Gordon (1949-   )
Type of plot: Family
Time of plot: 1895-1985
Locale: New York City and Ireland
First published: 1989

> *Principal characters:*
> ELLEN COSTELLOE MCNAMARA, the matriarch of the McNamara
>   family, who is dying of a stroke
> VINCENT MCNAMARA, Ellen's husband, who is returning home after a
>   ten-month stay in a nursing home
> MAGDALENE MCNAMARA, Ellen and Vincent's oldest daughter, an
>   alcoholic beautician who has not left her room in fifteen years
> THERESA MCNAMARA DOOLEY, the middle child, a medical secretary
>   and religious fanatic
> CAMILLE (CAM) MCNAMARA, Magdalene's only child, a divorce lawyer
> DAN MCNAMARA, Cam's cousin and law partner

The Novel

The Other Side traces an Irish American family, the McNamaras, through five generations, from the "old sod" to "the other side," as the Irish called America. Framed by the events of one day, August 14, 1985, the story spans ninety years, weaving the memories of various family members throughout to tell the tale. The book consists of five sections: The first and last parts introduce the family members and set the scene in the present; the second relates Ellen McNamara's memories of her life; the third explores the lives of second-, third- and fourth-generation McNamaras; and the fourth recounts the past from Vincent's point of view.

The novel opens as Vincent McNamara recalls the night some ten months earlier when his wife Ellen, ninety years old and cruelly debilitated from a series of strokes, rises from her bed and strikes out at him in a senseless rage. She knocks him down, breaking his hip and leaving him helpless as she wanders into the street in her nightclothes. Vincent, who summons help by hurling family heirlooms through the window, spends ten months in a rest home recuperating, while Ellen continues to fluctuate between rage, fear, and sleep under the care of a domineering nurse at home. The story returns to the present as the family gathers to celebrate Vincent's return from the nursing home.

As Ellen drifts closer to death, her memories of the past become stronger than her grip on the present, and she relives her life. Her idyllic existence as the only child of a beautiful mother and handsome, successful father degenerates into a nightmare as her mother is transformed by a series of miscarriages and stillbirths into a fat, gibbering madwoman while her father takes up with another woman. The remainder of Ellen's childhood is spent caring for and concealing her mother, nourishing a profound hatred for her once-beloved father, and plotting her escape to America by stealing from her father's business. Leaving her mother in the care of a hired girl, she arrives in America, taking jobs first as a lady's maid and later as a seamstress. Her anger and resentment are further nourished by servitude and miserable working conditions, and she becomes passionately interested in the union movement and politics. She falls in love with and marries Vincent McNamara and begins her life as wife and mother.

Vincent also escapes a miserable, poverty-stricken childhood in Ireland by emigrating to America. He accepts the first position he is offered, an unspeakably miserable job digging the New York City subway system, although he trained as an ironworker in Ireland. He later works as a signal repairman and machinist and becomes actively involved in union organizing until a heart attack forces him to take up a less stressful occupation and give up union activity.

Ellen and Vincent, although devoted to each other, fail as parents. Ellen dislikes her daughters and lavishes all of her attention on her only son, John. The oldest daughter, Magdalene, marries hastily in search of the affection she missed at home, is widowed early, and becomes an alcoholic, self-imposed invalid, leaving the responsibility of rearing her daughter, Cam, to her parents. Theresa, the second daughter, is cold, judgmental, and filled with hate. She passes her mother's coldness on to her own children. Their son John impregnates a girl and must marry her before going off to be killed in the war. Ellen intimidates her daughter-in-law into leaving the child, Dan, for her and Vincent to rear. It is only with these grandchildren, Dan and Cam, that Ellen is able to provide the maternal love that was withheld from her own children. Dan and Cam grow up much closer than most brothers and sisters, and they are loving toward and protective of their surrogate parents.

As the novel returns to 1985, Cam picks up a reluctant Vincent at the nursing home to return him to care for Ellen and to keep the promise made early in their marriage that she will die in her own bed. Dreading the ties of family obligations and complications after the easy sociability of the nursing home, Vincent nevertheless realizes as he enters the house and sees his wife again that home is where he belongs.

The Characters

Ellen McNamara embodies many of the worst aspects of Irish culture and experience. Although she is bright, opinionated, and outspoken by nature, her childhood taught her concealment, shame, insularity, and anger. She has not adopted the American Dream, the pursuit of happiness: "She'd never believed in happiness. The mention of it put her in a fury." Although a voracious reader, passionately interested in the outside world, she shrinks her own universe to claustrophobic dimensions, allowing none but family and the closest friends inside her home.

Vincent, on the other hand, embodies more positive aspects of the Irish character. Despite a difficult childhood in the old country, plagued by an older brother who hated him and drove him from home, he did not carry anger and bitterness with him to the new world. Although not as sharp and quick as his wife, he is kinder and more decent.

Outgoing and friendly, he finds life at the nursing home refreshingly sociable and relaxed after his intense and confined life with Ellen.

Theresa Dooley is the product of Ellen's coldness and indifference as a mother. A medical secretary and a charismatic Catholic, she poisons everyone around her with bitterness, anger, and jealousy. Believing she is blessed with the power to heal, she spitefully withholds this "gift" from her dying mother. Her children—John, a Vietnam veteran unable to hold a job or a marriage together; Sheila, an unlikeable, self-despising former nun; and Marilyn, with three failed marriages behind her—are heirs to the hatred and bitterness that flow through the family's bloodlines.

Her sister Magdalene has been ruined by this familial poison as well. Pretty and soft, the antithesis of her mother, she has become a professional invalid, a role in which she can both receive sympathy and have control over her surroundings. Equipped with a big-screen television with remote control and bedside microwave oven, she interacts with the world on her terms, gossiping on the phone, entertaining visitors, and perusing her wardrobe in the safety of her room.

The two favored grandchildren, Cam and Dan, have also been poisoned by the family hatreds, jealousies, and feuds, but they fare somewhat better than their parents' generation. They receive the love, attention, and interest that their grandparents withheld from their own children, and they thrive academically and professionally. Both, however, have failed marriages, Dan is divorced, and Cam is married in name only. Dan grieves for the family that might have been and the time lost with his daughters, and although he has lived with a woman for fourteen years, he does not marry again. Cam, a prisoner to her own "good girl" instincts, lives with and cares for her self-pitying "invalid" mother and cannot bring herself to leave the husband she pities but no longer loves. She has finally met a man she loves, but her feelings of duty to her mother, her grandparents, and her husband prevent her from committing herself to him.

Themes and Meanings

In *The Other Side*, Mary Gordon explores the dynamics of Irish American families, examining the characteristics that set the Irish American experience apart from that of other immigrants and their descendants. While visiting Ireland for the first time Dan McNamara thinks of his family that "they could never be happy, any of them, coming from people like the Irish. Unhappiness was bred into the bone, a message in the blood, a code of weakness."

Although they cannot escape their heritage, Ellen and Vincent represent two different reactions to it. Ellen rails against her past and everything connected with it, condemning the church, mocking her husband's fondness for Irish music, and reviling anyone who romanticizes Ireland or the Irish. Vincent, on the other hand, although he came from poverty and a hard family life, has not let hatred poison his life, and he has fond memories of Ireland and the Irish. He has allowed his background to enrich his life in the new land rather than poison it. He has accepted the new, but he has not forgotten nor rejected the old.

The Irish heritage has power over even the third and fourth generations of American McNamaras. Cam and Dan, who visit the "old country" together as adults along with Dan's children, Darci and Staci, have strong reactions to the "old sod." Dan, accepting and forgiving like his grandfather, does not like Ireland. He sees it as a source of anger, hate, and unhappiness, as does his daughter Staci. On the other hand, Cam, who like her grandmother is rigid and unforgiving, feels a strong attachment to the country of her grandparents' birth.

The novel's concerns transcend those of the Irish American family, however; the book addresses the more universal theme of the dynamics of family life. As the experience of several generations of McNamaras illustrates, family cannot escape the ties that bind; everyone in some way is "in bondage" to their family. Ellen never escapes the effects of her miserable childhood, passing them on to her children, who pass them on yet again. The struggle for individuality within the family unit never abates. Cam, feeling duty-bound to her mother, her husband, and her grandparents, cannot be herself. She feels tied to their image of her rather than to her own image of herself. Dan also takes upon himself the burden of putting up a good front and hiding his real emotions for the sake of keeping the family's image of itself alive.

Critical Context

Mary Gordon's work can be placed in three literary traditions: the Catholic novel, the Irish American novel, and the feminist novel. Each of her novels exemplifies at least one, and sometimes more than one, of these genres, but Gordon is most often considered a Catholic novelist. Her first two books, *Final Payments* (1978) and *The Company of Women* (1980), are the most explicitly Catholic of her work, dealing with the protagonists' struggles to reconcile their own spirituality with the traditions and dictums of the church hierarchy. Her third book, *Men and Angels* (1985), can be classified as a religious but not specifically Catholic novel, as the protagonist struggles with her relationship to a fanatical fundamentalist Christian.

Most of Gordon's work can also be seen in feminist terms. Both *Final Payments* and *The Company of Women* feature women not only questioning their relationship with the church hierarchy but also struggling against their dependence upon the strong male figures in their lives. In *Men and Angels*, the protagonist struggles to come to terms with the conflict between her career and her children, and *The Other Side*, while not directly confronting feminist issues, features several strong female characters.

Much of Gordon's work can be placed squarely in the tradition of Irish American fiction, alongside the works of such writers as James T. Farrell, Jimmy Breslin, John O'Hara, John Gregory Dunne, and Edwin O'Connor. *The Other Side*, in particular, concentrates on the Irish component of the Irish Catholic experience in America. Gordon's work conforms to critic James Liddy's characterization of Irish American fiction as "a dramatic, easily accessible story in which men and women with divided loyalties and sensibilities work out their fate." In a controversial 1988 article published in *The New York Times Book Review*, Gordon accounted for what she saw as a shortage of Irish American novelists by discussing the Irish traits of concealment, sexual puritanism, and fear of exposure, traits, she wrote, that contributed to this shortage. Many critics and writers, however, have disagreed with her assessment and have argued for the recognition of a rich tradition of Irish American literature.

Bibliography
Bennet, Alma. *Mary Gordon*. New York: Twayne, 1996. In this first book-length study of Mary Gordon, Bennet draws on personal interviews with Gordon as well as other primary and secondary resources to provide students and scholars with a comprehensive introduction to Gordon's work. Includes excellent resources in chronology, notes and references, bibliography, and index sections.
Cooper-Clark, Diana. "An Interview with Mary Gordon." *Commonweal* 107 (May 9, 1980): 270-273. In this early interview, Gordon discusses *Final Payments* as a Catholic novel and examines the religious novel in general. She considers issues relevant to *The Other Side*, including the Irish Catholic immigrant experience in America. She also reveals her own preferences in literature, her reaction to her critics, and what she likes best about her own work.
Gordon, Mary. Interview by Patrick H. Samway. *America* 170 (May 14, 1994): 12-15. A revealing glimpse of Gordon's childhood, Catholic education, and writing career. Although she does not specifically address *The Other Side*, this illuminating interview sheds considerable light on the major themes in her works.
_____. "Radical Damage: An Interview with Mary Gordon." Interview by M. Deiter Keyishian. *The Literary Review* 32 (Fall, 1988): 69-82. Gordon discusses her collection of short stories *Temporary Shelter* (1987). Commenting on writing about women and children, she asserts that "to write about women and children is to be immediately ghettoized. . . ." She also reveals her own literary likes (which include Marguerite Duras and the German writer Christa Wolfe) and dislikes (which include Joseph Conrad and John Updike).
Liddy, James. "The Double Vision of Irish-American Fiction." *Eire-Ireland* 19 (Winter, 1984): 6-15. An examination of Irish American fiction; helpful in understanding Gordon's work. Liddy discusses those writers he classifies as Irish American (James T. Farrell, Edwin O'Connor, Jimmy Breslin, and Mary Gordon) as well as those he does not (F. Scott Fitzgerald and Flannery O'Connor).
Mahon, John. "Mary Gordon: The Struggle with Love." In *American Women Writing Fiction: Memory, Identity, Family, Space*, edited by Mickey Pearlman. Lexington: University Press of Kentucky, 1989. A study of *Final Payments*, *The Company of Women*, and *Men and Angels* in terms of their religious motifs. Includes a bibliography of Gordon's work, including books, poems, articles, reviews, and stories, and a bibliography of writing about her.
Ward, Catherine. "Wake Homes: Four Modern Novels of the Irish American Family." *Eire-Ireland* 26 (Summer, 1991): 78-91. An examination of four Irish American novels by women, including *The Other Side*. Ward reveals "how later generations

try to escape the stultifying ties to family and church that had served the needs of their parents and grandparents but now threaten to overwhelm them." A straightforward evaluation of the novel as a study of the Irish American family.

Mary Virginia Davis

OUTER DARK

Author: Cormac McCarthy (1933-   )
Type of plot: Surrealistic parable
Time of plot: Indefinite, but probably the beginning of the twentieth century
Locale: Indefinite, but probably Southern Appalachia
First published: 1968

> *Principal characters:*
> RINTHY HOLME, a young mountain girl and new mother in search of
> her missing baby
> CULLA HOLME, Rinthy's brother and the father of her child; he
> abandons the baby in the woods shortly after its birth
> AN UNNAMED TINKER, who finds the child and takes it away, thus
> initiating the ensuing search
> THREE MEN OF DARKNESS, who appear at intervals throughout the
> journey and commit acts of brutality and mayhem

The Novel

Outer Dark is a story of sin and retribution, played out in folktale fashion against an indefinite time and place. It begins with the birth of a child, the incestuous offspring of Culla Holme and his sister Rinthy, who live in the mountainous recesses of Johnson County (no state is indicated). Culla, ashamed and frightened by his misdeed, refuses to summon aid for his sister, forcing her to give birth in the secrecy of their isolated cabin. When the child, a boy, is finally born after a long laboring, Culla takes the baby deep into the surrounding woods and leaves it, later telling Rinthy that it was sickly and died while she slept. Rinthy, however, refuses to believe her brother, especially when, after being led to the supposed grave site, she can find no trace of the baby's remains. Convinced that Culla has given the child to a wandering tinker, who appeared at the cabin shortly before the birth, Rinthy sneaks away from her brother in a blind search for the old man and her baby. When Culla discovers her absence, he follows after her, with no real understanding of his purpose in doing so.

The novel is thus constructed in terms of the encounters these two characters experience as they wander throughout a dreamlike and most often nightmarish landscape. The tinker disappears, known only by rumor, but Rinthy is led by a kind of innocence and faith that protects and sustains her. Culla, on the other hand, following in his sister's steps, becomes an Ishmael in this outside world, suspect and fugitive wherever he goes. His guilt concerning the child dogs him and takes on a universal identity. He is anathema to those he meets.

At intervals during Culla's wanderings there appear three dark figures—perhaps escaped murderers, perhaps malignant supernatural beings, perhaps even the demoniac shapes of Satan himself. Dressed in clothes stolen from the grave, these manifestations plague the land with atrocities, deeds for which Culla is inevitably blamed.

The leader, clad in black, proclaims himself a minister. His two followers are a psychopath named Harmon (the only one of the three with a name) and a mute, monstrous idiot. Emblems of horrifying evil, these three are also figures of judgment and retribution who face Culla with his overwhelming guilt and exact punishment in a final scene of inevitable justice.

The Characters

The characters in *Outer Dark* are drawn in broad surface strokes. The reader rarely enters their minds, and he is often left to guess at their motivations, which may be quite different from their stated purposes. For example, Culla Holme is ashamed of his incestuous coupling with his sister. When Rinthy is in labor, Culla refuses to summon outside help, even that of an old witch, a "midnight woman," because "She'd tell." "Who is they to tell?" Rinthy asks. "Anybody," Culla answers. Although he himself helps with the birth, he does so only at the last minute, after his sister has undergone great pain. Clearly he is giving her a chance to die, hoping that she will take the proof of their sin with her.

Culla's attempt to rid himself of the child after its birth is also marked by a combination of cruelty and cowardice. Rather than simply murder the child, he leaves it to die in the midst of the night swamp and flees in dread and panic from the sight and sound of his wailing son. Yet in his flight he becomes lost and circles unknowingly back to the scene of his guilt, where the baby still howls in outrage and accusation.

The pattern is repeated after Rinthy takes off in search of the child. Culla comes after, perhaps to find Rinthy, although he never asks of her from the strangers he meets on the way. Indeed, it is possible that Culla's following his sister is more a matter of fate than intent, and that his movement is still flight rather than search. Moreover, his journey continues to circle, and the book ends as he walks along a road leading to a swamp, likely the very one in which he was lost at the beginning.

Rinthy Holme owes much of her characterization to William Faulkner's Lena Grove in *Light in August*. Like Lena, Rinthy is, despite her obvious sexual experience, an innocent in the alien world. She has true love for her child, who causes her neither shame nor regret. When Culla tells her that the child is dead, she wants to see the grave, to lay her baby in the earth. When Culla confesses that the child is still alive, she simply sets out after it. Her breasts continue to make milk months after she begins her search; to her the milk is a sign that the child still lives. As she tells the skeptical doctor who examines her, "I don't live nowheres no more. . . . I never did much. I just go around huntin my chap. That's about all I do any more."

Again like Lena Grove, Rinthy Holme illustrates a deep yet simple faith in life. Because she does not lie or dissemble, she is met with general kindness by the strangers she encounters. They constantly offer her food, shelter, security. Only her love for her child keeps her on the road. Culla, however, is always held in suspicion. He is once arrested for trespassing, once threatened with hanging, always pursued by the possibility of punishment.

The third character to be considered in this novel is the tinker, an ambiguous figure at best. In some ways he is reminiscent of the archetypal Wandering Jew, doomed to roam without end. He straps himself in harness to pull his cart like an animal. He is associated with evil, enticing Culla with liquor and obscene books. Later he refuses to return to Rinthy the child he has found. Yet he is also the victim of evil. "I've seen the meanness of humans till I don't know why God ain't put out the sun and gone away," he tells Rinthy, and later he is murdered by the three strangers, who in turn take the child away from him. There is the suggestion that, in the end, Culla has taken the tinker's place as the eternal wanderer on nameless roads.

The most disturbing figure in the novel, however, is the bearded leader of the dark murderous trio. On two occasions Culla stumbles into his company. All others who encounter him are killed, but Culla, in a perverse way, is almost welcomed, as if he were expected. "We ain't hard to find," the man tells Culla. "Oncet you've found us." At the first meeting around their campfire, they force him to eat with them a black, nameless meat which he consumes with great difficulty and disgust. It is a terrible meal, a blasphemous communion with these creatures of darkness. The bearded man seems to know Culla's secret. "Everything don't need a name, does it?" he asks Culla, and later says of himself, "Some things is best not named." At the second meeting, after they have killed the tinker and taken the child, the leader acts as prosecutor and demands that Culla acknowledge his son, who is now hideously disfigured. When Culla once again denies the child, the bearded man cuts its throat and throws the small corpse to the mute, who apparently devours it. The act enforces a kind of terrible justice. The dark man is a figure of death, certainly, but also of retribution. He demands that payment be exacted for Culla's sin, and when the job is done, the three men disappear.

Themes and Meanings

The title of this novel comes from the eighth chapter of Matthew, in which Jesus cures a child because of the faith of his father, a centurion, but warns that those without such faith will be driven into the outer dark, the "place of wailing and grinding of teeth." In large degree this is the world of the novel. The sun rarely shines in this book. It is "bleak and pallid" when it does, and the sky is "colorless." It often rains, and much of the action takes place at night. There are numerous characters who wail in the outer dark, but Culla is the most obvious outcast. Unlike the father in Matthew, who comes to Jesus to heal his child, Culla denies his son in the presence of the judgment figure and thus causes the boy's death. Rinthy, although she, too, is denied her child, perhaps finds peace in the end when she falls asleep in the woods at the camp where the boy is killed.

The end of the novel, however, takes place years later. Culla is still wandering the "dead land," without faith or hope, on a road that leads to a swamp. He meets a blind man, whom he mistakes for a preacher. The blind man tells him that "they's darksome ways afoot in this world" but also offers Culla a form of reassurance. "I'm at the Lord's work," he says, and asks Culla what he needs. The blind man is the last of the searchers in the book. He is looking for "a feller . . . that nobody knowed what was wrong with. . . . I always did want to find that feller. . . . And tell him. If somebody don't tell him he never will have no rest." The man he seeks is Culla, but Culla turns away and hides, even though the blind man follows him with his silent, smiling stare. Culla, who never prays, never loves, never accepts, is left a solitary, tormented figure.

Thus, for all its grotesque violence and horror, *Outer Dark* is a seriously moral book. It argues for the existence of sin and evil, and it holds that the failure to admit sin is death, but it also suggests the possibility of grace, as evidenced by the blind man at the end, although such grace can blast the unprepared.

Critical Context

Outer Dark was Cormac McCarthy's second novel; his first book, *The Orchard Keeper* (1965), had won the William Faulkner Foundation First Novel Award for 1965. McCarthy has always been grouped with other Southern "Gothic" writers because of his penchant for violent and dark stories. One of the charges most often brought against him is that the arcane, polysyllabic vocabulary he sometimes employs is in direct imitation of Faulkner and serves to obscure rather than enrich his work. McCarthy, however, is a dedicated and serious writer who has developed very much his own voice and worldview. The so-called Gothic qualities of his writings come from a profound belief in man's spiritual and moral obligations. He is Catholic in background—he attended Catholic High School in Knoxville—and he infuses his Southern settings and characters with a stark religiosity. In this sense he is closer to Flannery O'Connor than to Faulkner.

Although appreciated more by critics than the general reader, McCarthy is one of the finest of modern American writers. His books since *Outer Dark*—*Child of God* (1974), *Suttree* (1979), and *Blood Meridian* (1985)—have shown him to be unswerving in his vision and artistry.

Bibliography

Aldrich, John W. "Cormac McCarthy's Bizarre Genius: A Reclusive Master of Language and the Picaresque, on a Roll." *The Atlantic Monthly* 274 (August, 1994): 89-97. Traces the evolution of McCarthy's fiction, from the publication of *Orchard Keeper* in 1965 to *All the Pretty Horses* in 1994. Offers brief analyses of *Outer Dark* and *Suttree.*

Arnold, Edwin T. "Blood & Grace: The Fiction of Cormac McCarthy." *Commonweal* 121 (November 4, 1994): 11-14. Arnold asserts that McCarthy's novels often explore the more negative aspects of the human condition in meaningful, religiously significant ways. He discusses several of McCarthy's works.

Arnold, Edwin T., and Diane C. Luce, eds. *Perspectives on Cormac McCarthy.* Jackson: University Press of Mississippi, 1993. This collection of ten essays explores the historical and philosophical influences on McCarthy's work, the moral center that informs his writings, and the common themes of his fiction. Includes an extensive bibliography.

Jarret, Robert J. *Cormac McCarthy.* New York: Twayne, 1997. Jarret offers a detailed examination of all seven of McCarthy's works, including *Outer Dark* and *Suttree*. His masterful study compares McCarthy's early fiction to the regionalists of the nineteenth and twentieth centuries, discusses McCarthy's shift of locale to the Southwest, and analyzes the distinctive aspects of McCarthy's writing.

Edwin T. Arnold

OUTERBRIDGE REACH

Author: Robert Stone (1937-   )
Type of plot: Adventure
Time of plot: The 1990's
Locale: Connecticut; New York City; the yacht *Nona* in the South Atlantic
First published: 1992

> *Principal characters:*
> OWEN BROWNE, the protagonist, a man seeking to reaffirm his
>   manhood, lost youth and lost dreams
> ANNE BROWNE, Owen's wife of twenty years, still in love but disturbed
>   by his changes and fascinated by Strickland
> MAGGIE BROWNE, the Brownes' teenage daughter
> RON STRICKLAND, a documentary filmmaker engaged to record
>   Browne's round-the-world sailing adventure
> PAMELA KOESTLER, Strickland's prostitute girlfriend and film subject
> HARRY THORNE, an honest businessman half in love with Anne
> MAD MAX, a ham-radio operator, Owen's human connection for much
>   of his voyage

The Novel

Building on his knowledge of the sea gleaned as a member of the U.S. Navy, a merchant marine seaman, and a yachtsman, Robert Stone in *Outerbridge Reach* tells an exciting but disturbing story of the challenges of transoceanic yachting, the heights and depths of human daring, the class conflicts beneath democratic façades, and the difficulty of fully understanding the behavior and motivations of others. The book is also a story of betrayal: of self, of family, of personal and corporate dreams.

The novel begins with Owen Browne testing a forty-five-foot Altan Marine sloop and having trouble with failing parts. Such weaknesses, the result of cutting corners and substituting cheap, unreliable materials for solid craftsmanship, will later prove his undoing on the long sea voyage he ultimately undertakes. He is inexperienced and uncomfortable at sea. Nevertheless, when the Hylan Corporation's head executive mysteriously disappears and therefore will not represent Altan in an around-the-world one-man yacht race, Owen decides to fill the gap, advertise the Altan product, and possibly win the race. Although he is undertaking a foolhardy venture, he convinces himself that this is the only way to regain his lost sense of self, the youthful self-awareness and pride of his military days. His wife, a far better sailor than he, doubts his ability to make the stressful voyage but supports his venture in hope that it will help him to regain the vigor and confidence of their early marriage. Superficially a perfect couple, they are estranged and drifting apart. Owen's humble origins have kept him far more aware of the class distinctions of the yachting crowd than she. The Brownes' daughter sees her parents' deception of self and spouse and refuses to bless

the farcical voyage, avoiding her father, refusing to see him off, and escaping telephone calls during the voyage—yet weeping for him. Owen, in turn, reveals ineffec-
tiveness with the cabinetmaker and others hired to prepare his boat. Harry Thorne and
his colleagues, the behind-the-scene movers considering how to save the sinking parent company, decide that Owen is the only Altan representative worth saving and give
his voyage the go-ahead.

Before Owen leaves, he is interviewed and filmed by a mean-spirited, embittered,
but clearly talented filmmaker, Ron Strickland, who is hired by Thorne to record the
preparation for the voyage, set up cameras for Owen to self-record his adventures, and
turn the whole into an advertisement for Altan yachts. Strickland, however, has other
film goals. A cynical, professional skeptic whose films destroy their subjects' pretensions, he sees Owen epitomizing the self-deluding officer class he had earlier satirized
in a film about the Vietnam War. He plans to expose the upper-middle-class emptiness
of Owen's family life, social position, and self. The novel alternates between the
Brownes and Strickland; the former are led to believe in his objectivity, while conversations between Strickland and his former film subject, Pamela Koestler, a prostitute
and drug user, reveal the real, destructive effect of the scenes. Strickland also becomes
sexually obsessed with Anne Browne and determined to break through her upper-
middle-class façade. While Owen is at sea, Strickland finally seduces and falls in love
with her. His love for her and her betrayal of Owen make Strickland see Owen in a
new light, and his sense of his film begins to change. She, in turn, feels that she cannot
telephone Owen at sea and as a result never speaks to him again, although she works
hard to maintain the role of devoted wife.

In the meantime, at sea Owen faces repeated problems (including a lockjaw scare).
Yet he falls into the rhythms of the sea and gains confidence and strength. Missionary
programs enacting biblical stories, especially ones related to betrayals and concealment, and Morse-code communication with a blind South African adolescent, Mad
Max, give Owen human contact. Thoughts of the boy's darkness make Owen think of
the whole world in hiding, concealed and concealing. He and his ship *Nona* lead the
race until furious driving rain and winds off Argentina reveal the internal flaws of his
craft: plastic instead of wood and a failing mast. When Owen realizes the dangerous
deception of his cherished advertising copy and his inability to complete the voyage
because of his faulty ship, he anchors off a small South Atlantic island and goes
ashore. The bleached bones of whales and the haunted house of nineteenth century
whalers make for an eerily surreal, hallucinatory experience.

By the time Owen renews his journey, he has opted for deception. Because of satellite transmission difficulties, the *Nona* is no longer trackable, so Owen begins a devious course of misleading reports of distances covered to make those back home think
he is still ahead of the race when, in fact, he is almost motionless in the water. He prepares two sets of nautical logs, one truthful, the other a fiction. Yet he realizes that "he
could no more take a prize by subterfuge than he could sail to the white port city of his
dreams" and that the strange confusions of Vietnam, where truth had been "a trick of
the mind that confounded logic," continue. Employing "instruments of rectitude"

such as compass, sextant, and rule to lie, he concludes, would "erode the heart and soul." He decides that there is no way out, that "there would always be something to conceal." After a final entry in his log, he steps overboard; as his ship sails on, he drowns.

When his deception and fate are discovered, the world rejects Owen as a cheat. Only Strickland sees into the heart of the matter and understands his basic honesty. This insight drives Strickland to try to make a film to restore Owen's reputation, but ironically, Anne and her company protectors steal back from him everything he could have used to redeem Owen. Only too late does Anne understand what Strickland could have shown the world: a man doing his best to meet the larger challenges of life but continually defeated, not by a lack of inner drive but by social concealment and deception that encompass everything from his boat to his own wife and daughter. Harry Thorne, the sponsor of Owen's voyage, one of the few honest men in the company, concludes that his trust has been misplaced. The novel ends with Anne considering making the voyage her husband failed and writing a novel about it.

The Characters

An Annapolis graduate and Vietnam veteran, Owen Browne was one of the golden boys of his generation. For him, the war years were the best years of his life, a time of excitement and danger but also of intense commitment, clear-cut purposes and loyalties, and a daily challenging of self physically, psychologically, and intellectually. Everything has been downhill since. He resigned his Navy commission to write advertising copy for a yacht brokerage in Connecticut. Though he excels at sales and copy, he has lost his self-respect and the respect of his wife and daughter. He feels estranged, isolated, discontent. Browne sees the round-the-world yacht race as an opportunity to experience the excitement and danger of his wartime years and to regain his self-respect. His inexperience sailing the high seas alone does not diminish his desire to do so.

Anne Browne, a lovely, intelligent woman from a wealthy nautical family, has been faithful but is hurt and disturbed by an unfulfilling sex life and by Owen's psychological distance from her; she longs to recapture the love of their youth. A successful, serious writer, she feels contempt for his advertising career. Though not convinced Owen can survive the voyage, she does nothing to stop him. Anne is trapped between loyalty to her husband and the fierce, fascinating sexuality of Strickland's continued and insistent attentions. Strickland's intensity, his driving sensuality, the sense he communicates of being on the edge, of dealing with harsh realities, both attract and repel Anne, and she ultimately succumbs. Yet she worries about appearances and proprieties; she is strong enough to reject Strickland when she thinks Owen is returning, and she later agrees to his being robbed and mugged to prevent him from finishing his film about her husband. She is a survivor who recoups financially at the end and who toys with redemption through repeating Owen's maritime struggle. When she reads a romantic quotation she had included in her final, unsent note to Owen, she cannot imagine the person she had been.

Maggie Browne, the teenage daughter of Anne and Owen, is a silent presence throughout, fearful, pouting, embarrassed, refusing to acknowledge her father's affection, but deeply loving him. She takes after Owen both physically and in her upright sense of character and fortitude. She is embarrassed and disappointed by his pretenses and lies and is heartbroken at his demise.

Ron Strickland is central to the testing of and understanding of Owen and Anne. He is an aging, embittered hipster filmmaker, obsessed by the Vietnam War, instinctively detecting pretense, hypocrisy, and human foibles. He prides himself on being able to see through "uptight" manners and find the core of darkness. Yet he is also an artist who can capture on celluloid the essence of the human condition, twisted and weak but somehow also pathetic and worthy of sympathy. He begins his film with the idea of tearing down the Browne family and showing the emptiness, fakery, and hypocrisy of their inner selves, but he ends up falling in love with Anne, admiring the innocence and vulnerability of Maggie, and vowing to do everything necessary to redeem Owen, to restore his honor by showing the integrity behind his lies and death.

Pamela Koestler, the star of one of Strickland's films, accompanies him during much of the filming. In fact, Strickland delights in introducing a kinky degenerate into the homes of what he considers "uptight" puritanical types. Pamela feels comfortable with Strickland's obsessions. Through her, readers see his darkest side.

Themes and Meanings

Outerbridge Reach is the story of a man staking his and his family's fate on a single decision that will either make or break him, pitting himself against the sea, society, and self, pushing himself to his limits—and failing. In the tradition of Joseph Conrad, Herman Melville, and Ernest Hemingway, Owen's battle against the sea represents all of humankind's challenges. In the harsh geometry involved, the sea, sky, and sailor form a triangle, with other concerns completely removed, all emphasis being placed on the ethics of winning and losing. Ultimately, Anne's final musings make clear the symbolism of the voyage: "The ocean encompassed everything, and everything could be understood in terms of it. Everything true about it was true about life in general." Within this tradition, Owen is the believer, the idealist shattered by the harsh discovery of emptiness and delusion. One of the final entries in his diary is from Melville's *Moby Dick: Or, The Whale* (1851): "Be true to the dreams of your youth."

Like Robert Stone's other novels, *Outerbridge Reach* questions the cost of pursuing the American Dream: Success turns to ashes, lives disintegrate, and nightmares come true. It is a story of failures of responsibility, of loyalties challenged and betrayed, of human weakness and limitation, the shattering of "lovely illusions." As such, it is meant to be a portrait of its time, an exploration of the deceptions and self-deceptions in the service of success that are commonplace in society, the workplace, and even the home. Owen's father taught him the importance of concealment and lies, a lesson with which he was never really comfortable. His Vietnam experiences were exercises in misleading statistics and lying as a mathematical art. His experience in the Hylan Corporation is with the illusions of advertising, illusions accepted so wholeheartedly that he believes them himself, staking his life and future on them, only to be faced with the fact that the beautiful ships he has praised in such glowing terms lacked the craftsmanship to endure. The deceptions are reinforced by the mysterious disappearance of the corporate head and the failure of the company in the wake of shady dealings and financial scandal. The love of his life fails him in his time of need, betrays him with another man, and ultimately founds her success on his failure. She asks her daughter not to judge Owen harshly, since few men ever test themselves the way he did, but even this is a lie of sorts. The story ends with cover-ups, deceptions, and self-delusions.

Mad Max, the blind shortwave fanatic tapping away to unknown listeners in Morse code, epitomizes the human condition—hopeful, optimistic, yet limited and some-how doomed. Blindness about motive and reason is quintessential Stone.

Critical Context

The excited reception of *Outerbridge Reach* suggests that many critics considered Robert Stone America's leading novelist, at least in the arena of the "big issue" novel that takes up the moral problems of the age. After a brilliant beginning to his career with *Hall of Mirrors* (1967) and *Dog Soldiers* (1974), his *A Flag for Sunrise* (1981) and *Children of Light* (1986) left some enthusiasts disappointed and hopeful that a new novel in the man-against-the-sea tradition would have substance enough to carry the weight of Stone's themes. Critics in general seem to feel this hope was justified, and while Stone has been criticized for windiness, he has also been praised for his bal-ance—counterweighting his customary social deviants with citizens solid to a fault—his lively and interesting prose, his evocation of place, and his masterful plotting of doomed relationships. Thus *Outerbridge Reach* gave new hope that a mature Stone would deliver the crowning works his youth promised, and that this sensitive recorder of the 1960's generation's angst and fears would produce new surprises and insights in coming years.

Bibliography

Bloom, James, D. "Cultural Capital and Contrarian Investing: Robert Stone, Thom Jones, and Others." *Contemporary Literature* 36 (Fall, 1995): 490-507. Presents a critical appreciation of Stone's *Children of Light* and *Outerbridge Reach*. Bloom examines the setting and story outline of *Outerbridge Reach*, as well as the narra-tive techniques of both novels. He also criticizes the apparent decay in standards re-lating to poetry, art, and culture.

Jones, Malcolm, Jr. "A Good Novelist's Glum Cruise." *Newsweek* 119 (February 24, 1992): 69. Jones believes Stone's great themes, convincing characters, and scenes "as sharp as rusty fishhooks" are marred by attempts to imitate the moral dramas of Nathaniel Hawthorne and Herman Melville. *Outerbridge Reach*, Jones writes, is best when Owen is fighting off insects, haunted by icebergs, beset by fervent radio preachers, and undone by sloppy craftsmanship that turns his boat into a coffin.

Leonard, John. "Leviathan." *The Nation* 254 (April 13, 1992): 489-494. Leonard notes some of the literary influences that seem to "hover" over Stone's novel, including Herman Melville and Joseph Conrad. He sees the novel as reflective of a spiritual quest and says, "Like Ahab, Stone hounds God—-and discovers his absence."

Pritchard, William H. "Sailing Over the Edge." *The New York Times Book Review*, February 23, 1992, pp. 1, 21, 22. Pritchard finds Stone's usual preoccupation with the underside of American life toned down in *Outerbridge Reach*, though Strickland, with his ability to penetrate to the false heart of pretentiousness and to expose ideals as trumpery, is typical Stone. Allusions to Melville, William Shakespeare, and nineteenth century poems add depth and irony, while the symbol of Outerbridge Reach "reaches further and deeper than anyone could have thought."

Stone, Robert. "The Genesis of Outerbridge Reach." *The Times Literary Supplement*, June 5, 1992, p. 14. Stone discusses the degree to which he based his story on personal experiences sailing in the Antarctic regions. He also describes the historical case of David Crowhurst, who decided not to sail around the world but to claim that he had.

_____. Interview by David Pink and Chuck Lewis. *Salmagundi* 108 (Fall, 1995): 119-139. The interviewers question Stone about the ways in which he kills off the characters in his novels, the "Stonian" universe, and his experiences as a writer. Useful for gaining a better understanding of the influences that shape Stone's writing.

Sutherland, John. "In Dangerous Waters." *The Times Literary Supplement*, May 22, 1992, p. 28. Sutherland places *Outerbridge Reach* in the tradition of Stone's other fiction, discusses his Navy and sailing experiences, and tendentiously considers the degree to which Crowhurst and others influenced Stone.

Weber, Bruce. "An Eye for Danger." *The New York Times Magazine*, January 19, 1992, pp. 6, 19-24. Weber summarizes Stone's life, including his friendships and adventures with Ken Kesey and the Merry Pranksters, his canon, the influence of Samuel Beckett, the serendipity of some Stone characters, the influence of the Crowhurst story, and Stone's spiritual quest as he studies perplexed men unsure of right.

Andrew Macdonald
Gina Macdonald

THE OUTSIDER

Author: Ernesto Sábato (1911-   )
Type of plot: Psychological novel of passion and crime
Time of plot: 1946
Locale: Buenos Aires and Hunter's ranch in the countryside
First published: El túnel, 1948 (English translation, 1950)

> *Principal characters:*
> JUAN PABLO CASTEL, the protagonist, a thirty-eight-year-old painter of
>   some importance
> MARÍA IRIBARNE, Allende Hunter's wife and Castel's lover, who is
>   much younger than Castel
> ALLENDE HUNTER, María's blind husband
> LUIS HUNTER, Allende's cousin and the possible lover of María
> MIMÍ HUNTER, Allende's cousin, a pseudointellectual

The Novel

   The Outsider is an intense psychological novel concerning a passionate crime narrated in the first-person-singular form, using techniques found in detective fiction. The opening line of the novel unveils the outcome of Juan Pablo Castel's desperate attempt to reach out of his inner confinement through a total physical and spiritual communication with María. The direct opening statement, "I am Juan Pablo Castel, the painter who killed María Iribarne," takes the reader through the sordid labyrinth of the protagonist's convulsed mind. The plot of the novel unfolds in a very simple way: A tormented artist enters into a passionate affair with the wife of a wealthy blind man. Frustrated by his inability to experience María's absolute love or to possess her, Castel murders her. The protagonist confides the recollection of his story to the readers in a direct, personal style, forcing them to enter his tunnel of absolute isolation.

   The painter first sees María at one of his art exhibits. She is the only person who discovers a minuscule detail of a painting entitled *Maternity.* Although the artwork centers on the figures of a mother and child, there is a small window in the upper left-hand corner of the painting. Through that window, one can see a scene in which an anxious woman on a desolate beach seems to be waiting for someone's response. Castel observes María's attraction to the remote scene and is certain that finally someone equal to him understands his cry for communication. While he is lost in a web of meditations, however, she leaves the gallery without giving a clue regarding her identity. The reader is then thrown into Castel's frantic search for María throughout the endless streets of Buenos Aires. By this time, one realizes that the anecdote is being told from the point of view of what could be considered a madman, the protagonist, and that his recollections are probably distorted images of an uncertain story. The series of hypotheses, questions, and digressions that go on in Castel's mind, however, intrigue and hold his interest through the last line of the novel. The next encounter with María, as well as subsequent ones in Plaza San Martín, La Recoleta, and the painter's studio, confirm the tumultuous nature of Castel's personality. The intense and cruel interrogation which María is forced to undergo at every meeting reveals the futile struggle of Castel to possess her. She seems reluctant to surrender to Castel's passion, fearing to cause him more harm. The only common thread between them seems to stem from the mutual understanding of Castel's art, specifically, the interpretation of spiritual isolation implied in the scene of the little window. From this point on, María's actions are presented in a blurred, incoherent way, increasing the mystery about her real self to Castel and to readers.

Her sudden departure for the country leaves Castel in greater depression. He is told by her maid that María has left a letter for him. Anxiously, the painter goes to her fashionable apartment on Posadas Street. While waiting in the library, Castel is confronted by the inexpressive stare of the eyes of María's husband, Allende. He acts courteously toward Castel and hands him the envelope. The extreme discomfort of the situation for Castel comes from the discovery that María's husband is blind. At this point, the author brings out one of the reiterated themes that occupy a great part of his creation, his obsession for the "subworld" of the blind. As Sábato has admitted, blindness produces in him a profound intrigue and repulsion at the same time.

Castel hardly pays attention to María's message, which reads "I am also thinking of you," and runs away from Allende's presence. Another unexpected discovery is the fact that María has gone to the country to visit her cousin, Luis Hunter. Hunter is a man publicly known to be a mediocre writer and a womanizer, well-known to certain circles of Buenos Aires society. Needless to say, María's frequent trips to Hunter's ranch become a new source of anguish for Castel. The rest of the novel fluctuates between Castel and María's exasperating meetings at his studio and the absences of María because of her visits to Hunter. Castel's repeated accusations and intense questioning seem to frighten her and even drive her away. In desperation, the protagonist tries to possess her through physical love. Every sexual encounter is now marked by hatred and violence followed by moments of remorse and humility on Castel's part. María seems saddened by the situation, avoiding all types of intimacy with Castel. Instead, she writes him brief and tender letters permeated with feelings of nostalgia and loneliness. The protagonist decides to see María at Hunter's estate. Once there, he observes suspiciously every minute action of Hunter.

The presence of Mimí Hunter, another cousin of María, only serves to reinforce Castel's feelings of alienation from the social environment. When María invites him to take a walk along the beach, however, Castel is overwhelmed by her closeness. Without listening to her confessions, he buries his head on her lap like a helpless child. Upon returning to the ranch, Castel continues to observe Hunter's reactions during dinnertime. Now he is convinced that Hunter feels jealous. Castel finds a way to hide on the second floor and listen to the voices of María and Hunter arguing in the dining room. Later, he seems to distinguish the sound of a woman's footsteps entering Hunter's room. Without any doubt about the love relationship between María and Hunter, he leaves the ranch at dawn. Once in Buenos Aires, he spends nights and days in a phantasmagoric world of bars, prostitutes, and fights. His mental incoherence becomes evident and is shown in the difficulties he finds writing an insulting letter to María, accusing her of being Hunter's lover.

From now on the author details, step by step, the deterioration of Castel's mind. The rhythm of the novel reaches its peak, transmitting to the reader the chaos and disorder of the protagonist's inner world. First, he goes to the studio and destroys his paintings with a knife. He tears the canvas of *Maternity*, with its little window, into small pieces, anticipating perhaps the final separation from María. He then drives wildly to the ranch in a borrowed car, waiting until dark to approach María. In this agonizing interval, Castel summarizes his relationship with her, concluding with the fact that María never shared with him the feeling of isolation. She merely looked through one of the windows of his tunnel out of curiosity and saw him suffering, helplessly waiting to end his tormented existence. He misunderstood her compassion for love.

The treatment of time in this last section of the novel conveys the fragmentation of reality experienced by the protagonist. In certain passages, the hour and the minute are faithfully recorded. Moreover, during the last twelve hours one finds every action of Castel precisely marked by the time, representing the compulsive nature of his sudden behavior. In other sections, time seems to be suspended. Castel, lost in his inner struggle, feels indifferent to outside reality. Such is the case of the long wait of Castel outside Hunter's ranch during a violent storm. When the light of María's bedroom goes on, Castel enters and stabs her to death. Before turning himself in to the authorities, the protagonist confronts an astonished Allende to whom he reveals that María has been his lover, Luis Hunter's lover, and the lover of who knows how many other men. Castel also tells Allende that he has killed her. In the concluding paragraph, Castel, now in jail, learns of Allende's suicide. He ends his story in abject isolation. The basic negative vision of life portrayed by Castel, the alienation of the protagonist from external reality, and the absurdist view of the world link this novel to the mainstream of twentieth century existentialism.

The Characters

Juan Pablo Castel is one of the most memorable creations of Latin American literature. From the very beginning of the novel, one is exposed to his frantic search for reason and order, his quest for some clue to the elusive reality of his chaotic existence. Every incident related to María causes a series of questions, digressions, options, and deductions. The writing and rewriting of letters confirm his belief in logic and precision. He constantly struggles between words associated with intuition, such as "feels," "imagine," and "sense," and those linked to the intellect, "reason," "order," and "think." This linguistic dilemma reveals the nature of the protagonist, torn between intuition and reason. Partly because of the narrator's point of view, the reader feels drawn to the protagonist. *The Outsider* is a novel about Castel's world, one in which external elements are insignificant. One is forced to imagine a great part of the stage and the characters of Castel's drama. María Iribarne is an elusive and engimatic figure never projected but as a suspect of endless, never-proved acts of deception. The reader becomes acquainted with María's reactions to Castel's actions but ignores her motives. When the character of Allende is introduced, both Castel and Sábato focus the emphasis on his annoying blindness. Hunter is merely described as an insignificant writer and a womanizer.

Mimí Hunter, a character that Castel despises at first sight, is introduced as a skinny and nearsighted woman in order to communicate an unsympathetic feeling to the reader. While reading the novel, one is compelled to accept the protagonist's distorted vision of the individuals around him and to share his detective-like suspicions of their actions.

Themes and Meanings

The principal theme of the novel is the isolation of man in a world ruled by reason and logic. Throughout the novel, the contradiction between the tormented, complex world of the protagonist and the hostile, external reality is present and obvious. It is important to point out that "objective" reality is only one more element in Sábato's narrative, whereas "subjective" reality permeates the total work. Thus, most of the action takes place in the tumultuous mind of Castel. The novel's original title, *El túnel* (the tunnel), reveals the inner confinement and entrapment of the protagonist, who has become totally estranged from his exterior world. His desperate attempt to liberate himself from such a condition leads him to believe that María has spent her existence in a similar tunnel, parallel to his own. Therefore, the fusion of both paths should bring about a total union. Physical possession and subsequent jealousy gradually become frantic obsessions for Castel and seem to be the only means of bridging their inner lives. Yet sexual closeness will soon prove to be a futile way of communicating. The theory that love, and finally sex, leads only to more extreme anguish and solitude has been analyzed by Sábato in a lucid essay entitled "Solitude and Communication" in *Heterodoxia* (1953; heterodoxy). In *The Outsider*, the disenchantment with physical love is expressed in the following paragraph:

> I will say right away that this was another of my many ingenuous ideas, one of those naïvetés which surely made María smile behind my back. Far from reassuring me, our physical relations upset me still more, brought new and tormenting doubts, painful scenes of misunderstanding, cruel experiments with María.

Soon it becomes apparent to the reader that Castel painted the little window in *Maternity* to represent his own limited exposure to the world—one of his tunnel's windows. Looking through it, he found María, who seemed in turn to be searching for a way out of her own secluded world. The painter perceived conflicting images of María in each one of their encounters, however, and the reader must ponder her real identity. She is presented as tender and passionate as well as detached and cynical. It is precisely this confusing perception of his lover that leads Castel to his gradual mental deterioration.

The painter eliminates María and with her his only hope of escaping solitude. At the end of the novel, when he is confined to jail, the reader sees him looking through the small cell window while listening to the sounds of outside, everyday life. The exterior world seems to him more remote and indifferent than ever. Castel comes to the realization that he has always been alone in his inner labyrinth and, what is more frightening, that he is doomed to remain alone in his own tunnel forever. Such is the fate of a man whose anguish and loneliness are oblivious to the rhythm of an orderly world where reason prevails.

Critical Context

When Sábato's *The Outsider* was published in 1948, his name instantly gained international recognition. The novel was translated into French, English, Polish, Portuguese, Swedish, Romanian, Japanese, Danish, and German. It should be mentioned, however, that Sábato's first public exposure was through his incisive essays published since 1940. These diverse essays have been collected in several volumes: *Uno y el universo* (1945; one and the universe), *Hombres y engranajes* (1951; men and gears), *Heterodoxia*, *El Escritor y sus fantasmas* (1963; the writer and his ghosts), *El otro rostro del peronismo* (1956; the other face of Peronism), *El caso Sábato* (1956; the case of Sábato), and *Tango: Discusión y clave* (1963; the tango: discussion and key). They are encyclopedic in nature and their topics cover art, literature, politics, philosophy, history, education, religion, science, mathematics, and literary style.

To understand the vastness of his writings it is necessary to remember Sábato's academic background. He earned a doctorate in physics in 1938 and worked at the Curie Laboratory in Paris as well as at the Massachusetts Institute of Technology. Many of his essays reveal his disillusionment with the sciences early in his professional career. After all, according to the writer, pure science has not been able to alleviate man's anguish at the prospect of death. In his essays and novels, Sábato shows the futility of expressing the subjective world of the individual—his feelings and emotions—through orderly and logical reasoning.

Other essays deal with the writer's convictions on the role of literature and that of creator in the crisis of the twentieth century. His disenchantment with Communism also becomes apparent in several political essays. The most controversial, however, are the ones related to Argentina's unstable situation before and after Juan Domingo Perón's regime.

All the themes of Sábato's essays are masterfully interwoven in his three novels. In 1961, thirteen years after *The Outsider*, Sábato finished his second fictional work, *Sobre héroes y tumbas* (*On Heroes and Tombs*, 1981), unanimously acclaimed by the critics. This national novel presents the same conflict found in *The Outsider*: the study of man in an irrational universe. Instead of projecting the vision of the world through the mind of a tormented individual, however, the reader is exposed to a panoramic view of the Argentine society—explored from a historical, demographic, and geographical point of view—by four main characters. In a certain way, his second novel completes a process which begins with total despair expressed in *The Outsider* and ends with bleak hope for the future of mankind in *On Heroes and Tombs*; a similar mood informs Sábato's less successful novel, *Abbadón, el exterminador* (1974). *The*

Outsider remains his most widely read creation and an outstanding example of the Latin American psychological novel with existentialist overtones.

Bibliography
Busette, Cedric. *"La familia de Pascual Duarte" and "El túnel": Correspondences and Divergences in the Exercise of Craft*. Lanham: University Press of America, 1994. Little in English is available on Sábato; this study reveals some of his overall concerns, expressed also in *The Outsider*. Includes bibliographical references.
Oberhelman, Harley D. *Ernesto Sábato*. New York: Twayne, 1970. A good basic introduction to the author and his works, part of the publisher's well-respected World Authors series. Bibliography.
Predmore, James R. *A Critical Study of the Novels of Ernesto Sábato*. Dissertation. Seattle: University of Washington, 1977. Although available only through Ann Arbor, Michigan's University Microfilms, this overview is one of the few available in English.

Susanna Castillo

THE OUTSIDER

Author: Richard Wright (1908-1960)
Type of plot: Psychological realism
Time of plot: 1950
Locale: Chicago, New York City, and Newark, New Jersey
First published: 1953

> *Principal characters:*
> CROSS DAMON, the protagonist, an intellectual, black postal worker
> GLADYS DAMON, his estranged wife
> DOROTHY POWERS, his pregnant, fifteen-year-old lover in Chicago
> ELY HOUSTON, the New York district attorney
> GILBERT (GIL) BLOUNT, a Communist official who is murdered by
>   Damon
> EVA BLOUNT, Blount's wife and Damon's lover after Blount's death
> JACK HILTON, Blount's subordinate who is murdered by Damon
> BOB HUNTER, a railroad porter and Communist organizer
> LANGLEY HERNDON, a Fascistic landlord who is murdered by Damon

The Novel

The Outsider is divided into five books, each of which focuses on a phase in the psychological development of its protagonist. "Dread," the first section, introduces Cross Damon, a well-read black postal worker, who is caught in a web of circumstances that exacerbates his sense of existential nausea: Dot, his fifteen-year-old lover, is pregnant and threatening to charge him with statutory rape; Gladys, his estranged wife, is squeezing him for money; his pious mother burdens him with guilt; and his tedious job stifles him. A fortuitous public transit accident in which he is believed to have been killed gives him the opportunity to escape his situation and "shape for himself the kind of life he felt he wanted." Yet, before he leaves Chicago, he impulsively murders a coworker who discovers his secret.

In "Dream," the second section, Damon struggles to create a new identity. Initially, he finds himself "alone at the center of the world of the laws of his own feelings," and in this dreamlike state he boards a train for New York City. On board he has a lengthy discussion with District Attorney Ely Houston, who is fascinated by Damon's belief that "man is nothing in particular" or "just anything at all." Damon concludes that "what man is is perhaps too much to be borne by man." In New York City, Damon adopts the identity of a dead man, Lionel Lane, and meets Gil Blount, a white Communist Party official who invites Damon to share his Greenwich Village apartment in order to incite the racist owner, Langley Herndon. Damon accepts, and his new social contacts make him believe that "the dream in which he had lived since he had fled Chicago was leaving him."

In the third section, "Descent," Damon explores the limits of his new psychological freedom but finds himself increasingly caught in a pattern of deception and violence.

After moving to Greenwich Village, Damon discovers that Blount's wife, Eva, feels betrayed and used in her loveless relationship. When Herndon initiates a violent argument with Blount, Damon comes to Blount's defense but ends up killing both men, symbolically acting out his rejection of opposite but equally inhumane ideologies. His descent continues, however, as he realizes that he is "trapped in the coils of his own actions," that through this double murder he has "become what he had tried to destroy."

In "Despair," the fourth section, the murders are investigated by Ely Houston. In a discussion with Damon that is reminiscent of that between Porfiry and Raskolnikov in Fyodor Dostoevski's *Crime and Punishment* (1866), Houston considers the possibility that both murders were committed by a third man, "one for whom all ethical laws are suspended," but he rejects this idea and mistakenly decides that Blount and Herndon killed each other. Damon and Eva soon become lovers, but her love is based on the naïve assumption that Damon is a victim, and he continues to lie to her in a vain effort to protect her from the "monstrousness of himself." Damon later murders Blount's associate Jack Hilton, who has evidence of Damon's guilt. This murder reignites the suspicions of the Party, and Damon is examined by Blimin, another high-ranking Communist. In his lengthy response to Blimin's questions, Damon expresses his belief that technological progress is immunizing men against the myths created to separate them from "the horrible truth of the uncertain and enigmatic nature of life."

In the final section, "Decision," Damon is once again called in for questioning by Houston, who is convinced of his guilt but cannot prove it. Houston confronts Damon with the wife and children whom he abandoned and blames him for the sudden death of his mother but is unable to make Damon react. When Damon later decides to unburden himself to Eva, she cannot bear the truth and commits suicide. In a final confrontation, Houston tells Damon that he knows of his guilt but has decided to let Damon punish himself. In effect, Houston refuses to give Damon's actions meaning. To Damon, this is "a judgment so inhuman that he could not bear to think of it." Soon afterward, Damon is gunned down by operatives of the Party and dies in Houston's arms.

The Characters

Because *The Outsider* is a novel of ideas, characterization is subordinated to exposition. Therefore, all of the characters, including Cross Damon, are types, representative of intellectual positions.

Cross Damon, although not fully believable, is a memorable character whose name suggests an inverted Christianity. As a character, Damon is informed by a variety of predecessors, such as Herman Melville's Ahab, Dostoevski's Raskolnikov, and Albert Camus's Meursault. Damon is a metaphysical rebel, an ethical criminal who attempts to create "the kind of life he felt he wanted."

Although Wright, through Ely Houston, suggests that a black intellectual such as Damon has a special objectivity, he wants Damon to be an existential Everyman who transcends racial distinctions. His protagonist, a former University of Chicago philosophy major, has been shaped by reading Søren Kierkegaard, Friedrich Nietzsche, Dostoevski, and others. Psychologically, Damon has developed dialectically, in opposition to the Christian guilt imposed by his mother and the oppressive tedium of his work. Wright emphasizes that Damon's anger and confusion are not a special condition of his blackness.

Few critics have been able to accept the contradiction between Damon's stoicism and his passion. On the one hand, Damon is a man of reason who rejects traditional codes of behavior. He reacts to his murders with cool analysis, and he shows no emotion when confronted with the wife and children whom he has abandoned. Like Camus's Meursault, Damon does not react to his mother's death. Yet, in other ways, Damon is a man driven by "hot impulse," egotistical desires that are very different from the utter existential indifference of Meursault. This contradiction in his personality is underscored by his surprising love for Eva Blount.

The other characters exist primarily to exemplify or elaborate portions of Damon's philosophy. Ely Houston is Damon's mirror image, a kindred spirit who shares his sense of metaphysical rebellion but who chooses to support the legal system. In fact, his beliefs match Damon's so well that the lines in their long colloquies could be interchanged.

Eva Blount is an impossibly idealistic and naïve character who can only see Damon as a fellow victim. When he reveals the truth of his actions to her and cannot explain his motivation, she kills herself in despair. Damon's love for her and his desire to protect her represent the humanitarian yearnings that hide behind his brutal acts.

Gil Blount and the other Communist officials are portrayed as inhuman manipulators using people for ideological goals. In this sense, Damon sees little difference between them and the capitalists whom they oppose. By murdering Blount and the fascistic Herndon, Damon strikes out at two essentially similar men, only to realize that his action is simply another misuse of power. Thus, Damon kills them in part because he sees a frightening reflection of himself in them.

Themes and Meanings

The central theme of *The Outsider* is Cross Damon's quest for freedom: "I wanted to be free . . . to feel what I was worth." Yet at the end of the novel, he admits that he has discovered "nothing."

At first, the protagonist feels existential nausea: "insulted at being alive, humiliated at the terms of existence." This sense of alienation leads him to accept a Nietzschean view of an amoral universe in which man is destined to become either an executioner or a victim. The transit accident allows him to create a new life, to act independently and to see "what living meant to me," but he discovers that the egotistical exercise of freedom destroys those around him, including the one person he loves.

One problem is that Damon's effort to live for himself collides with his basic humanitarian feelings. In fact, he despises the will to power that drives men such as Gil Blount, and his multiple murders do not free him; instead, he becomes, like Blount, a little god playing with others' lives. The idea of universal freedom, which is negated by the will to power, demands the discovery or creation of norms that will protect the freedom of others.

In like manner, Damon fails in his effort to live authentically. He dreams of becoming one of those "men who were outsiders . . . because they had thought their way through the many veils of illusion," but the new life he creates and his relationship with other characters are based on deception. He cannot overcome his conviction "that bad faith of some degree was an indigenous part of living."

As he is dying, Damon states that "alone a man is nothing" and wishes that he "had some way to give the meaning of my life to others. . . . To make a bridge from man to man," but he fails in this effort. Unlike Houston, he cannot accept social norms in which he does not believe, so he dies, like Joseph Conrad's Kurtz, with a final enigmatic reference to the "horror" of his life.

Thus, *The Outsider* explores the question of freedom but provides no hopeful answers. In the novel, opposing ideologies are rejected, society is shown to be based on pretense, human nature is portrayed as brutal, and the possibility of creating a meaningful sense of freedom seems remote.

Critical Context

The Outsider was the first of Wright's books to receive predominantly negative reviews. Reviewers were primarily critical of its characterization, particularly the absence of sufficient motivation for Damon's violence. The novel's mix of melodramatic action and lengthy rhetorical exposition seemed disruptive. Black reviewers believed that Wright's interest in existentialism indicated a separation from his roots. Also, most reviewers found the unrelieved pessimism of the novel unattractive.

The novel is clearly the result of Wright's involvement with existential thinkers following his break from Marxism in the 1940's. The novel seems to mark the low point of Wright's despair, for it lacks Camus's humanitarian hope or Jean-Paul Sartre's belief in social change. Later critics, however, have suggested that *The Outsider* is a rejection of existentialism or is even a Christian existentialist novel.

existential or not, *The Outsider* is a logical extension of Wright's earlier fiction and thought. In *Native Son* (1940), Bigger expresses in a less articulate manner the same sort of rage and dread felt by Damon. In "The Man Who Lived Underground," Fred Daniels, like Damon, wants to share his hard-earned knowledge with others. In "Art and Fiction," Wright maintained that personal freedom was conditioned on the freedom of others. Thus, in *The Outsider* Wright addressed familiar themes but consciously tried to move beyond the racial limitations of his earlier work.

Bibliography

Baldwin, James. *The Price of the Ticket: Collected Nonfiction, 1948-1985*. New York: St. Martin's Press/Marek, 1985. The essays "Everybody's Protest Novel" and "Alas, Poor Richard" provide important and provocative insights into Wright and his art.

Bloom, Harold, ed. *Richard Wright.* New York: Chelsea House, 1987. Essays on various aspects of Wright's work and career, with an introduction by Bloom.

Fabre, Michel. *The Unfinished Quest of Richard Wright.* Translated by Isabel Barzun. New York: William Morrow, 1973. The most important and authoritative biography of Wright available.

_____. *The World of Richard Wright.* Jackson: University Press of Mississippi, 1985. A collection of Fabre's essays on Wright. A valuable but not sustained full-length study.

Hakutani, Yoshinobu. *Richard Wright and Racial Discourse.* Columbia: University of Missouri Press, 1996. Chapters on *Lawd Today, Uncle Tom's Children, Native Son, The Outsider,* and *Black Boy,* as well as discussions of later fiction, black power, and Wright's handling of sexuality. Includes introduction and bibliography.

Kinnamon, Keneth, ed. *Critical Essays on Richard Wright's "Native Son."* New York: Twayne, 1997. Divided into sections of reviews, reprinted essays, and new essays. Includes discussions of Wright's handling of race, voice, tone, novelistic structure, the city, and literary influences. Index but no bibliography.

_____. *The Emergence of Richard Wright.* Urbana: University of Illinois Press, 1972. A study of Wright's background and development as a writer, up to the publication of *Native Son* (1940).

Walker, Margaret. *Richard Wright: Daemonic Genius.* New York: Warner Books, 1988. A critically acclaimed study of Wright's life and work written by a respected novelist.

Webb, Constance. *Richard Wright: A Biography.* New York: Putnam, 1968. A well-written biography that remains useful.

Carl Brucker

OXHERDING TALE

Author: Charles Johnson (1948-   )
Type of plot: Bildungsroman
Time of plot: 1843-1865
Locale: South Carolina
First published: 1982

> *Principal characters:*
>> ANDREW HAWKINS, the narrator, a slave
>> GEORGE HAWKINS, Andrew's father
>> MATTIE HAWKINS, George's wife and Andrew's stepmother
>> JONATHAN POLKINGHORNE, Andrew's first owner
>> ANNA POLKINGHORNE, Jonathan's wife and the biological mother of
>>> Andrew
>> EZEKIEL SYKES-WITHERS, a Trancendentalist and Andrew's tutor
>> FLO HATFIELD, Andrew's second owner and lover
>> REB, an older slave who befriends Andrew
>> HORACE BANNON, the "Soulcatcher," who captures runaway slaves
>> PEGGY UNDERCLIFF, Andrew's white wife

The Novel

Oxherding Tale describes the education a young slave, Andrew Hawkins, receives from a variety of people. It is through synthesizing the different views from these people that he becomes a complete person.

The novel itself opens with "the Fall," which is how Andrew describes his conception. During a bout of heavy drinking, Jonathan Polkinghorne, the owner of a South Carolina plantation named Cripplegate, and his favorite slave, who is also his butler, decide to swap wives for one night. The master slips into the slave's quarters, while the slave (George Hawkins) goes to the Polkinghornes' bedroom. The deception is uncovered by Anna Polkinghorne during the act of intercourse, and although she immediately screams, causing George to run from the bedroom, Anna has been impregnated. This act forces her husband to send George to work in the fields, thus causing him to fall in stature from a house slave to a field slave. George's new occupation is that of an oxherd.

Even though Jonathan would like the baby to be brought up as the Polkinghornes' own son since they are childless, his wife insists that Andrew be placed in the slave quarters as though there is no connection between the master and his slave. Consequently, Andrew is reared by George and his wife, Mattie, though Jonathan allows the boy to receive an excellent education with the promise of someday being free.

To tutor Andrew, Jonathan hires an itinerant philosopher named Ezekiel Sykes-Withers. Ezekiel professes to be a Transcendentalist, which means that he is more interested in theory than in real life. Andrew learns his lessons well from Ezekiel—mathematics, languages, abstract reasoning—but something is missing. Andrew finds what is lacking from his life in the person of a girl named Minty. When he asks Jonathan for his freedom so that he may purchase Minty and marry her, however, Andrew is sent to work for a woman, Flo Hatfield.

Flo, owner of a mine named Leviathan, takes the handsome boy as a lover and teaches him the philosophy of hedonism. Andrew enjoys the privileges of being Flo's lover for a year before he sickens of it. He escapes with another slave, Reb, a coffin-maker, who has become a father figure to him. On the road north, they meet Horace Bannon, the "Soulcatcher," who captures runaway slaves by emptying his own soul to allow the essence of the runaway to fill it. In other words, Horace—who is also a psychopathic killer—becomes "black" himself, taking on the characteristics and personality of his prey. He does not kill the runaway, he tells Andrew and Reb, until the slave begs for death because he can no longer stand the pressure of being on the run, of never fitting into a white society.

At Spartanburg, South Carolina, Andrew takes a job as a teacher. This is possible because his light complexion allows him to "pass" as white. Reb stays with Andrew for awhile, but finally he leaves for Chicago. Meanwhile, Andrew finds himself trapped into marrying the daughter of a local doctor. He comes to love Peggy Undercliff, however, and seems to be settled into Spartanburg as a respectable member of the white community.

Ironically, just as he feels safe, Andrew learns that Horace has set off to catch and kill Reb. Further complicating matters, Andrew attends a slave auction and discovers a very ill Minty. He buys her, but she soon dies. As he stands by her deathbed, Andrew feels forlorn and wonders how long he can continue the charade in Spartanburg. It is then that Horace appears. Andrew willingly accompanies the Soulcatcher to the woods, expecting to be killed. Instead, Horace tells Andrew that he could not catch Reb because the coffin-maker had gradually emptied his soul during his captivity; he had learned to expect nothing and to desire nothing. Reb had freed himself, literally and figuratively, by never attempting to fit into white society. Because he had finally encountered a slave he could not capture, Horace tells Andrew that he has retired from the slave-catching profession, leaving the schoolteacher to return to his life in Spartanburg. Andrew does just that, but he is wiser having learned from all his teachers—George, Ezekiel, Flo, and especially Reb.

The Characters

Andrew Hawkins, the narrator of *Oxherding Tale*, is an extremely intelligent, pragmatic man. He is always eager to experience all aspects of life and to learn from others. Although he comes across as a prig early in the novel—he feels himself superior to all the slaves and most of the masters—by the end of the story he has grown into a character with whom a reader can empathize. Charles Johnson certainly intended this feeling of empathy, as the readers of *Oxherding Tale* are to learn from Andrew's experiences just as Andrew himself learned from them. Andrew is not to be seen as a "real" character, however; instead, Johnson intends his protagonist to stand as a metaphor, a character whose adventures are allegorical. Woven into the character of Andrew are various philosophical threads that reinforce points Johnson wants to make in his novel. All this taken together means that Andrew never comes to life or seems like a real person.

George Hawkins, Andrew's father and first teacher, is nothing more than a stereotype in the novel. A radical black nationalist convinced that all whites are evil, he eventually leads a slave revolt at Cripplegate. Horace Bannon tracks him easily because George's soul is so full of hate that he can never hide. In the end, he begs Horace to kill him because the hate he bears is too much to carry any longer.

Ezekiel Sykes-Withers, Andrew's second teacher, is portrayed as a fool because he lives only for the abstract. He is devastated, for example, when he meets Karl Marx and finds that the German philosopher fails to share his own pessimism. Marx tells Ezekiel to enjoy life, to find a woman with whom he could be happy. Ezekiel, however, is "happiest" when miserable because he is convinced of the stupidity of the human race.

Flo Hatfield, Andrew's lover and third teacher, is a stereotype as well. Her only interest is in seeking all forms of pleasure. She indulges in excesses of food, drugs, and sex in an attempt to kill the pain of existence. For a time, this sort of life seems appropriate to Andrew, but he soon realizes that it is ultimately just as empty as the life led by Ezekiel.

Reb, a father figure for Andrew and his fourth teacher, is a member of the Allmuseri tribe from Africa. The Allmuseri, apparently a creation of Johnson's, believe that it is the duty of each individual in a society to immerse himself in the society as a whole, that individuality is, if not an outright illusion, at least an act of selfish egoism. Reb has learned that to survive in an alien culture he must eliminate his individuality through self-denial; he lives for each moment and for himself, in contrast to the other characters in the novel. Through the way he leads his life, Reb serves as an exemplar for Andrew. By the end of the novel, Andrew has learned his lesson well; it is understood that he, just as Reb had done years earlier, has freed himself.

Horace Bannon, the "Soulcatcher," represents the sum of all the people Andrew has met and the sum of all the lessons that Andrew has learned. Horace has a tattoo on his chest and arms, revealed to Andrew at the end of the novel, in which the entire story is seen in microcosm. It is through viewing this tattoo that Andrew realizes how Reb freed himself, for it is in the tattoo that Andrew sees the meaninglessness of physical life.

Themes and Meanings

Oxherding Tale is clearly not to be read as a novel about the brutality of slavery in the American South, although that element is certainly very evident. Instead, Charles Johnson would like his readers to see the novel as a parable about one man's attempt to free himself—both literally and figuratively—from a life full of traps. In other words, this is a novel that explores the existential truth of trying to lead an honest life, one that allows a person to be free spiritually. After experiencing many different "lives," Andrew comes to realize that Reb's philosophy is the most suitable for living in this world. His philosophy, which one critic has called "the phenomenology of the Allmuseri," is similar to Eastern religions in that it holds that the path to freedom lies through negation of the self.

Reinforcing this theme of finding one's true self is Johnson's style in the novel. It can best be termed "metafiction" because it eschews the traditional conventions of fiction—such as an author who remains aloof from the world he has created—in favor of experimentation. For example, there are two philosophical digressions in *Oxherding Tale* about the very nature of slave narratives and first-person narrators. These digressions seem to undercut the story itself, until a reader places them within the context of the overall fable that Johnson is relating. It is then that the true purpose of the digressions—their function as an "objective" commentary upon Andrew and his story that allows the reader to see the novel in a different light—becomes clear. In short, Johnson's metafictional techniques enable the reader to search for the true meaning of *Oxherding Tale* just as Andrew searches for the true meaning of his life. In summary, Johnson would like the novel as a whole to serve as a microcosm of human life; slavery in *Oxherding Tale* is meant to represent metaphorically the captivity in which human beings live until they manage to set themselves free through self-negation.

Critical Context

Charles Johnson started his career as a cartoonist and published his work in newspapers and magazines. Two collections of his cartoons and drawings were subsequently published, *Black Humor* (1970) and *Half-Past Nation Time* (1972). Eventually, however, he turned to fiction as a means of artistic expression. As he completed his master's degree in philosophy at Southern Illinois University in the early 1970's, Johnson studied with novelist John Gardner. He wrote and rewrote under Gardner until he produced what would become his first novel, *Faith and the Good Thing* (1974). That novel can be read as a folktale in which a woman named "Faith" sets out on a literal and figurative journey to find the meaning of her existence.

Following *Faith and the Good Thing*, Johnson published *Oxherding Tale*, which received favorable reviews from both popular magazines as well as from literary journals. He followed his second novel with a collection of short fiction, *The Sorcerer's Apprentice* (1986), and with a book of literary criticism, *Being and Race: Black Writing Since 1970* (1988). His growing reputation as one of America's most important writers was solidified in 1990 when he published *Middle Passage*, which was accepted by most critics as his best novel and which won the National Book Award. *Middle Passage* is the story of Rutherford Calhoun, a thief who meets members of the Allmuseri tribe who are being taken into slavery. He comes to admire their fortitude in the face of captivity and wants to learn how they deal with adversity. The novel then shows Rutherford's slow progress toward renunciation of materialism in favor of self-negation under the guidance of the Allmuseri.

A common thread throughout these novels is an interest in exploring the limits of human knowledge. Johnson, with his training as a philosopher, wants to know what is possible for people to understand about their own existence. Exactly why, Johnson asks, do we act and think the way we do? Although answers are not always readily available, Johnson argues persuasively in his fiction that to neglect to ask such questions, to go through life always accepting the way things are, is to live with blinders. According to Johnson, it is up to each individual to question his own existence in order to lead a full, free life.

Bibliography

Byrd, Rudolph P. "*Oxherding Tale* and *Siddhartha*: Philosophy, Fiction, and the Emergence of a Hidden Tradition." *African American Review* 30 (Winter, 1996): 549-558. Byrd shows the connection between *Oxherding Tale* and *Siddhartha* and demonstrates how Johnson was influenced by Hesse's novel. Both books share similar structure and intellectual concerns.

Coleman, James W. "Charles Johnson's Quest for Black Freedom in *Oxherding Tale*." *African American Review* 29 (Winter, 1995): 631-644. Coleman asserts that Johnson attempts to achieve freedom from the dominant and narrow tradition of written black texts. Johnson has stated that he centers his own writing around phenomenological theory. In this article, Coleman links the theory with Johnson's attempt at black textual revision.

Crouch, Stanley. "Charles Johnson: Free at Last!" In *Notes of a Hanging Judge: Essays and Reviews, 1979-1989*. New York: Oxford University Press, 1990. Crouch's insightful review of the novel shows that Johnson has created, using the nineteenth century genre of the slave narrative, a fascinating protagonist in Andrew Hawkins. Crouch finds Andrew and his search for some truth in his existence to be reminiscent of characters created by authors such as Herman Melville or Mark Twain.

Gleason, William. "The Liberation of Perception: Charles Johnson's *Oxherding Tale*." *Black American Literature Forum* 25 (Winter, 1991) 705-728. Gleason argues that *Oxherding Tale* is an explicit response to Johnson's own call for a rebirth and a rebuilding of African American literature.

Hayward, Jennifer. "Something to Serve: Constructs of the Feminine in Charles Johnson's *Oxherding Tale*." *Black American Literature Forum* 25 (Winter, 1991): 689-703. Hayward attempts to demonstrate that *Oxherding Tale* can be read as a metaphor in which polar opposites (white/black, master/slave, male/female) are reconciled through Johnson's use of metafictional techniques and African American tradition.

Johnson, Charles. "Philosophy and Black Fiction." *Obsidian: Black Literature in Review* 6 (Spring/Summer, 1980): 55-61. Johnson finds African American fiction a one-dimensional world populated with caricatures. Johnson goes on to argue that African American fiction writers should feel an obligation to strip away the "presuppositions" about black life in order to see the complexities that lie beneath. Johnson later expanded on the opinions in this brief essay in a critical book about African American fiction, *Being and Race: Black Writing Since 1970*.

Little, Jonathan. "Charles Johnson's Revolutionary *Oxherding Tale*." *Studies in American Fiction* 19 (Autumn, 1991): 141-151. Little's excellent essay argues that

Oxherding Tale breaks the constraints usually placed on African American fiction by dealing with issues, such as one man's struggle to find meaning in his own life, not normally seen in works by African American writers.

_____. *Charles Johnson's Spiritual Imagination*. Columbia: University of Missouri Press, 1997. A book-length study of Johnson's work offering an account of Johnson's artistic growth and the increasing spirituality of his imagination. Along with a discussion of *Oxherding Tale*, there are examinations of each of Johnson's major works.

Parrish, Timothy L. "Imaging Slavery: Toni Morrison and Charles Johnson." *Studies in American Fiction* 25 (Spring 1997): 81-98. Parrish asserts that although they offer differing views of the present, both authors understand that slavery's meaning cannot be recaptured, but only re-seen. Parrish compares the two works and the authors' philosophical approaches to them.

Jim McWilliams

PACO'S STORY

Author: Larry Heinemann (1944-   )
Type of plot: Magical Realism
Time of plot: The early 1970's
Locale: Vietnam and the American Midwest
First published: 1986

> *Principal characters:*
>> PACO SULLIVAN, a seriously wounded Vietnam veteran looking for
>> work and a new life after hospitalization and discharge
>> GALLAGHER, the raconteur company mate of Paco, capable of almost
>> any cruelty
>> ERNEST MONROE, a World War II veteran and proprietor of the Texas
>> Lunch, where Paco briefly works
>> JESSE, a hitchhiking Vietnam veteran with whom Paco is compared and
>> contrasted
>> CATHY, a college student and rooming-house neighbor whose sexual
>> teasing torments Paco

The Novel

Based in part on Larry Heinemann's experience in the Vietnam War, *Paco's Story* tells a representative tale of the brutality of war and the subsequent problems of a veteran's adjustment to life in small-town America. Heinemann presents this material through a narrative that focuses on Paco Sullivan's arrival in, partial adjustment to, and departure from the typical American crossroads town of Boone, a river town in the American Midwest. This strand of the narrative is punctured by scenes of the massacre of Paco's company at Fire Base Harriet, Paco's rescue and recovery, and earlier war incidents in which Paco was involved.

The novel, however, begins not with Paco but with a virtuoso introduction by and to the unnamed narrator, whose hip but elegant manner provides much of the novel's special flavor. The narrator insists that people do not want to hear another war story, and he is rather specific about just what they do not want to hear and why. Still, stories such as Paco's must be heard, and the narrator, who has cornered a listener whom he addresses as James, must tell it. Readers soon learn that the narrator is the ghost of a soldier who served with Paco in Alpha Company and who lost his life with all the others at Fire Base Harriet.

Paco arrives at the outskirts of Boone by bus, washes up at the Texaco station, and begins a hobbled walk toward town. Befriended by the garage mechanic, he begins a search for work and a place to stay. The townspeople are curious about Paco, and also suspicious. His faraway gaze (he is heavily medicated) and his cane-aided limp make him something of a freak; his presence brings the unpleasantness of the Vietnam War, about which few seem to know anything, into their midst. Most of the townsfolk—

those he meets at Rita's Tender Trap and Hennig's Barbershop—respond ungenerously to his requests for information about work. Soon, however, Paco meets Ernest Monroe, who gives him the job of dishwasher at the Texas Lunch and helps him find lodging at the nearby Geronimo Hotel (no doubt an ironic allusion to the serviceman's labeling Vietnam as "Indian Country").

The early scenes of Paco's progress in Boone, along with a detailed description of his wounding and rescue at Fire Base Harriet, underscore the various levels at which the war continues to affect Paco. Crippled and pain-riddled, he carries the physical consequences of the war everywhere he goes. He cannot leave it behind, because it has reshaped him. Although he wishes to get on with his life, to move forward, he carries his memories with him as well. Moreover, the war has shaped how he is to be perceived by others.

He remains a freak to most, not only because of his physical appearance but also because such a vision allows others to remove themselves from any connection with America's involvement in Vietnam. Ernest, an ex-Marine who survived World War II battles at Guadalcanal and Iwo Jima, is a fortuitous, benevolent presence through whose own story Heinemann is able to universalize his concerns with the human capacity to make war and survive it. Paco's earlier encounter with Mr. Elliot, a mildly crazed refugee from World War I Russia who runs the town's fix-it shop, also serves to establish a context for approaching the meaning of Paco's experience in and after Vietnam.

As Paco learns and repeats the harsh routine of his work at the Texas Lunch, it becomes clear that this unfriendly work helps him to hold himself together psychologically. The scalding water and irritating chemicals are nothing to what he has already endured, and the long hours of busing tables, soaking, rinsing, and scrubbing help to keep his memories and behavior under control just as much as the depressant drugs do.

The routine of Paco's short career at the Texas Lunch is disturbed by two encounters. One night, minutes before closing, a drifter named Jesse comes into the restaurant. Jesse has been on the road a long time, and he tells Paco and Ernest of his restless wanderings across the length and breadth of the United States. After Paco tells him (as he must tell everyone) about how he got his wounds and his limp, Jesse says that he, too, served in Vietnam, though at an earlier period of the war. Though he has suffered far less physical trauma than Paco, Jesse cannot settle down. He has spent the intervening years trying to discover America and, as he puts it, "looking for a place to cool out." As Jesse sounds off about the military-industrial complex and about the kind of memorial that might be appropriate for the Vietnam war, his rage pierces through his good-natured manner. He heads back to the road after giving a lesson on hitchhiking.

Even before Jesse shows up, Paco had noticed that his neighbor at the Geronimo Hotel, a college girl named Cathy, had been spying on him. Over a period of weeks, she pursued a tormenting game of allowing Paco to see her in various provocative stances and daring him to approach her. To his mind (and to the narrator's), she had even encouraged her boyfriend to a noisy lovemaking that would disturb and entice

Paco. This sadistic teasing culminates with a stealthy visit to Paco's room. When Paco discovers that Cathy has visited his room in his absence, he decides to return the favor. Once there, he discovers a diary in which she has set down her observations and fantasies about him. He reads about her dream in which, after lovemaking, he peels his scars off, laying them on her body, where they tingle and burn.

The diary entry wakes Paco from his own dream of belonging. He knows now that this is not the place to find what he needs. Taking the pay he is owed and leaving Ernest a thank-you note, Paco heads back to the Texaco station and boards a westbound bus.

The events during Paco's brief sojourn in Boone are accompanied by formal flashbacks (Paco's memories) and by less formal interjections of antecedent action by the narrator. Key scenes involve Paco's company-mate, Gallagher. Readers learn how Gallagher selected his tattoo and how he led his comrades in the gang rape and killing of a young woman who was a member of the Viet Cong. In one scene, Gallagher is allowed to tell a story of his own. In another, the medic who discovered Paco is placed in a bar, years later, to tell his version of Paco's story. In yet another background scene, Paco is shown in action as the company booby-trap man. In this way, Paco's life in Alpha Company is threaded through the events in Boone, counterpointing them and suggesting relationships between the present and the past.

The Characters

Paco Sullivan is soft-spoken, withdrawn, and polite. He wants peace, but he is unlikely to find it. Though the reader learns that (in war) Paco is capable of violence, the knowledge comes as a paradox about Paco and about humankind in general. While Paco's suffering, past and present, evokes the reader's sympathy, especially since many townspeople reject him or belittle him, that sympathy is checked by knowledge of his participation in the gang rape. His present state—in which his every movement brings pain, his dreams torment him, and drugs only make life tolerable—is perhaps overdrawn to the point of sentimentality. Paco's survivor's guilt is more successfully, because more subtly, handled. Paco lives just as much among the ghost of Alpha Company as he does among the living.

Ernest Monroe serves as a father figure and as a connection to America's war-riddled history. His present situation of responsibility and his active compassion suggest that the transformations of war need not be permanent. Ernest cannot forget, but does not live within, the traumas of his World War II experiences. He serves as one possible future for Paco.

Jesse is more obviously a foil for Paco. They have seen the horrors of the same war, and they have returned to the same inhospitable homeland, a country that does not seem to have a place for them. Heinemann employs the loquacious Jesse to articulate those perspectives of the Vietnam veteran that tight-lipped, drug-slowed Paco cannot or will not. A somewhat comic character, Jesse is also the conscious incarnation of a Vietnam veteran cliché. His tall-tale drifter manner has connections with frontier literature and legend.

Gallagher, prominent in the Vietnam flashback scenes, is a streetwise Chicagoan who is defined as the company killer and the company clown. For Gallagher, it seems natural to put on the attitudes and behavior that war demands. He seems made for it.

Cathy, the niece of the couple who run the Geronimo Hotel, is the most prominent female character in the novel. She, like the others, is defined (and defines herself) as a sexual object. Such portrayals of women are a perplexing ingredient in Heinemann's first two novels. Her diary provides one of the several versions or pieces of a story that Paco himself never fully tells.

Themes and Meanings

The devastation of war, its human toll, is one of Heinemann's primary themes, as is the arbitrariness of life and death in the combat arena. Paco's miraculous survival from an otherwise complete massacre cannot be seriously attributed to his will to live. The terms of his survival render him ghostlike, suggesting that in certain ways he remains among the dead whose spirits haunt him. Indeed, the dead quality of Paco's existence is heightened by the animated voice of the narrator, himself a ghost. Ironically, this story is one that only the dead can tell. There is a static and ghostlike quality, too, to Boone itself, as if Heinemann means to suggest that the United States has murdered or drugged itself, lost contact with its own most vital meanings and purposes. Technically, the ghost narrator provides the authority of a first-person (witness) narration along with the Olympian omniscience of third-person perspective. By defying (through blending) the pure conventions of narrative choice, Heinemann complicates his compact novel with concerns about how Paco's experience can be made sharable.

Critical Context

Though following his combat novel, *Close Quarters* (1977), at some length, *Paco's Story* fulfilled anxious critics' expectations that Heinemann was a major literary talent. By winning the National Book Award for fiction, *Paco's Story* assured itself a permanent place in the Vietnam War canon and perhaps first place in the important subgenre of the returned veteran. Moreover, with *Paco's Story*, Heinemann proved himself a stylist capable of a range of effects. The naturalism of *Close Quarters* is one ingredient in *Paco's Story*, in which fantasy and an intriguing narrational gamble figure importantly, as does a precise rendering of the material aspects of American culture. Heinemann is a master at blending the ordinary and the extraordinary in his evocation of the workingman's Vietnam and the workingman's America.

Bibliography

Anisfield, Nancy. "After the Apocalypse: Narrative Movement in Larry Heinemann's *Paco's Story*." In *America Rediscovered: Critical Essays on Literature and Film of the Vietnam War*, edited by Owen W. Gilman, Jr., and Lorrie Smith. New York: Garland, 1990. Anisfield argues that while the typical war narrative, including that of the returned veteran, depends on a violent, apocalyptic ending, *Paco's Story* defies this convention by closing with a largely passive, internal event. The rejection of

apocalyptic closure allows thoughtful examination of the war and its consequences.

Bonn, Maria S. "A Different World: The Vietnam Veteran Novel Comes Home."
In *Fourteen Landing Zones: Approaches to Vietnam War Literature*, edited by
Philip K. Jason. Iowa City: University of Iowa Press, 1991. *Paco's Story* is the
linchpin in Bonn's analysis of how veterans' fictions reflect the unusual conditions
of return for participants in this unpopular war. Bonn compares Paco's situation to
that of Philip Dossier in Heinemann's *Close Quarters* and Chris Starkmann in
Philip Caputo's *Indian Country* (1987), exploring how these novels treat the limits
and terms of reintegration.

Jeffords, Susan. "Tattoos, Scars, Diaries, and Writing Masculinity." In *The Vietnam
War and American Culture*, edited by John Carlos Rowe and Rick Berg. New York:
Columbia University Press, 1991. Jeffords finds a sinister pattern in which masculine suffering seeks retribution and relief in the raping of women. The polarization
of women and victims turns women into oppressors. Jeffords makes fascinating
connections among the various images of scars, tattoos, and other inscriptions.

Morris, Gregory L. "Telling War Stories: Larry Heinemann's *Paco's Story* and the
Serio-comic Tradition." *CRITIQUE: Studies in Contemporary Fiction* 36 (Fall
1994): 58-68. Morris argues that Heinemann's novel exemplifies a view of the Vietnam War based on the serio-comic tradition. This style utilizes a new relation with
the world, in which the atmosphere has a joyful relativity. Morris shows that Vietnam stories can reflect this relativity, in which imagination merges with deadly reality to create an atmosphere of carnival.

Scott, Grant F. "*Paco's Story* and the Ethics of Violence." *CRITIQUE: Studies in Contemporary Fiction* 36 (Fall, 1994): 69-80. Discusses the ethics of violence in
Heinemann's novel, particularly as it relates to the "selective seeing" characteristic
of the gang rape scene at the end of the novel.

Slabey, Robert M. "Heinemann's *Paco's Story*." *The Explicator* 52 (Spring, 1994):
187-189. Slabey demonstrates that Heinemann's work is characteristic of postmodern metafiction, which uses myth in a discontinuous, eclectic, and fragmented
manner.

Philip K. Jason

THE PALACE OF THE WHITE SKUNKS

Author: Reinaldo Arenas (1943-1990)
Type of plot: Family
Time of plot: The late 1950's
Locale: Holguín, a small provincial town in the rural Oriente province of Cuba
First published: Le palais des très blanches mouffettes, 1975 (English translation, 1990)

Principal characters:

FORTUNATO, the protagonist, an adolescent trying to escape from the misery of his family life during the time of the Cuban revolutionary struggle

POLO, Fortunato's grandfather, an embittered old grouch fed up with life who refuses to talk to any of the members of his family

JACINTA, Fortunato's superstitious and blasphemous grandmother, who is desperately searching for answers to explain life's hardships

CELIA, Fortunato's aunt, who is driven to madness after her only daughter poisons herself

DIGNA, Fortunato's aunt, who has been abandoned by her husband

ADOLFINA, Fortunato's aunt, a spinster desperate to lose her virginity

ONERICA, Fortunato's unmarried mother, who abandons him and goes to the United States

The Novel

The Palace of the White Skunks is a stylistically rich experimental novel that tells of the desolation, despair, and vicissitudes of a Cuban family prior to the 1959 Cuban Revolution. The novel, which deliberately and systematically undermines the conventions of the realistic novel tradition, is centered on Fortunato, a sensitive and restless young man living through a turbulent political period in Cuban history: the insurrectional struggle against the dictatorial government of Fulgencio Batista. Desperate to escape the disappointments and cruelties of his family (whom he refers to as "creatures" and "wild beasts"), as well as to escape from Holguín, a small, conservative rural town, Fortunato attempts to join Fidel Castro's revolutionary forces. This flight for freedom, however, ends tragically when the young man is arrested, tortured, and executed by the government police.

The novel is divided into three parts: "Prologue and Epilogue," "The Creatures Utter Their Complaints," and "The Play." In the fourteen pages that make up part 1, "Prologue and Epilogue," the reader is introduced to the self-pitying and squabbling voices of each character, all members of the same family. At this point, the crisscrossing of voices is so entangled that it is extremely difficult to decipher during a first reading. These fragments of voices, however, will be contextualized and expanded during the second and third parts of the novel. With the (con)fusion of what is traditionally the first word (prologue) and last word (epilogue) of the traditional novel, the suggestion is made that there is no first or final word on any given matter; rather, discourse is open-ended, without a finalizing period.

Part 2, "The Creatures Utter Their Complaints," constitutes the major portion of the novel. This section is divided into five "agonies" in which each family member takes turns articulating his or her own intimate sufferings. These accounts are presented as a rambling of voices that often conceals the identity of the speaking subject. Temporal-spatial realities are filtered through the turbulent voices of the family members, who do not concern themselves with providing objective reference points. It appears as if the same state of instability and crisis that is assaulting the country exists internally in each family member.

Part 2 also introduces fragments from newspaper accounts, bulletins of guerrilla activity, advertisements, film announcements, and beauty magazines; these fragments are juxtaposed alongside and serve to parallel the babel of voices of the family members. In "Fifth Agony," there appear twelve versions of the two most significant episodes within the novel: Fortunato's decision to escape from home to join the Castro-led rebels, and Adolfina's unsuccessful attempt to lose her virginity during a night on the town. The contradictions in the different versions of these two fruitless quests reveal the difficulty of attempting to record any reality faithfully. Yet this lack of precision is quite irrelevant to the emotional intensity, dreams, and desires of both characters. In the end, any reader searching for objectivity in *The Palace of the White Skunks* will be at a loss and will consequently miss the artistic and creative intensity of the novel. To appreciate this text, one must surrender to its hallucinatory situations, implausible incidents, and disjointed digressions.

In part 3, "The Play," the reader discovers the insertion of a play within the novel. This change of genre (from novel to drama) is accompanied by a significant change from interior monologue to dramatic dialogue. In this phantasmagoric theatrical representation, the family members become performers who reenact their own lives and obsessions. Immediately following the play, there appears "Sixth Agony," which recounts yet another version of Fortunato's escape. The omniscient narrator of this last agony describes the young man's torture and death at the hands of government soldiers. Earlier, however, this same omniscient narrator, traditionally a reliable voice, had expressed doubt over whether Fortunato had ever joined the rebel forces. Regardless of what indeed happened, it is significant that no version denies Fortunato's basic reasons for wanting to escape from home: hunger, poverty, repression, lack of opportunities, and the suffocating demands of his family.

The Characters

The Palace of the White Skunks is the story of Fortunato and of the young man's eccentrically frustrated and obsessive family: Polo, Fortunato's grandfather, who considers himself cursed for having engendered only daughters; Jacinta, Fortunato's superstitious and crazed grandmother; Digna, Celia, Onerica, and Adolfina, Polo's and Jacinta's daughters, all marginalized figures who desperately search for a space, either real or imaginary, in which to forget the misery of their existence. Together, on a structural level, the sisters function to articulate a psychotic and paranoic discourse that identifies the passive role assigned to women in Hispanic society. Their frustrated attempts to escape their suffocating fate only add to their sense of desperation. The sisters' children, Esther (Celia's daughter), Tico and Anisia (Digna's son and daughter), and Fortunato (Onerica's son), are all fatherless. On a spiritual level, Digna, Celia, Onerica, and Adolfina also are fatherless, since Polo rejects them because of their gender. Throughout the novel, these characters—or, rather, voices, for the text is constructed as a cacophony of voices—are given the opportunity to recount their own obsessive stories of despair.

In the novel, Fortunato pursues writing as a means to survive the continual oppression of his family and the conservatism of his hometown. He fabricates and invents imaginary refuges that take him away from his asphyxiating situation. The young man steals paper from his grandfather's small vegetable and fruit shop in order to write in secret, a labor of passion that he faithfully carries out under the most oppressive conditions. His wish is to record his family's experiences. For his identification with other oppressed individuals, however, he must pay a price. Fortunato's desire to bear his family's suffering, to understand, to feel their intimate pain and frustrations, places him on the path to destruction. The adolescent poet, whose existence is already marked by isolation and hopelessness, begins to fragment under the weight of misfortune. *The Palace of the White Skunks* challenges the notion of a single reliable voice that can faithfully telegraph reality to the reader, for the audibility of Fortunato's voice, a voice that wishes to see itself as the authentic representative of the family, is incessantly drowned out by the multiplicity of voices of other family members eager to tell their own sides of the story. Although first-, second-, and third-person narrative voices are utilized in *The Palace of the White Skunks*, the first-person point of view predominates within the text. This narrative "I" is shared by all the family members, producing a cacophony of voices in which each voice, at times unrecognizable, struggles in vain to be heard. Multiple narrative "I's" contradict one another, in this way not granting referential stability to any speaking subject. Thus, the text is reduced to a crisscrossing of affirmations and contradictions, denying the concentration of veracity into a single authoritative voice. In this Tower of Babel where no one understands anyone else, personal agonies are fated to echo and reecho within the chambers of the novel. That the characters, prisoners of their own suffering, yearn in desperation to find a receptive listener only underscores their alienation.

Themes and Meanings

The Palace of the White Skunks is embedded in a concrete historical event, the fight of the Sierra Maestra rebel forces against the Batista regime that culminated in Fidel Castro's revolutionary victory of 1959. Yet, the presentation of the characters' other levels of experience is never sacrificed for any type of accuracy or transparency, any hope to reproduce historical reality faithfully at a referential level of language. Arenas's concern is not to rewrite history but to subordinate history to fiction, thus allowing free inquiry into the nature of human existence. The novel does not support the concept of an "official" history of a collective consciousness that simplifies human experience by reducing it to facts or figures; rather, the book examines the enigma of individual human existence.

The ironic and ludicrous title, *The Palace of the White Skunks*, already alerts the reader to the unconventional story that follows. In this novel, the notion of a well-structured plot is subverted by the presentation of a narrative time-space of multiple possibilities that invites the reader to sort out the various narrative threads and, thus, to work out a larger meaning. The text requires a flexible approach to reading, a letting go of traditional expectations. The reader is asked to make the text intelligible in spite of its violations and transgressions, to accommodate the shifting codes of a multifarious reality. Hence, the initial image of death riding on a bicycle around the family home is presented as being equally "real" as the protagonist's frustrated attempt to join the revolutionary struggle. Fortunato's walking on the roof while stabbing himself, Esther and Fortunato's chats beyond the grave, demons and spirits dancing in the living room, the extreme poverty of the rural town, the insurrectional struggle against Batista, the grandmother's blasphemies and insults, Adolfina's sexual frustrations—all are presented side by side and contribute equally to the novel's textual validity.

Utilizing a narrative strategy that fragments the story into bits and pieces, *The Palace of the White Skunks* invites the reader to re-create a bewildering collage that, although it at first disorients, ultimately reforges the life-art connection on the level of the imaginative. In this, his third novel, Arenas provides the reader with a disturbing portrait of the poverty and misery that were present in rural Cuba shortly before the triumph of the revolution. While many Cuban novelists during the 1970's were writing testimonial realistic works that idealistically presented the revolution as the decisive moment that radically transformed Cuban society for the better, Arenas, undermining this rather utopian vision of history, portrays the revolution as the catalyst responsible for the death of his protagonist and the emotional destruction of a family.

In *The Palace of the White Skunks*, Arenas clearly had no intention of writing a closed, linear text that presented a coherent, objective representation of the empirical reality. The novel is a daring compositional experiment that subverts and challenges authoritarian and reductionist attitudes toward literature as well as life.

Critical Context

While living in Cuba, Arenas published only one novel, *Celestino antes del alba* (1967; *Singing from the Well*, 1987), and a few short stories. The author's refusal to articulate revolutionary propaganda in his writings forced the cultural policymakers of the Cuban Revolution—individuals who defined the function of literature as political and of immediate practical utility—to censor his texts and designate them as counterrevolutionary. After Arenas's fall from favor with the Cuban government, his work was no longer published on the island; moreover, his manuscripts were repeatedly confiscated and destroyed by the Cuban secret police. As a result, Arenas secretly began to send his manuscripts abroad. *The Palace of the White Skunks* thus first appeared in 1975 in French translation before appearing in its original

Spanish version, *El palacio de las blanquísimas mofetas*, in 1980.

   The Palace of the White Skunks is the second novel of a five-book sequence—*Singing from the Well, The Palace of the White Skunks, Otra vez el mar* (1982; *Farewell to the Sea*, 1986), *El color del verano* (1991; the color of summer), and *El asalto* (1991; the assault)—that constitutes a unique intradependent unit within the author's total novelistic productions. This quintet, which the author insisted on calling a *pentagonía* ("pentagony")—a playful but revealing neologism that underscores the despair and *agonía* (agony) suffered by the characters in each novel—reflects different historical periods of Cuban society as well as provides an imagined futuristic vision of the Cuban island and its people. In each novel of the series, the main character is destroyed—only to be resurrected under a new name in the subsequent text, where he suffers a whole new set of ordeals. With *The Palace of the White Skunks*, Arenas continued the family saga that he had initially begun with *Singing from the Well*. *The Palace of the White Skunks* explores the protean main character's adolescent world, a chaotic world of torment and spiritual hardship played out against a backdrop of revolutionary upheaval.

Bibliography
Arenas, Reinaldo. "Reinaldo Arenas's Last Interview." Interview by Perla Rozencvaig. *Review: Latin American Literature and Arts* 44 (January/June, 1991): 78-83. Arenas's last interview, granted shortly before his death in 1990, in which he talks at length about the novels of the *pentagonía*. The reader gets a sense of the author's humor and subversive spirit, essential elements of his writing.
Mujica, Barbara. Review of *The Palace of the White Skunks*. *Americas* 43 (January/February, 1991):60. Mujica praises Arenas's book for its textured, vivid images of pre-revolutionary Cuba.
Soto, Francisco, David William Foster, and Gary Soto. *Reinaldo Arenas*. New York: Twayne, 1998. Offers a critical introduction to the life and work of Arenas. Discusses Arenas's groundbreaking autobiography *Before Night Falls* as "an important milestone in American letters, for it was the first openly homosexual autobiography ever published." Relates this work to Arenas's entire oeuvre, including *The Palace of the White Skunks*.
Stavans, Ilan. "An Irredeemable Clan." *The New York Times Book Review*, January 20, 1991, p. 20. Stavans clearly observes how despair and desolation permeate the entire text, concluding that Arenas's characters, "like those of William Faulkner, are irredeemable, destined to suffer . . . we hear their tormented screams as they succumb to the perverse joke that has been played upon them by fate."
Wood, Michael. "No Sorrow Left Unturned." *The New York Review of Books* 38 (March 7, 1991): 21-23. A lengthy review of *The Palace of the White Skunks*. Wood states that Arenas "hasn't written any of this book ironically; he has written it lyrically . . . making excess and stylistic risk a kind of signature."

Francisco Soto

PARADISE

Author: Toni Morrison (1931-   )
Type of plot: Historical realism
Time of plot: 1976
Locale: The fictional town of Ruby, Oklahoma
First published: 1998

> *Principal characters:*
> DEACON (DEEK) MORGAN and
> STEWARD MORGAN, twin descendants of the town's patriarch
> CONSOLATA, a mystical woman who presides over a refuge known as
>   the Convent
> MAVIS,
> GRACE (GIGI),
> SENECA, and
> PALLAS, battered and abused women on the run from life who arrive
>   and stay at the Convent
> PATRICIA, a collector of genealogical information on Ruby's families

The Novel

Paradise, which focuses on the love of God, is Morrison's third novel in a trilogy of books dealing with various kinds of love. As the book opens, a violent, bloody massacre takes place at the Convent, a run-down refuge for broken women located near the small town of Ruby, Oklahoma.

The inhabitants of Ruby are descendants of a group of dark-skinned African Americans who migrated west in the 1870's from Mississippi and Louisiana. Hoping to be accepted in Fairly, a town of lighter-skinned blacks, they were turned away. This event becomes memorialized in the town's history as "The Disallowing." The nomadic group finally established a town that they named Haven. During the World War II years, however, the morals of Haven declined so much that the town elders became convinced that they should establish a new town, Ruby, named after the deceased sister of the town's two patriarchs, Deek and Steward Morgan.

The centerpiece of Ruby is the transported Oven, a brick kiln and shrine to the town's unity as well as the gathering place for town business and remembering. Ruby is a proud town, cloistered and protective of its immunity from the evils of the outside world. In this town, there is no tolerance for the less than righteous. Sin is either suppressed or secret.

Despite the town's stringent vigilance against the intrusion of sin and sinners, the weight of transgression and progress from the world outside—mostly sins of the flesh and a weakening of religious constraint—bears heavily upon the town. At the novel's beginning, the height of the mid-1970's social revolution sends the town's self-righteous and deluded leaders into a desperate and chaotic plot to destroy the blatant evil lurking west of Ruby: the Convent and its defiling inhabitants, the women Consolata, Mavis, Grace, Seneca, and Pallas. Ironically, the elimination of these women will also destroy the evidence of those who violated the town's blood rule, a code of sexual fidelity and purity.

The Convent serves as a central locale in the novel. The Convent is everything Ruby is not. It is a haven of acceptance and nurturing. It does not require judgment, nor does it require history or moral purity. Built originally by an embezzler with a taste for bizarre architecture and decadent décor, the Convent was later occupied by an order of nuns who ran a school for Arapaho girls. Consolata, herself rescued from a profligate life by Sister Mary Magna, the mother superior of the order, was brought to the Convent to live. As the school funding and church support eventually ran out, the girls all disappeared, and the residents of the Convent dwindled to Sister Mary Magna and Consolata.

Later, as Sister Mary Magna dies, Consolata is joined by four women who arrive at the Convent at the heights of their life crises. The lives of these women become inextricably entangled with those of the Ruby men, often as a result of adultery or promiscuity. Their lack of regard for the sexual psychoneuroses of Ruby men—so much in contrast to the quiet submission of the women of Ruby—mocks the moral piety of these men and inevitably leads the men to blame the women of the Convent for their own hypocrisy and sexual infidelity.

It is Patricia, Ruby's fair-skinned descendant, who figures out the malignant intentions of the men. She collects the enormous data on bloodlines of the original nine "8-rock" families, so named for their coal-black skin. She has gleaned information from her students, from conversations with her neighbors, and from her own copious notations of the interrelations and dead ends of the original bloodlines. The myth that no one dies in Ruby save those who leave, she discovers, depends on all generations being not only racially untampered but also free of adultery—the "deal" that Zachariah, the original patriarch, and Steward made with God. As the promiscuous sisterhood of the Convent invokes the destructive power of lust in the men, the women become a natural target.

The Characters

The stern voices of Morrison's two protagonists, Deacon and Steward Morgan, set the novel's tone. Inheriting the patriarchal leadership of Ruby by virtue of their wealth and bloodline, the two men rule over money, property, and ultimately the moral sanctity of Ruby's history. Insisting on a hard respect for an ethic of hard work, strength, and moral purity, they control of the town. Morrison uses their characters to resonate the voices of the past and emphasize the town's lack of its own voice for the present world. Anything that threatens to dishonor the town's ancestral covenant is condemned by one of the twins. Although they publicly inveigh against the sins of the flesh, however, both twins have privately violated the ethic that they so stringently guard. Their self-righteousness and the evil they do to maintain it is the catalyst for other Ruby men who lack the nerve to act. Their wives, Soane and Dovey, likewise epitomize the meek submission of the Ruby women to their men.

Consolata, who has been at the Convent since nuns rescued her from poverty in Brazil, presides over the company of bruised women at the Convent, which is still a respite for orphaned souls and wounded spirits. First comes Mavis, who has inadvertently allowed her babies to suffocate in a hot parked car. Driven to a private madness, she steals her husband's car and flees. Grace, the next to arrive at the Convent, comes to town in sleazy glory, arousing the lust of Ruby's men, most notably K. D., the last male of the Morgan line. Yet men are not her object; she seeks an elusive desert shrine to eroticism. Seneca, abandoned at age five and shuffled through a series of foster homes, comes to the Convent as a martyr. She feels that she can never do enough good to deserve goodness, and she wishes most of all not to offend others. She is patient with runaway Sweetie's dementia, she acquiesces to a brutal lesbian relationship with a dried-up rich woman, and she plays in the middle with the spatting Mavis and Grace. She learns acceptance through accommodation. Pallas, a teenage runaway, is found vomiting outside a clinic. She is delivered to the Convent, where Connie nurses her back to health and speech. Pallas eventually returns to her suburban life but finds it unchanged. Her father is preoccupied with moneymaking, and her boyfriend is still somewhere making art with her mother. It does not take long for Pallas to escape back to the Convent.

Consolata, the "consoler" of these women, is the thread that holds the novel together. Her story begins and ends the novel. Her beginnings are obscure, but her history is made clear toward the end of the novel. She has Christlike powers for healing and resurrection. After she is shot, the massacre is essentially over. The townspeople arrive, the others flee, and the hunters are diminished in their zeal. Her death involves suffering, and it is the result of her threat to those who should be least threatened by her. After her killing, she is laid on the kitchen table and covered. The next day, her body has disappeared; only the shroud of the sheet and a pillow remain. Her command to her followers is simple: "Follow me." They do, and because of their decision to do so, they may have risen above the earthly peril of the Ruby men and found life a better reality.

Themes and Meanings

Why do the men kill the women in the first place? The Convent women are survivors. With their spiritual and sexual freedom and their maleless environment, they manage to survive in better stead than the people of Ruby, who appear to be turning on one another. The line of the Morgans has come to a dead end. Though the men of Ruby interpret the peaceful and unfettered life maintained by Consolata at the Convent as sinful and dangerous, they must acknowledge their own attraction to and curiosity about the women. The truth to be extinguished is that the women, who can live simply and communally, succeed and survive, whereas the leaders of Ruby, who must exert control and rule over others by way of spiritual guilt and mercilessness, cannot do so without constant struggle to uphold the collapsing walls of isolation. Even then, there is sin among them—greed, jealousy, unforgiveness, lying, adultery, murder.

Morrison's overt symbols—the Oven, the Cadillac, the Convent—all point toward an objective world in which these symbols are endowed with powerful, historic ideas and values, sustained by the cultures that made them. The Oven at the center of town carries the town motto, "Beware the Furrow of His Brow." For the "8-rock" families, it serves as the axis of the community; it is the place to gather for food and for civil and social matters. Although the Oven has been preserved for years (it was transported brick by brick from Haven to Ruby), the young people wish to change it. By his own admission, the Reverend Misner admits that he was partly at fault for encouraging the young people to speak up and make changes.

Few women in Ruby ride in cars, but the women at the Convent have use of a Cadillac that gives them unlimited mobility and freedom. Their happiness and freedom must be resolved to evil if the myth of hard work, sacrifice, and denial is to work for Ruby. Morrison's tale is of the archetypal clash of good and evil, of moral righteousness fueling hatred and violence, and of good ultimately transcending evil.

Critical Context

Morrison has said that she intended *Paradise* as the third book in a trilogy dealing with various kinds of love. She covered maternal love in *Beloved* (1987) and romantic love in *Jazz* (1992); *Paradise* deals with spiritual love, the love of God. The heavy biblical themes and analogies support the epic tone of the Mosaic story: the exodus and wandering in the desert of the 8-rock families, the covenant and errand of the generations of 8-rockers, the fierce efforts to maintain an untainted blood line, and a temple (the Oven for some, the Convent for others). There is an Adamic patriarch and his two sons, one given to a brutal and self-righteous violence, the other more passive.

The novel, though, is more than a mere biblical parable; it has historical roots. Many African Americans uprooted from the oppressive sites of their slavery and migrated west to set up towns such as Ruby. Morrison uses her narrative technique, consisting sometimes of purely poetic diction, to represent a tangled connection between characters, thoughts, and events. Her characters tell the story from all of their angles, but most of all through their personalities and their imperfect, human vision. In the end, the reader will know more not only about the consequences of self-righteous vindication but also about redemption and love.

Bibliography

Grewal, Gurleen. *Circles of Sorrow, Lines of Struggle: The Novels of Toni Morrison.* Baton Rouge: Louisiana State University Press, 1998. A brief but perceptive discussion of Morrison's most important works, with emphasis on its relation to the American South. Bibliography and index.

Kubitschek, Missy Dehn. *Toni Morrison: A Critical Companion.* Westport, Conn.: Greenwood Press, 1998. A good survey of Morrison's life and writings; provides an interesting contrast to the similar volume by Jill Matus listed below. Bibliography, index.

Matus, Jill. *Toni Morrison*. New York: St. Martin's Press, 1998. A solid overview of Morrison's oeuvre to the time immediately preceding publication of *Paradise*. Index, bibliography.

Mori, Aoi. *Toni Morrison and Womanist Discourse*. New York: Peter Lang, 1999. A critical discussion of feminist themes in Morrison's works. Includes a good bibliography and an index.

Morrison, Toni. *Playing in the Dark: Whiteness and the Literary Imagination*. Cambridge, Mass.: Harvard University Press, 1992. Morrison presents a series of lectures outlining her literary theory.

Peach, Linden, ed. *Toni Morrison*. New York: St. Martin's Press, 1998. A collection of essays discussing Morrison's novels in a variety of contexts: as women's literature, as African American literature, and as twentieth century U.S. literature. Indexed, with an extensive bibliography.

Betty L. Hart

PARADISO

Author: José Lezama Lima (1910-1976)
Type of plot: Artistic education
Time of plot: The early twentieth century
Locale: Cuba, Florida, Jamaica, and Mexico
First published: 1966 (English translation, 1974)

Principal characters:

JOSÉ CEMÍ, the protagonist, a young poet
COLONEL JOSÉ EUGENIO CEMÍ, his father
RIALTA OLAYA DE CEMÍ, his mother
RICARDO FRONESIS and
EUGENIO FOCIÓN, friends of Cemí at the university
OPPIANO LICARIO, José Cemí's mentor, a poet

The Novel

Paradiso is both the story of a Cuban upper-middle-class family during the first quarter of the twentieth century and a *Bildungsroman* that traces a young man's path to artistic creation. Although the novel focuses on the protagonist, Cemí, and begins with a description of an asthma attack that he suffers in early childhood, from chapter 2 to chapter 6 it tells the story of his parents' families, their meeting, and his father the Colonel's early death at the age of thirty-three.

The death of the Colonel is the event that endows his widow, Rialta, and his son Cemí with a spiritual mission in life. She becomes convinced that the loss of her husband cannot have been meaningless and that her son, in some way, will fulfill his father's truncated destiny. Cemí seems to accept that destiny without question, but he does not know how he will fulfill it. Through a series of mystical experiences precipitated by Cemí's intense observation of objects and by his meditation about a particular image or idea, he comes to realize that he will make his contribution through the cultivation of poetry and the search for poetic images that will lead to truth. Poetry fills the vacuum left by the death of Cemí's father, and it endows that seemingly purposeless death with meaning.

The rest of *Paradiso* follows Cemí's education in art and in the ways of the world. Leaving behind the safety of family life, Cemí enters the outside world first at school and then at the university, where he is introduced to the allure of sex and the life of the intellect. In this stage of his education, his guides are his friends, Fronesis and Foción, and with them he explores all the vital issues that the embalmed lectures of the university professors never broach.

Having survived the dangers of this phase of his education (the pursuit of wanton eroticism and the abuse of intelligence as an instrument of power), Cemí is ready to undertake his poetic apprenticeship under the guidance of Oppiano Licario. This enigmatic character appears at several crucial moments in *Paradiso*. Licario, the only one present when Cemí's father died, accepts the Colonel's dying request: "I have a son. Get to know him, and try to teach him something of what you have learned through your travels, suffering, and reading." Licario becomes Cemí's poetic mentor and by the time he dies has led the young man to the very threshold of artistic creation. As Cemí sits alone, late at night in a café, he remembers his mentor's assurance that he is now prepared for poetic creation, and *Paradiso* ends with Licario's words: "We may now begin."

The Characters

All readers of *Paradiso* are struck by Lezama's unusual characterization. No matter what their social rank, age, or education, his characters all seem to speak in the same manner and with the same vast erudition. In fact, they all seem to speak exactly as the author himself does. In *Paradiso*, Lezama makes a total departure from the psychological character portrayal of the traditional novel. Lezama himself has explained that his characters are really metaphors that became too developed for poetry. That, he claims, is what led him to write his first novel, *Paradiso*.

The title *Paradiso* proclaims the author's tribute to Dante's *The Divine Comedy* and furnishes a clue to the proper understanding of Lezama's characterization. The characters of *Paradiso*, like those of *The Divine Comedy*, have an allegorical meaning. José Cemí, the protagonist, represents the search for the poetic image and truth. His last name is the word used by the Indians of the Caribbean for the images of their gods; at the same time, it seems to be a pun on the Greek work for "sign," an appropriate allusion in the case of a poet whose tools are letters and words.

Oppiano Licario, Cemí's mentor in the art of poetry, is described in the novel as the new Icarus who attempts the impossible. Licario plays a role in *Paradiso* similar to that played by Vergil in Dante's *Inferno*. Like Vergil, he is an experienced poet who guides Cemí, keeping him on the right path and away from dangerous dead ends and detours.

Fronesis and Foción symbolize reason and passion, respectively, but together with Cemí they define what Lezama considers to be the different aspects of the human personality. Fronesis, whose name means "prudence" or "worldly wisdom" in Greek, is noble, generous, and constructive. He becomes Cemí's best friend and a good model. Foción, petty, selfish, and destructive, is a friend whom Cemí never quite trusts, but at the university the three young men are inseparable. In the allegorical scheme of the novel, the presence of Foción is necessary to establish an equilibrium. As a poet, Cemí must encompass all of human experience; he cannot do this by heeding only the dictates of reason. The poet must also come to terms with passion, even in its darkest, most destructive aspects.

The characters who belong to Cemí's family seem to partake to a lesser degree of the allegorical aspect and come closer to being flesh-and-blood people; this is probably because they are closely modeled on the author's own family. Nevertheless, they still clearly have a trace of allegory in them. The Colonel seems to be an incarnation of the joy of living and of all the manly virtues: health, vigor, honor, and justice. Rialta is not only Cemí's mother but also the personification of Hispanic motherhood. After her husband's death, she lives totally devoted to his memory and to her children. She is Cemí's first guide, and she prepares him to face life with a mission.

The unorthodox characterizations of *Paradiso* must be understood as an aesthetic decision and not as a shortcoming. Lezama is fully capable of creating psychologically convincing characters, but he only displays this skill in the case of minor characters, such as Cemí's maternal grandmother, the cook Juan Izquierdo, the Colonel's father, and Rialta's brother Alberto, who are all as vivid and as unforgettable as the characters of a traditional novel.

Themes and Meanings

The principal theme of *Paradiso* is the power of poetic language to transform life. For Cemí, the quest for poetic images is also the road to spiritual salvation. For him, as for Lezama, the poetic image is a vehicle to reach truth and in particular divine truth. Although extremely unorthodox in his views, Lezama always maintained his adherence to Catholicism. *Paradiso* (and all of Lezama's work) must be understood in the context of the author's mystical concept of artistic creation. The artist must always attempt the impossible, for it is only by working at the limits of his capacity that he can hope to catch a glimmer of truth. The writing of poetry is therefore dependent on mystic revelations that often occur unannounced and that make use of the prosaic material of everyday life. *Paradiso* is a stylized autobiography in which Lezama utilizes the structures of the family novel and the *Bildungsroman* in order to expound his system of poetic mysticism.

Lezama's concept of illumination through difficult poetic images owes much to the practice of Zen Buddhism, in which, under the guidance of a Roshi (Zen master), the disciple meditates on paradoxes (*kōan*) that lead to flashes of insight. Similarly, the stages that Cemí must pass before he reaches the state of mind where artistic creation is possible recall the purification that a Buddhist must undergo through successive lifetimes before he can reach Nirvana.

Taoism also plays a major part in the characterization of Cemí; particularly important are the central concepts of yin and yang, the opposing but complementary principles that make up the universe. Cemí is in essence a personification of the yin and yang. Unlike his friends Fronesis and Foción, who are dynamic and represent either of these principles, Cemí is static because he contains them both. He is the balance of reason and passion, light and dark, heterosexuality and homosexuality. Cemí never engages in sex in *Paradiso* because he represents the principle of androgyny, which for Lezama means sexual self-sufficiency.

Sexuality in *Paradiso* functions as a parable of artistic creation and of salvation. Homosexuality represents a destructive turning upon oneself, symbolized in the novel by the image of the circle (for Lezama a symbol of false immortality). Heterosexuality is viewed in a positive light, but the concomitant procreation is considered an acceptance of mortality. Only asexuality is seen as compatible with artistic creation and true immortality.

From the point of view of twentieth century philosophy and literature, the most striking aspect of Lezama's worldview is his faith in language and in poetic expression. Where many others have seen language as a prison and poetry as mere wordplay, Lezama believes in their ability to reveal truth.

Critical Context

The publication of *Paradiso* launched Lezama into international fame. Prior to the novel's publication, Lezama was virtually unknown outside Cuba, where he was known as a major poet, essayist, and the founder of *Orígenes*, the most important literary journal in the years before the revolution. *Paradiso*, which was read and praised by leading Latin American writers such as Julio Cortázar, Octavio Paz, and Mario Vargas Llosa, earned a place for Lezama among the writers of the "Boom" of Latin American literature.

Although *Paradiso* has been hailed by novelists and critics as a seminal work that offers previously unsuspected rich avenues for the development of the novel, it has never enjoyed a wide readership. Indeed, the novel's great originality and richness has also been its bane; Lezama's highly metaphorical language, his idiosyncratic handling of characterization and plot, and his mysticism have presented insurmountable obstacles for many readers. *Paradiso* has also elicited heated polemics because of its treatment of sex and of homosexuality in particular, and it has been attacked on political grounds as well; upon its first publication in Cuba, it was received by some as a counterrevolutionary work.

Nevertheless, Lezama's first novel is firmly entrenched as one of the classics of Latin American literature. *Oppiano Licario* (1977), an incomplete continuation of *Paradiso*, was published posthumously.

Bibliography

Hassat, J. J. *Assimilation/Generation/Resurrection: Contrapuntal Readings in the Poetry of José Lezama Lima*. Lewisburg, Pa.: Bucknell University Press, 1997. Lezama Lima's prose often contains striking poetic images. Although this volume does not deal directly with Lezama Lima's fiction, it is a valuable resource for understanding the way Lezama Lima's poetry and prose influence each other and interact.

Pellon, Gustavo. *José Lezama Lima's Joyful Vision: A Study of "Paradiso" and Other Prose Works*. Austin: University of Texas Press, 1989. A definitive study of Lezama Lima's novel, it is an excellent full-length study that places his book within the context of his other works. Includes an index and a bibliography for further reading.

Pollard, Scott. "Canonizing Revision: Literary History and the Postmodern Latin American Writer." *College Literature* 20 (October, 1993): 133-147. Pollard examines the literary histories of Alejo Carpentier, Lezama Lima, and Carlos Fuentes.

He argues that these writers revise Western literary history in order to enhance the position of Latin American narrative within it. Of the three authors Pollard discusses, he particularly credits Lezama Lima with differentiating Latin American history from European history in his fiction.

Gustavo Pellon

THE PASSION ACCORDING TO G. H.

Author: Clarice Lispector (1925-1977)
Type of plot: Philosophical realism
Time of plot: The 1960's
Locale: An apartment in Rio de Janeiro, Brazil
First published: A Paixão Segundo G. H., 1964 (English translation, 1988)

> *Principal characters:*
>> G. H., the middle-aged sculptress who tells the story, a gregarious and
>> outgoing woman who shies away from intimate relationships
>> JANAIR, G. H.'s maid, who has abruptly quit and decamped
>> A COCKROACH, an insect who lives in Janair's wardrobe and whose
>> appearance precipitates G. H.'s spiritual crisis
>> THE CRYING MAN, a vaguely described ex-lover of G. H. to whom she
>> imagines she is telling her story

The Novel

Though the book is heavy with Christian allusions, especially to the Old Testament, what *The Passion According to G. H.* presents is a completely secular description of a spiritual rebirth. The trivial act of squashing a cockroach as she cleans her maid's room strangely rattles the story's narrator and leads her into a cascade of profound reflections on the scheme of things.

The book centers on a few hours in the life of the narrator, who is identified only as G. H., as she sits in her servant's room and thinks. The bulk of the text is taken up with a precise delineation of her thought processes as she reevaluates her life. This reevaluation, however, is not of the sort found in psychological novels, in which a character might reconsider past actions and resolve to make up for past lapses. What concerns G. H. is not any specific incidents but rather the tenor of her life. Thus, for example, thoughts on the animality of the cockroach lead her to ponder her own humanness, which, she learns, can be truly appreciated only by understanding its linkage to nature. This facet of her existence she has previously overlooked.

Abstruse as such a concentration on abstract issues may seem, the heroine's spiritual journey is correlated with the specifics of her present lifestyle, her relation to her maid, and her past history. Concurrent with the unraveling of her previous, faulty spiritual constructions occurs a gradual revelation of her material circumstances.

G. H.'s life is ripe for enlightenment because it is one of extreme artificiality. She is a rentier, that is, one who lives off the dividends of her investments. She sculpts, not as serious artistic activity but to pass the time. Her friends are fellow idle bohemians, isolated from the daily life of the average Brazilian, and G. H.'s relationships extend no further than friendships. She has no relatives or long-term interpersonal commitments. She is without real work, hobbies, or intimacies with others.

Such facts are scattered throughout the story, but G. H.'s connection to her maid, Janair, is given in a lump at the beginning. Though the servant had been employed for some time, G. H. knows nothing about her and has not been in her quarters since she was hired. Going into the room to clean up after the maid has abruptly left, G. H. is startled to find that the occupant had stripped the place of its clutter and sketched rude, primitive pictures on the wall, depictions that reveal Janair's hatred for her mistress. Finding her superficial understanding of her employee totally exploded sufficiently disorients G. H. so that she can begin a reconsideration of her relations with the world.

Forced to see one relationship in a new light, the narrator is enabled to more purposefully allow herself to look at major events from her past in a new light. Her casual killing of a cockroach in the maid's wardrobe leads her to remember an abortion she had undergone just as casually. Her quiet moments in the servant's quarters lead her to think back to quiet times with an ex-lover and to acknowledge for the first time the depth of the love they had, which was expressed best in silence. In keeping with the novel's philosophical bent, however, G. H. thinks of her abortion not to blame herself for the choice she made in eliminating her unborn child but rather in order to condemn herself for the offhanded, thoughtless manner in which she made the decision. This condemnation links to the central spiritual perception with which she leaves the room at the end: She must henceforth try to live without preconceptions so that she can approach every moment with heightened authenticity.

To crown and close this chapter in her life, these few hours in which she has thought and functioned more intensely than ever before, G. H. bends down and eats the cockroach. In this bizarre act of "communion," G. H. both thanks the bug for being the guide to her spiritual reinvigoration, and, more important, physically acts out her new rejection of traditional social stereotypes, such as the belief that insects are inherently disgusting. After this ritual, G. H. is ready to leave the room and confront life with an altered and enriched perspective.

The Characters

The Passion According to G. H. has an extremely tight focus. From G. H.'s viewpoint, the novel recounts what happened one morning while she worked and sat alone in her flat. Nothing about G. H.'s life is reported unless a memory of it turns up in this space of time—the reader learns nothing about the narrator's childhood, for example, since none of her mental associations lead to thoughts of it—and other characters are sketched only to the degree that they occur in her reminiscences. Aside from her maid, other people who appear in the book are not even named. The fact that the speaker laconically calls herself G. H. is thus a relative matter, since even this slight designation gives her more substantiality than is granted to other figures in the book. Lispector's strategy for describing her main character, then, is to keep personal details to a minimum without eliminating them altogether.

G. H. has had a shallow life, according to the details that do appear to describe her. Her life is taken up with such insignificant pursuits as gossiping and partying. Though she is a sculptress, she does not labor seriously at her art; though she is a social butterfly, she has no special confidantes or long-term love relationship. Yet she has, on occasion and only for brief spans, longed for a more profound connection to the universe. These details serve to anchor the character firmly in reality, so that what happens to her seems neither unbelievable nor an experience that would happen only to an extraordinary personality. On the other hand, Lispector's restrained use of specifics, so that next to nothing is told about G. H.'s current status or her life's former chronology, acts to direct readers' attention to what is of paramount concern to the writer: describing the gradations of consciousness that G. H. goes through in encountering a nova of philosophical epiphanies.

A cockroach, ironically, is the second most prominent character in the book. Like other characters in the novel, the insect is only described insofar as it is a contributor to G. H.'s awakening. Few details are given about the cockroach's looks or behavior. Rather, it is described generically. It is mentioned, for example, that the cockroach has a long pedigree, having been on earth since the time of the dinosaurs, and this thought draws G. H. into a lengthy reflection on history.

Janair, G. H.'s maid, is also incompletely known. The main information given about her is that she has rather grotesquely redone her room. The room changes do not cause G. H., who tells the story, to try to plumb the servant's motives; instead, G. H. merely observes how the shock of finding the changes affects herself.

Other characters without names, such as the doctor who performed G. H.'s abortion, are even less distinctly drawn. A single moment when they were in contact with G. H. is recalled, with neither the background to the scene nor its aftermath filled in.

Themes and Meanings

Before writing this novel, Lispector had lived extensively outside her homeland of Brazil, in the United States and in European countries, and she had a cosmopolitan, nonsectarian outlook. In depicting G. H.'s epiphany, though Lispector draws on Christian imagery and citations available to her from her unbringing, she presents the situation nondenominationally. She translates religious terminology into a secular vocabulary. In G. H.'s moment of truth, the name of God frequently comes up, but "God," G. H. explicitly states, is a word she is using to name the constantly emergent life force of the world, not a higher being attached to some religious creed. To someone like G. H., who has lived out of touch with nature and her own animal side, an awareness of this life force strikes with as much power as a religious revelation.

Part of the reason for Lispector's desacralization of this experience is to remove it from its doctrinal trappings. Above all, she wants to bring spiritual exaltation down to earth and make it seem realizable for anyone. Through such techniques as the use of homely details and realistic characterization, Lispector strives to indicate that every person who has ever thirsted for a richer life has the potential to undergo a genuine rebirth. Stated obversely, the book argues that no one has the right to shrug off such intangible events as are captured in the volume, since every person is liable to vital renewal.

Metaphysical experiences are often described in unconvincing and unsatisfying ways by those who went through them. Lispector confronts the issue of the possibility of representing near imperceptible happenings head on by having G. H. keep a written record. Everything in the novel describes the events of the narrator's extraordinary morning, but without revealing what has occurred since then, G. H. tells the reader that it is the day after her revelations; she is trying to write down what took place so that she will never forget the particulars. She runs into manifold problems in trying to find the words to embody what are resolutely nonverbal experiences. This is where re-definition comes in. Many words that she used to use, such as "God" and "love," no longer seem meaningful according to her new understanding of reality. Also, her wrestling with expression provokes her to constantly draw on biblical imagery, as when she describes the maid's room as a desert where a saint is tested. She does this not because the experience is especially Christian but because this imagery accurately conveys the subtleties of mental nuance felt by those undergoing spiritual ordeals.

Thus, though Lispector is intent on showing readers how close anyone is to mysti-cal discovery, this does not persuade her to downplay the complexity or ambiguity of such discovery. The writer is unflinching in accepting the challenges of attempting to put the ineffable into words.

Critical Context

The Passion According to G. H. can be connected to two intellectual currents of the period. The first was the rising prominence of "liberation theology" in Latin America. This theology was a Christianity, largely Catholic, that had become more concerned with social justice and trying to ensure the poor an adequate life than with getting them to take the sacraments and register doctrinal purity. This religious trend partook of some of the spirit of the Cuban revolution and of the urban guerrillas who fought corrupt dictators in many South and Central American countries, though it differed fundamentally from these movements in choice of means. Where the guerrillas de-pended on firepower, the liberation church eschewed violence in favor of preaching and having its leaders set examples of simple, dignified living in the communities of the impoverished. Though Lispector does not directly promote such ideas in her book, she shows she is influenced by them in her double act of translation. She places a woman's moment of life-shattering vision in a mundane setting, and she drops reli-gious phraseology in favor of everyday language. She translates a moment from spe-cialized religious experience to place it in the common stream of life. By this tactic, she follows the wave of liberation theology in an insistence on the relevance and worldliness of spiritual concerns.

Second, Lispector is inspired by continental existentialism, to which she had been exposed in the fiction of the twentieth century French philosopher and novelist Jean-Paul Sartre. Sartre's novel *La Nausée* (1938, *Nausea*, 1949) is highlighted by a scene that recalls the one in which G. H. is transfixed by a cockroach. Sartre's protag-onist is struck and horrified by the roiling, inexhaustible life revealed to him by a tan-gle of tree roots. Though his feeling is one of revulsion, Sartre suggests that such mo-ments are constructive, since one can live in authenticity and freedom only if one breaks the brittle surface of conventions—conventions that would ignore, for exam-ple, the life force in the tree and see it as merely another object. Lispector shares

Sartre's belief that the passageway to authenticity leads through a realization of the estranging foreignness of the natural world, though her vision is not so unrelievedly dark as his.

This novel continued to add to Lispector's reputation as a writer's writer. She did not garner as much popular support, as did many of her contemporaries in Latin American fiction. Though some of them, such as Julio Cortázar, and, to a lesser extent, Mario Vargas Llosa, were as tenaciously experimental as she was, their works had more conventional plots (though they were not always unfolded in a traditional way) and seamier themes, being concerned with such matters as sex or political corruption. Yet Lispector's reputation has continued to grow, as discriminating readers increasingly appreciate the exquisiteness of her writing and the depth and precision she brings to her treatment of philosophical and aesthetic issues.

Bibliography
Cixous, Helene. *Reading with Clarice Lispector.* Minneapolis: University of Minnesota Press, 1990. Chapters on *The Stream of Life*, *The Apple in the Dark*, "The Egg and the Chicken," and *The Hour of the Star.* The book includes an introduction by Verena Andermatt Conley, carefully explaining Cixous's critical approach to Lispector. Recommended for advanced students.
Coutinho, Afranio. *An Introduction to Literature in Brazil.* New York: Columbia University Press, 1960. A major Brazilian critic assesses Lispector's achievement, emphasizing her place in Brazilian literature and her powerful metaphorical and atmospheric fiction.
Fitz, Earl F. *Clarice Lispector.* Boston: Twayne, 1985. A useful introduction that includes a chapter of biography, a discussion of Lispector's place in Brazilian literature; a study of her style, structure, and point of view in her novels and short stories; and her nonfiction work. Includes chronology, detailed notes, and a well-annotated bibliography.
Lowe, Elizabeth. *The City in Brazilian Literature.* Rutherford, N.J.: Farleigh Dickinson University Press, 1982. Discusses Lispector as an urban writer, focusing mainly on *A cidade sitiada*, *The Passion According to G. H.*, and *The Stream of Life.*
Peixoto, Marta. *Passionate Fictions: Gender, Narrative, and Violence in Clarice Lispector.* Minneapolis: University of Minnesota Press, 1994. Written with a decidedly feminist bias, *Passionate Fictions* analyzes Lispector's frequently violent subject matter, juxtaposing it with her strange and original use of language. Special attention is paid to the nexus with Helene Cixous and to the autobiographical elements of *The Stream of Life* and *A via crucis do corpo.*

James Feast

THE PAWNBROKER

Author: Edward Lewis Wallant (1926-1962)
Type of plot: Psychological realism
Time of plot: The 1950's
Locale: New York City and surroundings
First published: 1961

> *Principal characters:*
> > SOL NAZERMAN, a Holocaust survivor and pawnbroker in New York
> > City's Harlem
> > JESUS ORTIZ, a Puerto Rican youth, Sol's assistant
> > MARILYN BIRCHFIELD, a Protestant social worker
> > BERTHA, Sol's sister, who came to the United States before the war
> > TESSIE RUBIN and
> > MENDEL, Sol's mistress and her father, both Holocaust survivors
> > GOBERMAN, a refugee and extortionist
> > MURILLIO, a racketeer who "launders" profits from illegal businesses
> > through the pawn shop

The Novel

The Pawnbroker is a stunning work that details the psychic journey of a tortured Holocaust survivor. A third-person omniscient narrator introduces and describes characters and circumstances that reinforce the main character's rage as well as those who help release him from it.

The novel's protagonist, forty-five-year-old Sol Nazerman, was a professor at the University of Cracow in Poland. Arrested by the Nazis for being Jewish, he was physically and emotionally tortured in an extermination camp where his wife and children died. At the beginning of the novel, Sol lives in Mount Vernon, New York, with his sister, her teacher husband, and their two children, and he supports them by running a Harlem pawnshop, a setting redolent of lost dreams and corrupted lives. Bertha, Sol's sister, tries hard to assimilate herself into American upper-middle-class life, while Sol's nephew Morton, like Sol, is a solitary soul who studies drawing.

Described as an intensely private, bitter man with no allegiances, Sol speaks mostly in cold monosyllables to his family and isolates himself from them. Sol's sleep is often interrupted by flashbacks to horrific experiences, as when his son drowns in the bottomless human feces in the cattle car en route to the death camp.

At the pawnshop, Sol hires a lively, amiable young assistant, Jesus Ortiz, who rapidly becomes more than a mere apprentice to Sol. Jesus wishes to learn the pawn business so as to open his own shop someday. Sol explains that the Jewish affinity for business and money comes from thousands of years of insecurity caused by anti-Semitism. A typical day at the pawnshop includes an endless series of junkies, prostitutes, and other desperate souls, each with an item to pawn. Sitting in his wire cage like a trapped animal, Sol coldly ignores their entreaties for more and gives each customer from two to five dollars.

Another important character is Marilyn Birchfield, a warm and caring social worker. She is not put off by Sol's coldness, and she senses the tortured person behind his impenetrable facade. Her friendly visits seem to quell Sol's inner rage slightly. Although he chafes at her kindness, Sol has a few moments of peace when they take a Hudson River boat trip; still, he dissuades her interest by likening a relationship with him to necrophilia.

The Holocaust is never far from Sol's mind. He frequently visits his mistress Tessie and her father Mendel, both of whom are tortured by their death-camp memories. It is loss, not love, that ties Sol and Tessie together, as each has lost both spouse and children at the camp. A less sympathetic survivor is Goberman, who betrayed his own family for food rations and who now threatens and manipulates other survivors to contribute to the Jewish Appeal. In another flashback to an episode in which a terrified inmate threw himself against an electrified fence, Sol recalls Tessie's idea that the dead are far better off. Therefore, when pawnshop owner and racketeer Murillio shoves the barrel of his gun down Sol's throat because Sol is angry that the pawnshop illegally launders money from Murillio's brothel, Sol encourages him to pull the trigger. Readers are then shown another flashback to Sol's horror at having to watch his wife's forced sex acts in a Nazi brothel.

After Mendel's painful death and Sol's traumatic flashback to his death-camp job of dragging gassed corpses to the crematoria, Sol treats Jesus more coldly. Sol even lectures Jesus that he trusts and believes in money only. This motivates the young man to conspire with some unsavory associates to steal cash from the pawnshop. When Sol thwarts the robbery by standing in front of the safe, Jesus moves to protect Sol and is accidentally killed by his co-conspirators. This crime—occurring on the fifteenth anniversary of the death of Sol's family—so stuns Sol that he suddenly feels great compassion and love for Jesus, reaches out to his nephew Morton for help in the shop, and begins to grieve his terrible losses.

The Characters

Wallant's major characters function both as well-developed individuals and as symbols that advance the novel's themes. His minor characters are never stock or one-dimensional, but their full development is necessarily subordinated to that of the major characters.

Since Sol rarely communicates verbally in more than monosyllables, readers learn about him mostly from the reactions of and comparisons with Jesus, Marilyn, Tessie, and Mendel as well as from omniscient narration, interior monologues, and nightmarish flashbacks. Wallant uses eye imagery for Sol, who wears the eyeglasses he removed from a corpse about to be cremated; this becomes symbolic of Sol's Holocaust-driven outlook on life. In addition to communicating the theme of the war's indescribable horrors, Sol's flashback to a family picnic in Poland shows him as a loving family man whose emotions and soul are later eviscerated by unimaginable depravity and deprivation. Indeed, the geographic, psychic, and professional parameters of Sol Nazerman's life are a study in violent contrasts: peaceful 1930's Poland versus Holocaust depredations; filthy death camps versus affluent Westchester, New York; Westchester versus decrepit and decaying Harlem; and erudite university professor versus heartless pawnbroker. Images of death and isolation permeate the scenes in which Sol appears. By contrast, river and water imagery is a positive force in readers' understanding of Sol. He finds momentary peace on his boat trip with Marilyn, and at the end of the novel, he metaphorically casts his agony into the water.

Jesus's garrulousness contrasts strongly with Sol's taciturnity, accenting their complementary teacher/student, father/son relationship. Although energetic conversation defines his character, Jesus's facial expressions and body language (often a smile and sprightly movement) give nonverbal cues to his youthful innocence, ambition, and sensitivity. These qualities lead the reader to affection for Jesus and to shock and grief at his violent, untimely death.

Wallant's balanced portrayal of Marilyn Birchfield, who represents both good and life in the novel, is defined through her talkativeness, her verbal hesitation, and her kindly inner thoughts as she attempts to draw out and soothe Sol's tortured psyche. Like Sol, Marilyn is associated with river imagery as a natural force that moves forward and diminishes pain. It is her invitation to a Hudson River cruise that helps Sol to commence the exorcism of his inner demons.

Name symbolism also colors the novel's characters. "Nazerman" could imply "Nazi" or "Nazarene" (early Christians of Jewish origin who retained Jewish rituals) while "Sol" could relate to either the sun or to the biblical kings Saul and Solomon. Jesus, a fatherless young man who was threatened by emasculation by a white gang, just as Sol was threatened by Nazi doctors, looks to Sol as a father or uncle—even though Sol, ironically, teaches his "pupil" only the most negative, materialistic view of life. Jesus's name has added resonance, since Sol begins to live after Jesus sacrifices his own life. By contrast, Marilyn Birchfield's purity, strength, and stability are suggested by her name, which connotes a field of birch trees.

Themes and Meanings

The Pawnbroker is a shocking and indelible portrait of the results of human behavior so sadistic that some who survive biologically do so only by committing emotional suicide. Taking place some fifteen years after the Nazi genocide, the novel suggests that although many millions were slaughtered, those who survived did so only with deepest agony, suppressed outrage, and resultant aberrant behaviors; one survival mechanism is the resolution never to be vulnerable to human feeling again. Sol Nazerman has so successfully cauterized his emotions that he is, though ambulatory, among the living dead. Through the macrocosm of Harlem and the microcosm of the pawnshop, Sol's memories of crime and despair at the death camps are reinforced. The novel depicts in flashbacks the excruciating pain and loss that engender Sol's volcanic rage, survivor guilt, and emotional shut down, through which he has lost the ability to give, feel, and receive positive emotion.

In fact, Sol's protracted fury embodies the axiom that if one hates long and deeply enough, one becomes the thing he hates. Though Sol has left the sadistic sociopathy of the death camp "kingdom," he has, perhaps unconsciously, set up his own unfeelingly mendacious pawnshop fiefdom, where he fosters Murillio's criminal corruption and sits in judgment, and often condemnation, of innocent and pathetic customers.

Yet Wallant's novel is more than a scathing indictment of human inhumanity and its terrifying, debasing consequences. It is also a testament to the healing power of human goodness in the persons of Marilyn, Jesus, and even Morton and Tessie. While Sol uses all of his energy to keep shut the door on his titanic pain, Marilyn, Jesus, and Tessie honestly admit to their pain but still feel and spread positiveness and love.

Through the deaths of Jesus and Mendel, Sol emerges from his agonized carapace and finds expiation in the courage to cry, to vent rage and self-poisoning hatred, to grieve his tremendous losses, and to help Tessie grieve hers. On the anniversary of their deaths, Sol realizes that the proper memorial for his lost family is not to consume himself in fury but to live. Wallant suggests that self-destructive wrath is almost as toxic and pernicious as human sadism and that real life and healing begin with self-forgiveness and reaching out to others. *The Pawnbroker* is about the complexities of grief and suffering and the self-exorcism of the demons of hate required for spiritual transcendence and redemption.

Critical Context

As a child, Wallant spent many hours in an uncle's pawnshop; later, he befriended a Holocaust survivor. The memory of these two life threads merge and blend in *The Pawnbroker*. In 1960, Wallant's first published novel, *The Human Season*, a celebration of human courage and strength, won the Jewish Book Council Fiction Award. *The Pawnbroker* was nominated for the National Book Award, and the film rights were purchased by director Sidney Lumet. Wallant died suddenly at age thirty-six, and his remaining two novels—*The Children at the Gate* (1963), which deals with the tension between intellect and emotion, and *The Tenants of Moonbloom* (1964), a comic revolt against the absurdity of life, were published posthumously.

The Pawnbroker evinces such stylistic influences as Fyodor Dostoevski, Thomas Wolfe, and Ernest Hemingway. Thematically, Wallant's work focuses on the deterioration of the American family (especially the delicate and difficult father/son relationship) and increasing individual isolation. Through use of both Jewish and Christian imagery, Wallant's most prevalent themes are confrontation with and responsibility for oneself and others and the possibilities of spiritual rebirth and regrowth.

The Pawnbroker was one of the first American literary works to so centrally deal with the Holocaust. Like Bernard Malamud and Saul Bellow, Wallant also emphasizes Jewish American alienation within society as well as an innate and profound humanism through which his protagonists, despite their agonized isolation, still work to rejoin the human family.

Although Sol, like the protagonists of Philip Roth's and Richard Elman's novels, is conflicted about his own Jewishness, Wallant does not diminish the unique horror of

Nazi genocide by displaying Sol's agony alongside Black, Hispanic, and Christian suffering. In fact, by placing Sol's humanity in front of his Judaism, Wallant clearly elucidates that human inhumanity transcends race and religion.

Bibliography

Baumbach, Jonathan. *The Landscape of Nightmare: Studies in the Contemporary American Novel*. New York: New York University Press, 1965. A chapter on Wallant's novels traces his protagonists' journeys from darkness to human feeling.

Becker, Ernest. *Angel in Armor: A Post-Freudian Perspective on the Nature of Man*. New York: George Braziller, 1969. A fascinating book on aberrant human behavior which offers a chapter of analysis of the psychopathology of Sol Nazerman.

Berger, Alan L. *Crisis and Covenant: The Holocaust in American Jewish Fiction*. New York: University of New York Press, 1985. Places the Holocaust as a central Jewish thematic focus in the works of Malamud, Bellow, Isaac Bashevis Singer, Elie Wiesel, and others. Includes a chapter on *The Pawnbroker*.

Bilik, Dorothy. *Immigrant-Survivor: Post-Holocaust Consciousness in Recent Jewish-American Fiction*. Middletown, Conn.: Wesleyan University Press, 1981. A far-ranging critique of *The Pawnbroker*, with comparisons to the works of Malamud and Singer.

Galloway, David. *Edward Lewis Wallant*. Boston: Twayne, 1979. The only full-length analysis of Wallant's life and works, an invaluable source for a close and perceptive reading of each of Wallant's four novels.

Hoyt, Charles Alva, ed. *Minor American Novelists*. Carbondale: Southern Illinois University Press, 1970. Hoyt traces the separateness and alienation of Wallant's protagonists, focusing on *The Pawnbroker*.

Pinsker, Sanford, and Jack Fischel, eds. *Holocaust Studies Annual, Volume 3: Literature, the Arts, and the Holocaust*. Greenwood, Fla.: Penkevill, 1985. A powerful essay by S. Lillian Kramer places *The Pawnbroker* firmly within the tradition of Jewish American literature.

Howard A. Kerner

PICTURES FROM AN INSTITUTION
A Comedy

Author: Randall Jarrell (1914-1965)
Type of plot: Satire
Time of plot: The 1950's
Locale: Benton College, a fictional school somewhere in the Northeastern United
    States
First published: 1954

> *Principal characters:*
> THE UNNAMED NARRATOR, a professor and poet
> THE NARRATOR'S WIFE, also unnamed
> DWIGHT ROBBINS, the president of Benton College
> PAMELA ROBBINS, the president's South African wife, who pretends to
>   be British
> GERTRUDE JOHNSON, a novelist and teacher of creative writing at
>   Benton
> SIDNEY BACON, Gertrude Johnson's husband
> FLO WHITTAKER, a liberal, public-spirited Benton wife
> JERROLD WHITTAKER, Flo's husband, a sociologist
> GOTTFRIED ROSENBAUM, a composer who teaches at Benton
> IRENE ROSENBAUM, Gottfried's wife, a former opera singer
> CONSTANCE MORGAN, assistant to the secretary of President Robbins

The Novel

Pictures from an Institution is divided into seven chapters, each of which is, in turn, divided into several numbered scenes. Randall Jarrell was enormously knowledgeable about music, and the novel has been likened to a musical composition in which the chapters are like movements and the scenes like themes, recurring point and counterpoint. The narrative begins at the end of a spring term at Benton, an exclusive college for women located somewhere within an easy distance of Harvard and Princeton Universities. The unnamed narrator eventually reveals himself as a teacher at Benton and a poet.

In the first scene of chapter 1, Constance Morgan is serving her last day as assistant to the secretary of Benton's president. From his office, Constance hears the voice of President Robbins bidding farewell to Gertrude Johnson and the voice of Gertrude Johnson bidding farewell to President Robbins. Both seem delighted to be parting.

By the third scene, the narrative flashes back to late in the fall, when Gertrude comes to Benton to replace a new teacher of creative writing, Manny Gumbiner, who proved in his own mind too "advanced" for Benton and, to Benton, simply "unexpectedly unsatisfactory." Gumbiner had succeeded Camille Turner Batterson, a genteel Virginian who had taught creative writing at Benton. Offered a chair at a Midwestern university, she had, to everyone's astonishment, accepted. When Batterson died the following March, a good many people felt that leaving Benton was the true cause of her death. Gertrude, a southerner of quite a different sort from Miss Batterson, cannot abide Benton, but she renders her life there tolerable by using the school and its inhabitants as material for her next novel.

The narrator reports that the friendship at first sight between Gertrude and the president did not survive their second look at each other. She is brilliant but insensitive, fiercely witty, and feels that no human being who is not a writer is worthy of her consideration. Her husband, Sidney Bacon, lives in the reflected light of her persona. He listens to her ideas with rapt attention, reads her manuscripts with expressions of awe, and constantly assures her that she is an extraordinary human being. He seems totally happy in this role. The narrator and his wife are old friends of the Bacons from the days when they all lived on Bleeker Street in New York City. Gertrude is always comparing Bleeker Street to Benton, much to the disadvantage of the latter.

The novel has little plot in the traditional sense. It covers six and a half months of an academic year. The setting for the first few pages of the novel is Benton at the close of school for the year. The rest of the novel is a flashback, beginning with Gertrude's arrival on campus and eventually returning, in chapter 7, "They All Go," to the nearly empty campus as summer begins. The narrator strings together scenes from academic life: dinner parties hosted by the president and Mrs. Robbins and various members of the faculty (including one particularly ghastly dinner hosted by Gertrude Johnson), student performances on Art Night, a pompous guest lecturer who speaks "for some years" one evening. In the final chapter, all the characters leave Benton, some for the summer, some forever—providing a firm conclusion, if not a resolution, to the narrative.

The novel contains almost no physical action. Its characters, however, are drawn with depth and precision. Initially, the vignettes that make up each chapter seem only obliquely related. Yet as a minor actor in one scene becomes a major actor in the next and vice versa, the mosaic of tiny pieces becomes gradually recognizable as a story. The chief unifying factor in the work is the tone of the narration. The narrator's observations and remarks are consistently elegant and witty. They are often ironic and not infrequently bitingly, even cruelly, satiric. On the other hand, the narrator clearly reveals feelings of affection mixed with his disdain for the prevailing ethos of this college for females. He provides the coda for the novel when, in the last chapter, he is preparing to leave Benton himself for another job elsewhere.

The Characters

The novel is, to some degree, a *roman à clef*. The author filled a part-time teaching position at Sarah Lawrence College in Bronxville, New York, during the 1946-1947 academic year. He worked sporadically on *Pictures from an Institution* from that time until 1954, when it was published in its final form. Appearing in the novel under fictional guises are Henry Taylor, then-president of Sarah Lawrence, and his wife; Jarrell's New York friends Jean Stafford, Hannah Arendt, and her husband, Heinrich

Bleucher; Sara Starr, the daughter of longtime Jarrell friends from Nashville, Tennessee, the place of Jarrell's birth; and the author himself. Which real person's behaviors and personality traits have been given to which fictional character is, however, problematic. For example, in *Pictures from an Institution*, Gertrude Johnson uses her six and a half months at Benton to gather material for a withering novel she will write about the place. The narrator looks somewhat askance at this behavior. In real life, though, it was Jarrell himself who used his year at Sarah Lawrence as Gertrude uses hers at Benton.

Characters are presented in the round, but since the novel is a satire, it is their foibles that are emphasized. President Robbins is a former Olympic diver, a Rhodes Scholar, and the recipient of an LL.D. from a college in Florida that also awarded a "doctor of humor" degree to Milton Berle. Mrs. Robbins affects British superiority, but she is a faux Englishwoman. She is liked by no one. The Robbinses have a little boy named Derek with a passion for snakes, and they also have Afghans named Yang and Yin that are described as "very pretty and very bad."

Other Benton couples prominently featured are Flo and Jerrold Whittaker and Gottfried and Irene Rosenbaum. Flo is the complete liberal-progressive activist. She subscribes to every left-wing shibboleth and belongs to every organization that idealizes the proletariat. She refuses to read any novel more than fifty years old because of the status of women depicted therein. She loves humanity and will love individual human beings if humanity is unavailable. She is as widely liked as Pamela Robbins is disliked. Her husband, Jerrold, is a sociology professor. For him, there are no discrete experiences in life. He deals with everything he encounters by generalizing it into part of some abstract theory, about which he then drones on endlessly. The Whittakers have two children: John, described by the narrator as a "good and agreeable, if inhuman, boy," and Fern, a "proto-Fascist."

Gottfried Rosenbaum is a professor of music and a composer of twelve-tone pieces. Gertrude comes to dislike him (as she comes to dislike almost everyone) and would like to refer to him as a "Nazi." Unfortunately for her purposes, he is an Austrian Jew, thus rendering that particular epithet unusable. His wife, the former Irene Letscheskinskaya, was a Russian opera singer. The narrator suggests that the Rosenbaums do not really live in Benton, for they have brought Europe with them to America. Constance Morgan is a young woman who comes to work at Benton after finishing college elsewhere. Although she is almost like family to the narrator and his wife, once she discovers the Rosenbaums and they her, she virtually becomes their adopted daughter.

Themes and Meanings

Pictures from an Institution is an unconventional realistic novel. Jarrell immediately signals his intent to give his novel the form of a musical composition, as its title is a reference to the composer Modest Mussorgsky's piano suite *Pictures from an Exhibition*. There are, incidentally, literal "pictures from an exhibition" in the penultimate chapter, "Art Night." Jarrell also slyly plays with the connotations of "institution." Benton College is, of course, an institution, but in common parlance the term is often used as a euphemism for a prison, reformatory, or madhouse. The novel is subtitled *A Comedy*, and it is a very biting comedy.

Jarrell was a professor of English all of his adult life, with the exception of his wartime service in the Army Air Corps. He taught in the Midwest, the East, and the South at both private and public colleges and universities. The main purpose of *Pictures from an Institution* is to satirize the complacency found at colleges such as Benton, where an education simultaneously insular and "progressive" is sold, at very high prices, to the parents of overprivileged young women. An examination of the usual goings on at Benton allows the author to attack a number of secondary targets as well.

Jarrell was erudite in the fields of music and painting as well as literature. He uses the music various characters favor to comment upon their sense of aesthetics. One art professor paints glowing animals in marshes and jungles, so his students paint glowing animals in marshes and jungles. Another makes ugly welded sculpture; her students, fetching in their goggles and masks, make ugly welded sculpture. Although Jarrell shows no pity for fools and charlatans, he is not inhuman. When, in the final chapter, Sona Rasmussen, the sculptor-welder, has made a wonderful statue of the East Wind from a railroad tie, the narrator is forced to reevaluate his assumptions about her and about other artists as well. Flo Whittaker's ritualistic compassion makes her a caricature, but not an insincere one. The narrator suggests that an appropriate statue for Flo would be a saint with her foot in her mouth. Even the waspish Gertrude Johnson has moments of insight during Sidney's brief illness, realizing how much she loves and needs her cipher of a husband. "Balance" is not a term usually associated with satire, but Jarrell attempts to give some of his characters, at least, their due.

Critical Context

Pictures from an Institution is Jarrell's only novel. He was known primarily as a poet and a literary critic who turned his wicked wit upon any work he deemed inferior. He was prolific—in addition to his poetry, he published four translations (three from German and one from Russian), edited six anthologies (five of fiction and one of modern poetry), and in the last years of his life wrote four children's books. *Pictures from an Institution* is very much a novel written by a poet. It is filled with striking metaphors and similes, and dazzling wordplay occurs throughout. The dialogue sparkles with wit; sometimes that wit stings, as when Gertrude, in a belligerent mood, decides to "smoke heads."

There are several indications, though none is definitive, that writing fiction proved harder for Jarrell than writing poetry. First, he published only one novel in a writing life of approximately thirty years. Second, Jarrell began work on *Pictures from an Institution* shortly after his year of teaching at Sarah Lawrence College and, despite the fact that the novel is of only moderate length, he required six years to complete it. Third, Jarrell's fictional technique may fail him at times. The novel is a first-person narrative, and the narrator's personality is well developed. However, he sometimes describes in great detail scenes at which he was not present and recounts conversations that he could not have overheard. These may represent lapses, or they may simply signify that Jarrell did not feel bound by the strictures of the naturalistic, or even the conventionally realistic, novel.

For a satire written in the 1950's by a left-leaning author (Jarrell was a Freudian and a Marxist in his thinking and the literary editor of the journal *Nation*), *Pictures from an Institution* is remarkably apolitical. It is replete with allusions to literary works, musical compositions, and paintings, but it contains few references to politics, even campus politics. The portrait of Flo Whittaker is that of an ideologue, a study of how the ideologue thinks and responds rather than a study of the ideology itself. Jarrell approaches his work not as a propagandist but as an artist.

Bibliography

Flynn, Richard. *Randall Jarrell and the Lost World of Childhood*. Athens: University of Georgia Press, 1990. The title of this evaluation of Jarrell's work is a play on the title of his 1965 collection of poems *The Lost World*.

Jarrell, Mary, ed., assisted by Stuart Wright. *Randall Jarrell's Letters: An Autobiographical and Literary Selection*. Boston: Houghton Mifflin, 1985. Jarrell alludes to *Pictures from an Institution* some forty-four times in his correspondence.

Pritchard, William H. *Randall Jarrell: A Literary Life*. New York: Farrar, Straus, and Giroux, 1990. Eighteen pages are dedicated to a discussion of *Pictures from an Institution*.

Quinn, Sister Bernetta, O.S.F. *Randall Jarrell*. Boston: Twayne, 1981. An entry in the Twayne's United States Authors series. Chapter 6, "Critic, Novelist, Translator," discusses *Pictures from an Institution*.

Rosenthal, M. L. *Randall Jarrell*. Minneapolis: University of Minnesota Press, 1972. Number 103 in the Pamphlets on American Writers series. Makes reference to Jarrell's "very witty novel" and "lively criticism" but concentrates upon his poetry.

Patrick Adcock

PICTURING WILL

Author: Ann Beattie (1947-   )
Type of plot: Family
Time of plot: 1989
Locale: Charlottesville, Virginia; New York City; Florida
First published: 1989

Principal characters:

WILL, a five-year-old boy around whom the story revolves
JODY, his mother, a talented and promising photographer
WAYNE, Will's unstable father, divorced from Jody
MEL ANTHIS, Jody's lover, devoted to Will
MARY VICKERS, Jody's friend
WAGONER, Mary's son and Will's best friend
D. B. HAVERFORD (HAVEABUD), a New York City art-gallery owner
SPENCER, the seven-year-old son of Haverford's former client
CORKY, Wayne's current wife
KATE, Wayne's lover

The Novel

In *Picturing Will*, the author presents the lives of three family members—mother, father, and son—in the late twentieth century. The first major section of the novel, "Mother," introduces Jody, who has managed to bring her life back to normal after her husband, Wayne, walked out and left her with their infant son, Will. Jody lives in Charlottesville, Virginia, and supports herself as a photographer specializing in weddings. She is an attractive and energetic woman for whose work the demand is increasing, but she is also an artist with an eye for the out-of-the-ordinary. She is on the verge of success, an obvious candidate for the attention of an art capital such as New York. Jody's devotion to Will is genuine. As she herself admits, he has been her salvation during the difficult days after Wayne's departure.

Enjoying the success of her photography business, Jody considers the proposal of Mel, her lover, to marry him and move to New York City. She hesitates to jeopardize the security of her present life and her independence as a single woman, but Mel is a good man who has developed an exceptionally close relationship with Will, and a move to New York would rescue her from routine photographic work. In many ways, Mel is even more understanding of Will than is Jody, while his sympathy for her work keeps prodding her to the challenge of New York. Jody's friend Mary Vickers, in a bad marriage herself, admires Mel and urges Jody to accept his offer. While Jody and Mary share the experiences of young motherhood, Mary poses for a photograph destined to show Jody's genius beyond doubt, and their sons Will and Wagoner become best friends.

With the intention of persuading Jody to move to New York, Mel arranges to show her work to art-gallery proprietor D. B. Haverford, who immediately sees the appeal of her photographs and agrees to a public show in his gallery. When they meet, he is as fascinated by her as by her pictures. She sees him as a mere businessman whose name she cannot bother to remember, so he is always "Haveabud" to her and to the reader, but she perceives that he could be the key to her professional future.

The second major section of the novel, "Father," centers on Will's father Wayne, now living in Florida with his third wife, Corky. It was the birth of Will, after he had unsuccessfully urged an abortion, that made life with Jody intolerable for Wayne, but as Will's father he of course retains visiting rights.

While Jody is absorbed in furthering her career in New York, Mel has willingly assumed the responsibility of driving Will to visit his father. This time, however, they are accompanied by Haveabud (whom Will is told he must tolerate because he is important for his mother's work) and Haveabud's young friend Spencer. Haveabud, once the promoter of Spencer's father, is sexually exploiting the seven-year-old boy. Will's only interest in the trip is the opportunity to visit Wagoner, now living in Florida with his mother, Jody and Mel having arranged for their reunion.

Wayne anticipates Will's visit with apprehension and dread, while Corky, trying to persuade Wayne that they should have a child, welcomes the opportunity to show him what a good mother she will be. She greets Will enthusiastically, amuses him with shopping, and carefully prepares his clothes and meals. Wayne makes the effort to please Will by taking him and Corky to the pool of a wealthy client whose garden he maintains, but he becomes more interested in having an affair with the wealthy owner. Wayne's most intense though brief affair during Will's visit, however, is with Kate, a mysterious woman who suggests that they conceal their last names from each other. It is this liaison that is his downfall. The police discover a pillbox with Corky's name that Wayne had accidentally let fall from his pocket into Kate's car; at the same time, they find a sizable amount of heroin in the abandoned car. From a window, Will sees his father being led away in handcuffs. As soon as his father is taken, he leaves for New York at once, without achieving the promised visit with "Wag" that was so important to him.

The final, brief section of the novel, "Child," presents Will twenty years later. The future of the family is revealed: Will has a self-absorbed, very successful mother and a devoted stepfather, Mel, Wayne having disappeared. Will himself now has a wife and son. As the novel ends, Will imagines that he is photographing himself and his son playing with the ball Mel has given them.

The Characters

This novel defines family members by their relationships to one another. All of their lives revolve around Will, both parents measuring themselves by their relation to, and responses to, their son. Because Will himself is too young to understand their motives, the reader sympathizes with him in his bewilderment, viewing the parents through Will's eyes even as the author allows the reader to see how the boy has changed their lives. He is a likable five-year-old who remembers his mother's counsel and tries to be a good son. He responds to Mel's love, appreciates Corky's kindness (they remain correspondents over the years), and ultimately becomes a loving husband and father. Throughout most of the novel, however, he is a child hoping to be reunited with his friend but unable to initiate the action.

Readers appreciate the difficulties of Jody's predicament and admire her determination to forge a new career and yet remain a functioning mother to Will. Gradually, though, her manipulation of others becomes apparent: She accepts Mel's love with reservations until the opportunity in New York persuades her to marry him, and she unhesitatingly photographs the private life of a real friend, Mary Vickers. Having made the mistake of marrying Wayne, she at first apprehensively and then more and more singlemindedly determines to realize her life as an artist. She sees only potential subjects for her camera. Even Will becomes mainly a subject for the cover of *Vogue*. Her selfishness transforms Mel from ardent lover to sacrificial husband. Haveabud she has shrewdly manipulated to forge a career. Like Mel and Will, the reader accepts her for the artist she is and the mother she has tried less successfully to be.

Wayne's deficiencies as a parent of course exceed Jody's coolness and self-serving calculation, for he is weak and despicable, a man totally unable to meet the responsibilities of fatherhood. Recognizing his own unsuitability as a father, he nevertheless blames Jody for insisting that Will be born. He reveals his inferiority when he accuses Jody of making it difficult for him to finish college, and he can only regard himself as victimized. Wayne's preeminent weakness, however, is women; he himself suspects it of bordering on addiction. Not surprisingly, it is a woman, Kate, who is his undoing.

Mel is Wayne's opposite. He has the decency and dependability that makes the family unit work. Will responds to him early, even before Jody is ready to make a commitment. Mel gives of himself, from the art show in New York that he initiated, to his protection of Will during his trip to Florida, and through the years that follow.

The character most like Mel is Corky. She tries to make Will's visit a happy one, and she displays wifely virtues that Wayne can never appreciate, particularly a determination to make family life work. Mary and Wagoner Vickers are serviceable friends to Jody and Will. Mary helps Jody to further her career, while Will remains a true friend until Wagoner's early death.

Haveabud is an opportunist ready to take advantage of anyone naïve enough to trust him, while Spencer is merely Haveabud's victim. Abandoned by both parents, he is a vulnerable child with no strong Jody and loving Mel to save him.

Themes and Meanings

The overriding theme of *Picturing Will* is surely the destruction of family life in the modern world. Beattie labors not only to present each member of a family but also to set the scene authentically with photographic detail. Her choppy sentences and rapid sequence of sketchily presented scenes reflect the fragmentation of a family. The scenes are mere flashes, like those from Jody's camera. A scene depicting grotesque masqueraders at a Halloween party that Jody is snapping, juxtaposed with that of a deer struck and killed by Mary Vickers's car on her way home, epitomizes the unpredictability of the moment, which Jody is quickly on the scene to record with her camera. As scenes keep changing rapidly, the reader is left, like Will, to decipher their significance. Will tries to fathom Haveabud's rape of a child and, later, his own father's arrest. Does his childhood amount to such experiences or to a photograph of himself and his mother taken for *Vogue* and persisting as a prominent display in his mother's home?

By the presentation of unconnected scenes, the author suggests that modern urban life is like a series of random pictures. Her splashes of realistic detail vivify the often excruciating relationships of Mel and Jody, of Haveabud and Spencer, of Wayne and Kate. The nature of Jody's art inclines her to see life as snippets, even her son as something to "picture." With good intentions, she becomes more and more a mere provider for her son, more like the hardworking but distant father of an earlier time. Is it possible, the reader wonders, for such a woman to succeed as a mother under such circumstances?

In its third section, the novel affirms the possibility of stable family life by telescoping twenty years, in the process establishing a sense of continuity to counter the staccato effect of the prior scenes, although the brevity of the section arguably diminishes its effectiveness. Also contributing to the sense of stability, however, are the characters of Corky and, in particular, Mel. They demonstrate the possibility of integrity and cohesion even amid the disintegrating forces at work in a megalopolis corrupted by too many versions of Wayne and Haveabud and increasingly served by people who, like Jody, fall short of the challenge of combining responsible parenthood with professional success.

Critical Context

Picturing Will was Ann Beattie's eighth book of fiction and fourth novel. She and her typical protagonist belong to what is sometimes called the Woodstock Generation. Their detachment and characteristically unfocused rebellion against the society their elders bequeathed them do not so much mellow as atrophy in middle age. Twenty years beyond the point of not trusting anyone over thirty, they face the ordeal of trusting themselves to be forty. They often can accept neither the commitment and responsibilities of parenthood nor the other miscellaneous obligations that society—now the society that they had a substantial part in forming—imposes on them. Yet if Jody's contemporaries in *Picturing Will* are the Woodstock Generation, the third section of the novel, in leaping to Will's adulthood, projects a hypothetical future, as if the author cannot wait for enough "real" time to elapse to make Will an art historian at Columbia University.

The six-page excursion into Will's future seems to suggest that if Will and his generation will not prevail, at least they will endure. Beattie's critics argue inconclusively about whether her photographic techniques work as well in long fiction as in her short stories. *Picturing Will* is a kind of album, perhaps suffering somewhat from the typically unselective nature of albums, but some of the pictures are vivid and true. They are not all beautiful by any stretch of the imagination, and some, such as the homoerotic scene Will is compelled to witness on the trip to Florida, are disturbing, but some, such as Will's discovery of Mel's diary, are touching. It is to Beattie's credit that she finds shards of hope among the wreckage of her generation, even as she avoids easy solutions to the problems arising from their improvisational lifestyles.

Bibliography
Beattie, Ann. "An Interview with Ann Beattie." Interview by Steven R. Centola. *Contemporary Literature* 31 (Winter, 1990): 405-422. This discussion ranges over Beattie's work up to and including *Picturing Will*. Her disclosures that the rough draft of this short novel required three years and that she discarded "at least fifteen chapters" provide an idea of the distillation involved. Centola's questions generally solicit useful information about Beattie's literary aims and techniques.
Hulbert, Ann. "Only Disconnect." *The New York Review of Books* 37 (May 31, 1990): 33-35. Hulbert sees Beattie as striving for "greater certainty" and more "authorial control" in this novel than in her previous books. The principals are less inclined to float aimlessly but have acquired a sense of duty. To a considerable extent, however, their liberation from the trammels of an earlier generation leaves them lonely and uncertain.
Lee, Don. "About Ann Beattie." *Ploughshares* 21 (Fall, 1995): 231-235. Although this article does not present a critical perspective of *Picturing Will*, it offers an interesting overview of Beattie's life and career.
Montresor, Jaye B. *The Critical Response to Ann Beattie*. Westport, Conn.: Greenwood Press, 1993. An illuminating collection of critical essays on the life and work of Ann Beattie. Includes an essay on the images of "good" mothers and fathers in Beattie's *Picturing Will*.
Murphy, Christina. *Ann Beattie*. Boston: Twayne, 1986. Although published before *Picturing Will* appeared, Murphy's book is valuable. A biographical chapter is followed by one on Beattie's "literary milieu," another on her early fiction, a chapter each on her six books before 1986, and finally one assessing her achievement. To Murphy, Beattie captures her age in fiction as successfully as J. D. Salinger, John Cheever, and John Updike did a somewhat earlier one.
Schneiderman, Leo. "Ann Beattie: Emotional Loss and Strategies of Reparation." *American Journal of Psychoanalysis* 53 (December, 1993): 317-333. A psychoanalytic interpretation of Beattie's work. Schneiderman offers illuminating insight into the way Beattie portrays depression.
Wyatt, David. "Ann Beattie." *The Southern Review* 28 (Winter, 1992): 145-159. Wyatt assesses Beattie's fiction from a more recent perspective than Murphy. His verdict is a largely complimentary one, though *Picturing Will* comes in for some negative criticism. Wyatt sees the novel as focusing on the cost of choosing art as the work of one's life, but he finds Beattie's presentation of art and life "too binary to satisfy."

Robert P. Ellis

PIGS IN HEAVEN

Author: Barbara Kingsolver (1955-   )
Type of plot: Social realism
Time of plot: The 1990's
Locale: The Southwestern United States; Seattle, Washington; and the fictional
   town of Heaven, Oklahoma
First published: 1993

    Principal characters:
        TAYLOR GREER, a young white woman, fiercely independent and
           devoted to her adopted daughter Turtle
        TURTLE GREER, a six-year-old Cherokee girl
        ALICE GREER, Taylor's sixty-one-year-old mother
        JAX THIBODEAUX, Taylor's devoted live-in boyfriend, a rock musician
        ANNAWAKE FOURKILLER, a young, idealistic lawyer for the Cherokee
           tribe
        LEDGER FOURKILLER, Annawake's uncle, a wise medicine chief
        JOHNNY CASH STILLWATER, a fifty-nine-year-old Cherokee who
           becomes Alice's lover
        BARBIE, a young woman who devotes her life to emulating a children's
           doll

The Novel

The third novel by Barbara Kingsolver, *Pigs in Heaven* is a warm, humorous, and thought-provoking story of the conflict between an adoptive mother and a Native American tribe over the destiny of an adopted Cherokee girl. The novel covers a time span of about six months and is divided into three parts: "Spring," "Summer," and "Fall." Generally, Kingsolver uses a third-person-limited point of view. Each scene is presented in the author's folksy third-person voice, and the view of the action is usually limited to the perspective of one of the five main characters, Alice, Taylor, Jax, Annawake, or Cash. At times, however, Kingsolver presents a scene from the perspective of a minor character (such as Annawake's coworkers Jinny Redbow and Franklin Turnbo) or briefly enters into the consciousness of a second character (such as Turtle or Lucky Buster) in a scene that is described mostly from a major character's point of view.

Pigs in Heaven is an unusual and provocative sequel that calls into question the moral certitudes of Kingsolver's first novel, *The Bean Trees* (1988). In that book, as the plucky young protagonist Taylor Greer drives southwest from Kentucky, she has a three-year-old girl thrust upon her during a stop on Cherokee land in Oklahoma. In this earlier novel, Taylor's act of accepting and rearing the girl seems unquestionably heroic, since the girl's mother is dead, Taylor has no desire to acquire a child, and, particularly, since it is revealed later in the novel that the girl has been sexually abused.

Much of *The Bean Trees* focuses on the special, nurturing love that develops between Taylor and the Cherokee girl, whom Taylor names Turtle because the girl attaches herself to her new mother with the tenacity of a turtle's jaws.

Pigs in Heaven, on the other hand, presents a different and unexpected perspective on the situation: that it might be better for Turtle (now six years old) to be taken from Taylor (who has settled in Tucson) and returned to Turtle's Oklahoma tribe. Annawake Fourkiller, a young Cherokee lawyer, is on a crusade to test the legality of adoptions that have taken numerous Cherokee children out of the tribe and into non-Indian homes. Annawake's legal weapon is the Indian Child Welfare Act of 1978, which gives individual tribes the right to rule over the legality of such adoptions—and even to take children back from families that have been rearing them for years.

Kingsolver leads into this central conflict with a dramatic and moving prologue. While Taylor and Turtle are visiting Hoover Dam, Turtle glimpses a man falling down the spillway, and Taylor and Turtle become national celebrities when the man is found and rescued. That national fame brings trouble, however, when Annawake hears about their appearance on a television show and begins to investigate the legality of Taylor's adoption of Turtle.

When Taylor feels her hold on Turtle threatened by Annawake's inquiries, she impetuously flees with Turtle from their Tucson home. Taylor's mother, Alice Greer, who was about to leave her unsatisfying marriage in Kentucky anyway, flies to Las Vegas to bolster her daughter's morale. As they are about to leave Las Vegas, the Greers acquire a bizarre traveling companion named Barbie. Alice then travels to the Cherokee nation to reconnect with a childhood friend and to try to bolster Taylor's legal claim to Turtle. Meanwhile, Taylor, Turtle, and Barbie head on to Seattle, where Barbie betrays their trust and Taylor is left struggling to eke out a living as a working single mother.

In addition to this main plot line, Kingsolver also develops two other plot threads involving Jax Thibodeaux and Cash Stillwater. Back in Tucson, Jax is badly depressed over the absence of Taylor and Turtle and has an affair with his landlady, Gundi, an eccentric bohemian artist. After two years in Jackson Hole, Wyoming, Cash Stillwater regrets his departure from the Cherokee nation (which he left out of grief and shame over the deaths and losses in his family) and eventually returns to Oklahoma.

As Alice is drawn in by the warmth of the Cherokee people and by a ceremonial "stomp dance" in Heaven, Oklahoma, she feels increasingly comfortable with the Native American way of life. Meanwhile, Annawake, who discovers that Cash is Turtle's grandfather, surreptitiously plays matchmaker to Alice and Cash, hoping that a romance between them will help to resolve the conflict over Turtle. The romance does develop, and Alice convinces Taylor to bring Turtle back to Oklahoma for a custody hearing. When Alice learns of Annawake's matchmaking, she feels manipulated and indignant, but despite this minor snag, Turtle's case is harmoniously resolved. Under a joint custody settlement, she will spend school years with Taylor and summers with

Cash. This compromise is further sweetened by the novel's final developments: Taylor plans to marry Jax, and Alice will marry Cash.

The Characters

Alice is the folksy, down-to-earth matriarch who embodies and repeatedly reflects upon a key issue for Greer females: their stubborn self-sufficiency. From Alice's mother Minerva Stamper (who ran a hog farm by herself) through Alice (who leaves two husbands) to Taylor (whose main goal in leaving Kentucky was to avoid the small-town girl's common fate of early pregnancy), Alice sees her female line as holding so tenaciously to their independence that it is difficult for them to establish and sustain relationships—particularly with men. The reader, however, takes pleasure in watching Alice reach out to provide maternal support for Taylor, Turtle, and even Barbie. Once Alice arrives in Heaven, she plays the role of an observer from the white world who enables the reader to appreciate the rich human and spiritual interconnectedness of the Cherokee culture.

Taylor, the chief protagonist in the novel, earns the reader's admiration for her independence, her pluck, and her devotion to her daughter Turtle. Early scenes involving the Hoover Dam incident establish the purity and power of this mother-daughter bond, as Taylor's staunch belief in her daughter's integrity enables her to prod disbelieving male officials into conducting a search for the accident victim her child has seen. Yet the reader also sees that Taylor's admirable qualities have their shadow side. Her self-reliance takes her out on a dubious limb when she flees with Turtle, disregarding the legal consequences and abandoning her support network in Tucson. The turning point in the novel comes for Taylor when she realizes that she and her daughter cannot be self-sufficient; Taylor agrees to bring Turtle back to the Cherokee nation and to submit to legal procedures that will determine what is best for her daughter.

Annawake Fourkiller is an idealistic young Cherokee lawyer who becomes the antagonist to Taylor, by virtue of Annawake's crusade to test the legality of adoptions of Cherokee children taken out of their tribe. Ironically, Taylor and Annawake share many character traits: stubborn independence, remarkable physical beauty, an indifference to that beauty and to the prospect of a committed relationship with a man, an intense bond with one other person, and ultimately the wisdom to listen to an older mentor. Parallel to Taylor's intense bond with Turtle is Annawake's deep feeling for her brother Gabriel, who was adopted off the reservation into a white family, was subjected to racist misunderstanding and abuse, and became a chronic criminal. Annawake's legal zeal is clearly traceable to her determination to prevent other Cherokee children from suffering as her brother has. The turning point comes for Annawake when her Uncle Ledger advises her to go beyond her tribal zeal and to consult her heart—the source of her eventual sympathy for Taylor and Alice.

Jax Thibodeaux and Cash Stillwater, though dissimilar in age and race, are alike in many of the traits that make them the obvious good choices of Taylor and Alice for their husbands. Both men are handsome, insightful, communicative, gentle, and humorous. Both are artists: Jax a rock musician with a band called the Irascible Babies,

Cash a craftsman who keeps his senses and memories alive by stringing colorful beads in traditional Cherokee patterns. Both have a melancholy streak, partly the result of their sad family histories, and both are warm and attentive lovers. Finally, in keeping with the feminist tone of the novel, both extend themselves beyond the limitations of traditional male roles: Jax is a softhearted homemaker who misses not only Taylor but also Turtle, and Cash's enjoyment of cooking is a revelation to Alice.

Themes and Meanings

The conflict between Taylor and Annawake, between the interests of motherly love and tribal community, provides Kingsolver with the foremost dramatic issue of the novel. From the beginning, the reader's sympathies are strongly with Taylor, fueled by her staunch belief in Turtle during the Hoover Dam episode and by the ways in which Taylor and Turtle have clearly become the central foci of each other's lives.

On the other hand, it is one of the greatest strengths of Kingsolver's writing that she makes the reader feel that the claims of Annawake and the Cherokee nation are not merely a matter of legal abstraction or political correctness but are also heartfelt concerns for both the tribe and the child. Kingsolver makes the reader realize that the unfortunate case of Gabriel is far from an isolated incident when Annawake cites the statistic that as late as the 1970's, a third of all Native American children were still being taken from their families and adopted into non-Indian homes. With children being removed in these numbers, the tribe's concern that such adoptions threaten its strength, and even its very existence, is clearly legitimate. Annawake makes the further points that there are invariably Cherokee extended-family members who want such children returned and would make good homes for them and that even if Cherokee children are being reared in loving non-Indian homes, such children would lack the strong sense of cultural identity that would strengthen them to confront the inevitable racism and stigmatization of white society.

The Cherokee position that Turtle may be better off with the tribe also gains strength from Kingsolver's treatment of the theme of poverty. Once Taylor and Turtle are on their own in Seattle, the reader sees that in white urban society, a single mother working a minimum-wage job faces virtually insurmountable odds in trying to pay for housing, food, medical care, and day care. In white society, poverty also brings Taylor the emotional burdens of isolation and guilt. In the Cherokee nation, on the other hand, poverty is no disgrace, and to ask for and receive help from others is the cultural norm.

Kingsolver's ultimate theme in *Pigs in Heaven* is that even though in its material poverty Heaven, Oklahoma, might appear to be anything but a heaven, it actually holds rich emotional and spiritual fulfillment for those people whose spirits are generous enough to see it. Her title refers to the Cherokee myth in which six greedy boys are turned into pigs and then into a star constellation as a warning about the dire consequences of selfishness. The novel suggests that when people hold too tightly to what they consider theirs, they risk ending up miserable and might even appear to be greedy swine. On the other hand, when they open their hearts to realize that everyone's interests can be reconciled, they then find themselves to be the happiest of creatures in a heaven on earth.

Critical Context

The ascension of *Pigs in Heaven* to national best-seller lists for a number of weeks testifies to growing interest both in Barbara Kingsolver as a writer and to the literary movement of ecofeminism that she represents.The distinctive focus of Kingsolver's books is on people who are marginalized by American society and on their struggles for economic, cultural, and emotional survival. Further, drawing on her academic training in environmental science, Kingsolver often focuses on her people's connections to the land and on the disastrous consequences that heedless abuse of the land can bring. Kingsolver's novels have been grouped with other works that draw connections between the exploitation of women and of the environment and that promote the healing that can occur when women are empowered and the Earth receives reverence and care. In addition to *Animal Dreams* and *Pigs in Heaven*, other notable ecofeminist novels include *Always Coming Home* (1985) by Ursula Le Guin, *Tracks* (1989) by Louise Erdrich, and *Mean Spirit* (1991) by Linda Hogan.

Even in the company of such distinguished writers, however, Barbara Kingsolver stands out by reason of the remarkable entertainment value of her fiction. Born and reared in Kentucky, she is a born raconteur, heir to the rich oral literary tradition of the South. Even as she is sharpening the reader's awareness of weighty social issues and profound literary themes, her narrative voice never ceases to entertain as a humorous and engrossing storyteller, a gifted creator of heartfelt characters, and a witty and poetic stylist.

Bibliography

Berkinow, Louise. "Books." *Cosmopolitan* 214 (June, 1993): 32. Berkinow praises the novel for its "breathtaking" story and racial themes. Among its many "unforgettable" characters, she particularly admires Alice for her "country-plain, no-nonsense sensibility." Overall, Berkinow finds the novel "profound, funny, bighearted."

Karbo, Karen. "And Baby Makes Two." *The New York Times Book Review*, June 27, 1993, p. 9. Karbo praises Kingsolver's ability to "maintain her political views without sacrificing the complexity of her characters' predicaments." On the other hand, she faults the author for not pursuing the issue of responsibility for Turtle's abuse.

Kingsolver, Barbara. Interview by Robin Epstein. *Progressive* 60 (February, 1996): 33-37. Kingsolver talks about how her feminist philosophy, childhood experience of being an outsider, and political activism have shaped her writing. Although she only briefly discusses *Pigs in Heaven*, the interview offers a good overall picture of Kingsolver's work.

Koenig, Rhoda. "Books." *New York* 26 (June 14, 1993): 99-100. Koenig praises Kingsolver's "lovely eye (and nose) for details" and judges her to be "a nice, well-meaning woman." Koenig, though, criticizes the novel for its "dopey benignity." According to Koenig, by making her major characters so well-meaning and good, Kingsolver eliminates her chances for suspense and for meaningful treatment of serious issues.

Lehmann-Haupt, Christopher. "Community vs. Family and Writer vs. Subject." *The New York Times*, July 12, 1993, p. C16. Lehmann-Haupt praises the novel for its "appealing homespun poetry" and "down-home humor." He also admires the "generosity and spiritedness" of its characters. On the other hand, he comments that "there isn't much conflict or tension in the story" and that "the reader begins to suffocate in all the sweetness."

Ryan, Maureen. "Barbara Kingsolver's Lowfat Fiction." *Journal of American Culture* 18 (Winter, 1995): 77-82. Ryan explores common themes in Kingsolver's novels.

Shapiro, Laura. "A Novel Full of Miracles." *Newsweek* 123 (July 12, 1993): 61. Shapiro praises Kingsolver for avoiding polemics and creating "a complex drama." On the other hand, she remarks that the novel is "less deftly plotted" than Kingsolver's earlier fiction because its resolution "relies on a somewhat unwieldy coincidence." Overall, however, Shapiro concludes that the novel "succeeds on the strength of Kingsolver's clear-eyed, warmhearted writing and irresistible characters."

Terry L. Andrews

PITCH DARK

Author: Renata Adler (1938-   )
Type of plot: Novel of manners
Time of plot: 1981, with flashbacks reaching to the early 1960's
Locale: Connecticut; Ireland, near Dublin; Orcas Island, off Bellingham,
    Washington
First published: 1983

> *Principal characters:*
>> KATE ENNIS, a writer and the narrator of the story
>> JAKE, her married lover

The Novel

The unconventional, oblique narrative method of *Pitch Dark* makes plot summary difficult and tentative, but the novel's division into three sections—"Orcas Island," "Pitch Dark," and "Home"—provides a helpful structure.

Kate Ennis, the narrator, tells the first part of her story from Orcas Island, but the events described take place in New England. "Orcas Island," like the other two sections, weaves together Kate's painful musings on her recent affair with Jake, her married neighbor, with a skein of incidents featuring people from Kate's past. Characters come onstage only to walk off forever, and promising themes sound once and fade away. Many of the quick shots of the past focus on college days (Harvard and Radcliffe, apparently, since one student is experimenting with psylocybin "under the guidance of [Timothy] Leary and [Richard] Alpert"), offering entertaining glimpses of teachers and fellow students.

The stream of Kate's consciousness darts here and there. Some passages turn into minilectures on themes from Ludwig Wittgenstein and Vladimir Nabokov, for example, while one sparkling gloss on Homer reveals that Penelope "did not unweave by night, and therefore by implication hardly ever wove by day." A puzzling reference on page eighteen to something called "London Exit" is amplified in a brief essay introduced fifteen pages later, but the "rich Italians" and the old people who "moved to the suburbs" are suspended in narrative limbo. Leander Dworkin, "the amplifying poet," and Willie Stokes, "the poet of compression," seem to have bright futures, but their complementary sensibilities wither away as they are buried in the narrator's flow of reminiscence.

Never far from Kate's mind is her recent break from her lover. Kate is apparently about forty, and in "Orcas Island" she has for some time improvised a home in a barn that is perhaps in rural Connecticut (it is a "long drive to the city"). Jake, a lawyer and a country neighbor, may be about fifteen years older than Kate—or at least she speaks of having planned to leave him on or about his thirty-fifth anniversary. Their affair has gone on for eight years, and much of the hurt that Kate feels centers on Jake's never having taken her anywhere on a trip. Jake has always traveled with his family to the

Caribbean for Christmas, but, as the Other Woman, Kate has had to subsist on his left-over time. ("Somehow not with me, not with me.") The "Orcas Island" section ends with Kate wondering, "But what am I going to do, what shall I do, now?"

Section 2, "Pitch Dark," is also composed on Orcas Island, but is set in Ireland, near Dublin. It is the most unified and coherent of the three sections, but was probably written separately and grafted on to the story of Kate and Jake. (In one scene in which she wants a name very like her own, the narrator comes up not with a variant of Ennis but with "Alder.") When Kate leaves Jake, she flies to Ireland, rents a car, and seeks out the estate offered her by a wealthy American acquaintance. Much of her journey is made in pitch dark, and it involves a very minor traffic mishap in which she is apparently used as the instrument of an insurance scam. Kate is unduly frightened by the incident and, thinking she is in trouble with the law, pursues a course of trivial evasive actions to avoid apprehension. Her brief stay at her friend's home is no more satisfying. The servants' boorishness evokes paranoid suspicions, and Kate makes a nightmarish drive to a dinner party with strangers. These events unfold with brief pauses for the echoing of several obscure verbal motifs, as well as the playing back in her mind of persistent questions about Jake and their romance. The section ends with Kate in London and Jake on the phone to her.

In section 3, "Home," Kate is living in a small house in a Connecticut town. The time is more than two years after her misadventures in Ireland. The Orcas Island interlude is behind her, and she is living comfortably with Jake. ("By then, we had long been to Orcas Island, New Orleans, God knows where.") Aside from the abrupt comments that allow the reader to piece together the happy ending to the love story, "Home" is, like "Orcas Island," a series of discontinuous accounts of local events, essays on legal matters (the whole novel reveals a preoccupation with the law and laws), more streams of reminiscence, lectures on literature (Thomas Wolfe and Gertrude Stein seen very clearly), and more. Much of it is witty, engaging chitchat despite its lack of unity—a judgment that applies to each section as well as to the novel as a whole. In sum, *Pitch Dark* tells an ordinary love story in a sometimes annoying, indirect way but decks it out with appealing side glances at whatever catches the author's alert eye.

The Characters

Pitch Dark rejects conventional characterizations, offering instead bursts of narrative from which the reader must deduce character. Kate Ennis emerges as a sensitive, intelligent, long-suffering heroine. The many digressions reveal where Kate comes from, where she is now, and where she hopes to be in the future. The characters are not so much described as experienced through Kate's consciousness. The Ireland story in the second section shows Kate in a state of paranoia, suggesting that her mental stability has been threatened by the upheaval in her love life. The sinister inscrutability of the servants and villagers in Ireland reinforces her sense of helplessness.

Jake is presented as an insensitive, vacillating, self-centered man who takes Kate's love for granted. His actions slowly force Kate to realize that his love for her is diminishing. When she seeks his assistance in some maintenance problems with her house and pond, he refuses even to share with her the names of reliable workmen he has used at his own place. This selfish disregard for her problems prompts these thoughts: "And though I know my heart cannot have been broken in these things, these things of my house and of yours. . . , I find that I am crying as I write. . . ." Similarly, he refuses to take her on any trips during those eight years of their romance. (She had had her heart set especially on a visit to New Orleans: "Would it have cost him all the earth, sometime in all those years, to take her to New Orleans for a week?") Jake remains, ultimately, a vague presence in the background. His importance is clear, but his character and personality remain thoroughly problematic.

Many of the other characters, brief as their bit appearances are, shine vividly on the page, but none of them takes on full flesh and blood.

Themes and Meanings

In an impressionistic collage of prose vignettes, Adler airs her views on social and political issues as well as mulling over such mundane topics as bad drivers and the possible evolution of the convention according to which a football quarterback wipes his hands on a towel draped from the hind parts of the center in front of him. Much of her political and social commentary presumably emanates from her personal experience in the 1960's, and her conservative slant is thinly veiled. The law profession is probed and condemned with a special vengeance that is closely connected with her alienation from Jake, as she seeks to rationalize a way to escape their futile love affair. She comments viciously on the legal system: "Here, on the other hand, with an ingenuity that should take an entrepreneurial schemer's breath away, there has evolved the following proposition: that a legal job no sooner comes into existence than it generates, immediately and of necessity, a job for a competitor. I can think of no other line of work where this is true."

Adler's main theme, however obliquely presented, is love, especially the love of a mistress for a married man. Her comments on this topic are poignant. "Is it always the same story, then?" she asks. It is always the case that "somebody loves and somebody doesn't." Sadly, she concludes that "someone is a good soul and someone a villain." It is obvious that in her own case Kate Ennis has cast herself in the role of the "good soul" and Jake in that of "the villain." She repeatedly asks, "But can we live this way?" She finally decides—or has decided at the novel's opening—that the answer is no, that the crumbs are not enough sustenance. It is then that she tries to make her escape. This prompts the repeated refrain, "Did I throw the most important thing perhaps, by accident, away?"

Critical Context

Critical response to Adler's style has been mixed. Like *Pitch Dark*, her first novel, *Speedboat* (1976), consists of a sequence of disconnected passages which force the reader to impose a pattern from his or her own imagination. Such a work is hardly a novel in the conventional sense of the term, but critical reaction to *Speedboat* was quite favorable on the whole. Adler's volume of essays *Toward a Radical Middle* (1970) also received excellent notices, and much of the commentary in her fiction should probably be related to her journalistic work. *Speedboat* had the advantage of being new, and its methods enjoyed the attention that attends on novelty, but in *Pitch Dark* her approach had to sway by its own innate virtues. Just how much pleasure a reader takes in these novels will depend finally on how much pleasure from conventional narrative continuity he or she is willing to sacrifice in return for Adler's freshness and distinct talent for the impressive quick sketch.

Bibliography

Conant, Oliver. "A Novelist's Lonely Song." *The New Leader* 17 (January 23, 1984): 17-18.

Epstein, Joseph. "The Sunshine Girls." *Commentary* 77 (June, 1984): 62-67.

Shattuck, Roger. "Quanta," in *The New York Review of Books* 31 (March 15, 1984): 3.

Tyler, Anne. "End of a Love Affair." *The New Republic* 189 (December 5, 1983): 27-28.

Len McCall

PLAINS SONG, FOR FEMALE VOICES

Author: Wright Morris (1910-1998)
Type of plot: Domestic realism
Time of plot: The early 1900's to the late 1970's
Locale: Madison County, Nebraska, and Chicago
First published: 1980

> *Principal characters:*
> CORA ATKINS, a Nebraska farmwife
> EMERSON ATKINS, her husband
> ORION ATKINS, his brother
> BELLE ROONEY ATKINS, Orion's wife
> MADGE ATKINS KIBBEE, the daughter of Cora and Emerson
> SHARON ROSE ATKINS, daughter of Belle and Orion, a music teacher in
>   Chicago and at Wellesley College

The Novel

Plains Song, for Female Voices contrasts the lives of two women of the Nebraska plains who seemingly have completely different ways of looking at the world. Cora Atkins comes west from Ohio in the early twentieth century to be a farmwife for Emerson Atkins and learns to accept the limitations of such an existence. Sharon Rose Atkins, Cora's niece, is appalled by the plains life and heads east to discover herself. The lives of four generations of Atkins women are interwoven in this plotless treatment of changes in a way of life.

Sharon's mother, Belle, is an Ozark hillbilly whose verbosity conflicts with the stoic silence of Cora, Emerson, and Orion, her husband and Emerson's brother. Belle's emotional isolation on the Atkins farm ends when she dies giving birth to her second daughter, Fayrene. Cora has only one child, Madge, the result of the first and last sexual act between her and Emerson.

The outgoing Sharon and the passive Madge develop a close relationship, but when Madge marries Ned Kibbee, Sharon feels betrayed by the cousin whose sole function has been to witness her accomplishments: "She was like a calf, bred and fattened for the market, and the buyer had spoken for her." A music scholarship in Chicago allows Sharon to escape such a fate.

Sharon later tries to save Blanche, Madge's oldest daughter, from the slavish life she associates with the plains and Cora, but Blanche turns out to be even more sluggishly passive than her mother. Meanwhile, after Emerson dies, Cora descends into madness, finally paying for years of labor and emotional abstinence; Madge becomes an invalid after a stroke and is cared for by Blanche.

When Cora dies, Sharon, now a teacher at Wellesley College, returns to Nebraska for the first time in thirty-three years to discover that she is considered a heroine by some Atkins women. Madge's daughter Caroline tells her, "we don't get married anymore unless we want to. We all had your example." Sharon sees that Cora's farm is nothing but a field of tree stumps and is frightened by the bleak emptiness, feeling more than ever her obligation to answer the questions Cora was never able—or willing—to ask.

The Characters

Cora and Sharon are the most fully developed female characters in Morris's fiction. On the surface, they are complete opposites, but they share some qualities. Perhaps recognition of these is part of what frightens Sharon.

The six-foot, humorless Cora accepts all the duties of a farmwife but one, biting through her hand on her wedding night, her scar becoming representative of the emotional distance between her and her bewildered husband and of her particular individuality and independence. As with the most complex Morris characters, Cora's strengths and weaknesses merge to become almost indistinguishable.

Cora is not very affectionate toward her daughter and the nieces she must rear after Belle's death. Unable to cope with emotional complications, Cora imposes order on her life by reducing it to a simple level that she can control: "Cora had little desire to see more than she had already seen, or feel more than she had already felt." She convinces herself that her life makes sense, that it is what God intends her to have: "Chickens, people, and eggs had their appointed places, chores their appointed time, changes their appointed seasons, the night its appointed sleep." All this, however, does not stop her from experiencing a strange sense of guilt for having peace of mind.

In Chicago for the 1933 World's Fair, she cannot bring herself to visit Sharon as there is no possibility of exerting control over her niece on her own ground. Cora's effort to live her life, limited though it may be, on her own terms ultimately gives her a considerable degree of dignity.

Sharon is admirable for the same reasons, though her life is hardly limited. She learns to overcome what Cora merely accepts. Sharon makes something of herself by breaking with her roots but has mixed emotions about the "half-conscious people so friendly and decent it shamed her to dislike them." She wants to understand why the people of the plains, especially the women, are as they are, how they can settle for so little, how they, like Madge, can find happiness in such a life.

The answer lies in the compromises made by all people, including Sharon. She forsakes some of the emotional attachments, such as relations with the opposite sex, that humans are supposed to need, but unlike her relatives, she is aware of what she has sacrificed. Her self-knowledge sets her apart from the other characters, creates her independence, her true escape from the emotionally barren plains. This self-knowledge makes it possible for Sharon to see beneath the surface differences between her and Cora. Sharon even defends her when Caroline says that Cora has been less than an animal for not complaining about her life: "She *could* have . . . but she simply *wouldn't*."

The main male characters are less fully realized as they are not of primary importance in the lives of the Atkins women. Emerson feels superior to Cora although she has many talents that he lacks: reading, writing, understanding how to order from catalogs, making their chickens productive, covering the kitchen floor with linoleum. The narrow-minded Emerson is not a negative creation, getting along well with all the other Atkins women, but as a husband, he assumes the passive role traditionally associated with wives. Orion, who understands Cora much better than his brother does and admires her, is capable of greater emotion as well; his wife's early death nearly destroys him.

Themes and Meanings

Plains Song, for Female Voices has been called a feminist novel; it is that and more. It presents, in Sharon, a woman of principles who forges her own identity, never even considering the conventional existence into which she could so easily settle, yet the novel avoids the clichés of sexual politics. Morris's women are recognizable human beings, not types illustrating this pathetic, or that heroic, behavior.

Morris, the least didactic of novelists, is especially interested in all of his books with the relationship of place and character. The Ohio-born Cora becomes the essence of the Nebraska plains; she and her farm are inseparable entities. The farm molds her personality just as much as she controls it. Sharon, on the other hand, rejects the plains because it dominates its inhabitants: "It seemed incomprehensible to Sharon that people continued to live in such places. Numbed by the cold, drugged by the heat and the chores, they were more like beasts of the field than people."

The home place, however, is an intrinsic part of an American's character and can never be completely ignored because of the tenacious hold of the past on American lives. At the end of the novel, Sharon realizes how much the past is a part of her: "Whatever life held in the future for her, it would prove to reside in this rimless past, approaching and then fading like the gong of a crossing bell." The inescapable influence of the past adds some irony to Morris's portrayal of Sharon's independence, for it is her plains upbringing which has created her desire to be different.

Failed and compromised American dreams are a frequent concern in Morris's fiction. Emerson and Orion pursue the dream west but fail to realize it. Even with Cora's help, they make but a minimal living from their farm, succeeding only in producing daughters who produce granddaughters to whom their agrarian heritage is meaningless. Only Sharon successfully pursues the American Dream, ironically by moving farther and farther east.

Critical Context

Morris's devoting his twentieth novel to a consideration of what it means to be a woman in twentieth century America is somewhat surprising, given the secondary status of women in most of his fiction. Women are presented as dominating their men in such works as *Man and Boy* (1951) and *The Deep Sleep* (1953), but beginning with *One Day* (1965), Morris's women gradually start to establish their distinctive qualities, developing a logical progression to Sharon Rose Atkins. He creates Cora and Sharon because he understands women better than he did previously, not because he wants to write a feminist tract. With the exception of *Love Among the Cannibals*

(1957), a rather sexy book by Morris's standards, he eschews the fashionable.

The ninth of his novels to be set at least partially in Nebraska, *Plains Song, for Female Voices* completes Morris's vision of the plains as a place with a profound grip on the emotional lives of its natives, these practical but passionless American dreamers. The Atkinses' failure recalls that of Will Brady, the doomed egg dealer of *The Works of Love* (1952). Despite his criticisms of the deficiencies of the American character, both male and female, Morris always finds something admirable in his protagonists' quests, as when Will Brady dies offering love to an indifferent world. Cora's endurance in a world of loneliness and alienation is no small achievement.

Plains Song, for Female Voices joins *The Works of Love, The Huge Season* (1954), *The Field of Vision* (1956), *Ceremony in Lone Tree* (1960), and *Fire Sermon* (1971) as one of Morris's most notable novels, primarily through his portrait of Sharon and his celebration of her individuality. The choice between living a reasonably safe, conventional existence, and one involving challenges and independence—or degrees of independence—is a difficult one for any inhabitant of Wright Morris's America.

Bibliography
Crump, Gail B. *The Novels of Wright Morris*. Lincoln: University of Nebraska Press, 1978. Crump explores Morris's novels and provides an overview and analysis.
Dyck, Reginald. "Revisiting and Revising the West: Willa Cather's *My Antonia* and Wright Morris's *Plains Song*." *Modern Fiction Studies* 36 (Spring, 1990): 24-38. Dyck compares the themes in novels by Cather and Morris.
Knoll, Robert. *Conversations With Wright Morris: Critical Views and Responses*. Lincoln: University of Nebraska Press, 1977. A collection of essays and interviews with Morris.
Madden, David. *Wright Morris*. New York: Twayne, 1965. Madden provides a critical and interpretive study of Morris with a close reading of his major works, a solid bibliography and complete notes and references. Useful for Morris's work through the early 1960's.
Morris, Wright. "Wright Morris and the American Century." Interview by James Hamilton. *Poets and Writers Magazine* 25 (November-December, 1997): 23-31. Morris comments on his career and his writing and photography over a period of fifty years. He discusses creative imagination and the influence of the American nation on his writing.
_____. "Wright Morris: The Art of Fiction CXXV." *Paris Review* 33 (Fall, 1991): 52-94. Interview by Olga Carlisle and Jodie Ireland. A lengthy interview with Morris on various aspects of his life and career.
_____. *Writing My Life: An Autobiography*. Santa Rosa, Calif.: Black Sparrow Press, 1993. Morris reflects on his life and career as a photographer, essayist, novelist and critic.
Waldeland, Lynne. "*Plains Song*: Women's Voices in the Fiction of Wright Morris." *Critique* 24 (Fall, 1982): 7-20. A study of Morris's portrayal of women in his novels.

Wydeven, Joseph J. *Wright Morris Revisited.* New York: Twayne, 1998. The first complete examination of the work of Wright Morris as a novelist and a photographer. Wydeven includes a portfolio of photographs by Morris along with a detailed analysis of the novels, criticism and memoir that Morris produced. Wydeven focuses on Morris's principal theme of the American Dream and the promise of the American West.

Michael Adams

PLATITUDES

Author: Trey Ellis (1962-   )
Type of plot: Romance
Time of plot: The 1980's and the 1930's
Locale: New York City and rural Georgia
First published: 1988

Principal characters:

DEWAYNE WELLINGTON, an unpublished novelist
ISSHEE AYAM, a successful novelist trying to revise Dewayne's novel
EARLE TYNER, a shy New York teenager, the main character in
   Dewayne's novel
EARLE PRIDE, a shy Georgian farmboy in Isshee's revision
DOROTHY LAMONT, a popular, even wild girl in Dewayne's version,
   who is modest and innocent in Isshee's
MAYLENE, Earle's mother, an urban socialite in Dewayne's version and
   a hardworking farm woman in Isshee's
DARCELLE, Dorothy's mother, the owner of a Harlem restaurant in
   Dewayne's version and an educated Southern woman reduced to
   prostitution in Isshee's

The Novel

Platitudes consists of two novels in progress and the correspondences between their respective authors. Both writers are African American, as are most of their characters. Dewayne Wellington's writing style is postmodern, hip, and urban. Isshee Ayam, whose work includes such titles as *My Big Ol' Feets Gon' Stomp Dat Evil Down*, *Hog Jowl Junction*, and *Heben and Chillun o' de Lawd*, is more traditional in terms of both her narrative style and her preference for what Dewayne refers to as "Afro-American glory-stories." She bears more than a passing resemblance to such authors as Toni Morrison and Alice Walker, while Dewayne is somewhat similar to novelist Ishmael Reed.

Dewayne's novel is about two black teenagers in 1980's New York City, both in private school: Earle, a shy, upper-middle-class "nerd," dreams of love and eagerly awaits his first sexual experience; and Dorothy, who frequents the city's hottest clubs, experiments with drugs and sex and hopes to get rich and leave Harlem. When Dewayne, stuck in the writing of his novel at chapter 6, solicits Isshee's advice, she disgustedly condemns his work as sexist. She also sends him a chapter based on his characters but reflecting her own beliefs about the appropriate functions and components of African American literature. This chapter, and those that follow, is located in rural 1930's Georgia, with Earle and Dorothy recast as farm children, poor but proud, who walk fifteen miles to school each day. In both works in progress, the two teenagers become friends and, eventually, lovers. Although the two authors have radically different styles and political agendas, they are headed for the same goal, and their chapters work in parallel to tell the story of Earle and Dorothy's rocky courtship and, later, Dewayne and Isshee's personal relationship.

In Dewayne's story, Earle, who seems to have no deeper connection to his African American heritage than watching reruns of *The Jeffersons* on television (his mother is a spokeswoman for South African Airlines), is led by chance and curiosity to explore Harlem. There, he finds himself in Dorothy's mother's soul-food restaurant. For middle-class Earle, Harlem is a dangerously exotic place where he must make an effort to conform to the stereotypes of black behavior he has learned from television. For Dorothy, who hums the theme song of *The Jeffersons* on the subway, Harlem is the place where she serves grits to her mother's customers while dreaming of getting out and becoming more "booj" (bourgeois) than her white friends.

Although Earle does not immediately impress Dorothy, her mother Darcelle tries to play matchmaker between the two, and when he gets a job in the neighborhood registering voters, Darcelle sends Dorothy out to deliver free sodas and encouraging words to the enamored Earle. Earle is not popular and has a number of typical adolescent problems, so when one of the popular girls in school invites him to a party, he is pleased and surprised. He is even more surprised when Dorothy, who goes to another school, is also at the party. Unfortunately, she has a date, but Earle's hopes remain high. In the following weeks, he and Dorothy begin to spend time together, going to films and amusement parks. The slowly developing romance between Earle and Dorothy is being paralleled in the correspondence between Dewayne and Isshee: He invites her to have dinner with him during the upcoming Black American Authors convention, and she accepts. Both Earle and Dewayne are hopeful and expectant, but when Isshee stands Dewayne up to go out with another novelist, he retaliates by writing a chapter in which Earle catches Dorothy with another man, having sex that is described in deliberately brutal and demeaning terms. As the lines between writers and written texts gradually blur, Dewayne punishes Isshee through Dorothy. Isshee's apology, a chapter in which her Earle and Dorothy make love tenderly and romantically, arrives and is accepted, clearing the way for Dewayne and Isshee to meet. They have dinner and talk, then go back to his apartment and begin to make love, but Dewayne finds himself unable to consummate this real relationship until he has resolved the romantic desires of Earl and Dorothy. Finally, after his characters have reconciled and made love, he is able to do the same with Isshee.

The Characters

Dewayne Wellington, the author of the more substantial of the two novels in progress, is revealed primarily through his writing and the ways that his novel reflects events in his personal life. It gradually becomes clear that despite the juvenile habits of his characters, Dewayne is a committed artist attempting to write with sensitivity and humor about the problems of teenage identity, sexuality, and love. It also becomes apparent that, in part because of a recent and bitter divorce, Dewayne harbors some resentment against women, perhaps black women especially. Earle and his novel are, in part, Dewayne's way of working through his own feelings about trust and intimacy;

when Earle is finally able to reconcile and make love with Dorothy, it is a healing experience for Dewayne as well, freeing him to pursue a relationship with Isshee.

Isshee Ayam is initially contemptuous of Dewayne's work in progress. She calls him a "No-Rate Hack," urges him to "learn a trade," and calls his writing "puerile, misogynistic, disjointed, and amateurish." She also stands him up for dinner and threatens to co-opt his novel, and her initial apologies are rather casual. She eventually begins to gain the reader's sympathy with a subsequent, more heartfelt apology. Just as important, it becomes clear that her initial dismay at reading Dewayne's first chapters reflects her sincere concerns about the portrayal in literature of African Americans in general and of black women specifically. When she realizes that Dewayne does not share Earle's sexism or indifference to his black heritage, she begins to read his work differently and to find more of merit in both the novel and the novelist.

Earle Tyner's experiences in high school and his first romantic encounters are believable and familiar, if somewhat predictable. Hiding pornography under his bed and dreaming of falling in love, Earle is an apt mixture of teenage awkwardness and maturity, hope and fear, love and hormones. Earle Pride, Isshee's farmboy version of this character, is somewhat more sensitive and less obsessed with sex, but the two characters are more similar than different, both looking for love and trust, like their creators.

In both versions of the novel, Dorothy is more confident and experienced than Earle. In Dewayne's version, while she enjoys slow dates with Earle, she also craves the fast life of New York clubs and college boys. In Isshee's version, she is both more innocent and better educated than Earle. She is not quite so fully developed a character as Earle, especially in Isshee's version, but the reader can gain some insight into her feelings about her life and dreams and about being black, poor, and pretty.

Earle's mother Maylene is a rather sketchily developed character. Her chief function seems to be to provide Isshee with an opportunity to rewrite her as a traditional black super-mother, in contrast to the nagging, self-justifying socialite in Dewayne's version.

Dorothy's mother is considerably more fleshed out in Isshee's version than in Dewayne's: The powerful black farm mother seems to be one of Isshee's main themes as a novelist. Like Maylene Tyner, Darcelle is transformed in Isshee's version into an indomitable life force, enduring poverty and the humiliations that go with it without losing sight of either her own dignity or her duty to her children.

Themes and Meanings

Generally speaking, *Platitudes* is about love, trust, and the trials of growing up. Earle's struggle to make friends, his teenage sexual fantasies, and his dismay at this mother's nagging are familiar elements of contemporary adolescence. So are Dorothy's mixed feelings about her mother's unglamorous business, her hopes of escaping poverty and its restraints, and her conflicting desires for romance and glamor. Other issues under examination include Dewayne's emotional problems as he moves past the resentment of his divorce and Isshee's tendency to have adversarial relationships similar to those she depicts in her novels.

On one level, this is a straightforward story of boy meets girl and the difficulties that arise when people with complex lives and conflicting desires begin to move toward one another. Romance requires obstacles, whether poverty and venal landlords or ex-wives and competing careers, and the fact that one of these couples is inventing the other two can be read simply as an elaborate courtship ritual.

Platitudes can also be read as a dialogue among different ways of representing, perceiving, and experiencing life for and by African Americans. The fact that most of the characters in Dewayne's novel ignore or actively reject their identities as African Americans is not an oversight on Trey Ellis's part. This indifference is consistently contrasted with Isshee's almost obsessive glorification of every aspect of the lives of her black characters, even their "weathered but jubilant and noble handmade cedar outhouse." Ellis uses gentle satire to make each position seem empty, both for the characters and the novelists who envision black identity so narrowly. Finally, as Dewayne and Isshee come to appreciate one another more, both as novelists and personally, a more balanced perspective, a middle ground, seems possible.

The dialogue between Dewayne and Isshee about African American literature, its traditions, purposes, and responsibilities, is carried out explicitly in the course of their correspondence as well as implicitly in their rival versions of Dewayne's novel. In an early letter, Isshee contemptuously dismisses Dewayne's "postmodernist, semiological sophism" and asks him if he has read James Baldwin or heard of "narrative and continuity." Dewayne responds not by defending his literary style but by revealing his marital and financial woes. This has the desired effect, however, of convincing Isshee that he is a "heartbroken human being" rather than an "insensitive cretin," and she concludes by revising her opinion not only of his novel but also of experimental or postmodern fiction in general, even confessing some envy for its "stylistic liberty." It is in this same letter that she suggests that they meet at the upcoming literary conference, suggesting a connection between their literary and personal lives that will continue and become complete by the end of the novel.

Critical Context

Trey Ellis's style in this, his first novel, is not identical to Dewayne's but is also postmodern and experimental. In addition to its postmodern flair, the book is obviously influenced by the development of the African American novel. While Ellis questions and gently parodies some of the assumptions and approaches of the more traditional African American novel, he also pays homage to it: Dewayne is a fan of Isshee's mainstream novels, while she lists James Baldwin, Alice Walker, and Toni Morrison (as well as T. S. Eliot and F. Scott Fitzgerald) among those writers who have influenced her most.

Ellis's purpose is not to reject or condemn literature that focuses on aspects of African American life but rather to argue that literature by and for African Americans need not focus exclusively on issues of race. In a 1989 article, Ellis describes the "New Black Aesthetic," a new literary trend being developed by black artists to whom he refers as "cultural mulattoes." These artists can embrace both African American culture and mainstream "white" culture, both Geoffrey Chaucer and Richard Pryor, "both Jim and Toni Morrison." Elsewhere, Ellis has stated, "In the past some wanted to force Black artists to only write about jazz and Africa and poverty. Black folks deserve and crave more choices." By contrasting Earle and Dorothy's suppression of their identities as black Americans and Isshee's obsession with blackness and black experience, Ellis seems to be suggesting that neither extreme is a tenable position, that both result in gaps and missed opportunities, and that a middle ground should be sought or created.

Bibliography

Ellis, Trey. "The New Black Aesthetic." *Callaloo* 38 (Winter, 1989): 233-243. Ellis describes the art and philosophy of art being produced by a new generation of black artists. Ellis calls these artists, including himself, "cultural mulattoes," able to appreciate and function in both white and black culture. He states that such an aesthetic is "not an apolitical, art-for-art's-sake fantasy" but a redefinition of "the black aesthetic as much more than just Africa and jazz."

Favor, J. Martin. "Ain't Nothing Like the Real Thing, Baby." *Callaloo* 16 (1993): 694-105. Martin reviews both *Platitudes* and Ellis's essay, "The New Black Aesthetic." Comparing both works, he focuses on the artistic impressions of black Americans, factors constituting African American experience and expression, sexism, and notions of racial pride.

Hunter, Tera. "It's a Man's Man's Man's World: Specters of the Old Re-Newed in Afro-American Culture and Criticism." *Callaloo* 38 (Winter, 1989): 247-249. Hunter perceives the black art world (and Ellis's criteria for the New Black Aesthetic) as male-dominated and misogynist. She comments that Ellis's article on the New Black Aesthetic disregards most class and gender differences among black artists, but she nevertheless praises his article for opening "a discourse with far-ranging implications."

Lott, Eric. "Hip-Hop Fiction." *The Nation* 247 (December 19, 1988): 691-692. Lott addresses the dialogue between literary styles in *Platitudes*, calling it Ellis's "call for a truce in the black literary world." He concludes, however, that the debate between Dewayne and Isshee is unbalanced and that Dewayne's "tale is the one finally endorsed; the various jokes on Isshee go unanswered."

_____. "Response to Trey Ellis's 'The New Black Aesthetic.'" *Callaloo* 38 (Winter, 1989): 244-246. Lott chides Ellis for oversimplifying complex literary movements and discussing authors with significant differences as if they were in complete agreement. Lott also states that Ellis's article largely ignores class differences among black artists and intellectuals.

Peterson, V. R. Review of *Platitudes*, by Trey Ellis. *People Weekly* 30 (November 14, 1988): 49. Offers a brief plot synopsis of the novel and praises the book as "a funny, intelligent first novel" and a "vibrant, comical tale."

Catherine Carnell Watt

PLAY IT AS IT LAYS

Author: Joan Didion (1934-   )
Type of plot: Nihilistic black comedy
Time of plot: The late 1960's
Locale: Southern California and Las Vegas
First published: 1970

> *Principal characters:*
>> MARIA WYETH, the protagonist, an unemployed actress
>> CARTER LANG, a film director, Maria's husband
>> BZ, Carter's producer and Maria's friend, a homosexual
>> LES GOODWIN, Maria's lover and the probable father of her unborn child
>> IVAN COSTELLO, Maria's former lover, a sadist
>> JOHNNY WATERS, a conceited young actor who goes to bed with Maria
>> KATE, Maria and Carter's brain-damaged daughter
>> BENNY AUSTIN, the business partner of Maria's late father

The Novel

The first thing that one notices about *Play It as It Lays* is its strange physical appearance. Joan Didion has said that her technical intention in the novel was to write "a book in which anything that happened would happen off the page, a 'white' book to which the reader would have to bring his or her own bad dreams." She accomplishes this goal by dividing her 214-page book into eighty-seven short chapters (some as short as a single paragraph). The fast, even violent, pace of the novel and the accumulation of many nearly blank pages instill a sense of vertigo in the reader.

Play It as It Lays tells the story of a young, third-rate film actress named Maria Wyeth. When Maria is introduced, she is remembering the events of the novel from the perspective of a mental institution. A native of Silver Wells, Nevada (a former mining community that is now the site of a nuclear test range), Maria is separated from her obnoxiously cruel husband, Carter Lang, and from her brain-damaged daughter, Kate. (Although Maria feels genuine maternal love for Kate, the child's condition makes it nearly impossible for that love to be demonstrated or returned.) When Maria once again becomes pregnant (probably not by her husband), Carter pressures her into having an abortion by threatening that he will otherwise prevent her from seeing the institutionalized Kate. Following her abortion, and other, lesser traumas, Maria finds herself in bed with Carter's producer, BZ. The purpose, however, is not love but death. BZ (who is a homosexual and thus not erotically interested in Maria) swallows a handful of Seconal and dies in Maria's comforting arms. Rather than follow his example, she keeps on living.

Unlike BZ, Maria is averse to examining life, philosophically or otherwise. (At the outset of the novel she says: "What makes Iago evil? some people ask. I never ask.")

She tells the reader that she keeps on living because she hopes someday to get Kate back and go someplace where they can live simply. Maria will do some canning and be a mother to her child. This "hope" is encouraging, however, only if there is a chance of its being realized, and by the end of the novel, one understands that Maria's dream is, in fact, hopeless. Viewed in this light, the closing lines of *Play It as It Lays* seem ironic indeed. Maria says: *"I know something Carter never knew, or Helene, or maybe you. I know what 'nothing' means and keep on playing. Why, BZ would say. Why not, I say."*

Maria may actually believe that she is living for Kate. The truth, however, as Didion's narrative perspective forces the reader to see it, is that Maria continues to live because she does not even share BZ's faith that freedom comes with death. Albert Camus once said that suicide was the only truly serious philosophical problem, because it comes down to judging whether life is worth living. BZ has answered the question in the negative. Maria, however, believes that there are no serious philosophical problems.

Although the novel begins with first-person accounts by Maria and two other characters (Carter and BZ's wife, Helene) and ends with a final word from Maria, the bulk of the story is told from a third-person-limited point of view. At its best, this technique allows Didion to move back and forth between a close identification with Maria and an ironic distance from her. Alfred Kazin has argued, however, that when her control becomes too obvious, Didion turns herself into a kind of literary director-auteur.

Upon first reading *Play It as It Lays*, one is likely to be struck by its spare, bleak, nihilistic tone. What becomes evident with successive readings, however, is the crucial function that irony and humor serve in this novel. One of the most hideously black comic scenes in *Play It as It Lays*, the contact between Maria and the man who is to take her to an abortionist, is also one of the most memorable in contemporary fiction. Maria meets her contact, a moral zombie in white duck pants, under the big red "T" at the local Thriftimart. To pass the time he hums "I Get a Kick Out of You" and begins to make inane small talk. Speaking of the neighborhood through which they are passing, he says: "Nice homes here. Nice for kids." He then asks Maria whether she gets good mileage on her car and proceeds to compare the merits of his Cadillac with those of a Camaro that he is contemplating buying: "Maybe that sounds like a step down, a Cad to a Camaro, but I've got my eye on this particular Camaro, exact model of the pace car in the Indianapolis 500."

Because Maria has strong maternal instincts, her abortion is the cause of much guilt and anxiety. It can also be seen as a symbol of the breakdown of the family and of traditional standards of morality. Yet what makes the episode of the abortion unforgettably grotesque is the image of that cretin in white duck pants babbling about the mileage that Maria gets on her car. Throughout *Play It as It Lays*, Didion employs just such comic touches to undercut the sentimental, self-pitying nihilism inherent in Maria's story.

The Characters

In many respects Maria Wyeth is a typical Didion woman—weak, confused, eccentric, and morbidly nostalgic for a traditional society with strong and loving fathers. Her only present link to that world comes in intermittent encounters with her father's old business partner, Benny Austin. None of the men with whom she is sexually involved is strong (they range from weak to brutal), and none could be described as either loving or paternal. Indeed, what Didion depicts is a kind of sexual conflict that pervades American literature. In *Love and Death in the American Novel* (1960), Leslie Fiedler speaks of the schizophrenia that informs American perceptions of sexual identity. He argues that just as women are frequently viewed as either virgin or whore, Earth Mother or bitch goddess; so too are men often depicted in terms of two extremes—as being either gentleman or seducer, rational suitor or demon lover. Accordingly, the protagonist in each of Didion's novels is torn between Apollonian and Dionysian lovers. In *Play It as It Lays* the author has given her single Apollonian figure three Dionysian rivals.

One of the most harrowing scenes in the novel occurs when Maria encounters an egocentric young actor named Johnny Waters at a typically decadent Hollywood party. Waters is the sort of individual who plays "Midnight Hour" repeatedly on the tape deck of his car, mistakenly calls Maria "Myra," and suggests that she "do it with a Coke bottle" when she rejects his sexual advances. Later, when he does get his way with her, he breaks an amyl nitrite popper under his nose just prior to orgasm, tells Maria not to move, and orders her to wake him in three hours—"with your tongue."

Another of Maria's Dionysian lovers is the vaguely demonic Ivan Costello. Because he lives in New York, Ivan is mostly a memory or a voice on the telephone. (He is in the habit of calling Maria up at night to say: "How much do you want it. . . . Tell me what you'd do to get it from me.") If anything, Maria's relationship with her husband, Carter, is even worse. Like Johnny Waters and Ivan Costello, Carter is a self-centered hedonist who treats Maria solely as an object. He has directed the only two films in which she has appeared, and when he thinks of her, it is invariably in cinematic terms. Remembering his life with Maria, Carter says: "I played and replayed these scenes and others like them, composing them as if for the camera, trying to find some order, a pattern. I found none."

As Didion's name typing would imply, Les Goodwin is a better but weaker man than Maria's other lovers. After aborting her unborn child (Les is probably the father), Maria fantasizes an idyllic life in which she and Les and Kate live in a house by the sea. In her waking moments, however, she realizes that such a life can never be. When she finally does get away for a weekend with Les, even that experience proves empty. Although they never mention it, the memory of their aborted child creates a permanent strain between them.

Next to Maria herself, the most important character in the novel is BZ. At the most superficial level, he is an example of the decadence of Hollywood. (While he is secretly indulging in sexual perversions, his mother pays his wife to stay married to him.) Gradually, however, the reader comes to see him as primarily a victim. He cares more for Maria than any of the other men do. When he tries to persuade her to join him in suicide, he is motivated by love, not malice. Also, in his attitude toward life and death, he serves as a necessary foil to Maria.

Themes and Meanings

If there is any positive theme in this otherwise nihilistic novel, it is suggested by Didion's title. *"Always when I play back my father's voice,"* Maria says, *"it is with a professional rasp, it goes as it lays, don't do it the hard way. My father advised me that life itself was a crap game: it was one of two lessons I learned as a child. The other was that overturning a rock was apt to reveal a rattlesnake. As lessons go those two seem to hold up, but not to apply."*

In expecting to find a snake under every rock, Maria is symbolically acknowledging the pervasiveness of evil in an essentially hostile universe. (She has suggested earlier that it is a universe in which one cannot even count on Darwinian logic to prevail.) So, how does one live in such an environment? By playing it as it lays, by never taking the hard way in anything. Although Maria has learned this lesson in childhood and continues to live by it, she concedes that such stoic acceptance (if that is what it is) does not really work. It is simply one arbitrary method among many for dealing with the void in which humanity is doomed to live. It is a lesson that seems to hold up *"but not to apply."*

Critical Context

When *Play It as It Lays* was first published, John Leonard wrote: "There hasn't been another writer of Joan Didion's quality since Nathanael West." This comparison is appropriate for several reasons. First, *Play It as It Lays* is a classic Hollywood novel in the tradition of West's *The Day of the Locust* (1939). The introduction of sound into motion pictures in the late 1920's and early 1930's created a need for dialogue that lured many talented writers to the West Coast. Several (like West) went on to write bitter, satiric novels about the decadence and meretriciousness of Tinsel Town. *Play It as It Lays* seems to be part of that tradition.

To categorize *Play It as It Lays* as merely another anti-Hollywood novel, however, is somehow inadequate. The action of the novel occurs less in Southern California than in an existential void (the white space off the page). Something more fundamental than Hollywood is the cause of BZ's despair and Maria's catatonic resignation. (Indeed, in several of her essays Didion has ridiculed writers who propagate the image of "Hollywood the Destroyer.") At least in this one novel, Didion's pessimism surpasses both the defiant humanism of Camus and the apocalyptic cynicism of West. Maria Wyeth is too passive a character to choose the ritualistic death of suicide or (like West's characters) go berserk at a Hollywood riot. She has been reduced to a state of moral and spiritual paralysis, in which even death seems a sentimental cop-out. Going beyond the comparison to West, Leonard finds an even more suggestive parallel when he notes that Didion's vision in *Play It as It Lays* is "as bleak and precise as Eliot's in *The Waste Land*."

Bibliography

Didion, Joan. "A Conversation with Joan Didion." Interview by Lewis Burke Frumkes. *The Writer* 112 (March, 1999): 14. Didion discusses her life, work, and writers who have influenced her. She also discusses her love of poetry, her methods of composition, and her marriage to writer John Gregory Dunne.

Felton, Sharon, ed. *The Critical Response to Joan Didion.* Westport, Conn.: Greenwood Press, 1993. Critical essays present a detailed study of Didion's various works, including *Play It as It Lays.* A biographical introduction, as well as a selected bibliography make this a valuable resource.

Fracasso, Evelyn E. "Exploring the 'Nightmare Landscape': Didion's use of Technique in *Play It as It Lays.*" *CLA Journal* 34 (December, 1990): 153-160. An analysis of Didion's narrative technique in the novel.

Friedman, Ellen G., ed. *Joan Didion: Essays and Conversations.* Princeton, N.J.: Ontario Review Press, 1984. A collection of essays on various themes and a discussion of her works.

Henderson, Katherine U. *Joan Didion.* New York: Ungar, 1981. A critical and interpretive study of Didion's works.

Winchell, Mark R. *Joan Didion.* Rev. ed. Boston: Twayne, 1989. An expansion and update of Winchell's 1980 Twayne's United States authors series volume. He provides a critical and interpretive study of Didion with a close reading of his major works, a solid bibliography, and complete notes and references.

Mark Royden Winchell